SECRET WARS

Also by Gordon Thomas

NONFICTION
Descent into Danger
Bed of Nails
Physician Extraordinary
Heroes of the R.A.F.
They Got Back
Miracle of Surgery
The National Health Service and You
Thames Number One
Midnight Traders
The Parents' Home Doctor
    (with Ian D. Hudson, Vincent Pippet)
Turn by the Window
    (with Ronald Hutchinson)
Issels: The Biography of a Doctor
The Day the World Ended
    (with Max Morgan-Witts)
Earthquake
    (with Max Morgan-Witts)
Shipwreck
    (with Max Morgan-Witts)
Voyage of the Damned
    (with Max Morgan-Witts)
The Day Guernica Died
    (with Max Morgan-Witts)
Enola Gay/Ruin from the Air
    (with Max Morgan-Witts)
The Day the Bubble Burst
    (with Max Morgan-Witts)
Trauma
    (with Max Morgan-Witts)
Pontiff
    (with Max Morgan-Witts)
The Year of Armageddon
    (with Max Morgan-Witts)
The Operation
Desire and Denial
The Jesus Conspiracy

Journey into Madness
Enslaved
Chaos Under Heaven
Trespass into Temptation
Gideon's Spies
Magdalene: Woman of the Cross/The 13th
    Disciple
Seeds of Fire
The Assassination of Robert Maxwell:
    Israel's Super Spy
    (with Martin Dillon)
The Secret Armies of the CIA
Secrets and Lies

FICTION
The Camp on Blood Island
Torpedo Run
Deadly Perfume
Godless Icon
Voices in the Silence
Organ Hunters
Poisoned Sky

SCREENPLAYS
Emmett
    (with Gordon Parry)
Enslaved
Organ Hunters
The Jesus Conspiracy
Chaos Under Heaven
Mambo
Underpass
Desire and Denial
Doctor of Hope
Citizen Maxwell
The Hostage
Tiananmen
Connections (with Declan White)

SECRET WARS

One Hundred Years of
British Intelligence Inside
MI5 and MI6

Gordon Thomas

THOMAS DUNNE BOOKS

ST. MARTIN'S GRIFFIN ⚋ NEW YORK

THOMAS DUNNE BOOKS.
An imprint of St. Martin's Press.

www.thomasdunnebooks.com
www.stmartins.com

The Library of Congress has cataloged the hardcover edition as follows:

Thomas, Gordon, 1933–
   Secret wars : one hundred years of British intelligence inside MI5 and MI6 / Gordon Thomas. — 1st ed.
      p. cm.
   Includes bibliographical references.
   ISBN 978-0-312-37998-8
   1. Great Britain. MI6—History.   2. Great Britain. MI5—History.
3. Intelligence service—Great Britain—History.   I. Title.
   JN329.I6T48 2009
   327.1241—dc22

                                                              2008035778

ISBN 978-0-312-60352-6 (trade paperback)

First St. Martin's Griffin Edition: February 2010

10 9 8 7 6 5 4 3 2 1

To Edith
Her love, patience, and understanding
reminded me each day that
writing this book was
all that much easier

CONTENTS

Directors of Intelligence Services. ix

Acronyms and Agency Names xi

Prime Sources. xv

1. Her Majesty's Secret Agent 1

2. The Flight of the Falcon 21

3. The Fairy Godmother's Spies 42

4. The Enemy Within the Gate 64

5. Ciphers and Bugs. 86

6. The Atom Spies 102

7. Moles Between Friends 120

8. The Winds of Hate 141

9. Partition to Perdu 161

10. Out of the Shadows 184

11. High Expectations. 203

12. New Targets 221

13. Glasnost in the Snow. 240

14. The Bamboo Curtain Spies. 262

15. A New World: Adjust or Die 280

16. Tango in the Basement 299

17. Route Nine Eleven 321

18. The Day Their Lives Changed 341

19. Back to the Future 361

20. For the Moment 381

   A Personal Note 399

   Select Bibliography 403

   Index 413

MI5: Founded August 1, 1909

1909–1940	Major General Sir Vernon Kell
1940–1941	Brigadier Oswald Allen "Jasper" Harker [acting]
1941–1946	Sir David Petrie
1946–1953	Sir Percy Sillitoe
1953–1956	Sir Dick White
1956–1965	Sir Roger Hollis
1965–1972	Sir Martin Furnival Jones
1972–1978	Sir Michael Hanley
1978–1981	Sir Howard Smith
1981–1985	Sir John Lewis Jones
1985–1987	Sir Antony Duff
1987–1992	Sir Patrick Walker
1992–1996	Dame Stella Rimington
1996–2002	Sir Stephen Lander
2002–2007	Dame Eliza Manningham-Buller
2007–	Jonathan Evans

MI6: Founded August 1, 1909

1909–1923	Captain Sir Mansfield Smith Cumming
1923–1939	Admiral Sir Hugh "Quex" Sinclair
1939–1952	Major General Sir Stewart Menzies

1952–1956	Major General Sir John Sinclair
1956–1968	Sir Dick White
1968–1973	Sir John Rennie
1973–1978	Sir Maurice Oldfield
1978–1981	Sir Arthur "Dickie" Temple Franks
1981–1985	Sir Colin Frederick Figures
1985–1989	Sir Christopher Curwen
1989–1994	Sir Colin McColl
1994–1999	Sir David Spedding
1999–2004	Sir Richard Dearlove
2004–	Sir John McLeod Scarlett

GCHQ: Founded January 1, 1946

1946–1952	Sir Edward Travis
1952–1960	Sir Eric Jones
1960–1965	Sir Clive Loehnis
1965–1973	Sir Leonard Hooper
1973–1978	Sir Arthur Bonsall
1978–1983	Sir Brian Tovey
1983–1989	Sir Peter Marychurch
1989–1996	Sir John Adye
1996–1997	Sir David Omand
1998	Sir Kevin Tebbit
1998–2003	Sir Francis Richards
2003–	Sir David Pepper

ACRONYMS AND AGENCY NAMES

AFI	Syrian air force intelligence, Idarat al-Mukhabarat al-Jawiya
AFS	Syrian air force security service
AIVD	General Intelligence and Security Service (Netherlands)
Alec Station	A "virtual station" within the CIA Counter-Terrorism Center focusing on Osama bin Laden and al-Qaeda
Aman	Israeli military intelligence service
ANA	Arab News Agency
ANC	African National Congress (South Africa)
ASIS	Australian Secret Intelligence Service (foreign)
BKA	Bundeskriminalamt, German internal security service
BND	Bundesnachrichtendienst, German secret intelligence service (foreign)
BOSS	Bureau of State Security (South Africa)
Box or Box 500	Slang for MI5 (from its wartime address of P.O. Box 500)
BSI	Burma Bureau of Special Investigations
CDC	Centers for Disease Control (U.S.)
CIA	Central Intelligence Agency (U.S.)
CNI	Centro Nacional de Intelligencia, Spanish foreign intelligence service
COI	Office of the Coordinator of Information (U.S.)
COMINT	Communications intelligence (U.S.)
CTC	Counter Terrorism Center (Pakistan)
CX	Secret Intelligence Service reports (U.K.)

DAS	Departamento Administrativo de Seguridad, Colombian intelligence service
DCC	Directorate of Covert Collection (South Africa)
DCI	Director of central intelligence (U.S.)
Delta Force	U.S. special operations commando unit
DGI	Cuban intelligence service
DGMI	Director General [Indian Directorate] of Military Intelligence
DGSE	Direction Générale de la Sécurité Extérieure, French foreign intelligence service (after 1982)
DIA	Defense Intelligence Agency (U.S.)
DIE	Romanian foreign intelligence service
DINA	Chilean foreign intelligence service (ANI since 2004)
DIS	Defense Intelligence Staff (U.K.)
DMI	Director of military intelligence (U.K.)
DNI	Director of naval intelligence (U.K.)
DS	Bulgarian intelligence service, Darzhavna Sigurnost
DST	French internal security service
ECHELON	A satellite program able to tap global phone, fax, e-mail, telex, and Internet traffic
ELINT	Electronic intelligence
ETA	Euskadi Ta Askatasuna, Basque terrorist organization
Fourteen Company	Secret British unit attached to MI5
FSA	Armed Forces Security Section (Norway)
FSB	Russian Federal Security Service
G-2	Military Intelligence Branch of the Irish Defense Forces
GC	(Guardia Civil) Spanish internal intelligence service
GCCS	Government Code and Cypher School (U.K.)
GCHQ	Government Communications Headquarters (U.K.)
GIC	Global Issues Controllerate (MI6)
GRC	Global Risks Controllerate (MI6)
GRU	Soviet military intelligence service
GSD	Syrian General Security Directorate, Idarat al-Aman al-Amm
HUMINT	Human intelligence
IMINT	Image intelligence
INSLAW	Washington, D.C.–based surveillance company
ISC	Intelligence and Security Committee (U.K.)
ISI	InterService Intelligence (Pakistan)
JIB	Joint Intelligence Bureau (Pakistan)
JIC	Joint Intelligence Committee (U.K.)
JID	Jordanian Intelligence Directorate

JSIC	Joint Staff Intelligence Center (U.S.)
JTAC	Joint Terrorism Analysis Center (U.K.)
KGB	Soviet intelligence service
Komman-datura	Russian army military headquarters
KYP	Greek Central Intelligence Service
Mabahith	Saudi Arabian internal security service
MBR	Russian internal security force
MECAS	Middle East Center for Arab Studies
MI	Syrian military intelligence, Shu'bat al-Mukhabarat al-Askariya
MI5	British internal secret service
MI6	British foreign secret service
MIT	Turkish intelligence, Millî İstihbarat Teşkilâti
MITI	Japanese agency for economic and commercial intelligence
MOD	Ministry of Defense (U.K.)
MOIS	Iranian Ministry of Intelligence and Security
Mossad	Israeli foreign intelligence service
MSS	Ministry of State Security, Chinese foreign intelligence service
NCIS	National Criminal Intelligence Service (U.K.)
NGA	U.S. National Geospatial-Intelligence Agency
NIA	South African National Intelligence Agency
NIB	National Intelligence Bureau of Burma
NIE	National Intelligence Estimate (U.S.)
NIF	Sudanese National Front Intelligence Agency
NIS	Norwegian Foreign Intelligence Service
NKVD	Soviet World War II intelligence service, renamed the KGB
NORAD	North American Aerospace Defense Command
NSA	National Security Agency (U.S.)
NSIS	National Security Intelligence Service (Kenya)
OFAC	U.S. Treasury Department's Office of Foreign Asset Control
OHS	Office of Homeland Security (U.S.)
OIS	Oman intelligence service
OSS	Office of Strategic Services (U.S.)
OZNA	Yugoslavian intelligence service
PDB	President's Daily Brief (U.S.)
PET	Danish intelligence service
PFLP	Popular Front for the Liberation of Palestine
PLA	Chinese People's Liberation Army
PLO	Palestine Liberation Organization
PROMIS	A software program that can be modified for intelligence operations

PSIA	Japanese Public Security Intelligence Agency
PSS	Palestinian Security Services
RAF	Royal Air Force (U.K.)
Red Cell	CIA analysts who provide "out of the box" analysis to the director
RCMP	Security Intelligence Service of the Royal Canadian Mounted Police
rezidentura	Senior Russian intelligence officer, usually based in an embassy
RUC	Royal Ulster Constabulary
SADF	South African Defense Force
SAS	Special Air Service (U.K.)
SASS	South African Secret Service
SAVAK	Iranian security service, Sazeman-e Ettela'at va Amniyat-e Keshvar
SBS	Special Boat Service (U.K.)
SDECE	French intelligence service (1946–82)
SEB	Czech security service
Shin Bet	Israeli internal intelligence service
SIGINT	Signals intelligence (U.S.)
Sigurimi	Albanian secret service
SIS	Secret Intelligence Service (U.K.)
SISMI	Italian Intelligence and Military Security Service
SKW	Polish military counterintelligence
SMERSH	Soviet NKVD's Section for Counterintelligence
SOE	Special Operations Executive (U.K.)
Stasi	East German intelligence service
SUR	Russian foreign intelligence service
SVC	Secure Videoconference Center (U.S.)
SVR	Russian Foreign Intelligence Service (Sluzba Vneshney Razvedki)
SWW	Polish military intelligence
TECHINT	Technological intelligence
TELINT	Telemetry (missiles) intelligence
TTI	U.S. Terrorist Threat Information Center
VEVAK	Iranian Ministry of Intelligence and Security
YAR	Yemeni security service

PRIME SOURCES

MI5 and MI6 are the oldest of modern-day intelligence services; only the Vatican spies and the Chinese Secret Intelligence Service (now MSS) can claim a longer history. My contacts with personnel in both services ranged over almost a half century and many are now deceased. While they all guard their secrets, there are those who now also accept that, while they are still bound to protect secrets that can threaten national security, a need for greater openness is valid. This book was possible because of them. They include:

Stanislaw Alexandrovich	Former KGB *rezidentura* in Tokyo
Ken Alibek	Deputy Director, Biopreparat, USSR Biowarfare program
Meir Amit	Former director-general, Mossad
Juval Aviv	Former Mossad field officer
Norman Baker	Former member of Parliament
Norman Bailey	Former analyst, National Security Agency
Ehud Barak	Former prime minister of Israel
Ari Ben-Menashe	Intelligence adviser to the Israeli government of Yitzhak Shamir
Cheryl Ben-Tov	Former Mossad agent
William Buckley	CIA station chief in Lebanon
Vera Butler	Intelligence analyst (Australia)
William Casey	Former CIA director

Eddie Chapman	Former MI5 double agent
Eli Cohen	Former Mossad field officer
William Colby	Former CIA director
David Dastych	Former CIA officer
Iuan Deake	Special Operations Executive officer (U.K.)
Éric Denécé	Director, Centre Français de Recherche sur le Renseignement
Rafi Eitan	Former Mossad director of operations
Marer Elmer	Head of Vatican security
Moshe Goldberg	Former Mossad field officer
Edward Gunderson	Former FBI agent in charge, Los Angeles
Efraim Halevy	Former director-general, Mossad
Isser Harel	Former director-general, Mossad
Charles Haughey	Former prime minister of the Republic of Ireland
Richard McGarrah Helms	Former CIA director
Barbara Honegger	Senior military affairs researcher, U.S. Navy
David Kelly	Director of microbiology, Porton Down (U.K.)
Annie Machon	Former MI5 officer
Robert D. Morningstar	Intelligence Specialist in photo analysis and computer imaging (U.S.)
Daniel Nagier	Former Israeli military intelligence officer
Gamal Abdul Nasser	President of Egypt
Victor Ostrovsky	Former Mossad officer
Dr. Vladimir Paschenik	Microbiologist, Porton Down (U.K.)
Andres Penate	Director-general, DAS
Viktor Alexandrovich Penkov	Former GRU officer in Paris
Carlos Rodrigues	Officer with DAS
Uri Saguy	Former head of Aman
Dr. William Sargant	Consultant psychiatrist and adviser to MI5 and MI6
John C. Stennis	Member, U.S. Senate Select Committee on Intelligence
Richard Tomlinson	Former MI6 officer
Colin Wallace	Former senior British Army Intelligence officer

Marcus Wolff   Former chief of Stasi
Peter Wright   Former MI5 officer

    Others asked for their identities to be protected. In all, over one hundred persons contributed to this book. Key sources were each interviewed a half dozen or more times. While respecting the sensitivity of the topics they discussed, the recall of those well-placed sources was often far more revealing than reading stacks of documents, sometimes stamped with SECRET or TOP SECRET, indicating this information must be kept classified for anything up to thirty or more years. Those anonymous sources made it clear this classification in the intelligence world is often no more than a means to conceal embarrassing mistakes. Another reason to respect their anonymity was that the book covers contemporary events.

1

Her Majesty's Secret Agent

On a morning in mid-March 2007, a dark blue car with a Scotland Yard Special Branch driver at the wheel made its way through the west suburbs of London toward the city center. The single passenger in the backseat, Sir John McLeod Scarlett, looked intimidating, the embodiment of the British establishment, a banker, perhaps, or the chairman of a large company. His customized suit, tailored by Gieves & Hawkes, a handsewn shirt with double cuffs and his Travellers Club tie enhanced the impression.

Scarlett was Her Majesty's Secret Agent, a spymaster who had long understood that the chessboard of intelligence gathering has no rules. Now fifty-nine years old, he still had the cultivated drawl from a prep school education (Epsom College) and three years at Magdalen College, Oxford, where he studied history before joining MI6, the Secret Intelligence Service, entering a world where deception and betrayal would remain the cornerstone of his work. For thirty-two years his talents at spying and counterespionage steadily brought him promotion until finally he became its chief, the fourteenth to hold the post, and early in the year he had been knighted by the queen. Married with four adult children, three boys and a girl, he enjoyed collecting history books, visiting medieval churches, and fine dining.

Those pleasant pastimes fitted in with the massive mahogany desk in his office, which once graced the cabin of Admiral Lord Nelson on *Victory* and behind which Scarlett's predecessors had sat. On the desk was a Victorian inkwell, its pot filled with green ink, and beside it the Parker fountain pen Scarlett used to sign all his correspondence. A desk communications console had direct links to the prime minister, the head of MI5, the director of the CIA, and the chiefs of Europe's intelligence services. There was also a button that activated a phone three thousand miles away on the desk of the director-general of Mossad.

The office furnishings were completed by a grandfather clock constructed down to the last flywheel by the first chief, Sir Mansfield Smith Cumming; almost a century later, it still kept perfect time. Cumming's order that all communications emanating from him were to be known as "intelligence product" and marked with the prefix "CX," an abbreviation for "Cumming Exclusive," remained in force. In his will he had bequeathed the agency a large oil painting of a group of French villagers facing a Prussian firing squad during the war of 1870, and as MI6 had moved from one headquarters to another around London, the picture followed. With it went the custom that Cumming was only addressed as Chief.

When Scarlett had been appointed on May 6, 2004 as director-general of MI6, the queen had addressed him as such. He called her the first time "Your Majesty" and thereafter "ma'am." Protocol with both was inbred.

Attached to Scarlett's console was a tamper-proof computer that contained the current state of MI6 missions across the world: in Moscow, Beijing, Baghdad, and Tehran; in the depths of Amazonia and the jungles of Central Africa; in the mountains of Afghanistan and Pakistan: in all those places where Scarlett and his senior staff detected terrorist threats to the United Kingdom. It was hugely expensive to maintain the field operations, often requiring a score of people to service a single field agent "down the pipe."

MI6 is Britain's external Secret Intelligence Service and has a worldwide mandate. MI5, the Security Service, is responsible for internal security. MI6 is answerable to Britain's foreign secretary; MI5, to the home secretary. Both service heads are appointed by the incumbent prime minister and are represented on the Joint Intelligence Committee (JIC), the link with the government. However, both the chief of MI6 and the director-general of MI5 also have immediate access to the prime minister of the day. The services work closely together in the current threat from global terrorism.

Since the al-Qaeda attack on the United States, September 11, 2001, however, budget considerations were no longer the main concern; MI6 was flush with money to conduct espionage, counterespionage, and electronic surveillance, whose gadgetry in 2007 remained the growth industry of the secret world. Scarlett's computer had a map listing the current state of the terrorist threat to the United Kingdom; on that March morning it was "severe," one level below "critical."

Superimposed over London on the map was the figure 35, representing the number of Islamic networks MI6 believed were in the capital. Eighty were identified as operating within the Muslim communities in the Midlands, in Leicester, Birmingham, Derby, and Nottingham. Further north in the conurbation of Leeds, Bradford, and Manchester, there were another sixty networks. West, in the port city of Liverpool, twenty networks had been uncovered. Across the border into Wales, ten were pinpointed not only in the cities of Cardiff and Swansea but in the Brecon Beacon mountains, where suspected terrorists had been spotted training before the London bombings in July 2005. Twelve other networks were in Scotland, and across the Irish Sea were two more.

Most of the networks consisted of two or three members; a few comprised up to a dozen men and women. After becoming radicalized, they had melted into their community as sleeper agents maintaining contact with each other at Friday mosque prayers and biding their time for instructions to carry out an attack. Their deep cover was protected through their daily jobs as schoolteachers, college professors, doctors and nurses, shopkeepers and salespeople. The popular image of the uneducated terrorist of the IRA had long gone. Al-Qaeda sought to recruit university graduates rather than the street-corner dropouts. While the jihadists waited to be activated, they observed any procedural, legal, or cultural weaknesses in their society that could be exploited.

The networks had produced Richard Reid, a British-born convert to Islamism who, in December 2001, tried to blow up a U.S. airliner bound from Paris to Miami with a bomb in his shoe. The July 2005 London bombers all belonged to a network; two, Mohammed Sidique Khan and Shehzad Tanweer, had trained as terrorists in Pakistan before returning to England to become sleeper agents. Four others had set up a poison factory in a peaceful suburb of north London, using techniques they had been taught by a chemist at an al-Qaeda training camp in Afghanistan before coming to Britain.

Even knowing the jihadists were there, taking action against them before they were about to strike was not easy. Neither MI5 nor MI6 had the power of arrest, and Britain's human rights lawyers made full use of the country's laws to challenge arrests made by the police.

In a briefing to his senior managers on the day he became director-general, Scarlett reminded them, "As we are in a global and totalitarian war against terrorism, we must continue to fully engage it on those terms."

In January 2007, a team of MI5 officers had flown to the war-torn African state of Somalia to try to obtain DNA samples from four British-born terrorists, who had been among a hundred jihadists killed in a U.S. bombing raid on an al-Qaeda training camp on the remote island of Lamu in the Indian Ocean. The men had been born and raised in Leeds and had told their families they were going to visit relatives in Islamabad. Instead they traveled to Somalia, joining other jihadists from France, Spain, Italy, and Germany. The passport details of the four Britons had provided an electronic footprint for their journey to Lamu, tracking them through Athens airport on to Mogadishu in the Horn of Africa. From there they had traveled to Lamu, arriving only days before the U.S. fighter-bombers struck. Immediately after the bombing their bodies were buried along with the other dead by their instructors, who then fled back to Mogadishu.

The MI5 officers had flown from London to Kuwait and then to an American carrier on patrol in the Arabian Sea, from which U.S. Navy helicopters took them to Lamu. For three dangerous days, guarded by a combined force of SAS and Delta Force commandos, the officers had helped to dig up bodies buried in shallow graves. On the fourth day they unearthed the four Britons. Each still carried his passport.

Their DNA samples were flown out to the carrier and processed on board before being flown to London so forensic pathologists could match them against other DNA obtained from the unsuspecting families of the dead men. Experts from MI5's technical support department, using the passport information, had located addresses for members of the dead men's families. An officer posing as a local health employee checking on contamination of the local water supply due to broken pipes after unseasonable flooding, had called on each address and taken swabs. These had been driven to London, where a Home Office scientist conducted comparison tests on the DNA recovered from the Lamu bodies. In each case there was a perfect match.

MI6 calculated there were still some 1,600 potential terrorists spread across Britain. It had been one of the first points Scarlett made to Gordon Brown, the prime-minister-in-waiting, during his initial intelligence briefing.

TONY BLAIR, IN THE SUNSET of his ten-year premiership, had been Scarlett's political mentor and protector in the jungle of Whitehall. Yet against Scarlett's advice, Blair had made an extraordinary choice and announced his early retirement from politics with two years of his term remaining. It left him a lame-duck leader, the object of media ridicule and fierce internal sniping within his own cabinet. Within MI6 there was speculation that when Blair left office, Scarlett would soon follow. Critics had not forgotten the damage he had brought upon MI6 following those halcyon days when the Blair Crisis Cabinet had met in the run-up to the Iraq War in 2003 and Scarlett had read aloud, from his buff-colored file with the red cross of St. George on its cover, the latest intelligence from Baghdad. Blair had given him a place at the cabinet table, as chairman of the Joint Intelligence Committee, and had seized upon every word of Scarlett's to support his own belief that Saddam Hussein possessed weapons of mass destruction, or WMD. The claim was enshrined in a document signed by Blair and presented to Parliament, one to which Scarlett had made a major contribution.

By the time the Crisis Cabinet became the War Cabinet after the invasion of Iraq, Scarlett surely knew Saddam had no warheads filled with smallpox to rain down plague on his enemies, no mobile chemical weapons laboratories roaming the Iraqi deserts at night to launch mass death, no nuclear rockets capable of being fired in forty-five minutes against the coalition forces mustering in Kuwait. There were no WMD of any kind to be found.

When it emerged that it had been Scarlett who pressed for the inclusion of what became known as "the golden nuggets"—the very reason Bush and Blair had gone to war with Iraq—and that those "nuggets" turned out to be fantasies based on highly dubious intelligence sources, Scarlett became the object of intense public criticism calling for his resignation.

Instead Tony Blair had appointed him as the director-general of MI6. Within the Secret Intelligence Service there was stunned disbelief. The appointment was seen by many officers as no more than repayment by Blair for Scarlett's support over WMD. That view was shared in the corridors of the Ministry of Defense and at Langley. One CIA officer who had been directly involved in the search for WMD told the author, "Until the golden nuggets, Scarlett had a good reputation. Not anymore. If Blair was Bush's poodle, Scarlett was Blair's donkey."

In Washington the issue of WMD had ensured Scarlett's footprint would be clear in all subsequent assessments of the Iraq War; he was the intelligence chief who had made a disastrous error.

John Scarlett now had an opportunity to show his peers that MI6, under his command, could carry out an operation that would become a hallmark of careful planning and derring-do and would restore his reputation in the secret world of intelligence and with the new government of Gordon Brown. For the rest—the media commentators on the Sunday morning talk shows, the retired analysts turned pundits—he would continue to dismiss them as "legless men trying to teach running." The operation would be a fitting climax to his long career.

ONE OF HIS OXFORD INSTRUCTORS was a talent spotter for MI6. After Scarlett had passed through its training school at Fort Monkton near Gosport in Hampshire, he was posted to Nairobi. Among his first calls was to the Oasis Club near the city's venerable Norfolk Hotel. The club had long been a favorite among Kenya's business and political communities and the city's foreign spies. Patrons could drink from dusk to dawn in its gloomy interior and risk taking a bar girl to one of the rooms out back after checking that her latest medical certificate promised she was free from AIDS.

Moshe Goldberg, a Mossad *katsa,* a field officer, had met Scarlett when he was familiarizing himself with the city and had invited Scarlett to have a drink in the club. Late in the evening they had been joined by a South African intelligence officer: Sober, the man was an amusing raconteur; drunk, he could become boorish and violent. When a barman brought them a new round of drinks, he accidentally spilled a glass over the South African's safari suit.

"The man lunged at him. Scarlett stood up and restrained him. The whole club fell silent. Scarlett quietly told the waiter to bring fresh drinks and turned to the South African and said this wasn't Cape Town. It was an object lesson in the use of confidence coupled to certainty," recalled Goldberg.

In Kenya, Scarlett used his social skills to good advantage; he was well read and enjoyed watching polo and partying. His reports to London were regarded as some of the best informed on the impact that the Russians and Chinese were having on Kenya. His time there was followed by a posting to Moscow, the most dangerous place for a spy.

Scarlett was completing his second tour in the Russian capital when, in January 1994, the KGB caught him meeting one of his contacts, Vladimir Sinstov, whom Scarlett had recruited the year before at an arms fair in London. Sinstov was the export manager for a Moscow weapons company. Russian intelligence officers had pounced on the two men in a café near the Kremlin. Scarlett had just paid Sinstov for the most recent details of arms sales to Syria and Iraq and the names of Sinstov's contacts in Budapest, Paris, and Damascus. Scarlett was expelled and Sinstov sentenced to ten years' hard labor in a Siberian gulag. He would die there. In all, Scarlett had paid him eight thousand pounds in the ten months they knew each other.

Scarlett was given a desk job at MI6 as director of security and public affairs. The post required him to act as the service's internal watchdog; his only role in "public affairs" was to ensure that as little as possible about MI6 appeared in the media. He imbued both jobs with what one former officer, Richard Tomlinson, described as "cold efficiency. A number of officers who did not measure up to Scarlett's yardstick suddenly found themselves out of a job."

IN 2001, PRIME MINISTER TONY BLAIR had appointed Scarlett as chairman of the Joint Intelligence Committee, the invisible bridge over which all important intelligence went to Downing Street. The appointment caused raised eyebrows within MI6. The incumbent head of the JIC, Peter Ricketts, was not only popular within the Secret Intelligence Service but also understood how to define the correct distance between intelligence and politics. Now, after only seven months in the post, Ricketts was sent abroad as Britain's representative at NATO headquarters in Brussels. The move was seen by many within MI6 as a demotion.

It also probably marked the time when Scarlett became a man to watch. Career officers like Mark Allen, long regarded as the service's most gifted Arabist, did not bother to hide his concerns. Like Scarlett, Allen had joined MI6 after graduating from Oxford. His worry was that Scarlett's appointment would lead to the "inevitable politicizing" of intelligence—not least because of Blair's longtime friendship with Scarlett. The prime minister had also graduated from Oxford, along with Nigel Inkster, the deputy director of MI6. Allen thought Inkster's overseas tours, including lengthy periods in the Far East that had given him considerable insight into Chinese intelligence—already a burgeoning threat—made him the ideal choice to replace the current chief, Richard Dearlove.

Dearlove had informed Blair he was "seriously considering" retiring to fulfill a lifelong ambition to become master of Pembroke College, Cambridge, one of the most prestigious positions in academia, and had told his old classmates at Monkton Combe School, near Bath, that he'd had his "fill of those places where the streets change their names depending on who is running the show."

Dearlove had given Blair no time frame for leaving, but he had gently indicated that when he did, Inkster would be a safe pair of hands to steer MI6 through the storms that required cool judgment. Instead

Blair had casually asked Scarlett, when the time came, whether he was ready to take up the challenge of being the next chief. Richard Tomlinson would later claim, "Knowing the kind of overly ambitious type Scarlett is, it could only have been an offer he could not possibly refuse."

Three days after Scarlett's appointment as JIC chairman, 9/11 happened. Scarlett saw how the grimly effective simplicity of the attack on the World Trade Center and the Pentagon had struck with numbing abruptness within the U.S. intelligence community. He wrote that what clearly emerged from the disaster was "a devastating pointer to U.S. intelligence failure."

Yet the signs had been there: the fall of the Berlin Wall in November 1989, the First Gulf War, Operation Desert Storm, Operation Iraqi Freedom, the collapse of Soviet Communism, the slide into anarchy in the Balkans, the emergence of al-Qaeda, the revolt of militants against the regimes in power across the Muslim world, and the rise of religious ideology into a powerful cohesive force that was daily expanding not only among the urban poor but to middle-class professionals.

"In none of these matters did U.S. intelligence provide its policy makers with information to allow them to use pre-emptive leverage on these events," wrote Scarlett.

He had gone on to argue that, for Britain, the most effective way to deal with the threat terrorism posed was to recognize that surveillance on a global scale was essential. In forty-eight hours Scarlett had pulled together all the multiple strands of British intelligence to provide Blair with a clear picture of the extent of the threat. He hand-carried his report to Downing Street in a buff-colored file bearing the red cross of St. George, an outward clue to his patriotism.

Now, in his third year as director-general of MI6, John Scarlett was satisfied he had proved his argument.

THE SWEEPING VICTORY of New Labour in the election in May 1997 had led to corrosive rumors within MI6. Some of them were damaging, suggesting that John Reid, a future home secretary and an admitted former member of the Communist Party, still had ties to Moscow. Files on other Labour politicians were dusted off and the contents circulated among MI6 managers. Jack Straw, a future British foreign secretary who had expressed misgivings about going to war with Iraq, and Peter Mandelson, who became a European Commissioner, each had a file, along with Cherie Booth, the wife of Tony Blair (a fact Blair later insisted he was not told by Scarlett). Other files included one on Mohamed al-

Fayed, the owner of Harrods and the future bête noire of the royal family over his claims Prince Philip had been involved in the death of Princess Diana. There were files on John Lennon and the rock bands the Sex Pistols and Primal Scream. In all there were a hundred files on celebrities, leading trade unionists, politicians, and human rights lawyers. Long-serving MI6 officers remembered that when Labour held power under Harold Wilson there had been deep distrust toward Downing Street because of the fear that Wilson, too, had links with Moscow.

In October 2008, it was MI6 who raised the issue of suspicious contacts when Gordon Brown invited Peter Mandelson to join his government as Business Secretary. Newspapers, led by the London *Sunday Times*, established that Mandelson had enjoyed a long relationship with a Russian billionaire oligarch, Oleg Deripaska, the world's tenth richest man and a close friend of Vladimir Putin, Russia's former president and later its prime minister. More disturbing for MI6 was that Deripaska had alleged links to a powerful Russian Mafia gang, the Izmailovo Organization, a fact the media seized upon to demand that Mandelson should resign. He did not. Deripaska denied any connection to the Mafia. But Mandelson's previous MI6 file had been upgraded to "Y-category"—the most secret category—and stored on the Secret Intelligence Service's Scope database, which can only be accessed by the heads of MI6, MI5, and GCHQ. Beyond them only the incumbent prime minister and foreign secretary have access to Scope.

Scarlett believed Tony Blair would be a different political master than Wilson. For him, the new prime minister was "refreshingly open, ready to listen and, though he had no real knowledge of how intelligence operated, he was ready to learn."

When Scarlett saw an opportunity to brief Blair on the work of MI6, Richard Dearlove readily acceded. In no time Scarlett was a regular visitor to Downing Street. Cherie Blair often cooked supper for him, dishing up her favorite Lancashire hot pot [similar to a Crock-Pot stew], and the Blairs became guests in the Scarlett home, eating off their walnut dining table. In June 2001, Labour was reelected with a majority of 179 seats, and the Scarletts were among their friends who danced the night away.

Despite Scarlett's efforts to build trust, however, mutual suspicions remained, with Labour politicians calling for a detailed account of MI6 spending and the Secret Intelligence Service arguing that revealing this would "prejudice its operational security." A Cabinet Office inquiry had concluded that MI6 "lacked focus" and had recommended some "downsizing as it appears to have run out of things to do." Scarlett had rejected this and crisply reminded Blair that the party's election manifesto had no "discernible" intelligence policy. Foreign Secretary Robin Cook, under whose political control MI6 came, had been among the fiercest critics of the service for "its lack of performance and often [being] a waste of taxpayers' money."

Once more Scarlett had used his skills to smooth over such attacks. Recognizing that the majority of Labour politicians who had come into office had previously little or no contact with MI6, he set out to host private dinners for them at which he revealed a heady mixture of what MI6 did: daring missions in the Balkans and the Middle East in those places where the streets had no names and it was kill or be killed. The stories were interspersed with racy tales of the human side of MI6: the officer who had paid for his divorce by pocketing expenses for a fictitious informer he had created for his reports drawn from the pages of the *Economist*. There was the spy who had sold fake British passports to a Middle Eastern businessman to sell on to drug dealers; when the documents were presented at Immigration, the holders were arrested. Eventually the businessman was murdered in a Beirut back street. Robin Cook later said, "Scarlett saw this as a win-win situation for Labour as all these shenanigans had happened on Prime Minister Margaret Thatcher's watch."

Scarlett promised to make sure there would be no repetition during his tenure. The guarantee, as he surely knew it would, had been passed back to Blair, further cementing the new relationship between Downing Street and MI6. This was regularly refreshed by Scarlett's skill at assiduously cultivating an air of mystique and conveying the importance of intelligence work. Selected senior politicians were invited to MI6 headquarters. Scarlett would give them lunch and smilingly see them off in their government cars for the short drive back to Whitehall.

ON THAT MARCH MORNING OF 2007, as Scarlett's car took him toward MI6 headquarters, the London Eye, the giant Ferris wheel that gently hoisted tourists into the sky for a panoramic view of the capital, and the towering arch over the new Wembley stadium were lost in the predawn. In April 2006, a plot to destroy them had been discovered on an al-Qaeda Web site by one of the scores of computer experts, collectively called the Surfers, who worked in the half-light of a large, open-plan, windowless room in Central London, the home of the Joint Terrorism Analysis Center (JTAC), which had opened in 2003. The Surfers could locate a radical Web site, spot a threat, and pass the data on to analysts in milliseconds. Along with MI6 and MI5, the CIA and Mossad were among those who received the "product."

A growing number of al-Qaeda Web sites operated out of Pakistan, a country that was both the epicenter of worldwide Islamic extremism and an important ally of the West. Its president, Pervez Musharraf, identified the struggle against terrorism as his top priority, but increasingly it was becoming clear al-Qaeda was a dominant force in the country. Musharraf had barely survived several assassination attacks. He was ousted from office in 2007.

From his redoubt somewhere in the mountains of the Northwest Frontier, Osama bin Laden had turned the streets of scores of cities and towns into a bloody battlefield in which non-Muslim minorities— Christians, Hindus, and Parsis—were killed. In adjoining Afghanistan, entire towns and villages had become "Talibanized," their populations given an ultimatum to support extremism or die. Village youths were ordered to attend training camps where they were taught to become suicide bombers and given travel documents to go to Europe and join the hundreds of highly trained and motivated extremists who were waiting to strike. John Kringen, head of the CIA analysis directorate, had warned, "We see more trained extremists. We see more money being spent to prepare them. And we see that activity rising."

The threats to the London Eye and the Wembley Arch had been traced to a Web site in Karachi. A priority signal from Pakistan's Counter Terrorism Center (CTC) confirmed the details; jointly funded by the CIA and MI6, the center was set up after the 9/11 attacks, supervised on the spot by officers from both services, and had become a well-run operation staffed by young Pakistani intelligence officers trained in either London or Washington.

Part of their equipment included ultrasophisticated direction-finding devices that could pinpoint a radical Web site's source to within a few hundred yards. It was a D/F (direction finding) team in Karachi that confirmed where the Web site operated. Two hours later a Pakistani police detachment accompanied by an MI6 officer raided the apartment. Six al-Qaeda suspects were bundled into a truck along with two Dell computers. Within the hour the officer had opened up a line in cyberspace to the Government Communications Headquarters (GCHQ) in Cheltenham and transmitted the contents of the computer hard discs. It took only seconds to do so. Another small victory in the war on terrorism had been achieved.

SINCE THE KARACHI EPISODE, thirty-two other plots had been uncovered by the Surfers. All had been initiated by groups across the Middle East, Asia, and the Muslim republics of the former Soviet Union. "But the enemy is not only at our electronic gate; it is within this country," Dame Eliza Manningham-Buller, director-general of MI5, had said in her last public speech on terrorism (she retired on April 20, 2007). Though she was careful not to identify any radical group, the claims were seen as being directly aimed at Britain's two million Muslims.

To deal with the enemy at that electronic gate, the Internet, Scarlett had expanded the Global Issues Controllerate (GIC), amalgamating six existing departments within MI6, and local station commanders in the Middle East, Western and Eastern Europe, and the Far East were absorbed into it as well. Some officers lost their jobs; others resigned in anger. Morale within MI6 began to sink. Rumors about Scarlett's methods when he had been stationed in Nairobi and Moscow surfaced. "Hard-nosed" and "cold" were two epithets attached to his name. A story circulated that he had failed to "properly protect" a valuable source in Pretoria, who had credible evidence that Pakistan was headhunting South African nuclear scientists to work on its own nuclear program.

The whispers did nothing to sway Scarlett's determination to mold MI6. The clearest evidence of his success was how money was poured into the GIC. It took up a significant amount of the MI6 annual budget of £2.5 billion. The funding came from the government secret fund, the Single Unified Vote, which covered the costs of running a modern-day intelligence service. Every major Western country had such a fund, but Britain's was second only to the vast sums that ensured the U.S. intelligence community would never face a financial drought.

Among much else, the MI6 budget paid for the regular attachment of Secret Intelligence Service officers to the CIA and to the Mossad. After GCHQ opened its own office, close to the National Security Agency (NSA) complex in Maryland, Scarlett had stationed a senior officer to deliver specific MI6 targets for NSA's satellites to track. As the majority of requests dovetailed with the NSA's own targeting, there was rarely a challenge from Fort Meade as to whether the cost and repositioning of a satellite would be worthwhile. These umbilical links with the NSA, the largest "spy in the sky" organization in the world, were further reinforced by the stationing of two Secret Intelligence Service officers at the NSA station at Menwith Hill in the north of England.

An uncertain future, which MI6 had faced at the end of the cold war with threatened budget and staff cuts, had all but vanished with the emergence of al-Qaeda. Scarlett's negotiating skills had persuaded the Treasury to end the long-running backstairs struggle between successive chancellors and intelligence chiefs. What Scarlett asked for he got. New staff was recruited and offices rented behind Harrods, the Knights-bridge store, and in Sloane Square, where the renegade spy Kim Philby had been interrogated. In all, a dozen locations were obtained for MI6 after Scarlett became chief. Money to pay for the expansion was dis-guised in the annual budgets of the Ministry of Defense and the Foreign Office. Supported by the Blair government's encouragement for out-sourcing, Secret Intelligence Service officers taking retirement were found berths in a network of private consultancies like Control Risks, which specialized in kidnap negotiations. Those companies provided useful cover for MI6's own secret operations.

Before Scarlett took over, MI6 had undergone major restructuring fol-lowing the end of the cold war, when the JIC decided to add terrorism and global crime—narcotics, economic espionage, and counterproliferation—to the Secret Intelligence Service's list of prime targets. Scarlett had in-sisted on the need to support the traditional role of the spy with state-of-the-art technology to defend Britain against the enemy at the gate.

Communication facilities had been expanded at Ayios Nikolaos on Cyprus to support covert operations in the Middle East, especially Iran. A joint facility with the CIA operating on the Pacific island of Guam had been upgraded to increase the monitoring of the Republic of China and North Korea.

The idea of using "front" companies behind which MI6 agents could hide had been a cherished one since the 1930s when the service's second chief, Hugh Sinclair, a film buff, had persuaded Alexander Korda to al-low his London Films company to provide cover for Sinclair's agents. In 1947, Marshall's Travel was purchased, followed by the Casuro Travel company.

Like all intelligence services, MI6 had recognized the value of black propaganda, and after World War II, its purchasing department bought the Britanova news agency to pump material into the Soviet Union and ANA, the Arab news agency, to do the same in the Middle East. On Scar-lett's direction, the global number of safe houses had been increased and their locations made known only to those agents who needed to use them. Each was fully maintained and swept regularly for bugs.

On that March 2007 day, John Scarlett headed a global organization employing 2,500 people full-time and twice that number on contracts. What had begun as a one-man operation in 1909 now had two helicop-ters and detachments from the Special Boat Service (SBS) and the Spe-cial Air Service (SAS) permanently on call. As well as Control Risks, there was the Bahamas-registered Sandline International, with offices in London's King's Road. The staffs of those organizations were known as "the King's Road Irregulars," ready to do MI6's bidding, knowing their activities would be protected by the Intelligence Services Act of 1994.

SINCE THE LONDON BOMBINGS OF 2005, there had been a major increase in security at Britain's air- and seaports, nuclear power stations, railway terminals, and major bridge crossings; as well as armed police, officers from MI5 and MI6 stood watch alongside Immigration officers. The most significant development had been the spread of closed-circuit television (CCTV) cameras. By 2007, over £500 million had been spent installing 4.2 million cameras, one-fifth of all CCTV cameras in the world. Every government building had its quota of unblinking lenses linked to a monitoring station inside the building. Shopping malls were fitted with cameras to warn of a terrorist attack. On the streets of London and other English cities and towns, a person was filmed on average three hundred times a day. Over three million citizens had their DNA samples taken and stored on police computers. They were told, "It is in the interest of national security."

No other nation, except China, equaled such surveillance. Sufficient film to encircle the equator was downloaded daily and analyzed, and "appropriate" images were stored for future use. A Home Office spokesman said, "The question of what is appropriate is decided on a national security basis."

A surveillance network was devoted to automatic license plate recognition: Its cameras tracked vehicles used by suspected terrorists or criminals and had the capability to handle fifty million plate readouts in a day in any weather conditions and transmit them to one of the scores of optical software recognition stations positioned across Britain. From snapshot to target recognition took seconds.

Hidden among this forest of silent watchers were the cameras deployed by MI6. It had doubled its film coverage since Scarlett became chief. Many of the cameras were sited on the approaches to predominantly Muslim areas and linked to a monitoring center in the south of London. The building resembled a warehouse and appeared no different from others bordering the River Thames. However, it was enclosed by a security fence strengthened to resist a Baghdad-style bomber, and from within the building came the low hum of an air-conditioning system cooling the computers. Day and night they sifted and matched many millions of pieces of information, slotting them into place among the billions of pieces already stored in the databases. The material included details about a person: address, employer, bank, salary, spending patterns. E-mails, faxes, and telephone calls all were stored and could be downloaded in milliseconds.

The technicians who worked in the building had the latest equipment to turn images into three-dimensional pictures, enhance the contrast between a person and his or her background, and, if need be, remove the person totally from the background for closer inspection. The vast monitoring station was an example of the shifting parameters of intelligence in the growing world of cyberwarfare, which marked MI6's own shift from espionage against the Soviet Union during the cold war to fighting the terrorism of al-Qaeda.

The demise of Soviet Communism saw the end of a recognizable enemy, the KGB and its associate service the GRU, military intelligence. They had more or less operated in the same way as MI6, or any of the other major Western intelligence services, turning up in the world's trouble spots: Berlin in 1961, Cuba in 1963, and the Middle East from 1967 onward. From time to time stories about their activities appeared in the media, among them claims about suitcase nuclear bombs and missiles with biological warheads.

Since 9/11 the claims were laid at al-Qaeda's door, and it became part of both MI6's and MI5's brief to track dual-purpose equipment that could be used to make a "dirty" nuclear bomb, from vacuum pumps used in hospital imaging scanners to the rods used in nuclear medical equipment.

In 2007, a significant portion of their work continued to focus on sourcing the funding of al-Qaeda. The money came from the many private Islamic charities in Britain, which were often funded by the fabulously wealthy princes of Saudi Arabia's ruling monarchy. An MI6 document in December 2006 claimed, "There are now over 300 members of the Saudi royal family providing money to al-Qaeda." With their mansions in the center of London and in the countryside around the capital, many of the princes were members of the Wahabi sect, named after the extremely puritanical founder of modern Islamic fundamentalism. From bank accounts in the City of London held by these petrodollar billionaires came the cash to endow new mosques and Muslim colleges and schools. Within their classrooms the first seeds of terrorism were often sown by imams. For every radical preacher who had been deported, another had taken his place. From this background came the London bombers. That knowledge had furthered Scarlett's belief that surveillance was the only way to preempt the threat.

"It is the most effective way to uncover the paymasters of terror and lead to the closure of those places which advocate terrorism," he had told Prime Minister Tony Blair at a Downing Street Christmas party in 2006. An MI6 operation had led a few weeks later to the closure of the Jameah Islamiyah faith school in its fifty-four acres on the edge of a beautiful English village in Sussex. The radical preacher Abu Hamza— now serving seven years in Belmarsh high-security prison in London for "promoting murder and taking part in terrorist activities"—had run a summer training camp for Muslims at the school. The details emerged after an MI6 officer had interrogated an English Muslim prisoner held at Guantanamo Bay. The youth had been a pupil at the school. The school's imam, Bilal Patel, admitted he had received £800,000 from wealthy Muslims living in Saudi Arabia. He refused to name them on the grounds it would be "beyond my religious beliefs to do so."

Shortly after the police raid on the school, an MI6 surveillance team had identified fourteen other Muslims in London who had links to the school. They included Abu Abdullah, who regularly preached at the city's notorious Finsbury Park mosque that he "would love to see our jihadists go to Iraq and kill British and American soldiers." All were arrested.

These successes had led to the installation of new surveillance equipment in 2007 in London and other cities where there were sizable Muslim communities; tall, weatherproof, matte-painted steel poles had been erected. Each was filled with fiber optics linked to a camera bolted to the top of the pole. Each camera contained eight powerful lenses to provide a panoramic view. Software enabled each camera to pinpoint up to fifty behavior traits. The moment a target was identified, a ninth lens mounted in the base of the camera zoomed in to follow every move by a suspect. It would then track him or her along a street or in and out of a building. Image clarity was ensured by each highly polished lens being continually adjusted by a computer chip inside the camera to compensate for exhaust fumes and other kinds of pollution.

AS WELL AS TERRORIST-LINKED SUSPECTS, the MI6 cameras monitored scores of foreign intelligence officers operating in London. Some working for the United States, Canada, and the member states of the European Union did so under diplomatic immunity, usually listed as a third secretary or press officer at their embassies. Others headed trade missions and tourist offices. On a list circulated within the intelligence community they were identified as coming from "friendly" nations. Some had been "declared" as intelligence officers to the Foreign Office and subjected to minimum surveillance.

Spies from less friendly countries, like the two agents operating out of the Syrian Embassy, were placed on an MI6 watch list making them subject to closer scrutiny, which included electronic surveillance. The list also named fifty-two officers from the Russian Foreign Intelligence Service (SUR), who made up a quarter of that embassy's staff list. None had been "declared."

What MI6 calls "intermittent surveillance" had enabled its officers to track the search by the Russian spies for biological weapons that the KGB had secretly planted in the English countryside during the cold war. Dr. Alexander Kouzminov, who held a senior post in the Russian biological warfare program, Biopreparat, and had moved to New Zealand after the collapse of the Soviet Union, claimed that the vials of deadly germs contained Ebola, anthrax, and smallpox and that some were designed to release toxins "to control human emotions and [were] capable of creating uncontrollable feelings of fear and panic among the population."

Kouzminov insisted he was never told where the vials were deposited, but he did reveal the operation had been controlled by a KGB woman officer, code-named "Rosa," who had come to work in England under the cover of being a research microbiologist. Kouzminov claimed he believed her real task was to locate targets, which included reservoirs and pharmaceutical and biological research centers. A thorough search of MI6's copious files on the KGB failed to turn up "Rosa," but early in 2007 a car bearing the license plate prefix given to all Russian diplomatic vehicles—2480—was seen close to Britain's biological research establishment at Porton Down in Wiltshire. Kouzminov confirmed "the establishment would most certainly have been a target for a Soviet biological attack," and he speculated the car was there "to recover embarrassing evidence, but there is also the possibility if the vials were located they could be sold to a terror group."

The prospect that al-Qaeda was planning an attack on Britain had increased after Meir Dagan, the director-general of the Mossad, had sent Scarlett and other European intelligence chiefs a document in which he concluded, "Al-Qaeda will soon be in a position to create artificially engineered biological agents which will spread disease on an unparalleled scale. There is an urgent need to check the backgrounds of all foreign students studying chemistry and biology at your universities. The same science they are taught can be adapted to create the world's most frightening weapons."

Tracking the spies of the People's Republic of China posed a more difficult and growing problem for MI6. By 2007, only a few of the forty-six agents so far identified worked out of their country's embassy. The others were undercover operatives, with no diplomatic cover, functioning as employees of China's banks in the City of London and as students or, in the classic espionage cover, as importers of one kind or another. Their prime task was to obtain economic, industrial, and defense information. University campuses and defense contractors had all been warned of the threat the spies posed in their hunt for British weapons and systems technology, but for every suspected Chinese operative uncovered and usually expelled, there appeared to be many more ready to take his or her place.

The growth of the Internet had given the Chinese Ministry of State Security (MSS) an even greater global reach and coincided with Israel signing a significant intelligence agreement with Beijing that "obliges both parties to work together in the investigatory process where a leakage takes place and also permits China and Israel to mount joint operations." It was an unsettling prospect for MI6.

Early in February 2007, Scarlett sent officers to America's top-secret nuclear research establishment at Los Alamos near Albuquerque, New Mexico, to check whether Britain's latest Trident nuclear submarine secret had been among those just stolen from the facility. Under a secret agreement between London and Washington made during the cold war, details of Britain's nuclear weapons were stored at Los Alamos when it was feared the Soviet Union would destroy Britain's nuclear arsenal in a preemptive strike.

The theft of highly classified discs had been discovered during a "routine" police check for drugs inside Los Alamos by the facility's police force. Hours later an FBI team swooped down on what it described as "a trailer trash mobile home" near the complex. The trailer was owned by a known drug dealer who sold drugs to Los Alamos employees, but hidden under a mattress the FBI found computer drives marked "highly classified material." They had been smuggled out of Los Alamos by a technician who worked in X Division, buried deep underground and only accessed by swipe cards whose codes changed every day. It was there that Britain's Trident secrets were stored. The woman insisted she had shown no one the discs, let alone allowed them to be copied. Despite intensive interrogation she did not change her story. She was finally charged with theft of government property. The MI6 officers flew home unable to resolve the matter of whether or not the hard disks had been copied by spies. Michael Anastasio, the director of Los Alamos, said in a telephone interview with the author, "My ability to discuss the matter is still constrained by the seriousness of what happened. The international implications here are far-reaching." David Dastych, a veteran CIA specialist in nuclear terrorism, added, "We should not forget it was the Chinese who stole the technology for the neutron bomb from U.S. labs."

ALL TOLD, IN 2007, there were over a hundred foreign spies in London. They included two who worked for ANI, Chile's Agencia Nacional de Inteligencia, the six operatives of SASS, the South African Secret Service based in well-appointed offices in their embassy overlooking Trafalgar Square, and the three officers from NIB, the National Intelligence Bureau of Burma. The Mossad had its own base in Israel's embassy in Kensington. In a northern suburb, North Korea's single spy worked under the guise of that embassy's second secretary. He was a regular guest at the parties hosted by the Foreign Office, Buckingham Palace, and foreign legations celebrating their national holidays. The North Korean stood out in his morning dress suit. Scarlett, who had met him at a Canada Day cocktail reception, remarked that the Korean reminded him of Oddjob, the servant in the James Bond film *Goldfinger*. Cuba, Sudan, and Zambia each had a spy who used diplomatic pouches to send reports that MI6 had long established were mostly based on material published in the British press. The spies of MITI, Japan's agency responsible for gathering economic and commercial intelligence, and those of Argentina, Mexico, and other Latin American nations were all represented in London. For many it was a posting that offered a good social life in between gathering data.

Ireland had a member of its country's small intelligence service at its embassy. He had played his part in identifying five Islamic terror groups based in Dublin and linked to al-Qaeda. They were Egyptian Islamic Jihad, al-Gama'a al-Islamiyya, the Algerian Armed Islamic Group, Hamas, and Palestinian Islamic Jihad. All were identified "as providing financial and logistical support to other terror organizations abroad." The names and details of the two hundred members of the groups went onto MI6 computers. Again it was Irish intelligence who first sounded the alert that young Muslims from the Middle East and Asia working in Ireland's booming information technology (IT) industry were being recruited to travel to Pakistan to learn the techniques needed to launch cyberterrorism, which could seriously disrupt Britain's airports, power stations, and communications networks. All their names were placed on an MI6 watch list, a copy of which was sent to the MI6 station in Islamabad. From there it was passed to Pakistani intelligence. In 2007, they arrested three Muslims from Ireland.

Al-Qaeda's links with Irish terrorism dated from the days in 2000 when its paymaster, Hamid Aich, operated from Dublin. The slim, darkly handsome, smartly dressed Algerian had three addresses in Dublin's upmarket suburbs. From these he had orchestrated funding for the 9/11 attack through the Mercy Relief Agency, an Islamic charity that was a front for al-Qaeda. Aich had left Ireland a few days before the attacks. He was probably killed in an American bombing raid on the Tora Bora mountains in Afghanistan in the hunt for Osama bin Laden.

On a regular basis Scarlett met with the CIA's London station chief over dinner, usually in a private room at the Travellers Club. The view was widely held by Scarlett's enemies that a secret would then be shared or a reputation discreetly tarnished. Those enemies were politicians and disaffected intelligence officers who believe MI6 has made secrecy an end unto itself to protect its activities and that Scarlett was the past master of this. More certain is that both men held a deep conviction that the European Union, and Germany in particular, had provided what Scarlett called "the rear assembly area which had led to a decade of Islamic terrorism." From Hamburg had come some of the al-Qaeda pilots who had launched the September 11 attacks.

In the privacy of the dining room the spymasters could use the language of their profession: "playback," the placing of false stories in the media; "flap potential," the risk of embarrassment to an intelligence service stemming from disclosure of an illegal or questionable activity; and "discard," an informer who had to be exposed in order to protect another more valuable asset. There was a lexicon of such words. Richard Tomlinson recalled that "learning the language was among the first lessons an agent had to master at MI6. Once taught we were warned never to use it except among ourselves and then only under secure circumstances because it would identify us as spies. We had to know about two thousand descriptions also used by the CIA, Mossad, the French, and, of course, the Russians." Tomlinson claimed that Scarlett, after his expulsion from Moscow, had regularly given the talk on Russian expressions: *dubok*, a dead letter box, and *Nashi* (youth organization), a defector, were among those Tomlinson recalled scribbling in his notebook.

Now, early on that March day in 2007, the most important operation by MI6 involving a defector during Scarlett's tenure as chief had come to its conclusion.

2

The Flight of the Falcon

On the bitterly cold morning of December 11, 2006, an Iran Air 737 passenger plane flew out of the Shiraz airport in the foothills of the country's Zagros Mountains. The cabin was full except for the front row, which was occupied by a solitary figure. General Ali-Reza Asgari had boarded last and would be the first to disembark, a gesture to his rank. With his black hair and trimmed mustache, he looked younger than his fifty-seven years, a birthday he had recently celebrated with one of the four wives he was allowed under Muslim law. Afterward he had flown from their home in Tehran south to Shiraz, his birthplace, to visit his parents' graves. It would be the last time he would pay them his respects, or see the snow-capped mountains beneath the 737 and, when the aircraft had banked, glimpse the Shatt al-Arab waterway that divided Iran from Iraq.

Since the overthrow of Saddam Hussein, the seaway had been heavily patrolled by U.S. and coalition forces to stop the smuggling of weapons from Iran to the Shiite insurgents in Iraq. An invisible line divided the Iranian and Iraqi coasts, and powerful, well-armed gunboats crewed by Revolutionary Guards patrolled the Iranian side of the line. There had been several incidents between the two forces, including the capture of a Royal Navy patrol after Iran claimed it had entered its waterspace. Following intense diplomatic pressure, the sailors had been released. Among the senior officers who advised this should be done, when the maximum propaganda value had been extracted, was General Asgari.

Asgari was a senior director of VEVAK, Iran's prime foreign intelligence service, with spies in over seventy capitals including London,

Washington, Moscow, and Beijing and using technology provided by Russia and China. Like MI6, VEVAK had no budget limitations, and like Mossad, it had its own assassination squad, which had struck in Europe and elsewhere to eliminate opponents of the regime. VEVAK had also recruited disaffected Pakistani intelligence officers whose al-Qaeda sympathies made them doubly welcome. Asgari's prime skill was a phenomenal memory, and he could memorize a complex document after one reading. He knew his talent made him a valuable asset.

Inside Iran's secretive theocratic regime he had played a significant role in fomenting Islamic revolution through terrorism and, most important, protecting its inexorable advance to creating a nuclear bomb. That process had reached the stage where it was seen as the major threat confronting Israel and its ally the United States. North Korea's nuclear program was moving only slowly forward in a nation close to starvation and watched with growing concern by its neighbor China, who had finally accepted that the Pyongyang regime was as aggressively volatile as Washington insisted. Pakistan's nuclear weapons had been reluctantly accepted by the West, not least because its missiles were aimed at India, its traditional enemy, and not at the West. However, since October 2003, when the Islamic Republic of Iran first announced it had been secretly producing highly enriched weapons-grade uranium, the mullah regime had become increasingly dangerous and unpredictable.

The threat of a nuclear-armed Iran had already dramatically shifted the balance of power in the Middle East, causing growing alarm in Washington and London, and leading to Israel increasingly threatening to launch a preemptive strike against Iran's major nuclear facility at Natanz, where hundreds of scientists and technicians were working around the clock to produce enriched uranium. In all, there were eight other nuclear sites fully engaged in creating the country's nuclear arsenal. At Saghand, miners were excavating tons of uranium which was transported to Ardekan for purification before being enriched at Natanz. There were also reactors at Arak, Bushehr, and Tehran. Asgari was one of the few persons who knew the exact state of production at the sites and when Iran would be ready to launch its own preemptive strike against Israel.

Before flying to Shiraz, Asgari had learned about America's plans for attacking Iran. Tomahawk cruise missiles would be launched from U.S. Navy ships and submarines in the Gulf to target Iran's air defense systems at the nuclear stations. The Tomahawks had an onboard facility that allowed them to be reprogrammed while in flight to attack an al-

ternative target once the initial one was destroyed. United States Air Force
B-2 stealth bombers, each equipped with eight 4,500-pound bunker-
busting bombs, would fly from the USAF base at Fairford in Gloucester-
shire, England. Each bomb could penetrate twenty feet of reinforced
concrete.

The details had emerged during a meeting at the Ministry of Defense in London chaired by General Sir Michael Walker, the chief of
Britain's defense staff. The meeting had determined that apart from
Britain and the United States, only Israel would support the attack. Its
three Dolphin-class nuclear submarines in the Gulf would help target
Iran's air defenses at the nuclear facilities with their combined total of
120 missiles. Diplomatic support for the attack would probably come
from Australia and Poland and possibly Germany, France, and Spain.
Less certain would be the role of other European countries. However, the
meeting concluded an attack could trigger devastating reprisals against
8,500 British troops based in Iraq and would certainly result in Iran cutting off oil supplies to the West. There would be an increase in suicide
attacks on Israel, and it would also bring China and Russia into confrontation with the West.

What had astonished Asgari was not that the details had been published in a respected London broadsheet, the *Daily Telegraph*—long ago
he had learned that disinformation was an integral part of espionage.
Was the report nothing more than that? His surprise was that it might be
part of the ongoing process by MI6 to test him, to challenge the truth of
his own judgment: that Iran was still "at least three years away from creating a nuclear bomb." He knew that much would depend on his view being believed.

Asgari had been in his twenties during the closing years of the shah's
reign and its failed attempts at industrial modernization of a nation.
While possessing 10 percent of the world's oil reserves, the majority of
Iran's people lived a life indistinguishable from that of their medieval
forefathers; millions were without electricity, running water, or paved
roads. The call for change had finally swept the Ayatollah Ruhollah
Khomeini to power in 1979 when he had returned from exile in Paris
preaching with the fervor of a new prophet.

Asgari had been standing outside the Majlis, the country's parliament, when Khomeini had been appointed *faqih*, the nation's pious ju-
rist, who would lead religious scholars to teach the people the true
meaning of *velayat-e faqih*, a harsh doctrine that previously even the twelve
Shiite Muslims who were the apostles of their faith had not spread. Con-
sumption of alcohol was punished by public flogging and adultery by

stoning to death. Punishments were enforced by the Revolutionary Guards. Eager to find his role in the new regime, Asgari had passed the entrance examination to the University of Tehran, the first member of his family to have a higher education. Three years later, with a degree in English and Arabic, he had joined the Guards' intelligence service. He quickly showed himself able to track down the remaining members of the shah's notorious security service, SAVAK—Sazeman-e Ettelaat va Amniyat-e Keshvar—watching its agents being hoisted on a rope into the air by a crane and left publicly to strangle to death.

Step by step Asgari moved up the intelligence ladder and transferred to VEVAK, where he was appointed a senior director in 1983. That year he was sent to Beirut as the Revolutionary Guards liaison officer with Hezbollah. He arrived in a city that had once been the pride of French colonialization but was collapsing into ruin. The Lebanese pound was as worthless as the scrip of the Weimar Republic. Over Hamra Street in the western suburbs, along the seafront Corniche to the alleys of Kantari in the west, flew the black flag of Hezbollah as well as the party flag of yellow and green. Asgari found their strategists eager to see the city, indeed the whole of Lebanon, lurch into irreversible destruction. From its ruins Hezbollah would rise to claim forever the land for Iran. Asgari had come to help make this possible.

He told the Hezbollah leaders they should start taking foreign hostages. Among the first was the CIA station chief in Beirut, William Buckley. On Friday morning, March 16, 1984, while the imams called the faithful to prayer, Buckley was kidnapped from his penthouse apartment in West Beirut. Four hundred and forty-four days of incarceration and torture later, the spy chief finally died in his cell deep beneath the ruins on June 3, 1985. Hezbollah announced his death with a press release.

Asgari had shown the Hezbollah bomb makers how to study a picture of a target and decide exactly the right amount of hexogen, a volatile explosive, which must be added to the equally unstable nitroglycerin to produce the required result. He watched them as, like the alchemists of old, they spoke a language rich with the words that brought death—oxidizers, desensitizers, plasticizers, and freezing-point depressants—and showed them how to select the right amount of explosive needed to collapse an underground garage or a high-rise apartment building. For the destruction of the U.S. Marine base near the Beirut airport, Asgari had recommended Composition B, a standard mixture of 60 percent hexogen and 39 percent TNT, to which should be added 1 percent of wax to coat and desensitize the explosive long enough for the teenage driver to hurtle his truck into the target. He told the Hezbollah leaders he knew that in Tehran people would be cheering the massacre and reminded his listeners that the war they waged was because their enemies had broken all the sacred tenets of their God. Later, as one of his last actions in Beirut, Asgari had organized the transfer to Tehran of the Israeli pilot Ron Arad, shot down over south Lebanon by the Syrian air force.

Returning to Tehran, Asgari found his status had been elevated to deputy director of VEVAK. He traveled to Damascus and other capitals to discuss common ground: how Iran could further promote terrorism. He went to Egypt, Tunisia, and other parts of the eastern Mediterranean, areas where a thousand years before the Shiites had ruled peacefully alongside their Sunni brothers before the religious schism drove them apart in the early centuries of Islam, an event, he told other intelligence chiefs, that opened the way for the infidel hordes to invade. Asgari assured his hosts that when Iran had its nuclear bomb the enemy would feel its heat, most of all in Israel.

Three months before Asgari boarded the flight from Shiraz back to Tehran, he had been summoned to the private office of President Mahmoud Ahmadinejad. Over coffee and sweet cakes in his midtown palace, the president had told Asgari he was being given a new responsibility—to uncover a traitor within the country's nuclear program. The night before, explained Ahmadinejad, he had experienced another of his dreams. In it, a traitor among the thousands of scientists and technicians working at the nuclear sites had been bribed, either by the Israelis or the Americans, to sabotage Iran's first nuclear bomb. That person must be found. Anything Asgari needed to uncover the traitor was his to command.

Not for a moment could President Ahmadinejad have suspected that General Ali-Reza Asgari was the Trojan horse in the program, the spy who now worked for MI6.

ASGARI HAD BEEN A "WALK-IN," a spy who had made the first approach. It had often happened during the cold war, but it was unusual for a defector from the Middle East to offer his services, and certainly for one of Asgari's status.

The first check on his motives had been for the MI6 station commander in Tehran to provide every possible detail of Asgari's background so as to create a picture, which had answered some of the questions posed in London. The consensus was that Asgari was a highly professional officer. Almost nothing was known about his family life except he appeared to be happily married with a comfortable lifestyle that went with his position. More checks needed to be made. Scarlett suspected that unless he received a response soon, Asgari could offer his services to another foreign intelligence agency; the CIA, French intelligence (DGSE), or the German BND no doubt would welcome him. Based on the few details about Asgari that had emerged, it was likely he would have thought long and hard about defecting. Until now his loyalty to his country appeared unchallenged. Was it purely self-interest or some other goal as yet unexplained that had driven him into the arms of MI6?

There was only one way to finally find out: A face-to-face meeting with his appointed controller was arranged. (In intelligence lingo, a controller is the intelligence officer appointed to "run" an "asset" or informer.) Again, where and when it took place would remain another closely guarded secret. The MI6 officer was reputed to have the same interrogation skills as the legendary Jim Skardon, who had winkled out the truth from Klaus Fuchs as to why the atom scientist had betrayed his own country to the KGB.

At their meeting it was agreed Asgari would be known as "Falcon." Codes and the methods of communication were settled. Contact times decided. Financial arrangements made. Thought had been put into the level of payment: too high and it might suggest to Asgari his services were being too eagerly sought; too low and he could be insulted.

Gradually the reason that he wanted to help became clear. He believed the West could no longer tolerate the extremism of Iran's rulers. He loved his country, but he no longer wished to see its people facing the same destruction Iraq had suffered. Caught publicly in lie after lie by the International Atomic Energy Agency, Iran's leadership continued to react to exposure by dragging its feet and reneging on commitments, but the West would never allow a nuclear Iran—a multilayered theocracy with atom bombs—to be established. Asgari had ended by saying he simply wanted to play his part in stopping the headlong rush to destruction. To do so he would reveal all he knew.

EXACTLY WHERE, WHEN, and by whom he had been recruited was known only to MI6's senior staff, and initially they wondered whether Asgari's motives were money driven; it was a common enough reason in the files of other spies who had switched sides. Was it that Asgari feared that the long reach of the CIA and Mossad was coming closer for what he had done in Lebanon and he hoped that by offering himself to MI6 he could negotiate his own safety in exchange for solid information? It was a possibility. Those questions and many more had been asked.

Asgari's answers produced a wide range of intelligence beginning with significant developments in the leadership of al-Qaeda in late October 2006. He revealed that before the first meeting with his controller, he had met Abu Jihad al-Masri a.k.a. Muhammed Khalil al-Hakaymah, who had just been appointed al-Qaeda's first full-time intelligence chief to coordinate all its major attacks and would also be responsible for training agents to penetrate foreign intelligence services. Al-Hakaymah had boasted he would teach the recruits how to beat lie detector tests and use biological and chemical poisons. The appointment placed him one step below Ayman al-Zawahiri, the organization's long-serving deputy. Both men were born in the slums of Cairo and were originally personally recruited by bin Laden. Al-Zawahiri had remained the acknowledged strategist of al-Qaeda while al-Hakaymah took charge of analyzing the methods of Western intelligence services. His emergence at the upper level of al-Qaeda was a clear sign of a new sophistication in how it would conduct its future operations.

Equally revealing was Asgari's detailed disclosure about another senior appointment in the organization's command structure. Saif al-Adel was al-Qaeda's liaison with the Tehran regime and had developed a close relationship with President Ahmadinejad. He also shared a mansion in the city's western suburbs with two of bin Laden's sons, Saad and Mohammed, acting as their mentor.

Saif al-Abdel had been a colonel in Egypt's special forces before he joined al-Qaeda to fight with the mujahideen against Soviet forces in Afghanistan in the 1980s. Since 9/11 he had remained on FBI/CIA lists of their top wanted terrorists accused of helping to plan the deaths of eighteen U.S. soldiers in Somalia in 1993 and the truck bomb attacks on U.S. embassies in Kenya and Tanzania in 1998.

Al-Abdel had given Asgari a valuable insight into bin Laden's failing health; his kidney condition needed regular dialysis, and he required constant medical attention. However, al-Abdel insisted bin Laden had lost none of his skills, not only maintaining his preeminent position as the world's most wanted man but also ensuring that to millions of Muslims he remained a heroic figure. He knew that his charisma was based not just on his success so far in eluding capture but on his personal reputation for probity, austerity, and dignity, all contrasting so starkly with the mismanagement bordering on incompetence in many Arab regimes.

Asgari had been frank about his own position on bin Laden: He had admired the way the terrorist put aside the temptation of personal wealth and demonstrated patience, brilliant planning, and outstanding managerial skills. This encomium, his controller recognized, was an indication of the admiration felt by a professional for a skilled enemy and provided another insight on the man who had unleashed global jihad.

Asgari had continued to provide valuable intelligence, which, among much else, raised questions about Pakistani president Musharraf's commitment to fighting terrorism. Asgari revealed that a number of Pakistani doctors had been sent to Afghanistan to treat wounded Taliban fighters before taking them across the border to Pakistan to receive additional surgery in, among other places, one of Quetta's main hospitals. Musharraf had sent a personal message to congratulate the doctors.

The MI6 commander in Islamabad had been ordered to investigate the truth of the claim and had found it to be accurate. He found patients wearing the turbans of the Taliban in various stages of postoperative recovery. Some had openly boasted that once they were fit, they would return to the battlefields of Afghanistan. The news gave credibility to another claim by Asgari, that his own agents in Pakistan had established that Taliban leaders, including Mullah Mohammed Omar, were living under the protection of the Pakistani intelligence service in the country.

Weeks later had come further news from Asgari that the Continuity IRA, the extreme Irish terror group, was providing its expertise to supervise the making of ultrasophisticated roadside bombs in three arms factories in the Lavizan suburb of Tehran. The Irish terrorists had traveled from Dublin to Frankfurt and onward to Damascus. From there they were brought in an Iranian military aircraft to Tehran. Originally used in the conflict in Northern Ireland, the bombs had left British soldiers dead or injured in the province and brought terror to the streets of Belfast. In the summer of 2006, the black art of the bomb makers became an effective weapon for Hezbollah fighting Israeli armor. Adapted to be fired from antitank missiles, the bombs had created fireballs, traveling at over 1,000 feet a second to strike advancing Israeli tanks. Asgari had described how the weapons were shipped from Iraq and Afghanistan to Syria and then to southern Lebanon.

Again, his claims were checked in London and matched what MI6 had in its copious file on the Continuity IRA activities.

This was not the first time the Continuity IRA had sold its bomb-making expertise. In 2001, three of its members went to Colombia to train that country's terror group, FARC. When arrested by DAS, Colombian intelligence, on a tip from MI6 and sentenced to long terms of imprisonment in a Bogotá court, the trio were helped to escape by the terror group. They eventually were smuggled back to Ireland. There, despite attempts by the Colombian government to have them extradited to serve out their sentences, the Dublin government refused to comply.

Spanish intelligence officers had also learned that in the late summer of 2006, Continuity IRA members met with terrorists of a South African group called PAGAD. Originally called People Against Gangsterism and Drugs, it was formed in 1995 to rid the streets of South Africa of drug dealers, but its ideology changed due to the strong influence of the million-plus Muslims in the country, and it developed strong links with the Tehran regime. The meetings with the Continuity IRA took place at Sotogrande, in southern Spain, a favorite holiday resort for Irish tourists. The Spanish officers established that PAGAD wanted to recruit the terrorists to come to South Africa to work in their training camps in the hinterland beyond Durban, but the proposal collapsed with disagreement over the financial terms.

Asgari's controller was satisfied with the quality and steady flow of information the Falcon provided.

LIKE ALL SUCH RELATIONSHIPS THEIRS, no doubt, had been awkward at first because MI6 had decided it wanted Asgari to remain in Iran; he was too valuable to be allowed to simply defect. The growing crisis over the nuclear program required that MI6 have the most up-to-date intelligence. The risk of discovery for Asgari was that much greater, leaving him open to making a fatal mistake. A prime responsibility for his handler was to ensure that that did not happen.

Ari Ben-Menashe, who ran several informers for the Mossad, described what is involved to the author, "When you initiate an asset into working for your service, you tell him only what he needs to know to protect himself and you. You want to know his secrets, but you don't tell him yours—or if it is vital to do so to keep him on your side, you tell him 'false flags' that sound totally convincing, but he cannot really check. You constantly remind him he does nothing without your approval. You give him a personal code—a word or a short sentence—which only the two of you know. From the outset you must establish he works only for you. He will probably at some stage need you to play the part of confessor, reassuring him. Even a trained agent, for all his experience, is entering a world filled with a new kind of deception. He is betraying his colleagues who trust him. As a result he can become suspicious of the trust you offer. Will you betray him once you judge there is no more information to be obtained? You must be totally reassuring on this point. Ultimately your relationship with an asset is always going to be that of Orpheus without the love or music."

It is as good a description as any of the relationship his controller had with General Ali-Reza Asgari.

In the long history of MI6 operations in Iran, no double agent was better placed or more politically astute than Asgari. Not only was he superbly placed to judge the quality of information he provided, but he displayed the cool nerve of the quintessential double agent of World War II.

AFTER THE END OF THAT WAR, MI6 had a new head of station in Tehran, Christopher Montague Woodhouse, a product of the English prep school system who had served with partisans in Greece, in the Special Operations Executive (SOE), the equivalent of the American Office of Strategic Services (OSS). His MI6 personnel file noted he was "a shining and rare example of someone who has a sophisticated understanding of the political requirements of his mission." Woodhouse had predicted, "Since the communists' post-war efforts have so far been directed towards expansion in eastern Europe and the Far East, it is not hard to guess their next probe will be in the Middle East where they have scarcely yet scratched the periphery. The weakest spot seems to be Iran."

Before leaving London, he had been briefed by a seasoned MI6 officer, Ann Katherine Swynford Lambton, who had spent her war years at the British Embassy in Tehran as a press attaché, a cover for her post. In Tehran, Woodhouse had kept track of all the corrosive whispers of what was happening in London, of career officers disillusioned with the first postwar Labour government. "It was the time of the tragic reduction of Britain and the shrinkage of its prime minister (Clement Attlee) into a sphinx without a riddle," he would later recall. For George Young, another senior officer, it was "depressing to work for politicians who could only say 'you can't do that' or 'proceed with caution.' "

The embassy compound in Tehran covered sixteen acres of barbered lawns, sculpted flower beds, tennis courts, a croquet green, and a swimming pool, all protected from the local population by a high wall. "No point in making them envious," Woodhouse had remarked. It was a time when poverty was rife and nepotism widespread in the country, and the massively overstaffed Iranian civil service was poorly paid. The nation's wealth was concentrated in the hands of the landowning class: merchants, the upper echelon of society, "old money," and the senior ranks of the army. Among the wealthiest were the directors of the Anglo-Iranian Oil Company (AIOC), who had recently reaffirmed its arrangement, entered into in 1933, that a portion of its profits would go toward the economic and social development of Iran under the benevolent guidance of London.

Woodhouse arrived at a time when the political climate had become increasingly unstable. The leading nationalist politician, Prime Minister Mohammed Mossadeq, had called for the nationalization of the AIOC. There had been an attempted assassination of the shah, and in a report to London, Woodhouse categorized the situation as one "where the cult of bullets and knives has entered Iranian politics with a vengeance." He added he didn't have to look far for the driving force behind the ideological foment. The Soviet Union's embassy was only a street away from the British compound. "Very handy for us to keep an eye on what the blighters are doing," Woodhouse had told his staff.

His officers were as opinionated as they were skillful at their work. One had created a network to report on the links between Iranians and the Communists. Another cultivated a relationship with the Iranian chief of the security police, spending nights playing cards with him in the back room of a teahouse. Others had a background of military service in the war. A good-looking former RAF officer of White Russian extraction had used his sociable manner to date a wealthy merchant's daughter whose ambition was to be married and living in the English countryside.

George Young, the oldest member of the MI6 station, had a caustic wit and contempt for the Arab nations. At an embassy dinner party he would mercilessly lampoon their eating habits and attitudes. "While the European has been building, the Arab loots and tears down." Not even the gentle remonstrations of Woodhouse could halt Young in full flow, but the wealthy Iranian guests encouraged his comments, and Young was always the first to be asked back to their mansions for reciprocal hospitality. It was Young's way of building his own network. One of his assets was Robin Zaehner, a lecturer in Persian history at Tehran University, someone, Young reported to Woodhouse, who had "all the eccentricities of a mad professor with his pebble glasses and squeaky voice." Young decided he would be the ideal choice to run a discreet campaign to alert his students and, through them, their parents to the dangers of Soviet penetration in the country. Zaehner also set out on a crusade to secure the overthrow of Mossadeq by "all means possible." Woodhouse obtained London's agreement that MI6 would fund Young's enterprise, but the ambassador, Sir Francis Shepherd, was not to be kept informed.

Soon a powerful group of opinion makers—lawyers, engineers, bankers, doctors, and journalists—had begun to spread the word that the longer Mossadeq remained in office, the greater the risk that Iran would pass into Soviet control.

THAT POSSIBILITY BEGAN EARLY IN WORLD WAR II when Moscow sent intelligence officers to Iran to establish contacts with nationalists opposed to Britain's control over the oil industry. Partly because they had minimal understanding of Iranian culture, the Russians achieved little, and the MI6 chief, Stewart Menzies, despite a strong anti-Bolshevik mood among his senior officers, decided the presence of the Soviet spies posed no serious threat.

Menzies, the third man to be appointed chief, was an Old Etonian who spent his weekends riding with the Beaufort and Quorn hunt, and he would sometimes discreetly claim to his country house hosts he was the bastard son of King Edward VII. As well as creating a frisson of excitement, it added to the mystery he liked to cultivate. When war started he spent a part of his day reading the communications of the French, Belgian, Norwegian, and Dutch intelligence officers working with their governments in exile in London. He arranged that all their orders to resistance groups working in their occupied countries were transmitted from MI6.

Key field officers in the Secret Intelligence Service had been arrested by the Gestapo in Austria and Holland soon after the outbreak of hostilities and their networks destroyed. As the Nazi blitzkrieg overran Poland, still more agents were captured or managed to flee to neutral countries. In Madrid and Lisbon they set up listening posts. As Paris fell, further agents were arrested. In a matter of months MI6 was in a state of disarray, to be saved only by the code breakers of Bletchley Park. They were a brilliant but eccentric group of mathematicians, working in an English country house, who had unraveled Germany's top-secret codes in one of the greatest espionage successes of this or any other war. In August 1940, MI6's Radio Security Service had started to pick up Abwehr (German military intelligence) transmissions, and the cryptologists at Bletchley Park, Station X, had broken the German cipher codes transmitted on their Enigma code machine. The Bletchley cryptologists called their system Ultra, and it gave MI6 an extraordinary insight into the secret world of German espionage, becoming the most powerful single weapon in the intelligence arsenal Menzies was rebuilding.

Later Menzies would also establish a working relationship with the newly formed American OSS, the forerunner of the CIA, after it became operational in July 1942. Young and enthusiastic, its staff had almost no working experience about the intelligence world, but Menzies was impressed by their strong Christian commitment and the way they spoke of God being on the side of America and the OSS being created to fight the forces of evil.

The station chief of the OSS, Allen Dulles, was based in Bern, Switzerland. On a visit to see him, Menzies was astonished to see a bold nameplate on Dulles's office door alerting all visitors as to whom he was and what he did. Years later, CIA officer William Buckley told the author, "Dulles told me it was his special way of showing he did not have to make a mystery about his work because he could outspy them all." After that meeting Menzies arranged for OSS agents to work alongside his own officers, and, in turn, MI6 opened its own office in New York to coordinate joint Ultra-based operations in the Atlantic and Pacific, which led to the sinking of U-boats.

However, Menzies found he had lost the battle for MI6 to have control over running the resistance in Occupied Europe. That became the role of the Special Operations Executive, to which some of his best officers had been assigned. Nightly, Lysander aircraft flew from their base at Tempsford, Bedfordshire, into France to drop SOE agents and supplies. Nevertheless, in London, Menzies still had the ear of Prime Minister Winston Churchill, who had an endless fascination with the dark world of intelligence. Every evening the chief brought to the prime minister's wartime underground bunker in Whitehall the latest Ultra ciphers, and the two men would sit sipping whiskey—Menzies explaining, then Churchill firing questions. Dawn would often be breaking as the chief walked back to his own office. Senior politicians and military commanders who did not have such access made no secret of their envy.

When the war ended they voiced their feelings to the new Labour government that, in the early years of hostilities, MI6 "product" had been inconsistent. Another issue also brought an unwelcome focus on the Secret Intelligence Service. Menzies had approved its role in delaying refugee ships carrying the survivors of the Holocaust from Europe to Palestine (in 1948 it became the State of Israel). There were sabotage attempts and delays in processing paperwork. This caused outrage among Britain's sizable Jewish population, and Menzies was forced to call a halt to the activities.

He also saw the arrival of the Central Intelligence Agency as a threat to MI6's supremacy. Massively funded, the CIA represented the very public-spirited determination of the Truman administration that the

United States would not be outsmarted by either the old European empires of Britain and France or the new Soviet one. CIA agents and analysts had gained hard-won experience during the war. To these were added academics and lawyers. Surely, America had never before had such a peacetime intelligence organization staffed with able people eager to serve their country. In all, there were over 5,000 personnel working for the agency (in 2007 the number was 23,500). MI6 had barely 1,000 on staff. Inevitably the CIA became the senior partner in its relationship with the Secret Intelligence Service. There was talk in Whitehall that further alarmed Menzies: the idea that MI6 should merge with MI5, in which that service would have the dominant role. All this ultimately contributed to his decision in July 1952 to retire. Menzies was sixty-two years old at the time; he died in May 1968, still riding to hunt.

By then Iran had become the focus of two power struggles. One was the expansion policy of the Soviet Union; the other was between the United States and Britain over the latter's determination to remain a world power, even with a diminishing empire. Iran had precipitated the conflict with the events that had begun in Tehran under the regime of Mohammed Mossadeq and his plans to nationalize the Anglo-Iranian Oil Company.

IN 1952, THE EFFORTS OF MI6's station in Tehran to remove Mossadeq were controlled by its new chief in London, John Sinclair, known throughout the Secret Intelligence Service as "Sinbad" from having served in both the Royal Navy and British Army. He had spent a miserable two years in submarines in World War I suffering from continuous seasickness, but a distinguished career in the army had culminated in his becoming deputy chief of the general staff in 1944, when Sinclair had been one of the planners for the Normandy invasion.

The reports Sinclair received from Woodhouse in Tehran were increasingly worrying. Mossadeq had steadily undermined the authority of the young shah, Mohammed Reza Pahlevi, who had ruled since 1941 under British guidance. Sinclair suggested Woodhouse should play up the dangers of Soviet political influence on Mossadeq, and the shah was a ready listener at Woodhouse's regular briefings on the matter. Woodhouse also began to slip in warnings that the United States would like to have "a closer interest" in the country's oil industry. For Britain it was important the oil industry remained in British control, so as to prevent Soviet expansion into the Gulf and the Indian Ocean, through which the fuel flowed from the refineries in the south of the country to Britain and its empire.

In 1951, Mossadeq nationalized the Anglo-Iranian Oil Company, arguing Britain received far more of the profits than Iran. Shortly afterward, U.S. Secretary of State John Foster Dulles visited the Middle East and reported the nationalization was "further proof that British influence is declining in the region and Soviet influence gaining." He decided Washington must launch a political/diplomatic drive in all Arab countries to show that America was "not on the side of the British and French empires." For the moment, however, he was determined to retrieve the Anglo-Iranian Oil Company from what he called Mossadeq's "grubby little hands" and ensure America would benefit, though MI6 would front the operation. The urgency to launch it was clear from the dispatch Monty Woodhouse sent to London, "My agents have gathered evidence from their contacts within the Iranian government that Mossadeq is planning to bring the Russians into the oil fields."

While Sinclair enjoyed his favorite summer pastime of watching cricket, Woodhouse had a free hand in planning a coup d'état. There was something of the Lawrence of Arabia about him. He traveled north in the embassy car to persuade the tribal leaders to oppose any Soviet invasion. They told him they needed money for weapons. He persuaded the RAF at Habbaniyah, its largest base in the Middle East, to provide Sten guns and rifles from the base's arsenal. The embassy air attaché, the indomitable Beverley Barnard, conjured up an old Dakota. The weapons were loaded and flown to the tribesmen. Along with guns and ammunition boxes were bags of gold sovereigns, part of the contingency money Woodhouse stored "in case of an emergency." They were given to the tribesmen, and every coin distributed was noted and details sent to the MI6 accounts department as "essential expenses." Within two months the plan to oust Mossadeq was in place, and he was eventually removed.

A nationalized oil company, the National Iranian Oil Company, was formed. British Petroleum, formerly Anglo-Iranian, held 40 percent and Gulf, Mobil, Standard Oil of New Jersey, Texaco, and Standard Oil of California a combined 40 percent. Royal Dutch Shell held 14 percent and companie Française de Pétroles 6 percent. Until 1951, Britain had controlled all Iran's oil fields. Woodhouse noted, "Another sign of the growing power of the United States here. But the Reds have been kept at bay, at least for the moment."

Among those who had listened to the animated table talk about these events were the parents, uncles, and grandparents of the future

General Ali-Reza Asgari in his home in Shiraz. In the years that followed, first at college, then rising through the ranks of the Revolutionary Guards and finally VEVAK, he had remained fascinated by the way Britain and the United States, after ousting Mossadeq, had each struggled to obtain supremacy in Iran. Nowhere was this more evident than in the relationship between MI6 and the CIA. Joint operations had become a thing of the past; mutual trust and respect were replaced by suspicion on both sides.

In Washington, the State Department in 1951 supported the view of the CIA's then deputy director, Allen Dulles (he would become director two years later), that in his wartime contacts with MI6 he had learned to be wary. Dulles was a committed Anglophobe from the days he wrote a college term paper supporting the Boers of South Africa in their war with Britain. In his view, shared by his brother, Foster, "British imperial policy must not be allowed to compete with American political and commercial interests." Allen Dulles had told his colleagues that for too long MI6 had used Iran as its exclusive playground to operate as it wished. The CIA would try to ensure it would no longer have that freedom. Intelligence would not be shared unless there was a strong common interest to do so, such as the threat the Soviet Union posed in the region.

At college, Asgari had read T. E. Lawrence's *Seven Pillars of Wisdom*. Its description of the role intelligence had played in using the Arabs to overthrow the Turks had convinced him MI6 had been the most powerful intelligence service, and remained so, in the region. He read elsewhere how it had later manipulated the shah and helped the Ayatollah Khomeini gain power and had then gone on to try unsettling the mullahs after Iran revealed its plans to become a nuclear power. In intelligence terms, Asgari saw MI6 as cool, calculated strategists. That conclusion may well have been the moment his thoughts of secretly working for it were sown. A passage in Lawrence's book had stayed in his mind, "All men dream, but not equally. Those who dream by night in the dusty recesses of their minds wake in the day to find that it was vanity: but the dreamers of the day are dangerous men, for they may act their dream with open eyes, to make it possible." After he had been recruited, General Asgari had selected key words from the passage to let his MI6 controller know when he needed to contact him.

Returning from praying at his parents' graves in Shiraz, he had activated this code so he could say he wanted to defect.

───────

ASGARI'S REQUEST HAD EVOKED an immediate response from his controller. Was he in danger of being arrested? Several hours passed before the answer came. Asgari could not be certain, but the Internal Vigilance Department in the Revolutionary Guards may have started making inquiries about him. His controller was certain that Asgari was experienced enough not to have made a slipup, but in the increasingly paranoid atmosphere of the Iranian regime, investigations were routinely started without even a hint of suspicion.

The first of several meetings with MI6's director of operations and the head of the Iran Desk were held in Scarlett's office, in what was widely acknowledged to be the most magnificent headquarters of any spy agency. Designed by Terry Farrell, the doyen of postmodern English architecture, the building overlooked the Thames on the south side of Vauxhall Bridge. Rising four tiers, it resembled a wedding cake clad in honey-colored concrete panels with triple-glazed sea green windows on the lower floors. Several large atria—conservatories off which led nooks and crannies where staff could hold private conversations—rose through the building. One floor was reserved for Scarlett and his assistant directors. It was distinguished by a row of yew trees shipped from Tuscany and acclimatized in Scotland; four tons of soil filled their containers, and a system fed and watered them. At ground level more trees, box hedges, wisteria climbers, and lavender bushes surrounded a gazebo, and fountains sprayed water. The effect was of an English country garden. A total of £460 million had been spent on the building by the time it opened in 1993; its security fittings included bombproof windows and a range of antibugging devices to deflect spies outside the building. The cost of all this had been met from the Single Unified Vote budget.

In the run-up to Christmas 2006, the meetings in Scarlett's office had continued. It was decided that Asgari's exfiltration would require the help, in the first instance, of Mossad and possibly others later. Scarlett had pressed the button on his communications console linking him directly to the office of the Mossad's director, Meir Dagan, in Tel Aviv.

Despite their clashes over occasions when Mossad and MI6 had intruded on each other's territory without prior agreement—the Israelis running an operation in Britain without telling MI6, and Secret Intelligence Service agents arriving in Gaza unannounced—Scarlett respected and had come to like Dagan. A muscular man with a firm handshake and a face that radiated authority, Dagan was now in his fifth year as *memune* and had agreed to stay on a further eighteen months to deal with the growing threat Iran's nuclear program posed to Israel. Like Scarlett, he worked a long day, often seven days a week. His routine was

one he had developed fighting battles in the Yom Kippur War and in
Lebanon, leading his men from the front with distinction. Like Scarlett,
he didn't suffer fools and stood on his record.

Both men shared a passion for history and the lessons to be learned
from wars won and lost. At their first meeting, Dagan reminded Scarlett
that the first known intelligence operation was when Moses sent Caleb
and his men into Canaan to find out if its people possessed a plentiful
supply of poisons and disease-spreading germs, which could be used
with devastating effect on the Jews, who had already endured much in
their flight from Egypt. Caleb had found nothing to threaten the Is-
raelites entering the Promised Land and returned with news that Canaan
flowed, as the Bible says, "with milk and honey." Meir Dagan, a gifted
artist, had given John Scarlett one of his own landscape paintings, a
small watercolor depicting Caleb giving Moses the good news.

Now, three thousand years after that historic moment, Dagan immediately agreed that Mossad would help in the exfiltration of Asgari. He
proposed the "exit strategy" should either be through Turkey or Syria,
both countries Asgari visited on a regular basis. Mossad knew he went to
Syria to discuss the latest intelligence on Israel gathered by Syrian agents
in Lebanon. In Turkey, Asgari often met with arms dealers from the Rising Sun, Eastern Europe's most powerful criminal family, run by Semyon Yukovich Mogilevich. The organization specialized in providing
arms stolen from the former Soviet arsenal. MI6's Iran Desk knew of
these contacts because Asgari had kept his controller fully apprised and
revealed that Mogilevich traveled on an Israeli passport, a fact Dagan
had confirmed to Scarlett. The passport had not been canceled because
it enabled Mossad to more easily track Mogilevich's movements. It was a
classic example of what Meir Amit, the legendary Mossad spymaster,
had once told the author, "Common interests always circumvent borders in the intelligence world." In Istanbul, Asgari also had private business to attend to: He had a financial interest in a small but lucrative
company importing fine-quality olive oil to Iran.

Using this information, MI6 devised a plan to bring out Asgari.
Then, in early January 2007, a problem surfaced. Asgari demanded a
cast-iron, irreversible guarantee he would not be extradited to the United
States to face trial for his involvement in the massacre of the U.S.
Marines in Lebanon. Until he received such an undertaking, he would
not move. By now Asgari's value to MI6 was all too clear. He had already
answered such important questions, put to him by his controller, as
where Iran obtained its uranium, revealing that it had a total of over
four thousand tons of uranium reserves and had secretly imported ura-

nium from the Democratic Republic of Congo, where export controls are nonexistent, as well as from Somalia and Kazakhstan. The information confirmed what MI6 suspected. Scarlett was told by the head of the Iran Desk that Asgari almost certainly knew even more. The significance of bringing him out became more important.

If the operation were successful, the Mossad would want its share of Asgari's "product." While the Israeli service had its own deep-cover spies in Iran, none was close enough to the inner core of the regime to provide insights into Mahmoud Ahmadinejad's mind-set: to be able to discover the conversations he had with his closest confidantes; to learn how he responded to challenges; to realize his desire to justify himself, perhaps his need for expiation. Such information would be invaluable not only for the Mossad's analysts but for the list of assassination targets for the Kidon assassination and kidnapping unit, and the time could come when Ahmadinejad would be moved up the list for "action to be taken." Certainly, in the eyes of many Israelis his threats against them had made him increasingly dangerous, but nothing would be done without the written authorization of the incumbent Israeli prime minister. "Such sanction is essential to ensure any action is legitimate. The Kidon is no different from the executioner in any other country," former Mossad director Meir Amit told the author.

Scarlett's next call had been to Washington. Porter Goss, who had replaced George Tenet as head of the CIA—a move deeply unpopular with senior staff at the agency—had suddenly resigned over accusations of possible "irregular behavior" coupled with a turf battle with John Negroponte, the politically shrewd director of U.S. national intelligence, a post created by President Bush to oversee all U.S. intelligence gathering after 9/11.

Scarlett's contacts with Negroponte had been limited, but after a telephone conversation there was agreement that Asgari would be given his guarantee that he would not be prosecuted over the death of the U.S. Marines in Lebanon provided MI6 shared his revelations with the CIA. Scarlett agreed. Then another issue arose. Asgari wanted two of his wives—Ziba Ahmadi and Zahra Abdollahpour—and his two sons and a daughter to be brought out as well. There were urgent discussions within the MI6 team. While it was feasible to smuggle out so many people, what should the family be told before leaving Iran forever? How could it be certain they would not say something to a relative or close friend, so betraying the whole operation? There were no ready answers; everyone agreed the risk was high. In the end, Scarlett signed off on bringing out the entire Asgari family.

On February 18, 2007, Asgari told them he had booked a family holiday in the Black Sea resort of Samusun. By then MIT, Turkish intelligence, had been informed of what was happening. Turkey is a member of NATO and has close military links with the United States, Israel, and Britain. At the same time, it also maintains strong cultural links with Iran. These had been taken into account by the MI6 planners before seeking the help of MIT, who set up a surveillance operation on the hotel where the family was on vacation to ensure no Iranian intelligence officers were tracking them.

On February 21, Asgari took an Iran Air flight from Tehran to Damascus. For the next six days he spent his time in meetings with Syrian intelligence officers and Hezbollah leaders, discussing the possibility of a new war against Israel being launched by Hezbollah in the summer of 2007.

This was the high-risk point of an operation already fraught with danger, one that would require Asgari to display more vigilance than usual during his stay in Damascus, knowing his every move from the time he landed would be watched; no matter how trusted he or any other foreigner was by the regime, it was standard practice to conduct such surveillance. Even Iran had fewer security services than the fifteen in Syria, which between them monitored every aspect of the country's political and cultural life: No newspaper or magazine could publish and no radio or television program broadcast before approval; even subjects to be raised at community "discussion clubs" had to be vetted.

The most important Syrian intelligence service was the ruthless Shu'bat al-Mukhabarat al-Askariya, military intelligence. It had its own interrogation center in a Damascus suburb with underground cells and torture chambers. Women and even children had died there. The Mukhabarat ultimately controlled all the country's strategic and tactical intelligence and had a global mandate to track down the growing number of Syrian dissidents in Europe and the United States. When they could not be dealt with, their families in Syria were subjected to the full force of the Mukhabarat's methods.

Among those Asgari had come to see in his office in the presidential palace was the head of military intelligence, the squat, bemedaled General Hassan Khalil, a spymaster inured in the Islamic tradition of *taqiya*, the art of concealment and dissimulation.

On February 28, 2007, Asgari told his hosts that on the way back to Tehran he planned to stop over in Istanbul to update himself on his olive oil export business. He arrived in the city and went to the Ceylan Hotel, where a reservation had been made in his name. After dinner he took an evening stroll to where another room had also been reserved at the nearby Hotel Ghilan. Both rooms had been booked by one of the Mossad agents who had arrived in the city. Hours before, Asgari's family had been put on board an Alitalia flight to Rome, clutching their new British travel documents.

On the evening of March 1, Asgari left the Ceylan Hotel. His bed was turned down, his clothes left hanging in the wardrobe, his toiletries neatly laid out in the bathroom. He would never be seen again in Istanbul. During the night, equipped with a new British passport and an appropriate number of entries to show its holder was a regular traveler, Asgari was driven to the border with Bulgaria by a Turkish intelligence officer. Waiting at the border crossing was an MI6 officer. He took Asgari to Sofia International Airport. Together they caught a flight to Rome. In the early hours, Scarlett had been awakened with the news that Asgari was on his way to London. Scarlett was driven by his Special Branch officer to MI6 HQ. By then Asgari's family was already waiting in a safe house selected by one of the MI6 "housekeepers" for their stay in Britain. A security-cleared tutor had been chosen to give the family English lessons. In Tehran, the Iranian Foreign Ministry issued an urgent request to Interpol to "locate General Asgari, who has gone missing. He may have been kidnapped by foreign agents." The Falcon had flown.

At a meeting in his office, John Scarlett read out the request. There were smiles from the dark-suited men gathered around the conference table.

3

The Fairy Godmother's Spies

On a sunny spring morning in April 2007, Eliza Manningham-Buller, the director-general of MI5, arrived for work at seven thirty. Her punctuality was legendary: She was never late for a meeting and never let one overrun its allotted time. Her appointments were kept with the precision of her wristwatch, a gift from her father, a former Lord Chancellor.

During World War II her mother, Mary, had been assigned to collect messages sent from spies in Nazi Germany to MI5. It was only after joining the Security Service that she discovered her mother's contribution. Her father had told her "the whole business of espionage was slightly sordid," Eliza admitted after her retirement later that April. Another surprising insight was her confession that within the family she was known as a hard-rock fan who treasured her collection of Rolling Stones and White Stripes recordings. With her conservative dress style, measured words, and occasional booming laugh, she was far removed from the woman who could hum and jig to the music as she cooked Sunday breakfast for her grandchildren.

Few of her colleagues knew much about her life outside the office, other than that she was married to David, an Irish Catholic and a former moral theology instructor who had become a successful carpenter and brought five children to their marriage. She had none of her own when she wed at the age of forty-three. They had a farm in the Cotswolds, and after Sunday lunch she would settle down to solving crosswords and Sudoku puzzles.

In her fifty-eighth year, Manningham-Buller was a tall, vigorous woman with a helmet of steel gray hair, piercing eyes and a strong voice that emerged from behind one of the Laura Ashley neckscarves she favored to brighten her formal clothes. One of her critics in MI5 told the author, "She has an imperious way of looking down her nose when someone annoys her. Rebuke delivered, she walks away like a galleon in full sail." Others recall her small kindnesses, asking after a sick child or spouse or recommending a restaurant for an anniversary celebration. Oleg Gordievesky, the former deputy head of the KGB at the Soviet Embassy in London whose defection she helped, recalled she was "bright, sharp, and full of color."

There was also still a hint of the schoolteacher she had once been: her ability to reduce a problem to its bare essentials and deliver her solution in a crystal clear voice. "Persistent" and "impatient" were the labels most frequently applied to her, and she could fire off facts with unerring accuracy: On that April morning, MI5's staff numbered 2,848, and the figure had steadily increased in the weeks following 9/11. A quarter of the staff were now under the age of thirty, 6 percent came from ethnic minorities, and between them they spoke fifty-two languages. Her counterterrorism staff was at various stages of investigating thirty-four terrorist plots against the United Kingdom, a third of which appeared to have originated overseas in Pakistan, Yemen, and Sudan. MI5 could call upon 117 intelligence services worldwide to assist in unraveling the plots.

Her salary was £175,000 a year. She had virtually immediate access to the prime minister and her political boss, the home secretary; no other woman in the secret world of intelligence had such power to commit her vast secret budget to fight whatever she decided was a threat to Britain.

Yet in fourteen days, on April 20, Eliza Manningham-Buller would no longer hold the post of director-general of the Security Service. No longer would she have the responsibility for dealing with the expanding menace of Islamic terrorism, one far more dangerous than anything she had imagined when she joined MI5 thirty-three years previously and the IRA had been the threat.

Since 9/11, terrorism in all its forms had come of age, and Britain was a prime target for its exponents as well as a haven for their supporters—the Islamic fundamentalists allowed to preach and publish their extreme views within the country.

Jonathan Evans, Manningham-Buller's deputy soon to succeed her, had used Home Office figures to estimate that as many as four hundred thousand British-born Muslims had journeyed between Britain and Pakistan in 2006 and that a growing number had made their way up into the Northwest Frontier provinces and crossed into Afghanistan. G-Branch, responsible for counterterrorism, had told Evans there was every possibility that at least 10 percent had "some links with al-Qaeda, either as sympathizers or as sleeper agents in Britain." For Manningham-Buller, the stark truth was that "more and more people are moving from passive sympathy towards active terrorism through being radicalised or indoctrinated by friends or families, in organised training overseas, by images on television, through chat rooms and websites."

She had kept the pressure of protecting the sixty million citizens of Britain under careful control: It came from the external criticisms in Parliament and the media over bungled operations; the leaked reports of turf wars with Scotland Yard's Counter Terrorism Command and the pungent criticisms of former MI5 officers. Dame Stella Rimington, the Security Service's first woman director-general (1992–96) had written, "The putting together of all the pieces of information, however big and small, that come in from all sources, the following up of leads, all the classic spy catching techniques, are also necessary against terrorist targets. It appears, looking at it from the outside, that this sort of investigation may not have been sufficiently thorough."

If Manningham-Buller was stung by the oblique criticism of her leadership, she had hidden it. Instead, she cooly replied, "Success cannot be advertised and failure cannot be explained."

Manningham-Buller had defined her work in one sentence, "The purpose of the Security Service is the Defence of the Realm and nothing else." For thirty-three years she had devoted herself to doing so.

Her career high points had included leading the MI5 team investigating the 1988 bombing of Pan Am flight 103 with the loss of 270 lives over the Scottish town of Lockerbie in one of the first terrorist outrages. A year later she had been posted to Washington as MI5's liaison officer with the CIA and FBI during the first Gulf War in 1990. The first time she walked through the main lobby of the CIA, she took care to avoid stepping on the agency's emblem inset into the marble floor—a sixteen-pointed star on a shield with the head of a bald eagle in profile on top, set in a circle, with CENTRAL INTELLIGENCE AGENCY on the top rim and UNITED STATES OF AMERICA on the bottom. Her sidestepping was her way of showing respect for an agency she openly admired. She had been impressed by the way the agency's main cafeteria was partitioned into separate sections: one for staff, the other for visitors, so as to avoid any chance of an officer being identified. Her own standing allowed her to dine in the separate restaurant on the seventh floor where the director and his senior officers ate.

Returning to London to get married, she was appointed as the Security Service's director of Irish counterterrorism, a new post created after MI5 had replaced Scotland Yard's Special Branch in tackling the IRA. The only clue to her success emerged when David Bickford, a former chief legal adviser to MI5, said, "She tore the guts out of the IRA's active units with a succession of brilliant operations which ensured there was sufficient evidence for prosecution." Shortly afterward, she took control of all surveillance and technical operations and expanded MI5's relationship with foreign intelligence services. The can-do mentality she had developed while in Washington went down well with the Australian and Canadian secret services. The day after 9/11, she flew to Washington to liaise with the U.S. authorities; within hours she had advised her boss, Sir Stephen Lander, to place a ring of protection around the Houses of Parliament. When he retired in 2002, she was the first choice to replace him. Now, in two weeks, a career that David Bickford had described as "being in her genes" would be over. She had no plans to write her memoirs, as Stella Rimington had done, or go on a lecture tour. For her, the days would be spent down on her farm. The only dark shadows she wanted to see were the rain clouds scudding over the land.

She had planned her farewell party with her usual attention to detail: choosing a pastel shade for the invitations, each name written in her copperplate handwriting and sent to all the heads of European intelligence services, men she often called by their first names, like August Hanning, the former head of Germany's BND, with whom she still exchanged Christmas cards after he retired in 2005. All had swiftly accepted her offer. She invited members of the Washington intelligence community; a number had said they would be more than happy to come. Friends from the Ministry of Defense and MI6 had promised to turn up. In all, there would be over fifty guests enjoying a buffet supper, vintage champagne, wines, and a wide range of hard liquor.

Although she suspected that behind the warm handshakes, ready smiles, and raised glasses, there would also be the unspoken questions. *Why was she leaving?* Had she simply decided to retire from the long days of always being on call, of having to advise how to tackle fresh targets, to constantly make new assessments, and to brief the prime minister and the home secretary? In the end, had it become too great a burden to bear? There also had been growing speculation that she had been forced out of office by the mandarins in Whitehall and the media. After the

2005 London bombings, there had been a firestorm of headlines accusing MI5—accusing her—of being unaware that Islamic radicals, born and bred in the country, had been operating, in the words of one newspaper, "under the nose of our spy catchers." Another tabloid had suggested MI5 should have adapted the techniques of *Spooks,* the popular TV series about espionage, where everything was knowable and solvable by a handful of actors.

The jibe had been the first time she had publicly responded to criticism. "Real intelligence work is not like *Spooks* where everything is solved by half a dozen people who break endless laws to achieve their results—and all in one episode. It is potentially quite damaging for the suggestion to prevail that we are totally above the law," she said.

In the real world of intelligence, *her world,* the gleaning of information drew together the pieces, often painfully slowly, by assessing, judging, being objective, using integrity and a skeptical eye. "Even in the end it never told the whole story," she had said.

There was always going to be a decision to be made between gathering sufficient evidence to secure a successful court prosecution and having to disrupt a plot where public safety had suddenly become paramount. As she prepared to leave MI5, Manningham-Buller knew the risks would increase and the further Britain was from the last terrorist action, the closer was the next.

AMONG THEIR ASSIGNMENTS, foreign spies on their first posting to London were often sent to identify the headquarters of MI6 and MI5. Some confused the buildings because of their proximity. Others wondered if they were only fronts and the intelligence services really operated elsewhere. A Burmese officer reported to his Rangoon headquarters that MI5 worked from Freemasons' Hall in Covent Garden, the city's market quarter. In fact, the BBC had used the building for exterior shots for *Spooks.* The agent's mistake was understandable; Freemasons' Hall and MI5 headquarters have a distinctive similarity.

Carlos Rodriguez, an officer with DAS, the Colombian intelligence service, recalled, "Seeing the buildings, whose occupants I had dealt with from Bogotá over such mutual problems as drug-running and terrorism, was a reminder that behind their walls were people who are serious players on the international intelligence chessboard."

Thames House, MI5 headquarters since 1994, is situated on the corner of Horseferry Road and Millbank and overlooks Lambeth Bridge. The building was designed by Sir Frank Baines and shows the influence of the Imperial Neoclassical style of Edwin Lutyens, the designer of the Cenotaph in Whitehall. By 1929, Thames House had risen over what had once been a slum quarter of the city, a massive structure in Portland stone hailed as "the finest office building in the British Empire." Stella Rimington, the first woman to be appointed MI5's director-general, saw Thames House as "a great pale ghost." Others who worked there said the exhaust fumes from traffic and the smell of the river penetrated the inner recesses of Thames House.

For outsiders who had business with MI5, there was a ritual to be observed: First, hand in their passport to one of the guards in the entrance hall and then be walked through the security barriers to take an elevator to the appropriate floor. Each level had its corridors with offices on either side, each door shut and marked with letters that gave no indication who worked there.

The Mossad agent Moshe Goldberg recalled his visit, "I was shown into a conference room with a great view of the Thames. Sandwiches, coffee, and soft drinks were laid out on a table. A man in a dark suit and tie greeted me warmly and left. Moments later a side door opened and Dame Eliza came in. We shook hands and she led me to the table and began to serve me like a country-house hostess. We sat in armchairs facing each other, and she asked how were things in Israel and how she admired our intensive farming. I already knew she had her own farm where she kept chickens and alpacas from South America. Then suddenly she was all business."

Visitors to the building were often astonished by the furnishings. Dominating the spacious entrance hall is a six-foot sculpture of the MI5 crest, which had cost £25,000 and was a statement every inch as bold as the CIA emblem in the Langley lobby. Close to the Thames House sculpture stood a piece of modern art that rumor had it once came from the Tate Gallery. Certainly many tourists heading for the gallery had been sufficiently confused to enter Thames House in search of artwork; MI5 had been forced to post on its Web site that visitors were not allowed— but still they came.

Martin McGuinness, one of the leaders of Sinn Fein, the political arm of the IRA, had strolled into the building having mistaken it for Labour Party headquarters. It was the height of the IRA bombing campaign in Britain and, after giving his name and affiliation, he said he had come to see his "contact." There was near panic until a senior officer emerged from one of the elevators and politely directed McGuinness farther down Millbank. Still, for weeks there persisted a belief in Thames House that McGuinness had been on a scouting trip.

Over £500 million had been spent creating a headquarters that rivaled the grandeur of the MI6 building. The money for Thames House had gone for, among other extravagances, £150 a square yard for carpeting the staff restaurant, and resurfacing the squash court in the basement after the floor was laid at the wrong temperature and buckled. A gymnasium had also been added, along with parking space for eight hundred cars for the staff. There was an Italian piazza and two well-appointed bars. The overall decoration was pristine whites and ice grays, mingled with frosted glass panes. Private dining rooms on the fifth floor were where the director-general and senior staff entertained important guests. Each room was paneled with the finest dark walnut, polished to reflect the hand-carved tables and chairs and the deep blue of the carpeting.

Down below in the subbasement was the Registry, where state-of-the-art monorail minicarriages electronically carried files to each of the eight floors. In 2007, the Registry contained over 750,000 files, some of them dating back to the Security Service's creation in 1909. Of these, 45,000 files related to administration and policy, 50,000 concerned subjects ranging from the Arctic to Zululand, and 85,000 dealt with persons or groups of people who had received "protective advice," including the royal family, cabinet ministers, and the archbishop of Canterbury. The balance of well over half a million files dealt with persons who at some time during almost a century had been the subject of Security Service investigation; many were long dead, but their files remained open. Half of the files had been placed on microfilm and were often given a restricted category to which MI5 staff only had access "for specific research purposes." Personal files were buff colored. In 2007, they numbered over twenty thousand names. Blue files contained intelligence on all Britain's political organizations and its Islamic groups. The top security rating was for the Y files—locked boxes—which contained the most highly classified information on spies and defectors and required the signature of the director-general to be opened.

Millions of pounds sterling had been spent on information technology, some of it made specifically for MI5. One system was called PROMIS. Devised by the specialist software company INSLAW in Washington, D.C., it was designed to help MI5 fast-track suspects. The software could locate the millions of secret documents stored in the Registry. Nevertheless, for all its information technology, MI5 had failed to conquer the threat from al-Qaeda that exploded in all its fury in the London bombings of July 2005.

The day after the attacks, Eliza Manningham-Buller spoke to all her staff in Thames House, her words ringing out, "What we feared would happen has finally happened. It was only a matter of when. We cannot focus on everything because the sheer scale of what we face is daunting. We won't always make the right choices and we recognise we shall have scarce sympathy if we are unable to prevent another atrocity. While we will develop new techniques, new sources and new contacts, much will still be obscure and radicalisation will continue. The al-Qaeda threat to the United Kingdom, to Europe, to the entire world is serious, is growing and will, I believe, be with us for a generation."

Two years later her rallying call would be judged as her acknowledgment that the London bombings were MI5's greatest failure in its prime role as defender of the realm.

ON AN APRIL DAY IN 2007, a number of operations were at various stages in Thames House.

The director of counterterrorism had spent part of his morning studying the latest report from a team of MI5 officers—the Watchers—conducting surveillance in the northern city of Bradford. Their presence was a further indication of the ever-growing threat from Islamic terrorism, whose advocates had moved to the country from the Middle East, Pakistan, and Afghanistan. Many had fought against the Soviets in Afghanistan in the 1980s, and their reminiscences had excited young British-born Muslims. Most came from respectable, hardworking families who had ensured their children went to the mosque and obtained good grades at school, but the arrival of the Afghan veterans, accompanied by radical preachers, had seen a dramatic change within their communities. Osama bin Laden became a hero among their youth, and an increasing number were soon radicalized, the more so after Muslim charities had paid for them to visit Pakistan and travel to its Northwest Frontier, where al-Qaeda had its base.

Hundreds of youngsters returned home filled with the belief they must contribute to bringing fiery Islamism to Britain. They attended Friday prayer meetings where radical preachers took their texts from the International Islamic Front for Jihad Against Jews and Crusaders, which Osama bin Laden had created in 1998. The rantings of the imams sounded as unintelligible as the even louder responses they evoked. In the period immediately preceding 9/11, the preachers became even more outspoken in their support for terrorism. After an occasional visit to a mosque, an MI5 officer would return to his office and send a memo to Scotland Yard's Special Branch hoping that perhaps it might have someone who understood what was being preached, but the Branch, like MI5, was focussed on the IRA. The radical preachers were left to continue their conversion of young Muslims. Soon, every mosque in Britain had its collection boxes to support Islamic causes in Kashmir, Chechnya, and Palestine, and cries from the faithful resounded with an ancient call for jihad, holy war.

Nowhere was it heard more loudly than from the lips of two acknowl-edged leaders of Islamic militancy in Britain: Abu Hamza (in 2008 he continued serving a seven-year jail sentence for promoting terrorism) and Sheikh Omar Bakri, the Syrian-born cleric who founded the ex-tremist al-Muhajiroun organization and had been deported from Saudi Arabia in 1985 for his views. The Home Office granted him sanctuary in Britain after he claimed he was a "political refugee." With Abu Hamza firmly established as the demagogue of the Finsbury Park mosque, Bakri began to operate at street level, cruising the city's Muslim quarters to gather recruits. In no time he boasted he had signed up over seven hundred volunteers to join Osama bin Laden in creating a worldwide caliphate. Bakri also began to post fatwa, religious opinions, in which he warned of death for anyone who cooperated with the intelligence services. Still MI5 took no action. A memo referred to Bakri as "another ranter." Only two years later was he finally deported to wage a war of at-trition over the Internet from his Beirut bolt-hole.

Long before, Hamza's Finsbury Park mosque in Regent's Park, Lon-don, had continued to attract and recruit more Muslims. Zacarias Mous-saoui, the "twentieth hijacker," arrested in America before the attacks of September 11, 2001, had worshipped there, as had Richard Reid, the "shoe bomber," along with Ahmed Ressam, who had been intercepted in December 1999 when he tried to smuggle bomb-making equipment from Canada into the United States to blow up Los Angeles airport dur-ing the millennium celebrations. The 9/11 attacks had not only stunned America and its entire intelligence community but had triggered an alarm bell in MI5. Manningham-Buller had asked her own staff to ur-gently investigate whether their sources in the Muslim communities indicated that the U.S. attacks were a precursor to a similar one in Lon-don.

The one question she repeatedly asked was: Could it happen to Lon-don? Could the carnage be repeated in the capital, striking at the prin-cipal symbols of Britain's hegemony, its global commercial and financial power, and call into question the certainties and beliefs that had con-tinued to survive long after the British Empire had become a fading memory?

"It was catchup time," recalled Annie Machon, a former MI5 counterterrorism officer, to the author. Although the Security Service also found itself confronting civil liberties groups opposed to some of those "catchup" methods. In August 2002, Home Secretary David Blunkett had issued an unprecedented public apology to British Muslims about "information sweeps conducted by MI5 in Muslim communities." Amnesty International protested about "serious violations of human rights of British nationals held in Guantanamo Bay." The criticisms were ignored in Thames House. The answer was to come on July 7, 2005, when British-born Muslim suicide bombers struck in the very center of London, killing fifty-two and leaving seven hundred injured, many of them seriously.

Now, two years later on that April day in 2007, the MI5 Watchers in Bradford had already established that the men they were secretly observing had also been regular worshippers at the Finsbury Park mosque before they had moved to Bradford. Their number included Pakistanis, Tunisians, Moroccans, and Algerians—all united by a common hatred of the West. They had held another of their regular meetings in a dingy-looking house after attending prayers at one of the mosques whose minarets dotted the city skyscape. The group included two halal butchers, a man who ran a taxi service with his cousin, and a bookseller who traded in Islamic texts and pamphlets. It was his business that had caught MI5's attention.

An informer, one of several the Security Service had recruited since the London bombings, had been asked by his case officer to purchase a selection of the most radical booklets and CDs on offer. Fluent in Arabic and Urdu following his crash course in both languages, what the officer discovered was sufficient for him to alert his director. The material was not only inflammatory but had recently arrived in Britain, almost certainly smuggled in by one of the English-born jihadists who regularly traveled between Bradford and Islamabad. With genuine British passports, they passed freely in and out of the country. Upon their return, Immigration officers at Heathrow Airport did not have the linguistic skills to read the booklets, and the CDs were disguised as music discs available at any Pakistani market stall. The messages of hatred were inserted between the tracks. A skilled Pakistani technician would extract the words and transfer them onto another disc. Their message, which the case officer had translated and passed on to the director, along with the booklets, described how to make and release cyanide gas in shopping malls.

The director faced an immediate dilemma. Should the bookseller be arrested at once, or should he be placed under surveillance to see who else could be identified as members of such a plot, which would enable them to be brought to court? The risk of waiting was high. Launching a gas attack was terrifyingly easy. Cyanide compounds in powdered form mixed with acid could create hydrogen cyanide gas, the same gas used in executions. To wait could result in scores, possibly hundreds of innocent people being gassed in a shopping mall. Yet the possibility of foiling the plot and striking a major blow against al-Qaeda's growing infiltration into Britain was compelling.

The director had decided a full-blown surveillance operation must be mounted. The bookseller would go on a watch list, his every coming and going tracked, his every meeting logged, his every conversation recorded. A team of Watchers was assembled. They included two experts from technical support; affectionately known as "the buggers," they were skilled in planting a variety of listening devices: under a suspect's car, on the outer walls of his home and the mosque he attended for Friday prayers, in restaurants where he ate, and at his workplace. The bugs were sensitive enough to pick up whispers and had sufficient range to reach one of the surveillance vans positioned to cast a highly sophisticated electronic net over a wide area.

With the team were three members of another highly specialized unit that had been created after the London bombings. They were recruits from various Muslim communities who had volunteered to help to infiltrate terrorist cells. After two years of difficult and dangerous work, they had become skilled at their task and had worked their way into key positions to provide vital intelligence. The three selected for the Bradford operation were among the very best. Nevertheless, to obtain the kind of information required, they could be forced to partake in some act of terrorism.

"If an asset was arrested, the plan would be to extradite him from custody, telling the police as little as possible why he was there. Sometimes this required the intervention of a chief constable of the arresting officers or even the head of the Scotland Yard Anti-Terrorist Branch. But it was a priority. The asset's usefulness would, of course, be over. He would be debriefed and, if possible, found another job far away from where he had operated," recalled Colin Wallace, a former British Army intelligence officer who had worked with MI5/MI6 in Northern Ireland. There was also the question of when to act upon a piece of information that could save lives but carried the high risk of putting a valuable source's life in danger. The matter was one of many constantly before the director of counterterrorism as he continued to monitor the Bradford surveillance operation.

IN THE MEANTIME, officers also under his command were updating security at places where other attacks could be launched. These included terrorists hiring a private plane from one of the flying fields around London and crash-diving it into Big Ben or the Houses of Parliament. Since the London bombings, RAF fighter-bombers were on "immediate take-off readiness" to be over London within sixty seconds of a plane being spotted as a threat. If it refused the command to leave the area, it risked being shot down. Another threat predicted was a suicide bomber driving a truck of high explosives into Britain's largest nuclear plant, in Cumbria. Guards had a standing order to open fire if such a truck failed to stop. The possibility of a "dirty bomb" created from radioactive rods stolen from a hospital nuclear medical department and wrapped with TNT was another constant concern, which required weekly checks with all those departments.

On that April morning, the latest report from the Watchers in Bradford indicated the cyanide gas plot was still at "the chatter stage." But for how long?

IN SAFETY AND SECURITY, officers continued their steady telephone trawl of contacting the country's forty-eight university campuses to discover the latest number of students who had joined Islamic societies, many of which promoted radical views. In 2006, several former students arrested for plotting to blow up transatlantic airliners had belonged to those societies. One, Anjem Choudray, was a graduate from the University of Surrey before he became a recruiter for al-Muhajiroun (the Emigrants, a radical Islamic organization). Evidence obtained by MI5 had finally led to the organization being proscribed by the home secretary. A student at Brunel University, Dhiren Barot, identified in 2006 as Osama bin Laden's U.K. "commander," was currently serving a forty-year prison sentence for planning terror attacks.

Muslim undergraduates at Oxford, Cambridge, and Imperial College London—universities with a long association with the Ministry of Defense—were subjected to special scrutiny. Some had been secretly photographed by MI5 officers distributing leaflets with such titles as "Jihad in Britain" and "Blair and Bush are the Most Wanted Terrorists." Guest speakers at Islamic society meetings invariably began with a standard disclaimer, "We are not here to promote Osama bin Laden, though we support him, which is not a crime. But we recognize his leadership and we ask: How can he be a terrorist? What defines what is wrong and what is right? Certainly not our repressive government and its Security Services." They had been advised to use the words by a human rights lawyer.

Stored in the antiterrorism department were files of al-Qaeda sympathizers who had tried to enlist in MI5, offering their services as translators for some of the ninety languages and regional dialects now spoken in Britain. Three of those who had tried to join were British-born Pakistani police officers serving with Scotland Yard. In 2006, they had made visits to Pakistan, traveling to the Northwest Frontier, where Osama bin Laden had established his latest headquarters. On their return the officers had been closely questioned by MI5 officers and denied any links to terrorism, but their names were placed on a watch list. An MI5-led raid on a suspected supporter's house had unearthed an - English-language translation of an al-Qaeda tactical manual, *The Management of Savagery*, written by one of al-Qaeda's strategists. It urged, "Infiltrate the police forces, the armed services, the different political parties, the petroleum companies, private security companies and broadcasters like the BBC." Inside was a handwritten note, "To be used when recruiting at universities."

The London *Daily Mail*, with good connections to the Security Service, claimed that one police officer had been in possession of Internet images of beheadings and roadside bombings in Iraq. "He claimed he was trying to 'enhance' the debate about the war. Classified intelligence reports raising concerns about a police officer's background cannot be used to justify his dismissal," reported the newspaper.

Omar Altimimi, jailed for nine years for hoarding manuals on how to carry out car bombings, had applied to work as a janitor in the Greater Manchester police force before his arrest, and there was growing concern that terrorists were trying to infiltrate other public-sector organizations. Since the London bombings, vetting procedures had tightened, but background checks depended on overseas agencies in Pakistan, Africa, and the Middle East to do them locally. There was increasing anxiety many of these organizations had already been infiltrated by al-Qaeda and allowed radical Islamists to go undetected.

Meanwhile, MI5 had launched its own recruiting drive in 2007, advertising for the first time in the London subway and on buses for intelligence officers and support staff. It needed five hundred additional men and women to cope with the expanding terrorist threat. Linguists were still a priority, followed by surveillance officers and technology experts. Ads had also been placed in women's health clubs. Those who applied found themselves facing six months of security checks. Many felt the intrusion into their privacy was unacceptable and withdrew their applications.

MI6 had also launched a campaign to fill its vacancies for case officers, targeting officers, and reports officers, "Women university graduates who possess a high degree of personal integrity, interpersonal skills and are resourceful will be most welcome to apply." A profile had been created of a "typical officer" called Isobel. In the advertisement she was young and married. MI6 gave her breaks for maternity leave, allowed her to take her husband and two children to work in Asia and paid for her children to go to an international school, and let her work a four-day week. The claims brought cynical smiles from real-life intelligence officers. "Isobel was created by somebody who had never worked in intelligence," said one.

The Mossad had also started recruiting. Its advertisement in a number of Jewish newspapers was simply stated. "The Mossad has openings. Only in your heart will you know if you are capable of thinking differently, of doing more than you could." It was far more effective than the outcome of creating "Isobel." By January 2007, over six hundred applicants—half of them women—had responded.

Unlike any other intelligence service, the Mossad expected its women to be prepared to use sexual entrapment in their work. Meir Amit, the service's former director-general, explained to the author what was involved, "Sleeping with the enemy. Using sex for the good of her country. All Mossad women know the risks involved. To do what is asked of them takes a special courage. If she is married, as many are, she must betray her marriage vow. But she is not a prostitute. She is living up to the ideal of her chosen profession—intelligence work."

An example of what was expected of a female Mossad agent was described by Cheryl Ben-Tov. Born in Orlando, Florida, she was recruited a week after she returned from her honeymoon in Spain. Only on the flight home did her husband, Ofer, tell her he was a senior Israeli intelligence officer. Like all Mossad recruits, she underwent a series of tests to evaluate her social skills and her IQ. Mossad psychologists taught her she must trust no one except her colleagues. She was tutored in deceit, learning to use methods that violated all she had once believed in. She learned how to draw a gun while sitting in a chair and how to memorize as many names as possible as they flashed across a small screen. She was shown how to pack her Beretta inside her pants and how to cut a concealed opening in her skirt for easy access to the handgun. She learned how to break into a hotel room and steal documents from an office. She used sex to pick up a male tourist in a nightclub, steal his wallet, then slip him a fast-acting drug developed by Mossad chemists consisting of a cocktail of amphetamines that would leave no trace in the bloodstream. The intention was to leave the victim, when he recovered, believing he had been robbed.

For three months a team of Mossad instructors refined her skills to use sex to coerce, seduce, and dominate. Other skills were drummed into her. She learned how to use cotton wadding in her cheeks to change the shape of her face, how to steal a car, how to pose as a drunk, and how to create a dead letter box—a hiding place, such as under a tree, where a coded message could be left by prior arrangement. The Mossad's favorite way to indicate a message was waiting to be collected was by painting a small mark on a preselected lamppost or placing a small stone beside a grave. Another technique Cheryl learned was to sit on a park bench "in a casual and relaxed way," she recalled, "then I would pin a note under the bench and leave." Her Mossad trainer, who had been watching her from a distance, would later retrieve the message: a classic dead letter success.

After graduating she traveled to Madrid, returning to the hotel where she had honeymooned with her husband, but this time she went with an instructor. Her appearance altered by the disguises she had been taught, she was sure none of the hotel staff recognized her from her previous visit. She carried out scores of missions for the Mossad before she became an instructor at its training school in the Israeli seaside resort of Herzliya, close to Tel Aviv.

Ari Ben-Menashe, a former adviser to the Israeli government on counterterrorism, has painted a graphic portrait of what the Mossad expected from its recruits, "The work calls for calm, clear, farsighted judgment and a balanced outlook. People want to join the Mossad for all kinds of reasons. There is the so-called glamour of being a spy. Some like the idea of adventure. Some think joining will enhance their status, small people who want to be big. A few want the secret power they believe the Mossad will give them. None of these are acceptable reasons for joining."

IN G9C, THE SECTION in MI5's/(international Counterterrorism) G-Branch that specializes in tracking down threats from al-Qaeda suicide bombers, the search continued to try to establish the existence of videos made by bombers waiting to strike. The possibility of such a library had been raised after the tape of one of the London suicide bombers, Mohammed Sidique Khan, bore striking similarities to those made by the two English-born Muslims who blew up a Tel Aviv nightclub in Israel two years earlier. All had been filmed against a wall decorated with identical geometric designs that G9C officers discovered were favored only by young jihadists in Britain. All three suicide bombers had also worn headbands identical to those displayed by other radicals who had returned to Britain from Pakistan and had boasted on Islamic Web sites they were ready to die. A detailed examination of the tapes offered further clues. All used phrases in common, and each bomber appeared angry, as if he wanted to maintain order within his own psychological universe and what he was doing was a response to a threat to his own culture, his own people, his own life. In each case the bomber's eyes showed symptoms of being drugged, but MI5's pharmacologists found it impossible to decide what drugs had been used. A trusted Muslim source had raised the possibility that Khan's video had been made a year before the 2005 bombings and had been stored—ready to be passed to al-Jazeera, the all-news Arab television channel, after his death. More certain was that, like the tapes of the other two suicide bombers, Khan's speech had a remoteness about it. The delivery was flat and bore no relation to the words spoken. "They were all like actors who are working from the same script," a source told the author, but where those tapes were remained as elusive as ever.

IN 2007, THE EIGHT FLOORS OF Thames House were divided into branches. A-Branch contained operational support units, including A1A, Technical Operations, which specialized in covert entry—burgling premises to place bugging devices—and using CCTV. Its work was shared with A1F, which dealt with long-term surveillance of embassies, foreign trade missions, offices of various foreign banks, and travel agents who specialized in trips to the Middle East and Asia. From a small office at the back of A-Branch worked film and still cameramen who specialized in covert photography, and locksmiths and safecrackers trained to pick every known lock.

On a separate floor was D-Branch. Its officers dealt with nonterrorist organizations such as crime families and drug-running operations. Christopher Benbow, a drug dealer, had come to D7's notice when he was overheard boasting in a London nightclub in 2006 that he knew where the world's most accessible nuclear facility had stored more than two tons of enriched uranium and weapons-grade plutonium behind a rusty barbed-wire fence protected by a handful of guards. Once a jewel in the former Soviet arsenal, the National Science Institute at Vinca, ten miles south of the Serbian capital, Belgrade, was closed in 1984 and its reactor switched off. Since then the forty-eight-acre site had fallen into decay. MI5's international terrorism branch, G2, had checked. Benbow had been telling the truth. There was only a caretaker staff at the site, and while death from fatal radiation sickness for those stealing the fissionable material would be questioned, the facility was still "a dream target for terrorists."

The man Benbow had spoken to was Gilbert Wynter, an enforcer for Britain's most powerful crime family. When he was not carrying out the orders of its godfather, Terry Adams, Wynter was always on the lookout for opportunities to increase the family's estimated £200 million fortune it had acquired from drugs, money laundering, and trafficking in foreign girls for the thriving sex market in Britain. Wynter had a fearful reputation: He had once butchered a man with a samurai sword and had served a five-year prison sentence before Adams appointed him as his enforcer and helped to make him the most feared man in the country's underworld. Wynter reported what Benbow had said about the Vinca site to the godfather.

Terence George Adams dressed and spoke like the chairman of an international corporation; he wore custom-made Armani suits and had a voice that rarely rose above a modulated tone. He lived in a mansion in the exclusive Barnsbury suburb in north London, where Tony and Cherie Blair had once occupied a Victorian home. His home was tastefully decorated and filled with antique furniture and objets d'art from Paris, Rome, and Moscow—cities where his criminal activities had earned him respect. His cultured tastes in art and rare books and his liking for fine food and wine enhanced his image. He rented a box close to the Royal Enclosure at Ascot races where he and his wife, Ruth, entertained financial highfliers from the City of London. Both were devout Roman Catholics; the bishops of the church were regular guests at their table, and Adams gave lavishly to church charities. Their wealthy neighbors, even if they suspected how Adams made his money, waved respectfully as he drove past them in his favorite black London taxi, one of twelve vintage cars he owned.

For thirty of his fifty-two years, Adams had built his empire, first from extortion rackets in the London produce markets, then by organizing armed robberies and trafficking in drugs and humans. His organization was known in the underworld as the A-Team, dealing swiftly with rivals who tried to usurp its position. Adams was rumored to have authorized over twenty killings, but not one had been traced directly back to him, furthering his air of invincibility and fueling the underworld's belief that Adams had detectives, lawyers, and prosecutors on his payroll. Anyone considered to be an informer was likely to be left permanently crippled.

By the year 2000, Adams was head of a family organization with links to Colombian drug barons, Mexican criminals, and the New York Mafia. They all helped him to flood London with high-grade cocaine.

Christopher Benbow was one of Terry Adams's distributors. His proposal that "the Boss" could become even richer by dealing in nuclear material intrigued Adams enough not to dismiss it in the way he had disregarded other proposals as "fool's talk." What the godfather did not know was that Scotland Yard's senior officers had held the first of their meetings with MI5 under the chairmanship of the Security Service's deputy director, Jonathan Evans, to discuss a plan to end Adams's operation. Evans had made his reputation with the Security Service in fighting the IRA and the Belfast criminal families who armed and sheltered them. He had proposed to the Yard detectives that a combination of officers from D-Branch and A-Branch would create a special unit to obtain the evidence to destroy the Adams organization. Evans had warned it would need months of patient undercover work to achieve this. The ultra-secret operation would be code-named Trinity.

By the summer of 2006, a team of officers from both branches was ready to move. They rented a house near Adams's mansion. Posing as mechanics, two surveillance technicians replaced the regular service engineers who checked Adams's fleet of cars. The pair placed listening devices in the mansion's master bedroom, the adjoining gymnasium where Adams performed his daily workout, and the lounge where he met criminal associates who came to pay their respects and hand over large sums of money from drug sales. While Adams had the mansion regularly swept by a private security firm for any bugs, the MI5 team was satisfied it would have required all the furnishings to be removed before their devices were discovered. Some of the bugs were no larger than a pinhead; others were concealed in door hinges and under-floor heating vents.

Recordings built up a picture of Adams's activities: how he would franchise out to other gangsters the right to say they were his associates while they ran their own criminal activities. Being part of the Adams organization guaranteed them respect, but those who used the connection without having first paid a substantial fee were harshly treated: One local gang leader in Essex had his legs broken and would spend the remainder of his life in a wheelchair, which Adams actually purchased so that his victim would "have a permanent reminder of how he had stepped out of line," one tape recorded. Other tapes contained details of where drugs were stored. Still, Christopher Benbow's proposal that Adams should go into the business of selling nuclear materials from the Vinca site did not produce a response. Adams sent a message to Benbow, through Gilbert Wynter, that he was still thinking it over.

Meanwhile, D7 officers, posing as middlemen with links to al-Qaeda, had used the information on the Adams transcripts to begin negotiating with Benbow for the nuclear material so he could be arrested for trafficking. He confirmed he had access to strontium 90, a radioactive isotope and an important element in nuclear fallout. He wanted a million pounds sterling for a dozen ounces of the lethal material, the type stored at the Vinca facility. Nuclear scientists told the D7 officers that was sufficient to create havoc in a city the size of London. Benbow was asked to provide a small sample of what he had to offer. He refused, saying he was not an expert in handling such material, and asked them to deposit half of the money in his numbered account in a Credit Suisse branch in Switzerland as an act of "good faith." Then, while the D7 director considered the next move, Benbow left London. The D7 officers believed he had gone home to Tampa, Florida. Two days after they arrived there, they spotted Benbow meeting a group of Arabs on a yacht in a Miami marina. Photographs of the encounter were taken and transmitted to London. The men with Benbow were on file as al-Qaeda contacts.

In the weeks that followed, Benbow traveled to Bogotá, Colombia, before flying back to Eastern Europe. The original D7 officers had been joined by those from G-Branch's G2P unit—which specialized in nuclear counterproliferation—and officers from G9C, who dealt with Islamic extremists. In Budapest, Benbow met with members of Europe's leading crime family, the Rising Sun.

The Rising Sun specialized in money laundering, contract hits, and drug trafficking and was run by Semyon Mogilevich who, with the help of the newspaper tycoon Robert Maxwell had obtained an Israeli passport, which enabled him to travel around the world to set up no fewer than fifty legitimate companies, fronted by surrogates, in places where money and a no-questions policy were opposite sides of the same coin: Cyprus, Lichtenstein, and the Cayman Islands. In 2007, David Dastych, a former CIA officer who had been tracking Mogilevich, told the author he had obtained "good evidence that through those front companies, Mogilevich has begun to place large amounts of money in the U.S. trying to influence the 2008 elections."

MI5 knew the organization had long been trying to traffic in nuclear

materials, and for the intelligence officers trailing Benbow there was a
more pressing question: Had Benbow been trying to cut a deal with the
Rising Sun? Yet once more he was on the move, this time to Spain's
Costa del Sol to meet two members of the Terry Adams organization.
The meeting had taken place in Marbella, the Spanish resort that had
become a haven for drug and arms dealers. At the meeting on one of
the luxury yachts moored in the raffish Puerto Banús marina, Benbow
had again been secretly recorded saying he had been offered "a load of
drugs" from a "good source." He wanted the Adams family to "unload
the drugs" for him on a fifty-fifty deal. He finally revealed the drugs
were from al-Qaeda, his payment for providing the terrorist organization with the nuclear materials. Now he was ready to sell the drugs to
Adams.

The Adams gang members became suspicious, sensing that despite
his heated protest—all recorded on tape—Benbow might be part of a
police sting operation. While the drug dealer had been moving around
South America, Terry Adams had been finally arrested in London, leading to his trial and a seven-year prison sentence for his multifarious
criminal activities.

Failing to make a deal in Marbella, Benbow flew back to Tampa. Waiting for him at the airport were FBI agents who charged him with trafficking in nuclear materials. In February 2007, Benbow was sentenced
to life imprisonment; he would serve his time in America's top-security
prison. Benbow's life sentence was overturned on appeal and he is currently in Butler Federal Penitentiary in Terre Haute, Indiana, awaiting
retrial.

AN UNEXPECTED RESULT from the Benbow operation was the discovery of a plot by al-Qaeda to crash the Internet in Britain, an act
that would have effectively closed down the London Stock Exchange
and brought total chaos to the country's international trade. The country would have come to a standstill with airports, seaports, railroads, and
communications systems no longer able to operate.

At the outset of the Benbow surveillance, a two-man team from A4,
MI5's Internet surveillance unit, had been assigned to work with GCHQ.
Its seven thousand staffers monitor all electronic traffic in and out of
Britain; from its doughnut-shaped headquarters near Cheltenham, it han-
dles billions of messages a day. Among them are those "tasked" for inter-
ception by MI5 and MI6. Benbow had gone on GCHQ's interest list.

The dozens of e-mails Benbow sent to his contacts trying to off-load the fissionable material were routed initially through the Telehouse Europe building in London's Docklands, which handled all the country's commercial Internet traffic. Messages on the GCHQ interest list were automatically sent from Telehouse Europe to Cheltenham. In Benbow's case GCHQ copied them to the A4 team.

One of Benbow's first e-mails had been sent to a Web site, one of the millions stored on the Telehouse computers. The message had been redirected from the first site to a second one not known to the A4 team. After a search that involved MI5's H1 unit, whose officers dealt with information technology, the second Web site was pinpointed as operating from a house in Ealing Broadway, a suburb of London and home to a large Middle Eastern population. Some of them were already on an MI5 watch list, but the operator of the second Web site was not.

While D7 officers had continued to track Benbow's movements, an electronic watch was placed on the Web site operating from the Ealing address. The house phone was interrupted, allowing for a "bugger" from Technical Operations to pose as a British Telecom engineer checking a problem. He installed a bug in the phone that was powerful enough to hear a conversation anywhere in the house. Another surveillance officer had rented a room across the street to use the electronic equipment known as the "vacuum cleaner" to gather up the conversations. Once a day they were collected by another officer and brought to Thames House for analysis.

A group of terrorists, after carrying out a reconnaissance of Telehouse Europe, were recorded in the house intending to storm the building and blow themselves up with sufficient explosives strapped to their bodies to topple it. With the planned attack only days away—coincidentally when Benbow had failed to enlist the support of the Adams gang in Marbella—officers from Scotland Yard's Anti-Terrorist Branch raided the house in Ealing Broadway and arrested the plotters.

THE SECOND FLOOR OF THAMES HOUSE included scientists and technicians who created new gadgets to track suspects. Displayed behind a glass-fronted case were some of the devices acquired from other services. They included a king-sized cigarette loaded with a single .22 caliber bullet developed by the CIA. The cigarette had been field-tested on a German double agent in postwar Germany during the notorious MK-ULTRA experiments, a secret CIA program to control human behavior and find ways to carry out assassinations. The cigarette bullet, while not a part of the main program, was devised as a sideline by CIA chemists. After killing the double agent, the weapon was "deemed fit for purpose" but never actually used again.

A tool kit containing a file, two cutting blades, and a grinding tool had been devised by the Stasi, the former East German intelligence service, for insertion in an agent's rectum. The MI5 researchers had tried to adapt the tube to carry microfilm, but it was still uncomfortable to use. A more workable device was the CIA's "exploding flour," intended to cause "destructive mishaps" when used to bake bread or cakes. The results were passed to MI6, whose own technicians used the idea to create explosive carrots and cabbages as leave-behind weapons in Eastern Europe during the cold war.

The third floor of Thames House housed the open-plan operations room for major emergencies, like the 2005 London bombings and the hunt for the 2006 bombers who had attempted to blow up transatlantic flights. It was maintained at a state of "battle readiness" for the key personnel needed to handle a significant threat. Plasma screens, whiteboards, and maps were pinned to the walls. There were workstations for the analysts and linguists. Other areas housed behaviorists, psychologists and psychiatrists—collectively known as "the specialists"—who created profiles of suspected terrorists. The profilers had their own section with desk consoles linking them to their counterparts in Scotland Yard, MI6, GCHQ, and, if need be, the country's regional police forces.

4

The Enemy Within the Gate

Since the War on Terrorism was declared by President Bush in 2001, the number of legal advisers in MI5 had grown from a small number until, in 2008, they numbered over one hundred men and women. Some had been headhunted at law school, others selected from legal firms in the City of London. All were handpicked not only for their legal skills but for intellectual precision and a highly sophisticated grasp of Britain's constantly changing legal system. Several had a grounding in European law and that of Islam.

At their first interview, lawyers were told they must have an aptitude for "logical and lateral thinking." Officially they would be working for the Home Office or Ministry of Defense. In reality their office would be in Thames House, working "within the framework of the Official Secrets Act." In 2008, the starting salary was £50,000 with regular raises. An essential condition of employment was that they should not reveal they worked for the Security Service. To add to the cloak-and-dagger element, their interview before MI5's senior legal adviser ended with the reminder "Discretion is what protects the Service and you," recalled one young attorney. He failed his final interview when he said he would be uneasy if he had to confront ethical matters.

The lawyers were there to shield MI5 from the equally skilled attorneys who operated among the multiplicity of caveats of human rights legislation. Increasingly those complex laws had been used to fiercely challenge the power of government in Britain and had led to lengthy court battles over extradition and basic democratic rights. A number of verdicts had been appealed to the highest court in the land, the House of Lords, and then to Europe's Court of Human Rights. Some cases had taken years to resolve. There had been public anger at the freeing of some suspects and outrage at the vast sums of money spent to win their freedom. MI5 had come under increasing criticism for failing to present reliable court evidence, and the role of its lawyers was to ensure that all its operations were as legally sound as possible to avoid accusations of wrongful arrests.

Yet, despite all its legal protection, the Security Service continued to fail. During 2006, its security and counterespionage branch had received what it later termed "credible intelligence" that a house in south London, occupied by a Muslim family, contained a cyanide bomb capable of "killing thousands of Londoners," subsequently reported one newspaper. Over two hundred Scotland Yard officers, many armed, a Chemical Biological Warfare Unit, and MI5 agents raided the house in Forest Gate. No bomb, nor any evidence of terrorist activity, was found. The building had been wrecked. The cost of refurbishing the family home came out of the Single Unified Vote, the secret budget for both MI5 and MI6. In June 2008, Scotland Yard confirmed it had paid £210,000 to refurbish the building and £60,000 compensation to the family.

Criticism over the operation led to Director-General Dame Eliza Manningham-Buller offering to resign. Home Secretary John Reid did not accept it; he was quoted as saying, "These things happen." A few months later he announced his own departure, shortly before Tony Blair ended his ten years as prime minister. The Forest Gate fiasco was not the only cloud hanging over Manningham-Buller. She knew that a final government report by the Intelligence and Security Committee (ISC) into the London bombings of 2005 would hold MI5 culpable. When it was published in March 2007, the criticism was damning. Page after page listed the failures of MI5: the failure of its Watchers to conduct "continued professional surveillance" on two of the suspected bombers; its failure to pay "close attention" to "credible information" the FBI had provided after arresting an al-Qaeda operative in New York who had admitted an attack on London was being planned; its failure to keep Scotland Yard's Anti-Terrorist Branch (now the Counter Terrorism Command) fully informed of the impending threat; its failure to inform the provincial police force where the suspects lived of details which MI5 had uncovered twelve months before the bombings. On every page the damning conclusions of failure were catalogued.

The ISC report raised serious questions. How could the Security

Service have failed to predict a threat far greater than that ever posed by the IRA? Why had it failed to realize al-Qaeda was infinitely more dangerous than the Irish terrorists, far better organized and protected within its own communities? Where was the "risk management" for which MI5 was supposedly famed? It had not helped that Eliza Manningham-Buller had told government ministers MI5 "could not be certain it knew the identities of no more than half al-Qaeda suspects in Britain who are linked to the organisation." She likened al-Qaeda to "a piece of crochet. It is complex, interwoven and impenetrable. You think you have a grip on one bit of it, then suddenly the whole thing unravels in your hand."

Within MI5 the issue of training was raised by senior career officers who felt they often had to show inexperienced recruits how to do the job. Annie Machon, who had worked in counterterrorism, said her "basic training" had only been a "couple of weeks."

One of the most difficult jobs was learning surveillance. A minimum of two teams, four officers each, was needed to follow a suspect on foot, two up front, two trailing behind. Across the street was a backup of four more officers. From time to time the teams switched places, to lessen the chance of being suspected by the target, on the command of a senior officer directing the operation through a throat mike linked to the teams' microchip earpieces. A veteran of such operations told the author, "Multiply the number of suspects to be watched by the number of terrorists involved in the London bombings and we just didn't have enough properly trained officers for the job. It becomes even harder when a target is driving. A minimum of four cars are needed in interchange positions on the road. Each vehicle needs a different number of people in a car—say, two men, a man and a woman, a single male driver, two women. This helps reduce the target's suspicion he is being followed. For the London bombings we would have needed sixty people working twelve-hour shifts. That would be one hundred and twenty officers a day, working every day for weeks, even months."

It was not only the shortage of an adequate number of properly trained surveillance teams that caused debate within the Security Service. The analysts blamed the failure of counterterrorism officers to uncover sufficient evidence to allow what one analyst called "at least a sensible prediction of what was afoot. It is very easy to slip into the fallacy of thinking that the failure to find evidence is evidence of its absence. This is clearly what happened in the London bombings."

Eliza Manningham-Buller's previous skills at news management—she would dine a carefully chosen national newspaper editor or the BBC security correspondent to disclose just enough detail to give a favorable spin on some recent MI5 operation, and charm malleable journalists with her stories of successful operations—left her sheltering behind the admission, "Further attacks by Islamic extremists are unavoidable. The reality is that we will not stop them all."

The cloud of failure settled ever darker over Thames House and touched the lives of everyone who worked there. The relationship between the Security Service and the outside world, never easy, reached a new low. Pointed questions were asked in Parliament as to how MI5 had produced such a catastrophic failure. There were calls for a reassessment of what MI5 stood for and even more calls for Eliza Manningham-Buller to resign. On April 20, 2007, she did so, driven for the last time by her Scotland Yard driver from Thames House. It was an inglorious end to a career that had looked so promising all those years ago when she joined MI5.

ELIZABETH LYDIA MANNINGHAM-BULLER, Eliza to family and friends, was born on July 14, 1948. The war in Europe had ended in May 1945, leaving the people of Britain still slowly recovering three years later from their exhaustion. Undernourishment remained a problem: Meat, cheese, sugar, and tea were strictly limited; the year Eliza was born the bacon ration was still one ounce a week per person; bread, which had escaped being controlled during the five years of war, was now rationed by the new Labour government. Bombed-out buildings were everywhere, and the grime of destruction permeated furniture, clothes, skin, and hair. London, like all the country's major cities, had rat-infested slums, and the stench of pollution hung like an endless pall above industrialized areas. Over a third of the nation's twelve million houses had no bathtub or hot water. There was insufficient coal to fuel the power stations. The black market thrived.

Despite that, the guns were silent, the bombers grounded, the warships at anchor, the searchlights switched off, and the soldiers, sailors, and airmen were wearing their cheap demobilization suits. It was a time for the children of the Depression, who had come of age overseas, to begin their journeys into civilian life; young veterans and their fiancées married in the thousands, glad to have survived injury and joined together in a passion their parents had never publicly shown. They held hands in the theaters as they watched *Brief Encounter* and *Kind Hearts and Coronets,* and afterward went to a Lyons Corner House for tea and toast. It was a time of a new language: Youngsters were called "teenagers" after the phrase had crossed the Atlantic; shiploads of GIs returning home spoke Cockney rhyming slang and promised all the girls they left behind they would return. In London's Fleet Street, the newspapers ran articles about what the future held, saying that while "readjustment" was inevitable, it could be solved by making a happy home. The only difference was finding a home in the bombed-out streets of the capital and all the other cities that bore the ravages of war.

A quarter of London lay in ruins, and the erection of ten thousand Nissen huts, which had billeted troops before they set sail for the beaches of Normandy, had barely met the housing needs. Newlyweds were squeezed into their parents' homes listening to the wireless reports from across the Atlantic about American brides dressed in the New Look, while their sisters in England had to make do with one dress a year, four ounces of knitting wool, and two yards of material—enough to make one-third of a petticoat or one-fifth of a nightgown. Victory, proclaimed a speaker at London's Hyde Park Corner—the traditional home of protest—had brought survival, but little else. Then came the terrible winter of 1946–47 when Eliza's parents, like millions of others, found themselves living in temperatures below zero from one month to the next as blizzards piled layer upon layer of record-breaking snowfalls across the country. England was gripped in frozen paralysis: Industry closed down; electricity was limited to five hours a day; unemployment rose to six million.

Few people realized that was also the time when world leadership began to move from the dying British Empire to the muscular power of the United States. It started when President Harry Truman, in July 1946, signed a congressional bill authorizing a fifty-year loan of $3.75 billion to His Majesty's government to liquidate America's obligation to rebuilding the United Kingdom after the war (the loan, with accrued interest, was finally paid off in 2007). In accepting the money, Britain, once proud and expansionist and beholden to no nation, bent its knee in gratitude for its dollar transfusion after a six-year struggle against Nazi Germany. All else followed: the acceptance that America was the first postwar superpower, and with it the dominance of the Central Intelligence Agency as the largest and best-equipped secret service in the world.

The government had decided that high-rise apartments were the answer to the housing problem. There were protests on the streets by couples who found themselves transplanted from their family homes to live in the grim structures. Their anger was not assuaged when the leading Labour Party thinker, Evan Durbin, announced, "These places are good for selective breeding."

Meanwhile, MI5 was in a state of transition. Hundreds of employees, who had hunted down Nazi spies and collaborators in the blacked-out streets, were returned to civilian life. Others were posted to military units in Occupied Germany to hunt war criminals and identify Nazi intelligence officers.

By the time Eliza was born, a wartime ally, the Soviet Union, had begun to cast its own shadow over Europe. The first wind of the cold war had started to blow.

In Moscow, Stalin had delivered the first of his hard-line speeches to a huge rally in Red Square, in which he denounced democratic coexistence and promised he would lead a worldwide revolution of the proletariat. Truman had responded by telling Congress that America would "meet our obligations to the free world." His words became known as the Truman Doctrine, a determination to "roll back" Russia to its prewar borders. From Moscow came the first serious riposte: blocking road and rail traffic between West Berlin and West Germany. Britain and the United States responded with an airlift into West Berlin using the city's two airports, Templehof in the American sector and Gatow in the British. West Berlin was home to two and a half million people, and keeping them alive needed four thousand tons of supplies a day—requiring the landing of one plane every minute and forty-six seconds around the clock. It had never been done before in the history of aviation: Coal would be flown in to keep the city's ovens and lights burning. With the overloaded planes came the spies, turning the city into the first postwar capital for intelligence gathering. In London, among those who closely followed events and gave evidence to the government on how to avoid confrontation with the Russians was Eliza's father.

He was Reginald Manningham-Buller, a minister in the Churchill wartime government before becoming attorney general and Lord Chancellor. Eliza grew up, she later said, as "one of the best informed children in the country just by listening." Her father had been dubbed with the unflattering sobriquet of Bullying-Manners, which was attached to Eliza—a chubby child who became a plump teenager, a weight problem that would follow her through life—starting when she went to school with Princess Anne at Benenden, one of England's most prestigious private academies. Eliza's privileged education gave her entrance to Oxford, where she studied English at Lady Margaret Hall. She also impressed her adviser with a shrewd analysis of the growing threat Communism posed to world peace. At the dinner table her father said, "The enemy is inside our gate." It was a phrase that Eliza would use decades later in her own description of al-Qaeda.

In her final year at Oxford, Eliza had a career interview. She had thought of teaching. Her adviser asked if she would like to do "something more interesting like working for the government in an unusual capacity." She went home and discussed it with her father. He said: "No, absolutely not. We don't need a spy in the family!" She returned to Oxford for her final semester and took part in the college production of *Cinderella,* playing the Fairy Godmother (by 2007 she was godmother to thirty children).

After Oxford, she taught at the exclusive Queen's Gate school in London. Her pupils included the future celebrity television chef Nigella Lawson. Later MI5 also "approached" her, but Nigella's father, then the chancellor of the exchequer, had given his daughter similar advice, "Steer clear of the intelligence people."

IN THE 1970S, MI5 WAS on a recruiting drive to deal with the threat of domestic Communism; over fifty thousand citizens were filed in the Registry as Communist Party members. Career officers who had been let go at the end of the war were recalled to MI5's new headquarters at Leconfield House near Hyde Park, but soon overcrowding became a constant problem and substations sprang up around the city. That inevitably led to competing fiefdoms and a culture where information was not always shared. People often did not know exactly who did what. This was especially true in counterintelligence; agents used to working under deep cover on their own were reluctant to share with other departments what they had discovered. An ingrained suspicion of Whitehall did not help, particularly toward Labour politicians.

The recruiting drive focused on universities like Cambridge and Oxford. Both were turning out graduates who had returned from the war and received the free higher education promised to them by the Labour government. Young men from Welsh coal-mining families and women who came from farming stock had acquired a maturity during their university years and recognized that a career in intelligence would give them an insider's view of how the world was developing and the role they could play in shaping it. The shrewd MI5 recruiters appealed to the patriotism of those they approached, and the phrase "Do it for king and country" was often a clincher. Joining the Security Service would not match the financial terms that industry or the banking world offered, but the job would be far more interesting than studying balance sheets. As the process of intelligence collection itself became more sophisticated—phone tapping and eavesdropping—the caliber of recruits became higher: Engineers, electronic experts, and scientists signed on after being selected by campus instructors who acted as talent spotters. The arrival of graduates at MI5 gave the Security Service a group of officers with analytical reasoning and the ability to act calmly under pressure in operations that were anything but calm.

While MI6 operated a long-established number of written and psychological tests, including weekends spent at some country retreat with members of the Civil Service Selection Board to "see how a chap would fit in," recalled Lord Carver, chief of the Defense staff, MI5 preferred its own talent-spotting methods. Stella Rimington would recall that in those postwar days "recruitment was mainly through friends and contacts—the 'tap on the shoulder' style. It was a fairly mysterious process, and young people who signed on were told not to tell their wives—and some men never let on to their wives what they did."

There was one area that was never oversubscribed: Transcriptions. Scores of well-bred women typists and clerks were needed to type secretly taped conversations for careful storage, and only those with special clearance handled the Y transcripts. From time to time a young woman was promoted to another part of A-Branch, such as the Watchers or the Technical Operations department. Both units tracked enemy spies with the few gadgets available, mostly a variety of telephone-tapping devices. Even more exciting for the daughter of a wealthy family was to be promoted to C- or D-Branch, which dealt with sabotage and secret operations. Finally, for a young woman who liked traveling, E-Branch offered an opportunity to work at MI5 stations around the empire in Hong Kong, Singapore, New Delhi, Canberra, Washington, Ottawa, Bermuda, and Johannesburg. There was a long-held belief that only those who had slept with senior officers were given the choicest postings.

NOWHERE WITHIN MI5 did anyone suspect that an unprecedented scandal, deeply buried, was moving slowly but inexorably to the surface. It involved Sir Roger Hollis, who after ten years as director-general had resigned. Few lamented his departure. "Authoritarian" and "as cold as a bank manager refusing a loan" were two of the judgments. His harshest critics were the service's counterintelligence officers, over Hollis's reluctance to focus more clearly on the KGB infiltration of Britain's trade unions and the Labour Party. Each time Hollis had smiled his Cheshire Cat smile and said, "Let them run a little longer. Time is on our side," according to Peter Wright, a veteran MI5 officer since 1955.

With Hollis's departure in 1965, the suspicions continued. Was he a Soviet mole? Initially the idea was dismissed by Hollis's successor, Martin Furnival Jones. He later admitted that if the whispering campaign continued and was proven to be baseless, it would do serious long-term damage to the Security Service. Nevertheless, a group of career officers, led by Wright, pored over Hollis's personal files, looking for any clue of a contact with the KGB. Was it possible that the son of a bishop, who had risen through the ranks, was secretly recruited in the 1930s when he had been in China working for the British American Tobacco Company? Wright believed it was, but there was no proof to support his suspicion. The only question in Hollis's long career was over his affair with his secretary. A check on her background showed she was no more than her file claimed: the daughter of a businessman with no known connection to any Communists or, for that matter, Fascists.

The internal inquiries might have ended, but Wright, later to become assistant director of MI5, let the London station chief of the CIA know, "We are ninety-nine percent certain that Sir Roger was a Soviet spy." The claim was sent directly in the U.S. Embassy overnight diplomatic pouch to the State Department in Washington. From there it was hand-carried to President Lyndon Baines Johnson by John Alex McCone, the director of Central Intelligence. After reading the station chief's report, Johnson ordered McCone to carry out an unprecedented investigation "into the whole of this British intelligence setup. MI5, MI6, the lot." McCone ordered two senior agents to London. They were given full access to MI5 and MI6 after claiming they were there to establish common ground to fight the KGB. Their report, later copied to MI5 and MI6, produced a furious reaction for its suggestion that both services had been penetrated by the KGB. Martin Furnival Jones felt "a sense of great betrayal," while in Washington, McCone ordered, according to a CIA memo, "a careful cooling-off period of all but the essential contacts we need to have with the SIS and MI5."

In a last attempt to uncover Hollis, Peter Wright headed a joint MI5/MI6 investigation into the KGB's alleged penetration. It produced no evidence that Hollis was a Soviet double agent—though the claim has persisted to this day. Long before then, Hollis had died at his home in Wells in Somerset, broken by the smears he continued to face. Wright had also left MI5, an embittered man at his failure to unmask Hollis. He ultimately tried to do so in his memoir, *Spycatcher*. The book caused a political storm, largely because Prime Minister Margaret Thatcher tried to halt publication, allowing it to become a global bestseller. It was a revenge of sorts for Wright, who lived out his life as a Tasmanian livestock farmer.

By then McCone had been replaced at the CIA by Admiral William F.

Raborn, an old-fashioned patriot who had no direct knowledge of the intricacies of international intelligence affairs. He had made it a condition that "unless there was an absolute crisis, he should not be disturbed on weekends, when he played golf from dawn to dusk," recalled Raborn's deputy Richard McGarrah Helms to the author. Another assistant to Raborn said, "In those days we had digraphs for everything. I was the guy who wrote down the true name for the director. One day Raborn sent for me and bawled, 'I asked you for this cryptonym to be translated.' I told him, 'Admiral, but I have done that.' He replied, 'You damn well haven't! What is KUWAIT cover for?'" Raborn remained in his post as DCI for barely a year. Into his place stepped Helms, an Anglophile who had served with the OSS in Europe and had been a founding member of the CIA. He told the author: "I recognized the value of having a good relationship with British intelligence. They've been around a lot longer than we have. I found their reports concise, more to the point. If they said something was 'probable' it meant it was between 50 and 75 percent accurate. 'Almost certain' meant from 75 to 100 percent. We picked up on that quickly."

By the time Helms was reassuring both Martin Furnival Jones and Dick White, the director of MI6, that matters were back on an even keel with the CIA, Eliza Manningham-Buller had again been approached by MI5. She had now spent three years as a teacher, and the work had begun to pall. At the family dinner table there were often American visitors—lawyers, diplomats, and sometimes men who never really explained what they did, let alone admit they worked for the CIA or one of the other U.S. intelligence agencies—and the talk was of the threat the Soviet Union posed. After one of those dinners, Eliza was taken aside by her old Oxford adviser, a regular guest, and asked if she had reconsidered joining MI5, adding that her father no longer had objections.

Her adviser said he thought she would do rather well working in intelligence. Eliza Manningham-Buller had smiled—a brief and decisive movement of her lips, gone as swiftly as it had appeared—accompanied by a little nod, itself a reminder of that evening on stage when she had waved her wand over Cinderella. On April 24, 1974, she signed the Official Secrets Act and became the latest recruit in MI5.

IN HER CONSERVATIVE CLOTHES and sensible shoes, with hair cut in an old-fashioned style and only a touch of lipstick to enliven her face, Eliza Manningham-Buller reported for her first day in MI5. She was twenty-five years old and ready to play her role as a spy.

Her destination was Number 1 Curzon Street, a bunkerlike building, built in the 1930s; its basement had served as an air raid shelter for the royal family in nearby Buckingham Palace during the blitz. She would work in Transcriptions, the starting point for every woman recruit. Situated in the basement and overheated by radiators that frequently became air-locked, with carpets not replaced since the war and walls painted a depressing green, the room was laid out like the floor of a clothing manufacturer: rows of worktables and bright lighting; instead of the clatter of sewing machine treadles, the staccato sound of keyboards filled the room. Patrolling it was the middle-aged Head of Transcripts, who only spoke to a typist when a transcribed tape was handed back and a new one passed over. The Head addressed each typist as "young lady," allowed no one to eat at her desk, and insisted on a transcript being handed over to the Head while a typist took a comfort break: One visit to the lavatory was permitted during an eight-hour shift. Talking between typists was discouraged and any discussion about the content of a transcript strictly forbidden. The working conditions were a test of resolve. Some gave up and left. Those who stayed became united in a determination that one day they would move off the bottom rung of the ladder Transcriptions represented.

The typed pages were checked by the Head for spelling mistakes before being delivered to a Security Service building in nearby Bolton Street. Months passed before Eliza Manningham-Buller learned that the Stalinist-style structure housed the offices of various antiterrorism branches, which dealt with threats that still emerged from the Indian subcontinent after the partition of Pakistan and Kashmir: Militants from both countries protested with acts of violence over what they saw as the unfair apportioning of geographical boundaries. As the empire steadily reduced in size, other nations over which the Union Jack still fluttered became more threatening in their demands for independence from their colonial masters. Combating them was the task of counterespionage officers working at 40 Gower Street, who also received the output from Transcriptions. Those who worked in the basement were bound by a common triumph: All had survived the positive vetting process.

The process was set up by the 1948 Labour government over its mounting suspicion that Communists would try to gain employment in sensitive government jobs and pass on defense secrets to the Soviet Union. Every applicant for work in Whitehall, defense establishments, and even the BBC had to undergo the process. Those identified as a "security risk" found it almost impossible to later obtain worthwhile permanent employment. The BBC had an office—Room 105—in

Broadcasting House where all those who applied for staff jobs had their names sent to B-Branch in MI5. Talented film editors, journalists, directors, and producers were refused employment on its recommendation. No reason was given to an applicant, and there was no appeal against the decision. The process continued until 1985 after the Former Home Secretary, Lord Rees, revealed he had no knowledge of the secret checks. Only the director-general of the BBC and two senior executives now remain subject to vetting, as they are required "to ensure the broadcaster carries out its duties during a national emergency." However, positive vetting has remained for all applicants who wish to join MI5, MI6, and GCHQ, which also deals with selecting safe houses and the internal security of all MI5 buildings. GCHQ also holds the files on staff below the rank of department head; those of senior officers are held in the deputy director-general's office. His own file is in the director-general's safe.

Despite her unblemished family background, Eliza Manningham-Buller had undergone the vetting process designed to discover, among much else, if she had a history of mental illness, had concealed a criminal record, including a driving conviction for drunkenness, or had indulged in any activity that could expose her to blackmail. Her family and a list of friends she had provided were discreetly asked about boyfriends—or girlfriends. Lesbianism, like homosexuality, was then a barrier to joining the Security Service. "Sexually MI5 is worse than being in a convent or monastery," recalled one agent, who left the Security Service when it learned of her liaison with another woman. In August 2008, the Security Service turned 180 degrees and began to recruit homosexuals.

The officer assigned to Eliza's vetting wanted to be assured she possessed what was known in B-Branch as TLR—trust, loyalty, and reliability. Dr. William Sargant, a consultant psychiatrist to MI5, recalled to the author, "A candidate would be invited to spend a weekend at a country house, and I would cast an eye over him or her. I would then write a report, noting whether the chap or girl drank a drop too much, was too talkative, or too familiar with others in the house party." Peter Wright likened those weekend gatherings to "members of a gentleman's club, who all suffered from the extraordinary belief that the upper classes were trustworthy in all matters of security and the lower classes were not."

Though Eliza Manningham-Buller had sailed through her vetting, nevertheless, like other daughters of the upper class, she still had to spend eight hours a day wearing headphones and typing tapped telephone conversations between Warsaw Pact diplomats in London. When she was uncertain about a word, she consulted her Russian-English dictionary, and with a speed of eighty words a minute, she was regarded as the typist to handle rush transcripts.

Her father had told her that a nation's intelligence service reflected its national morality and that spying was an essential part of the political process in a democracy like Britain's. After her first months in Transcriptions, she came to see that what other people might call "dirty work" was important for the security of the nation. Her work had also given her insights into the resourcefulness of those who had obtained the tapes. They had been recorded on bugs placed in manholes, chimneys, or window flower boxes. The skills of the unit who planted the devices had stirred Eliza Manningham-Buller, and she was determined one day she would be allowed to partake in dealing with what she typed instead of passing the pages over to the draconian Head for distribution. While many members of Transcriptions saw the job as only a stop on the road to marriage, Eliza Manningham-Buller spent her evenings in the Registry library absorbing the history of MI5, determining one day to leave her mark on the Security Service. Her enthusiasm had been noted and placed in her personnel file.

THE ROLE OF INFORMATION GATHERING began to play a serious part in Britain's defenses during the first Elizabethan reign. Until then it had been left to a diplomat or courtier to report anything important he heard. Few had any knowledge of what that could be, and as they were expected to purchase information out of their own purses, they paid little attention to what was said by the hundreds of ill-informed agents who usually offered only tittle-tattle and supplemented their income by passing it on to anyone with influence at court. Misinformation was rife.

That changed with the appointment in 1573 by Queen Elizabeth I of Sir Francis Walsingham as her secretary of state. He was perfectly suited for the most powerful position at court. All his working life he had dealt in secrets: the secrets of illicit liaisons among courtiers, the secrets of those who bribed and stole, the secrets of the queen's bedchamber. In his steady climb up the royal ladder, he had noted them all. So obsessed was the pinch-faced secretary that he removed all correspondence from his desk before admitting anyone to his salon and trod softly through the corridors of the palaces to surprise courtiers in their offices. He was the queen's quintessential spymaster-in-waiting.

Within months of his appointment, Walsingham had recruited scores of informers and made them sign a document that was the forerunner of the Official Secrets Act. In turn, they were promised royal protection for carrying out his orders. He began by ordering them to spy on Britain's Catholic families and priests, whom he suspected of plotting against Elizabeth. Soon his agents were traveling into France and Spain to report on the strength of their navies and armies. It was the foundation of military intelligence gathering. Walsingham had also expanded his domestic spy network so that he had spies in every city, town, and hamlet; their activities led to dozens of men and women ending up on the axeman's block.

The defeat of the Spanish Armada saw the end of foreign threats against Britain, and there was no real further work for Walsingham's agents. Many returned to their former moneymaking ways: stealing, blackmailing, and pimping. Walsingham died in 1590, nearly bankrupt, having virtually funded his spying operations from his own pocket. For all her praise of his undoubted triumphs, including discovering that Mary, Queen of Scots, had plotted against her, Elizabeth was miserly in her financial contribution to the upkeep of Walsingham's network.

When in 1653 Oliver Cromwell became Lord Protector of England, Scotland, and Ireland, he sent scores of his agents into Europe to obtain intelligence on the military strengths of the old adversary Catholic Spain before launching a war that routed the enemy. He spread word that superior intelligence had enabled him to do so, and England became regarded as the best-informed nation in the world. Nowhere were Cromwell's spies more active than in Ireland, where famine had created huge hatred for the English landlords and the agents they had recruited as spies. Later, when the Fenians emerged in the 1840s, many were hanged on roadside gibbets, each bearing a placard denouncing him as a traitor.

Meanwhile, the London government had passed the Secret Service Fund, which would remain unchallenged for another two hundred years. The money was misused: Members of Parliament misappropriated it to finance election campaigns, and one Tory prime minister, Lord Bute, used £80,000 to bribe MPs to support his policies. Another prime minister, William Pitt, insisted the fund was essential for his government to deal with the threat of domestic subversion following the French Revolution. For all his rhetoric, few people believed Pitt; there was a growing mood in the country that financing information gathering was only another means for politicians to indulge in corruption.

By the mid-nineteenth century the government's network of spies still remained decentralized and unstructured. When the Fenian bombing campaign began in 1883 and escalated in 1885, there was no proper intelligence organization to tackle the new violent campaign by Irish Republicans seeking independence from Britain. Only after the Boer War did the War Office finally recognize the need for a properly organized secret intelligence service. The 1911 revision of the 1889 Official Secrets Act—which had placed the burden of proof on the state—charged that any suspect must now prove his or her innocence. Out of the new act would emerge MI5 and MI6, both with sufficient powers that Parliament could not challenge.

THE FIRST DIRECTOR-GENERAL of MI5 was Vernon Kell. His father came from a military family, and there was no question that his son would follow the tradition of going to Sandhurst and then join his father's regiment, the South Staffordshires. His mother, however, was determined the boy would learn skills beyond soldiering. She taught him German, Italian, French, Polish, and Russian, languages in which he was fluent when he joined the regiment. In 1900, on a visit to Ireland, he met and married Constance, the daughter of a Cork landowner. By then the asthma that had developed in childhood had worsened, and his work as the regiment's interpreter was interrupted by bouts of illness.

Within months of the marriage, Kell was posted to China, where he fought in the Boxer Rebellion. He returned to England in 1904 and, his health deteriorating, was transferred from the Staffordshires to a desk job in the War Office. His initial responsibility was to investigate the Irish Republican Brotherhood (IRB), the secret military organization that had grown from the Fenian movement and was operating alongside the Irish Parliamentary Party, the political group demanding Home Rule. He was simultaneously concerned with the threat posed by the stirrings of Kaiser Wilhelm's Germany. These were Kell's first encounters with intelligence gathering, and he showed an aptitude for spying, though by then less pleasant traits had emerged in his character: He was arrogant, chauvinistic, and imbued with racism, characteristics found in many of his superiors.

His work came to the notice of Winston Churchill, the home secretary, and shortly after his thirty-fifth birthday, Kell became the youngest departmental head in the War Office. The department was called Military Operations Five, the forerunner of MI5. In a room in the War Office, he and his staff shared two large desks and a filing cabinet, and Kell had an annual budget of £7,000—a substantial sum at the time—to pay his nine men and carry out counterintelligence operations. He had two qualities that appealed to Churchill: a growing belief that German spies were an increasing menace to the security of Britain and a gift of understanding how military bureaucracy worked. "The less those above you know, the better for us," Kell endlessly repeated to his staff. He insisted the needs of government must always outweigh any effects spying had on people's private lives. With only limited resources, however, surveillance was little more than a "watch and follow him" process, tradecraft an unknown skill, and "intelligence product" no more than handwritten reports signed by Kell.

The Boer War of 1899–1902 had shaken the British military establishment out of its Victorian complacency and revealed disturbing deficiencies in its preparations for another conflict, this time against the expanding military might of Kaiser Wilhelm's forces. An added concern was that Germany could also strike at England by attacking Ireland and forcing London to send more troops to defend its closest outpost of empire.

Until the arrival of MI5, intelligence from Ireland was under the control of Scotland Yard's Special Branch, which relied on informers who, like Cromwell's spies, were English landowners on the country's east coast and paid their workers to provide tips. These were passed on to the British Embassy in Dublin and added to the diplomatic bag sent to the Foreign Office in London. They included clippings from Irish newspapers and "interesting names" of passengers on the nightly ferry to Britain.

Kell's spies operated against an increasing nationalism; newspapers like Lord Northcliffe's *Daily Mail* found a wide readership for its arguments that Germany increasingly threatened the Royal Navy's supremacy, and the *Weekly News* offered to pay every reader who could prove he had seen a spy £10, a small fortune. Kell arranged for all the letters to the newspaper to be forwarded to him. Soon he needed a second filing cabinet to hold them. It was the start of the MI5 Registry, but the letters did not lead to the arrest of a single spy.

By 1914, Kell had created a file of sixteen thousand aliens, eleven thousand of them German. The Registry was constantly updated so that by the outbreak of the Great War in August of that year, thirty-seven German suspected agents had been identified. The Registry had also played its role in MI5's first counterintelligence success.

Kell had assigned one of his officers to uncover sabotage plots at naval dockyards. The officer's suspicions fell on a German journalist, Max Schultz, who had rented a houseboat on the river at Exeter. Schultz spent most of the day reading the local newspapers and paying visits to Plymouth and Portsmouth harbors, photocopying articles for a New

York magazine he claimed to work for. No one suspected Schultz was an agent of the kaiser's spymaster, Gustav Steinhauer.

The magnificently mustached German had served first as a Pinkerton detective before becoming the kaiser's personal bodyguard. Operating out of an office in Potsdam, Prussia, Steinhauer ran an intelligence operation that was both daring and inventive. His targets were the London docks and the Plymouth and Portsmouth naval yards; these were all key Royal Navy establishments from where the kaiser believed would come Britain's response to his plans of going to war. To keep the German High Command apprised, Steinhauer had created a complex communications system. Prewar German visitors to Britain carried his orders in letters that they posted to Schultz and other deep-cover agents in the country; bearing English postal stamps and franking, they attracted no attention from anyone. The spies had a list of names including waiters, hairdressers, and housemaids through whom they could respond to Steinhauer.

He created a code for each spy to send encrypted information to Potsdam, posting the letters to names and addresses in France and other European countries where Steinhauer's other spies forwarded the letters to him. The system had worked perfectly until Schultz decided the information he had was so urgent he mailed it directly to Steinhauer on the day an MI5 officer was visiting Exeter on a routine check. A clerk checking outgoing foreign mail showed him the envelope, and the officer took it back to London, where it was opened by Kell, who ordered Schultz to be arrested. Fearing he faced imprisonment for spying, he agreed to collaborate and explained how the code worked. The network was rolled up.

The outbreak of World War I led to spy mania sweeping Britain. No police station escaped daily reports of German agents operating in the area. Pigeon fanciers came under suspicion of using their birds to fly messages to Germany. On September 14, 1914, Basil Thomson (later Sir Basil) head of the Special Branch and usually a man of carefully chosen words, told the *Daily Mail*, "It is positively dangerous to be seen feeding a pigeon. A foreigner walking in one of the London parks has been arrested because a pigeon was seen to fly from the place where he had stopped." No German spy was known to have used a pigeon during the war.

Under Kell's lobbying at the War Office, MI5 grew from its roomful of men to having 135 persons on the payroll, including chemists able to unravel the secrets of invisible inks and the first cryptologists, who broke codes written as business telegrams that had raised the suspicions of cablegram censors. With a new budget of £100,000, Kell based an officer in Holland after a spy, Karl Lody, confessed his "postbox" was in Rotterdam. Traveling on a stolen American passport, Lody had entered Britain and was arrested the next day sketching the defenses around Portsmouth harbor. He was executed on November 6, 1914, by a firing squad in the Tower of London. In the months to come, other spies would follow him, each refusing the offer of a blindfold before being shot. By 1916, Kell had effectively destroyed Germany's intelligence penetration of Britain; in the remaining two years of the war, only five more spies were captured and executed at the Tower. By then MI5's Registry had expanded to contain 137,000 names, making it the largest record of facts in the empire. Not only names and addresses but personal habits, work details, and marital status were recorded, along with the pub where a man drank, the shops where a woman bought her clothes, and which school her children attended. Using details from other government departments, a suspect's life from birth onward was chronicled. A person could sail to India, South Africa, and the farthest reaches of the empire and, in a matter of weeks, the details of where he or she had gone and with whom he or she stayed would all be in the Registry.

Kell had secretly entered into an arrangement with the U.S. Secret Service and the French Deuxième Bureau to give them details about their own nationals kept on the Registry. In return, they provided copies of intercepted wireless transmissions indicating American and French workers were encouraging their British counterparts to disrupt the war effort. Kell planted stories in the newspapers that "German gold" was financing the unrest. The most alarming report was that MI5 had uncovered a plot to assassinate Prime Minister David Lloyd George by killing him with a poisoned dart to be fired from an air rifle while he played golf. The plotters were identified by Kell as "German sympathisers," but they were never found.

Using such tactics, wheezing and coughing in and out of government offices, Vernon Kell persuaded his superiors to increase his staff to eight hundred. Women were recruited to read all the nation's mail; a team was trained by a professional burglar to break into the embassies of neutral nations to open safes and photograph documents, while another unit worked in London's central telephone exchanges to monitor conversations, and agents provocateurs stirred up pacifist meetings to allow the Special Branch to arrest people.

In the name of patriotism Kell created fear among those who did not agree with the war and its continuing loss of tens of thousands of lives in the trenches of France. In the corridors of power in Whitehall he was a hero. Yet, despite his powerful intelligence-gathering organization, he was totally remiss in anticipating what was happening in Ireland. The Easter Rising of 1916 in Dublin revealed a huge deficiency in MI5's intelligence capability with the failure of the Security Service's Irish network of informers to warn what would happen on that Sunday. While the Rising lasted only a few days, the sheer violence of the response of the English garrison would unite the Irish people in total support of the Republican cause. No longer could MI5 easily recruit spies within the movement, and Michael Collins, the director of intelligence for the Sinn Fein movement seeking independence, with its armed wing, the Irish Republican Army, organized a daring attack on Kell's spies based in their Dublin Castle fortress, killing twelve agents. For Kell, it was a grim reminder there was more to contend with than the threat from German spies.

The Bolshevik Revolution in 1917 gave him a chance to redeem MI5's reputation. Discovering the revolutionaries were attracting support within Britain's own armed forces, he once more sent agents provocateurs into the military bases to search for pro-Bolshevik leaflets. A number of soldiers caught distributing them were court-martialed. Sensing the Bolsheviks would have further support among the working classes, Kell created MI5's first team of Watchers, deep-cover agents who unearthed what he called "subversives" in the Trade Unions. The election in 1924 of Britain's first Labour prime minister, Ramsay McDonald, was worrying for Kell, as a number of the party's leading members had been under MI5 surveillance. On Kell's advice, McDonald excluded them from his cabinet, but it would mark the start of a long-running suspicion between the Labour Party and MI5.

Kell had learned that during the Great War, America had its own cipher-breaking unit code-named the Black Chamber. Jointly funded by the State and War departments, it was run by Herbert Yardley, a professional poker player whose brief was "to read the code and cipher telegrams of foreign governments by such means as we could devise and if we were caught it would just be too bad," he later recalled. Using skills that had won him a small fortune at card tables, Yardley devised a number of systems to break the ciphers of a dozen countries, including those used by MI5 to communicate with its spies throughout the empire. Following America's entry into the war, Yardley told the State Department he could unlock the diplomatic code the Vatican was using to communicate with its nuncios, the pope's diplomats, in war-torn Europe after a War Office official had told Yardley there were fears the Holy See was pro-German. The offer was not taken up. By the end of hostilities, Yardley and his cryptologists had unscrambled over fifty thousand cryptograms, and the Black Chamber continued operating until it was finally closed down in 1929 by Henry Stimson when he became secretary of state and delivered the immortal line "Gentlemen do not read each other's mail."

Kell had been rewarded with a knighthood after the end of World War I, but peacetime cost-conscious politicians had less need for the Security Service, and his budget of £100,000 was reduced to £25,000. He needed a new enemy to hunt. It was provided in a letter from Admiral Reginald Hall, who had worked for Kell, asking him to develop a system secure from Yardley's skills and stop Washington reading London's peacetime codes. Hall wrote: "Hard and bitter as the battle has been, we now have to face a far, far, far more ruthless foe. A foe that is hydra-headed and whose evil power will spread over the whole world. That foe is Soviet Russia."

IN 1924, KELL SELECTED one of MI5's genuine eccentrics to run the most successful penetration between the interwar years. Tall, with a bulbous nose and a comedian's chin, Charles Henry Maxwell Knight liked suits cut from herringbone-patterned cloth and hard-toed shoes. His first wife had committed suicide after dabbling in black magic with the occultist Aleister Crowley. Remarried, Knight chose to live alone in one of the most expensive apartment buildings in Central London, Dolphin Square, and paid the rent in the name of "Miss Copelstone," one of his aliases. On his rare visits to MI5 headquarters, he insisted he should only be addressed as M. Asked by Kell to explain why, Knight replied, "Six have C; you have M." C is the designated name for the chief in MI6. Knight chose M after his middle name. The matter was not raised again.

Knight's apartment, at various times, contained a small bear that he led around on a chain, a baboon that spent its days sitting on a couch, several grass snakes, and a cuckoo that had been bought from Harrods. The menagerie was paid for by MI5; Knight insisted it was part of his cover as a zoologist. He may have had his quirks, but his skills at building up a network were remarkable. His agents were youthful, the men handsome and the women attractive, and all possessed what Knight also required: private incomes. "The idea of having to pay for someone to spy for his country is not on," he once told Kell. Recruited from the nightclubs Knight had made his second home—methodically collecting receipts and charging all his expenses to MI5's finance department—his network consisted of playboys, debutantes, and writers. None was allowed to visit his apartment. Instead he divided them into cells, run from their own homes, which he regularly visited to acquire their latest intelligence. Their brief was to uncover Communists.

The deeper Knight's network penetrated their cells, the more Kell became convinced that Bolshevism remained the main threat MI5 must confront. While the danger from Irish terrorism was still there, it was no longer a prime concern, and Kell—now in his thirtieth year as head of MI5—had judged that Hitler was not going to launch a new German intelligence offensive against Britain. Russia was the enemy. His fears were fed by Knight. Both men shared an interest in ornithology, and often Knight would produce a matchbox holding insects that spymaster and spy would avidly discuss before turning to the latest threats of Communism. They would jump on and off buses to make sure they were not being followed before going to their rendezvous in the lobby of one of the hotels in Cromwell Road, where MI5 was now headquartered.

THERE WAS ALSO GROWING SUPPORT for Hitler among influential English nobility, who had come through the Great War with their land-holdings and way of life intact, and wanted it to remain so. The chaos of the Weimar Republic and the way America had opted out of the League of Nations had deepened their belief that Hitler was the strongman needed to control Europe and that Britain should support him. At summer garden parties and coming-out balls for their debutante daughters after being presented at court, the approval for Hitler grew. Here was a führer who had built the autobahns and created a powerful army that could travel along them to defend the borders of his country, a leader who had gone to the aid of Spain's General Franco when his Falangist forces were threatened with defeat by his Communist opponents, a politician who had repeatedly said when he attended German military maneuvers that his tanks and planes were only there to defend the Reich should it ever be attacked. In Britain it was a view supported by Sir Oswald Mosley, the head of the British Union of Fascists, whose blackshirt uniform he had modeled on the one worn by Italian Fascists. In the East End of London and the poorer districts in other English cities, Mosley directed his venom particularly against the Jews, demanding their expulsion, a cry that won discreet approval from such aristocrats as the duke of Westminster, Britain's wealthiest landowner, and the duke of Bedford.

Winston Churchill's warning that Hitler's Condor Legion in the Spanish Civil War had given German aircraft invaluable practice for blitzkrieg tactics and that the country's broad autobahns were ideally suited for German armored forces to speed over the borders into neighboring countries was seen as the words of an alarmist within the country mansions.

Though Hitler had swallowed the Czech rump, there was a mood among the landed gentry that he was not going to go further and a number of them decided to travel to the World's Fair in New York in the summer of 1939 to accompany another Englishman with an indecisive manner: King George VI, by the Grace of God, of Great Britain, Ireland, and of the British Dominions Beyond the Seas, King, Defender of the Faith, and Emperor of India. He was accompanied by his queen, the former Elizabeth Angela Marguerite Bowes-Lyon. Both were the personal guests of President Roosevelt. Before the royal couple arrived, the president had sent a polite reminder to Berlin that America would welcome the führer's guarantee that "weak nations will not be attacked." Hitler told an adoring Reichstag he had no plans to invade the United States. The promise came after his propaganda chief, Dr. Joseph Goebbels, had described Roosevelt as a "pettifogging Jew," adding, "The completely Negroid appearance of his wife shows she is half-caste."

The slander barely produced a stir within the United States; Europe, for many, was far away, and the fulminations from Berlin's Wilhelmstrasse were of little consequence, any more than Hitler's demand for Danzig and the nonaggression pact with Russia he had signed. There were some Americans, however, who saw the British Empire was no longer the world's most powerful stabilizing force; while the Royal Navy still ruled the seas, if Hitler extended his reach into Poland and then France, Britain would be trapped on its island. To their astonishment, when they raised such matters with the visitors accompanying the royal party, they were told there was nothing to worry about. Hadn't Neville Chamberlain come back from his meeting with Hitler in Munich with that piece of paper he had waved in the air as he stepped off the plane and solemnly said, "We have achieved peace for our time"? Kell had also been one convinced by the words.

It was widely reported in Fleet Street newspapers the next day.

5

Ciphers and Bugs

On a July morning in 1940, a middle-aged man stood at the deck rail of an American liner and watched the sun rise over the Old Head of Kinsale; the sight of the headland never failed to emotionally stir him. A century before, William Donovan's grandparents had sailed from the nearby Irish port of Cobh, two more of the impoverished and often uneducated emigrants seeking a new life in the New World. The Donovans had saved enough for two steerage tickets.

Now their grandson—a successful Manhattan lawyer—was traveling in a deluxe cabin and was a guest at the captain's table. A further sign of Donovan's importance was that in the captain's cabin safe he had placed a sealed unmarked package. Before sailing from New York, Donovan had given the captain strict instructions that despite the ship flying the American flag at its stern, the symbol of its country's neutrality, if it was attacked by one of the German U-boats that had started to patrol the North Atlantic, the package must be destroyed. Inside was a letter addressed "for the personal attention only" of Prime Minister Winston Churchill, which was signed by Cordell Hull, the secretary of state of the United States. It pledged America would assist Britain "in all ways possible." The offer of help was conditional upon Donovan being satisfied that British intelligence "had bared its breasts to him"—a phrase the puritanical Hull had hesitated using until Donovan said it was the kind of language Churchill would appreciate.

For Britain the war had started badly. Poland had been occupied in four weeks; Holland surrendered in six days, quickly followed by Belgium. The British Expeditionary Force had conducted a humiliating evacuation from the beaches of Dunkirk, and shortly afterward France fell. All England could depend on was the Spitfires and Hurricanes winning the dogfights over the Channel and Churchill's resonant voice delivering the ennobling words of Shakespeare's *King John: This England never did, nor never shall, lie at the proud foot of a conqueror.* The pledge had roused in Donovan another wave of emotion, furthering his own determination that, while night had fallen over Europe, his voyage would ensure one day there would be a new dawn over the continent.

Donovan was unusual among Irish-American Catholics, who were mostly Democrats; he was a committed Republican and an Anglophile who saw no point in keeping alive the past memories of British rule over the Republic. In 1918, Donovan had been awarded the Medal of Honor for his battlefield bravery in France during the Great War but had returned home after the armistice convinced peace would not last. Unlike many Americans in the interwar years, he was not an isolationist but was convinced Germany would rise again, this time to threaten the United States. His views had attracted the attention of President Franklin Delano Roosevelt, and Donovan had made, in the late 1930s, regular trips to Europe, visiting the Sudetenland, Yugoslavia, and Italy at Roosevelt's request to observe German maneuvers. After each trip he told Roosevelt he was ever more convinced Hitler was preparing for war.

At a meeting in the White House in June 1940, Donovan reminded the President, Henry Stimson—now secretary of war—and Cordell Hull that Hitler's empire was already bigger than Napoleon's and it was not enough for Americans to admire how the first four notes of Beethoven's Fifth Symphony—the three dots and the dash of the Morse code for *V,* which the BBC used to symbolize Victory as the precursor for all its radio programs—was a reminder beamed into Nazi-occupied Europe that all was not lost. Nor was it a sufficient contribution for Americans to have welcomed into their homes the thirty-two thousand children evacuated from England.

What was vital was for the United States to have access to intelligence of where the relentless advance of Hitler's field gray columns would go next. Already their conquests had shown the isolationists what to expect: the Stuka bombers hurtling down on fleeing hordes of hapless refugees, the shooting in the streets of civilians in Warsaw and Rotterdam, the trainloads of Jews heading east, the tramp of jackboots of troops singing, "Wir fahren gegen England"—"we're driving against England." Donovan had turned to the silent Oval Office and said again, "We must have some form of intelligence to protect our own shores."

Donovan had spoken with the quiet passion of his belief that any aid the United States would provide, while it set about forming its own intelligence organization, must be offset against what it would learn from Britain's intelligence services. "These are organizations which have helped rule an empire," Donovan had concluded.

The president asked only one question. In what form did Donovan envisage American aid? The answer had been swift. Money, ships, aircraft, and eventually men to fight. Roosevelt had gently reminded the feisty Irishman that the United States was not at war.

"Not yet, no," Donovan had replied. "But we will be, Mr. President. Everything I've seen of Hitler tells me that."

At the end of that June meeting, Hull had written the letter for Donovan to hand-carry to Churchill, which made it clear that America's cooperation would be a foreign policy priority for the Roosevelt administration, providing William Donovan was satisfied after his visit to London.

Now, on that July morning in 1940, as he watched the Old Head of Kinsale, a headland on the south coast of Ireland, disappear into the morning haze and the ship continued its zigzagging course toward Southampton, William Donovan prepared for a series of meetings in London.

Within a month later, he had dined with Winston Churchill and King George and had learned of Britain's top-secret invention of radar, had seen its fighter planes coming off the production line, and had visited its coastal defenses, having been briefed on the successful propaganda war both MI5 and MI6 were already conducting in Europe, and how the SOE (Special Operations Executive, the organization Churchill had authorized to be created to "set Europe alight") had already begun by infiltrating its saboteurs into enemy-occupied France. Donovan had even been allowed to visit the secret base at Tempsford in Bedfordshire from where they flew on their hazardous missions. In daylight the place looked like any other farm in the area; at night the hayricks and animal pens were rolled back for the Lysander planes to emerge and fly agents into France.

THE SUREST SIGN OF THE TRUST in which the soft-spoken Donovan was held by his hosts came when Churchill personally authorized he should be shown the highly secret interrogation center that had been prepared for captured Nazi generals—"and captured they will be," the prime minister had repeated, waving one of the Cuban cigars Donovan had brought as a personal gift.

The center had been prepared by Stewart Menzies, one of the first decisions he made after becoming MI6's third chief two months after Britain entered the war. On a Sunday morning in early August as he drove Donovan out to the center, Menzies had said, "My entire career has been preparing for war with Germany. But I still don't understand what has driven its people to fall in behind Hitler, especially his military leaders. They are anything but stupid. How could a nation who had produced Luther, Kant, Goethe, and Beethoven have allowed it to happen?"

He hoped Trent Park would provide an answer. Set in the rolling hills of Enfield in the countryside just beyond the northern limits of London, the Combined Services Interrogation Center (also shared by MI5) had once been Henry IV's private game reserve. Centuries later, the Sassoon family had built a magnificent mansion in the grounds, and kings, peers, and industrialists had enjoyed its hospitality. Menzies had decided it was the ideal place for his interrogation center.

For weeks MI6 technicians had worked to hide tiny microphones, devised by the BBC, in the mansion's bedrooms, lounges, and dining rooms. Menzies's prisoners would be free to go where they wished on the grounds and enjoy the best food available under the restrictions of Britain's rationing. They could listen to music and read books removed from the German embassy in London or view films. They would live out the war in comfort. Menzies had calculated the relaxed atmosphere would be conducive to his prisoners talking among themselves, hopefully revealing far more about Hitler's plans than their interrogators could obtain.

MI6 analysts had drawn up profiles of priority targets to be captured: full-blown generals, divisional commanders, brigade führers, general staff officers, and senior officers in the Waffen-SS and Kriegsmarine. In all there were close to a hundred names on the list. Allowing for death by natural causes or in battle, Menzies expected to have over fifty German military leaders to secretly monitor. He hoped that, unlike open interrogations in which answers could be distorted and questions circumvented, discussion between prisoners who did not suspect they were being secretly recorded could provide valuable information, including clues to morale on the German war and home fronts and even insights into the military thinking about Hitler.

Menzies had ordered that the microphones must be left on all the time, and a small team of German and Austrian exiles was recruited to monitor all the prisoner conversations. Each listener had undergone a training course in German military terminology, and as soon as a prisoner said something important, a gramophone recording was made. These were transcribed by a special unit Menzies had created. Until senior officers from Hitler's military elite arrived, captured junior officers were held at Trent Park to test out the monitoring system. Prisoners were given a daily English-language newspaper. Lord Beaverbrook, the owner of the *Daily Express* and a key member of the Churchill coalition government, had arranged for his editors to create a special edition containing fake stories of thrilling British victories—events still some way off. Their content had aroused satisfying concern among the prisoners.

Donovan saw Trent Park as having exciting possibilities. When he returned to Washington, he asked Stimson to prepare a similar camp ready for the time America entered the war. The site chosen was at Clinton, Mississippi. In all, thirty-one German generals would eventually be brought there for interrogation. Like those at Trent Park, their secretly taped conversations reflected on their roles in the war and what the future held. The intelligence revealed the overall direction of German politics and strategy and captured discussion of the failed assassination attempts on Hitler in July 1944, the Holocaust, and other war crimes.

The transcripts of the secret conversations would remain one of the last intelligence secrets of World War II until August 2007, when Sönke Neitzel, a professor of modern history at the University of Mainz, published them. They still make shocking reading and effectively end the legend that the Wehrmacht had fought a "clean war" and that war crimes were the sole responsibility of the Nazi political leadership, the SS, and the Gestapo. Even General Dietrich von Choltitz, captured at the fall of Paris and later acclaimed as a hero for disobeying Hitler's order to destroy the city, admits on his transcript that he had "systematically carried out orders for the liquidation of Jews in the Crimea in 1941–42."

IN 1940, VERNON KELL was sixty-seven years old and in fading health; at times his asthma attacks were so severe he was close to choking. His mustache had grayed, giving his face a gaunt appearance. He was working extra-long hours, but had developed a poor appetite. In May of that year, close to midnight, Kell was summoned to Churchill's office in the Admiralty. He was kept waiting for an hour before being called before the prime minister. Churchill, puffing on a cigar, said, "Kell, I need someone else to run my intelligence service." For a moment, breathing wheezily, Kell stared wordlessly at the man who had abruptly ended his long career. The prime minister looked up from a document he had resumed reading and, realizing Kell was still there, repeated, "You are dismissed. Go." There was no handshake, no offer of a farewell drink. Nothing. Kell turned and walked from the room, a broken man. The next day, Constance, Lady Kell, gathered her own staff of volunteer workers together and, not troubling to hide her bitterness, said, "Your precious Winston has sacked my husband."

Kell retired to the village of Emberton deep in the Buckinghamshire countryside and dug up his cottage flower beds to grow vegetables for the war effort. He became a special constable whose duty was to watch out for poachers hunting rabbits and patrol the village to ensure the blackout was observed. Few of his former staff visited him before he died on the cold morning of March 27, 1942. Lady Kell received no condolences from Churchill or his ministers. Kell's place had been taken by Jasper Harker who was head of counterintelligence at MI5. He stayed less than a year (1940–41) before Kell learned that his permanent successor was David Petrie, a soft-spoken sixty-one-year-old who had been a shrewd intelligence officer as head of the Indian Political Service. A large man, wide across the shoulders, and thick-necked, he made it clear he sought approval from none of his staff. In India, he had a reputation as a methodical and careful officer in his steady conformity with expectations. Churchill's order was short and clear, "Petrie, I want you to give the Security Service strong leadership. Whatever you need to do—do it."

PETRIE'S FIRST MAJOR DECISION after his appointment as director-general was to move the Security Service to two separate locations. Transcriptions, counterespionage and other departments would be housed in the unlikely setting of Wormwood Scrubs, one of London's main prisons, its prisoners having been transferred to other jails and the execution chamber sealed. According to Petrie, "The sight of our stylishly dressed ladies coming to work in Transcriptions soon ended any semblance of secrecy in the neighbourhood." Staff occupied cells connected by narrow galleries and came and went across the exercise yard. As cell doors had no inner handles, if a door was closed no one inside could get out during an air raid alert. Life was more pleasant in the Registry, now installed in the medieval splendor of Blenheim Palace. "Beautiful girls and eligible young men created something of a party atmosphere," Petrie recalled.

After an incendiary bomb struck the prison, it was decided to move operations to St. James's Street in the heart of London's nightclub area. Revelers turned out in the early hours found themselves dodging motorcycle messengers bringing files from the Registry or returning them to Blenheim Palace. In the planning stages of the preparations for the Normandy landings, a dispatch rider left the flap on his saddlebag unsecured and top-secret plans were scattered along his route. Scores of policemen retrieved them; not one document was lost. The hapless messenger, however, was assigned to a Scottish outpost.

MI5 rounded up thirty German spies in the opening months of the war. They were interrogated at Latchmere House, the specially prepared center in the village of Ham Common on the outskirts of London. The sprawling Victorian house that had served as a World War I military hospital was now MI5's prime center for questioning captured enemy spies and was under the command of another of those unusual characters who had found their way into the Security Service on the eve of war.

Born in Egypt at the turn of the century, Robin Stephens had been commissioned into the Gurkhas, the elite regiment of Nepalese troops in the British army who are renowned for their ferocity in battle. With his mastiff's chin, a monocle, and close-cropped hair, Stephens was renowned for his ferocious temper and his ability to curse in seven languages, all of which he spoke fluently. He also had a deep-seated antipathy toward Jews, homosexuals, and Germans, in that order. Nevertheless Petrie, steeped in the mores of the empire, had recognized these made Stephens the ideal person to run Latchmere House. There was also another quality. Stephens was an astute judge of character, acquired, he insisted, from his years of studying the complex minds of the Gurkhas he had commanded, and from his reading of Freud and Jung.

On the first day he assumed command of Latchmere House, he told his staff he would not tolerate any physical violence against prisoners.

"We are here to crush a spy psychologically. Crush his mind into small pieces, examine those pieces and then if they reveal qualities useful to the war effort—like becoming double agents—they must be mentally rebuilt. Those who do not have the qualities we require will end up on the gallows or before a firing squad in the Tower of London."

He had concluded his briefing with a reminder that would remain on his file in MI5. "A breaker is born, not made. He must have certain inherent qualities: an implacable hatred of the enemy, a certain aggressive approach, a disinclination to believe and, above all, a relentless determination to break down a spy's psychological defences, however good they are, however long the process takes. And you must never lose your temper. But display no chivalry. Indulge in no gossip. Offer no cigarettes. A spy should be kept at the point of a sword."

He had set about putting his words into action. Latchmere House was surrounded by multiple strands of barbed wire. The cell-like rooms where prisoners were kept were bugged. Food was basic. At nine thirty sharp in the morning, Stephens, after a hearty breakfast, and dressed in his Gurkha uniform of a lieutenant colonel, would march into a cell with the overhead bulb glinting off his monocle and begin the process of unraveling the truth about a suspect before, if finally satisfied, turning him over to others to train him to become a double agent. Stephens could spend long hours over many days and sometimes weeks before he was satisfied a man could either be useful or sent to the Tower.

Eddie Chapman, a London-born petty criminal, captured when the Germans had overrun the Channel Islands, would remember his first encounter with Stephens after he had been parachuted back into Britain by the Abwehr and had promptly offered to work for MI5 as a double agent. "Even standing in the cell door Stephens created an atmosphere of a court, and I was ordered to stand up and answer his questions as if he was a judge," he recalled to the author. Stephens had broken the silence in a bristling tone, "I am not saying this in any sense of a threat, but you are held here in a British Secret Service prison, and it is our job to see we get your whole story. Do you see?" Chapman saw. For the rest of the war he was the most effective double agent MI5 ran.

The harsh conditions in Latchmere House had led to several suicides in its cellblocks. Fifteen spies failed to pass Stephens's grilling and were hanged or shot in the Tower. Fourteen agreed to become double agents, using their German radios to send false information to Berlin. Known as Operation Double Cross, it became the start of long-distance disinformation. Petrie also approved a plan for RAF planes to fly over the Channel and drop pigeons carrying false information in the hope they would fly back to dovecotes owned by Nazi sympathizers in France and spread confusion. Any bird flying back to Britain with its message faced the risk of being killed by one of the falcons of the Bird Interceptor Unit set up by MI5 on the south coast of England. It was under the control of Lord Tredegar, one of the country's leading falconers.

IN JULY 1941, WILLIAM DONOVAN CONTINUED to urge President Roosevelt to create an intelligence-gathering organization that would confirm the news Donovan constantly received from his close contacts with MI5 and MI6. Germany had overrun Europe and acquired Russia as its ally. Was Hitler preparing to leap the Channel? While not doubting the resistance Britain would put up, both Stewart Menzies and Petrie had admitted the possibility of an invasion could not be discounted. If Britain fell, would the Royal Navy be scuppered like the German Fleet had been at Scapa Flow at the end of the Great War? Or would it sail to the safety of one of the empire's ports in South Africa or Australia? Supposing Germany had built a long-range bomber capable of hitting the East Coast of America? To all those questions Britain's intelligence services had offered continued reassurances: Churchill would not surrender; there was no evidence to suggest Germany had an aircraft capable of flying the Atlantic; the Royal Navy would continue to sail out of British ports to protect the lifeline convoys from America. Was it not time, Donovan urged Roosevelt, for the United States to have its own intelligence officers who would provide the president with independent confirmation?

Roosevelt finally agreed, and Donovan was appointed director for the Office of the Coordinator of Information (COI). It would be the first time the United States had a peacetime, civilian intelligence agency solely with a military purpose. In approving its creation, Roosevelt had publicly signaled America was turning its back on isolationism and could not—would not—any longer stand aloof from what was happening in Europe. The news was received by MI5 and MI6 with delight, and Churchill entertained both his intelligence chiefs at dinner. On December 7, 1941, while the COI was still in its birth pangs, Japan struck at Pearl Harbor. Three days later Germany and Italy declared war on the United States. A year later the Office of Strategic Services was created to launch an undercover war in Europe. There was further rejoicing within MI5 and MI6 at the arrival of a powerful ally to support its own missions on the Continent.

ONLY THE SLIGHTEST LIMP in his left leg indicated the clubfoot Allen Welsh Dulles had been born with; in spite of corrective surgery, it had left him with less than perfect balance. Bill Buckley, who at the time was a desk officer in the CIA Directorate of Operations and became a trusted confidante, said that in quiet moments Dulles brooded over the deformity but had made his family swear a solemn promise never to discuss it with outsiders. Clover Dulles, his wife, said the request marked Allen's entry into the world of secrets. A slightly bowed figure with bushy eyebrows, Dulles presented the appearance of a campus professor. People often said the smoke emerging from his briar pipe offered the first visible clue to his suspicions over some troubling matter: When the smoke emerged white, he had not yet decided; when it turned black, he had. Dulles had told Buckley it was nonsense, but he allowed the fable to continue without contradiction.

Dulles was now fifty years old in 1943, a graduate of Princeton and George Washington University Law School, and had served in the U.S. diplomatic service before resigning to become a schoolmaster in India. It was there he developed a lasting dislike for Britain and its empire. "It has a contempt for all but its own," he had written to his brother, John Foster Dulles, later the secretary of state. Allen Dulles returned to New York to become managing partner in Sullivan & Cromwell, one of the most respected law firms in the city, one that came to the notice of William Donovan. Both found they shared the conviction that the United States must have its own intelligence agency. Over dinner one night in Donovan's upper Manhattan penthouse, he proposed Dulles could run U.S. secret intelligence in Europe while Donovan continued to work on setting up the OSS. He had learned that Dulles already had some knowledge of intelligence work. After America entered the Great War, he had been sent by Washington to Austria, where the Bolsheviks were planning their revolution. One was Vladimir Ilyich Lenin, who had asked to meet Dulles; ignoring the request, Dulles dismissed Lenin as "not very important." Years later Dulles would ruefully recount, "If I had seen Lenin, maybe I could have changed the course of history." Lenin had returned to Russia and launched the revolution that did change the world.

Nevertheless, the prospect of being a one-man secret service appealed to Dulles, and he arrived in early 1943 in Bern, Switzerland, with a $1 million letter of credit drawn on the Bank of America and a trunk containing two suits, half a dozen shirts, and an extra pair of customized shoes built to disguise his clubfoot. There was also the codebook Donovan had provided. Dulles spoke good German and made no secret of why he had come to Bern. The Swiss burghers laughed good-naturedly: spies didn't behave like that. Dulles had chosen Bern not only for its fine food and wines but also for its young women. He had already developed an insatiable sexual drive, and many a typist in New York had shared his bed. In Bern he enjoyed similar success; more than one *Mädchen* fell for his charm.

His arrival, however, caused concern among the small local foreign intelligence community in the country. An MI6 officer operating as the British consul, a German Abwehr agent running a bookshop, and a Russian NKVD agent with the unlikely cover of an importer of caviar all set about trying to gain Dulles's friendship in the hope of passing him false information. Dulles listened politely as he swallowed schnapps and ate roast venison in the town's restaurants while they told their stories, and not for a moment did he allow them to think other than that they had duped him.

With the instinct that came to serve him well, Dulles shared what he was told with the director of Swiss intelligence, who was strongly pro-American and divided his dislike equally between the British and German spies operating in Switzerland. By the time the OSS began to rampage through Occupied Europe, Dulles was ideally placed to play a decisive role in sabotage and espionage operations against the Third Reich. His own speciality was black propaganda, and he created hundreds of different leaflets and documents for the French Resistance to circulate. The Swiss intelligence chief helped him to find a printer in Geneva who had fonts of German and French type and a stock of printing paper from both countries to give more credibility to the forgeries. The results spread havoc across the Third Reich.

It was a life in which Dulles thrived: He was only answerable to Donovan; he could come and go as he pleased and lavishly entertain his girlfriends or a potential recruit to his network. In turn he sent a steady stream of encoded cables to Washington, which he believed contained valuable intelligence that MI6 was not privy to. The thought of, as he later put it, "putting one over the Brits" was especially satisfying, so he was understandably astonished in April 1943 to receive a coded cable from Donovan, "Your work is being discounted one hundred percent by the War Department." A second cable followed in even stronger terms, "Be advised your material disagrees with reports we have received elsewhere. Your information is now given a lower rating than any other source. This seems to indicate a need for using the greatest care in checking all your sources."

Dulles had become a victim of MI6 manipulation. To the Secret Intelligence Service he was what one report described as "a Yankee-doodle-dandy blow-in who has little to provide in real intelligence." With London awash with governments-in-exile intelligence organizations, the feeling in MI6 was that a newcomer like Dulles did not have the commanding grasp of how the deadly secret war must be fought. Two years before the United States had entered the war, MI6 had already built up its own network of spies and informers in Occupied Europe. An MI6 report said, "Dulles seems to get too excited about small successes."

Nevertheless, to keep track of what he was reporting, the Bletchley code breakers had been ordered to use their skills to decipher Dulles's cables. The transcripts were sent to MI6. Among those who read them was Kim Philby, a Soviet mole in the Secret Intelligence Service. Though he saw nothing in 1943 to alarm him, Philby reported Dulles's activities to his Soviet controller in Moscow, where the news caused concern that, as the Red Army slowly but surely pushed back the Nazi invaders from its homeland, Dulles might pay serious attention to the growing propaganda Goebbels was disseminating that the Soviet thrust west was really intended to occupy land beyond the German borders. Philby was ordered to discredit any claims by Dulles's informers that supported the view, and he began to raise questions with that slight stutter at Stewart Menzies's Monday morning senior staff meetings: Was Dulles being spoon-fed stories that fed his own anti-British mentality?

Finally Menzies ordered the MI6 station chief in Washington to warn his War Department contacts of the danger of taking intelligence at its face value at the expense of analysis. The alert was intended as a warning shot across Dulles's bow, but it failed. Dulles had ignored Donovan's messages and cabled back he always trusted his own judgment and did not intend to stop doing so, adding that he was certain the criticisms of his sources "come from a place that is not always accurate as I have discovered." There were no more cables challenging him.

Dulles's own spies were more than Nazi propagandists, and not least remarkable was the level they operated at and the risks they took. Bern had its quota of Gestapo agents who kept close watch on all visitors from the Reich to the town. One was Fritz Kolbe, a senior diplomat in the German Foreign Ministry who, on one of his early visits, had approached an MI6 officer and volunteered his services. The offer had been relayed to London, and Sir Claude Dansey, the deputy director of the Secret Intelligence Service, had rejected Kolbe as "too obviously a plant." Kolbe had then turned to Dulles, who spent weeks establishing Kolbe was genuine before he started to accept the copies of secret telegrams Kolbe smuggled out of Berlin. Dulles was astonished at the quality of the intelligence, and Kolbe became his most important asset. Within eighteen months, the diplomat provided over fifteen hundred documents, which by 1944 continued to reveal priceless insights into Hitler's plans. In May of that year, Dulles cabled Washington, "I feel we will miss genuine opportunities if we disregard what I am getting."

As well as Kolbe, there were other important agents in Dulles's still small but increasingly significant network. One was a member of an anti-Nazi underground organization. The man revealed to Dulles the plan to assassinate Hitler. In July 1944, the plot almost succeeded, but as a result the German borders were closed, and Kolbe could no longer visit Switzerland. Dulles's other informers fell silent. Only after the war ended did he learn they had been executed. By then the spymaster had become convinced the Soviet Union was the threat about which they had warned. He had returned to Washington in 1945 determined to continue supporting their claims.

On March 5, 1946, Dulles had listened on the radio to Churchill using for the first time the metaphor "Iron Curtain," which would become part of the lexicon of fear that cast its shadow over the world. In a rousing speech, Churchill warned of the threat to democracy posed by the Soviet Union. Dulles had been in Washington when, on March 12, 1947, Truman developed the theme in his address to a joint session of Congress. Truman knew he would scare his listeners with his demand for $400 million to launch what became known as the Truman Doctrine to fight Communism. Still he was determined to defend Europe against Soviet subjugation. "The United States must not hesitate, otherwise we may endanger the peace of the world and we shall surely endanger the welfare of our nation." Dulles had been present when the Joint Chiefs of Staff had briefed the CIA in June 1948 on what was required of the agency: early warnings of Soviet military schemes.

Since then Dulles had been at the center of secret operations to deny Moscow its plan to spread Communism and dominate the world. Even before the Berlin Blockade had started he was in the beleaguered city, supervising the unleashing of anti-Soviet propaganda across Europe. In many ways he had arrived too late to stop the brain drain from Germany; over a thousand German scientists and technicians had been captured by the Russians in the fall of the city and shipped to the Soviet Union, many never to return. All atomic research facilities, the rocket-testing station in Peenemünde, and the optical instrument plants in Thuringia had all been dismantled and shipped by train to Russia under cover of the Potsdam Agreement, which gave Moscow the right to claim reparations for loss the Soviet people suffered during the war. A quarter of all Germany's equipment in the metallurgical, chemical, and machine industries was uprooted.

When Dulles arrived in West Berlin in late May 1945, his counterpart in East Berlin, Lavrenti Beria, chief of the NKVD, had set up his headquarters in the city's Soviet zone in the suburb of Karlshorst. Dulles had already assisted in launching an operation against Beria in which he had helped to smuggle out of Germany, under the nose of the NKVD, Werner von Braun and his team of rocket scientists, who had launched the V-1 and V-2 rockets against London in the dying months of the war. He had recruited Wehrmacht General Reinhard Gehlen, who had been responsible for gathering Germany's military intelligence about the Soviet Union, and arranged for him to be secretly flown to Washington on September 20, 1945, along with eight cases secured by steel combination locks Gehlen had personally buried in the Bavarian Alps as his bargaining offer to the Americans. The trunks contained thousands of documents from Abwehr informers inside the Soviet Union and a list of OSS operatives who were claimed to be members of the U.S. Communist Party (a claim never pursued). There was also detailed information on the lifestyles of Stalin, the Soviet Politburo, and Russian military commanders. Most important of all was the Soviet Order of Battle in the run-up to the German collapse, which indicated there were plans to occupy countries beyond the German borders. Finally, Gehlen's treasure trove contained details of his own network of spies. He offered to mobilize them to work for the United States under his command as a new Bundesnachrichtendienst (BND, the Federal Intelligence Service), which became a key element in the CIA's war against the NKVD's Section for Terror and Diversion (SMERSH, from *Smert Shpionam*, a Russian phrase meaning "Death to Spies").

Once more Dulles's dislike and often deep distrust of Britain made him take steps to ensure that in none of these operations would MI5 or MI6 play a major role. They would only become what Dulles termed "minor beneficiaries" in intelligence obtained from the Gehlen boxes.

THREE YEARS BEFORE, ON FEBRUARY 4, 1945, with Allied victory in sight and their armies prepared to capture Berlin, Stewart Menzies and Allen Dulles were among Allied intelligence officers in the delegations of the Grand Alliance—the United States, Britain, and Russia—gathered to agree to the shape of the postwar world. On that cold day in Yalta, the ancient playground of the tsars, fifty nations had by now joined the Allied cause, and sixty million of their troops had been mobilized.

Even as Churchill and Roosevelt expressed the pious hope the killing would soon be over, the number of dead was about to increase. Over dinner the night before, Stalin had requested that Dresden be destroyed to stop German reinforcements being moved to the front line against the Red Army. Menzies had asked one of the British delegation, Field Marshal Lord Alexander, what the intelligence was for Stalin's claim. Alexander had spread his hands and shrugged. A few days later, over twelve hundred RAF and U.S. bombers devastated Dresden: 39,773 bodies were officially identified; 20,000 were listed as "burnt beyond recognition."

By the end of the conference, Stalin had steamrolled his way to achieving all he wanted: the unconditional surrender of Hitler and a Germany that could never again threaten Russia as it had twice done in the past thirty years, together with a wide swath of Eastern Europe that would subordinate its sovereignty and turn it into client states of Moscow. It signaled the creation of the Soviet Union.

The nightmare Churchill had feared, and which he hoped the Yalta Conference would resolve, had become a living threat that dogged his footsteps through the Vorontsov Palace, where the British delegation was staying, as he came and went from his meetings with Stalin and Roosevelt. The climax had come when Churchill had met Stalin to try to salvage something for Britain. "How would it do for you to have ninety percent predominance in Romania, for us to have ninety percent of the same in Greece, and go fifty-fifty about Yugoslavia?" the prime minister asked. Stalin had stared impassively listening to the translation of the proposal.

Churchill had written down the figures on his sketchbook and handed it to Stalin, who glanced at it and handed it back without a word. Churchill then added, "Fifty percent each for Hungary and seventy-five twenty-five for Bulgaria in Russia's favour." Once more Stalin had studied the paper. He smiled for the first time, produced a blue pencil, then made a large check mark on the page. No mention was made of Poland, for which Britain had gone to war, or Czechoslovakia or the division of Germany.

So had begun the carve-up of Europe, something Britain had resisted from the days of the kaiser, of Napoleon, of the Sun King Louis XIV, and even before the Spanish Armada in the sixteenth century. No single power had dominated Europe as Russia would do now.

Before his flight back to London, Menzies had told Dulles, "Stalin will not only have a powerful army to make this work for him, he will also have the backup of his intelligence service. And mark my words, we will be the prime targets. Britain and the United States in that order."

The first victims of Yalta were the Soviet prisoners of war who had taken up arms against the Red Army. They were transferred to the Russians, along with Russian-born Jews pulled from the concentration camps and an unknown number of displaced persons caught up in the devastation of Europe. Forced into Soviet arms at gunpoint, many committed suicide. Within days of the end of the Yalta Conference, Poland became another part of the Soviet Union, along with East Germany.

Back at his retreat at Warm Springs, President Roosevelt had somehow summoned up enough strength to grip the arms of his wheelchair
and croak, "We can't do business with Stalin." Hours later he was dead.
His failure early on to recognize that Stalin was what Secretary of State
John Foster Dulles called "an authentic monster" would become part of
the president's legacy.

6

The Atom Spies

In the early hours of June 13, 1944, a terrifying new sound filled the sky over London. More frightening than the drone of German bombers during the blitz, it was the sound of jet engines powering fuselages each containing 1,800 pounds of explosive. The pilotless bombs sounded like giant insects sent to fulfill the vengeance Hitler had promised for the firebombing of Hamburg. As fearful Londoners looked skyward, the venomous sound stopped, followed by the bomb plummeting to earth and exploding. Within two days, forty-five more flying bombs had swarmed over London to deliver their lethal payloads against terraced houses and office buildings.

On the night of June 17, after another 217 missiles had struck the city, Churchill summoned Menzies and Petrie to join his air force tacticians to answer one question: How could central London, the heart of the war effort, be protected? The Air Ministry analysts had calculated the bombs were aimed at central London, from where Britain's war effort was directed against Nazi Germany.

Among those gathered around the War Room conference table was yet another of the extraordinary men recruited by MI5. He was John Cecil Masterman, in many ways the perfect upper-class Englishman. With his cultivated accent and foppish manners, he had the handsome looks women found appealing. A distinguished history professor at Oxford, he had played hockey for his country and, in his spare time, wrote detective thrillers, the nearest he had come to the intelligence world until he had been recruited to head the Twenty Committee, who ran the double agents who had survived the interrogations of Robin Stephens in Latchmere House. Where Stephens's defining trait was his monocle, Masterman liked to sleep on the floor of the barber's shop at his club, the Reform. "I would lie awake listening to the doodlebugs overhead followed by a thudding silence, hoping that in the next silence I would not be destroyed," he recalled.

Masterman had chosen the twenty symbol for the committee because it appealed to his academic wit. The figure in Roman numerals, XX, symbolized the double-cross.

On that warm June night when the All Clear siren announced another raid was over, Churchill's question to Masterman was blunt: Could his double agents successfully feed information to their German controllers that would make the technicians at the rocket launch sites adjust the target coordinates?

In the silence of the conference room, everyone knew what that would mean. To move the present coordinates too far from central London would arouse immediate suspicion among the Germans.

Everyone knew the double agents had already played an important role in fooling the Germans over the question of where the D-Day landing would take place, and no one doubted that before the war ended, there would be further need for their skills. Equally, if the attacks on central London continued, the consequences would be devastating. But if the technicians at the launch sites could be persuaded to shorten their ranges in the belief they were overshooting the original target, it would make a significant difference. It would mean the rockets would fall on an already battered East End of the city and the countryside beyond, which had so far largely escaped death and destruction. Was Churchill ready to dramatically reduce the threat to central London— the seat of government—by approving a plan that, if it became public, would have enormous political repercussions for allowing one part of the city to be spared and another area sacrificed?

The eastern part of the city had a large Jewish population of tailors, shirt- and shoemakers, and pastry cooks and their families. Despite the powerful voices they had in the government, Churchill and his air chiefs had so far not been persuaded to direct some of their Lancaster bombers to bomb at least the gas chambers in the concentration camps along their routes to destroy German cities. A cabinet decision had been made that the camps were not a priority target. If they learned of it, would British Jews see the decision to divert the doodlebugs as another example of what they regarded as indifference to the fate of their relations in Auschwitz, Dachau, and Bergen-Belsen, the liberation of which would finally begin to unmask the first horrors of the Holo-caust?

Churchill authorized the deception to proceed. Masterman assigned Eddie Chapman, his top double agent, to carry it out. Chapman's biogra-pher, Ben Macintyre, would record: "To the hard-headed men of military intelligence, the plan was clear and logical." The part Menzies and Petrie had in approving it has remained hidden from scrutiny in the highly clas-sified files of both services.

The urgency of Chapman's mission intensified daily. On July 1, 1944, Chapman had sent his first radio message to his Abwehr controller, insist-ing the rockets "are still overshooting their targets." The next doodlebugs began to fall short, plummeting into the East End and the farmland be-yond. Masterman was exultant. "The deception was a very real triumph, saving many thousands of lives," he said later.

Chapman's messages to his controller were destroyed on Petrie's or-ders, who was only too well aware of the outcry that would ensue if in-habitants of East London discovered Winston Churchill had sacrificed their loved ones to protect the center of the capital. The doodlebug campaign ended in August 1944 and had killed 6,184 people.

AS ALLIED VICTORY in the war became more certain, David Petrie sent officers to liaise with MI6 and American intelligence teams advanc-ing off the beaches in Normandy into France. Each team carried a "Pur-ple Primer," a school composition book listing names of German and French nationals suspected of collaborating with the Nazis. Among them was P. G. Wodehouse. During the war the British-born writer had broad-cast on German radio. After his capture in Paris he was interrogated by a member of MI5's legal department who decided there was insufficient evidence to prosecute successfully. Wodehouse was allowed to travel to New York, where he vowed he would never return to England. Other collaborators did not escape so lightly. John Amery, a committed Fascist and the son of the politician Leo Amery, was found in an internment camp near Rome. He readily admitted being a Nazi supporter and was brought to London, tried at the Old Bailey, and sentenced to be hanged. William Joyce, the notorious "Lord Haw-Haw," suffered the same fate. Working with French, Dutch, and Norwegian intelligence services, MI5 officers rounded up British prisoners of war who had vol-unteered to serve in the SS Legion of St. George on the Russian front. They were handed over to the army and sent to military prisons in England. After the war they were allowed to disappear into a world that had forever changed.

THROUGHOUT THE WAR, the reading list of MI5 counterintelligence officers included the *Daily Worker* (later renamed the *Morning Star*) and pamphlets published by the Communist Party of Great Britain. They were a reminder that though the Soviet Union had since June 1941 become an ally in the fight against Nazism, there remained within the Security Service a feeling that Communism would pose the threat to a lasting postwar peace. It was a constant theme for David Petrie at his Monday morning meetings with his assistant directors. One was Roger Hollis of F-Branch, MI5's future director-general, who would become the subject of an unprecedented hunt to discover if he was a Soviet double agent. An event that began on a winter's day in 1945 would help to fuel the investigation.

Hollis had barely unlocked his office door in Leconfield House, the new home of MI5 in London's Mayfair, when he signed for a sealed envelope messengered over from MI6. Inside was a buff-colored file and a typed letter from Kim Philby, the head of IX Section, which dealt with international Communism. Hollis had met Philby at interservice conferences to discuss the threat of Communism.

Philby was the son of Sir Harry Philby, and the boy had been raised in a world where Britain still ruled almost a quarter of the earth's surface and the most important document in his father's fancooled palatial office, as a senior member of the Indian Raj, was his British passport.

Sir Harry was one of those charged with implementing London's decisions, one of a band of brothers, no more than two thousand, who made up the Indian Civil Service. They lived in magnificent mansions and traveled in style on the Hyderabad Express, with its private compartments where champagne was served from ice-cold silver buckets before eight-course dinners in the dining car reserved only for those in the service of the Raj. Growing up, Kim had spent his holidays indulging in the great pastimes of the British in India, playing cricket and polo, or tennis on the family's well-kept grass court, and, when he was old enough, sitting with his father on their veranda while white-robed servants served "sundowners," the first whiskies of the evening.

Then suddenly the dazzling vision of a life of marble palaces, tiger hunts, bejeweled elephants—the world of the Philbys—was no more.

No one knew what was the cause; no one ever would. There were whispers in the Raj's clubs in Bombay, Delhi, and beyond to those in Lahore and Simla that there had been a serious falling-out between Sir Harry and his superior. "Maybe he had made a pass at the man's *memsahib*, his wife," wrote one grande dame to a cousin in England. Harry Philby was known as "a bit of a dog." One day Sir Harry was there, another of those Englishmen with a braying voice that caused Mohandas Gandhi to suggest, "The English were descended from donkeys and not, like the rest of mankind, from monkeys." Then Sir Harry was gone, on a liner out of India. At the Egyptian port of Suez, he had disembarked.

Embittered and hostile toward Britain, he traveled to Saudi Arabia and found a ready listener in Ibn Saud, the founder of the Saudi royal family, who had come to believe he was being cheated by Britain over oil rights. Sir Harry used his undoubted negotiating skills to enable American companies to obtain the concessions.

By then Kim—named by his father after the hero of Rudyard Kipling's novel of espionage and adventure—had become a foreign correspondent for the *Times* of London after graduating from Cambridge and had been sent in 1937 to cover the Spanish Civil War. His shyness and fluent Spanish made him a welcome figure among General Franco's Fascist forces. None suspected Philby had already been recruited as a Russian spy while at Cambridge University.

His first assignment from his Moscow controller, an officer of the GRU—Russian military intelligence—was to send reports on where Franco intended to attack Republican forces. Among the targets Philby identified was Guernica, the historic Basque capital.

Franco gave the order for the Luftwaffe Condor Legion to destroy the town, an act that drew worldwide condemnation and led to Picasso's greatest antiwar painting. Shortly afterward, Philby was wounded by a Republican artillery shell supplied from Russia. Returning to England in 1939, he was told by his Soviet controller to apply for a job in MI6. He passed the vetting process and was assigned to the Secret Intelligence Service's Iberian section; one of his colleagues was Graham Greene. Years later, the novelist recalled, "When Kim became head of the section, he covered up any mistakes we made. He had that skill of appearing totally loyal to his staff while, of course, his real loyalty was to Russia."

The GRU had long recognized the importance of recruiting spies from the traditional universities of Oxford and Cambridge in Britain, perceiving that clever and ambitious undergraduates, if caught early, could be persuaded to join the Communist cause and continue to serve it throughout their high-flying careers, which their degrees virtually guaranteed. There was the added bonus of the attraction both campuses had for Americans who could be exploited. Whittaker Chambers, a *Time* magazine editor, and Alger Hiss, a State Department official who had attended the Yalta Conference and was the secretary-general of the founding session of the United Nations in San Francisco, had both visited Cambridge.

Philby had access to MI6's own Registry, from which he passed details of officers and informers across the world to his controller. After Britain and the Soviet Union became wartime allies, Philby received a new assignment: to find out if Churchill and Roosevelt planned to make separate peace with Germany, so allowing Hitler to use all his military power to attack the Soviet Union. Philby reported that within MI5 and MI6 were a number of senior officers not opposed to the idea. In March 1943 a German spy, Otto John, working for Admiral Wilhelm Canaris, the head of the Abwehr (military intelligence), secretly traveled to Lisbon to meet a small MI6 team that included Kim Philby. John revealed that a group of German High Command officers was ready to open peace negotiations with Britain.

Philby returned to London and wrote a report to Stewart Menzies, in which he described the plot as "no more than a ploy to buy time for the Nazi war effort. If we go along with it, we are expected to reduce our bombing raids and focus more on the Pacific War. We would also have to agree to stop our supplies of arms to the Red Army. Otto John is unreliable and bordering at times on being a fantasist. This is a view shared by Allen Dulles in Switzerland."

Philby's report was sent to Winston Churchill, who wrote across it, "No Action." Stalin's fear of a separate peace treaty was dead.

IN HIS LETTER DELIVERED to Hollis on that winter morning, Philby did not indicate why he had passed the file along. Neither did he reveal he had urgent business in Istanbul.

A Russian intelligence officer, Konstantin Volkov, based at his country's Istanbul embassy, had approached the British Consulate saying he wanted to defect. In return for receiving asylum he would reveal the names of a Soviet spy ring operating within the "very heart of your government. One is an intelligence officer. Two more are employed in your Foreign Office." The startled consul had sent a priority-coded telegram to Prodome, the Foreign Office cable address, quoting Volkov's claim. The details were passed to Stewart Menzies, who asked Philby to investigate. He realized at once that he was the intelligence officer identified

by Volkov; the others were Donald Maclean and Guy Burgess, both Foreign Office diplomats and also Russian spies. Maclean had been photocopying top-secret documents for Moscow since 1938. Philby caught the
first flight to Istanbul. By then Volkov had vanished.

On arriving, Philby used a pay phone to send a message to his contact in the Soviet Embassy. Istanbul remained a center for intelligence
gathering, with Russian and Allied agents using shortwave transmissions
to report to their controllers in London, Washington, and Moscow. MI6
had stationed a team from its Radio Security Service to monitor other
wireless transmissions. After Philby's arrival there was a succession of
coded messages from the Soviet Embassy to Moscow about Volkov's disappearance. While Philby made every show to his colleagues of trying
to locate Volkov, he kept his Soviet controller informed of where the
diplomat could be hiding. After a week Philby sent Menzies a report,
"Regret no sign. Am giving up. Returning to London."

Days later a Soviet military transport made an unscheduled landing at
Ankara airport and a heavily bandaged figure was carried on a stretcher
onto the aircraft. Konstantin Volkov was on his way to Moscow to meet his
certain death. Kim Philby's role in leading Volkov to his captors would remain undetected.

THE FILE PHILBY HAD SENT HOLLIS also involved a defector. Igor
Gouzenko was a twenty-six-year-old cipher clerk at the Russian Embassy
in Ottawa. Due to be posted back to Moscow with his pregnant wife,
Gouzenko had become aware of the harsh conditions back home: The
incoming messages that passed through his office painted a picture of
near-starvation and draconian police behavior. Gouzenko had decided
he and his wife must remain in Canada, and in exchange he would offer
a number of documents he had carefully hidden for just such an emergency. He hoped if they were published, they would reveal the truth behind Soviet propaganda the embassy sent out to the Ottawa media,
describing life in the Soviet Union. He had also included a GRU codebook listing the names of Soviet informers.

In his cheap suit, the slightly built cipher clerk had walked into the
office of the *Ottawa Journal* and offered his story. Despite poor English
and an excitable manner, Gouzenko attempted to translate the documents he pulled from a shopping bag. The more he tried, the more he
sounded like another of those cranks who regularly turn up in every
newspaper office. The reporter brought him coffee and sent him on his
way. Furious, Gouzenko walked over to the Canadian Parliament build-

ing and tried to see the minister of justice. Again, he was turned away. Visibly upset, he returned home to find his wife screaming from behind the front door of their apartment and the Russian military attaché and two other diplomats from the embassy trying to gain entry. Meanwhile, a neighbor had summoned the police, and two officers arrived. The Russian diplomats left, having failed to persuade Gouzenko to accompany them, but their presence had been included in the police incident report and, because of their diplomatic immunity, was passed on to the head of the local Security Intelligence Service of the Royal Canadian Mounted Police.

Recognizing it wasn't every day that "three Soviet diplomats try to break down the front door of one of their staff," he sent the details to Sir William Stephenson, who oversaw all MI5 and MI6 intelligence operations in North America from his New York office. The MSS chief added that he had retained the documents Gouzenko was carrying and that the clerk and his wife were in protective custody while a decision was being made on how to respond to the Russian ambassador's repeated requests for the couple to be returned to his custody, claiming Gouzenko had stolen diplomatic material from the embassy. It had been enough to alert Stephenson, and he had flown to Ottawa to interview Gouzenko. He then telephoned Hollis, saying he should come to Ottawa.

Stephenson was another of those rich and powerful men who found themselves attracted to the twilight world of spying. A noted amateur boxer—commentators said he could have turned professional—he had gone on to make his fortune from industry. On a visit to New York he had met William Donovan. The Irishman and Scot found much in common, a passion for sports and the subtleties of the law, and became close friends not least because Donovan had become Stephenson's personal lawyer. When Donovan returned from his visit to London, which had led to America's collaboration with MI5 and MI6, the two men had dined at Donovan's New York club. Over lunch Stephenson had confessed he was bored "just making money." Donovan had proposed he might consider "something a little more exciting." He had then shared with the industrialist details of the deal he had orchestrated between American and British intelligence. "Any chance of a berth on the ship?" Stephenson had asked. There was: Within days Donovan had persuaded Churchill to appoint Stephenson as MI5 and MI6 coordinator with the COI.

By the time Stephenson met Hollis at the airport, Gouzenko had been transferred to the former Special Operations Executive camp on the shore of Lake Ontario. It had trained British agents for missions into Nazi Germany. Ivan Drake, who was an agent, recalled to the author,

"The place was designed to create unholy terror in anyone who thought they were up to serving in SOE. In one corner of the base was a compound where special interrogations were conducted on suspected double agents or spies."

It was there Gouzenko was held and subjected to techniques in which he was deprived of sleep, denied food, and threatened he would be handed back to the Soviets because he was really trying to plant false information. Hour after hour he was questioned by Hollis, but Gouzenko stuck to his story: The documents were not fake, and he would readily cooperate with his interrogators in return for being allowed to remain with his wife in Canada. After a week, Hollis decided the cipher clerk was telling the truth and the documents he had stolen were genuine.

Gouzenko was reunited with his wife and moved to a comfortable MSS safe house near Montreal, having been given a code name, Corby, and promised asylum in Canada. His wife later gave birth to a daughter. By then Gouzenko had confirmed the identities of more than twenty GRU agents operating in Canada who were listed in the codebook. "Elli" was Kathleen (Kay) Willsher, who worked in the British High Commission's Registry in Ottawa, a position that gave her access to sensitive security files on Canadian, American, and British intelligence officers in Canada. Another alias revealed someone even more important. "Alek" shielded the identity of Alan Nunn May, a British physicist who had worked on the Manhattan Project to produce the atomic bomb. It would emerge that he had secretly passed to his Russian controller samples of the uranium isotopes crucial to the weapon. After the war ended, Willsher was sentenced to three years hard labor and Nunn May to ten years imprisonment.

The verdicts alarmed Washington and sowed suspicion that a deal had been made in which the two spies would reveal the full extent of their treachery in return for their light sentences and, in doing so, would enable MI5 and MI6 to plug any holes in their internal security. Even Donovan found it hard to explain away how Willsher and Nunn May had escaped the fate—either long imprisonment or even the death sentence—that they would have faced in America. He had asked Stephenson a blunt question: Had either British intelligence service something to hide? Stephenson insisted they had not. Elsewhere in Washington, though, other questions persisted. Why had MI5 and MI6 failed to spot the treachery of Nunn May and Willsher until it was pure good luck that a Russian cipher clerk had raised the alarm? Had there been a cover-up within the Secret Intelligence Service or the Security

Service, not only to protect their reputations but for an even more sinister reason? Was there another Soviet mole inside British intelligence? If so, how high did he go in the hierarchy of either service?

Within MI5 the breaking of the Canadian spy ring was seen as a personal triumph for Hollis. Kim Philby sent him a note of congratulations.

DAVID PETRIE RETIRED AS MI5 DIRECTOR-GENERAL IN 1946, having conducted a dignified campaign to ensure the new Labour government, which had swept to office that year, did not amalgamate MI5 with MI6. He failed, however, to get his deputy, Jasper Harker, appointed to replace him. Harker had not succeeded in convincing Clement Attlee, the new prime minister, that he had the attributes to head the Security Service. "He has to have the technical qualities required for intelligence work. He must be able to control a team of individualists engaged on important secret work. At the same time he must have a lively appreciation of the rights of the citizen," insisted Attlee. He decided the man best suited was Percy Sillitoe, whose career had mostly been in police work in South Africa and Northern Rhodesia (now Zambia). In 1943, Sillitoe had been appointed chief constable of Kent. His MI5 deputy was Guy Liddell, who had served under Kell beginning in 1919 and was regarded by his colleagues as an outstanding counterintelligence officer. Though he himself was not homosexual, Liddell preferred the company of those who were. For the puritanical Attlee, it was a choice he found "most regrettable."

Liddell's first impression of Sillitoe was equally unflattering. "In his country brogues he looks like a farmer on a day out in London after chasing poachers and minor criminals through the lanes of Kent. Not exactly training for serious intelligence work," Liddell had told a friend at the Chelsea Palais, a well-known homosexual haunt. Liddell began to ridicule Sillitoe using Latin epigrams and coded references his superior did not grasp. Sillitoe later wrote, "On occasion I felt like a small boy, unwillingly let into a closed world." The words reflect his failure to exert his authority over his staff.

BOTH WINSTON CHURCHILL AND FRANKLIN ROOSEVELT had paid close attention to intelligence gathering during the war. Roosevelt's prime interest was in spies and covert operations, and he liked nothing better than to hear from Allen Dulles about OSS operations in Europe.

Churchill, while also gripped by tales of derring-do, had a deep understanding of how signals intelligence (SIGINT) had played an important role. The mathematical skills needed to break a code held an abiding fascination for the prime minister; in the early hours of the morning, he would sit in his bed and study how a cipher had been cracked. He considered it "much more fun than trying to solve a crossword."

Roosevelt's sudden death in April 1945 had changed the future path the U.S. intelligence community would take. "Had he lived, FDR would almost certainly not have closed down America's wartime intelligence agency, OSS, before there had been firmly established a peacetime replacement," concluded intelligence analyst Christopher Andrew. More certain is that Roosevelt's successor, Harry Truman, was not only less interested in intelligence, but he also had a set of different priorities in how he wanted his spymasters to operate.

Truman was also concerned about the wartime expansion of the FBI's powers and in his first meeting with J. Edgar Hoover, the agency's director, had brusquely told him it was "not altogether appropriate" for him "to be spending federal funds merely to satisfy curiosity concerning the sex lives of members of Congress."

The new president was equally unimpressed by the links the OSS had with MI5 and MI6. It was part of his complex personality that he found it hard to accept the idea of America maintaining an organization primarily concerned with Europe. What was needed, he said, was a new organization that would operate under "presidential direction." His decision, ratified by the National Security Act of July 26, 1947, confirmed the prime position of the Central Intelligence Agency in the fledgling U.S. intelligence community. However, Truman had agreed to the continuation of America's SIGINT collaboration with Britain after Acting Secretary of State Dean Acheson sent him a top-secret memo on September 12, 1945 (still only partly declassified), in which he reminded the president of "the possible hostile intentions of foreign nations" and "recommended you authorize continued collaboration between the United States and the United Kingdom in the field of signals."

At the end of the war, one arm of British intelligence—the Code and Cipher School—had emerged with its reputation enhanced. They were the Bletchley Park code breakers whose Ultra machines had broken the German codes for its U-boats. Renamed in 1946 as Government Communications Headquarters, they were relocated from their rural surroundings of Buckinghamshire to a featureless group of buildings in the drab London suburb of Eastcote. It was there that the cryptographers continued trying to decipher the coded messages of Soviet spymasters to their agents. The Russian intelligence service had been founded in 1917 as the Cheka and became known successively as the GPU, OGPU, GUGB, and in the war as the NKVD. (On March 13, 1954, it was retitled the Komitet Gosudarstvennoi Bezopasnosti, the KGB, and in 2005, it once more underwent a name change to become the FSB, the Federal Security Service.) To the Politburo and millions of Russians it remained the feared "Sword and Shield of the Party"—the shield to protect the Communist Party oligarchy, the sword to impose its will within and outside Russia. In 2008, three interrelated intelligence services continued to operate: the FSB, the SUR (foreign intelligence), and the long-established GRU (military intelligence).

Britain's and America's code breakers, who had worked closely together to break Nazi and Japanese codes, continued their collaboration on an equal partner basis. However, America under the Truman administration had emerged from the war as the most powerful nation on earth, and the arrival of the CIA—with its financial powers and technical skills—had led to its domination in other areas of the Anglo-American intelligence alliance. Meanwhile, after the uncovering of the Nunn May Canadian spy ring, both MI5 and MI6 had become what Allen Dulles called "services living on their reputations."

It was left to a GCHQ code breaker to partly save the day for MI5. Soviet intelligence used a one-time-pad system for encoding radio messages that, if properly used, made them virtually unbreakable. As the NKVD expanded its networks around the world, however, it took to distributing duplicate sets of pads to its agents. Arthur Martin, a wartime wireless intercept operator who was GCHQ's liaison officer with MI5, discovered what the Russians were doing, which led to the first major postwar code-breaking operation, code-named Venona. Using Martin's skills, Venona began to track the activities of a Soviet network in Britain and the United States. The work was also substantially helped by the NSA. Painfully slowly the information surfaced from the decodes; often they were no more than fragments of words. Pieced together they began to reveal how widespread Soviet espionage was in both countries, including its continued penetration of the atomic bomb program.

While the Venona code breakers continued their work, MI5's hunt for Soviet spies involved other branches: counterintelligence, the liaison unit with the empire's intelligence services, and the section tracking the activities of domestic political parties. In 1948, over a hundred civil servants in Whitehall were repeatedly questioned and never told why they had come under suspicion. Over twenty of them had their employment terminated; several had held senior positions during the war. Eighty-eight were transferred to other work and their security clearance reduced to the lowest category. Desks were suddenly vacated and a once trusted employee assigned to some outpost of the government. Families were split and there were a number of divorces.

Neighbors whispered that a man who had been a stalwart of their community had turned out to be "a Commie." The Registry files continued to expand, and scores of women found their next promotion was to work under the vigilant eye of its head, who made sure every file had its correct place in the indexes kept on cards in rows of wooden drawers. By 1949, thousands of new names had joined all the others on file.

Four years after a U.S. Air Force B-29 bomber, the *Enola Gay*, named by the pilot after his mother, had dropped the world's first atomic bomb over Hiroshima on August 6, 1945, the Registry contained the most personal details of over half a million ordinary British citizens, yet the system still failed to discover the identity of the Soviet spies in its midst. In Washington, there was consensus that the moles were after more of the secrets of the bomb. The uncovering of the Canadian ring increasingly raised fears within the CIA and FBI that further betrayal would also be traced to Britain.

AT 4:00 A.M. ON SEPTEMBER 3, 1949, Rear Admiral Roscoe H. Hillenkoetter was awakened by a telephone call at his home in the Georgetown neighborhood of Washington, D.C., bringing news he had dreaded. The fifty-two-year-old director of central intelligence (DCI), the third to hold the position, had left instructions that the moment there was confirmation he was to be called no matter what the hour. Two years into his job, after a career as Admiral Nimitz's intelligence chief in the Pacific war against Japan, the scholarly DCI continued to study the writings of Marx, Lenin, and Stalin. Their books had pride of place on his night table. The more he read, the more convinced Hillenkoetter became that the Soviet Union was determined to become America's military rival. To prepare for this, he had built a network of informers within the Soviet satellite nations: From East Germany through Poland, Hungary, and Bulgaria all the way into Russia, they risked their lives to send messages that eventually reached his desk. One had revealed that Russia was almost ready to explode an atomic bomb. Confirmation came from an intercept by one of the Venona code breakers. Frustratingly, there still had been no clue when or where the test would take place. Now, on that sultry morning in Washington, Hillenkoetter knew.

Six thousand miles away from where he had been awakened, the technicians aboard the USAF Long Range Detection Squadron aircraft checked their instruments one more time. The readings continued to show a radioactive cloud was drifting over the remote northwest area of the Soviet Union. On its present track the cloud would pass over northern Canada and out into the North Atlantic before reaching the British Isles. In the coming days Canadian and Royal Air Force planes were scrambled and began to fly in and out of the cloud collecting samples, which were sent to the Atomic Energy Commission and laboratories at Los Alamos and Harwell, Britain's atomic energy research center. The scientists all came to the same conclusion: Between August 26 and 29, the Soviet Union had detonated an atom bomb. Though it had less destructive power than the weapon that had devastated Hiroshima, CIA director Hillenkoetter nevertheless concluded, "The weapon is intended to secure a Soviet-dominated Communist world and the possibility for a direct attack upon the United States must be considered to have increased."

By then Venona had achieved a major breakthrough.

FROM THEIR EASTCOTE BUILDINGS, GCHQ decryption teams reached into Europe, with offices in Berlin and Gibraltar; in Tokyo, the British Embassy compound housed a team, and another was in Hong Kong. By 1949, every embassy within the empire had at least one cryptologist on its staff. Copies of all the intercepts were sent to MI5 and MI6 and shared with the National Security Agency department working on Venona. Its code breakers probed for Soviet spy rings in North America and Canada. To cover the South Pacific, the NSA and Eastcote jointly operated a station at Shoal Bay, near Darwin in Australia's Northern Territory, under the control of MI5's Far East expert. A fluent mandarin speaker, he cracked a number of coded messages from Moscow to its embassy in Canberra, revealing that several Soviet networks were operating in the country. As a result, Roger Hollis was sent to Australia to advise on the creation of the Australian Secret Intelligence Service (ASIS).

On October 9, 1949, a Fort Meade code breaker deciphered a message that indicated there could be another mole working in the Anglo-American atom bomb project. The revelation came at the time Mao Zedong's Communists had driven Chiang Kai-shek's Nationalists from power; it had been a revolution over which Washington had no control, and Americans were told that one in five of the world's population were now under Communist domination. On both sides of the Atlantic, the code breakers began the huge task of going back through every Soviet message ever located in the hope of discovering clues to the mole's identity. Many of the intercepts had not been properly decrypted at the time due to a shortage of skilled operatives. Now, the NSA and Eastcote had a total of 12,500 highly skilled technicians and the latest decoding machines.

The message the NSA cryptologist deciphered on that October day had originally been sent in 1945 to a Soviet agent based in New York. It contained a copy of a private telegram from Churchill to Truman about how to deal with Stalin in the postwar years. The telegram reflected the early days of the war when Roosevelt had said, half jokingly, he felt at times he found it easier to strike a deal with Stalin than to make one with Churchill.

While Churchill recognized that the bravery of the people of Stalingrad during its siege had created something close to hero worship in many Americans, the telegram reminded Truman that the evidence of the Stalin-induced famine in the Ukraine and the horror of the gulags was "every bit as bad as the Nazi concentration camps." America's prewar isolationism must not be allowed to return, urged Churchill. While due respect should continue to be paid to how the Soviet Union had fought hard against Nazi Germany, it must be leavened with reality: Global politics demanded that America must recognize that in Joseph Stalin was a tyrant as evil as Hitler had been.

What electrified the cryptologist was the telegram's revelation that an informer continued to be "invaluable." But who was he, or she? The code breaker continued his patient search. A week later he unearthed another clue. The indication came from a decrypt that revealed the spy had a sister at an American university. But which one? Was she a student or a teacher? Or employed in some other capacity? A third message contained a request for an update on the latest scientific terms being used in "the project." The cryptologist recognized the words. They had been identified in other decoded messages as referring to the Manhattan Project.

The FBI checked every campus in the United States. It took weeks to identify Kristel Fuchs as "probably" the mysterious sister. She had been a student at Swarthmore College. Another check turned probability into certainty. Her brother was Klaus Fuchs, a German-born scientist who became a British citizen in 1942. An outstanding mathematician and physicist, he had worked on the Manhattan Project and now had a senior post at Harwell. Fuchs and his sister had arrived in Britain as refugees from

Hitler's Germany in the mid-1930s. At the outbreak of war, like so many other Jews who had fled, they were interned, but once Fuchs's scientific background came to the notice of the authorities, the pair was released. Klaus Fuchs went to Los Alamos; his sister went to college. After the war both returned to England, Kristel to live a quiet, blameless life, while her brother continued his secret research at Harwell.

Given the FBI's growing belief that Klaus Fuchs was the most highly placed Soviet mole working at the heart of the Anglo-American atom bomb project, there was an immediate embarrassment for MI5 when his file was retrieved from the Registry and pored over by Guy Liddell and Roger Hollis. The file contained an entry that Klaus Fuchs was "very probably a Soviet spy before he was interned." There was no supporting evidence for that judgment, only a note stating, "The requirements of the war effort overrode all other considerations." Hollis and Liddell realized that if the FBI or CIA discovered this truth, it would have disastrous repercussions on the entire relationship MI5 had with the agencies. They decided to show the file to Percy Sillitoe. The director-general had read it in silence. Liddell insisted that "for the good of the service" the facts must be kept secret from the Americans. Sillitoe agreed. Hollis then suggested the secrecy should be extended to include Prime Minister Clement Attlee. Again, Sillitoe agreed. "Fuchs must be interviewed" was Sillitoe's only contribution to the next move.

Hollis and Liddell drew up a short list of persons who possessed not only good interrogation skills but also knowledge of Soviet recruiting methods. The chosen officer would have to ensure that Fuchs would never be given the slightest hint he had been unmasked because a Soviet code had been broken; he might be able to pass on the news to his controller before he was arrested. He could be successfully prosecuted only if he were persuaded to confess.

Hollis and Liddell finally settled on Jim Skardon, with his record of getting wartime Nazi spies to confess. Skardon's technique was to sit with a suspect for hours, allowing him to direct the conversation, but always slipping in a deadly question that would lead to an admission; his methods were regarded in MI5 as a master class on how to elicit a confession. Skardon had nodded sympathetically when, at their first meeting, Fuchs admitted that for years he had lived "in a state of schizophrenia." Gently pressed, the spy revealed he had been torn between his "love" for Britain and his "loathing" for the part he had played in the destruction of Hiroshima. Over weeks, Fuchs had revealed the full extent of Soviet penetration of the Anglo-American atomic bomb project, speaking in a low voice, pausing to allow Skardon to make his notes, and readily elaborating when asked, never for a moment admitting the gravity of his betrayal. Early on he identified two Americans, Julius and Ethel Rosenberg, as being members of the Soviet network in America, and Harry Gold as his courier at Los Alamos. A naturalized American born in Switzerland to Russian parents, Gold initially denied any knowledge of Fuchs or the Rosenbergs and insisted he had never been anywhere near Los Alamos, but a search of his home in Philadelphia uncovered evidence of hotel bills in Santa Fe, near the facility.

On February 10, 1950, Klaus Fuchs was tried at the Old Bailey, pleading guilty to four charges of passing information to the Soviet Union. The trial lasted eighty-five minutes. No mention was made of his MI5 file and its damning statement that almost a decade before he had been suspected of being a Soviet spy. Lord Goddard, Britain's chief justice, imposed a sentence of fourteen years. Ethel and Julius Rosenberg were executed by electrocution for spying, after a final demonstration outside the White House in which picketers protesting the sentence struggled with demonstrators bearing placards that read TWO FRIED ROSENBERGS COMING RIGHT UP. Gold received a thirty-year sentence largely because he had cooperated with the FBI.

In Washington, the conviction grew that Fuchs had been the linchpin of one of the most successful operations in the history of international espionage. He had been in a position to describe in detail the gaseous diffusion process for separating uranium-235 and uranium-238. "The Russians could hardly have learned more about our nuclear weapons had they been full partners in the undertaking," Roscoe Hillenkoetter had growled. The information the Soviet Union now had was worth far more than the original two billion dollars America had invested in a program that had given Soviet physicists the theoretical knowledge needed to detonate their first bomb on that August day in 1949. It exploded a little more than four years after America's entry into the atomic age with its test explosion in the New Mexico desert. Two trusted Britons, Klaus Fuchs and Alan Nunn May, had allowed Russia to close the gap and had hastened the start of the cold war by at least eighteen months.

The CIA and FBI asked rhetorical questions echoing those raised when Nunn May was unmasked. Why had Fuchs, a sensitive, intelligent, and idealistic man who lived through the Nazi period, embraced Communism, a belief system that would remake the world in Moscow's image? How had Fuchs evaded detection for so long? Or successfully managed to hide his allegiance to the Soviet Union? Why had no one in MI5 or MI6 noticed anything suspicious during his positive vetting process, which had given him an open door to the secrets of the Manhattan Project and later the clearance to work at Harwell? Within the CIA grew a conviction that both services had too easily allowed spies like Nunn May and Klaus Fuchs to penetrate, unchallenged, the very core of America's defenses.

7

Moles Between Friends

On an October morning in 1950, two men bounded down the aircraft steps before the transport's engines had stopped spinning. Collars upturned against the bitterly cold wind whistling over the tarmac of the Royal Air Force base at Northolt, to the west of London, they hurried toward the waiting government car.

The shorter of the pair was General Walter Bedell Smith, the new director of central intelligence. He had been appointed by President Truman, and Congress's approval came a week before he had boarded the overnight flight to Northolt. His reputation was that of a soldier who had risen through the ranks to become General Dwight Eisenhower's chief of staff in Europe and later U.S. ambassador in Moscow. Like his predecessor, Roscoe Hillenkoetter, Smith had made a close study of Stalin and concluded, "Here is one sonofabitch." Smith's reputation for making such judgments was coupled with his short fuse around fools and an obsession for perfection he shared with his own hero, General George Patton. On that October morning he was fifty-five years old and recovering from an operation to remove stomach ulcers. Surgery had left him weighing under 130 pounds, making his already prominent ears jut out even more. In the way he walked there was a menace that suggested if someone was not part of the answer he wanted, then he was a part of the problem. With him was his deputy, Allen Dulles.

Behind them they had left Washington in the grip of the cold war, which had spread to the other side of the world. In the last weekend of June 1950, Communist North Korean forces had invaded neighboring

South Korea all along the 38th parallel. Truman had immediately committed American warships, warplanes, tanks, artillery, and ground troops to go to the aid of South Korea, but the soldiers were untried in battle, and their only antitank weapons were ten-year-old bazookas virtually useless against the Soviet T-34 tanks Moscow had gifted North Korea. The U.S. forces had dug in around Pusan, one of the many unfamiliar names suddenly appearing in American newspapers in a succession of ever more depressing headlines for their readers. General Douglas MacArthur, the seventy-year-old hero of the Pacific war, had flown out of his Tokyo headquarters in his C-54, the *Scap,* to Seoul and pledged to drive back the enemy. But the enemy pressed forward into the winter of 1950–51, one even colder on the battlefront than that which had greeted Smith and Dulles when they landed in Northolt.

During the flight they had spoken about the need to destroy what Smith had called "Stalin's plan for world domination." As the plane crossed the Atlantic, both men had pondered the lack of warning the CIA had received about the impending attack. "Are we looking here at another Pearl Harbor?" Smith had asked. Dulles had no answer. But he later predicted (in a document declassified in 2003) the Korean War was a precursor for what he believed would be the real conflict in Europe against Communism.

TWO YEARS HAD PASSED SINCE THE FIRST AMERICAN TRANS-PORT had landed at Berlin's Tempelhof airport to break the stranglehold the Soviet blockade had on the embattled city. The last vestige of Stalin's popularity had turned to fear in the West as Bulgaria and Romania became the latest to be absorbed by the Russian expansion. From the Arctic Circle to the Baltic Sea flew the Russian flag. Soviet troops had seized control of northern Iran, and Moscow had declared a new parliament in Azerbaijan, which immediately granted it oil-drilling rights. Twelve battle-hardened Soviet divisions were massed on Turkey's eastern border. Italy's Communist Party was ordered to follow the hard line of the Kremlin's ideology, to oppose Truman's Marshall Plan to rebuild Europe, after Stalin had attacked it as an attempt by the United States to subjugate the continent economically and politically. A wave of strikes, street demonstrations, and battles swept up from Naples to Rome and on to Milan to be joined by two million workers in France in support.

In Washington there was a swift response. As well as into Germany, Marshall aid poured into France and Italy. With it came U.S. experts in the black art of propaganda, to use their skills against Communism, and bankers with cash to make secret payments to non-Communist political parties. Across Western Europe, the two forces of Communism and democracy mobilized under opposing banners. With them came the spies: the agents of the NKVD spreading into every corner of the Soviet satellites and beyond into Western Europe, Britain, and the United States. Opposing them were the officers of MI6, MI5, and the Central Intelligence Agency.

In one of his interviews with the author, Richard Helms recalled those turbulent times, "We were on a fast learning curve. Sure, we had the funds, the backing, and the people, and we no longer had to depend absolutely on the British to help guide us. We had to pick our own way and do it pretty damn quick."

Truman's order to carry the fight against Communism into all those countries where it was perceived as a threat to democracy had led to the CIA seeing its brief as "[to] go where we are needed and look where we want," recalled Helms. He also recognized that both MI5 and MI6 had accepted there "was a new player on the block" and that the CIA was ready to challenge the split Stalin had announced between capitalism and socialism, describing them as "two systems that cannot peacefully coexist." The American chargé d'affaires in Moscow, George Kennan, sent a telegram to Secretary of State James Byrnes that said, "Marxism is the fig leaf of [the Russian's] moral and intellectual respectability. Without it, they would stand before history, at best, as only the last of that long succession of cruel and wasteful Russian rulers who have relentlessly forced their nation to ever new heights of military power to guarantee external security for their internally weak regime." Truman couldn't have agreed with him more. The president had also recognized that while Soviet survival depended on Soviet aggression, it could not be defeated solely by the United States. To overcome world Communism's determination to achieve global domination required the help of its wartime ally Britain. Smith and Dulles had come to discover whether the Anglo-American alliance had been more severely damaged than had been suspected.

THE SUSPICIONS OF BOTH MEN had increased with a further serious breach of security over MI5's failure to carry out a proper vetting process on a nuclear physicist, Bruno Pontecorvo, who had been a colleague of Fuchs's at Harwell. A Jewish refugee from Mussolini's Italy, he was one of the few scientists in the world who knew the type of nuclear reactor needed to produce the most powerful weapon in the world. After Fuchs had been arrested, Pontecorvo had been interviewed in the same room, O55, in the War Office where Fuchs had finally confessed. However, his MI5 interrogator had failed to find any gaps in Pontecorvo's history, and his high-level security clearance remained intact.

Now, days before Smith and Dulles landed at Northolt, Pontecorvo and his wife and children had slipped out of London to travel to Moscow. Only then had MI5's failure emerged.

Pontecorvo and his wife were ardent Communists who had fled from Italy to the United States in 1938 and then traveled to Britain before the war started. Why the physicist had done so would remain one of the omissions in his MI5 file that was never addressed. His family had once more moved back to the United States, buying a house in Connecticut and living a quiet life as model citizens. From time to time, Pontecorvo would visit them before returning to his laboratory across the border in Canada, where he was working on the top-secret Manhattan Project. When the Nunn May spy ring had been uncovered through the Igor Gouzenko defection, Bruno Pontecorvo had never aroused suspicion. The Canadian Security Intelligence Service (RCMP) had assumed that before being sent from England in 1943 to work on the project, the scientist would have passed his positive vetting. The RCMP never checked whether its assumption was correct. However, the FBI had become curious about the physicist's lifestyle, traveling back and forth to his Connecticut home and maintaining another apartment outside Toronto. Certainly his salary did not allow for such expenditure. Was he perhaps receiving funds from a family legacy in Italy? Or from some other source? RCMP had made no checks. Why, after the war ended, when he had gone to work at Harwell, had Pontecorvo kept the Connecticut house while he had brought his family back with him to England? Again, RCMP had sought no answers. These intelligence failures meant other questions were also never explored.

Long before coming to Canada, was Pontecorvo already a Soviet sleeper agent who had been recruited at university after his scientific skills were noted? Had he been ordered to go to London before the war, where he would be in a good position to offer his services and learn about Britain's nuclear research? With his specialist qualifications, Pontecorvo would have been a welcome asset for Britain's defense industry, and he would be coming from the United States with a doting wife and loving children; their decision to settle in a country braced for war would show others the courage Winston Churchill called for in the nation.

No one had asked why the family gave up the security and bright lights of neutral America to live in blacked-out London. No one, it turned out, had asked any questions.

To their neighbors in Connecticut, retaining the house seemed a symbol of the family's wish to one day return and become American citizens. Instead Pontecorvo had become a British citizen in 1948. In one of those bureaucratic twists and turns, the news of his citizenship finally made its way across the Atlantic. Perhaps it was no more than a need to record in some file that a former resident of the United States was now a British citizen. In any event, the Pontecorvo house remained empty.

Given that the property, like any other, accrued taxes, which had gone unpaid, and given who Bruno Pontecorvo was—his name had briefly surfaced in the mass media hysteria following the atomic destruction of Hiroshima—the FBI had finally visited the house. What they discovered astonished the agents. The house contained a small library of books and pamphlets that extolled the virtues of Communism. For the FBI this was further proof that what the newspapers called the "Red Peril" had burrowed a little deeper into the United States. The discovery was sufficiently important for J. Edgar Hoover to send a letter to the British Embassy in Washington detailing what his agents had uncovered.

The letter arrived on the desk of Kim Philby, now the Embassy's first secretary and, in reality, MI6's liaison officer with the CIA and FBI. His position was one of the most important of all the Secret Intelligence Service's overseas postings and effectively placed him on the same level as the ambassador, allowing Philby to sit in on all U.S./U.K. policy meetings and read all the intelligence traffic between both countries. Just as he had when he realized the danger he faced when the defector Konstantin Volkov had offered to name him as one of the Soviet moles in Britain in exchange for his own asylum, Kim Philby had taken decisive action. He knew he could not send the letter to London so that Pontecorvo could be questioned; nor could he destroy the document, as Hoover might later ask what action London had taken. Philby had buried the letter deep in the embassy Registry. What he had not anticipated was that before boarding the flight to Northolt, Allen Dulles had been given a copy by Hoover. It was now in his briefcase in the car in which Stewart Menzies was driving Dulles and Smith from Northolt to London.

THEIR BELIEF THAT ANOTHER MOLE was operating within MI5 or MI6 had been fuelled by yet another transcript from the Venona code breakers, who had discovered a Soviet spy had been operating within the British Embassy in Washington during the last year of the war. The only clue to his identity in the intercept was a reference to his code name, "Homer," and an indication he was still active. J. Edgar Hoover had ordered the FBI to conduct an unprecedented check on the embassy's locally recruited domestic staff, believing they were the most likely to have been employed by one of the Soviet spies operating out of their own embassy in Washington. Like the RCMP Security Intelligence Service in the Pontecorvo case, Hoover had made the mistake of assuming the members of the diplomatic staff at the British Embassy had passed a security check in London before being posted to Washington with a sufficient clearance to give them access to U.S. secret intelligence material.

Philby, who had arrived in September 1949 in Washington, had begun regular lunch meetings with James Angleton, a founding member of the CIA after a brilliant wartime record with the OSS in Italy. They were often joined by an FBI agent, Bill Harvey, appointed by Hoover to run the hunt for Homer; when speculation turned to his identity, Philby encouraged the idea that if there was a mole—and he stressed it was a big "if"—then most likely it would be among what he called, with his disarming stutter, "the carpet cleaners and bottle washer brigade."

Philby began to sense Harvey and Angleton's growing suspicion that Homer was better placed in the embassy than a mere domestic. Guy Burgess and Donald Maclean, two of the founding members with Philby of the Soviet spy ring operations, were now diplomats on the embassy staff, and their presence had undoubtedly made life tense for Philby. Burgess had charmed his way into sharing Philby's house, and soon it became renowned for heavy-drinking parties and homosexual guests. Eventually the gatherings came to the attention of the ambassador, who recommended that Maclean, whose forays among the city's male prostitutes were now attracting public comment, should be posted to the Cairo embassy. Shortly after arriving in the Egyptian capital, Maclean went on a drunken rampage while a guest at an American's apartment, causing extensive damage. The embassy settled the claim, pleading Maclean had suffered a nervous breakdown brought on by "personal problems." He was flown back to London and hospitalized under the care of Dr. William Sargant, the psychiatrist both MI5 and MI6 used on sensitive cases. Meanwhile, Burgess was carousing even more heavily in Washington, and his drunken anti-American outbursts at parties became more scandalous. By the summer of 1950, his behavior had led to Robert Mackenzie, the security officer at the embassy, recommending Burgess should be recalled to London.

Against this background Allen Welsh Dulles and Walter Bedell Smith had flown to London.

IN THE THREE DAYS THEY SPENT IN LONDON, Dulles and Smith held several meetings with Stewart Menzies and Percy Sillitoe. Dulles had decided, with Smith's agreement, for the moment to hold back the copy of Hoover's letter about Pontecorvo. "We wanted their cooperation rather than cause embarrassment," Dulles would later recall to Bill Buckley.

Meanwhile, Guy Liddell, the deputy director of MI5, had undertaken a review of the Venona transcripts about Homer and had established the mole had regularly traveled from Washington to New York on the fifteenth and the thirtieth of alternate months. Liddell concluded the journeys had been to meet his controller. A check with the embassy's travel office revealed the only person whose trips fitted the schedule was Donald Maclean.

Smith and Dulles had urged that Maclean should be brought in for questioning and, if need be, flown back to Washington for further interrogation. Menzies had demurred. He felt that more could emerge if Maclean was placed under surveillance, as it could lead to discovering the identity of his Soviet controller and possibly even the names of other moles. The Special Branch was given the task of following Maclean around London. In yet another error, the surveillance did not extend to Maclean's country house in Surrey, and only his London apartment telephone was tapped.

Satisfied they could do no more in London, the two Americans returned to Washington. Before doing so, Dulles had finally handed Menzies a copy of Hoover's letter about Bruno Pontecorvo. After reading it, the MI6 chief murmured, "I doubt if this would have made any difference. Only now do we know our Italian was long ready to fly the coop."

In November 1950, Philby's Soviet controller asked for a meeting, itself a high-risk request, but indicative of the urgency and importance of what he had to say. Philby had to find a means to warn Maclean he was not only under surveillance but could be arrested. The Soviet *rezidentura* in London had discovered this from one of his own sources. The source has remained undisclosed to this day, though the suspicion remains that he was a police officer at Scotland Yard. Philby was instructed that he must convey to Maclean he should leave Britain. Realizing that passing on the order could also implicate him, Philby had sent the warning to Anthony Blunt.

Blunt was another founding member of the Soviet spy ring recruited at Cambridge, where, like Burgess, Maclean, and Philby, he had been a member of the elite Apostles Society. After leaving Cambridge Blunt established himself as an art historian and became the Queen's Surveyor of Pictures, an archaic title that gave him not only regular access to Her Majesty but free run of the royal palaces and a seat at the table of one of the frequent state banquets. He developed a circle of friends that made him undoubtedly the best-connected spy in the Soviet ring and ideally placed to become the group's recruiter, using his connections to draw a number of people into working for the Soviet Union. At some stage, though, his belief in the righteousness of what he was doing had come to trouble him: The doubts grew after he was knighted by the Queen in 1956. Among those who attended his investiture were Dick White, who would become chief of MI5 and later MI6, and Guy Liddell; both were Blunt's friends. Their presence would add to the embarrassment of their Services when, in 1979, Prime Minister Margaret Thatcher told a stunned House of Commons that Blunt had been a longtime Soviet mole but that, in return for providing MI5 with "valuable information about other Soviet spies," he had been given immunity from prosecution. However, he would be stripped of his knighthood. Shamed and humiliated, Blunt faded into obscurity. In Washington, the feeling continued that the way Blunt had been so leniently treated was further proof, in the bitter words of Allen Dulles, that "British intelligence and the Establishment it represents will do anything to protect its own kind, even if the country's security is threatened."

Blunt had been identified, in the wake of the defection of Burgess and Maclean, as the Third Man by the British press. Dulles had become convinced there was a Fourth Man: Kim Philby. Dulles disliked everything about Philby: his excessive snobbery over food and wine, his condescending mannerisms, the way he spoke of "my tailor in Savile Row." He was "just so damned Brit he could have stepped out of the Raj," Dulles would later tell Bill Buckley.

During the 1950 Christmas holiday in Washington, Philby sought a second meeting with his Soviet controller to warn that he now believed it was vital for Maclean to leave England. Philby was, on his own later admission, "increasingly worried" that the net was closing on him and that if Maclean was interrogated, he would implicate him and probably Guy Burgess, who was nowadays drinking even more heavily, more openly flaunting his homosexuality, and more loudly abusing all things American. Having had no response from London to Robert Mackenzie's recommendation that the virtually uncontrollable Burgess should be sent home, Philby decided there was an urgent need to put distance between himself and his fellow spy; at the same time, back in London Burgess could personally warn Maclean of the danger he faced. To ensure Burgess's compliance, Philby warned him of the risks he faced if he continued to remain in Washington. He instructed him to collect three speeding tickets in one day and each time abuse the traffic cop until threatened with arrest, which he could, of course, comfortably challenge, but which would be a flagrant breach of his diplomatic immunity. As expected, the ambassador ordered Burgess to leave the United States within forty-eight hours, and Philby escorted him to the airport.

Burgess was found a job in the Foreign Office. Philby's warning must have had an effect. Burgess led what was for him a sober life; he was rarely seen in his old Soho club haunts and declined invitations to gay parties.

ON FRIDAY, MAY 25, 1951, Menzies had decided there was finally enough evidence to have Maclean questioned. The interrogation would begin on the following Monday. That Friday evening Burgess drove to Maclean's house in the Surrey countryside, from where they traveled on to Southampton to catch the evening ferry to France. The following Monday morning, Kim Philby was awakened "at a horribly early hour" by Geoffrey Paterson, MI5's Washington liaison officer, explaining he had just received a Most Immediate telegram from London. Philby hurried to the embassy to be met by an ashen-faced Paterson. Philby recalled what happened next, " 'Kim,' he said in a half-whisper, 'the bird has flown.' I registered dawning horror (I hope). 'What bird? Not Maclean?' 'Yes,' he answered. 'But there's worse than that. Guy Burgess has gone with him.' At that my consternation was no pretense." Had Maclean told Burgess he should also defect? Or had another mole in MI5 warned both men?

Had Burgess acted on the spur of the moment, the act of a man increasingly mentally unstable? Or did he realize once Maclean fled, his own role as a spy would be uncovered? There was a further extraordinary twist to the drama. Burgess had left documents in his apartment that identified Blunt as a Soviet mole, but these documents were never recovered because, it was later claimed, of a "strange decision" by Guy Liddell to ask his old friend Anthony Blunt to help with the search of Burgess's apartment. "The wily aesthete quietly pocketed the incriminating documents while Special Branch searched elsewhere for evidence. Blunt then burnt the evidence," one intelligence source later claimed to the author.

On June 13, 1951, three weeks after Burgess and Maclean had fled,

Bill Harvey, the FBI agent in Washington, sent a copy of a long memo to the head of Special Operations. In a piece of commendable deduction, he wrote that Philby was one of the few who knew the exact status of the Homer investigation that had finally unmasked Maclean. He had also been involved in the Volkov case in Istanbul. Dulles had given Harvey copies of the messages from the British consul in the city in which the luckless Russian had offered up the names of a British intelligence officer and the two Foreign Office employees who were all Soviet spies in return for his own asylum in Britain. Harvey had concluded from Volkov's claims that he was referring to Burgess and Maclean and that, given their close friendship with Philby, he must be the intelligence officer. *Kim Philby was a Soviet spy!* Five days later, on June 18, Angleton sent a separate memo to Walter Bedell Smith that reached the same conclusion. The CIA director couriered both documents to Stewart Menzies with a one-line note: "Fire Philby or we break off our intelligence relationships." Smith could do no more. Dismissing Philby would be a matter for MI6, but Menzies claimed there was "not enough hard evidence to do so."

Within a week Philby was back in London. He knew that there was little more than suspicion to link him with Maclean; they had never been close. It was different with Burgess. They had occupied the same house, and both were counterintelligence officers who had shared the same secrets. In Washington, Smith had raged. How could no one have been suspicious about Burgess? If nothing else, why had no one taken notice of his anti-Americanism? And now Philby! How many more moles did the Brits have?

On arriving in London, Philby found many of his colleagues simply could not believe that, with a glittering career behind him and widely tipped within the Secret Intelligence Service to one day become its next chief, he could possibly have ever been tempted to be a Soviet spy. The officer Menzies had chosen to interrogate Philby was Dick White, the director of counterintelligence. While he was a competent officer, he did not have the probing skills of Jim Skardon, who had elicited the confession from Klaus Fuchs. Philby knew that as long as he calmly maintained his innocence and dealt with any evidence offered against him, using his own considerable experience to avoid being tripped up, he would be safe. Philby was finally allowed to resign from MI6 even though White remained convinced of his treachery. It was the fear of undoubted scandal that allowed Philby to resign. It is known in MI6 as CYAS—the Cover Your Ass Solution.

Having survived other interrogations by Helenus Milmo, a former

MI5 officer, and finally Skardon, and still lacking any real evidence to bring him to trial, the foreign secretary, Harold Macmillan in 1955, told Parliament that Philby was an innocent man. The spy promptly called a press conference at his mother's apartment to celebrate "my absolution." On January 23, 1963, Kim Philby left Britain forever to make his home in Moscow. Five years later he published his memoir, *My Silent War,* which confirmed his treason, a betrayal that damaged Anglo-American intelligence for many years to come.

He had become a heroic figure for Soviet intelligence, perhaps the greatest spy it had ever recruited. His activities had also generated an obsessive fear in MI5, MI6, and the CIA about the skills of the KGB and raised a troubling possibility each time a defector arrived in British or American hands: If Philby had successfully operated for decades as a Soviet spy, then any Russian defector might be a KGB plant.

On May 14, 1988, Kim Philby was given a funeral with full KGB honors in Moscow before being buried in a cemetery in the western suburbs of the city. Guy Burgess had died in 1963, a discontented drunk living in reduced circumstances, ignored by the KGB, but still clinging to his Marxist beliefs. Donald Maclean tried his hand at writing and enjoyed a small success with his book analyzing British foreign policy. He pined for England and hoped one day to return. The wish would never be granted.

There are those in the CIA and FBI who still believe they have not totally recovered from Philby's massive act of treachery—his high-level Washington connections had extended to the upper echelon of the intelligence community. Most of the time he had operated alone, a loner in the world that is occupied by the double agent. No one will ever know how many deaths he had caused through those who trusted him.

ON JULY 14, 1952, STEWART MENZIES, the third chief of the Secret Intelligence Service, in the post for almost thirteen years, sat behind his desk to write a letter in the traditional green ink. He was sixty-two years old, and despite his graying hair, he looked a decade younger. As the longcase clock struck noon, Menzies began to write in the neat copperplate hand he had learned at Eton. The hour was the time he had always reserved for composing important personal letters. This one was different from all the others: The single page contained his resignation. Later it would be murmured around MI6 and beyond in Whitehall that he had resigned because of the bruising experience following the debacle over the Soviet spy ring. The truth was more personal. His second wife,

Pamela, had recently died after a long illness. Months later he had re-married, the daughter of a millionaire financier, and he wanted more time to spend with his new bride, Audrey, and to indulge his passion for horse racing, which she shared. There was not a racecourse in the country they had not visited in between the trips he had made to Washington to restore the confidence of the CIA and FBI in the Secret Intelligence Service.

Walter Bedell Smith and J. Edgar Hoover had accepted his regrets over what had happened and agreed Menzies's nomination for Philby's replacement in Washington was the perfect choice. He was John Bruce Lockhart, who had worked with the CIA from its inception and whose personal friendship with Smith and James Angleton had flourished from those postwar years when Lockhart ran MI6 operations in Germany. Like Menzies, his strength was in understanding the politics of how America operated, and Menzies knew Lockhart would manage to feel his way through Washington's corridors of power. On his first meeting with Smith, he had told the CIA director, "Walter, what happened with Philby and those other bastards is the greatest betrayal I know. My job here is to make sure there is a way past that."

Where Kim Philby had been insidiously charming, Bruce Lockhart was openly frank. He said if he could do something, he would; if not, he would say why. Even Dulles had found him "a Brit you can get along with."

It is certain none of that was contained in Menzies's resignation letter. But shortly after noon, wearing the light gray flannel suit he wore on fine summer days, he left his office and strolled through the crowds to his club, White's in St James's. Sharply at twelve thirty he strode into the bar and invited his friends to join him in a round of pink gins to celebrate "my freedom." No one asked any questions; they knew what Menzies meant. He had long ago promised them that when he retired, he would stand them the first round. Then, over more drinks, he had led them in his favorite pastime, trying to pick out which horse would win on the afternoon card published in the only newspaper allowed in the bar, the *Sporting Life*. Not once since Philby had been allowed to resign from MI6 had Menzies mentioned the name of the man he had once regarded as a friend, to whom he had sent Christmas cards and for whom he had bought drinks at the bar. It was as if the traitor had never existed.

Stewart Menzies continued this weekday ritual until shortly before his death due to pneumonia in the King Edward VII's Hospital for Officers on May 28, 1968. Some of his obituarists said he had left a legacy that would influence the way MI6 operated in the future; others said he would be remembered as the spymaster who failed to recognize the truth about Kim Philby until it was too late.

By then the hapless Percy Sillitoe, decked out with a knighthood, had announced in 1953 that he was retiring as director-general of the Security Service. That night Guy Liddell and his friends drank champagne and made arch remarks about Sillitoe's revelation of intending to run a sweetshop in the Sussex resort of Eastbourne. However, before standing behind a counter selling his favorite toffees, Sillitoe had delivered a surprise: He would be making a six-month tour of MI5 stations scattered through the empire, traveling whenever possible on board luxury liners. The image of the man Guy Liddell still called "the plodding policeman" making his way across Africa and Asia to some of the remoter Security Service outposts had caused Sillitoe's deputy to smirk as he and his friends quaffed their champagne. But Sillitoe had one further piece of news that infuriated Liddell. The new director of MI5 would be Dick White, the friend of Anthony Blunt and the interrogator who had failed to elicit a confession from Kim Philby.

For the second time in his long career, Guy Liddell had been passed over for the top job. It was a bitter blow for him to bear, the more so that he had been a mentor to Dick White.

IN THE EARLY HOURS OF NOVEMBER 1, 1952, seismographs around the world recorded a massive eruption that centered on the tiny atoll of Elugelab in the Marshall Islands of the South Pacific. Within minutes the first reports were in the hands of every intelligence chief in the West: Some were awakened by aides; others were coming to the end of another working day. All the reports confirmed the United States had finally exploded the world's first hydrogen bomb. The sixty-five-ton weapon had been given the homely name of "Mike," and the detonation came in the last year of the Truman presidency. For days Mike had been fussed over by scientists from Los Alamos as it waited in a shed on Elugelab surrounded by beta-ray spectographs and containers of uranium and hydrogen. At dawn, local time, the time-counters inside Mike reached zero and the first man-made star rose twenty-five miles into the stratosphere, its blue-gray cloud blotting out the sun, while below, Elugelab was incinerated before sinking into the suddenly boiling ocean around it. On the seabed Mike created a mile-long, six-hundred-foot-deep canyon, another first for the nuclear age. Scientists in various capitals used local landmarks to illustrate the damage the forty-mile-wide fireball could have done: vaporizing Manhattan or central London, Paris, and Madrid. "Not since the Creation has there been a more awesome sight," an eyewitness wrote; he was sixty miles from the explosion. On August 8, 1953, two days after the anniversary of the atomic bomb attack on Hiroshima, Russia's prime minister, Georgi Malenkov, announced, "The United States no longer has a monopoly on the hydrogen bomb." A top-secret investigation was launched into how Russia had achieved this. The results of the closed-door inquiry still remain shrouded in secrecy. To this day the one certainity is that Bruno Pontecorvo, the scientist who had betrayed Britain, had arrived in Russia in time to lend his expertise to enable Malenkov to make the claim. The nightmare envisioned by Albert Einstein had materialized. "General annihilation beckons," he told reporters.

The prediction came at a time of major changes in the leadership of both MI5 and MI6.

THE APPOINTMENT OF JOHN SINCLAIR AS MENZIES'S successor was a single step up from his position as deputy chief. Sinclair had held the position since 1945 when he replaced Claude Dansey, who had rejected Allen Dulles's prime intelligence source because he was "too obviously a plant." With a knighthood and a new wife, a glamorous divorcée, Dansey had retired to Bathampton, a pleasant country town in Somerset.

Sinclair, whose father-in-law was the archdeacon of Canterbury, was an avowed opponent of godless Communism, though his only direct contact with Russia was when he served in the North Russia Campaign in Murmansk in 1918. What he witnessed had left him unimpressed with Communism's failure "to produce consumer goods," a lack that would "eventually lead to their economy imploding." The news that Moscow had its own hydrogen bomb did not change his view.

He was yet another of the eccentrics who find their way into the upper levels of British intelligence. With an offbeat sense of humor and a liking for music-hall comics, he usually lunched at his desk—a piece of cheese and soup from a thermos he brought from his house in Queen Anne's Gate, one of the most sought-after addresses in London. On weekends, he and his wife and their children drove down to their country cottage in Hazelmere, Sussex, and never missed the Sunday morning Anglican service in the village church. Back in London, Sinclair walked to work and unfailingly paused for a friendly word with a vagrant who wore regularly whitened cricket boots all year long. Sinclair never asked why, and when one day the man was no longer there, he discovered he had died the night before. Sinclair sent flowers to his funeral, the only floral tribute on the grave.

His own good relationship with the CIA, fostered by Lockhart, had encouraged Sinclair to enter into a global division of intelligence gathering with the CIA, in which MI6 would deal with the Far East—still the rump of the empire with Singapore, Malaysia, Burma, and Hong Kong in its keep—while the CIA concentrated on Thailand, Laos, Vietnam, Cambodia, and Indonesia, all countries where Soviet influence was on the increase. Both services would jointly handle Europe. This had resulted in another venture in which MI6 had joined the CIA in its long-running operation against the Soviet Union in the Balkans. Partisans from there had been trained at Fort Monkton, the Secret Intelligence Service's own training school near Portsmouth. Dozens of agents were sent back into the Balkans only to be caught by the KGB.

In 1953, MI6 contractors successfully tunneled under the Imperial Hotel in Vienna, the headquarters of the Soviet *kommandatura* in Austria from where telephone and teleprinter lines were linked to Moscow. Every day over 150 reels of tape were made and couriered from the MI6 station in the city to London by RAF aircraft for linguists at GCHQ to translate. So successful was the operation that Sinclair and Allen Dulles, who in February 1953 had become the new head of the CIA, decided on an altogether more ambitious operation, to monitor communications traffic in and out of the most important base the Soviet Union had: the Red Army's Central Group headquarters at Zossen-Wünsdorf in East Germany, through which all military and intelligence data flowed to and from Moscow. The operation would enable Britain and the United States to know the Warsaw Pact's battle plans in advance and where and when they should deploy their own NATO forces accordingly.

Surveyors expert in tunneling spent weeks in West Berlin before settling on a location near the border with the Soviet zone. From there engineers from the U.S. Corps of Engineers would have the task of tunneling half a mile into the zone, and every foot they advanced would have to be undetected. Code-named Stopwatch, the project became fully operational in December 1953 after a number of meetings in London under the direction of George Young, who had returned from Turkey to become MI6's director of requirements.

The minutes of the meetings were taken by George Blake, a soft-spoken young officer who had just joined the SIS. Born in Holland, the thirty-six-year-old had an unusual background. His father was an Egyptian Jew with a British passport, and one of his cousins was a founding member of the Egyptian Communist Party. During the war, Blake had fought in the Dutch resistance before escaping to England to serve as a lieutenant in naval intelligence, working under Ian Fleming, the creator of James Bond. Fleming recommended that Blake should apply for a job in MI6; he was hired and given a crash course in Russian before being posted to the Foreign Office's Far Eastern Department, where another newcomer was Guy Burgess. In September 1948, Blake was sent to the MI6 station in Seoul, South Korea. He was still there in 1950 when he and all the other embassy diplomats in the city were captured by the North Koreans when they invaded. Freed in a prisoner exchange, Blake had returned to London and had been assigned to Young's department. Blake's duties were to take notes and to circulate the minutes on a need-to-know basis, detailing the most secret intelligence operation since the plans for the D-Day landings. They included the blueprint of a building at Zossen-Wünsdorf, which looked like a radar station for aircraft flying into Tempelhof, West Berlin's airport.

Beneath the complex, a shaft was sunk thirty feet leading to a tunnel fourteen feet wide. To hide the huge amount of earth being excavated from watchers inside the Soviet zone, a huge warehouse was built above the tunnel. Trucks arrived at the building carrying large, empty crates clearly identified as parts for the radar station and left with the boxes filled with soil. In all, over three thousand tons of earth were smuggled away. The top of the tunnel had to be close to the surface in order to give the monitoring teams who would work there ideal conditions in which to operate, yet strong enough to support the weight of traffic passing overhead in the Soviet zone. There was also a need to ensure that the chamber where the tapping apparatus would be installed was sufficiently insulated to prevent it acting like a huge drum and making the intercepts unintelligible.

Progress had once been temporarily slowed when an iron-shod horse trotted overhead, sending down vibrations. Another time there was a continuous succession of thuds. These turned out to be the result of the Vopos, the East German police, setting up a temporary automobile checkpoint directly over the tunnel; the vibrations were caused by Vopos stamping their feet on the frozen ground to keep warm.

To ensure the tunnel had extended to the required distance—a precise 1,475 feet to gain maximum effect for the intercept equipment—two CIA officers in U.S. Army uniform made one of the regular trips into East Berlin the Western Allies were allowed in return for Soviet patrols being permitted to enter West Berlin and arranged to have a flat tire at the calculated point where the tunnel should end. Before driving away they left a tiny radio transmitter that sent the information to the tunnel engineers: They only needed to dig another foot to complete a remarkable engineering feat. On February 25, 1955, the work was finished. It had cost $30 million and had been the most expensive construction in the secret war against the Soviet Union. British telephone engineers set up the twenty-five tons of equipment needed to simultaneously intercept up to five hundred separate communications from the Red Army base. These were transmitted to buildings in Washington and Regent's Park in London where linguists, each fluent in Russian and German, worked around the clock to translate and send the information to the CIA and MI6.

No one suspected the KGB had successfully penetrated the operation. George Blake had been recruited by the Soviet Union while a prisoner in North Korea, and since then his every career move had been planned for him by his Moscow controller. The self-effacing Blake had carried on where Kim Philby, Donald Maclean, and Guy Burgess had left off. In 2007 Blake was honored on his eighty-fifth birthday with the Order of Friendship.

In the early hours of Sunday, April 22, 1956, the tunnel was discovered when a team of Soviet engineers, checking storm damage to underground electricity lines across East Berlin, uncovered its existence. It was a blow from which John Sinclair never recovered, and he resigned. In retirement he divided his time between serving on the board of an Anglican seminary and as chairman of a Church of England organization that provides housing for retired country parsons. Shortly before his eightieth birthday and his golden wedding anniversary, he died. An anonymous obituarist in the London *Times* referred to Sinclair's "inability for security reasons to answer some of the criticisms made long after the events."

IN THE WAKE OF THE DISCOVERY OF THE TUNNEL, the first questions asked by the CIA and MI6 were how long the Soviets could have suspected its existence and whether they had used the tunnel to feed false information. Checks on every incident logged eliminated any possibility that the Russians, apart from the temporary traffic checkpoint, had set up a surveillance operation in the vicinity of the tunnel. Other checks confirmed that in the eleven months the tunnel had operated, the decryption and analysis of the material showed it to be genuine, proving the accuracy of intelligence provided by informers in East Germany about Russian troop movements not only throughout the country but in other Warsaw Pact countries. A wealth of other detail revealed the relationships between Soviet military commanders and insights into Eastern Bloc politics. "It was often like being in the same room with the Soviet planners listening to their every move," Allen Dulles recalled.

Nevertheless, a worrying question remained. Was it possible the KGB had a spy in the project who was of sufficient importance for the decision to have been made in Moscow that his security outweighed taking any action over the tunnel before its accidental discovery?

The intuitive skills of Bill Harvey were called upon. The former FBI agent, who had been the first to deduce Kim Philby was a spy, had resigned from the bureau to join the CIA's Office of Special Operations and been given the responsibility of tracking down any Soviet mole who could be buried inside any CIA-related operation. Harvey had come to Berlin to see if he could dig one up. He spent weeks trawling through the names of all those in key positions with access to how the intercepts were handled. The hunt took him back and forth to London. In the end, he turned up no suspects and concluded the tunnel operation had not been penetrated.

During his time in Berlin, Blake had been encouraged to develop contacts with the West German intelligence service, BND, to learn more about its operations that could interest MI6. Blake's agent was Horst Eitner, who was also a KGB asset. Blake did not inform his Soviet controller of his contact, a mistake that would cost him dearly.

In 1960, Blake was posted to the Foreign Office language school in the foothills outside Beirut to learn Arabic for his next assignment. A year later, he received a request from MI6 to return to London. On April 4, 1961, he made his way to the Secret Intelligence Service's personnel department on Broadway, near St. James's Park. He was directed by a security guard at the door to a small conference room in nearby Carlton Gardens overlooking the Mall, where he faced a formidable team of interrogators. The four counterintelligence officers laid out the evidence they had gathered. There was the confession of Horst Eitner, who had denounced Blake as a KGB agent. There was the admission of a Polish intelligence officer, Michael Goleniewski, who had defected from Warsaw with copies of MI6 documents that had been leaked to the KGB and passed on to Polish intelligence. Blake had been one of the few names on the original distribution lists. There was the evidence that he had been the minutes taker at all the planning meetings for the Berlin tunnel.

For two days George Blake had been confronted with fact after damning fact. Each time he had calmly denied the accusations. Then, in a dramatic moment on the third day, one of his interrogators, John

Quine, the head of MI6 counterintelligence, sat back in his chair and, barely disguising the contempt in his voice, accused Blake of betraying his country for money. There was a sudden silence in the room. Then Blake erupted. He had never taken any money. "All my actions have been based on sound ideological reasons," he shouted. It took two further days to listen to his confession.

On May 3, 1961, Blake pleaded guilty to five charges of espionage at the Old Bailey. He was sentenced to forty-two years' imprisonment by Lord Chief Justice Goddard, the longest prison sentence ever given to a traitor. But he served only five years. In October 1966, he escaped from Wormwood Scrubs prison by using a nylon ladder reinforced with steel knitting needles to scale the prison perimeter wall. To this day no one knows exactly how Blake had managed to elude prison searches, the police, and his hunters from MI5 and MI6 before he reappeared in Moscow a year later. Like Philby, he sat down and wrote his autobiography, *No Abiding City*, coached by the KGB on what to say. In 1990 he updated the book, calling it *No Other Choice*. No publisher in the West was interested in publishing either version.

WHILE BILL HARVEY HAD UNSUCCESSFULLY tried to discover if a spy had betrayed the tunnel, the new director of MI6, Dick White, had tried to make certain that any treachery by a Soviet mole would not be laid at the door of the Security Service. His well-placed sources in Washington had told him Carl Nelson, an officer in the CIA's Office of Communications who had been closely involved in the creation of the tunnel, had ruled out the possibility that a mole could either be a German who had worked on the project at the construction stage or any CIA officer involved in the operation of the tunnel. Given that MI5 had only been the recipient of the harvest of intelligence material in the time the tunnel had functioned, White concluded that any traitor could be in MI6, but he was careful to keep his view to himself. He had already failed to uncover Philby's treachery and had been severely criticized to the point where he had considered resigning from the Security Service. Instead he had been appointed director-general after Percy Sillitoe went off on his world cruise.

White's promotion had not only surprised the forty-seven-year-old but was urgently needed. With his boyish good looks and impeccable manners, Dick White had found no trouble in attracting women before eventually marrying the novelist Kate Bellamy, a divorcée with two daughters; she would bear him two sons. His bachelor days over, he found the extra salary that went with his new post a welcome boost to meet his increased household expenses.

White had joined the Security Service in 1936, a graduate of Oxford and the University of Michigan and UCLA. Vernon Kell had assigned him to counterintelligence and asked Guy Liddell to be White's mentor. The veteran intelligence officer quickly realized that White's natural skill at analysis and his ability to think through a situation before acting made him an ideal spy catcher. During World War II, White had distinguished himself by the number of Nazi spies he identified as well as his ability to recognize the Abwehr's signals intelligence when he had served with General Montgomery's Twenty-first Army Group in Europe in the closing months of the war. Now, as director-general, he realized that to succeed in the war against the KGB required a new structure within MI6. The old "divisions" Kell had created became "branches," smaller, interrelated units, each with its own specific responsibility. He also expanded the role of MI5 from a primarily domestic service into one that had fully staffed stations throughout the empire to uncover and counter subversion and guerrilla warfare. MI5 operations in Malaya, Borneo, Kenya, and Cyprus had led to striking results against Communist-led insurgencies.

White was also the first British intelligence head to recognize the importance of the Mossad, Israel's fledgling intelligence service, in providing MI5 with intelligence in the Middle East, and he had flown to Tel Aviv to meet with its new director, Isser Harel. The physical contrast between the two men could not have been more stark: the tall, fair-haired White with his athlete's stride and the diminutive Harel, barely four feet eight inches tall, who had jug ears and spoke poor English with a heavy Central European accent; his family had emigrated from Latvia in 1930. Despite the long flight from London, White's suit bore no creases, while Harel's clothes looked as if he had slept in them. But the two men found common ground in the threat posed by Arab nationalism simmering in the region's capitals. Harel had smiled his snaggletoothed smile and said the Mossad had its spies in every hostile capital and they provided a stream of priceless information, which he would be happy to share with MI5. Before Harel escorted White back to his RAF plane, he presented his guest with a dagger bearing the engraved words of a psalmist, "The Guardian of Israel never slumbers." Later Harel would present a similar inscribed dagger to Allen Dulles when he traveled to Washington to meet the CIA chief. He explained to the author, "I had a small supply of daggers for those I trusted."

The gift led to the creation of a partnership between the Mossad and

MI5 and MI6 and also created the first "back channel" between the services through which both sides would communicate either by code or telephone. The channel effectively bypassed the normal diplomatic contacts between the Foreign Office and the Israeli Foreign Ministry. It was a remarkable achievement given the ambivalence of many Israelis over Britain's role in the 1948 War of Independence and the way it had tried to halt Bricha (from the Hebrew for "escape"), the unprecedented operation to bring the Holocaust survivors out of Europe. Jewish relief agencies in the United States had bought—often at highly inflated prices—every available seaworthy ship. Tens of thousands of Jews had been crammed onto their decks to make their journeys to the shores of Israel. There had not been an operation like it since Dunkirk in 1940. Not a word of reproach had Isser Harel made to Dick White over Britain's attitude before Israel gained its independence in 1948.

If White had been surprised, and no doubt grateful for it, at Harel's diplomacy, it was nothing like the astonishment he must have felt when, in July 1956, he was called to the Whitehall office of Sir Frank Newsome, the permanent undersecretary with daily responsibility for political matters involving MI5 and MI6. The meeting began with Newsome's reminder that White had a duty to do whatever the prime minister asked of him. White had wondered if, after all, Anthony Eden wanted his resignation over his role in the Soviet spy scandals. Instead Newsome had said: "Mr. White, the PM wishes you to become the new chief of the Secret Intelligence Service." A quick congratulatory handshake and a refill from the vintage single malt whiskey Newsome kept for special occasions sealed the appointment of MI6's new chief. Dick White would be the only spymaster to this day to have run Britain's two intelligence services.

Three thousand miles away from London in the desert heat of Cairo, a young lieutenant colonel, who four years previously had played his part in the downfall of the country's corrupt King Farouk before the monarch fled the city with his collection of pornography and most of the country's gold reserves in ingots, had become the leader of a junta of like-minded nationalists. His name was Gamal Abdel Nasser, and he was about to create a crisis that would engulf the intelligence services of Britain, France, and the CIA and change forever the political balance of the region.

8

The Winds of Hate

There had been ample warnings for the MI6 officers in Cairo, which they failed to grasp. The Egyptians increasingly resented the physical presence of British troops and their support system of English civil servants and had come to regard their country's own politicians with contempt. Nowhere was that feeling stronger than among the younger generation who had hurled abuse at King Farouk's royal yacht as it took him into exile in Naples, his loot from the national bank stacked in the hold, each box containing twelve gold bars. Yet throughout successive Ramadans and the holy pilgrimages to Mecca, the warnings continued to be ignored by the Secret Intelligence Service commander, John Collins, and his officers as they sipped their sundowners under the electric fans of the Gezira Sporting Club in the fashionable Cairo suburb of Zamalek.

Fourteen years earlier, Field Marshal Bernard Montgomery had relaxed in the club while planning how his Eighth Army would drive Erwin Rommel's Afrika Korps out of North Africa. Now, it was a favorite place to gather for not only the spies of MI6 but those from the CIA, NKVD, France's SDECE, and Israel's Mossad.

"The Brits had their own corners near the billiard room, the Americans had colonized a place near the entrance to the restaurant, and the rest had their own spots. Walking into the club you got a pretty good idea of the current state of 'the Great Game.' If the Russians had something going, they would be doing some serious drinking. If the French had pulled off something, there was champagne on the table," recalled Wolfgang Lotz, one of the two Mossad agents in the city.

His own cover as the owner of a riding school gave him the perfect reason to visit the club; many of its clients were racehorse owners. His targets were the wealthy Egyptians who sipped the crushed fresh grapes and vodka cocktails. One was the deputy head of Egyptian military intelligence and the chief of security for the Suez Canal Zone. He had provided Lotz with his first intelligence success, handing over the complete list of Nazi scientists then living in Cairo who had used concentration camp victims for their wartime experiments. Each was systematically executed by Mossad's assassination squad, the Kidon, sent from Israel and led to their targets by Lotz.

The CIA outnumbered by four to one State Department diplomats in the city. The Soviet Embassy's NKVD officers concentrated on Cairo University, seeking students they could recruit by offering them free tuition at Russian universities. The German BND officers chose the coolness of the Egyptian Museum as a favorite place to meet their informers, listening to their latest information as they strolled past the ancient wonders of Egypt. Other foreign spies had their favorite meeting places: on board one of the Nile ferries, in the Zoological Gardens, outside the central bus station, or at a sidewalk café on the road leading to the City of the Dead, the Muslim cemetery near the old city wall.

"For a spy, Cairo was in every sense a perfect posting. The Egyptians are natural information hoarders. Get a good one in the right position in government and half your work is done," Eli Cohen, another Mossad agent, told the author. Luke Battle, American ambassador to Egypt from 1964 to 1967, was less enthusiastic about the CIA's attitude to its work in the capital. "Too happy-go-lucky, and when things went wrong, its people thought they could sweep it under the carpet," he recalled.

A similar attitude permeated the MI6 station. The end of the Mandate in Palestine in 1948 and the emergence of Israel as a sovereign state had meant the loss of a powerful base for the Secret Intelligence Service. Cairo was the obvious replacement, still enabling it to monitor Soviet activities around the region and ensure the Suez Canal did not fall into Russian hands but remained the vital link between the United Kingdom and the Far East, guaranteeing the flow of oil. As long as Britain controlled the canal, any threat of "a bunch of Muslim hotheads causing a problem," Collins had assured London, was "not a serious matter."

On June 22, 1952, three thousand Egyptian soldiers led by two hundred of their army's finest officers and under the command of General Mohammed Neguib had swept through the city, taking control of the radio station and seizing power in a classic coup. A month before,

Collins had sent a telegram to the Foreign Office in London, "The army is loyal to the king." On the day of the coup, the MI5 station did not have one file on Neguib.

Another warning that Collins had ignored was the arrival in Cairo of Kermit Roosevelt. The grandson of President Theodore Roosevelt and the man Kim Philby had called "the quiet American," Roosevelt had been the OSS chief in the Arab regions during World War II. He had been sent to Egypt in the wake of the coup by U.S. Secretary of State Dean Acheson to effectively start the process that would see the transfer of power in the area from the Old to the New World, from Britain to the United States. Like Allen Dulles, Roosevelt had little liking for the British Empire and the failure of its policymakers in Whitehall to recognize reality: A new political climate had blown in on the desert winds.

Roosevelt had come to Egypt to develop secret channels, already started by the local CIA station chief, James Eichelberger, with the anti-British officers who had taken part in the coup. Eichelberger was a veteran Arabist, speaking the language and understanding the culture. He had money to spend and used it to buy American influence with the officers. His anticolonialism gained him many friends.

One was the ultra-nationalist Gamal Abdel Nasser. In his early thirties, with the charismatic oratory of a born rabble-rouser, Nasser had been the strong arm behind Neguib and the perfect choice for Roosevelt to unfold his plan to. The United States would support the new government with as much economic aid as it needed in return for a guarantee that Egypt would have political stability "oriented toward the free world." The United States would replace Britain as Egypt's principal banker, armorer, and defender.

They had met late at night in Farouk's old office. Seated behind the king's desk, Nasser cut an imposing figure in his crisply laundered khaki uniform with his colonel's pips on its epaulettes. He had listened in silence, his coal-black eyes never taking their gaze off Roosevelt's shiny face until he finished speaking. He recalled what followed to the author, "I stood up, walked round the desk and shook Roosevelt's hand, and said his words were the most wonderful I had heard. I said that one day he would have a monument in his honor in Cairo."

Roosevelt arranged for the first tranche of money from the CIA slush fund, which in the end would total $12 million, to be transferred into an account Nasser had designated. Bribery would be a hallmark of Roosevelt's activities in the country, "the quickest and guaranteed way to buy influence," he once said. In turn Nasser kept his promise, later using part of the money to build the Cairo Tower, an ugly monument on an island in front of the Nile Hilton—Nasser called it *el-wa'ef rusfel,* Roosevelt's erection.

As a boy, Nasser had grown up in a Cairo slum and learned to hate the luxurious lifestyle of those who lived on the British bases in the Suez Canal Zone, where officers used their fly whisks to flick Arab servants who did not move fast enough. His anger at such behavior had boiled over when, still a teenager, he had led a street demonstration outside one of the camps and had been horsewhipped by a soldier before being cast into prison. He emerged to enlist in the Egyptian army, his months in prison having firmly allowed his hatred of Britain to fester and grow. Soon he gathered a small coterie of like-minded officers who dreamed of the day Britain would be ousted, and Roosevelt's proposal perfectly suited that aim, the more so because the American had shown him a State Department document revealing that Britain now planned to establish a power axis of Iraq and Jordan, a move that would increase its own hold in the region. Roosevelt had concluded their meeting in Farouk's office by saying that for Nasser to achieve his ambition to be free of what he called "the British yoke," he needed a stronger leader than Mohammed Neguib. In 1954, Neguib was maneuvered into resigning, and, propelled by a powerful campaign in the *Akhbar el Yom* newspaper owned by a CIA agent, Mustafa Amin, Nasser became Egypt's president.

A month later Nasser had once more caught the MI6 Cairo station unprepared. Using Roosevelt as his conduit, the new president said he was prepared to enter into a binding agreement in which he would continue to regard Britain as "a close and important ally," providing British troops left the Canal Zone by no later than June 1956.

In London the proposal was seen as a "possibility." Within the Foreign Office there was recognition that Britain's "global status" was already marginalized and could become totally eroded if the United States and the Soviet Union continued to create their own power bases in the Middle East. In a prescient note, George Young, who had been one of the planners of the ill-fated Berlin tunnel, wrote, "The hard truth is that a course of action could be forced on us as a consequence of failure to make positive decisions at an early stage." Young asked the questions that later many others would pose, "How did the British government get into this fix? Why didn't it sort out its Middle East policy long before Nasser arrived?"

While Young fumed, in London the Suez Group (later the Egyptian Committee) had been formed after Nasser became president. Its objective was to oppose any removal of British troops from the Canal Zone, and its members included intelligence officers who served on the Joint Intelligence Committee, the link between MI6 and Downing Street. JIC saw the intelligence reports from Cairo and discreetly passed them on to the Suez Group. Collins's analysis dismissed the idea, cautiously promoted by the British Embassy in Cairo, that Nasser represented "the new voice of Egyptian politics" and should be given a sympathetic hearing. Collins labeled Nasser as "a despot fulminating against Britain and offering his fawning support for the United States. He is not to be trusted, let alone taken seriously."

The parliamentary members of the Suez Group began to attack the government of Anthony Eden for "selling out British imperial interests," stomping the corridors of Westminster and speaking of "Nasser and his bloody wogs." A senior member of the Foreign Office, Geoffrey McDermott, later claimed, "Half a dozen of the top MI6 officers went in for extreme right-wing politics and believed Britain would only remain a world power by maintaining control over the Suez Canal."

By the time Dick White had settled into his post as the new chief of MI6, decisions were being made to rearrange the intelligence relationships with France's intelligence service and Israel's Mossad and to exclude the CIA from the secret planning beginning to develop in the summer of 1956 to secure the Suez Canal for Britain.

ONE OF THE FIRST APPROVALS DICK WHITE had given after becoming chief was to circulate a document that read like a help wanted ad. The officers he needed were those who understood, "It is the modern spy who has been called upon to remedy the situation caused by deficiencies of ministers, diplomats and generals. Men's minds are shaped, of course, by their environment and we spies, although we have our professional mystique, do perhaps live closer to the realities and hard facts of international relations than other practitioners of government. We are relatively free of the problems of status, precedence, departmental attitudes and evasions of personal responsibility. We do not have to develop, like the Parliamentarians conditioned by a lifetime, the ability to produce the ready phrase, the smart reply and the flashing smile. And it is not surprising these days that the spy finds himself the guardian of intellectual integrity."

It was intended to remind all agents what was expected of them in the wake of the Philby and Blake debacles.

Yet White feared, when he moved from MI5, he had left behind yet another mole. The source for his concern was impeccable. Arthur Martin was the GCHQ liaison officer with MI5 who had played an important part in unmasking Klaus Fuchs through the Venona project and was the classic mole hunter: Cold and focused, he triple-checked every detail before finally setting them all down in the bald language taught at GCHQ. Martin had identified Graham Mitchell, the deputy director of MI5, as a "very possible" Soviet mole.

Martin had spent weeks reviewing the admissions Philby had made during his interrogation by White and had deduced that the skills Philby used in deflecting responses suggested he was highly trained in avoiding making admissions and appeared to have been advised of what to expect. Martin concluded Graham Mitchell had provided the warning.

Dick White had listened respectfully to George Martin's conclusions even though they often highlighted his own failures to have nailed Philby. He had known Martin for sixteen years, and they had become close friends after Martin married White's secretary, Joan Russell-King. White, however, faced a dilemma: The Soviet spying scandals had left a debilitating mood within MI5, and the discovery of a further mole would seriously undermine confidence within both the Security Service and MI6, which could lead to a rupture with the CIA, the Mossad, and European intelligence services, especially those of France and West Germany. Yet to ignore Martin's conclusion, if it were proven true, would have a disastrous effect on his own position and make a mockery of the document he had circulated. White had agreed to Mitchell being placed under surveillance by a team of MI6 officers: The telephone at his home near Chobham Common, a scenic spot on the outskirts of London, was tapped, and a team of Watchers followed his movements. Despite Martin's suspicions, no evidence was found against Mitchell.

MEANWHILE, THE SUEZ CRISIS had deepened. White had been in a delegation Anthony Eden had led to the Middle East to try to coax governments in the region—including Iran and Iraq—to sign a treaty in which Britain would guarantee to come to the defense of any country attacked; the threat was identified as coming from the Red Army poised on Russia's southern border and situated to capture the oil fields of Iran and Iraq. Eden had planned to sign the pact in Baghdad on the eve of becoming prime minister on April 4, 1955, and to make the trip a total success, he needed to have Nasser's signature on the treaty document. For Eden it would bind Egypt to Britain and justify keeping their troops in the Canal Zone.

While White went off to meet with the local MI6 station, Eden was closeted with Nasser for several hours. Precise details of their discussion are still classified today as "Secret," but it would emerge that Eden's patrician manner had led to a disaster. Nasser had said Egypt would not be a signatory of the Baghdad Pact. Eden and his delegation had flown home with the prime-minister-elect furious about Nasser being "no more than a Soviet puppet."

Even before the BOAC flight had touched down in London, Nasser had begun to show he was "not a person to be kept under the thumb of Britain," he later told the author. He ordered the Egyptian General Staff intelligence branch to mobilize the *fedayeen* it had trained and positioned in the Gaza Strip to be launched against Israel. It was the start of what would become a series of wars by the Arabs against the Jewish state. Simultaneously, Baghdad's decision to sign on to Eden's pact prompted Nasser to foment unrest in Iraq. Within hours there were demonstrations on the streets of Basra and other Iraqi cities. Most disturbing of all, Nasser signed his first arms deal with the Soviet bloc for a large quantity of weapons from Czechoslovakia. The deal, worth $400 million, included eighty MIG-15 fighters, forty-five Ilyushin-28 bombers, and one hundred of the latest Russian tanks.

After Eden had flown out of Cairo, Kermit Roosevelt had taken up a virtually constant presence in Nasser's entourage, advising him on how to handle the mounting confrontation with Britain. He told the president to say to the new British ambassador, Humphrey Trevelyn, that the arms deal was no more than "to redress the balance of the military threat Israel posed to Egypt" and that after seventy years of being dominated by Britain, Nasser was not going to allow Eden to decide who Egypt should deal with, either politically, economically, or militarily.

In Washington, Secretary of State John Foster Dulles and his brother, Allen, met with President Dwight D. Eisenhower and told him that, despite Kermit Roosevelt's attempts to get Nasser to support the United States in the cold war, it was becoming increasingly clear "the Egyptians and the Russians are working together to bring the whole Middle East into Communist hands."

Trevelyn's Most Immediate telegram to the foreign secretary, Selwyn Lloyd, was copied to Dick White, who realized that Nasser, like Syria, was ready to allow Egypt to become a Soviet satellite. It was then the first question was seriously raised about assassinating the Egyptian president.

In the MI6 Registry was a copy of a CIA manual written by Dr. Sidney Gottlieb, the director of the agency's Technical Services Division. Its eighty-eight pages were titled "Assassination Methods," and it was the first handbook for state-sponsored murder. It included a warning: "Decisions and instructions should be confined to an absolute minimum of persons and ideally only one person will be involved whose death provides positive advantages."

In London, Harold Caccia, a former head of the JIC and a veteran MI6 officer, buttonholed White and drawled, "Look, old boy, we really will have to do something about this fellow Nasser. Maybe we'll have to get rid of him." White had passed the matter over to George Young to see what "was possible." Young, a seasoned veteran of "life at the raw end," cast around and settled on the station commander in Rome. The two spies met in the MI6 safe house near the city's Spanish Steps, and came up with a plan. He had met two anti-Nasser Egyptians who assured him they had the support of a number of senior army officers increasingly concerned at Nasser's deepening relationship with the Russians; they outlined their proposal for the Egyptian army to arrest the president, after which Egypt's former prime minister would be sworn in to lead a new pro-West government. The proposition was put to Dick White. He went to see the foreign secretary, who, after a short discussion, rejected the idea.

In the summer of 1956, the issue of what to do with Nasser had become a renewed matter of urgency. In Washington, the Dulles brothers agreed Nasser had to be taught a lesson that would seriously damage his public credibility with his own people and show them where their future really lay, "instead of cozying up to the Russian bear, being shielded by the wings of the American eagle," Allen Dulles had said in a rare moment of poetic license.

The previous winter, his brother had agreed the United States would lend Egypt $56 million to build the three-mile-wide Aswan Dam on the upper Nile. Six months later Nasser had given diplomatic recognition to Communist China and announced a state visit to Moscow as well as trading $200 million worth of cotton to Czechoslovakia. On July 19, 1956, John Foster Dulles canceled the American loan for the dam.

With funding withdrawn from a project that Nasser had boasted would be his lasting legacy, the Egyptian president turned his vitriol on the United States. He railed on Cairo Radio, "I look at the Americans and say: May you choke to death on your fury! We shall build the high dam as we desire! The annual income of the Suez Canal is one hundred million dollars. Why not take it ourselves?"

Every day 1.5 million barrels of oil passed through the canal, 90 percent destined for Western Europe, providing two-thirds of the fuel needed by the Continent for heat and production. The canal was the lifeline that linked Britain and France with Iranian oil, their Far Eastern markets, and distant colonies, as well as reducing the need to totally rely on the longer route around South Africa's Cape of Good Hope.

In London the idea that Nasser should be assassinated was increasingly a matter of discussion. MI6's legal department concluded that under its royal prerogative to defend the realm, it would be permissible to murder a head of state when the very security of Britain was under dire threat. The CIA assassination manual was consulted, and George Young met with CIA officer James Eichelberger, who had been transferred from Cairo to the agency's London station by Allen Dulles to "keep a close eye on what the Brits are doing." Over dinner at the Travellers Club, Eichelberger and Young spoke about murdering Nasser. Afterward, the CIA officer hurried to his office in the American Embassy and sent a coded cable to Allen Dulles. "He talked openly of assassinating Nasser instead of using a euphemism like liquidating. He said his people had been in contact with suitable elements in Egypt and the rest of the Arab world and with the French who were thinking along the same lines."

Eichelberger had also discussed Young's conversation with the CIA station chief, Chester Cooper, whose duties included monitoring Prime Minister Eden's ailing health. Cooper's own contacts in Downing Street had told him Eden was barely surviving with less than five hours of sleep and a dependency on drugs, which "appears to have affected his judgement." Cooper had then revealed to his contacts in Downing Street that the question of assassinating Nasser had also been raised by Eden after he had learned that the French SDECE had formed a special unit to murder Egypt's president. Code-named RAP-700 and under the command of Paul Leger, who had served in Egypt, the unit had already sent an assassin, Jean-Marre Pelley, to Cairo. No record would survive of any attempt to kill Nasser.

Encouraged by Eden's near obsession with ridding himself of the Egyptian president, MI6's Q Department (in Technical Services) was tasked to find a way. The unit had a deserved reputation for creating weapons and munitions for sabotage in World War II, and its postwar activities had been clearly defined by Stewart Menzies as "providing covert support where British national interests are threatened."

The department was under the command of Frank Quinn, an army officer who had joined the Secret Intelligence Service in 1946 to create methods to kill that could not be traced back to MI6. So far Quinn's skills had been used to murder Soviet informers and double agents in postwar Germany and had earned him an Order of the British Empire to go with his Military Cross. However, he recognized that assassinating a head of state required a more sophisticated method than planting a bomb under a traitor's bed. Having read the MI6 profile on Nasser, Quinn settled on poison as a way to exploit the president's weakness for the popular Egyptian Knopje chocolates, which were offered to him after each meal and kept in a box on his desk. A dozen boxes of the confectionery were sent by diplomatic bag from Cairo for Quinn to experiment on.

Porton Down, Britain's chemical and biological warfare establishment, was asked to recommend a suitable poison: It must be odorless, have a long shelf life, act immediately, and simulate a heart attack. Shellfish toxin was recommended. A vial of the deadly substance was hand-carried from Porton Down to Quinn's laboratory. Before he could inject the poison into the chocolate, he had to make sure the sealed wrapping on each piece would raise no suspicion. There could be no sign of tampering, not only with the wrappings but with the actual chocolates. Quinn had devised a method of using a heated plate to remove the base of a chocolate square before injecting the poison, but each time he replaced the base, it left a telltale mark; he finally achieved the correct temperature for the plate that would leave no trace. He handed over the remaining boxes of poisoned chocolates, but he never learned what happened to them.

By then another plan to kill Nasser was under discussion. Two officers from Technical Services had driven to Porton Down to explore the feasibility of using nerve gas. The scientists offered three varieties: Tabun, Soman, and Sarin, which had been tested on animals at a former RAF airfield on the remote coast of Cornwall. All the nerve agents were recommended as suitable to be released through the ventilation system providing air-conditioning for Nasser's office. White had presented the idea to Eden. The prime minister rejected the plan on the grounds that it would result in the deaths of innocent people. For once the ethics of being a party to possible mass murder had overcome Eden's desire to kill Nasser.

Quinn—later immortalized as Q in the Bond films—continued his search for a suitable weapon. One was a modified cigarette packet that the CIA's Dr. Gottlieb had developed as an addition to his assassination manual: The packet contained a poisoned dart. Gottlieb's counterpart at Porton Down, Dr. Ladell—whose first name nobody ever used, simply calling him "the Sorcerer"—had tried out the dart on one of the flock of sheep kept in pens at the establishment. His report read like a horror movie script, "The sheep begins to buckle at the knees and it starts to roll its eyes and froths at the mouth. Slowly the animal sinks to the ground, its life draining away." Quinn rejected the idea because the result could easily be traced.

Meanwhile, the Mossad had been working with scientists at the Institute for Biological Research in the Tel Aviv suburb of Nez Ziona, who tested the efficacy of chemical and biological weapons for the Kidon unit, the Mossad's assassination squad. The scientists concluded the best way to kill Nasser was to exploit his vanity. The president, despite his liking for chocolates, was concerned about his weight and insisted he would have no sugar in his coffee, only an artificial sweetener. The tablet had been tested on a captured Arab who had shot dead an Israeli soldier. Victor Ostrovsky, a former Mossad officer, later claimed to the author, "We all knew that a prisoner brought to the institute would be used as a guinea pig to make sure the weapons the scientists were developing worked properly." After waiting several weeks for a chance to poison Nasser's coffee, Isser Harel used the back channel to call Dick White and say the plan had been abandoned due to a lack of opportunity.

MI6's own plans had also fallen by the wayside, but they had left unanswered questions. Peter Wright, the renegade intelligence officer, claimed MI6 was so eager to kill Nasser that the vital question of "plausible deniability had never properly been thought through." Wright believed White had taken every plan to the prime minister, for whom Nasser had "now become a continuous fixation." At every opportunity—at cabinet meetings, meetings with senior Foreign Office officials, and his regular contacts with Dick White—Eden had asked in one form or another the same question: How much longer do I have to endure Nasser? The CIA station chief in London, Chester Cooper, had concluded in a report to Allen Dulles, "There is a mood little short of madness about Eden over Nasser." The evidence in the MI6 files clearly points to Anthony Eden becoming the first peacetime British prime minister to sanction the cold-blooded murder of a head of state.

ON JULY 26, 1956, IN THE PORT OF ALEXANDRIA at the Mediterranean end of the Suez Canal, Nasser announced he would nationalize the waterway. Foreign correspondents, among them the author, noted the president was calm; none of them knew Nasser had just received a briefing from his intelligence service that there appeared to be no real threat of a military response by Britain. Nasser's trusted aide Ali Sabri briefed reporters that the nationalization should be seen as "purely a decision by us to buy out the shareholders."

In Downing Street that evening, Dick White was among the guests at a dinner hosted by Anthony Eden for King Faisal of Iraq and his long-serving chief minister, Nuri es-Said. The meal was interrupted by a tele-gram from ambassador Humphrey Trevelyn in Cairo, which Eden read aloud; it summarized Nasser's speech. There was a stunned silence. Nuri es-Said spoke directly to Eden, "Prime Minister, you have only one course of action and that is to hit hard and hit now. Otherwise it will be too late." Eden gave his toothy smile, "Have no fear. Nasser will not be allowed to have his hand on our windpipe." Eden had spoken calmly, a certainty in his voice that had not been heard for some time. Chester Cooper, another guest, wondered if the prime minister had swallowed more of his pills before the meal.

White remained behind after the others left, and soon members of the Egyptian Committee—chaired by the cabinet secretary, Norman Brook, and comprising a small number of ministers and civil servants—arrived. By the time they settled around the Cabinet Room table, the calm demeanor of the prime minister had been replaced by an emo-tional outburst. Eden was almost shouting as he called Nasser a "Muslim Mussolini. I want him removed and I don't give a damn if there's anar-chy and chaos in Egypt."

The attitude of the others was equally ebullient and there was swift agreement that there must be a "firm response" to Nasser's decision to take over the canal. Guidelines for further action were minuted by Dou-glas Dodds-Parker, a former operative in the wartime SOE who now worked closely with MI6 as undersecretary of state for foreign affairs. He wrote on his pad: "Target of guidelines. A show of military strength preceded by suitable covert action to include countering Cairo Radio propaganda and redress criticism of our own role. The response to Nasser to be code-named 'Musketeer.'"

It was decided that only a small number of Whitehall officials on a need-to-know basis would be made aware of the committee's decisions. The most important one was that the United States should be excluded from the circulation of Musketeer plans. The meeting ended in the small hours with a clearly exhausted Eden finding enough strength to de-liver a Churchillian peroration, "We shall go it alone without the Amer-icans!"

It was a decision that would have far-reaching consequences, the first being that Chester Cooper sent Allen Dulles a signal, "It appears our cousins [MI6] have crawled into their shell."

In Washington, the Dulles brothers conferred and decided it was unlikely even the physically ill and mentally tormented Anthony Eden would take any foolhardy action.

THROUGHOUT THE SUMMER IN LONDON, PARIS, AND TEL AVIV, the plan to recover the Suez Canal gained momentum. George Young had handpicked Nicholas Elliott, a Hebrew-speaking veteran intelligence officer, to fly to Tel Aviv to liaise with the Mossad. So secret was Elliott's mission that he had strict instructions to avoid all contact with the British ambassador in Israel, who, like other Foreign Office envoys in the Arab capitals, was unsympathetic to the Jewish state. Rafi Eitan, the hands-on Mossad director of operations, recalled to the author, "They looked on us as a bunch of terrorists who had fought them during the British Mandate."

Elliott's first task was to arrange a secure radio link and ciphers with which the Israeli prime minister, David Ben-Gurion, could communicate through the back channel with Eden. Isser Harel had arranged for Elliott to have his own office in Mossad headquarters, the first time a foreign intelligence officer had been given such a privilege, and the two men became firm friends. After the communication circuits with London had been tested, Elliott received a coded message in early August to explore with Harel whether the Israeli Defense Force was sufficiently prepared to launch an attack across the Sinai Desert into Egypt. Rafi Eitan, who attended the discussion in Harel's office, recalled to the author, "I told Elliot our people would go into Cairo if needed."

In London on their own secure telephone link, Eden and French foreign minister Guy Mollet agreed there would have to be "good grounds" for Israel to feel sufficiently concerned to launch a preemptive attack against Egypt. The Mossad should plant a number of stories in the foreign media that Israel was once more being threatened with an attack orchestrated by Nasser. "It was a slim enough excuse, but it would have to do, and any such plan would require high-level agreement with Israel that Britain and France could intervene as peacekeepers," recalled Rafi Eitan.

In London the Egyptian Committee, still operating within its own wall of total secrecy, had approved another idea. The SAS would move into Cairo and kill Nasser. The committee received an assurance from the SAS that such a plan was not only "highly feasible" but would have the essential total deniability. In the meantime, the Secret Intelligence Service had also honed another plan to use its own black propaganda radio stations based in Cyprus and Aden to broadcast threats of attack against Israel by Egypt.

As August waned into September, the drums of war beat ever more loudly in the Middle East over the airwaves being manipulated by MI6.

Then, as the planning for the Suez intervention gathered its own momentum, MI6, along with other Western intelligence services, found its attention focused eastward on Hungary. Tens of thousands of students had taken to the streets of Budapest, demanding withdrawal of Soviet troops, the release of all political prisoners, and the establishment of an "independent Communist regime." The MI6 troubleshooter John Bruce Lockhart had been ordered by Dick White to fly to Budapest to monitor events. By the time he arrived, many thousands of angry workers had joined the student demonstrations shouting the same demands. In a cable to Dick White, Lockhart wrote, "What had seemed impossible a month ago may well happen."

In Paris and London, Guy Mollet and Anthony Eden had agreed that the Tripartite Agreement signed in 1950 gave Britain and France a legal right to occupy the Canal Zone if war broke out between Israel and Egypt. Dick White was ordered by Eden to increase the propaganda being pumped out by the MI6 radio stations, and the Mossad mobilized its media contacts across the world to plant even more dire stories of the impending threat to Israel posed by Nasser. It was a classic example of the black art of media manipulation.

AS THE STIFLING HEAT OF AUGUST IN WASHINGTON gave way to cooling breezes off the Potomac, the only concern for its population was whether President Eisenhower would be given a clean bill of health when he went into Walter Reed Army Medical Center for his regular checkup. Events in Europe and the Middle East seemed a long way away to Americans planning their Labor Day break.

Only in the CIA and the State Department were the Dulles brothers increasingly troubled about the studied silence from both the Quai d'Orsay in Paris and the Foreign Office in London. It was, in Allen Dulles's words, "a sign that the damned Brits and the French could be cooking up something." Yet all attempts to get responses from MI6 or the SDECE were met with bland reassurances. There was nothing going on.

IN THE EARLY EVENING OF OCTOBER 22, 1956, an Israeli Air Force transport and an RAF plane from the Queen's Flight emerged from the low cloud base to touch down at a military airfield near the French town of Sevres. On board the flight from Tel Aviv was David Ben-Gurion, Defense Minister Shimon Peres, and Chief of Staff General Moshe Dayan. From London had come Foreign Secretary Selwyn Lloyd and Patrick Dean, his deputy undersecretary. (Dean, just promoted by Eden, was a founding member of the still secret cabal around Eden that had spent months plotting to bring about the downfall of Nasser.) Both groups had previously agreed their entourages would be kept to the minimum to preserve the total secrecy surrounding the meeting. Dick White and the MI6 station chief in Paris, Rodney Dennys, provided the intelligence presence for Britain; Isser Harel was the Mossad representative.

"There was an air of both tension and expectation," Harel recalled to the author. "We knew broadly why we were there, of course, but we had no idea of exactly what was on the table."

Waiting on the tarmac to greet the two delegations was the French prime minister, Christian Pineau, and Guy Mollet. Both wore the tired faces of men who had spent long nights in discussion, receiving telephone calls from UN Secretary-General Dag Hammerskjöld, who wanted to avoid conflict with Israel, and from Shimon Peres, who had been politically noncommittal. Other calls had come from Egypt's foreign minister, Mahmoud Fawzi, the day before the secret mission to France, offering reassurances that Egypt had no hostile intentions toward Israel. Guy Mollet had listened politely to Fawzi's request that France should convey this promise to Tel Aviv.

The arrival of the groups at that military airfield on a cold October night was proof those entreaties had failed. Their presence owed much to the skilled organizing by Pierre Boursicot, the head of the SDECE, who was the Paris point man for Operation Musketeer and supervised the meticulous planning for the French role in the proposed invasion of Egypt. No detail had escaped his attention. His limousine led the convoy out of the airfield; Isser Harel sat beside him. Behind came the three cars carrying the diplomats. In the last car were White and Dennys. Arriving at the château chosen for the conference, they found Boursicot had arranged a spread of kosher, French, and English dishes and soft drinks. Champagne was being kept on ice in the kitchen ready for the celebration if there was agreement among the group of colluders, who would have created a war without the slightest approval of their governments or the United Nations. For Isser Harel "there was something medieval about the situation."

However, there was a time limit for them to reach consensus. The historic meeting was scheduled to end at midnight so the Israeli delegation could be back in Tel Aviv before dawn, when their absence would be noticed.

The château's main salon, exquisitely furnished, its walls adorned with long-forgotten faces encased in gilt frames, had been chosen by Boursicot as the conference room. Adjoining it was a room that was now occupied by GCHQ and Israeli technicians who had arrived earlier in the day to set up a joint communications link with London and Tel Aviv.

Across the Atlantic, the National Security Agency had already pinpointed transmission tests emanating from the château and had recorded from midevening onward a sudden increase in coded signals traffic. Cryptologists at Fort Meade, who had been placed on standby, began trying to decipher the messages, but there was no way they could break the codes. Allen and John Foster Dulles both concluded the volume of signal traffic could be the precursor of Israel asking for French support to be allowed to launch an attack on Jordan if the Iraqi army invaded the Hashemite kingdom. That possibility had been part of the Mossad disinformation campaign.

By midnight, agreement had been reached in the château. Israel would launch a ground attack on Egypt across the Sinai Desert and aim to reach the Suez Canal within twenty-four hours, a promise Moshe Dayan had shortened to "if not sooner." Britain and France would then issue an ultimatum to Nasser that he should allow their troops to enter the Canal Zone as temporary peacekeepers, after which the Israeli forces would withdraw to the Sinai side of the waterway. If these proposals were not accepted by Nasser, "without further warning" there would follow a full-scale Anglo-French invasion of Egypt to reoccupy the Canal Zone. The protocol was written in French with English and Hebrew translations attached as annexes. One by one the ministers signed the document, each having given a solemn undertaking that its contents would forever remain secret. At Boursicot's signal, waiters came into the salon carrying trays of champagne to celebrate the collusion.

IN THE LAST WEEK OF OCTOBER, the CIA station in Tel Aviv sent a Most Urgent flash to Washington. Israel was mobilizing. More than a hundred thousand troops were poised on the border with Egypt. John Foster Dulles sent equally urgent cables to Paris and London, demanding an answer to the same question: What was happening? From both capitals the response was couched in the careful language that had long been the stock-in-trade of diplomacy. The Israeli troop movements would probably turn out to be another of the maneuvers the IDF liked to carry out. John Foster Dulles conveyed the responses to Eisenhower, who was about to undergo his medical tests in Walter Reed Army Medical Center. It was Sunday, October 28, 1956, when the president dictated a note from his bed to Ben-Gurion asking for the reason why his forces had been mobilized. He handed it to Dulles for transmission with the words, "You know, Israel and barium make quite a combination."

The next day Israeli forces crossed the border into Egypt. "We had planned to the last tank track," Moshe Dayan said later to the author, and had code-named the attack Operation Kadesh. In typical style, Dayan had led from the front, watching his tanks swiftly roll up the Egyptian forces with minimal losses. Even the CIA's Middle East Watch Committee in Washington, which had started to receive U-2 photographs of the buildup of military forces in Israel, was stunned at the speed of the Israeli advance. Still, even as the tanks rolled on toward the Suez Canal, there was a reluctance within the Watch Committee to believe this was any more than Israel alone on the warpath in a well-planned strike.

The months of secret planning between France and Britain, between Ben-Gurion, Eden, and Mollet, between the Secret Intelligence Service, the SDECE, and the Mossad, had stayed their secret; they had deliberately kept their most powerful ally in the dark. Eisenhower saw it as a great betrayal. In London, Eden addressed the House of Commons. He stood at the dispatch box not bothering to hide the satisfaction in his voice. "We have asked both sides to lay down their arms and have asked the Egyptian government to agree that Anglo-French forces should move temporarily into key positions around the Canal in whatever strength may be necessary." He had taken the words from the château protocol, which he had then burned in the fireplace in his Downing Street apartment. However, a copy of the document would survive in the SDECE Registry, and it is there to this day.

After news of the invasion, Eisenhower had been driven back from the hospital to the White House. He authorized a statement to be issued under his name that the United States was "pledged to assist any victim of aggression in the Middle East." It was a clear warning shot to the colluders.

In Cairo, Nasser appeared on a balcony to address applauding crowds. Echoing Winston Churchill's speech in 1940 as Britain faced invasion from across the Channel, the Egyptian president roared into his microphone, "We shall not surrender. We shall fight the enemy wherever they appear." He ended his mob-rallying oration with a demand that any collaborator must be hunted down and killed.

When no response to the ultimatum had been received in London or Paris, RAF Canberra bombers attacked Egyptian airfields around the canal. Eisenhower made a special announcement, broadcast to the nation, demanding that "all hostilities must cease." Four days later the White House learned that British and French troops had set sail from Cyprus and that British paratroopers had landed in the town of Suez.

By then, in the basement War Room in the White House, Eisenhower had studied the reconnaissance photographs from a U-2 spy plane that had made several passes over the Egyptian air base at Cairo West. He was shocked by the scale of the destruction. Allen Dulles ordered the photographs to be wired to Dick White in London with a note, "Is this what Britain intended to do?" Riled by the tone of the question, the MI6 chief cabled back, "The RAF say this is the quickest bomb damage assessment they have had."

On November 5, 1956, the first British and French paratroopers landed near the canal; two days later the Anglo-French invasion force of one hundred thousand men came ashore.

That evening Nikolai Bulganin, Russia's president, warned Eden, Mollet, and Ben-Gurion that unless they withdrew their forces "immediately," he would order Soviet nuclear missiles to be used against them.

Eisenhower warned if that happened, the United States would retaliate with its own nuclear rockets targeted on Russia. Bulganin backed down and turned his fury on subduing the Hungarian Uprising, the Red Army leaving the streets of Budapest carpeted with the bodies of martyrs. Eisenhower ordered $20 million of Mutual Security Act funds to be spent on food and medicine for Hungarian Uprising aid and allowed 21,500 refugees to be admitted to the United States and given jobs and homes. Meanwhile, he ordered pressure to be maintained on France and Britain to withdraw from the Canal Zone. Oil supplies were halted from U.S. companies in Latin America for both Britain and France. In London there was a growing wave of jingoism accompanied by anti-Americanism. Newspapers like the *Daily Express* thundered that the "special relationship" had never been special, only a means for the United States to get control over the canal. That mood was reflected inside MI6. George Young bitterly accused the United States, "When its own Allies acted in pursuance of what they believed to be in their national interests, it took the lead in preventing them, and went its own way."

Eisenhower had ordered dollar support for the British pound and the French franc on international exchanges to be stopped, leading to a serious run on both currencies. On November 23, 1956, Anthony

Eden, visibly gripped with illness, once more raised the question of having Nasser assassinated. He asked Dick White to explore the possibility. It was the last order he gave the chief before he left for Jamaica to recuperate at the home of Ian Fleming—the creator of James Bond, who had a license to kill, though never a head of state. The wish to assassinate a head of state would be part of Anthony Eden's legacy. By December 22, 1956, the invaders of the Suez Canal, having only advanced a few miles up the waterway, finally withdrew from Egypt under the relentless pressure from the United States. In their place came a United Nations peacekeeping force to actually carry out the cover role that had been created at the French château just two months earlier.

The humiliating blow to Britain and France probably marked the end of their last attempt to regain control of the Suez Canal. In Tel Aviv, Nicholas Elliott felt "shame" at the way his secret mission had ended, feeling that Eden should have called Bulganin's bluff about launching nuclear weapons. His view failed to take into account Eisenhower's deep anger, only matched by Allen Dulles's own feeling, that British and French diplomacy, like the British and French intelligence services, was "mired in shoddy deception."

It was not until March 1957 that Dick White felt it safe to make a visit to Washington without "running the risk of fireworks" to talk with Allen Dulles on what he admitted was a damage-control mission. By all accounts he succeeded. By then Nasser's relationship had become ever more linked with the Soviet Union, and it remained so until his peaceful death in 1970, when Anwar Sadat succeeded him as president. Long before then, Anthony Eden had resigned, and Dwight Eisenhower and Allen Dulles died in 1969, the year before Sadat took office. Dick White would remain in office until 1968 before retiring to live in a timber frame house he had built in Sussex and spend his retirement writing poetry. He died on February 21, 1993, and at his memorial service one of the Bible lessons was read by the then director-general of the Security Service, the first woman to be appointed to the post, Stella Rimington.

IN JUNE 2007, ASHRAF MARWAN, an Egyptian billionaire who had married Nasser's daughter Mona and had been one of the president's key advisers during the Suez War, was found dead outside his high-rise apartment in central London. He appeared to have fallen from the balcony while conducting an animated conversation with a person never identified. The death of the seventy-two-year-old industrialist reopened the mystery surrounding him. Gad Shimron, a former Mossad officer, revealed that Marwan had been a longtime informer for the service and after Nasser's death had been appointed national security adviser to president Anwar Sadat, who was shot dead in 1981 while reviewing a military parade in Cairo. Since then, Marwan had become convinced he was going to be assassinated and had lived his life in London as a well-protected exile.

Nevertheless, who would want to kill him? Shimron claimed Marwan had finally lost the trust of the Mossad because it suspected he was a double agent for Egyptian intelligence. The charge was dismissed by a senior Mossad officer who spoke to the author, "There are enough people who are a problem without killing an old man long past his sell-by date."

In October 2008, MI6 joined Scotland Yard's Specialist Crime Directorate in reopening the investigation into Marwan's death. His widow, Mona, had revealed her husband had been writing a book, but the incomplete manuscript and documents he had removed from his bank safe deposit box had, she discovered, "disappeared" shortly before his death. While Mona did not know their contents, she told the respected London *Observer* newspaper she believed they could be associated with her husband's fear he would be murdered. "He told me that three times," she said to investigators. By November 2008, their inquiries had spread to Washington, Cairo, and Tel Aviv.

9

Partition to Perdu

On one of those bright summer mornings in July 1969, which Londoners said compensated for the delays on the Underground as it shuddered and swayed beneath the capital, among the underground passengers was Stella Rimington.

In her striped Indian silk blouse and fashionable miniskirt, which showed off her tanned legs, with her long hair coiled into a bun beneath her pillbox hat, she looked ten years younger than her thirty-four. She was about to start on a new journey, very different from the one she had recently completed to the top of the Khyber Pass, looking toward the towering peaks of the Himalayas. Then, she had been filled with a sudden feeling of uncertainty, because she was leaving India. Would she be successful in holding down a permanent job with MI5 in London—not as a secretary but as a spy catcher? Her enemy, as in India, would be Soviet spies, only instead of typing up reports of their activities for her MI5 boss in Delhi, she would be on the first rung of tracking them down herself. It was a heady prospect, which filled her with excitement as the train rumbled under the streets of London.

Passengers were reading newspapers filled not only with the continuing threat of the cold war but the successful NASA mission of the Apollo 11 manned flight to the moon. A feat so extraordinary it had involved twenty thousand contractors employing three hundred thousand skilled workers. It was capped by Neil Armstrong planting his size 9½ boot on the lunar surface and pronouncing, "That's one small step for [a] man, one giant leap for mankind."

Stepping off the train to continue her journey to her first day at work in Leconfield House on Curzon Street, Stella Rimington could well have echoed Armstrong's words. The claustrophobia that had blighted her teen years had passed, and there had been no recurrence of the migraine attacks she decided were caused by the large amount of estrogen in her contraceptive pills, which had left blotches on her face and a dark line above her upper lip.

Rimington was slightly built; her face had its many fine points, dominated by often quizzical eyes. She was married to a childhood sweetheart, a high-flying civil servant who, four years previously, had taken her to India in his post as economic first secretary at the High Commission in Delhi. At first, life had been no different than that of any other diplomat's wife in a foreign posting to the subcontinent: the endless round of cocktail parties, dinners to host, dances to attend. By day there were English lessons to be given to slum children in the suburbs, or an English child to be coached for the entrance exam to a boarding school back home; in between, one might help out in the servants' clinic in the High Commission compound. On the surface nothing much had changed in the enclosure since Sir Harry Philby had been a regular visitor.

Beyond the immaculate lawns and flower beds, the remains of the Raj were being steadily demolished. Statues of the Empress Queen, Victoria, had been pulled down; roads named after the Emperor King, George, now bore the names of Gandhi and Nehru. Every week ships sailed for England, Australia, and Canada, their deck rails lined with members of the Anglo-India community: law officers, doctors, and teachers glad to be leaving behind them a growing anti-British feeling fed by Indira Gandhi. Stella Rimington would later write in her memoir of those times, "She was no friend of the British, nor for that matter, the Americans; her support was for the Soviet Union and as the British left, colonies of Russians moved in."

LONG BEFORE THE RIMINGTONS' ARRIVAL, India had been an important posting for MI5 and MI6. Some of their officers had been recruited from the ranks of the army and navy intelligence corps; others had transferred out of Scotland Yard's Special Branch; a number had been "tapped" at Oxford and Cambridge. After training they had been sent to India to defend the subcontinent against any threat of insurgency and ensure *Pax Britannica* continued to imbue its leaders in London with the unshakable conviction that they belonged to a race born to rule, and nowhere more so than in India.

Before airliners had shortened the journey, the spies had arrived by ship to stand on a steamer's deck and stare in awe at the vaulting Gateway of India, a towering arch of yellow basalt rising above the Bay of Bombay; it was the very visible symbol of the greatest empire the world had known. No one could believe that one day, and soon, the arch would be no more than a pile of forgotten stone, a reminder that like other, lesser, empires the British Empire had passed.

Stepping ashore, the spies, like all newcomers, had been engulfed in the endless confusion of the city's Victoria Station. The heat, the aroma of spices, and the stench of urine were overwhelming as men in sagging dhotis and flapping nightshirts and women in saris, bare arms and feet jangling with gold bracelets, struggled to pass the Sikh soldiers in scarlet turbans, emaciated *sadhus* in orange loincloths, and deformed children thrusting out their stunted limbs for *baksheesh*, the universal begging cry.

It was this world that Allen Welsh Dulles—the fifth and longest-serving CIA director—had loved until the day he died. Going to his grave he had said as much to Bill Buckley, in between his bouts of coughing from pneumonia; he was still filled with a deep dislike for what Britain had done to destroy the Indian subcontinent. "There was something almost touching in the way he said he was glad to have lived long enough to see the 'Brutish Empire,' as he called it, consigned to history," Bill Buckley told the author.

It had been the role of both MI5 and MI6 to have helped it survive for so long. Its agents had traveled into the wastes of the Deccan and danced the nights away at the magnificent imperial balls in the Himalayan summer capital of Simla, or watched cricket being played on the manicured grass of Calcutta's Bengal Club and sat down with subalterns in their dinner jackets in the steamy jungles, joining in the toast to whichever monarch was on the throne in distant London. The spies had infiltrated everywhere to intercept the first hint of a threat against the realm.

In the MI6 station commander's office in Delhi had been a framed quotation by Winston Churchill, "The loss of India would be final and fatal to us. It could not fail to be part of a process that would reduce us to the scale of a minor power." He had delivered those words to the House of Commons in February 1931, and for sixteen years they held true, until August 14, 1947, when Jawaharlal Nehru had addressed the new Indian Constitutional Assembly in New Delhi with words of a similar highly charged ring.

"Long years ago we made a tryst with destiny, and now the time comes when we shall redeem our pledge. . . . At the stroke of the midnight hour, when the world sleeps, India will awake to life and freedom. A moment comes . . . when we step out from the old to the new, when an age ends, and when the soul of a nation, long suppressed, finds utterance."

As Allen Dulles had hoped, India had finally been freed from the British Empire.

BY THE TIME THE RIMINGTONS had arrived in Delhi, the cold war was well entrenched on the subcontinent, with the almost daily arrival of flights from Moscow of men and women ready to place a harsher imprint on the romantic India of Kipling. The new arrivals had no interest in cricket, polo, or tiger hunts in Assam, or black-tie dinners in the unbearable heat of summer in the Northwest Frontier or during fierce winter snowstorms that rolled down from the Himalayas. For the Russians, the maharajas who had helped rule the subcontinent for Britain had no role to play in Soviet plans to gain control over India.

The battalions of Soviet advisers had been well prepared by lecturers at Patrice Lumumba University in Moscow on India's culture, its history, and, more recently, its partition. The instructors spoke of how, and why, in their hour of triumph its people had turned on each other in a mockery of what their greatest leader, Mohandas Karamchand Gandhi, had preached about nonviolence; instead, with equal brutality, Muslims and Hindus had slaughtered each other as the subcontinent had been geographically divided on religious lines. Muslims would go north to the new nations of Pakistan and Kashmir, where they could continue to practice the faith of Allah, the One and Merciful. The Hindus would remain in India to follow their religion, which worshipped God in almost any form they chose to see him: in the sacred cows who roamed the streets; in ancestors, sages, spirits; in the flowing River Ganges and its lesser tributaries; in the fiery tongues of the six-armed God and the Goddess, each with a holy snake coiling from the sacred head; in elephants who could fly to the clouds and venerated monkeys; and in multiple phallic symbols. Hinduism, the faith of Brahma, Shiva, and Vishnu, is eternally in search of the balance in life, the attainment of the Absolute, chosen from a staggering pantheon of over three million divinities. Muslims, however, prostrate themselves on the mosque carpets in the direction of Mecca, chanting together Koranic texts.

The godless Soviet Communists had sent their own experts on Islam and Hinduism to guide their minions about the pitfalls of religion in India: military advisers, industrial advisers, political advisers, commercial advisers, and financial advisers. Many of them had the same calculated fervor of the missionaries who had once failed to proselytize British India.

With the advisers had come agents of the KGB and the GRU. From Madras to Bengal and beyond into the Punjab, East and West Pakistan, and Kashmir, the spies had spread throughout until there were more Soviet spies there than in Eastern Europe. Tracking them were the officers of the CIA, mostly young, often on their first posting out of training school. They had believed they were winning the cold war when over 750,000 Pakistanis had welcomed President Eisenhower to Karachi and a million Indians in Delhi had held aloft banners acclaiming him as "the Prince of Peace." They had tossed so many bouquets into his open car that he stood, as he was paraded through the streets, calf-high in blossoms.

The hardened men of MI5 and MI6 in their offices in the High Commission in Delhi had witnessed similar exultation before when Lord Louis Mountbatten, the last viceroy of the Raj, had presided over untold millions as the new flag of India had been raised on August 15, 1947, the high spot of the new nation's independence celebrations. It signaled the greatest disengagement in history of one nation from another. The separation of the two nations also meant that MI6, like other foreign intelligence services, had to set up new networks to operate in both countries.

IN THIS STILL DANGEROUS WORLD, Stella Rimington had become quickly bored with the routine of a diplomat's wife and increasingly aware there was more to life than in the lives other wives led. For them a major decision was choosing what dress to wear at a party or when to book a court for tennis. With a good English degree from Edinburgh University and an interest in world events—she had followed closely the Suez Crisis and the Soviet invasion of Hungary—Stella Rimington wanted more than just being "identified in terms of my husband's job—a First Secretary's wife. I felt I was just frivoling around. I was wondering how to solve this when one day in the summer of 1967, as I was walking through the High Commission compound, someone tapped me on the shoulder."

He was the MI5 station chief in India, he wanted a secretary, and would Stella like the job? She had not hesitated, filling in her positive vetting form that allowed her past to be probed. When London had

responded positively, she accepted a salary of five pounds a week and
was shown how to use the combination lock to enter the area in the High
Commission where both MI5 and MI6 officers worked. Her job was typing up reports, which left for London in one of the diplomatic bags,
hand-carried by a Queen's messenger who placed his bag on the first
class aircraft seat beside him.

Most of the reports concerned the KGB and GRU spies who operated from the magnificent white palace that housed the Soviet Embassy
in Delhi. On the same street was the more modest building housing the
Chinese legation and its spies. Some of them spent their days parked
across the road from the High Commission, noting down in their pads
everybody who came and went.

The Rimingtons had already been exposed to entrapment, targeted
by a lecturer at Delhi University who had inveigled them to meet a Russian diplomat. A quick check revealed the lecturer was a Communist
and the diplomat a KGB officer.

Now, after a lifestyle that still had an echo of the Raj about it, the
Rimingtons were back in London, and Stella, no longer merely a typist,
was about to embark on a life as a full-time MI5 spy. She believed India
had given her the self-confidence and maturity to do the job.

STELLA RIMINGTON WAS ASSIGNED a cubbyhole in Leconfield
House, one of several in a partitioned, windowless room. On her desk
was the latest issue of the *Morning Star* and an instruction to comb the
newspaper for names on whom a file should be opened. She was to
concentrate on rural Sussex, long a bastion of the landed gentry and, it
seemed to her, an unlikely refuge for a Soviet sympathizer.

Three floors above where she picked her way through the turgid
prose, Martin Furnival Jones, the director-general of MI5, continued to
build his list of KGB operatives who had penetrated the very core of
Britain: its armed forces, trade unions, and industry. Not until 1971
would Stella Rimington discover that her own culling of names had contributed to the expulsion of seventy Soviet intelligence officers accused of
espionage. The operation that finally led to their exposure had all the
makings of a cold war movie thriller.

In 1970, Oleg Lyalin, a low-ranking KGB officer stationed at the Russian Embassy in London, had been caught by MI5 Watchers engaging in
an affair with a married secretary at the Soviet trade delegation office in
London. The MI5 team had secretly filmed and recorded the couple's
passionate lovemaking. An MI5 counterintelligence officer had con-

fronted Lyalin and, after showing him the evidence, had played on the KGB officer's understandable fear that he and his mistress would be returned to Moscow once their superiors learned about their affair.

Lyalin's response had astonished the officer. In return for a guarantee that he and his lover would not be unmasked, he would spy for the Security Service. All he would require in return was that MI5 would provide him with a safe house where the couple could continue their assignations. An apartment was found in the Fulham area and wired for sound and picture. For eight months Lyalin had met with his MI5 officer and provided valuable information on the activities of other KGB officers in the country.

Then, on August 15, 1971, disaster struck. After an afternoon of sex in the apartment, fueled by the generous supply of alcohol MI5 had provided, Lyalin drove off only to be stopped by a police patrol for drunken driving and taken to the nearest police station, where he demanded that the duty commander should phone Lyalin's MI5 officer. Thirty minutes later, the KGB operative had been freed from custody and taken to an MI5 safe house in Sussex, the very county where Stella Rimington had been putting together her own list of local Communists. For days Lyalin was debriefed by a team of senior MI5 officers. After he had, in the words of Furnival Jones, been "squeezed dry," Lyalin was reunited with his lover for one last night of passion. The next day the couple was given a choice: If they wished, they could begin a new life together and be provided with fresh identities and passports. The woman, the mother of two children, allegedly chose instead to return to her family. Purportedly she was among the expelled Soviet intelligence officers and their families who were escorted aboard a Russian ship carrying them back to the USSR. However, the BBC reported that Lyalin and she had begun a new life under aliases in Britain. The BBC also reported that Lyalin died in 1995. The only photograph of him kept in an MI5 file shows a face remarkably like that of the screen actor Ronald Colman.

ALL MORNING ON THAT FEBRUARY DAY IN 1972, Frank Steele, a veteran MI6 officer, had followed the Russian through the damp streets of Dublin. He had watched him enter a dilapidated tenement building in Gardiner Street on the north side of the city that housed the offices of Sinn Fein, the political wing of the outlawed Irish Republican Army. Afterward, the Russian had walked across O'Connell Bridge over the River Liffey back into the city center. From time to time he paused to photograph buildings and Dublin's famous Georgian doors. On his application form for accreditation by the Irish Tourist Office, he described himself as a journalist working for *Pravda*, Russia's most influential newspaper. The attached photo with the form showed a round-faced bespectacled man in his middle years. Steele had sent a copy to Century House, where MI6 was now headquartered at 100 Westminster Bridge. The photo was identified as Aleksander Feoktisov, a KGB officer who had served in West Berlin and under cover later as a press officer with the Soviet delegation at the United Nations in New York.

Since the expulsion of the Soviet spies from Britain, the Soviet consulate in the Irish Republic had suddenly been upgraded to embassy status and a steady stream of genuine Russian journalists and trade missions had flown into Dublin airport. Their arrival had been welcomed by the Department of Foreign Affairs as proof of Ireland's growing importance in a world where the United States and the Soviet Union continued to glare at each other through the jaundiced prism of the cold war. With Europe as its crucible, Irish politicians optimistically saw their country acting as peacemaker between the superpowers; while such a role would no doubt irritate their neighbor, Britain, the support of Moscow in the long-held Republican dream of uniting Northern Ireland with the South would be a powerful help in lifting what one Irish politician had called "the English yoke from Ulster." Charles Haughey, a radical nationalist with a deep-seated dislike of the English, had that February day entertained Feoktisov at lunch in the Irish parliament, the Dáil, and spoken animatedly about the hope that Moscow would lend its support in "removing the British army of occupation from the North," Haughey later confirmed to the author.

Steele's presence in Dublin was to follow up a claim made by Major General Jan Sejna, the former First Secretary of the Czechoslovakian Communist Party at the Ministry of Defense and former Chief of Staff to the Minister of Defense, who had defected in 1968 and had undergone an extensive debriefing in Washington. After some hesitation, Richard Helms, the CIA's eighth director, had agreed MI6 could send two officers to question Sejna. He had told them the KGB had been secretly funding the IRA with money transfers from a number of Swiss bank accounts to those in Irish banks. Part of the money had been spent on sending IRA gunmen for training by Czech intelligence. After lengthy questioning, the MI6 officers had decided that Sejna was telling the truth.

———

WHILE HELMS HAD A GENUINE respect for the Secret Intelligence Service, it did not extend to John Rennie, who had been appointed its sixth chief in 1968. Helms knew the nearest Rennie had come to hands-on intelligence work was during the run-up to the invasion of the Suez Canal, when he had been in charge of the black propaganda broadcasts from MI6 radio stations based in Cyprus and Aden to counter the powerful rabble-rousing calls from Cairo Radio.

Rennie had survived the corrosive criticism sweeping through Whitehall following the failure of Suez because his establishment friends had not deserted him. They had remained steadfast from his days at Balliol College, Oxford, and had guided him into the Diplomatic Service, at every rung of his ladder ready to catch him at the first sign of falling. He had married a Swiss from a wealthy family, and his powerful friends had been there to toast their happiness. During World War II, Rennie had been sent to New York to work in the British Information Service; later he had been posted as a commercial first secretary at the Washington Embassy and then as minister at the Buenos Aires embassy. In neither post had he shone, but he had done enough to satisfy his well-placed allies in Whitehall.

He became assistant secretary of defense at the Foreign Office and continued to give the impression that if he knew something he would not let on what it was; the general assumption around the Foreign Office was that he might know even more. The impression was sufficient to get him appointed to be the new chief of MI6 in 1968. With it had come an invitation to visit Richard Helms, who had been appointed director of the CIA two years earlier.

Two of the most powerful spy catchers in the Western world could not be more different. Helms was fifty-three years old on the day he was sworn in at the White House. The Marine Band was playing his favorite World War II melodies; gray hair neatly trimmed, his body muscular from tennis, there was about Helms in everything he did and said a can-do attitude. Rennie was a year younger than his Washington host, the son of a wealthy manufacturer of matchsticks; his hair was thinning, and his expensive formal suits did not quite hide his paunch. Helms drove himself to work in his Cadillac, arriving each morning on the dot of six thirty. Rennie preferred the comfort of his chauffeur-driven limousine, arriving at Century House at the civilized hour of 9:30 A.M. Helms almost never took a day off from the office and never a full weekend; he had been known to turn up at his regular hour on Christmas Day to check what was happening in Operations. Unless there was a good reason for Rennie to be called into the office, his weekends were sacrosanct, devoted to painting: His work had been exhibited at the Royal Academy and the Paris Salon. Both had married independent-minded wives, Rennie a second time, after his first wife died, to a widow a year before he became chief. Helms had been married to the same woman for twenty-seven years.

On the day they had met at Langley, Helms commanded twenty thousand people, over half of them spying overseas, their every requirement met from a budget of over a billion dollars in 1968 (it trebled by 2007). Rennie had a total staff of close to fifteen hundred in sixty stations around the world and a budget when he met Helms of around £250 million.

Their first meeting failed to impress Helms. He had wanted to know how Rennie intended to deal with the KGB. Rennie had been vague. "We have to anticipate which way the tide is running. Europe is changing, that sort of thing," Helms later recalled. He put the response down to Rennie not having hands-on experience.

The MI6 chief had returned to find himself being pressed by Prime Minister Edward Heath to get seriously involved in Northern Ireland, which had long been the preserve of MI5. "The Secret Intelligence Service does not operate in England, Scotland, or Wales. A bad precedent would be established if we begin to do so in Ulster," Rennie had told the prime minister. Heath had not been satisfied. He had read the report of the two MI6 officers who had interrogated Sejna and wanted MI6 to get involved.

Unknown to Heath, the Secret Intelligence Service had already received help in dealing with what Rennie called "the Irish problem." Nine years before he had taken office, the Mossad had sent Rafi Eitan, its director of operations, to Belfast to track links between the IRA and Hezbollah. In the summer of 1986, Sean Savage, a senior member of the Irish terror group, had been spotted by a Mossad undercover agent in Beirut.

"He was on a shopping spree for Arab arms for the IRA. Ties with the IRA posed a direct threat to Israel. The Irish group had expertise Hezbollah could benefit from. They had access to funds in the United States which would help Hezbollah develop a financial base it did not yet have to attack Israel. Terrorism was already on the boil: hijacking, kidnapping statesmen, an embassy held at gunpoint. An alliance between two ruthless organizations was a pressure Mossad had to diffuse— and quickly," Eitan told the author.

His visit to Northern Ireland had left him concerned. The Royal Ulster Constabulary (RUC) was incapable of defeating the IRA. More wor-

rying was that MI5, a service he had long respected from his own days as
a Mossad agent in London, appeared unable to penetrate the organization. "That could be the only reason why several cargoes of arms had
been run ashore on the west coast of Ireland as part of the deal which
Savage had made in Beirut. Only MI6 could stop further shipments, but
they would need hard evidence," recalled Eitan.

In October 1987, Mossad spies had tracked the Irish cargo ship *Eksund*, which had 120 tons of weapons on board, as it made its way from
Libya to the Atlantic and on to its final destination, the windswept
shores of Donegal in the Irish Republic. From there, they would be
smuggled into Northern Ireland: cases of surface-to-air missiles, rocket
launchers, machine guns, explosives, and detonators.

Eitan decided the *Eksund* should be stopped well before it reached
Ireland. The ideal place would be off the coast of Brittany. Neither the
Irish government, MI5, nor the RUC would be briefed on what was going to happen. Only the Mossad, French intelligence (DST), and MI6
would be told. It was agreed that credit for the operation would go to the
Secret Intelligence Service. Its officers were part of the team that stopped
the ship.

The *Eksund* and its crew were arrested and its cargo impounded. It
was the start of the Secret Intelligence Service working in Northern Ireland.

FRANK STEELE WAS APPOINTED MI6 director of operations in Ulster, reporting to Howard Smith, a former ambassador in Moscow who
would concentrate on the political minefield of Ulster. Rennie had told
Steele he could not yet run locally recruited agents, as he had in the
Middle East and Sudan, but must initially only use his considerable experience in conflict situations. Steele had speed-read into the history
and cultural divides of the province and recognized that counterintelligence operations would have to be supported by shrewd political assessments. The rambunctious Ian Paisley and the fast-talking Gerry Adams
would be formidable foes in the battle for the "hearts and minds" Rennie had spoken about in his briefing to Steele.

Intelligence officer Colin Wallace—one of several sources for the
author in what became known as "Ulster's secret dirty war"—later elab-
orated on the problems MI6 faced, "In an already crowded intelligence
field, there was the danger of everyone falling over each other. The army
people had learned most of their counterinsurgency tactics in Malaya,
Aden, and other parts of the empire, and these didn't work in the back

streets of Belfast and Londonderry. And, as well as the RUC, there was also the SAS and MI5 running their own operations. On top, the CIA and officers from the BND and French intelligence were in town to see if they could pick up anything of interest to them. Then there were the Amnesty people collecting evidence about torture: 'white noise,' sleep deprivation, hooding, forcing a suspect to stand against a wall for hours and not move. Those tactics might have worked with Arabs, but they were no use against IRA guys conditioned by a history of hating the English to resist such methods."

MI6 had slipped unannounced and uninvited by the other security forces into the province and based itself between Belfast and Lisburn in a location that even today remains unknown. Its officers familiarized themselves with names that were only beginning to emerge in the international headlines: Armagh, Newry, Coleraine, and Londonderry. They began building their own contacts: a bartender, a schoolteacher, a pastor, anyone who could provide information on the IRA, especially its links with the Eastern Bloc and Middle East terrorists and its developing ties with urban guerrilla groups across Europe.

The Secret Intelligence Service's patient information gathering was disrupted when the army and the RUC swept into the province's republican areas and began to hunt for IRA suspects, but their intelligence was faulty and enabled a number of key members of the organization to escape to their hideouts in Donegal or Monaghan, in the Irish Republic. Bitter argument ensued between the RUC and the army commanders over what Steele called "another shambles." The rough-and-ready tactics of soldiers breaking down front doors and threatening women and children led to scores of young men and women joining the IRA. It marked a turning point in Rennie's hope of winning the support of nearly a million Catholics and shocked many Protestants.

While barbed wire, walls, and vehicle checks creating a visible barrier between the two religious communities became part of daily life, Steele's officers resumed their business of gathering information, mostly within the Catholic community; every source was stored on MI6 computers and routinely sent to Century House for further analysis. Slowly the first insights emerged into how the IRA was financed from supporters in the United States and Libya, as well as the KGB. Accounts were opened in Belfast banks, including the Protestant Ulster Bank, and in the Dublin-based Bank of Ireland and Allied Irish Bank. The IRA had also developed contacts with foreign terrorist organizations like the Basque separatist group ETA, the Italian Red Brigades, and the Popular Front for the Liberation of Palestine (PFLP).

More worrying was that the IRA had begun to develop into a power-ful guerrilla force, equipped with walkie-talkies and high-powered ra-dios tuned to police frequencies, as the province moved to the threshold of civil war, which would eventually lead the IRA into open confronta-tion with guns blazing, knowing that they had the discreetly sympathetic ear of Moscow. That February day in 1972, when Frank Steele had tailed Aleksander Feoktisov through Dublin before the KGB agent had sat down for lunch with Charles Haughey—himself to become a loyal sup-porter of the IRA—had borne fruit.

From its contacts, the IRA had learned the value of an impenetrable cell structure where betrayal guaranteed execution by one of its death squads; how to forge passports; and the need to exploit the religious background of most IRA members, who remained worshippers at Mass and made their confession regularly. A number of their priests, while es-chewing violence, regarded the IRA as freedom fighters.

A year into MI6 operations, Steele informed Rennie the time was coming when the armed struggle against the IRA could not be won and said it seemed "just pragmatic to talk to their leadership." At a London conference chaired by Secretary of State for Northern Ireland William Whitelaw, and attended by Rennie and his MI5 counterpart, Michael Hanley, supported by military commanders in Northern Ireland and se-nior RUC officers, Steele's proposal was fiercely rejected.

Shortly after the London meeting, a small group of senior IRA men had traveled across the border to Dublin and caught an Aer Lingus flight to Frankfurt, where they boarded a flight to Beirut. They were guests of Dr. George Habash, the Palestinian Christian who had given up his medical practice to run the Popular Front for the Liberation of Palestine. He had quickly established it as the most sophisticated terror-ist organization in the Middle East: Its operatives had been taught by their KGB instructors how to use invisible inks, codes, and letter drops, and Hezbollah and other terror groups admired their bomb-making skills.

Habash had assembled terror groups for his summit in a Lebanon refugee camp from as far afield as Spain's ETA Basques, the Japanese Red Army, and the Italian Red Brigades; all had come to hear his vision of a globe-wide terror network. Among those who applauded Habash's plan was a slim, guitar-strumming South American with a ready eye for women and unlimited access to money from his doting mother, an at-tractive divorceé popular in London diplomatic circles. His name was Ilich Ramirez Sanchez—later to be renowned as Carlos the Jackal and to become the bête noire of every intelligence service in the world. On the closing evening of the summit, he had astonished the IRA delegation by playing Irish folk songs before they sneaked back into Belfast to spread the word that the IRA must be part of Habash's revolution. His summit marked the start of a decade of unprecedented terror.

IN THE SPRING OF 1973, Frank Steele had left Northern Ireland and returned to his old hunting ground as MI6 director for the Middle East. His first call was on Zvi Zamir, then the director-general of the Mossad. Following Rafi Eitan's visit to the Ulster province, a close working relationship had developed between the two services. Zamir and Steele had recently discussed a security matter involving Israel's prime minister, Golda Meir, who was due to travel to Rome for a long-planned private audience with Pope Paul VI.

Zamir had taken personal charge of her security and had called Steele from the Israeli Embassy in the city to ask whether there was a possibility the IRA would become involved in an assassination attempt on the prime minister. The ramifications of such an attack were incalculable. Already one terror group, Black September, had attacked the Israeli Embassy in Bangkok, hoisting the PLO flag over the building and taking six diplomats hostage. The terrorists had demanded that Israel release thirty-six PLO prisoners or they would execute their hostages. In the end, the Thai government had persuaded the terrorist group to accept safe passage out of the country in return for freeing their captives. It was an all too rare peaceful ending to a terrorist outrage.

Zamir's fear was that Black September would now seek to assassinate Golda Meir. Would it be possible, Zamir had asked Steele, for the terror group to use a surrogate as an assassin who would be less physically recognizable and would have every reason to be in Rome, using the guise of being a priest come to pay respects to the Supreme Pontiff? Steele had promised to have MI6 carry out a thorough check. No sign was found that any IRA operative was in Rome. The papal audience passed without incident.

Before Steele had left Northern Ireland, however, there had been a vague report that a known contact of Black September had met a member of the Official IRA in Dublin. Steele had suggested his replacement, Craig Smellie, should check this information.

Smellie had been MI6's operations director in Nigeria, which had become another target for the KGB to infiltrate, using it as a springboard to support newfound African nationalism and exploit tribal rivalries. Yakov Cohen, a Mossad *katsa* in Lagos, recalled to the author, "The

Soviets were like us in Nigeria. They would work with anyone who would work with them. It meant both of us knew what was going on." Nigeria provided over 60 percent of Israel's oil supplies in return for arms, which had been originally supplied by the United States to Israel. Smellie's job had been to keep a close eye on both KGB and Mossad activities and ensure neither disrupted the trading links Nigeria had with Britain.

Smellie had handed over the possibility of a link between the IRA and Black September to his new deputy, Fred Holroyd. Close to six feet tall with a girth almost to match, the middle-aged officer's sartorial taste went little beyond his brown tweed suits and a yellow vest usually seen on a huntsman. When he spoke he popped a monocle into his left eye; when listening he left it hanging over his double chin. With his booming laugh and a rapidly turning index finger when something excited him, he was a cartoon figure. Holroyd was based in Dublin, and his task was recruiting informers; with a generous expense account, he entertained them in some of Dublin's finest restaurants, but despite his considerable charm he failed to attract many guests to go beyond a free dinner. As well as living the life of a bon vivant under the cover of having inherited a family fortune, he had also been asked by Smellie to find ways to compromise IRA operatives in the Republic so as to cause embarrassment to the Irish government, which appeared to MI6 to tolerate their presence. However, Holroyd's luck changed.

Working the bars in the city center he had encountered two brothers, Kenneth and Keith Littlejohn. Both had come over from England hoping to make a better living. Over drinks Kenneth had told Holroyd, "We're up for anything." Keith added, "The trouble is that the bloody Irish don't like Brits." Holroyd had sensed an opening, and a few days later he had invited the Littlejohns to dinner at the city's leading hotel, the Shelbourne. With Holroyd was John Wyman, an MI6 officer who was already running several informers in the Republic; he introduced himself as Douglas Smythe and told the brothers he might be able to help them "on the business side."

As the wine flowed, the two intelligence officers satisfied themselves the Littlejohns had not only a contempt for the Irish but also a positive hatred of the IRA. Over nightcaps in a quiet corner of the hotel bar, Wyman had proposed the brothers could work for him. The work would be unusual and with an element of risk, but the financial reward would be considerable. The Littlejohns would carry out bank robberies in the Republic that would be blamed on the IRA. The offer was immediately accepted.

Further meetings with Wyman were held in Phoenix Park, where details of the robberies were refined. It was at the end of one of those meetings, Kenneth Littlejohn later claimed, "Smythe said he would like us to carry out political assassination of IRA leaders. He gave me a list that included Seamus Costello and Joe McCann." It was agreed McCann would be the first target. Before the Littlejohns could assassinate the IRA man, however, he was shot dead by a British patrol in Belfast.

The brothers now took action on the original proposal of making their fortune by bank robberies. They raided the Allied Irish Bank in Dublin, stealing £67,000, until then the biggest bank robbery in Irish history. The Littlejohns fled back to England but were arrested and returned to Dublin. Though they named Holroyd and Wyman, both officers were barred by MI6 from appearing at their trial. Kenneth Littlejohn was sentenced to twenty years and Keith to fifteen. Two years later Kenneth Littlejohn escaped from Dublin's Mountjoy Prison.

In December 1972, two explosions rocked central Dublin. Initially the IRA was blamed, but the Irish Special Branch established the bombers had been aided by MI5 in planting the devices. By then Holroyd had left the country, but on December 19, the Irish police had sufficient evidence to inform the British ambassador that unless he withdrew his first secretary, Andrew Johnstone, on the grounds he was "a senior British intelligence officer," there was a risk of diplomatic ties between the two countries being broken. It marked the end of officially sanctioned Secret Intelligence Service operations in the Republic, though it remained in Ulster operating on a strictly controlled leash. To all intents and purposes, MI5 was back in control of Northern Ireland.

For John Rennie, the Littlejohn debacle was a bitter blow and he became severely criticized for lack of judgment.

There was a more personal crisis for Rennie, a devoted father, to face. His eldest son, Charles, and his daughter-in-law had been arrested in a commune in possession of heroin and tried at the Old Bailey, standing in the same dock where spies had learned their fate after being caught. The Foreign Office had contacted all Fleet Street newspaper editors requesting they should not link the couple with the MI6 chief. It was too good a story, though, and the editors contacted foreign correspondents in London who fed the details to their newspapers. The German weekly *Stern* published them and opened the floodgates for the British media to follow. Rennie resigned, leaving his five-year tenure knowing he would be largely remembered as the chief who failed to tame the IRA and left MI6 in disarray.

BY THE MID-1970s, STELLA RIMINGTON had moved up from being a "junior assistant officer" devoting her mornings to reading the *Morning Star* and had joined the Registry in her capacity as a "desk officer" working with one of several teams conducting ongoing investigations. Not only was the hunt for Communist spies still a priority, but she was also keeping a lookout for any suspected double agents within MI5; those who had betrayed the Security Service had cast a deep shadow over Century House, which continued to permeate the building. Years after the fact, the names of Burgess, Maclean, and Philby still managed to arouse anger in even the most mild-mannered officers.

However, Rimington's access to files was strictly monitored and dependent on her place on the invisible ladder she was slowly, but steadily, climbing. It was so different from those days at the university when she had been encouraged to ask questions; here she had been told only enough for her to make limited intelligence decisions.

AS THEY PASSED HER IN THE CORRIDORS, clutching their files, coming from or going to some meeting on another floor, Rimington suspected many of her colleagues had climbed as far as they could on their particular ladders. There was about them a cultivated air of being manly enough to take the demanding pace of life in Century House, and when it was finally time for them to go home to a wife and family, she wondered if they were satisfied enough to have done in their day what was required of them. Some, she suspected, caught a train out to the suburbs, while others went to enjoy a drink at one of the pubs around Century House; drinking was part of the culture at MI6. She supposed it had always been. Rimington had never yet spoken to the director-general, Michael Hanley, but she had heard about his temper, which empurpled his face even more, and a running joke was that he wore his dark glasses in the building so he would not be recognized. A similar mystery surrounded the counterintelligence officers who came and went, but she no longer felt the need to "still romantically dream about the Great Game."

The reality had proven otherwise. MI5 was still a man's world, filled with veterans from the Colonial Service who had learned their intelligence skills in the far-flung empire—in the Solomon Islands, Kenya, and Singapore and around the Pacific Rim. Inside Century House they formed small groups in the dining room, huddling together as if they were still expecting an attack from native insurgents, and had been given names like the Sudan Souls, the Rwanda Regulars, and the Malayan Mafia. They had joined as fully fledged "officers" and often behaved with the same attitude, calling the women staff "other ranks." For their part, those who worked as filing clerks in the Registry were often debutantes or daughters of Whitehall mandarins and high-ranking military officers. With their endless tales from the social world they inhabited outside the office, they were known as "the girls of the night."

Times were changing for Rimington, though, and with her grip growing more firmly on her career ladder came more responsibility. By 1974, she was a fully fledged officer and, in turn, worked in countersubversion, counterespionage, and counterterrorism—her targets were the Soviet and Eastern Bloc spies operating in London. Part of her work was to assemble a case for the Foreign Office to cancel a visa application by a Russian with nondiplomatic status.

Her work became a life of keeping watch on dead letter boxes, which KGB spies had placed in tree trunks in the royal parks for their own informers to leave documents and collect their regular payments, or spotting chalk marks left on lampposts and empty milk bottles placed beneath a park bench signaling an informant needed to speak to his Russian controller. Rimington followed GRU officers to various libraries where they spent hours photocopying technical and scientific journals, all freely available to the public. "We speculated that they stamped the material 'Secret' to give it more importance before sending it back to Moscow," she later recalled in her autobiography, *Open Secret*.

BY THE LATE 1970s, STELLA RIMINGTON was deputy director of the Soviet section and had full access not only to data from MI5's own spies and moles but also to intelligence product from the listening devices the Security Service's "buggers" had planted in and around the Russian Embassy in London, its trade mission offices, the hotel rooms used by visiting dignitaries from Moscow, and the offices of Tass and *Pravda*, whose journalists often doubled as KGB agents. The intensive surveillance mirrored that to which British Embassy staff in Moscow and foreign visitors in Russia were subjected. From time to time, Rimington also saw the images from America's U-2 spy planes, which were useful to compare with other intelligence that crossed her desk.

The sleek, uniformly black-painted aircraft depended for success entirely on their ability to rise beyond the reach of Soviet radar on flights from their base in Peshawar, Pakistan, across Afghanistan and the Hindu Kush into Soviet airspace on a course that passed over the Aral Sea and its secret military bases before flying over the rest of Russia to Barents Sea and finally landing at another U.S. airfield at Bodo in Norway.

It was the images from those long flights that interested Rimington. They were a part of the classic intelligence cycle that had now become part of her working life: collection, analysis, dissemination, and action. U-2 flights were a major asset in intelligence gathering—each plane with its seven infrared cameras was capable of continuously photographing a strip of earth over fifty miles on each side of the aircraft's fuselages, where one "take" was three thousand miles long and produced four thousand printed frames. However, there was another even more sophisticated tool for Rimington and her fellow spy catchers to call upon. It combined all the major intelligence-gathering techniques—ELINT, electronic intelligence; SIGINT, signals intelligence; IMINT, imagery intelligence; HUMINT, the human ability to analyze what was discovered—and had resulted in the first new electronic language of the cold war, one that eventually would distinguish the local Cyrillic words of central Asia from the multifarious dialects of China. It was the language of space, where America's satellites spun in silent orbit.

The linguists creating it were at the stage of what one described in 1974 as "getting the baby to talk right." Nevertheless, they had come a long way from that evening when, in the homely surroundings of a barbecue, one of the most powerful men in the Western world had chosen to reveal some of the details about satellite surveillance.

IN MARCH 1967, LYNDON JOHNSON, the president of the United States, used his barbecue fork to rap on the roasting spit from which he had been carving slices of beef for his guests at a cookout on the ranch of a friend in Nashville, Tennessee. Each guest had been carefully chosen for his or her loyalty and discretion.

He jabbed his fork at the night sky and asked a question, "You all remember what happened up there ten years ago?"

They did. How could anyone forget that a decade earlier a Russian sphere, no bigger than a volleyball, had circled the earth every ninety-six minutes at a constant speed of eighteen thousand miles an hour and emitted a continuous beep as it spun through space? Millions of Americans, like the rest of the world, had looked up in amazement. Until then, the United States was accepted as the birthplace of postwar scientific innovation: from the atom bomb to the Salk vaccine, from keyhole brain surgery to mind-healing drugs, in hundreds of ways American scientists had set the bar higher. Now Moscow had gone one dramatic step further; it wouldn't be until twelve years later that astronaut Neil Armstrong would step onto the moon and deliver his memorable words about taking one big step for mankind. The beep-beep in space on October 4, 1957, had shown that the Soviet Union had already achieved the conquest of space with its *Sputnik,* literally a fellow traveler.

Johnson told the cookout gathering he had a piece of news that once more put the United States ahead.

"We've spent thirty-five, more likely forty billion dollars, on what I'm gonna tell you. What our scientists have done is worth ten times that. We now know where the Soviets have their missiles and launching sites. We've seen their faces as they wait to push the button on key sites. We know where the North Koreans have their radar installations and looked inside their buildings unaware we are looking at them. We know where the terrorist camps are in Libya and Syria and we've seen the make of their Russian weapons. We know all this because of something special."

Johnson paused, looking into their faces, the consummate actor who had held the attention of millions while on the campaign trail. Then, spearing a slice of meat, he waved it skyward.

"What we have is real-time space photography! We are back in front."

Even if some of his listeners did not fully understand what he meant by "real-time space photography," they still clapped. *America was back in front.* That was all that mattered.

PRESIDENT JOHNSON HAD NOT TOLD them how those billions had been spent on positioning a necklace of American satellites in deep space, some halfway to the moon, others in low orbit, recording images of events as they happened, each robot spy with highly tuned mechanical ears listening in all directions. They could eavesdrop on a conversation between military planners inside the Kremlin walls or photograph the aged leaders of the People's Republic of China as they walked through their Zhongnanhai compound in Beijing, with the aid of tubular steel frames or sticks fashioned from the rain forests bordering Burma and China. The satellites could indeed monitor missile silos in Russia's Ural Mountains; air bases minutes' flying time from Western Europe; armaments factories hidden along China's border with Mongolia; and factories producing chemical weapons to the north of

Pyongyang, the capital of the virtually inaccessible North Korea, which the silent watchful satellites had effortlessly penetrated. Each of their multiple cameras was tasked to collect images from all parts of the world under Communist control. A new railroad spur, unfamiliar vehicle tracks around a factory, freshly dug earth near a military base: It was these, not the majestic topography of Asia and the Soviet Republic, the cameras focused on.

The satellites were listed by one word in the new lexicon of intelligence gathering: TECHINT. It was the catchall term for a system that enabled Soviet rocket designs still on their drawing boards to be silently uplifted into space without their designers having the remotest idea what had happened, the license plate of a suspected KGB officer to be photographed from halfway to the moon, or secret short-burst radio transmissions to be tracked and isolated in a jungle village in North Vietnam where a Chinese Secret Intelligence agent was operating. Some satellites were situated over the seas of China and Russia, geopositioned along the 22,300-mile-high orbit where they moved in time with the earth's own orbit.

This vast system was so secret that no one person—including the president of the United States, the chairman of the U.S. Joint Chiefs of Staff, the director of central intelligence, or the two heads of MI5 and MI6—allowed to share in the end product knew how it was collected and what the system's overall budget was (in 2006, it was estimated to be $600 billion).

The Byzantine system had a language permeated with homely code names behind which hid the blackest of black operations: Magnum, Chalet, Jumpseat, Oxcart, Idealist, and Keyhole were some. The full details of their discoveries were known only to a select few—the intelligence chiefs, military planners, and a few U.S.-friendly presidents and prime ministers of the Western world. With the information, they could better deal with the diverse threats from the Soviet Union and China and create responses. But before intelligence reached them, it had been downloaded and analyzed by specialists. They were the Deep Black Operators, who worked with the secrets from space espionage gathered in the void where the silent sentinels watched and listened.

THE SIX-STORY STRUCTURE on the corner of First and M streets in the southeast quadrant of Washington, D.C., resembled a warehouse and appeared no different from all the others around the capital's old Navy Yard on the bank of the Anocostia River. It was, however, enclosed by a Cyclone fence and guarded by armed marines. On the Pentagon list of properties, it was identified as Federal Building 213. There were other indications that the nondescript structure housed some of the most important elements in America's strategic defense global network. The first was the blue-and-white sign above the main entrance: NATIONAL PHOTOGRAPHIC INTERPRETATION CENTER. The second was the massive air-conditioning plant bolted to one side of 213. Seventy-five feet long, the unit rose through floor after floor, past bricked-in windows, to cool the computers inside the building. Some of these were the size of a room, others of a house. The real monsters ran the length of an entire floor. Day and night the computers sifted and scanned billions of pieces of information downloaded from the satellites and automatically eliminated atmospheric effects such as those caused by electrical storms over the Gobi, sandstorms over central Asia, or typhoons off the coast of China. Once that work was done, the images were transferred to the photo interpreters.

The dozens of technicians working shifts in Federal Building 213 handled between them an average daily input of two million images downloaded from the U.S. satellites. They had been the first to see the infuriated face of a Soviet general in East Germany when the Berlin airlift had started, and the first to observe the Cuban missile crisis unfold and then collapse with the departure of the Russian ships carrying their rockets back home. There was a running joke among the technicians that they would be the first to see Doomsday.

Each operative had a workstation equipped with an infrared scanner, rather like a microscope, to search every dot of each image that appeared on his or her screen. Each dot was checked against a previous image of the same subject, if available. A laser copier was used to produce a hard print, and when a set was completed, the images were posted on a viewing screen, not unlike one used by a surgeon to study X-rays before an operation, for a final check. The entire process took seconds before the prints were electronically transmitted to the Office of Imagery Analysis at Langley and the Defense Intelligence Analysis Center at Bolling Air Force Base. With the images went a technical report: the position of the satellite, the time and date the images were collected, and the atmospheric conditions. The details would proceed through "the community," the generic term for all the U.S. intelligence agencies, and on to the screen of the appropriate director. It was a continuous process.

Already, however, the race to challenge the supremacy of America in its use of the vacuous blackness of space to gather intelligence was well under way. By 1980, the Soviet Union had launched fifty satellites into orbit and developed the capability to transmit digital imagery in real time. Its global coverage was linked to its photo interpretation stations at Lourdes in Cuba and at Cam Rahn Bay in Vietnam (both facilities were closed down in 2002 as the economic crisis deepened in Russia). Meanwhile, France was creating a global satellite system with bases on Mayotte in the Indian Ocean and in its former colony of New Caledonia. In a joint venture with Germany's foreign intelligence service, BND, the French DST had set up a station at Kourou, French Guiana, to download intelligence on Latin America. The DST also had yet another collection site at Domme in the pleasant countryside of the Dordogne. Hundreds of satellites were either remaining geostationary or silently hurtling around the earth in the name of national security.

10

Out of the Shadows

From 1973 to 1985 three chiefs had sat behind the massive mahogany desk in their office in Century House to direct the Secret Intelligence Service. They were Maurice Oldfield, Arthur Temple Franks, and Colin Frederick Figures.

Oldfield was a Derbyshire farmer's son and claimed his corpulent figure, which gave him a striking resemblance to Alfred Hitchcock, came from eating too much red meat as a boy. He had learned to play the organ in the village church, collected a degree in medieval history from Manchester University, and liked to quote his favorite passage from Macaulay, "A perfect historian must possess an imagination sufficiently powerful, . . . yet he must control it so absolutely as to content himself with the materials which he finds, and to refrain from supplying deficiencies by additions of his own."

In intelligence work, Oldfield told recruits, it was those deficiencies they were precisely expected to supply. He had learned that in World War II when he was an army intelligence officer in Cairo and tried to understand Rommel's intentions. Later, when he had joined the Secret Intelligence Service as a counterintelligence officer, he had applied the same question to the Russians. Seeking answers had taken him first as a station commander to Singapore, responsible for several other stations around the Pacific Rim, and then to Washington, D.C.

His warmth, witticisms, and confirmed-bachelor charm assured that his hostess always sat him next to the prettiest woman at the table, but he invariably went home alone, his secret safe that he was a homosexual. Early on during his time in Washington, an FBI unit had caught him accosting a "rent boy," or teenaged male prostitute. The matter had been reported to J. Edgar Hoover. He had kept the report and ordered no further surveillance to be conducted. Oldfield's peccadillo would join all the others in the director's file on sexual deviants.

In 1973 Oldfield was appointed as chief by Prime Minister Edward Heath, another confirmed bachelor and a talented organ player. Within MI6, Oldfield continued to be admired for the way he had guided the government of Harold Wilson through its first foreign policy crisis when in 1974 the Greek junta had seized control of Cyprus and drove its president, Archbishop Makarios, out of office; Oldfield had arranged the prelate's escape to Malta. It was a fitting conclusion to his career, and he retired in 1978. In retirement he started to write a biography of the first chief but gave up the task in 1979 when Margaret Thatcher asked him to become her intelligence supremo in Northern Ireland. It was there his homosexuality was finally uncovered. Once more he had been caught with a rent boy by a police officer, and there was no Hoover to cover up the matter. Oldfield was immediately ordered to London. In a tense interview with the government cabinet secretary, Robert Armstrong, Oldfield confessed his long-standing sexual proclivity and that he had lied on his positive vetting form about it, an omission that laid him open to blackmail. His security clearance was immediately withdrawn. Nine months later he was dead—the cause was officially given as a heart attack—and buried in the family plot in the village church graveyard at Over Haddon. The organist gave a reprise of what had been Oldfield's favorite hymns to play.

CHIEF FOR FOUR YEARS, 1978 TO 1981, Arthur Temple Franks had come to the post through a tried-and-trusted route: a wartime SOE operative in Europe, followed by three years in Tehran during which he had played a role in placing the young shah on the Peacock Throne. Back in London he became controller for the Middle East, watching over a territory that extended from Egypt and Syria to the mountains of Afghanistan and the deserts of Saudi Arabia.

Finally he had been made the head of the London station, a position that put him in the front line against the KGB. In his office was a framed quotation from Lenin, "We must thoroughly, carefully, attentively and skillfully exploit every fissure among our enemies." That was Franks's leitmotif, and he became a firm believer that any suspected KGB spy operating under diplomatic cover should be immediately expelled. His call echoed through the corridors of the Foreign Office, but it came at a time when once more Whitehall was carrying out financial cutbacks.

Franks saw them as part of a new government move to amalgamate MI6 into MI5. The idea had been bruited about at meetings of the Joint Intelligence Committee, where the Downing Street representative expressed the fear that there was a campaign to destabilize the government. Certainly the Tory press continued to publish anti-Labour stories that appeared to come from inside the intelligence services. Franks had deflected any threat of amalgamation by accepting the cutbacks. It was enough to appease Downing Street.

One budget cut resulted in the virtual closure of the Tehran station. Acting on Foreign Office orders, the British ambassador, Sir Anthony Parsons, had refused to allow the one remaining MI6 officer to even work out of the embassy. He operated out of modest rented accommodations with minimal overheads and depended on SAVAK, the shah's secret service, to brief him on what was happening in a country whose oil supplies were vital to Britain. Much of SAVAK intelligence would turn out to be worthless and would leave the Secret Intelligence Service, not for the first time, blinded to what was really happening behind the scenes in Iran, where Islamic fundamentalism was already starting to brew in the backstreets of Tehran and spill over into the villages.

On October 12, 2008, Sir Dickie Franks died. He was eighty-eight years old and right to the end of his life he had continued to make regular visits to the Traveller's Club in London to reminisce with old colleagues and discuss current events in the Middle East.

FRANKS WAS FOLLOWED BY COLIN FIGURES as the ninth occupant of the chief's chair on the tenth floor of Century House. In many ways he was the quintessential spymaster: soft-spoken, immaculately dressed, and a member of the Travellers, long the favorite club of MI6. He had been "tapped" at Pembroke College Cambridge by his tutor and had gone directly into MI6 after obtaining his degrees in Russian and French. His linguistic abilities flagged him as a future Soviet Bloc specialist and, after an initial training post in Gemany and a junior slot in the Amman station from where he witnessed the Suez debacle, he became station commander in Warsaw.

His operational successes in his three years in Poland established him as a highflier who knew how to recruit and run foreign spies. Three of them were well-placed Polish intelligence officers, "walk-ins," volunteering their services. One was code-named "Noddy," and his information included material he had picked up during his frequent visits to Moscow. Initially there had been suspicion Noddy was a KGB-orchestrated deception, but Figures had authenticated him, and time and again he proved his worth. Contact with him in an environment such as Warsaw was dangerous, a matter of fleeting, brush-past meetings and the familiar tradecraft of dead drops, but Figures and his agent had survived.

Posted to Vienna, Figures continued his work of recruiting agents in that dangerous world of letter drops and secret meetings. His favorite film was *The Third Man,* a movie some colleagues said fitted Figures's own character as its hero flitted through the streets of Vienna. One of the many contacts he had made in that city was Simon Wiesenthal, the legendary Nazi hunter. His time in Vienna coincided with the 1968 Soviet invasion of Czechoslovakia; his assessment of how the Prague Spring would end had accelerated his promotion. He became deputy chief in 1979 before finally taking over from Franks in 1981.

In the early summer of that year, Figures decided to make a visit back into the field—this time into Afghanistan. The Soviet Union had invaded the country two years before, and its presence had once more reminded Figures of the adage "You can't buy the loyalty of an Afghan, only rent it."

Even for a fit fifty-six-year-old, his trip was a physically demanding one into the mountains of the Hindu Kush to meet some of the leaders of the mujahideen, the Afghan resistance movement. Figures had suitably dressed for the occasion wearing a flat *pakol* hat and a *shalwar kamiz,* the traditional baggy shirt and trousers of the mountain men. For two days Figures and his guide, whom he had met in Peshawar with the local MI6 station chief, had made their way across rivers swollen with snowmelt from the mountains and through steep-sided passes. Their target was a young mujahideen fighter known as "the Mountain Lion" for his skills in attacking the Russians. In between endless cups of green tea and helpings of roast mountain goat, Figures and the Lion had worked out a mutual alliance. The Lion had explained he needed modern communications equipment to warn him when Soviet bombers approached or their tanks came rumbling over the lower ground, and for his fighters to be trained to run a modern guerrilla war. In return they would eventually drive out the Russians. Figures said if the Lion could get his best men to Peshawar, he would arrange to have them flown to England where they would be properly trained. Within two months, over a hundred mujahideen had been secretly flown to Scotland to undergo training in the remotest parts of the Highlands before, just as secretly, being flown back to Peshawar to show the Lion all they had learned.

It was an appropriate climax to the career of a chief many within MI6 regarded as someone who reflected the sterling qualities that had imbued the first chief. When Figures retired in 1985, he took with him two personal items on his desk: his wedding photograph and a portable radio on which he listened to a cricket Test match commentary. He died on December 8, 2006, aged eighty-one. On his bedside table was his radio, ready to bring him the next ball-by-ball report.

IT WAS THOSE THREE MEN—OLDFIELD, FRANKS, AND FIGURES— each so different, who had guided MI6 through the aftermath of the invasion of Suez, the fallout from the treachery of Kim Philby and the other Soviet moles, and the rebuilding of a relationship with the CIA. The bad times, if not forgotten, had been forgiven by Washington in a mutual determination to win the cold war.

It would not be easy. The shah had been driven out by the Islamic regime of the Ayatollah Khomeini in 1979. North Vietnam was establishing control over the rest of Indo-China. The long dictatorship of the Somoza family in Nicaragua had been swept away and in its place had come a regime backed by Moscow. Fidel Castro had begun to threaten again that he would allow Cuba to be a Soviet satellite.

Wherever MI6 and the CIA turned, a new crisis seemed to be erupting—but, time and again, there had been insufficient warning: none when the Polish government imposed martial law and the country's army struck against Solidarity; none before a Marxist, Maurice Bishop, seized power on the tiny island of Grenada and immediately opened diplomatic ties with Cuba and Moscow. Both would provide him with weapons to "resist imperialist aggressors."

These failures were born out of earlier ones. Until the inglorious end of the Korean War in 1953, the CIA still had two hundred officers in Seoul. "We had our own bars and girls and a brothel on either side of our office on Pasteur Street, the CIA headquarters in the Cholon suburb of the city," Bill Buckley recalled to the author. "Most of the agents depended on intelligence from local Korean spies. Most of it was made up. But as the end drew near, nobody seemed to care."

In 1953, anxious to pinpoint Russia's role in Korea, the CIA had sent one of its senior officers undercover to the American Embassy in Moscow. Within a week, the man had been seduced by his housemaid— a KGB colonel—and was secretly photographed making love to her. Before the KGB could mount a full-scale blackmail operation, the hapless officer had been recalled to Langley.

If a lesson needed to be learned from that incident, others were to follow. The CIA intelligence that led to the invasion of the Dominican Republic in 1965—claiming it was on the verge of becoming a Soviet satellite—was so inaccurate, a furious President Johnson said the agency had a serious "credibility gap."

By the end of the Vietnam War, there were yet a thousand CIA operatives in Southeast Asia and a staggering three thousand analysts across the United States trying to decide how the Pentagon could still win the war. "Most were a bunch of college graduates who'd read books about the Pacific war and thought MacArthur's tactics would still work," remembered Buckley. One was Bill Gates, whom the CIA had sent to Whitman Air Force Base in Missouri to study the best way to launch nuclear weapons against North Korea. "I knew then the war could not be won," he later said.

SHORTLY BEFORE HE LEFT OFFICE, JOHN RENNIE had been forced by yet another Treasury review of MI6 spending to cut back on intelligence gathering on the South American continent. The station that had spied on Portuguese-speaking countries was amalgamated with the Spanish-speaking station based in Buenos Aires. The resulting reduction of staff—coupled with a curious CX message (Cummings Exclusively, i.e., Chief Executive) from Rennie to his Buenos Aires commander, Mark Heathcote, to give "priority for intelligence gathering, but in a low category"—had led to London being sent little more than translated newspaper reports.

Heathcote had learned the value of high-level contacts when he served as an MI5 deputy station commander in Northern Ireland. Those he had developed in Buenos Aires were also well placed—but not close enough to the small group of junta strategists planning to invade the Falkland Islands. Up to the very day of the invasion in 1982, Heathcote's sources continued to insist Argentina would not attack, despite strident reports in the anti-British local media "that the Malvinas are ours." Had Heathcote's contacts simply misread the situation? Or had they been part of a carefully constructed plot to outwit London so that by the time the islands had been captured, it would be too late for Prime Minister Thatcher to send her forces halfway across the world to recapture them? If so, they had totally miscalculated the Iron Lady. Hers was a very public victory when the Royal Navy returned home having hoisted the Union Jack to fly once more over the Falklands.

There had also been another success, one so secret that only a handful of senior officers in the Secret Intelligence Service knew the details.

IN LATE SEPTEMBER 1974, Robert Browning, the MI6 station commander in Copenhagen, sent an encrypted message to Century House that signaled the achievement of the supreme goal for MI6 during the cold war, one even the CIA had failed to achieve. It was to have a spy not only deep inside the KGB, but of sufficient seniority to have access to the inner thinking of the Politburo, able to fill the vital gap between information acquired by Soviet satellites and the planning by the Kremlin strategists that would follow. A spy who could do that was beyond price. From that September day, the Secret Intelligence Service had such a man, a volunteer and not a recruit, the most precious of all double agents.

His name was Oleg Gordievsky, and he was a senior political officer in the KGB's First Chief Directorate. He spoke several foreign languages, including fluent English, and had risen to be a *rezidentura,* the KGB equivalent of a station commander in a foreign country. Along his climb, he had become disenchanted with a political system that mocked all his attempts to rationalize that what he was doing would only better the Russian people. The torture of suspected enemies of the state before their executions by a single bullet in the head, the locked cattle trucks taking prisoners to the gulags of Siberia: All this, and more, had eroded his belief in the system, bleaching from his mind the promise made when he had entered the Foreign Intelligence School in the forests outside Moscow. There he had been taught surveillance, ciphers, recognition signals, and radio communications and had taught himself how to spot a *stukach,* an informer planted among the students to report their private conversations and try to trick them into criticism of the state, an offense punishable by death. He had become comfortable with his pseudonym and learned how to avoid any real friendships. He had been repeatedly told to see himself as an essential cog in an essential machine that protected Russia.

After graduation, Gordievsky had been posted to the KGB's First Chief Directorate, housed in the Lubyanka, the massive edifice on Red Square, to learn about the mentalities and ways of foreigners and how they could be lured into working for the KGB. Then he had been transferred to the directorate's most prestigious branch, Department Twelve. From its headquarters in the forests outside Moscow, its agents went to the farthest corners on earth working under cover as diplomats, members of trade missions, visiting lecturers from the Soviet Academy of Sciences, or university professors who attended international conferences and sought permission to conduct research at prestigious campuses. From their ranks came the *rezidentura*. That had been the position Oleg Gordievsky held when he finally decided to work for the Secret Intelligence Service.

For eleven years the KGB officer had fed MI6 details of the Warsaw Pact's strength, its nuclear capability, its megatonnage, its missiles, and the most secret of all its weapons programs: using germs to create a biological Armageddon to be launched against the West. Gordievsky's priceless information was frightening but also reassuring: The Soviet Union was still "some years away from posing a serious threat."

GORDIEVSKY'S INTELLIGENCE—PAGES OF HIGHLY classified Kremlin documents and transcripts of KGB instructions to agents, together with his own analysis of their importance, along with the MI6 evaluation of the data—was sent to the CIA in a sealed bag within the U.S. London embassy's own daily diplomatic bag to the State Department. The sealed bag was delivered to Aldrich "Rick" Ames by a State Department courier, and Ames only removed the contents behind the locked door of his office. It was a routine he had diligently followed since he had been assigned to the Soviet/East European Division of the Directorate of Operations, and by 1985 he was the CIA's acknowledged expert on the Soviet Union. His reports often ended up on the desk of the incumbent president. But that was for the future.

AMES'S FATHER, CARLETON, had served in the directorate as a field officer in Asia for two years in the 1950s, but his work had been judged "negative because of a serious alcohol dependency." Recalled to Langley, Carleton was given a desk job and had retired in 1967 at the age of sixty-two; he died five years later of cancer.

By then his son had joined the CIA as a filing clerk and had shown sufficient promise to be selected for advanced Russian-language training before being sent as a junior officer to Turkey and later Mexico. At the same time, his first marriage was crumbling and not helped by the same drinking problem that had dogged his father. Ames became drunk at a CIA Christmas party and was found seminaked with a CIA clerk making love in her office. It marked the end of his marriage, though his annual career review described his work as "superior and invariably exceeding work standards."

His next posting had been to Mexico City, where he met Rosario Dupuy, the vivacious cultural attaché at the Colombian Embassy and a member of the local diplomatic association, which included the local KGB *rezidentura*. Ames, by now already close to becoming an alcoholic, became besotted by Rosario and lavishly entertained her, taking her on weekends to resorts around the Caribbean. Coupled with those costs were the financial demands of his first wife over their divorce settlement, which had led Ames to a rapid accumulation of debt. Pressed to settle by his bank and fearful he would lose his job if his financial position was discovered by the CIA, Ames wondered how he could resolve the mounting crisis.

He was recalled to Washington and assigned to handle sensitive intelligence reaching the Soviet/East European Division. Studying the amount of documentation on his desk, most of it from Gordievsky—though his identity had been removed in London—Ames realized here was the solution to his problems.

On a warm Washington evening Ames remained behind the locked door of his office and took his first treacherous step, writing a letter that described how two Soviet Embassy officials had approached the CIA in Mexico and Turkey to offer their services and how the agency had decided they were really double agents working for the KGB. To the letter, Ames had attached a copy of the CIA classified directory that gave the name and position of all its officers working on clandestine operations. He had highlighted his own name and placed beside it the alias he had assumed in Turkey and Mexico when meeting Soviet officials. At the end of the letter, he had asked for a onetime payment of $50,000.

The next morning, April 16, 1985, Ames strolled into the Soviet Embassy in Washington and left the letter at the reception desk. It was the start of a crippling series of blows to the CIA's Soviet operations and had a serious effect on MI6's activities behind the Iron Curtain.

A MONTH AFTER DROPPING OFF THE LETTER, Ames was invited to lunch by Sergei D. Chuvakhin, a diplomat at the Soviet Embassy, who was listed by the State Department as an adviser on arms control. It was routine for diplomats to meet and discuss alleged violations of the arms treaty.

Arriving at the embassy, Ames was escorted by Chuvakhin to a small room where a man handed him a sheet of folded paper. The note said Ames would be paid $50,000 and, in return for further information, each time a similar sum would be paid. Chuvakhin would arrange their meetings. With a quick smile, the man left the room, and Ames shook hands with Chuvakhin, sealing his betrayal of the United States. Two days later the two men met on the bank of the Anacostia and Ames received his $50,000 in dollar bills. The sum settled all his debts, but Ames saw a way to ensure that never again would he incur them. His position as head of the agency's counterintelligence for the Soviet Union would guarantee that.

On June 13, 1985, Ames began to provide the KGB with what eventually would be the largest amount of sensitive CIA documentation ever passed to the Soviets. He wrapped his first delivery in a newspaper and placed the packet in his briefcase. Walking out of the Langley headquarters, he knew that the risk of being stopped for a spot-search had ended during the tenure of George Herbert Walker Bush, the CIA's eleventh director. "We must trust our people," Bush had said.

Ames's delivery to Chuvakhin on that summer day marked the start of a betrayal that eventually compromised over one hundred CIA and MI6 intelligence operations against the Soviet Union and led to the execution of ten senior Russian military and KGB officers, along with the imprisonment of many more. Ames was a textbook case of a traitor with multiple character weaknesses—alcohol abuse, arrogance, and impulsiveness—yet those well-documented traits in his personal file had not aroused suspicion in the CIA that he could be the traitor in its midst. Ames's supervisor had given permission for him to continue his contacts with Chuvakhin after being told by Ames he was trying to recruit the Russian to work for the CIA. Over expensive lunches, the two men concocted reports that Ames would later present to his supervisor of the progress he was making in turning Chuvakhin. Each meeting ended with Ames receiving another $50,000 for his latest revelations about CIA operations and the names of its agents in charge, together with the identities of the agency's latest double agents in the Soviet Union.

If there had been any suspicion about the new bank accounts Ames had opened, he had a ready answer: They were deposits to handle the substantial sums his new wife, Rosario, was receiving from her family inheritance and her director's benefits from the family business in Colombia. The CIA station in Bogotá was never asked to check out the claims, and no one in Langley wondered how Ames could afford a luxurious home and a lifestyle well above his income. In the end, Ames would receive a total of $2.5 million in payment for his treachery.

IN LONDON, NO ONE IN THE SECRET INTELLIGENCE SERVICE had an inkling of Ames's betrayal until the morning of February 21, 1994, Presidents' Day, when a team of FBI agents arrested Ames as he left his suburban home. Handcuffed, he was driven to the Alexandria, Virginia, jail, a gray-haired, bespectacled man close to his fifty-third birthday, who had celebrated the last nine of them as a Soviet spy. A search of his house revealed a further 144 classified documents packaged and ready to be delivered to Chuvakhin.

On April 28, 1994, Aldrich Ames and his wife pleaded guilty to conspiring to commit espionage and to evading taxes. Ames was immediately sentenced to life imprisonment without parole. Under a plea agreement, Rosario Ames was sentenced to five years and three months in prison for conspiring to commit espionage and evading taxes on $2.7 million obtained by her husband for his illegal activities.

In the fallout from his treachery, six former CIA officers and five more still in service, including the chief of the clandestine service, Ted Price, would receive letters of reprimand—the agency's version of a slap on the wrist.

In MI6 there were wry smiles at the unmasking of Ames. In the past the service had been severely criticized in Langley over its failure to uncover Soviet moles, a failure regarded in the upper echelons of the CIA as an aberration bordering on criminal negligence. But not even Kim Philby had created more damage than Aldrich "Rick" Ames.

EARLY IN JULY 1985, OLEG GORDIEVSKY asked the Secret Intelligence Service to urgently exfiltrate him from Moscow. Two months before, he had suddenly been recalled from London, where he had been appointed the KGB *rezidentura*; during his time there, he had continued to supply MI6 with important intelligence crossing his desk at the Russian Embassy in Kensington. His new handler was John Scarlett, since Robert Browning had abruptly resigned after being posted to Belfast— he regarded the move as a downgrade from working in Copenhagen, where he was heavily engaged in dealing with KGB penetration into Western Europe.

Gordievsky told Scarlett he was worried that a former MI5 officer, Michael Bettany, who had offered his own services to the KGB before being uncovered by the Security Service's best mole hunter, Eliza Manningham-Buller, had told the KGB of Gordievsky's activities. Scarlett was reassuring: Bettany was now serving a twenty-three-year prison sentence in solitary confinement, and there was nothing in his case file to indicate he knew anything about Gordievsky's duplicity. Nevertheless, Scarlett had promised that the Moscow station would be alerted to look for a signal that the double agent must be urgently exfiltrated. To activate it, all Gordievsky would do was stop at a street corner leading to Red Square carrying a bag of groceries he had bought at a nearby market. Then he should go home to his apartment. It could have come from the pages of a le Carré novel.

Gordievsky triggered the signal the day after a team of KGB interrogators had questioned him for hours, accusing him of being a spy. He had calmly dealt with them, using the skills he had acquired at the intelligence school to resist the grilling. Nevertheless, the next day he had stood at the street corner with his shopping bag. Within an hour Viscount Asquith, the MI6 station commander in Moscow, had sent a priority encrypted message to Century House, one that confronted Christopher Curwen with his first challenge as the newly appointed chief. He was fifty-six years old, the tenth to hold the post, and this was the climax to his thirty-year career in the Secret Intelligence Service. He had served in Thailand and Kuala Lumpur and, along the way, married and divorced a Vietnamese psychotherapist, taking a second wife, his secretary, when he was station commander in Washington before returning to London as deputy chief. When Colin Figures had been appointed intelligence coordinator to the cabinet, Curwen was the first choice to succeed him. Now, on that July morning in the office that had been his for less than a week, Asquith's message landed on his desk.

Curwen sent for Scarlett. The two men spent an hour discussing the mechanics of the operation. Flying Gordievsky out was impossible. Smuggling him by ship was equally out of the question. The only way to bring him out was by road. If at any stage the operation was uncovered, there would be serious political fallout; the Russians would almost certainly expel the entire MI6 station in Moscow and possibly even arrest British Embassy staff who did not have diplomatic protection.

Curwen already knew the importance of Oleg Gordievsky. Summaries of his intelligence regularly appeared in the MI6 Red Book, a top-secret file hand-carried every morning to Downing Street and, since she became Prime Minister in May 1979, the first document Margaret Thatcher read when she awoke at 5:30 A.M. She had demanded it should be a no-holds-barred report, and in recent years it had often contained embarrassing revelations about MI6: how its lack of advance warning had almost led to defeat in the Falklands War; its failure to discover the Pentagon planned a full-scale invasion of Grenada until American troops were actually storming ashore in the full glare of U.S.

network television; the humiliation of a senior officer in the Paris station caught fabricating reports from a nonexistent informer in French intelligence and claiming substantial sums to pay his contact, the money supporting the officer's own high life. The deception was discovered by Richard Dearlove, a future chief. Colin Figures, Curwen's predecessor, had decided the only way to avoid a public scandal was to offer the officer the chance to resign and arrange for him to take up a senior position with a City of London bank.

On that July day when Curwen and Scarlett considered how best to bring out Oleg Gordievsky, both knew the operation would require Thatcher's approval. After the Paris scam, she had made it clear she wanted to know "the embarrassment level" of any operation.

She was on her annual visit to stay with the Queen at Balmoral, the royal retreat in Scotland, which every prime minister was expected to make in the late summer. Curwen arranged to catch the next flight to Scotland to brief Thatcher. While the Queen walked her corgis in the Balmoral grounds, the prime minister and her spy chief sat sipping the finest whiskey in the house.

"Whatever the risks, we have to bring him out, Prime Minister," Curwen concluded.

"Then do it. I will call Geoffrey and tell him."

Geoffrey Howe was the foreign secretary and the political boss of the Secret Intelligence Service.

Before leaving Balmoral, Curwen had obtained Thatcher's agreement that Gordievsky's escape and resettlement package, including a British passport, would be worth the risk because of the intelligence he possessed.

PET, the Danish intelligence service, which had a long-standing relationship with MI6, suggested a safe house in Skovlunde would be a secure place to hide Gordievsky once he was out of the Soviet Union while final arrangements were made to bring him to London. However, Gordievsky feared that, in the manhunt that would undoubtedly follow his flight, there was still a risk he could be identified by colleagues he had served with during his time in Denmark.

Asquith was well aware that the longer it took to settle the escape plan, the greater the risk of the KGB hauling in Gordievsky for a further grilling. With all the confidence he could summon, but may not have felt, Asquith arranged for Gordievsky to be firmly told there would be no further debate: He must do exactly as ordered, and the operation would take place on the last weekend of the month.

On a Friday morning, Asquith notified the Russian authorities he was driving a pregnant member of the embassy staff to Helsinki for urgent specialist medical treatment. While the authorities might well sniff at what they would take as a snub to Moscow's own medical facilities, both Asquith and his passenger had diplomatic immunity, which also covered the station commander's Saab. Asquith concluded that even the KGB would not risk a serious diplomatic incident by stopping the vehicle.

Meanwhile, Gordievsky continued his daily routine of jogging in a park near the main Moscow rail terminus. If he were tailed, he would shake it off; he had shown he could do so ever since he had become a double agent. His one-way ticket to Leningrad would be waiting at a long-established drop. After collecting it, he boarded the Saturday early morning train to Leningrad.

When the train stopped at a small station outside the city, waiting there was Asquith. Gordievsky, carrying no luggage, left the train, just another Russian taking an evening stroll. When he reached the Saab, its CD plates clearly displayed, he calmly lifted the lid of the trunk and lay down inside. Asquith locked the trunk and drove on, crossing the border at Viborg into Finland.

Despite the high risks when, as Asquith later said, "a hundred things could have gone wrong," the operation had passed without incident. Waiting across the Finnish border was the Helsinki station commander, Margaret "Meta" Ramsay. She drove Gordievsky to Oslo, from where he caught a flight to London the next day.

Waiting for him at Heathrow were Curwen, Scarlett, and MI6's principal Kremlinologist, Gordon Barrass.

AFTER LUNCH SCARLETT DROVE Gordievsky and Barrass to Fort Monkton, the MI6 training school at Gosport on the south coast. For several weeks he was debriefed, and his revelations created a fifty-page document titled "Soviet Perception of Nuclear Warfare." A copy was sent to William Casey, the director of the CIA, the thirteenth to hold the position. Casey was so impressed with what he read he showed the papers to President Reagan. It was said later that having read it aloud to his wife, Nancy, the president exclaimed, "I'm going to tone down my Evil Empire attacks, otherwise it will trigger even more paranoia in Moscow."

For the first time, a copy of Gordievsky's debriefing was not sent to Langley to be pored over by Ames. "Let's just keep it in-house for a while," Curwen told the debriefing team. No one would ever know how many other Soviet double agents working for the CIA had been saved from execution by his decision.

A few days after his debriefing ended, Gordievsky was brought to Century House for a celebratory lunch in Curwen's private dining room. The guests included Foreign Office Soviet Bloc analysts, the head of MI5, Michael Hanley, and the director-general of GCHQ, Peter Marychurch. They had all read copies of the debriefing, but like any appreciative audience, they wanted more.

Gordievsky did not disappoint. With the flair for name-dropping, which later became his hallmark, the double agent rattled off the names of an English national newspaper journalist, several senior trade union leaders, and three left-wing members of the Labour Party. He described them as "agents of influence who can be counted on to promote the Soviet position." It was a neatly aimed description that would further confirm the feeling among his listeners that the Labour Party's continued contacts with the Soviet Union left much to be desired.

The luncheon marked the start of a new career for Gordievsky. Coached by his MI6 mentor, he developed a skill for public speaking, delivering lectures which promoted the danger the Soviet Union posed and the KGB's important role in its policy making. He named names and, when the occasion required, produced KGB documents to support his attacks on his former service. He became a conduit for MI6, giving expression to what they wanted to reveal in selected newspapers and broadcasts. It was a bravura performance and one that largely echoed the use the KGB made of Kim Philby.

By 2007, long divorced from his Russian wife, Leila, and living a comfortable life with an English boarding school housemother in a house MI6 had helped to find, Gordievsky continued to publicly attack the Kremlin of President Vladimir Putin. Much of what he said was provided by the Secret Intelligence Service.

IN APRIL 2008, MI6 CHIEF JOHN SCARLETT was told that Gordievsky was publicly claiming he was the latest victim of a poisoning attempt by a Russian hit man who visited his home and that Scarlett had ordered the alleged attack to be covered up.

The claim was dismissed by the Secret Intelligence Service as "absurd and without foundation" and that Gordievsky was suffering from "acute stress" over the attacks on other high-profile defectors in Britain in recent months.

There is an unwritten rule within Britain's intelligence services that when one of its heads retires, he or she has no further contact with their successors on any matter relating to an ongoing case. After Gordievsky learned Scarlett had ordered there should be no investigation by Scotland Yard's Special Branch into his claim, however, he telephoned Dame Eliza Manningham-Buller, the former head of MI5, at her country home in Wiltshire where she raised pedigree chickens and llamas.

She had used Gordievsky as a prime source. So valued was his information that he was awarded, at Manningham-Buller's request, one of Britain's highest honors by the Queen in October 2007, the Most Distinguished Order of St. Michael and St. George (CMG) for "services to the security of the United Kingdom."

Jonathan Evans, director-general of MI5, met with Scarlett. What transpired at that meeting remained secret, but sources suggest neither can have been pleased to have Dame Eliza demanding to know what was going on. Pressure then came from another quarter. Lord Butler, the head of the inquiry into intelligence failures in the run-up to the war in Iraq, asked Evans and Scarlett why the Gordievsky claims had not been investigated.

An intelligence source described how, "Hell then broke loose over why Manningham-Buller had taken time out from feeding her animals to get involved in current decisions within the intelligence services and why Lord Butler had intervened.

Certainly the old spy was a close friend of Alexander Litvinenko, the former KGB officer who was murdered in London in 2006 by a dose of the deadly radioactive substance, Polonium.

Gordievsky later confirmed in his telephone call to Dame Eliza Manningham-Buller that he feared he had been poisoned by Thallium, a highly toxic substance used in rat poison and long a favorite with KGB assassins. When Gordievsky's claim first emerged in April 2008 in the *Mail On Sunday*, a newspaper with good intelligence contacts, he accused MI6 of "abandoning me. I realized that it wanted to hush up the crime."

But forensic tests carried out at Porton Down, Britain's chemical-biological warfare research establishment on Salisbury Plain, failed to identify any traces of poison in his body.

"I was forced to contact Dame Eliza and she helped me very much, but I am caught between MI5 and MI6 and the Special Branch. It is internal politics," Gordievsky told the *Mail On Sunday*.

The one certainty is that his claims caused anger within the upper echelons of both intelligence services, and he had ruptured his long-standing relationship with Scarlett, the most powerful intelligence chief in Britain.

What has puzzled intelligence officers is why Oleg Gordievsky has chosen to wait until now to go public on an incident he claimed happened almost six months ago.

It was on a November morning in 2007 that police were called to his house when his secretary could not gain access. He was found unconscious and rushed to the Royal County Hospital in Surrey. Two weeks later, after he was released, he flew to Vienna for a winter holiday. The hospital has steadfastly refused to discuss what treatment Gordievsky received. The police said they had no comment to make on the mysterious story of the spy who came in from the cold and has managed to do what the KGB never achieved during its time operating in Britain—cause dissent between the current security services' chiefs and one of their distinguished predecessors.

LONG BEFORE THE DISCOVERY OF AMES'S TREACHERY, the possibility of another mole had led to the closure of both the Moscow and East Berlin stations to protect the remnants of the CIA's once powerful network of double agents behind the Iron Curtain. For William Casey, their loss added to his fear that his tenure as director (1981–87) was already blighted.

Physically Casey was a shambling figure with a jowly face, permanently red-rimmed eyes as if he never slept enough, and a voice usually a little more than a mumble, but from his slack mouth came shrewd judgments. After his retirement, he gave a series of interviews (some to Bob Woodward of the *Washington Post*, others to the author). In them he characterized Ronald Reagan as "a man before his time with big visions." President Gerald Ford was "the wrong man at the wrong time." William Webster, the FBI director, had "swallowed a law library and whenever I proposed anything not quite in the book, he'd almost choke on it." Nahum Admoni (head of the Mossad, 1982–89) was "a Jew who'd want to win a pissing contest on a rainy night in Gdansk." Alexander Haig, secretary of state, was "an opportunist who knew how to rule by division." British intelligence was full of "people who knew how to bend the rules, usually to their benefit."

Bill Buckley, who became Casey's close friend, believed there was no better man to lead the CIA. "He had the classic can-do mentality which was once the trademark of the agency until disillusionment set in."

The possibility of another mole within the agency had helped create the sense of failure in Casey as the KGB continued to roll up CIA operations.

Following his transfer on Reagan's order from directing the National Security Agency to serving as Casey's deputy, Admiral Bobby Inman saw Casey as, "little more than a buccaneer." On their first meeting Casey had mumbled, "I want more can-do, less can't say." Officers who had served on the dark side in the Directorate of Operations were pitched into retirement. Careers were suddenly ending, not because of suspected treason, but for what Casey saw as a lack of zeal. On October 14, 1985, Casey addressed a closed meeting of those who remained in the directorate, "The Soviet Union has already trained about six hundred people in terror and paramilitary methods. A Soviet connection may seem very shadowy to some, but it seems very close to me. The terrorists are now in Cuba and Nicaragua and I need to know who sent them. Then we cut the threat off at source." He made it clear he needed new blood to do this, people who were ready to do what he wanted.

Casey's demand, following the CIA's failure to have correctly assessed Ames psychologically, would lead to another disaster for the agency.

Edward Lee Howard had joined the CIA in 1981 around the same time as Casey. International terrorism had begun its work of destruction, which would eventually zero in on the United States, and Casey had bought into the argument made by the Directorate of Operations that the Soviet Union was providing the funds for organizations as disparate as the Irish Republican Army, the Red Brigades in Italy, Germany's Baader-Meinhof Gang (a.k.a. Red Army Faction), and the various Palestinian groups. They were being trained in camps in Albania, Romania, and Bulgaria, but the details were sketchy. Casey wanted officers, capable of operating under deep cover, to try to discover exactly where the camps were so they could be destroyed—CIA officers would lead teams of mercenaries to carry out what would be total deniability "black ops." These operations were planned so as to give the president of the United States, in the case of the CIA, solid grounds for denying knowledge of covert activities he may have been briefed on. William Colby summed up black ops as "where it is understood that those participating may have to exceed their original instructions in the heat of action." Deniability, according to MI6's historical files, harks back to Henry II's query about Thomas Becket, "Who will rid me of this turbulent priest?" The cleric shortly afterward was murdered in Canterbury Cathedral. But the king's question raises an unresolved issue: Did his words actually *order* the murder? Deniability and black ops have remained gray areas to this day in the intelligence world.

Howard was one of the first chosen. A fluent Russian speaker, he was sent for two years of training with the Green Berets before joining the

Directorate of Operations. He was told his first mission was to work in the American Embassy in Moscow as a press attaché, a position often used as a CIA cover, and develop contacts with terrorist groups living openly in the Soviet capital to learn more about the training camps. To help him, he had been allowed to read the files of the CIA's few Soviet contacts in Moscow who so far had evaded detection. One was Adolf Tolkachev, a scientist working in the arms industry.

Before leaving for Russia, Howard was asked to take the standard polygraph test all operatives joining the directorate undergo. Howard's results revealed he had a serious drinking problem and was a habitual liar and a petty thief. His contract was immediately terminated. Casey was not told, according to a subsequent inquiry.

In April 1985, Howard flew to Vienna before his passport could be canceled. In his luggage was the name of the KGB officer in the city, which he had found in one of the CIA files he had been allowed to read. Like Ames, he had brought with him evidence of his willingness to commit treason: a photocopy of Tolkachev's file and the names of his CIA case officer and others working out of the American Embassy in Vienna. Within twenty-four hours of his meeting with the KGB officer, Howard was on a Russian military flight to Moscow.

Tolkachev was interrogated and tortured in the Lubyanka basement before finally being led out into a courtyard and executed by a firing squad.

By then Howard was living in a Moscow apartment close to where Guy Burgess would live out his days (Howard died in 2002). The damage he had done was reflected in a memo Casey wrote to the deputy director of operations, Clair George, saying he was appalled "even at a possibility by an officer committing espionage for the Soviet Union."

What infuriated Casey was that Howard had been, for a time, one of their own. The CIA had trained him. Yet he had betrayed the agency and his own country. Was he simply a drunken malcontent, acting out of revenge? Or was it something deeper that caused Howard to lose his loyalty? Seeking the answers would consume Casey during the rest of his tenure.

Yet on August 1, 1985, there appeared to be hope at the end of the spate of horror stories.

11

High Expectations

On the first Saturday in August 1985, another broiler of a day after Washington had gone almost a month without a breeze, Bill Casey lumbered into the Directorate of Operations. He often visited over a weekend, after that day in April 1983 when the American Embassy in Beirut had been totally destroyed by a massive car bomb.

Among the sixty-three people dead were seventeen Americans, including the CIA station chief, Kenneth Haas, and his deputy, James Lewis, and an old Beirut hand, Rob Ames. Not only was it the agency's greatest single loss, but the explosion had destroyed its files and its ability to gather information in Lebanon.

Nahum Admoni, the Mossad's director-general, sensed it had left the CIA "almost naked in intelligence terms, and we promised to find some clothes."

Seven months later, a Hezbollah suicide bomber drove an even more powerful bomb into the U.S. Marine barracks at Beirut International Airport. Over two days, pieces of 241 bodies were recovered from what the FBI investigators calculated was an explosion on the kiloton scale normally used to measure the impact of a nuclear weapon. Despite Admoni's promise to "find some clothes," no foreign intelligence service in the battle-torn city appeared to have had any prior warning. Casey had asked his analysts to come up with an overview of where the responsibility lay for the attack. The three foreign intelligence services the CIA had a working relationship with in Lebanon were the Mossad, the French DGSE, and MI6. All had come to the conclusion that while

Iran funded Hezbollah, the ultimate responsibility lay with the KGB working through its surrogate, Syria. Casey presciently told Reagan that one day the United States would have to deal with the Damascus regime.

"One way to do it, Bill," replied Reagan, "is to ensure that Israel wants for nothing."

The president had not forgotten the debt he owed to the Jewish support he had encountered on his journey to the White House; he had often come close to tears when introduced to a Holocaust survivor and heard another harrowing account of the concentration camps.

By that Saturday morning in August, Casey had decided, "You deal with Admoni like a difficult putt: You just hope there's nothing on the turf you haven't reckoned with."

As he entered the Directorate of Operations, Casey asked the duty officer if there was anything on the screen to cheer him. The officer handed him a decoded message. After reading it, Casey called a staff meeting in his sixth-floor suite.

SIX WEEKS BEFORE, HEZBOLLAH, the Party of God, had added to its tally of airport hijackings by taking over TWA Flight 847 as it climbed out of Athens and set course for Rome and New York. One of the passengers was a U.S. Navy diver. He was about to fall asleep when the terrorists took charge of the plane, shouting for all the passengers to hand over their passports. When the diver's military travel document was discovered, he was frog-marched to the front of the cabin and shot in the head. Ninety minutes later, after the plane landed at Beirut International Airport, the body was tossed from the cabin. Lying on the sun-baked concrete, it marked the beginning of trading American hostages for American arms.

JIMMY CARTER, IN HIS LAST desperate effort to remain in office—having long failed to impress the voters with his attempts to emulate John F. Kennedy's hairstyle and speech patterns—had authorized a secret operation to rescue the sixty-four diplomats, marines, and staff at the American Embassy in Tehran, who had been taken prisoner on November 4, 1979, by the Islamic regime of Ayatollah Ruhollah Khomeini. Carter's director of central intelligence (DCI) was Stansfield Turner.

He had been a full-fledged admiral, NATO's commander in the Mediterranean, which included the Sixth Fleet, and was the third admiral in the history of the CIA to stand at the helm. When he came on board, he knew almost nothing about how the agency operated but had decided he would run it the same way he ran a ship: Any order he gave would be obeyed without question. The attitude had made him the ideal spy chief for Carter; further, both men shared a fascination with the mechanisms of how satellites supplied information. Soon Turner's lack of experience in dealing with the dark side of intelligence gathering had involved him in a situation he had never encountered at sea. The head of the clandestine side of the agency had asked him to resolve a problem. "He came to me and said they had an agent close to the top of a terrorist organization, but he had been asked once more to prove his loyalty by murdering a top-ranking politician. I was asked to authorize that. I said no, pull him out. The United States could not be a party to murder," Turner would recall.

The issue had intensified his battle within the CIA for technology to have a bigger slice of the budget than human intelligence gathering. He came down heavily on the side of the technocrats. Among the spies there was anger and disillusionment.

Yet before the Tehran mission got under way in April 1980, it was doomed. There was no proper intelligence on the situation in Tehran, and the CIA had virtually been excluded from the mission's planning. Carter had dismissed the agency early in his presidency as "overloaded with analysts, administrators, and technical-intelligence collectors."

That very intelligence would have been vital for the rescue to have a chance of success. Carter had entrusted the mission to the navy; its helicopters were ordered to fly in with a transport plane of U.S. Marines and rescue the hostages from where they were held in the center of Tehran. No one in the White House had established whether the helicopters had a suitable navigation system for the long flight over the desert sands or where and how they would be refueled, let alone how they would fight their way out of one of the most anti-American cities in the Middle East. Well short of Tehran, two helicopters had crashed into the transport, killing eight marines, and the mission ended in the sands of Iran, along with Carter's hopes of remaining in office.

On the day of Reagan's inauguration, Ayatollah Khomeini released the hostages, a final snub to Carter and a reminder to the new president that Iran would remain a problem for the United States.

Up to his resignation in January 1981, Stansfield Turner argued that human intelligence had its limitations. "While technical systems would cost infinitely more money than human ones, reading another country's messages through intercepts and listening to its leaders talk to each other through a concealed microphone can reveal intentions, often with greater accuracy than an agent reporting," he later wrote.

Just as Reagan capitalized on Americans' relief over the return of the Tehran hostages, so Bill Casey had promised a new dawn for the CIA. He would once more make its spies the prime secret instrument of foreign policy. The satellites would still be out in the deep black of space, but the agents would have more freedom to task them. There would be no more blind-alley ventures like the Tehran fiasco. So Casey promised, and his promise was believed.

CASEY HAD BEEN REAGAN'S CAMPAIGN MANAGER for the election, drafting his keynote speeches about being tough on terrorism, and as CIA director his advice continued to be sought by the president on the TWA hijacking.

"I'll talk to Admoni. I'll get him to persuade his government to release their Lebanese prisoners," promised Casey.

Reluctantly, first a hundred, then two, and finally three hundred Arab prisoners in Israel's jails had been bused across the border into Lebanon. By then Reagan had approved a second deal to provide Iran with two shipments of five hundred American TOW antitank missiles; it was the start of the Iran-Contra Affair or Irangate. Shortly afterward Ali Akbar Hashemi-Rafsanjani, the speaker of the Majis, Iran's parliament, had arranged for the TWA passengers to be freed. An American president and his intelligence chief had struck a bargain with one of the most dangerous terrorist groups on earth.

"Hezbollah was controlled by Iran. Iran needed arms to fight Iraq. To get back their people, all Reagan had to do was provide the weapons. So much for election promises to be tough on terrorists," said Ari Ben-Menashe, a senior Mossad officer, who became involved in Irangate as a middleman in Washington in later negotiations with Iran for more arms shipments.

There was one hostage Reagan desperately wanted freed in return for those weapons. He was Bill Buckley, the Beirut station chief, whom Casey had sent to the city to rebuild the CIA station after the embassy bombing. Buckley had been grabbed on March 16, 1984, and since then every Sunday, Casey, a devout Catholic, went to a church near his home in Georgetown and lit a candle and prayed for Buckley's release.

Now, on that Saturday morning in August 1985, Casey had something else to occupy him after reading the decoded message from the CIA station chief in Rome that Colonel Vitali Yurchenko, a senior member of the KGB at the Russian Embassy in the city, wanted to defect.

Casey recalled, "The news was as if my Christmas had come early." For hours he sat with his senior officers in his sixth-floor suite and brainstormed. Was Yurchenko genuine or was he a KGB plant? It was agreed the only way to settle the matter was to bring him to Washington.

AS THE SUMMER OF 1985 WANED IN LONDON, it was yet another time of change for Stella Rimington. Her marriage was over, and she had set up a new home for herself and her two daughters. It was not easy being a single parent approaching middle age and holding down a new post as director of countersubversion. The role extended her already long working day, yet she could not explain to teenagers that being a spy catcher was not a nine-to-five job like those of other mothers. Secrecy had been so ingrained in Rimington that her children had no idea what she did; neither did her small circle of friends outside those in MI5.

John Lewis Jones, the director-general, had been caught in the crossfire following the unraveling of Michael Bettaney's spying for the KGB. Jones had tried to reassure Casey that Bettaney had been discovered before he had done any serious damage. Casey knew this was unlikely; any intelligence from within MI5 would be highly valued by the KGB.

Jones, a lackluster and persnickety pedant, had long appeared to his staff as often less concerned with the content of a report reaching his desk than with whether it was perfectly typed; if not, he would send it back for retyping. Jones also found it difficult to delegate, yet he did not have the managerial skills to control the complexities of MI5's departments.

These deficiencies emerged during his cross-examination by the Security Commission panel over the Bettaney case. After disclaiming any personal failure for the spy's grotesque betrayal and pointing out it was one of his own staff, the formidable Eliza Manningham-Buller, who had unearthed the traitor, Jones had fallen back on breathtaking complacency, effectively saying treachery was not new to any service and it would be "completely wrong to judge MI5 over one case." In mounting disbelief, the committee listened as Jones continued to sidestep and shrug off the probing questions. Finally there were no more. Jones had sat for long moments in the silent room where his answers had exposed his limitations in running the Security Service he had been in charge of for four years. Shortly afterward he resigned and faded into what could only have been a grateful obscurity.

He had been replaced by Antony Duff, the chairman of the Joint Intelligence Committee. Duff was sixty-five years old when he took over the running of MI5. His brief from Prime Minister Thatcher was to exorcise the near collapse of morale that Jones had left as his legacy. There was no better choice than the avuncular Duff: In his dark striped suits and starched-collar shirts, he had a direct way of looking, a reminder of his days peering through a periscope when he had been one of the youngest submarine commanders in World War II.

In his first week in Century House, he visited every office, shook occupants by the hand, asked what they did, and promised he would carry out any improvements they recommended. No one could remember a previous director-general doing so. The fear that had permeated the Security Service that there were still more moles to be unearthed lifted, and in its place came what Stella Rimington called "a strong communal loyalty." Her only personal criticism of Duff was the way he addressed women on the staff as "dear."

By day Duff worked the phone, calling the heads of foreign intelligence services and sending messages to his station commanders around the world. He regularly dined with members of the JIC and lunched with Christopher Curwen at a restaurant near MI6. He often strode into the Home Office to see the home secretary and afterward returned to his own office to dictate more memos for his secretaries to type and dispatch; they were among some of the busiest in Century House. In all Duff said or did, there was the sense of a man on a mission: to restore the Security Service's reputation.

He spent nights reading the key files his department heads had recommended. He realized one of the problems he faced was that under Jones the old-boy network had operated, in which officers had been promoted not on merit but with whom they drank. Duff had many quietly retired and replaced by younger recruits, and he promoted more women than ever before. Among the first to move up was Stella Rimington. Duff put her in charge of B-Branch, to run counterespionage.

Duff and Casey had a friendship going back many years, cemented by a common interest in the history of naval warfare, and one of the first calls Duff made on his appointment was to discuss with him not only the ongoing threat from the KGB, but the emerging one posed by Islamic fundamentalism. They agreed London, with its history of offering asylum, could face a problem.

IN A CORNER OF THE EXECUTIVE DINING ROOM on the seventh floor at Langley, Bill Casey had invited an unusual guest to lunch, KGB Colonel Vitali Yurchenko. It was the first time an officer from a hostile intelligence service had been allowed into the building, but from the time Yurchenko had said he wanted to defect, Casey had taken a close interest in the case, studying the debriefing reports as soon as they reached his desk and on several occasions preparing follow-up questions he wanted answered. He had also read the reports of the psychologists who regularly assessed Yurchenko, noting his "genuine readiness to cooperate." The more Casey read, the greater was his conviction Vitali Yurchenko was "the genuine article."

As a corporate lawyer, Casey had been an astute judge of character, looking at a client across his desk and deciding if he was telling the truth, a gift on the campaign trail with Reagan that had helped him spot many a liar. Casey believed he had not lost that skill as he discussed the day's specials on the lunchtime menu.

"The crabs come from Alaska, where your submarines patrol off the coast," he mumbled.

"And where your listening posts track them," Yurchenko replied.

The exchange set the mood for the meal: Casey, the relaxed host, using his recall of all Yurchenko had revealed during his weeks of questioning, and his guest once more answering questions already posed by others inside the CIA safe house, a stone-walled lodge deep in the woods of Maryland.

Yurchenko had produced a steady stream of revelations about KGB operations around the world, providing an updated look at the way Soviet intelligence operated since Yuri Nosenko, a senior KGB defector, had arrived in the United States in 1964. Nosenko had answered many questions—but had he been telling the truth when he claimed the Soviet government had ordered President Kennedy assassinated?

Casey had heard the rumors that Nosenko had said the assassination had been orchestrated by the KGB as part of a deal with Castro in exchange for Cuba becoming a full-time Soviet surrogate. Years later Richard Helms had repeated the claim during a congressional committee hearing into the assassination. "The Soviet government ordered President Kennedy assassinated," he testified in a document declassified in 1998. It was a view shared by Lyndon Johnson in the sunset of his presidency, "Kennedy was trying to get to Castro, but Castro got to him first." Was that an old man's anecdotage: Johnson's desire to leave his own judgment on the assassination?

Casey had a strong belief the death of Kennedy still remained unresolved when he sat down with Yurchenko and asked his guest if he could confirm the KGB had brainwashed Lee Harvey Oswald to become an assassin. Yurchenko had said if such a file existed, it would be beyond his level of security clearance.

For Casey, the answer reaffirmed his view that his guest was telling the truth about other matters.

LIKE EVERY INCOMING DIRECTOR, Casey had read the file on another murder, which had been plotted not by the KGB but by the CIA, to protect its own attempts to ultimately create an assassin through brainwashing. The program was code-named MK-ULTRA and would remain the most sinister ever undertaken by an organ of the United States government.

In the cabin where Yurchenko had been questioned, a group of CIA officers had met in November 1983 to discuss Frank Olson, an agency biochemist whose specialty was the airborne distribution of a range of lethal aerosols. He was also an expert on the use of LSD as a behavior-manipulating drug, which had been tested on American mental patients in hospitals and on prisoners. Within the Directorate of Operations it was decided the tests should be performed on suspected double agents held in U.S. Army detention centers in postwar Germany. Classified as "expendables," they could be drugged and given large quantities of electroshocks to see if their minds could be sufficiently altered to obey any command of their controllers. Allen Dulles was convinced that both the Russians and the Chinese in the Korean War had successfully brainwashed their prisoners.

Olson, who had never witnessed the results produced by the drugs he had created in his laboratory, had gone to Bavaria to observe the expendables being drugged to the point of death, after which their bodies were buried in the forests around the *Schloss,* a Bavarian-style mansion where the experiments took place.

On the way back to Washington, Olson had stopped over in London to describe what he had seen to Dr. William Sargant. The psychiatrist was involved in the MK-ULTRA program, in which the United Kingdom was a major participant with the United States. On Olson's previous trips to England, Dr. Sargant had taken the biochemist to Porton Down, Britain's biological/chemical research establishment, where British servicemen were unsuspecting guinea pigs for the program. The soldiers believed they were participating in research to find a cure for the common cold.

"On his return from Bavaria, Olson kept saying he had witnessed murder and that he had a moral duty to report what he had seen," Dr. Sargant later told the author.

After Olson flew back to Washington, Dr. Sargant also performed what he saw as his duty. He informed his MI6 contact of what Olson was planning to do and said his mental behavior suggested the biochemist was a security risk to the program. All else followed from that: the call from Dick White, the MI6 chief, to Dulles; the meeting between Dulles and Dr. Sidney Gottlieb, the clubfooted director of MK-ULTRA.

Back at Fort Detrick, the U.S. biological center where Olson worked, he was summoned to a lodge in the Maryland woods. Waiting for him were Dr. Gottlieb and several other members of the Directorate of Operations. Over dinner they questioned Olson about his trip to Bavaria and listened while the biochemist expressed his deep concern at what he had seen. "I think the whole thing should be stopped," Olson concluded.

The evening had become increasingly tense, and at some point Dr. Gottlieb turned to George Hunter White. He was a former OSS operative whom Dr. Gottlieb had appointed to deal with any threat to MK-ULTRA's secrecy.

White handed Olson a glass of Cointreau, his preferred after-dinner drink, which had been spiked on Dr. Gottlieb's order with LSD. Olson quickly began to display signs of being disoriented. The first stage of the plot devised by Dr. Gottlieb to deal with Olson moved up a gear. The increasingly disturbed biochemist was driven to New York to be examined by a therapist, Harold Abramson, whom Dr. Gottlieb had also recruited to work in MK-ULTRA. Abramson diagnosed Olson to be "in a psychotic state, filled with paranoia." Olson was taken back to the Statler Hotel in Manhattan. Seven hours later he was dead—seemingly having jumped through drawn curtains and a double-glazed window from the tenth floor onto the sidewalk. Part of his skull bore a mark as if it had been struck by a powerful blow not caused by the impact with the sidewalk. During his OSS career in Europe, George Hunter White had established a reputation of killing enemy spies and double agents with a single blow from his clenched fist.

For decades the truth of Olson's murder by White had remained a CIA secret, dismissed instead as suicide caused either by "work pressure" or "personal problems." Then, in November 1998, a New York public prosecutor, Steve Sorocco, began to investigate the possibility that Frank Olson had been murdered.

By then White was dead, but Sorocco believed he could still run a successful case against Dr. Gottlieb for arranging the killing. The prosecutor amassed evidence from scores of sources, some of them circumstantial, many offering a sobering insight into the CIA's obsessive pursuit to control human behavior, and its failure to create an assassin. But as Sorocco's case moved slowly but surely to trial, Dr. Sidney Gottlieb died in March 1999. Sorocco had no choice but to close the file.

Now, on that October day in 1985, Casey had one further question on the case. He asked Vitali Yurchenko how far the KGB had gone in trying to create a successful assassin by brainwashing. The defector looked across the table and shrugged. "There are things our scientists have succeeded in doing, but they knew early on that it would not be possible to successfully brainwash a person. They gave up long ago."

Casey pressed, "And the Chinese?" Again, Yurchenko shrugged. "The Chinese? We never knew with the Chinese."

It was another of the honest answers for which Casey had hoped.

IN THE DAYS FOLLOWING YURCHENKO'S return to the lodge after his luncheon with Casey, the psychologists who were part of his debriefing team had noted how cheerful he was; he spoke positively about his future life in America, perhaps even taking up the offer of a consultancy with the CIA that Casey had mentioned. Over the ensuing weeks his excitement diminished and he became more withdrawn, spending lengthy periods in his room watching television, then going alone for a walk in the woods.

The psychologists decided Yurchenko was experiencing feelings not unusual for a defector: a growing realization of being permanently cut off from his past; an uncertainty about whether he really could make a new life in a culture so different from that which was familiar to him.

Nevertheless, Yurchenko had continued to deliver important intelligence, including information about Russia's biological warfare system. The Soviet Union was among the 140 signatories to the 1972 Biological and Toxin Weapons Convention, pledging "never to develop, produce, stockpile or otherwise acquire or retain" biological agents for offensive military purposes. Despite that, Russia had a program, Biopreparat, whose highly secret institutes continued to research and produce vast quantities of bioweapons like bubonic plague—the medieval Black

Death—weapons-grade tularemia, typhus, and the deadly botulinum toxin. Biopreparat had stockpiled sufficient germs to kill every man, woman, and child on earth, along with every animal and every fish in the sea.

For hours only Yurchenko's voice had filled the living room in the lodge, his every word recorded, as he took his listeners on a journey of biological death stored in facilities sited on Russia's borders with Finland and Poland, deep in the Ural Mountains, and beyond to the frontiers with Iran and Afghanistan and to Vladivostok on the Sea of Japan. In all there were thirty-eight facilities holding untold billions of spores and pathogens.

At the end of each session, Yurchenko had gone to his bedroom to call his girlfriend, the wife of a Soviet diplomat stationed in Ottawa. At first their conversations were personal, filled with sexual overtones, and were bugged for the psychologists to analyze. They were surprised at Yurchenko's strong sexual drive, knowing his rather prim manner. Over time, his optimism that his girlfriend would join him gave way to uncertainty. Finally she told him she would not do so, but he should return to Moscow where they could talk about their future.

Sensing his mood change, the psychologists had told the debriefers to cancel their next session with Yurchenko. The next morning, however, he had emerged for breakfast very much his old self, confident, answering each question fully, and seeming to have no worries. He had taken the debriefers through a number of assassination operations the KGB had successfully carried out. One had been on Georgy Markov, a Bulgarian dissident employed by the BBC in London. Markov had been on the way to work when a KGB agent had touched his leg with the tip of an umbrella. Within hours he was dead. The autopsy revealed Markov had been poisoned by ricin. Yurchenko identified the agent as Lev Aleksandrovich Shulikov, a KGB officer based at the Soviet Embassy in Paris. He had returned to Moscow the day after killing Markov. He is identified here for the first time.

When the morning session was complete, Yurchenko had declined lunch and gone to his room to call his girlfriend. There was no reply. He spent the rest of the afternoon alone, refusing a suggestion to take a stroll in the woods or watch a football game on television. The psychologists wondered if this mood change had been triggered because Yurchenko feared he could face a fate similar to Markov's, even though the CIA had promised he would have a new identity to guarantee the KGB would never find him.

On the morning of Friday, November 1, 1985, Yurchenko emerged from his room once more his cheerful self. He had made no phone calls in the night and appeared to have rejected his girlfriend's proposal to join her in Moscow. After breakfast, as he went to his usual chair by the fireplace to prepare to answer more questions, his debriefers had news for him. His questioning was finally over. To celebrate they were taking him to dinner for what one officer called "a real slap-up meal."

The CIA team had booked a table at the Au Pied de Cochon, one of the finest restaurants in the Georgetown area of Washington. Over cocktails the conversation was about the plans for Yurchenko to begin settling into his new life, going window shopping with one of his hosts, buying American-cut clothes, and later meeting one of the agency officers who specialized in relocating defectors. Over the meal there were jokes about the strength of American bourbon compared to that of Russian vodka, and Yurchenko had led the praise for the food, insisting it could never be equaled in any Moscow restaurant. Suddenly he stood up and turned to one of his hosts and asked, "What would you do if I walked out? Would you shoot me?"

The question had been greeted with laughter. "Have another drink, Vitali," one of the officers suggested.

"No. No, just answer the question." Yurchenko had smiled. "Would you shoot me?"

"We don't treat defectors that way," came the reply.

Yurchenko looked around the table. "I'll be back in fifteen or twenty minutes. If not, don't blame yourselves."

He walked out of the restaurant. No one moved to stop him. His hosts felt this was some sort of test Yurchenko was running to compensate for all the tests they had put him through when establishing his credibility.

The twenty minutes passed, and there was no sign of Yurchenko. One of the CIA officers said, "Jesus H. Christ, the Soviet Embassy is only twenty minutes away!"

Recalling the conversation, William Colby, a former director of central intelligence who was a prime source for the author, spoke of "the feeling those guys must have had of being up the creek without a paddle. You take the fella out to dinner and then he just walks out."

Yurchenko had taken a cab to the Soviet Embassy. An FBI surveillance unit saw him enter, but no one would ever know what transpired inside the building. Three days later, dressed in an ill-fitting Russian suit, Yurchenko appeared on live network television from the Soviet ambassador's office to recount an astonishing story. He had been kidnapped in Rome, drugged, and flown in a military plane to Washington. For weeks he had been held in a drugged stupor and questioned by men he believed were CIA interrogators. As abruptly as he had appeared, he departed the office, leaving unanswered questions. How had he been drugged? By injection? Tablets? Liquid? How could he have answered questions while drugged? How had he escaped from his captors? How had he made his way to the embassy? Was this a plot by the KGB to embarrass President Reagan on the eve of his summit with President Mikhail Gorbachev to settle the Arms Control Treaty?

Two days later Vitali Yurchenko was on a flight back to Moscow, never to be seen again in public. No one would ever know his ultimate fate. More certain was the embarrassment for Casey, who had assured his contacts in Congress after his lunch with Yurchenko that the defector was "probably the most valuable asset we have." Reagan, with his folksy manner in overdrive, had told the White House Press Corps, "I think it's awfully easy for any American to be perplexed by someone who could have lived in the United States and yet would prefer to live in Russia."

AS THE 1980s DREW TO A CLOSE, MI5 continued to be embroiled in the IRA's murderous campaign in Northern Ireland, while at the same time trying to root out the spies of the KGB and the Polish intelligence service who continued to aggressively target scientific and industrial companies working on military contracts.

As well as burnishing her credentials as director of counterespionage and becoming the first woman to be addressed on in-house correspondence as "K" (her internal prefix for correspondence to all departments), Stella Rimington worked even longer days and passed her weekends in a succession of meetings to discuss such matters as recruiting officers "with quite a rare mixture of talents; a good brain, and good analytical skills." She also required recruits who would think on their feet "in difficult and dangerous situations" when there would be no experienced officer to support them. She set high standards, and many failed her demands. Those who passed found themselves working the same punishing schedule she had set for herself.

For many in MI5, Rimington was seen as possessing formidable qualities similar to Margaret Thatcher's, dismissing a weak argument with a chilling curtness and showing impatience with a presentation that veered from the essentials. Rimington also had a temper, which could be triggered by trivialities: pigeon droppings on her office windowsill, or an office cleaner who had dusted the portrait of the Queen on the wall and not realigned it in exactly the same position as previously. Her concise memos and the crisp way she spoke when making decisions were a reminder that if you were not able to offer a solution to a problem, you were part of it. Years later she would say, "When the adrenaline flows, it makes you focus better, and I think I have always been a bit bossy."

Within the Security Service the effect from what was known as the Stalker Inquiry became another issue for Rimington. In 1984, John Stalker, a senior police officer on the Manchester force with an unblemished record for investigating serious crimes, had been appointed to investigate growing newspaper claims of a "shoot to kill" policy in an SAS-trained unit of the Royal Ulster Constabulary. The enormity of the allegation, if proven, would have huge political ramifications both in the North and at Westminster: It meant the largely Protestant police force was engaged in cold-blooded murder of Catholic republicans.

Matters had come to a head when a teenage boy was shot dead in a hay shed in which MI5 had been asked to place a surveillance tape recorder after being told by the RUC it was an IRA meeting place. Stalker wanted to check unconfirmed reports that the tape contained the sounds of the shots and the voices of the youth's killers, but at every turn to track down the tape, he was thwarted. When he finally approached Christopher Curwen, the MI5 director-general firmly denied any involvement by the Security Service. Shortly afterward, Stalker's investigation was halted, and he retired from the police force, supplementing his pension by appearing in double-glazing advertisements on television. Later he became one of the many investigators into the deaths of Princess Diana and her lover, Dodi al-Fayed: Stalker drove a car at the same speed along the road taken when the couple had been driven to their deaths. Stella Rimington, whose position as K gave her an insight into the activities of MI5 in Northern Ireland, made no reference to the Stalker Inquiry in her memoir, *Open Secret*.

WHILE THE IRA REMAINED essentially a domestic problem for MI5, terrorism was a growing global issue, and London had increasingly become the headquarters for extremist Islamic preachers who, through a network of organizations, were dedicated to spreading hatred: hatred of Israel, hatred of America, hatred of the West, hatred of all democracies that valued tolerance and freedom, the very ideals that had given the extremists freedom to operate.

Labour prime minister Harold Wilson was regarded with continued deep mistrust within MI5. Its file described him as a "dangerous social-ist who has ties to an East/West trading organisation" and said "a num-ber of East European émigré businessmen [were] among his closest associates." The welcome Wilson had extended to Middle and Far East-ern businessmen, with their large infusions of capital into the British economy, had deepened the often barely concealed suspicion.

Soon mosques were filled with Islamic fundamentalists wanted for ter-rorism in other countries. The governments of France, Algeria, Egypt, Jordan, Saudi Arabia, and the United States hired expensive lawyers to ar-gue in London's High Court that the terrorists should be deported to face trial for their alleged crimes in those countries. Defense attorneys time and again successfully opposed deportation on the grounds it would be exposing their clients to persecution and ultimately death.

In their mosques a new name was added to the expanding pantheon of Muslim heroes and thinkers. The newcomer who began to be men-tioned at Friday prayers was the son of an illiterate laborer from the im-poverished area of Hadhramaut in Yemen, who moved to Saudi Arabia and had become a millionaire when the ruling al-Saud family gave his construction company the contract to maintain the Holy Places in Mecca. There had been enough money to send his son to the respected Azhar University in Cairo to study the great Islamic scholars. The student also had his father's natural business acumen and became a senior manager in the family business after graduating. Later, unlike the Saudi royal princes who spent their money in the playgrounds of Europe, he had gone to support the mujahideen in their war against the Russian-backed regime in Afghanistan. Then, on his twenty-third birthday, in a move that settled his future, he had crossed into Pakistan and set up his own recruiting agency to fight the Russians. He called it Sijill al-Qaeda, or Register of the Base. Soon it became known as al-Qaeda, the Base. Its founder was Osama bin Laden.

THE KIDNAPPING OF WILLIAM BUCKLEY had faced Casey with an unprecedented crisis. In a short time he had lost two heads of station, something that had not happened to the CIA even during the height of the cold war. Casey had begun to work the phones: He called Duff in his office in London, Admoni in his Tel Aviv headquarters, and the heads of France's DGSE, Germany's BND, and SISMI, the Italian Intelligence and Military Security Service in Rome. All promised to mobilize their resources in Beirut.

An NSA satellite began to gather images and phone calls from the alleys of West Beirut and downloaded them into their banks of computers at Fort George G. Meade to be transcribed, cross-checked, and separated into Arabic, the Farsi dialects of Iran, and the French patois of Beirut. More information arrived from the world's leading centers for evaluating Middle East terrorism: the Jaffee and Dayan institutes at the University of Tel Aviv. Ariel Merari, the head of the Center for Political Violence at the University of Tel Aviv, recalled to the author, "We tried to provide insights into the mind-set of the kidnappers and how they were motivated by hatred, and why offering a ransom for Buckley would not work."

Details came from surprising quarters. King Hussein of Jordan sent a hand-couriered report from his own intelligence chief that gave a vivid description of how other hostages were being held: isolated, chained, hooded, and moved from one underground cell to another in West Beirut. Prince Bandar bin Sultan, the Saudi ambassador to the United States, provided a street plan of the area, but warned any rescue attempt would fail.

On May 7, 1984, fifty-two days after Buckley's kidnapping, a video was delivered to the American Embassy in Athens. The tape showed Buckley undergoing torture. The absence of sound made it all the more obscene—that, and the way the cameras zoomed in and out of Buckley's damaged body. He held before his stomach a document marked MOST SECRET, proof his briefcase had been carrying sensitive intelligence. His face showed signs of drugging: his eyes were lusterless and his lips limp. Also, his wrists and neck bore abrasion marks as if he had been bound with either a rope or chains.

The second video came on May 30, sent to the American Embassy in Rome. It showed Buckley with his arms punctured by needle marks. His legs shook and spasmed on the ground—his central nervous system, damaged by torture, had left him unable to control his feet—as he pleaded to be exchanged under a guarantee that the United States would remove all of its influence from Lebanon and make Israel do the same.

Copies of the transcript of Buckley's words were sent to George Shultz, the secretary of state. With the document went a lengthy position paper written by a CIA analyst, Graham Fuller, a specialist on the Middle East. He argued that a full-scale withdrawal by the United States or Israel was "impractical," but it might be possible to obtain Buckley's freedom by using Iran as a broker: The mullahs needed more weapons to continue their war with Iraq. To provide the arms could be the answer.

Shultz summoned the Israeli ambassador to discuss the matter. The diplomat asked for time to consult with Tel Aviv. A response came within hours: Israel would have no objection to equipping Tehran with the latest weapons. According to Ari Ben-Menashe, who would later shepherd the weapons into Iran, "Israel was happy to see Iran and Iraq continue to bleed each other white in their war."

Four hundred and forty-four days after he had been captured Bill Buckley was dead, choked on his own phlegm from the pneumonia that finally ended his life on the evening of June 3, 1985, in the underground cells in the Basta neighborhood in Beirut.

THE DETAILS OF HIS DEATH had come from David Jacobsen, the director of the American University Hospital in the city, who had himself been released after seventeen months in captivity in the jail. He had told Casey, "Buckley was delirious. There was just a long, long silence. I did not see him die, though he was in the next cell to me, because I was hooded. All I heard was the sound of Bill's body being dragged out."

On December 15, 1986, Casey arrived at his office on the seventh floor. As usual he looked again at the file on Buckley. More than once he had wondered if he had done everything possible to save him. Suddenly Casey collapsed, the victim of a brain seizure brought on by the undiagnosed lymphoma in his brain, and was rushed to Georgetown University Hospital. On January 29, 1987, Bob Gates, his deputy, arrived at his bedside.

"Hello, Bill."

Casey's mumble could not be understood. Gates explained he had been asked to deliver a letter from President Reagan. Casey lay back on his pillow and said nothing. Gates offered to read it to him. When he had finished, there were tears in Casey's eyes. The letter was his resignation. To confirm it, all he had to do was sign on the dotted line. Casey was too weak to hold the pen.

"The hell with it," said Gates, pocketing the unsigned letter.

The next day President Reagan offered Gates the job of acting director of central intelligence. They both knew it would not be permanent. He had been too close to Casey; Reagan wanted a new man to run the agency. Gates remained for five months in the post.

On May 6, 1987, Casey died of pneumonia following brain surgery to remove his tumor. He had served his country for six years and a day. President Reagan and former president Richard Nixon lead the mourners.

By then the Buckley file had been sent to the basement Registry. All that visibly remained of his service to the CIA was a silver star that the Langley engraver had embedded in a wall of the Langley lobby, joining the others who had fallen during active service. Close by was the marble plaque inscribed with the words of the Apostle John: AND YE SHALL KNOW THE TRUTH, AND THE TRUTH SHALL MAKE YOU FREE.

Bill Buckley recalled to the author that when he had seen the inscription on his first day at Langley "I wondered about that. I really did."

12

New Targets

At an early hour, 6:30 A.M., in November 1989, only the tip of the Washington Monument was visible in the emerging dawn, and across the Potomac the headstones still remained in darkness on Arlington Cemetery's hill. The two men seated in the back of the black government car each knew someone who had died in battle. The Oldsmobile had bulletproof windows, an armor-plated body, and antimine flooring. Only the official car of the president of the United States had similar protection. The Oldsmobile came with the job of director of central intelligence.

The older of the two men, William Hedgcock Webster, had held the job since March 1987 as President Reagan's choice to replace Casey. The soberly dressed sixty-four-year-old lawyer had been a public prosecutor and a district judge in his birthplace of St. Louis, Missouri, before running the FBI for nine unblemished years. For special agent in charge Edward Gunderson, "Webster was so squeaky clean, we called him the Rule Book Man." In Washington, Webster knew there were people waking up on that cold November morning wondering how much longer he would keep his job at the CIA.

Webster was the fourteenth to hold the position, and he faced a cold welcome at Langley. From the day he walked across the lobby, past the armed guards and glanced at the Apostle John's wall tablet before entering the elevator reserved for him, Webster must have sensed the hostility he attracted. Throughout the seven floors, he was seen as the former judge who had come to pronounce sentence on the agency survivors from the Irangate scam.

The Tower Commission, appointed by President Reagan to investigate the arms-for-hostages deal, had found his administration riddled with incompetents who had often come close to criminality as they had allowed the deal with Iran to cast an unprecedented blight on the United States. It had resulted in the buildup of anti-Americanism across the Muslim world after the discovery of the crucial role Israel had played in the scam, and in dismay among America's European allies, seriously affecting how the world saw the Reagan administration.

The darkest shadow fell across the CIA after the Tower Commission judged the agency had been deeply involved in secretly negotiating with an avowed enemy: Iran, providing it with planeloads of the latest American weapons, which were supposedly intended for Israel; collaborating with the Jewish State to fly the arms to Tehran; organizing secret payments to Arab wheeler-dealers, "fixers" described as "having the morals and cunning of alley cats." Five more years were to pass after Buckley's murder and Casey's death before the last hostages held in Lebanon by pro-Iranian militias were freed.

Ari Ben-Menashe, one of the Israeli middlemen in Iranscam, recalled, "I was told time and again in Langley, 'go ahead, let the Iranians and Iraqis kill each other. We'll help you to help them do that.' And my friends in the CIA did just that."

Webster had been appointed to remove those remaining friends of the fast-talking Israeli and, at his nomination hearing, was left in no doubt that Congress expected him to bring the agency back into line. No more Casey thumbing his nose at Congress. No more illegal operations. Webster was never to forget that while he was the president's chief intelligence adviser, he also worked for the people of the United States. His first decision had been to fire Clair George, who had been Casey's head of clandestine operations, running them with a mixture of calculated cunning and controlled charm. There was no place for that kind of guile in Webster's CIA, any more than he liked being called "Director." He preferred to be addressed as "Judge." Soon a large number of intelligence officers, who between them had served in every continent and had acquired a thousand years of experience, had left with Clair George. Many of the six thousand who remained on the payroll had dubbed Webster "Boring Bill"; he was ridiculed as the Southerner with no idea how things worked at Langley. "He just didn't understand that spying around the world wasn't the same as running the FBI with its agents in button-down shirts who shaved every morning," said one of George's team when he was told he was no longer needed. Others had started taking bets on how long the Judge would survive before he went back to Missouri, taking his small-town attitudes with him.

SEATED BESIDE WEBSTER IN THE OLDSMOBILE was Colin McColl who wore a suit that had the cut of the sharper end of Savile Row, where the tailors offer their swatches of cloth to the marketing managers of British industry. Indeed, McColl had something about him of the style of the salesmen who had roamed the world of the empire: the plummy voice and the raconteur's collection of jokes and anecdotes gathered from places whose names had long changed in the atlas. With his stories went a rack of designer ties hanging in his wardrobe along with the Australian bushwhacker's hat he had picked up on one of his trips, which he still liked to wear on weekends when he hosted cookouts in his back garden in the Oxfordshire countryside.

Even in repose there was the air of the actor about him, a reminder of those times he had been a leading man in amateur dramatics at Oxford and later dominated stages as far apart as Warsaw, Geneva, New York, and all those other places where he had served. Only his carefully chosen inner circle of friends knew that the affable, smiling McColl was one of the most brilliant officers in the Secret Intelligence Service. Even they did not know the precise details of what he had achieved; only within the upper ranks of MI6 was he known as the spy's spy.

McColl at the age of sixty-three had only recently been appointed head of the Secret Intelligence Service, but unlike the CIA director, the chief had long ago begun his journey into the dark and dangerous world he had chosen after being "tapped" at Oxford and sent to the School of Oriental and African studies at London University to learn the Thai language. Next came a course at Fort Monkton—the MI6 training school—to acquire all the essentials of his chosen profession, from codes and dead letter boxes to weapons handling. His instructors graded him as "highly proficient," the highest mark they could give.

Equipped with all the skills they had shown him, McColl had been sent out into the field. In New York he had tracked the money men who supplied funds for the IRA to buy weapons and recruited his own Irish informers to report on Sinn Fein's fund-raising dinners and identify the wealthy guests who flew to Ireland on its national airline, Aer Lingus, carrying in their hand luggage bundles of dollar bills that were handed over at Shannon Airport to the IRA. McColl had flown the route himself to see how poor airline security was at Kennedy Airport or with the Irish police at Shannon.

In Warsaw and later Vienna, McColl's reputation was furthered when he again began to recruit informers in locations where the KGB had established a ruthless reputation for murdering double agents. Soon he was seen as one of its top agents in the SovBloc unit.

Years later former MI6 agent Richard Tomlinson told the author, "Being in SovBloc meant you lived on the tightrope every moment of every day. Someone who could do that had to be very special."

McColl was a skilled flutist, and the haunting sounds of the instrument drifted out of his office. For McColl, the flute was a calming influence, relaxing him as he continued achieving one successful operation after another against the KGB.

He had uncovered some of its money launderers in Geneva and discovered that the respected Credit Suisse bank was unwittingly being used by them to finance links with organized crime families and Middle East terrorist groups. The money was also funneled through Bulgaria's intelligence service, Darzhavna Sigurnost (DS), to kill Soviet dissidents in the West.

It was while tracking KGB operations that McColl discovered that Robert Maxwell, the British newspaper tycoon and owner of the mass circulation tabloid the *Daily Mirror*, was not only spying for Israel's Mossad, having refused a request to work for MI6, but had also established business links with Eastern European criminal gangs. Most remarkable of all were Maxwell's contacts with Vladimir Kryuchkov, the head of the KGB. Maxwell had used a combination of his business contacts throughout Eastern Europe and his power as a publisher to reach Kryuchkov, and they had finally met in the Lubyanka, the massive KGB citadel in Moscow.

Their first encounter survived in the memory of one of Kryuchkov's aides, Colonel Vyacheslaw Sorokin, who had been recruited by MI6, "Maxwell was very boisterous, and at the end of the meeting he said his newspaper would tell the world how much the Soviet Union was changing. Afterward Kryuchkov said Maxwell was going to be very useful to the KGB." From then on a British Airways flight from London regularly brought gifts for Kryuchkov from Maxwell: crates of vintage Scotch whiskey and Krug champagne, a cashmere overcoat, sets of solid gold cuff links, and a hi-fi set with the finest opera recordings. All were duly noted and the information was passed on by Sorokin to his MI6 contact. The conclusion was that though Maxwell worked as a Mossad informer, he was primarily motivated to promote himself as a major dealmaker in the Soviet Union. Nevertheless, like many other British businessmen and politicians, Maxwell was placed on the surveillance list that MI6 shared with MI5.

While the collapse of the Berlin Wall had caught many analysts, including those in MI6, by surprise, McColl was not one of them. Neither did he share the view that the intelligence world would become an easier place in which to operate now that the threat of a superpower confrontation had vanished.

With an already burnished career, McColl was recalled to London to continue his progress along the path that would eventually lead him to the top. He became interested in the technological revolution, which was creating new openings for intelligence gathering, and the possibilities excited him more than any other subject. For McColl, drugs, money laundering, and terrorism became an increasing threat. To defeat them would require a full understanding of the new technology available to the traditional spy.

Margaret Thatcher had asked him to ensure that MI6 had a guaranteed place in conquering this new frontier of espionage and to use it to exploit the collapse of the Soviet Union and the unification of Germany, as well as to ensure that the fledgling democracies in Czechoslovakia, Romania, Bulgaria, Poland, and Hungary created new intelligence services that would support MI6.

McColl had gone to his office and played his flute. The mournful notes had long been a running joke in the Seniors Club, the drinking den in the MI6 basement, where it was said that McColl played his instrument while he marshaled his thoughts to lead MI6's many enemies to their doom.

On that November morning, McColl had flown to Washington to discover how the latest surveillance weapons in space could do that.

TEN MILES NORTHEAST OF WASHINGTON is the largest and most powerful surveillance organization in the world. Opened in November 1952, a direct descendant of the World War II cryptologists and the Bletchley code breakers, the National Security Agency summed up its role on the heraldic insignia in its lobby: a bald eagle grasping a key in its talons, representing the NSA's hold on global eavesdropping and the secrets it gained through technology that no other organization could remotely rival.

Standing on the hundreds of acres of Fort Meade, its anonymous buildings rise over the Maryland countryside, and though their purpose has finally been acknowledged, NSA is still said in Washington circles to stand for "No Such Agency." Those who work there prefer to call it Sigint

City, their in-house reminder that they work at the cutting edge of codes and ciphers in the most secretive agency in the U.S. intelligence community.

They run the world's latest single group of supercomputers, all built specifically to NSA blueprints, operated by the largest number of mathematicians gathered together in one organization, along with thousands of cryptologists and analysts. Just to do their work had required $40 million per year in electricity in the first five years NSA operated; in 2007, the *annual* cost was calculated at $60 million. The NSA annual budget is a blank space on the financial surveys that serious newspapers publish on the costs of running U.S. intelligence. A best-guess estimate places its annual spending at $30 billion or more a year. A single satellite can cost a billion dollars; NSA had fifty-four in 2007. Its thousands of computers are all unique to the agency, often the end product of years of research and development, to handle the ever-increasing volume of communications. The computers are linked to storage systems, each holding a petabyte of data, eight times more than the entire word count in the Library of Congress or the British Library. Part of the budget pays for the NSA in-house Supercomputer Research Center, which specializes in crypto-computing and creating faster processing techniques.

Speed is the vital key to analyzing material and the driving force behind all that the NSA does. Computer speed has moved from billions of operations per second to a quadrillion—petaflop speed, which only the fastest of the superfast microcomputers can achieve.

Another segment of the budget goes to developing programs that can interdict foreign databases. Everything that happens at the NSA, William Colby, the former CIA director, said, "makes lightning look slow. One time there was a program that could translate seven languages at five hundred words a minute. Next time I checked, a month later, it had doubled its capacity and halved its translation time."

There was a longtime boast in Sigint City that, if tasked, its computers could capture the first birth cries of a baby and follow the infant through life to its death no matter where on earth it went. True or not, it was part of the can-do philosophy of those who worked in Sigint City, where nothing was impossible. Day and night, depending on their shifts, they left their homes, each with its patch of lawn out front and a barbecue pit at the back, in one of the feeder colonies that surrounded Fort Meade and took the turn off from the Baltimore-Washington Parkway to pass through the guarded gateway into a world so secret—so black—that not one of the staff knew everything that happened at Sigint City.

They spent their time working in over thirty categories of information gathering: All were secret, some more secret than others, and still more so secret that the workers did not know where the information came from, only that after it was downloaded and analyzed it was sent to such diverse organizations within the U.S. intelligence community as the CIA, the National Intelligence Council, and the Weapons and Space Intelligence Committee. There were over a dozen such taskmasters, each with its own priority demand on Sigint City. Together they formed the outer ring of the System, the collective name for the NSA's multifaceted attack on the communications of every foreign government and their diplomatic and military organizations. No code remained safe from the cryptologists. It might take them days, even weeks, but ultimately their mathematical skills would triumph.

Once words were spoken by telephone or sent by encrypted fax or e-mail into the void of space, they were silently grabbed by the NSA technology at Fort Meade or one of twenty-five listening posts around the world: from Waihoapai in New Zealand and Kojarena in Western Australia to the northern border of Finland, the System gathered up the information. A million words a second. Seventy billion a day. Every day. Every week. Every month. No one knew the size of the "take." Like almost everything else at the NSA, such figures were secret.

Those who worked in this compartmentalized world operated in a framework of acronyms from COMINT, communications intelligence, to TELINT, telemetry intelligence (data transmitted by missiles); there was an INT, an identification number, for every multitask performed in their Byzantine world. A small committee did nothing else but review, change, and create new names to reduce the risk of security leaks.

The National Security Agency's global reach was continually extended. New satellites were launched into space, new telemetry systems introduced, new tracks selected for near-polar orbits, and new stations opened.

Two had come on stream that November day in 1989 when William Webster led Colin McColl past the twenty-two thousand parking spaces for the workforce (in 2007, it numbered thirty-eight thousand, each with his or her allotted space).

MCCOLL AND WEBSTER WERE RECEIVED that morning by Vice Admiral William Studeman, USN, the NSA's twelfth director. Washington politics dictated that the agency should be headed by either a navy or army man, as the NSA came under the ultimate control of the Department of Defense; the feeling was that only a military figure would know how to keep in check some of the more temperamental of the cryptologists and mathematicians, "near geniuses who live beyond all the usual rules," President Truman had once called them.

Some were veterans from Bletchley Park who had opted for a higher salary and a better life for their families in America when the NSA opened; their work in breaking the German Enigma code made them legendary figures in the communities around Fort Meade. Their neighbors included specialists on loan from Britain's GCHQ; others had moved from Canada's Communications Security Establishment, set up after the postwar Soviet spy scandals in that country. Some came from Australia's Defense Signals Directorate and the New Zealand Government Communications Security Bureau; both had already developed close ties with the NSA. The agency grouped them all under the umbrella of UKUSA, a long-standing secret agreement between Britain and the United States.

Under the agreement, GCHQ is the coordinating center for gathering electronic secret intelligence from Europe, Africa, and Russia west of the Ural Mountains. The NSA covers east of the mountains, including Japan and China, as well as North and South America and the Caribbean. Australia and New Zealand monitor the South Pacific and Southeast Asia. This global-eavesdropping network ensures there are no gaps in coverage.

On their workstation screens at Fort Meade, people had watched the dramatic fall of the Berlin Wall in 1989 and listened to President Mikhail Gorbachev say that Russia still had "its proper place as a superpower." For his listeners it was sufficient reason for them to continue spying on an old enemy. At GCHQ the annual budget was increased to £600 million, making it by far the largest slice of the British intelligence funding, and it also received money to work on NSA black projects from funds hidden inside the costs of other U.S. defense projects.

WITH HIS MUTED TEXAS accent and his "sexual orientation" listed as "straight" in his naval records, Studeman had taken over the NSA weeks after the fall of the Berlin Wall. His background as a hard-nosed intelligence officer had preceded him. He had served as operations intelligence chief with the Seventh Fleet during the Vietnam War before becoming commander at the Naval Operational Intelligence Center in Washington. His reputation was of a man who made good judgments quickly.

His staff saw Studeman as a reassuring and calming figure after the bitter rows that engulfed his predecessor, General William Odom, who had finally been dismissed when he had fought for, and failed to get, funding to create a new generation of billion-dollar satellites able to survive a nuclear war in space. It had been deemed "inappropriate" by his paymasters, but there had been money to expand ECHELON.

No other surveillance net in the NSA was as secret and all-inclusive as what was regarded to be the jewel in its crown: ECHELON could access the satellite traffic from every computer and telephone on earth. ECHELON read customer accounts from banks, patients' records from hospitals, and details of business deals supposedly secret. It could access these and much more: The private e-mails between Princess Diana and Dodi al-Fayed were routine pickups by ECHELON in the closing weeks of their doomed relationship.

Tens of millions of tearful regrets, angry demands, and abject apologies daily carried over the world's telecommunications networks were sifted, and those deemed to be significant (like the Diana/al-Fayed correspondence) were stored in the NSA electronic archive, capable of holding five trillion pages of text. Studeman had called the system "probably the largest processing environment in the world."

ECHELON used its own software program, Dictionary, to compute billions of names, phrases, and telephone numbers in every nation on earth. Access to the Dictionary program was more password-protected than any bank vault, and it could comb through hundreds of millions of messages in nanoseconds.

It was those capabilities that had brought Colin McColl to Fort Meade to learn more about the important role an NSA base in the north of England played in ECHELON.

THREE THOUSAND MILES ACROSS THE ATLANTIC the NSA leases, at a peppercorn rent, 550 acres of what was once sheep-grazing land in Yorkshire, a gift from the British Ministry of Defense in 1959. On the contract it is identified only as Project 8313. The land was later named Royal Air Force Station Menwith Hill—the word comes from the ancient Saxon for "stony ground"—though the only connection with Britain was a token RAF liaison officer and a detachment of Ministry of Defense police who continued to patrol the high-wire alarmed fences in 2007 and will do so for the foreseeable future.

In every sense Menwith Hill is a transplanted part of America: Its supermarket sells the best cuts of U.S. meat and stocks American liquor and candies. Its chapel conducts services for Catholics, Jews, and Protestants, who take turns worshipping in the all-purpose building. Its gym facilities include basketball, and there are fields for baseball and soccer. Visitors are not allowed on site, and the base's two thousand employees continue to be briefed to tell any curious locals they are there on "military duties."

In the pubs, when the sheep had gone and the buildings were erected, the talk was that Menwith Hill was intended to be an Early Warning Station against an attack by Soviet bombers; in 1960, the newspapers were full of such stories. Later there were rumors Menwith Hill was going to track flying saucers. There had been a number of claims of strange objects in the heavens.

When the Americans arrived the reports grew as, behind the guarded fences, rose what looked like gigantic golf balls. Some were taller than many buildings in the nearby town of Skipton: huge white structures, some clustered together, others standing alone like discards from a science fiction film set.

No one suspected then what they really were: radomes, the very core of ECHELON's role as a global eavesdropper. Each radome was positioned by experts from the NSA in a carefully aligned course known as the Runway, which allowed them to intercept the messages from communication networks. Coated in toughened Teflon to shed the rain that swept in across the North Sea, the golf balls were each equipped with computers to interdict the networks as they bounced their messages around the globe so they could be unwittingly swallowed up into the radomes.

The initial budget for the radomes was $26 million; within a year a further $15 million had been added to what the U.S. Department of Defense called "support expanding classified missions." A number of those missions could not be remotely classified as addressing a threat to national security either for the United Kingdom or for the United States. Conversations by Jane Fonda, Dr. Benjamin Spock, and the Black Panther leader Eldridge Cleaver, all prominent opponents of the Vietnam War, were monitored at Menwith Hill.

By 1980, the base was the exclusive user of two systems, Silkworth and Moonpenny; both names had been chosen by the Naming Committee at Fort Meade. Both systems used specially designed satellites stationed over target areas to intercept specific long distance microwave radio communications. By 1984, Silkworth had become sophisticated enough to monitor conversations between a company and its branch offices or between military installations in a targeted country. A year later it had perfected the technique of recording intercom conversation inside a building. Meanwhile, the Moonpenny system had managed to

burrow into the satellite communications used by other nations to intercept the signals from their satellites as they were transmitted to their
ground stations. Russia, Israel, and the Arab group of nations that ran
the Arabsat satellite all had their supposedly secure messages intercepted and their coded words broken by the computers at Menwith Hill.

During his visit, McColl was told by Studeman that Menwith Hill
could handle "about two million intercepted messages an hour. Of
these, all but thirteen thousand were discarded. Of these, about two
thousand were sent on to Fort Meade, of which around twenty were selected for analysis." It meant that in 1989 Menwith Hill intercepted 17.5
billion messages, of which 17.5 million were analyzed. There is "every
reason" to believe, confirmed a former employee at Menwith Hill, that
the figures for 2007 were "substantially higher."

IN THE COMING DECADE, MENWITH HILL would remain the dominant user of ECHELON, with additional programs called Sire and
Steeplebush. In one year, 1993, it helped U.S. firms win $26.5 billion in
overseas contracts by alerting the governments in Third World countries that ministers were taking bribes. The contracts were awarded to
U.S. companies. The French prime minister, Edouard Balladur, found
himself at the losing end of a $6 billion deal for arms and the sale of the
European Airbus to Saudi Arabia when Silkworth intercepted messages
showing that Airbus agents were offering bribes to a Saudi official that
led to the deal going to Boeing. In 1994, ECHELON intercepted phone
calls between France's Thomson-CSF and the Brazilian government
about a $1.4 billion contract for a surveillance system to be installed in
the Amazon rain forest. The details were passed by the NSA to the
American Raytheon Corporation, which was given the contract. In the
Philippines, Malawi, Peru, Tunisia, and Lebanon, the work of Silkworth
and Moonpenny ensured that contracts that would have gone to European firms went to U.S. corporations. In 2007, Brian Gladwell, a former
NATO computer expert, said, "In cyberspace we now have a situation
where state-sponsored theft of commercial information is a growth industry."

AFTER SHE BECAME DIRECTOR of counterespionage, one of the
changes Stella Rimington had promoted, not without meeting resistance,
was to alter MI5's method of recruiting. Her appointment to a post previously held only by men was seen by many of her male colleagues "as a step

too far, and I heard tell of mutterings about it in the men's toilets," she recalled. Ignoring the whisperings, she pressed on with her campaign for MI5 to place carefully worded advertisements in newspapers and magazines making it clear women were welcome to apply.

She realized there were also problems to consider. Women who responded to the advertisements were likely to be in their early twenties, and while they would have the required intellectual skills, their own personalities would still be developing. From her own considerable experience, she recognized that to work in counterintelligence or analysis needed maturity and an ability to make judgments that could have far-reaching effects.

There were also the personal demands on those "working on the dark side of the house," where officers in counterintelligence or espionage operated. The sentiment in the male-dominated Security Service was that few women could accept the long hours, separation from friends and family for long periods, and the risk of violence on some operations. Even Rimington's persuasion had not entirely succeeded in overcoming the objections to employing women. Still, she was convinced that for MI5 to develop, more women must be recruited and encouraged to go for the highest positions.

ANNIE MACHON WAS TWENTY-THREE YEARS OLD when she took the Foreign Office entrance examination. She was ambitious in that quiet way that went with her island background; she had grown up on Guernsey, one of the Channel Islands. While not exactly beautiful in the way the small publishing house she worked for depicted women on their book jackets, she had a fine bone structure, long blond hair, gray-blue eyes, and a shy smile. She also possessed a Cambridge degree in classics and a working knowledge of French, German, and Russian. Working for the Foreign Office would satisfy her desire to serve her country.

Instead, she received a letter from the Ministry of Defense suggesting there was another job she might find more interesting. All she had to do was call a given telephone number. Her first reaction was "Christ! It's MI5!" All she knew about the intelligence world she had learned on those evenings she had sat in a cinema and watched a Bond film or, on a visit home, sat with her father to view the BBC dramatization of John le Carré's *Tinker, Tailor, Soldier, Spy*. Nevertheless, she made the call.

MI5 had "first stop" offices around London where "doubtfuls" were quickly separated from "possibles," candidates who could be sent on to the next stage of recruitment. Each office was furnished with a standard government desk with a chair on either side, a strip of carpet on the floor, and lighting as cheerless as the window drapes. One office was above a theatrical agency, which booked acts for provincial nightclubs, another near the produce market of Covent Garden, and a third on Fulham Road.

Annie Machon had been invited to an office on Tottenham Court Road, an area of downmarket shops and fast food restaurants. Seated behind the desk was a youngish woman wearing a long hippie-style skirt. The early stages of Machon's interview followed the lines of a typical job application: her personal history, family background, education. Then came more probing questions. Why had she applied for the job? Did she have any real idea of what it involved? What were her expectations if she was offered a position? Despite her educational qualifications and language skills, would she accept a comparatively modest salary? Did she understand promotion could be a slow process? Did she have ethical views (i.e., moral objections to the job)? Did she have any views on trade unions? Would she refuse to join one or take part in any strike action?

She had answered truthfully: She did have an interest in politics; she was not a member of any union; salary was not a prime consideration, it was job satisfaction that mattered; she had no ethical views; she had never met anyone with links to Communism, nor had she been approached by any foreign intelligence agent. Finally the questions stopped.

She had looked at the interviewer. "Could you tell me who I would be working for?"

The woman had reached for a document on the desk. "Please read this."

Annie read a copy of the Official Secrets Act. It was confirmation of her earlier guess that the letter from the Ministry of Defense had been sent on behalf of MI5.

"Do you understand what you have read?" asked the woman.

"Of course."

"Then please sign it."

Annie Machon did so and handed back the document. "Signing the document was like being admitted into one of those secret societies I'd read about," she recalled to the author.

The woman sat forward and spoke quietly. "If you are accepted, you will be looked after. The job offer will be with the Security Service."

The woman explained that its role had changed considerably and that MI5 had "virtually ceased to investigate Communists, anarchists, and right-wing extremists, which for years newspapers called 'the enemy within.'" She smiled. "Things have moved on a great deal since then."

Annie Machon had nodded, uncertain what to say, fascinated by what she had been told.

Having glossed over the reality that MI5 continued to deal with all enemies of the state, no matter what label was attached to them, the interview once more moved back to Annie.

"You will have to undergo EPV, enhanced positive vetting, the highest level of security clearance," the woman said. She explained it would be necessary to provide the names of four persons from "different phases of my life until a full picture of my character had been made," Annie later recalled.

The vetting process included an interview about Annie Machon's sex life, and this time her interviewer turned out to be "a sweet old lady who, despite being just like my grandmother, had a gently probing technique." Only when she had passed that final inquiry into her intimate life would she be recommended for two days of examinations by the Civil Service Section Board, during which she would undergo interviews with a member of MI5 and a psychologist who put to her a series of questions originally prepared by Dr. William Sargant.

All her interviews went well, and Annie Machon was accepted into the Security Service. For her the future looked infinitely more exciting than working in the Foreign Office.

THERE WAS NO HINT ON THAT JANUARY DAY IN 1991, having met Stella Rimington's expectations by displaying the qualities a woman needed to rise through the ranks and become a trusted officer, that Annie Machon would become MI5's most celebrated whistle-blower.

Her exam results had been sufficiently high to fast-track her into the countersubversion branch. Despite the assurance at her first interview that Communists were no longer a key target for MI5, she found herself working on the files of Communist Party members and updating the files of Labour Party politicians campaigning in the 1952 election. MI5's bête noire of "Reds under the bed was still very much alive in MI5," Annie Machon recalled to the author. She did what she was asked, and her meticulous reports earned praise from her branch director.

For two years Annie Machon worked as a desk officer, dealing not only with suspected Communists but with the threat the Irish Republican Army posed with their bombing campaign, which had spread from Northern Ireland to Britain. While combating them was work she well understood, she felt increasing unease at the way the Security Service created hundreds of files on "ordinary citizens" who, in her opinion, showed they presented no threat to national security.

So had started her mounting distrust that, while the IRA was a dangerous enemy of the state, the basic civil liberties of too many people were being abused by the way MI5 operated in a supposedly democratic system. Increasingly the conflict between what she was ordered to do and her ethics grew. By then she was in a relationship with a colleague, David Shayler.

With long hair and a sense of his own importance, Shayler had worked in MI5's counterterrorism branch heading up the Libya Desk, and his briefings to senior civil servants had earned him commendations in his personal file. His work had also brought him in contact with the Secret Intelligence Service, and Shayler learned of a plan by Libyan dissidents to assassinate the country's ruler, Colonel Mu'ammar Gadhafi.

The sense of drama that often surrounded Shayler once more emerged with the details of the plot from his source in MI6, an equally dramatic figure who insisted on being referred to as PT16B. The plot fueled Shayler's sense of being part of an extraordinary event that, if successful, would undoubtedly change the political map of the Arab world. The leading actors—apart from PT16B—were "Tunworth," an alias that could have been plucked from a spy thriller, who was a high-ranking Libyan government official, and a group of Libyan extremists called al-Islamiya al-Muqatila, the Islamic Fighting Force. PT16B had held secret meetings with them and Tunworth on Malta, and a final agreement had been reached in which Tunworth would receive four payments totaling £100,000 to cover "the costs" of the assassination. The money had been paid by MI6 through several bank accounts the Secret Intelligence Service operated around the Middle East. After the money transfer, a three-page memo was circulated to the Joint Intelligence Committee, Sir John Adye, the director of GCHQ, and Patrick Walker, the director-general of MI5, who sent a copy to Shayler.

Months later, Shayler learned from PT16B that the assassination attempt on Gadhafi had failed. At what would turn out to be their last meeting, speaking with what Shayler described later as "a kind of note of triumph," he was told by PT16B, "Yes, we almost did." "My reaction was of total shock. This was not what I thought I was doing in the intelligence service. Tens of thousands of pounds of taxpayers' money had been used in an attempt to assassinate a foreign head of state," Shayler recalled.

When he told Annie Machon, they both decided to resign from MI5,

and Shayler launched an unprecedented campaign to expose what the
Mail On Sunday, a mass circulation tabloid, called "a woeful tale of bungles, cover-ups, botched assassinations and witch hunts against law-
abiding citizens." He appeared on the flagship BBC program, *Panorama,*
to reveal the Gadhafi story.

The Foreign Office reciprocated with a campaign to dismiss Shayler's
claim as "completely nutty." A spokesperson told reporters, "It is incon-
ceivable that in a non-war situation the Government would authorise the
bumping off of a foreign leader." Nevertheless, the BBC reported that
Shayler maintained, "MI6 had operated out of control and illegally."
Whatever the truth of the plot, it would remain buried in the archives
of MI6.

Meanwhile, the couple had fled Britain to hide out in an isolated
farmhouse in France, where Shayler began to write a spy thriller and
Annie Machon found herself playing the traditional role of housewife:
cooking, cleaning, and tending to their needs.

Inevitably the tensions between them deepened. "We had got to know
each other in the artificial hothouse atmosphere of MI5, so we never
had a relationship outside that world. There were things I found out
about David which were unwelcome," she said in 2007. By then, they
had gone their separate ways and had long disappeared from the headlines until, in the summer of that year, David Shayler announced he was
God. The tabloids had a field day. Annie Machon said his claim was a result of the pressures from a life in intelligence. She continued to try to
promote her own account of her time at MI5.

WHILE ANNIE MACHON was getting her first glimpse of MI5's multifarious targets, in Washington, President George Herbert Walker Bush
had his focus on one target: Iraq's dictator, Saddam Hussein.

In the early stages of the Iran-Iraq War, Donald Rumsfeld, then Reagan's special envoy, had flown to Baghdad carrying in his luggage secrets that no previous American administration had shared in peacetime
with a foreign nation. They included NSA satellite images of Iran's battlefield deployment and licenses that allowed Iraq to have unfettered
access to America's arsenal of germs and chemicals developed as a defense against a Soviet threat.

The pathogens were supplied by the American Type Culture Collection, which houses the world's largest collection of germ strains in its
Virginia laboratories. Licenses for Iraq to obtain the pathogens had
been granted in 1988 by the U.S. Customs Department at Rumsfeld's re-

quest. The official reason was they would be used for "defensive purposes." In reality, Saddam would launch them against his enemy: the Kurdish population living on Iraq's border with Iran, who supported the Tehran regime. By then U.S. policy had become tilted against Iran, and the White House was blinded to the threat Iraq posed.

Charles Allen, a senior analyst at the CIA had delivered an assessment on July 20, 1990, stating that the chances for war with Iraq were better than ever. "I did sound the warning bell. Surprisingly, there were very few listeners. . . ." Four days later on July 24, 1990, William Webster had driven from Langley to see President Bush's satellite images of two Iraqi divisions—over 24,000 troops—camped on the border of Kuwait. Bush called his three personal contacts in the Middle East: the president of Egypt, the king of Saudi Arabia, and the CIA's longtime asset in the region, King Hussein of Jordan. Each reassured him: There was no intelligence to suggest Iraq would attack Kuwait.

It was only when Saddam's forces struck with a full-scale onslaught against Kuwait that he became Public Enemy Number One in the White House. Webster made sure the CIA's President's Daily Brief (PDB), was always topped by a report reflecting the mood in the Oval Office that any invasion of Kuwait was only the beginning of Saddam's dream of becoming Allah's avenger, chosen to free the Arab world from foreign domination.

In mid-August 1990, the PDB was headed by a report that Saudi Arabia was about to be attacked, the ruling dynasty deposed, and the country's oil riches turned over to its people. In London, Colin McColl asked the MI6 station commander in Riyadh to assure the king it had no intelligence of such a threat. The original report had come from a Saudi dissident dismissed by MI6 as a fantasist.

While MI6 had a network of contacts, who were mostly arms dealers, their information was often seen as suspect or self-serving, and its sheer volume at times overwhelmed the analysts charged with assessing it. Since the invasion of Kuwait, they were receiving up to a thousand reports a week: press cuttings, transcripts of broadcasts, verbatim texts of eyewitness accounts from inside Iraq. Several contained claims Saddam had a biological warfare arsenal.

Many reports were sent to the office of Dr. David Kelly; with his measured stride, his carefully barbered salt-and-pepper beard, a commanding gaze from behind his spectacles, and a clipped accent, he could pass for an off-duty submarine commander. Instead he was head of the microbiology department at Britain's Chemical and Biological Defense Establishment at Porton Down.

In the still largely secret world of how to combat the threat from biological weapons, Dr. Kelly was the voice of unchallengeable authority
regularly consulted by MI6 and MI5. When Dr. Kelly first became involved in advising the intelligence services, he found himself intrigued
by the difference in his own training as a scientist and the way their analysts worked. For them facts were often aimed at some distant, unwritten goal, while he had been trained to make his deductions from
experiments he would either create or at least re-create from the acceptable work of others. Without that yardstick everything else was suspect, often producing in him a strong skepticism.

Gradually he came to accept the ways of the analysts. Their methods
were designed to try to draw facts out of darkness, something they did
with surprising accuracy. From informers' reports, snatches of overheard conversations in some foreign country, and satellite images relayed from halfway to the moon, the analysts would make sense of
information and invite him to add his own careful judgment in support.

In Tel Aviv, the possibility that Saddam would launch rockets with
nose cones filled with anthrax and even smallpox had created understandable fear. Shabtai Shavit, the Mossad's director-general, was uncertain whether Iraq actually possessed rockets capable of carrying the
warheads into Israel. Gerald Bull, the maverick armaments designer who
had offered to build a supergun for Saddam, the range of which could
reach Israel, had been assassinated by a three-man team from Mossad's
Kidon unit. Bull was shot when he opened the door of his apartment in
Brussels, the Kidon taking turns emptying their 7.65 mm pistols into his
head and chest. Once the team was back in Tel Aviv, the Mossad's Department of Psychological Warfare fed stories to the media that Bull had been
murdered by an Iraqi hit squad because he had reneged on the deal with
Saddam Hussein. His supergun was now in pieces in the Iraqi desert, but
could Saddam still have biological or chemical weapons?

Shabtai Shavit knew the only way to be certain was to send a spy
into Iraq. The man was code-named "Shalom"—after the Mossad's legendary Shalom Weiss, who had been a member of the team that had
captured Adolf Eichmann—and was a veteran of dangerous missions.

Born in Baghdad, the eldest son of a Jewish shopkeeper who had
brought the family to Israel after Saddam seized power, Shalom had
been spotted during his obligatory service in the Israeli Defense Forces
and sent to the Mossad training school at Herzliya before undergoing
specialist training at Mossad's facility in the Negev Desert.

Shalom had completed his training to pass as a Sarami, the oldest of
the Islamic Sufi sects. At night he had slept in the Negev, eaten the food

nomads lived on, and drunk the brackish water from desert wadis. In the scorching midday sun, Shalom had run—to increase his physical stamina. At intervals during his rigorous routine, he had been assessed by a Mossad psychologist to ascertain his level of stress.

Shalom had spent a month toughening his wiry body to face the demands of what lay ahead. In the past he had been sent into Yemen and Saudi Arabia. For his mission into Iraq's western desert, Shavit had told him this was where he would most likely come across the tracks of mobile rocket launchers, which had escaped detection by the satellites due to swirling dust storms. This time there would be the added danger of having to get close enough to photograph the missile launchers.

On moonless nights an instructor had taken him deep into the Negev and rapidly shown him a sheaf of photographs of vehicles including prints of missile carriers. Shalom had to correctly identify each one at two-second intervals.

Afterward a helicopter of Israel's Special Forces, its rotor blades muffled, had flown him to the Iraqi border, and Shalom had disappeared into the pitch-black of night.

13

Glasnost in the Snow

On January 4, 1991, President George H. W. Bush made another of his speed-dial calls from the Oval Office to Israel's prime minister, Yitzhak Shamir. They had been in regular touch since Iraq had invaded Kuwait. Bush had been warned about Shamir's anti-American views, which were rooted in a belief that the United States had done little to stop the Holocaust under the presidency of Roosevelt, who had agreed with Churchill that bombing the Nazi concentration camps to give the prisoners a chance of escape was not a wartime priority.

The G. H. W. Bush administration held a well entrenched concern inherited from the Reagan presidency that Shamir had authorized passing on to the Soviet Union many of the important secrets contained in the five hundred thousand pages of documents that the Mossad's spy Jonathan Pollard had stolen while working at the U.S. Navy's most classified establishment at Suitland, Maryland. With his highest possible security clearance, Pollard had transmitted over 360 cubic feet of documents to Tel Aviv.

"It was a double blow. It had cost us every worthwhile secret we had. And it had been stolen by a country supposed to be our ally," William Casey told the author.

Before Pollard's treachery, the CIA had become overly dependent on the Mossad providing intelligence on the Middle East, though increasingly much of it was slanted to favor Israel, resulting in the CIA often misreading the situation. On that January day, though, Bush and Shamir had found an accord in dealing with Saddam Hussein.

DESPITE THE FRENETIC PACE OF EVENTS in Washington and London, time seemed to pass in slow motion as the world waited to see if there would be war with Iraq. The deadline for Saddam Hussein to withdraw from Kuwait had been set by the United Nations for Tuesday, January 15, 1991—and interpreted in Washington as expiring at noon Eastern Standard Time on that day.

American and coalition forces were massing in Kuwait, while in Baghdad Saddam continued to shout defiance over Iraqi Radio.

In London, the Joint Intelligence Committee met daily to assess how the war would directly affect Britain. The consensus was that the likeliest threat would be a series of terrorist attacks by Iraqi "sleeper" agents in the country using biological or chemical weapons. Porton Down, the U.K.'s main military research facility, sent a team of specialists to London equipped with a range of antidotes. Dr. David Kelly, a biological weapons expert, camped out in the basement of the Ministry of Defense, catnapping in between endless planning meetings.

"It was agreed that we only had enough antidotes to deal with an attack on London, and then we would only be able to deal with people essential to the city's defense. We knew we could do nothing about other cities if they were attacked," Dr. Kelly recalled.

MI5 and MI6 drew up a list of "known Saddam sympathizers," and over seven hundred were deported following an intensive MI5 surveillance operation under the direction of Stella Rimington, who had just been appointed to one of the two deputy director-general posts in the Security Service. Her new position made her the first woman to hold such high office in the Security Service, and at times Rimington still found that some of her male colleagues "had difficulty treating a senior woman like a human being." Exceptions were Colin McColl and John Adye, the director-general of GCHQ, who recognized Rimington had a critical role in the defense of the realm.

Elsewhere the countdown to war continued: An internment camp was set up on Salisbury Plain to hold any more Arabs caught in the surveillance operation, and cells were put aside in the prison at York. Not since World War II had such precautions been taken.

WITH FIVE DAYS REMAINING for the deadline with Iraq to expire, intelligence continued to flow into the Oval Office from the CIA. Despite all expectations William Webster had kept his job as CIA director, seeing off powerful figures in the administration. One was John Sununu, the former governor of New Hampshire who had pushed hard for Robert Gates to run the CIA. Instead George H. W. Bush appointed him as deputy national security adviser and left Webster where he was in the CIA on the advice of Brent Scowcroft, a gaunt, monklike figure who had run the Washington office of Kissinger Associates, a consulting firm created by Henry Kissinger, the former secretary of state; the organization had unrivaled links to China. Scowcroft had supported Webster from the time he had run the FBI (1978–87) and recognized that as CIA director, the Judge would be a powerful ally in a plan that had been secretly created after Saddam had invaded Kuwait.

It had evolved after James Lilley, the U.S. ambassador to China and a CIA officer who had served in Laos, Taiwan, and Beijing, had produced evidence that revealed the role China had played in equipping Saddam's army by supplying a thousand tanks, nine thousand antitank weapons, 150 F-7 jet aircraft, and twelve million shells and mines, along with four billion rounds of small-arms ammunition.

China had also provided Iraq with large quantities of lithium-6, a key component in the manufacture of a nuclear bomb. Throughout 1990, the China National Nonferrous Metals Import-Export Corporation had shipped several dozen bottles of the grayish white granular substance to Baghdad. Each bottle contained 250 grams of lithium-6 encased in lead, bearing labels stating the contents were for use in Iraq's medical laboratories. A planeload of Chinese nuclear scientists and technicians, many of whom had helped China successfully test its own hydrogen bomb, had flown into Baghdad's Saddam Airport.

Central to the plan was a decision by President G. H. W. Bush that China's arming of Iraq would not become an issue in the war "to restore Kuwait's democratic right" to exist as a sovereign nation. Within the administration, those who spoke of America being ready to fight a "just war"—one that would be short and decisive, a Panama perhaps, but never another Vietnam—rarely paused to consider that democracy, as they understood it, had never existed in Kuwait. At best the Gulf Kingdom was a family-run dictatorship that employed foreign labor under harsh conditions, and abuses of human rights were commonplace. In many ways Kuwait was as repressive as Iraq or the People's Republic of China. China, as a permanent member of the U.N. Security Council, had the power to veto and effectively wreck Bush's determination to go to war unless Saddam obeyed the January 15 deadline; the Iraqi dictator had become a casus belli for the president, and at times the rhetoric from the White House matched that emanating from Baghdad.

With the collapse of Marxism-Leninism in Eastern Europe, China saw itself as the one remaining bastion against democracy. Yet in its role as Communism's great survivor, the People's Republic had given the Bush administration a hold which had become known in the upper echelons of the White House as the Tiananmen Trump.

For fifty days in 1989, Beijing students, encouraged by a million and more of their fellow citizens, had occupied Tiananmen Square and demanded the regime introduce basic democratic rights, an appeal that had held the entire world in thrall. The Chinese regime had pondered in their secluded Zhongnanhai compound close to the square what to do about the continuing protests. Their decision came with numbing ferocity. The People's Liberation Army, the government's army, swept into Tiananmen Square on the night of June 3–4, 1989. When they left, helicopters were alleged to have scooped up the bodies in nets and carried them into the Western Hills outside Beijing where they were set on fire and cremated. Estimates of the dead ranged from a few hundred to five thousand. No one would ever know the exact number.

In Washington, President Bush issued a carefully worded rebuke over the massacre. The Chinese understood Bush. His mind-set was closer to theirs than most other Western leaders' were. His words were seen for what they were: the very minimum of protest he had to make to assuage public anger across the country. Unknown to his fellow Americans, the anonymous diplomats from the State Department's China Desk had begun to meet their counterparts from the People's Republic of China Embassy a few blocks from the White House. They made their separate ways along Jackson Place to the door of number 716, a government-owned brick town house with a long history of clandestine meetings. The 113-year-old building had been where Nelson A. Rockefeller had run his investigation into the CIA's notorious domestic activities in the 1960s and former agency director Admiral Stansfield Turner had briefed President Carter about how China had allowed the CIA to station listening posts on its northern border to spy on Russia in the days when Moscow was still perceived as America's main enemy. The precise cut and thrust of the discussions, who suggested what, who asked for time to take further instructions, would remain a matter of conjecture. "All I will say is that it was like playing poker blindfolded," one of the participants told the author.

What the Bush administration wanted from the deal was crucial to Operation Desert Storm: the exact location of every Chinese Silkworm missile site in Iraq, details of every other weapon provided by China, and the whereabouts of the lithium-6. In return, Washington would end all U.S. trade restrictions imposed after the Tiananmen Square massacre and would support China's entry into the World Trade Organization and GATT (General Agreement on Tariffs and Trade) and secure for China a full resumption of World Bank lending, which had also been suspended after the student slaughter. In New York, Secretary of State James Baker met with Zhang Tuobin, China's minister of economic relations and trade, and said, "It is time to put the recent past behind us."

AFTER DESERT STORM WAS LAUNCHED, Wang Dan, one of the student leaders at Tiananmen Square, appeared before the People's Intermediate Court in midtown Beijing on January 23, 1991. He wore the sweatshirt and black baggy pants that had been his distinguishing uniform on Tiananmen Square on the night of the massacre nineteen months before. Since he had last been seen in public, he had lost weight, and his glasses kept slipping down his nose as he stood, head bowed, looking shrunken and older than his twenty-two years. The senior of his three judges, middle-aged men dressed in Mao jackets, said he was accused of attempting to overthrow the government. Wang Dan offered no defense. The senior judge said one of the court's duties was to "redeem criminals" by sentencing them to be "reeducated" and shown the way back into Chinese society through a "full understanding of Marxism." He would serve a sentence of four years or until the court was told he had "redeemed" himself. He wound up serving about two years but was later rearrested and again imprisoned for approximately three years (1995–98).

The trial had lasted only three hours—far less time than it took to reach the final agreement between the State Department and Chinese diplomats that the Bush administration would make no public criticism of Wang Dan's trial or the others that followed. On that one day, seventeen student leaders had been sentenced to imprisonment.

BRITAIN'S INTELLIGENCE SERVICES had increased surveillance of China over the following years largely because of China's activities in Africa. In April 2008, MI6 asked for one of the Royal Navy's nuclear Trident-class submarines to track a floating arsenal of weapons and bombs dispatched by the Beijing regime in China on board a rust-stained freighter, the *An Yue Jiang*, to the pariah state of President Robert Mugabe's Zimbabwe. On board were one thousand rocket-propelled grenades, two thousand mortar rounds, and three million rounds of ammunition. MI6 agents in South Africa believed the arsenal was intended to further cow Zimbabwe's starving population.

Denied landing rights by dockers in South Africa's Durban port, the freighter began to wander around the South Atlantic while Chinese officials in the home port of Ningbo sought other ports in Africa where its cargo could be unloaded and sent by road to Zimbabwe. Intelligence sources in London confirmed that secret approaches had been made to Equatorial Guinea, Benin, and the Ivory Coast. None, however, allowed the ship to dock and offload its weapons.

Tom Casey, a State Department spokesman in Washington, said, "We think that under the present circumstances and the current political crisis in Zimbabwe, now is not the time for anyone to be increasing the number of weapons and armaments available to that country. We will press African nations to refuse the *An Yue Jiang* docking rights or to face worsened relations with the United States."

At 450 feet long and weighing 16,000 tons, the black-hulled Trident submarine covered with sonar-absorbing anechoic tiles tracked the freighter and sent short-burst communications to the Admiralty in London. Naval intelligence sources said the possibility "cannot be ruled out" that the ship could travel to Venezuela, whose maverick leader, President Hugo Chavez, has a good relationship with China and is an opponent of the United States.

"Chavez is a skilled player on the international stage and he could say he was offering to refuel the ship on humanitarian grounds. The weapons could then be transferred to a Venezuelan registered ship and repackaged for Zimbabwe," one ship's broker at Lloyd's, the world's largest shipping broker, told the author. The Trident—one of four in the fleet which is based in Faslane on Scotland's Clyde—continued to track the freighter until it suddenly hurried back to its home port in late May 2008.

A month later MI6 analysts had once more involved GCHQ in confirming that China had built a major naval base deep inside caverns on the South China Sea island of Hainan. Using high-resolution satellite images, the analysts decided the base could contain up to twenty of the latest C94 Jin-Class submarines, each equipped with antisatellite missiles and nuclear-tipped rockets. Knocking out the satellites would effectively leave Taiwan, Japan, and other countries around the Pacific Rim without a key warning system. An attack would also disrupt vital communications between U.S. battle squadrons in the region and Washington. The Trident on patrol off Africa joined the U.S. Pacific Fleet to help establish a clear image of what was happening inside the secret base. Naval intelligence officers in London and Washington confirmed that the discovery of the base would present "a significant challenge to U.S. naval dominance and protection to countries ringing the South China Sea."

The base, a.k.a. Yulin, was sited at Sanya on the southern tip of Hainan Island. The island came to the attention of Western intelligence in April 2001, when a U.S. EP-3 spy plane trying to test the island's electronic defenses was forced to land there by Chinese fighters, one of which crashed in the sea, killing the pilot.

The twenty-four U.S. crewmen on board, including specialist technicians, brought the first international crisis to the administration of George W. Bush.

One of the advantages of the base is that Chinese submarines can sail from there already submerged into deep Pacific water—exceeding fifteen thousand feet—making their detection that much harder.

In comparison, Britain's Trident submarines have to remain on the surface when they leave their base in northwest Scotland and cannot submerge to patrol depth until they are beyond the Irish Sea. Intelligence analyst Alex Neill at the Asia Security Program in London, which works closely with MI6, said the Sanya base "is a clear indication that Beijing is preparing for wider operations in the Far East and very possibly beyond." Another Ministry of Defense analyst, who cannot be named for security reasons, believed "this could be the prelude to China preparing for a nuclear response."

More certain is that Chinese defense spending could be as high as $200 billion. Kerry Brown, a China analyst at the Royal Institute of International Affairs in London, said the secret base is part of "a sea denial campaign which will prevent the United States intervening in any conflict with Taiwan. The base's submarine fleet will use their antisatellite missiles to ensure that U.S. satellites over the Pacific would be 'blind' and unable to keep the Pentagon in touch. The fact is that China is determined to challenge the power of the U.S. Pacific Command. The Sanya base is just a start."

Meanwhile GCHQ satellites had confirmed that agents of the Chinese People's Liberation Army, the PLA, posing as monks, had triggered the riots which left hundreds of Tibetans dead or injured. GCHQ analysts believed the decision to do so was deliberately engineered by the Beijing leadership to provide an excuse to stamp out the simmering unrest in the region, which was already attracting unwelcome world attention in the run-up to the 2008 Olympic Games.

For weeks there had been growing resentment in Lhasa, Tibet's capital, against actions taken by the Chinese authorities. Monks had led acts of civil disobedience, demanding the right to perform traditional incense-burning rituals. With their demands went cries for the return of the Dalai Lama, the fourteenth to hold the high spiritual office. Committed to teaching the tenets of his moral authority—peace and compassion—the Dalai Lama was fifteen years old when the PLA invaded Tibet in 1950 and was forced to flee to India in 1959, from where he has run a relentless campaign against the harshness of Chinese rule. He received the Nobel Peace Prize in 1989, the year of the Tiananmen Square massacre, but critics have criticized his attraction to film stars. Newspaper magnate Rupert Murdoch has called him, "A very political monk in Gucci shoes."

Discovering that his supporters inside Tibet would become even more active in the months approaching the Games, MI6 officers in Beijing learned the ruling regime would seek an excuse to move and crush the unrest. That fear was publicly expressed by the Dalai Lama. GCHQ's satellites were tasked to closely monitor the situation.

The images they downloaded from satellites provided confirmation that the Chinese had used agents provocateurs to start riots, which gave the PLA the excuse to move on Lhasa to kill and wound. What the Beijing regime had not expected was how the riots would spread, not only across Tibet, but also to Sichuan, Qinghai, and Gansu provinces, turning a large area of western China into a battle zone.

The Dalai Lama called it "cultural genocide" and offered to resign to bring peace, however, his followers did not listen to his "message of compassion." Many of them were young, unemployed, and dispossessed, and they rejected his philosophy of nonviolence. For Beijing, the need to urgently find a solution to the uprising became one of growing embarrassment during the spring of 2008, but once more, as had happened in the past, the demonstrations in Tibet abruptly stopped.

The Chinese prime minister said he was prepared to hold talks with the Dalai Lama. An hour before this announcement, Britain's prime minister Gordon Brown declared he would meet the Dalai Lama on his visit to London. This was the first time either leader has proposed to meet the Dalai Lama. Brown treated the visit as that of only a religious leader and insisted on meeting the Dalai Lama in a bishop's palace and not, where he would normally receive distinguished leaders, in Downing Street. Many people saw it as a snub.

THE BRIEF GULF WAR had ended with Saddam Hussein still in power. White House policy, not CIA intelligence, had dictated the outcome of the conflict. President G. H. W. Bush had promised the American people the fighting would last less than one hundred hours when ground operations started in earnest on February 24, 1991, and he called an end to the hostilities on February 27, 1991. Webster was told to have the CIA track Saddam's movements; the agents knew he had six Winnebago RVs and three were located and destroyed. The others, with Saddam supposedly in one, were not traced until months later, when they were found abandoned close to the border with Syria. Meanwhile, in Washington, Bush had publicly urged the Shiites in the south of the country and the Kurds in the north "to put aside Saddam and bring Iraq back into the family of peace-loving nations." While the U.S. and coalition forces stood by, there were mass uprisings by a people poorly armed. They were crushed by the Republican Guards. Overnight in Washington the call to rid Iraq of its "evil dictator" changed to "Bring home our victorious boys," a slogan that was designed to ensure G. H. W. Bush's stay in the White House. Bill Clinton still became the next president.

ON AUGUST 2, 1991, a C-160 Transall, painted white and displaying the bold markings of the United Nations, landed at Saddam Airport outside Baghdad. Dr. David Kelly, the biological weapons expert, led his team of twenty-eight weapons inspectors off the aircraft. Like Dr. Kelly, each man who would help him to search for biological weapons had been chosen for his expertise: microbiologists, biotechnology experts, and munitions and safety specialists. They came from half a dozen countries and between them spoke double that number of languages, including Arabic. Accompanying them were members of the SAS and Delta Force, as well as MI6 and CIA officers. They, too, had been specially selected, and their task was to deal with any threat to the inspectors.

Dr. Kelly had previous experience of conducting such an investigation. He had carried out the inspection of Russian factories and laboratories in the Biopreparat program after the signature of the still secret trilateral Russo-Anglo-American Treaty outlawing all such weapons following the collapse of the Soviet Union. That inspection had been conducted in a spirit of cooperation, but Dr. Kelly had warned his team they should expect hostility from the Saddam regime, which had been forced by the United Nations to facilitate the inspection, and Kelly had spent the summer preparing for what he realized would be a potentially dangerous mission. "The sites we wanted to check could be contaminated with biological or chemical agents or booby-trapped with bombs or mines," he told the author when they met in the Baghdad Sheraton Hotel.

With an attention to detail that had made him the first choice to lead the team, Dr. Kelly had briefed them on the "dirty tricks" they should expect from their Iraqi government minders.

"From the first day onward they used every way to delay or mislead us by refusing to produce documents and then claiming the listed items, such as vaccines, were part of a defensive program against biological attacks by Israel," recalled Dr. Kelly.

Salman Pak, to the southeast of Baghdad, was the first on his list of suspected biological sites. Ignoring the protests of his minders that the visit should be "properly arranged," Dr. Kelly led his team there. Waiting for them was Dr. Rihab Taha, the director of the facility. In her early thirties with a broad forehead, pointy chin, and bouffant hairstyle, Taha "vacillated between nervous wariness and prickly defensiveness. She had good English, having acquired a PhD in toxicology from the University of East Anglia. But when my questions didn't appeal to her, she would burst into Arabic and start to cry. Quite the little actress," Dr. Kelly recalled.

Dr. Taha had clung to her story. The biological research work at Salman Pak had been in its infancy and had been destroyed by the precision bombing in the first stage of the war. She had waved her hands and shouted, "The evidence for you to see is all around you."

For five days, meeting growing hostility from the Iraqi minders, Dr. Kelly and his team picked over the bomb rubble, noting that what could have been an aerosolization chamber, signs of animal cages, the remains at chemical storage areas, shreds of protective clothing, and pieces of filters indicated the research had been far more advanced than Rihab Taha had claimed. "Our problem was that after the end of the war there had been time for her to hide the truth. I had a strong suspicion there was a potential gun—but it was not smoking" was how Dr. Kelly saw it.

Then, to his surprise, Dr. Taha had tried to bargain. From a locked cupboard in her own office, she produced bottles of bacterial microorganisms. "They are part of the supplies Mr. Rumsfeld arranged for us to have in those days when we were an ally of America," she said, not bothering to hide her bitterness.

Dr. Kelly had inspected the still sealed vials.

"We did not use them. It is not the kind of work we did here," she insisted.

Dr. Kelly had pointed at the labels on the bottles: anthrax, botulinum, gangrene, tetanus, and tularemia. He noted them and her explanation for their presence.

"The Americans said we could use them to create vaccines against Israeli weapons. What you see here is the full extent of our biological military program."

She thrust a sheaf of paper at Dr. Kelly and asked him to write a note confirming he accepted that as the truth. He declined.

Meanwhile, other UN teams sent to search for chemical and nuclear weapons were given priority over the hunt for biological weapons, and the logistical support Dr. Kelly was promised—cars, radios, and an increase in security after shots were fired at his team—failed to materialize. The mood in New York among senior UN personnel was that his work had less urgency and was less likely to yield results. On his last day in Baghdad, Dr. Kelly told the author, "They've closed the door on understanding the full extent of Saddam's biological program."

Dr. Kelly returned to London certain another opportunity would come. From all he had heard and seen, he was convinced Saddam would continue his program of creating biological weapons. To prove it would require further visits, taking more risks in an increasingly hostile country, and dealing with all the other pressures from his work. Not for a moment did he think during that August in 1991 he would become the victim of those pressures.

FROM HER BEDROOM WINDOW, Stella Rimington had watched the Moscow River first ice over and then become covered with an unbroken field of snow, and across from her vantage point in the British Embassy, the cobblestones of Red Square had disappeared in the first snowfalls as the long Russian winter arrived. Only a few days had passed since she had left behind London and the constant arguments to ensure that the budget for MI5's new headquarters at Thames House came in on time, a responsibility that was another addition to her substantial workload.

MI5's caustic director, Michael Hanley, had fumed to Rimington about the insensate demands of the Treasury to "substantiate and justify all expenditure." Once more Whitehall was in the grip of cutbacks, and resource management echoed throughout the corridors of the intelligence services. Rimington had regularly accompanied Hanley in the past year to what he called "damned Star Chamber meetings" where ministers probed every expense.

Standing at that window in December 1991 somehow made them worthwhile. The constant financial nitpicking, she had told herself, was more than made up for by coming to Moscow as a guest of her old enemy, the KGB.

The invitation had come as unexpectedly as the sudden total collapse of the Soviet Union. While its spies had been a prime target for Rimington virtually from the day she joined MI5 and were, of course, still there, the end of the cold war meant the service was urgently in need of a new purpose.

Many KGB spies saw no future in a society whose leaders had agreed to form a commonwealth of independent states, though few had any clear understanding of what that meant. Beggars on the streets spoke of glasnost as if it were the cure for the growing economic breakdown, where babushkas sold cups of homemade gruel and Moscow's Gum department store had little on its shelves; a world where schoolgirls offered their bodies to the first tourists who had come to see the once "evil empire" and paid for shabby sex with fistfuls of rubles that changed in value daily.

Some of the KGB men found jobs in Libya, Iran, and Latin America as "advisers" to their intelligence services. Other colleagues remained, hoping for the best, expecting the worst. The KGB had a deserved history of violence and criminality. Blackmail and extortion were a means for many of its officers to supplement their meager state salaries.

Stella Rimington had come to Moscow to show them how they could adapt themselves to serving a fledgling democracy and learn that while intelligence gathering was still important in the defense of that democracy, it was compatible with the laws and controls that must inevitably form part of it. She would give them advice on how to recruit and train new personnel to replace the cold war veterans who, so she believed, "were tainted by their activities under Communism."

It was not purely goodwill that had prompted her visit. The idea had been Prime Minister Margaret Thatcher's when she had invited Colin McColl to lunch and had explained the advantage for both MI5 and MI6 in supporting the diplomatic initiatives with the new commonwealth. She had told Mikhail Gorbachev he was the sort of man she "could do business with," and that included helping to develop a new KGB that would no longer spy on Britain and, at the same time, would provide valuable information for its intelligence services. Rimington saw the sense of what Thatcher had said but nevertheless felt "it was as if suddenly everything was turned on its head, but nothing was impossible."

She had briefed herself thoroughly on the changes under way in the KGB but had come to Moscow still not certain what to expect. In her twenty years of combating Soviet espionage, she had never for a moment anticipated she would be a guest of honor in KGB headquarters, part of which contained the Lubyanka Prison. The new head of the KGB, Vadim Bakatin, appointed after the failed coup against Gorbachev the previous August, had already begun the process of breaking up the old KGB and creating a new agency to deal only with intelligence and counterintelligence. The KGB border guards had been transferred to police control, and the directorate responsible for protecting the leadership was no longer part of the new agency.

That wintry morning as Stella Rimington prepared for another meeting with the Russians, she felt that between them "we could crack the problems of terrorism and organized crime for all time."

NO ONE, INCLUDING RIMINGTON, was aware that in a cave in the Tora Bora mountains of Afghanistan, Osama bin Laden continued to fulminate against the "infidel forces" that had launched Desert Storm and the Saudi royal family who had allowed them to set foot in the Land of the Two Holy Sanctuaries. On his thirty-fourth birthday, he promised the small but growing number of followers gathered to congratulate him he would soon deal with the "apostasy" of Arab rulers who were cooperating with the West before dealing with the "infidels."

IN THE AMERICAN EMBASSY in Moscow during Christmas week in December 1991, Ambassador Robert Strauss put down the telephone and turned to the CIA station chief. "Bakatin wants me to come over. Says he wants to give me a present. Maybe it's a crate of that vodka they served at dinner for Rimington," Strauss recalled saying.

"Let's hope she doesn't get sucked in by all this talk of change," replied the veteran spy.

For every foreign diplomat and intelligence officer in Moscow, the continuing sheer speed of what was happening was breathtaking. Outside the blocks of apartments where embassy staff and their families lived, the surveillance cars were no longer visible. Diplomats had their calls swiftly returned from the Foreign Ministry by suddenly friendly voices. When Strauss emerged from Spaso House, his official residence, there was no longer a Zil limousine following. And, one time, as the CIA station chief made his morning run along the bank of the Moskva River, a member of the MBR, the Russian internal security force who usually ran some distance behind, came alongside and, in excellent English, spoke about sports on what would be the last day the CIA chief would see his tail.

Strauss had enjoyed several meetings with Bakatin over leisurely lunches and dinners when the final toast had been to a new Russian-American friendship. The ambassador did not doubt the KGB's hopes, but he remained concerned that the alacrity of what was happening could derail such optimism.

To collect his gift, Strauss had driven to Bakatin's office in the Kremlin. The last time he had been there was to see Vladimir Kryuchkov, a stocky man with a strong smell of cigar smoke on his breath and a chest full of medals for his service to Russia, a reminder of his fourteen years in the First Chief Directorate. To Strauss's surprise, Kryuchkov had initially accepted the reforms Gorbachev had introduced, but he quickly became resistant to them, recognizing they would be the end of the KGB he knew. Even so, he had refused to become involved in the coup to overthrow the Russian parliament, where Boris Yeltsin had continued to implement changes. Nevertheless, Yeltsin had replaced Kryuchkov with Bakatin, who had quickly demonstrated his support for reform by inviting Stella Rimington to Moscow.

Before she had arrived, Bakatin had ordered that the wife and daughters of Oleg Gordievsky should be allowed to travel to England to join the double agent who had done more damage to the KGB than any other traitor.

"I hoped it would be a clear signal to London that for us it was no longer business as usual," Bakatin later said. Soon, in a mood to placate the hard-liners who still had influence in Moscow, Yeltsin was persuaded to replace Bakatin with a new head of the restructured intelligence organization more to their liking. He was Yevgeni Primakov, and the KGB was renamed the SVR (Federal Intelligence Service).

On that December morning, there was no hint to Ambassador Strauss that Bakatin would become a victim of the plotters in their Kremlin offices. He had been his smiling self, offering coffee and freshly baked cookies from the Kremlin kitchen to his guest. The small talk had been about unseasonably early snowfalls and the ambassador's plans for the holiday season. Suddenly Bakatin stood up.

"And with that," Strauss recalled, "he went over to his safe and pulled out a big file and a suitcase. He opened it, and it was filled with high-tech devices. Then he turned to the file and took out what looked like blueprints."

Strauss had looked at them, wondering what they could be. Bakatin had smiled broadly at him, indicating the blueprints.

"Mr. Ambassador, these are the plans we used to bug your embassy." He pointed to the suitcase. "These are the listening devices we used. They are your gift."

Strauss was too astonished to speak. Bakatin picked out a bug from the suitcase and handed it to the ambassador. "Your CIA chief would, I am sure, be most interested to see these. So I want you to have them. There will be no, as you say, strings attached."

Strauss later told James Adams, the former Washington bureau chief of the London *Sunday Times,* he feared "some kind of entrapment" and refused to accept the suitcase and the file. He returned to the embassy and discussed the matter with the CIA station chief. Encrypted signals to Langley resulted in Strauss collecting the gift. It was sent in the diplomatic bag to Langley, and for months CIA technicians studied the bugs and the blueprints. Despite signs that Russia would continue to move toward creating a more democratic intelligence agency, Congress decided to spend $220 million on building a new embassy fitted with state-of-the-art antibugging devices.

STELLA RIMINGTON, FOR ALL THE ENDLESS BANQUETS in the splendor of the Kremlin's salons and the glowing tributes to her for having achieved such a high position in MI5, would be returning to London with one abiding memory. She had already filed through the Stalin mausoleum, passed the tourists posing with his look-alike (his arm around the shoulder of each visitor, somehow a lethal reminder of the hold over the entire nation Stalin once had) for a few rubles, and had been driven to Chekhov's house and attended the Bolshoi ballet, sitting in one of the gilt armchairs in the front row of the prime seats reserved for guests of the government.

Each had a place in her recollection, but her last evening in Moscow had also evoked a memory, one less agreeable. Rimington, with the style of the thriller writer she hoped one day to become, set the scene.

"In the dark, cold, and snowy night," she had been driven in the British ambassador's Rolls-Royce to what she took to be an old KGB safe house. She found it difficult to avoid feeling that she had "somehow slipped into a James Bond film and that reality had become confused with fiction."

As she removed her snowboots inside the dacha, the forbidding figure of Yevgeni Primakov appeared at the top of the shadowy staircase, the low lighting giving his face an ethereal look. When he spoke, his voice had a husky tone as if he had a permanent cold. He explained the house had once been the office of Lavrenti Beria, Stalin's confidante, whose reputation as one of the most ruthless spies in the Russian secret service had survived long after his death. Primakov had trained as a journalist for *Pravda,* a cover for his later work as a KGB intelligence officer in Cairo, Damascus, and Baghdad.

"We went upstairs to a lamplit sitting room furnished with heavy curtains and behind which anything could have been lurking. We had a brief, rather cool discussion. I asserted that there was much scope for cooperation on security matters, like terrorism and serious organised crime. However, if there was to be true cooperation, the level of espionage on the U.K. should be reduced," Rimington recalled.

Her request drew a stinging rebuke. The idea was "ridiculous," said Primakov. His spies would continue to operate "for the defence of Russia how they chose." Rimington decided it was time to leave, and with the briefest of good nights her host disappeared behind the curtains, completing her impression she had indeed stepped into a Bond set.

DURING THE 1991 CHRISTMAS PARTY SEASON, the speculation inside Century House revolved around who would be the next director-general. Patrick Walker, the incumbent, would be sixty years old the following February. During his three years in office, he had tried to strike a balance between reforms and Prime Minister Thatcher's constant demand at the outset of her first term to be aware of what she had called "the enemy within."

Walker was very aware that each step he took to continue the reforms his predecessor, Antony Duff, had introduced—encouraging younger persons to join the Security Service and expanding the circulation of Eyes Only files beyond the upper echelon of government so junior ministers could be better informed—had to pass the scrutiny of Thatcher.

No other prime minister since Churchill had taken so close an interest in MI5. Every morning Thatcher had received a summary of overnight intelligence reports, which she read over breakfast and returned to Century House with her comments underlined in blue ink; phrases like "beware of this" or "take immediate action" regularly appeared. When an item particularly interested her, she would note it down and raise it at the next meeting of the Joint Intelligence Committee. She was the only prime minister to have attended those secret conclaves on the second floor of the Cabinet Office. On more than one occasion she had reminded her somewhat startled listeners they must not forget that "the enemy within" could still be lurking within both MI5 and MI6. Her chancellor of the exchequer, Nigel Lawson, who had headed off his own daughter, Nigella, from being a spy, once said, "Margaret was positively besotted by Frederick Forsyth's thrillers about spies." At her private meetings with Walker, Thatcher had frequently asked if some secret he had told her could be trusted in other hands. She would add, "There are forces at work you must watch."

While there were grounds for her concerns, some were based on the fantasy of others. There was Peter Wright's bizarre claim that the former Labour prime minister Harold Wilson had been a Soviet spy—a paranoid view that led to Wright, once a rising star in MI5, being branded mad and dangerous by his colleagues before Walker had fired him. There was more reason for her to worry about those who followed the trio of betrayers—Philby, Burgess, and Maclean, brilliant men who had sold out their country. How had they survived discovery for so long? She had read their files and was, she admitted, none the wiser. More recently was the dowdily dressed Cathy Massiter, who had assiduously worked alongside Stella Rimington and then astonished everyone by one day resigning and appearing in the newspapers to say she had been ordered to conduct "inappropriate investigations" into trade union leaders and supporters of the campaign for nuclear disarmament. Then David Shayler had run his campaign that MI6 had tried to assassinate Colonel Gadhafi.

Not only Margaret Thatcher but also Patrick Walker wondered who else was waiting to emerge and cause further embarrassment to those charged with the defense of the realm.

Patrick Walker had a sharp, analytical mind developed from his days as an intelligence officer in the Colonial Service and then in Northern Ireland when the IRA had run rampant. He had no real answer, though, as to how it was possible for men and women who had offered their services to defend their country to betray it. Perhaps it was something in their makeup that had escaped attention during their psychological screening, he had surmised.

Certainly the question remained unresolved in his mind when Stella Rimington reported to the Monday morning senior staff meeting before Christmas. After she had delivered a crisp account of her trip to Moscow, the discussion turned to the continuing growth in global crime networks, including those in the Russian federal republics, and the need to combat them as a priority.

One group was the Rising Sun, Moscow's largest criminal family run by Semyon Yukovich Mogilevich, a Ukranian-born Jew who had established over fifty front companies around the world through which to launder vast sums of money from his activities in drug trafficking and gunrunning to the Middle East. Walker authorized an investigation to establish whether Mogilevich's companies had any links in the City of London.

The meeting moved on to discuss the continuing arrival of still more

Islamic groups in London. He wanted an assessment of the threat they posed.

One after another, Walker had made his requests. Thirty minutes after its start, the meeting ended. As his staff started to leave his office, Walker motioned for Rimington to remain seated. When the door closed on the last of her colleagues, he stood up and walked to her, hand extended.

"Congratulations, Stella. You are to be the next director-general."

She had not known what to say. She could only think that no one asked her if she wanted the job and wonder what Walker would have said if she had refused. He spoke again: "By the way, Stella, your name will be publicly announced. I'm sure you understand why."

She did. She would be the first woman to head the Security Service. She knew it would cause a media sensation.

THE INTENSELY PRIVATE RIMINGTON found herself at the center of a maelstrom of headlines for which neither she nor MI5 was prepared. She became the "Housewife Superspy," "Queen of All Our Secrets," and, inevitably, "MI5 Wife in Secret Love Split," a tabloid headline to give a little spice to her separation from her husband some years before. The *Sunday Times* hired a private investigator to access her bank account and even found a small sum it claimed had been deposited by the head of the KGB. Another newspaper ran a competition asking readers to provide the best story about the "Woman of Mystery." The new director-general found herself chased like any celebrity, being photographed unloading her weekly groceries from her car, and some of the newspaper photos carried black bands across her eyes to heighten the mystery of who she was. They saw it as fun, the cheeky side of Fleet Street. Rimington was less amused: IRA terrorism was a serious threat, and she knew killing her would be almost as great a triumph for the IRA as its bomb attack on Margaret Thatcher at the Grand Hotel in Brighton. While there was nothing she—anybody—could do to stop the media interest, she began to take precautions that, until then, she had never needed to implement, employing the tricks she had been taught in her surveillance course on how to avoid being followed.

Within MI5 her appointment was on the whole welcomed, especially among the growing number of women who had moved up from being secretaries and clerks to full-fledged intelligence officers, largely due to her encouragement.

Among the first to congratulate her was Jonathan Evans, who had worked in counterterrorism in Northern Ireland before returning to Century House and well understood how the IRA targeted security officers. Evans was a sympathetic listener, a throwback to his days at Bristol University when he had studied classics and was always ready to offer a helping hand to any student who was having a problem with a term paper. One of his professors later recalled Evans as "someone who would have made a good lecturer, perhaps even gone on to a professorship." Instead, Evans had joined MI5 in 1980 and had moved steadily up through counterterrorism to take charge of in-house security and later, after his return from Ulster, to advise the Home Office how to better protect visiting dignitaries.

A quiet and polite man with a receding hairline, which made him look older than his years, Evans had been one of the young officers marked down for fast-tracking, and he had been appointed to implement the policy changes Walker had left unfinished.

In his spare time, he had chosen a subject to study: the politicizing of modern Islam. He became fascinated with how it developed from the power struggle between the House of Saud monarchy and the fundamentalism of Ayatollah Khomeini and how later Saddam Hussein, a secularist, had mobilized Iraq's religious groups to keep them out of Khomeini's control, a decision that had led to the seven-year war between their nations. From the mishmash of groups that emerged from that conflict, Evans had become intrigued by al-Qaeda and its messianic leader, Osama bin Laden.

In 1991, bin Laden had set up his "Base" in a huge, well-guarded compound outside Khartoum, which was protected by the Sudanese military regime. As well as al-Qaeda's original Afghan freedom fighters, who had driven out the Russian troops, bin Laden's reputation had attracted tribesmen from Somalia and Yemen to join him. He called them the "true mujahideen" who, in the name of the Prophet Mohammed, would overthrow the Riyadh regime. Every day as he repeated this promise, standing beside him was his most important associate, the portly Egyptian academic Ayman al-Zawahiri, the cleric who reminded his daily religious classes of the tenets of jihad: that once Islam is attacked, every Muslim must be ready to give up his life in its defense. He told his students that in all Sheikh bin Laden said, he was preparing them to resist an attack on Islam being prepared by America, the Great Satan.

The photographs of both bin Laden and al-Zawahiri were among the first images Jonathan Evans placed in the file he opened on al-Qaeda.

EVANS'S INTEREST IN THE GROUP had been furthered in 1989 when he had met Dr. David Kelly during a visit to Porton Down. The microbiologist had just returned from Montreal, where he had assisted the Canadian RCMP intelligence service by confirming that thirty-two metric tons of growth bacterial medium could be used for biological warfare purposes. It had been discovered in a warehouse along the St. Lawrence Freeway and was destined for Iraq; its export license described it as "for medical purposes only." The warehouse had been leased from a Sudanese businessman with an address in London. He had been interviewed by Scotland Yard detectives and insisted he had rented the warehouse to a Khartoum-based charity to send medical equipment to Iraq. By the time MI5 had discovered the charity was part of al-Qaeda, the businessman was back in Sudan.

Both Evans and Dr. Kelly saw the incident as a sign that the increasingly powerful al-Qaeda and Osama bin Laden could not be dismissed as fanatics simply looking for a cause. From his research, Evans knew that within the group were doctors, engineers, and men like that businessman who had, until now, remained outside the traditional circles of Arab political power. Al-Qaeda promised Utopia and an end to those Arab regimes soiled by corruption and moral bankruptcy from their close ties to the West.

DR. KELLY'S TRIP TO CANADA was one of many he undertook to advise government organizations on how to provide defenses against deadly toxins, viruses, and bacteria in the hands of hostile nations and terror groups. He had met other experts and shared their experiences. Nothing, though, had prepared him for the telephone call he received in the second week of October 1989 from Royal Navy Surgeon-Commander Christopher Davis of the Defense Intelligence Staff. An expert on chemical and biological weapons, Davis asked Dr. Kelly to come to his office in the Metropole Building near Trafalgar Square in London. When Dr. Kelly arrived, Davis greeted him with a broad smile.

"We've got a walk-in. Our first primary source inside the Soviet BW program. Name of Vladimir Pasechnik. We need you to help debrief him."

Dr. Vladimir Pasechnik was one of Russia's most senior biochemists in its biological warfare program. His own specialty was DNA sequencing, highly sophisticated research that played an important role in developing weaponized germs. Now, in one of those classic spy novel moments, the fifty-three-year-old biologist had strolled out of a drug industry fair in Paris in 1989, telling his colleagues he was going to buy souvenirs for his wife and children back home in Leningrad. Instead he had hailed a taxi and asked to be driven to the British Embassy. Until then he had made no contact with a foreign country's embassy. After he had told a startled receptionist he was a Russian scientist who wanted to defect, he was shown into a waiting room with its formal portrait of the Queen on one wall.

A junior diplomat arrived. Pasechnik produced his official Soviet Ministry of Defense ID and some documents in Russian. The diplomat took them and left. Moments later the embassy's MI6 resident officer came in. He questioned Pasechnik, taking shorthand notes. Davis had shown Dr. Kelly a transcript. It began with Pasechnik's words, "I am part of Biopreparat, a large secret program which is devoted to research, development, and production of biological weapons in the USSR. I worked with *Yersinia pestis*."

Dr. Kelly had paused and looked at Dr. Davis. Neither man said a word. Dr. Kelly continued to read the priority message and realized Pasechnik was not only that rarity—an important walk-in defector—but he would be able to fill in the gaps NSA satellites could never close: what was going on inside the laboratories. He could explain the command structure, who gave the orders, who carried them out, how the Soviet Union had managed to breach the Biological Warfare Convention it had signed in 1972, where it had concealed its laboratories and storage depots for its weapons, and how many were there—and tell them how far he had gone with weaponizing *Yersinia pestis*, known to the world as the plague, the Black Death that had wiped out a third of the population of Europe in 1348, transmitting its spores by a pneumonia-like cough. Plague would be a "wildfire weapon," intended to spread death in an uncontrollable manner.

As soon as he set eyes upon the Russian, Dr. Kelly liked what he saw, he would recall. Pasechnik was squat with a wrestler's torso and a seamed face, but it was his hands that fascinated Dr. Kelly: They were farmer's hands, thick fingers with skin leathered by the elements. He spoke almost no English, but a translator was on hand and Pasechnik had already been given his MI6 code name, "Truncate." Dr. Kelly had no time to wonder how the name had been chosen; from his expectations, Pasechnik had so much information to impart, it would take weeks to analyze it.

Vladimir Pasechnik had been the chief director of the Institute for Ultra-Pure Biological Preparations in Leningrad (now St. Petersburg). Working with a variety of superbugs, the four hundred scientists and technicians at the institute had been adapting cruise missiles to spread the plague and smallpox. It was that which had finally decided Pasechnik to defect.

"I want the West to know. There must be a way to stop this madness," he had told the debriefing team.

For hours at a time, sipping black coffee laced with cognac, Pasechnik described how, instead of producing the pneumonia-like cough that had decimated medieval Europe over a period of many months, unmanned Soviet craft, flying close to the speed of sound, would kill millions in a matter of minutes as they distributed their deadly payloads.

"The really terrifying thing was that I knew Vladimir was telling the truth. There was no waffle. When he didn't know something, he said he didn't know. That's what made what he was certain about even more terrifying," Dr. Kelly later said to the author.

Pasechnik's brief had been to engineer germs and bacteria against which "the West would have no defense." He received an annual salary of less than three thousand dollars. For this he had worked seven days a week, with only a brief annual vacation. Pasechnik had corrected, confirmed, and clarified how the Russians had re-created their old biological warfare program after signing the convention document in 1972. At the end of his debriefing, Dr. Kelly echoed the words of all those who had listened for the past three months to Pasechnik's story, "It was truly horrifying."

14

The Bamboo Curtain Spies

In 2002, the American Embassy compound in Beijing occupied most of one side of Xiu Bei Jie in the city's foreign legation quarter. Tall iron railings separated the ill-kept roadway, the city's responsibility to maintain, from the pathways and lawns the embassy gardeners tended as carefully as those outside any federal building in Washington. During the hours of daylight, Chinese passersby stopped and peered through the railings, perhaps envious so much ground was landscaped when it could be put to good use rearing ducks or raising crops. They were not allowed to linger too long before being moved on by the rifle-toting soldiers in olive uniforms and forage caps; they were most numerous around the compound's entrance, watching everyone who came and left.

The real surveillance took place from the cars parked opposite, day and night; the vehicles contained agents of the Chinese secret intelligence service (MSS), who were in radio contact with one of several MSS buildings scattered across the city. Counterintelligence was on West Qiananmen Street. Foreign intelligence operated from a modern building near the city's main railway station. The training school was behind the Long Distance Telephone Office on Fuxingmennei Avenue. Political analysts were housed near the Workers' Stadium, overlooking the road to the international airport.

Most secretive of all was the Investigation Bureau, situated in a building close to the southern end of the lake in Zhongnanhai, the leadership compound in the lee of the Forbidden City, from where the emperors had ruled for seven hundred years. One of the first decisions the survivors of the Long Walk had made after Mao Zedong proclaimed a new China on October 1, 1949, was to turn Zhongnanhai into one of the most fortified enclaves on earth. There were guard posts cut into trees, each niche just large enough to hide a man, and in the wooden pavilions dotting the parkland, and concealed in shrubbery. Sensors, trip wires, and CCTV cameras completed the security. No aircraft was allowed to overfly the compound's 250 acres, and only the sound of helicopters ferrying the old men to and from their summer palaces in the hills to the west of the city disturbed the peace of Zhongnanhai.

From its building, the Investigation Bureau controlled agents in every Chinese Embassy who operated under diplomatic cover, often as first or second secretaries. Few Western spy agencies had such high-ranking spies. The bureau reported to the Central External Liaison Department, an entity with no equivalent in any other intelligence organization. It was unique not only in its size, estimated by the CIA to be over one thousand employees, but in the multiple roles it performed; among them was supervising internal security and espionage on a worldwide scale.

The department processed every visa application and made the final decision on the level of checks to be made on an applicant's background and, if a visa was approved, which MSS department should be assigned to see what use the visitor could be to China after arrival in the People's Republic. The department decided the correct level of secrecy to be applied to even the simplest of operations: whether a woman should be used to seduce a foreign businessman; whether he should be placed in a hotel room equipped with an adequate range of bugging devices. It oversaw the intelligence branches in all other government and civic organizations. The entire apparatus of Chinese intelligence was interlocked and tightly controlled.

A standard Foreign Office briefing to each British ambassador appointed to the Beijing post explains, "Chinese intelligence activities are usually cautious, often operating within a legal framework and essentially low key. There is not the preoccupation of the Russians with using blackmail or bribery. The Chinese approach is more subtle and those who work for MSS are invariably highly motivated and totally incorruptible. That is one reason why 'defectors' from the Chinese side must be treated with caution."

The department's tradition of espionage reached back over twenty-five hundred years and it took pride in its agents' reputations for rarely being caught and seldom deported. An estimated ten thousand spies and support staff had been under the command of Qiao Shi for the past sixteen years.

Qiao was unusually tall for a Chinese, almost six feet. His stoop made him appear shorter; rumor had it a spinal deformity came from spending too many hours as a child studying the Chinese language, driving himself to learn and memorize the radicals and the differing thickness of the strokes, which required fine penmanship to distinguish between the phonetics and recensions they represented.

Even the most senior of the Leadership treated Qiao Shi with respect. No one would have dared to point out that for a man in such a powerful position he was a poor dresser: Often his clothes looked as if he had gone to a tailor's shop in one of the city's *hutongs*, backstreet alleys, and bought the first suit on display. People assumed there was a purpose in his lack of sartorial style, other than eccentricity. Foreign diplomats, who remembered him from the time he had served in the Foreign Ministry, recalled his entire career had been one of adroit, low-key moves; he had climbed through one department to another with the minimum of notice. Each move enhanced his reputation. He had traveled widely—London, Paris, Berlin, Madrid, and New York had all been on his itinerary. One day he had been a diplomat, the next entrenched as a head of state security; from then on, few knew where he went or whom he saw.

The one essential certainty was that Qiao Shi knew all the secrets, peccadilloes, and personal shortcomings within the Leadership. He knew who was already corrupt, who could be corrupted—and, most important, he knew the exact condition of Deng Xioping's health. Deng had survived Mao's paranoia to rule China with consummate skill, which had been proven with his handling of the student rebellion in Tiananmen Square, when he had correctly calculated foreign governments would not really protest. Three months after the massacre he had welcomed two former U.S. secretaries of state, Henry Kissinger and General Alexander Haig, and President George H. W. Bush's brother, Prescott. They had come to reassure him China was America's most valued partner in the coming decade.

Haig was there as chairman of Worldwide Associates to discuss joint ventures with CITIC, the banking arm of the Chinese government. Kissinger was also engaged in similar discussions with CITIC. Prescott Bush had been retained as a consultant by Asset Management to invest an initial $60 billion in joint venture developments. One was to build a country club. Qiao Shi's spies had monitored all these activities. James Lilley, the former CIA chief in Beijing and now the American ambassador to China, told the spies in Spook City (slang for Beijing), "It's business as usual."

IN THE AFTERMATH OF THE TIANANMEN SQUARE MASSACRE, Qiao Shi ordered hundreds of his spies to be demoted. Some were posted to become guards in labor camps along the borders with Mongolia and Manchuria; others were dispatched to one of the MSS bases far from Beijing. All were judged to have failed—during the fifty-five days of Beijing's student protest—to identify the "troublemakers" on the square, though six prisons overflowed with thousands of captives awaiting trial for their part in the demonstrations. Over 270,000 people had their Party membership canceled after MSS agents who had survived Qiao Shi's purge traveled across the country to interview them. In the Yangtze Delta, those among its sixty million people who had raised their voices in support of the students were shipped off to labor camps in the largest roundup since the Cultural Revolution.

Other agents had been sent abroad to discover who among the millions of Chinese expatriates in the United States, Europe, and Britain had provided money and other support for the students. Once they were identified, their families back home were punished. Many were ordered to pay substantial fines and had their social welfare benefits withdrawn for a period.

Qiao Shi had also ordered an unprecedented increase in surveillance. As well as cameras on university and college campuses, tens of thousands more were sited in every building in every city, town, and village, on buses, trains, and river steamers, and alongside roads. Systems architects were ordered to design technology that would collect and analyze personal information, turning the classroom, office, and factory floor into a surveillance zone with electronic equipment checking every minute of the working day, silently recording performance rates and even toilet breaks. Existing surveillance equipment was upgraded to be "wiretap friendly."

Privacy International, a London-based human rights group, claimed that in the wake of Tiananmen there were some three hundred new interlinked databases, a network in which every foreigner became caught in a nationwide surveillance web recording what e-mails they sent or received, where they changed their currency, what kind of rental car they used, where they stayed, who they met. The data were analyzed at the Central External Liaison Department. Surveillance became part of a burgeoning industry that spread into all levels of commerce as an instrument of pacification, intimidation, obfuscation, propaganda, and control.

Intelligence officers in Spook City and Beijing's other diplomatic missions established that some seven hundred students arrested during the Tiananmen Square demonstrations had been executed and their vital organs—kidneys, hearts, lungs, and eyes—sold to wealthy Chinese in need of transplant surgery. The organs were removed in a well-established ritual. The usual form of execution was a bullet in the base of the skull, but if eyes were needed a prisoner was shot in the heart. Those scheduled to have their organs removed were not tortured and were given special diets to improve their physical condition before execution. Immediately afterward, a corpse was transferred to a nearby operating room and the organs removed.

Since the Tiananmen demonstration, the Nangiang Hospital in Canton had been designated as the country's main center for transplant surgery for foreign patients. In the first year after the protests, Amnesty International claimed over one hundred such operations had taken place on Chinese who had traveled from the United States. The hospital had a special medical wing for foreigners and advertised its unique services in the Chinese-language media. A heart replacement cost $20,000, a liver $6,000, a kidney $5,000; eyes cost $3,000 each. A spokesman for the hospital told the author, "There is nothing unethical about what we do. These are criminals whose organs we use. There is no need to obtain their consent when anyway they will be executed."

IN THE TWO YEARS AFTER TIANANMEN, QIAO SHI had expanded the worldwide operations of MSS. He had begun by reinforcing the London station with some of his best officers. Since the creation of the People's Republic, Britain had remained a prime target due to its expanding computer- and science-oriented industries. MSS had paid the fees for Chinese students to complete their postgraduate studies at Cambridge, Oxford, and other universities with high-quality research facilities in the technology field. They were then encouraged to apply for jobs in the high-tech industry, where many firms had sensitive defense contracts. Students who were accepted were trained by MSS officers on how to steal secrets from their employers and bring them to MSS safe houses in London's Soho quarter and other cities with Chinatowns.

MI5 had established that by 1992, MSS had twenty-four agents in Britain; as well as those with diplomatic cover, others operated from Chinese trading companies and travel offices. (In 2007, MI5 put the number of MSS agents at forty-six, the largest number of foreign intelligence officers operating in Britain.) In a two-year period—1989 to 1991—the Security Service believed £14 billion worth of secrets had been stolen by MSS.

QIAO SHI HAD TRANSFERRED KAO LING, the head of all MSS operations on the African continent, from his base in Zanzibar to continue his undercover role as the correspondent for the New China News Agency (NCNA) at the United Nations in New York. His task was to write favorable stories about American corporations that were investing in China, and he found a ready welcome in every major corporation in the country; many had defense contracts, and Kao Ling acquired a considerable amount of data for scientists and technicians in Beijing to analyze. The White House had encouraged American companies to "draw China back into having technical and military ties with us and enable their nation to move forward." Two years after Tiananmen, $2 billion worth of contracts were signed between both countries.

Kao Ling had been replaced in Africa by Teng Cheng, who had served in Thailand, Laos, and Havana. His down-slanting eyes gave the middle-aged man an appearance some women found attractive, and he had acquired several mistresses around the continent. The Mossad's profile described him as "the most efficient agent MSS has in Africa. He will corrupt anybody, but is beyond corruption himself."

Teng Cheng had strengthened MSS not only across the width of Africa but in Sudan, where, a Mossad undercover agent reported, Teng Cheng had met Osama bin Laden. Their discussion had revolved around the defeat of the Red Army in Afghanistan, followed by Teng Cheng's offer that China could provide any help al-Qaeda wanted. Bin Laden had declined.

MSS had been expanded in every Pacific Rim nation, including Australia and New Zealand. In Europe its spies were increased in Bern, Switzerland, and in Paris. Agents had been posted to every country in Latin America and to Iran, Iraq, and Syria. Qiao Shi's officers were entrenched in Turkey, Spain, and Germany, working as chefs or waiters or in any job that would provide the cover for their real work of gathering technical information for analysts in Beijing. They were the foot soldiers of China's ambition to become the technocrat superpower of the next millennium.

EARLY IN 1992, TENG CHENG had flown to Johannesburg to try to discover more about a highly secret program which had been part of the apartheid regime for twelve years.

Wouter Basson had been too small physically to become the rugby player his policeman father had hoped and did not possess the voice of his mother, an aspiring opera singer. She had encouraged him to enter medicine and perhaps one day become famous like Dr. Christiaan Barnard, South Africa's renowned heart transplant surgeon. Basson had other, less ambitious hopes, wanting to become a gynecologist, but his dream of going to London for training ended when his parents said they could not afford to pay his tuition fees at St. Mary's, the major teaching hospital that had agreed to accept him.

Basson had been a high achiever at one of Cape Town's private schools and passed with the highest exam marks to enter the medical school at the University of Pretoria. His friendly smile was reserved for whites only; "blacks are there to only serve you, not to socialize with," Basson had been heard to say. Imbued by his father from an early age of the virtue of apartheid, Basson was already a committed nationalist when he arrived on campus. Other students said he grew a full beard to give himself more the look of a bush Afrikaaner, to go along with his habit of chewing *biltong,* a cured stick of kudu meat, and drinking his share of the strong local beer. Girls found his quick wit and charm attractive, and he had a full social life.

Like every public medical school, Pretoria's had a staff member on the lookout for likely candidates for the country's intelligence services: the military intelligence Directorate of Covert Collection (DCC) and the Bureau of State Security (BOSS).

After qualifying as a doctor, Basson had served as an intern at HF Verwoerd, the country's leading teaching hospital. It was there his interest in deadly pathogens began. At medical school there had been brief mention of them, but in the hospital he met doctors who had served in the Special Forces and used the germs against South Africa's enemies in southern Rhodesia (now Zimbabwe), Angola, Namibia, and Mozambique. Basson was told the attacks were "defensive" and a response to the arrival in Angola of Cuban troops equipped with Soviet biological weapons. "Man, it made sense for us to take defensive precautions," Basson recalled his fellow doctors telling him.

Soon afterward, like all young men of his generation, Basson was called up into the South African Defense Force (SADF). With his medical qualification he was allowed to choose a subject in which to specialize, and his original thought of becoming a gynecologist was replaced by a desire to study for a master's degree in physiology and physiological chemistry. It was an opportunity to learn more about how germs could be weaponized, to overcome all the enemies who surrounded South Africa. Using them would be defensive, not offensive, against terrorists who had already shown they would slaughter women and children in their hatred for the republic.

Growing germs was easy; the process "seemed like brewing beer for a trained chemist," Basson recalled. Yet from what he read, "there appeared to be lacking within SADF a grasp on the essentials of biological engineering: Germs needed to be freeze-dried and weaponized before being stored in readiness to launch against an enemy."

In the bush of Rhodesia and other countries north of the Limpopo River, SADF Special Forces had only poisoned water wells and food storage *rondavels*. To entirely terrify an enemy the germs should be distributed by air, as the Japanese had done against the Chinese in the 1930s and as the Nazis had done experimentally in World War II. Basson found that SADF had never explored the possibility of how to distribute a weapon that could silently penetrate the natural defense of the human respiratory system, bypassing the hairs in the nose and the cilia along the windpipe, going directly to the lungs and overcoming its moist tissues to bring death. Anthrax could do that. Again, however, from what he read, there was not a spore of it in South Africa, and no one in the SADF had considered weaponizing microbes, even though a small canister of anthrax had sufficient potency to kill millions. Why had no one used it? Not even the Soviets had done so at the height of the cold war. Was it because of the fear of retaliation? Was that why South Africa had signed the convention outlawing biological weapons? There were endless questions for which Wouter Basson found no answers.

By the end of his military service, the proud owner of a master's degree in his two chosen subjects, the young scientist knew more about the potency of weaponized pathogens than anyone else in the republic. He did not suspect his interest had been noted by his commanding officer, Surgeon-General Nicol Nieuwoudt, or that a meeting had been held at the headquarters of SADF at Speskop, outside Pretoria, chaired by the SADF chief, General Constand Viljoen, and attended by Lieutenant General Pieter van der Westhuizen, chief of military intelligence, and Nieuwoudt. It was decided Basson should be given the rank of a brigadier and head a top-secret program code-named Project Coast. A few days short of his thirtieth birthday, Basson was called before the three officers and told by General Viljoen, "No one in the SADF knows anything about chemical or biological weapons except you, but we need them. Though you have not been trained in espionage, it will fall to you alone to obtain the ingredients to produce them. You can use any methods you like, choose who you wish to work with, and have an open-ended budget, but under no circumstances is the SADF to be linked to your work. Is that clear?"

Nieuwoudt had later driven Basson out into the veldt ten miles north of Pretoria and pointed to an old farmhouse near the Rooderplaat Dam from where Project Coast would operate. Nieuwoudt explained the site had been selected because it was far enough away from the city to ensure a margin of isolating safety. It would be ringed by electrified fences; police patrols would be on alert around the clock, and their dogs had been trained to kill. Just as Wouter Basson had requested, there would be Level Three containment laboratories, and all the equipment on his extensive shopping list would be provided. Everything would be in place by the time he had obtained the deadly toxins.

Nieuwoudt had turned to Basson with a "look of pride" in his eyes and allegedly said, "Wouter, you have been appointed to create an entire range of weapons which will kill or immobilize the terrorists in the bush, their leaders in our cities who organize their campaigns against us, and all their fellow travelers, the Marxists and Communists who threaten the very survival of our country."

In a similar tone, at a Nuremberg rally, Adolf Hitler had promised to ensure the future of the Third Reich for a thousand years.

BASSON HAD BEEN PROVIDED with a government-chartered jet to fly him anywhere in the world, a credit card with unlimited authorization, and access to bank accounts set up in a dozen countries. It was his open door to the world of toxicologists and microbiologists. He traveled to London, Washington, and Paris to conduct meetings in some of the best hotels in the world. Every night he wrote up his notes. Some dealt with his secret visits to Libya's two chemical production complexes at Rabta and Trahunan deep in the desert. Hidden beneath the sands were the laboratories developing Colonel Gadhafi's biological weapons.

A Mossad undercover agent in the Rabta plant had noted Basson's visits, and in Tel Aviv Mossad director Shabtai Shavit agreed Basson's name should be added to the list of potential targets for the Kidon. Its members began to gather information on his private life, his friends, and his offer to provide his own skills to help Libya enhance its biological warfare capability. All he wanted in return was the strains of germs Libya had obtained from Iraq, which originally Donald Rumsfeld had agreed should be provided to Saddam.

Soon the packages of freeze-dried germs arrived at Project Coast laboratories. Its Biosafety Level Three containment rooms were deep underground, along with the cages that held primates and beagles; the animals were required for testing the germs. The pathogens included a selection of the forty-five strains of anthrax stored at Rabta: from Trahunan came vials, sealed in lead containers, holding cholera, botulinum, and the most lethal of all biological agents, the plague. By the middle of 1992, Project Coast had also received quantities of the Ebola and Marburg viruses. Weaponizing the germs, in the words of Defense Minister Magnus Malan, could "*los die probleem*"—solve the problem. In a memorable sentence, Wouter Basson justified what he did (to the South African Truth and Reconciliation Commission later investigating Project Coast), "I've got one daughter and one day the blacks will take over and if my daughter asks me what did you do to prevent this, my conscience will be clear."

By the middle of 1992, Basson and his small team of like-minded scientists had begun to weaponize their cache of germs. They mixed anthrax into the gum of envelopes to be sold in street markets catering to blacks; botulinum and thallium were mixed into beer barrels sold in township *shebeens*; paratyphoid was inserted in deodorant sprays marketed to the African community, and its favorite peppermint-flavored chocolate was spiked with snake venom from the mamba. Project Coast's laboratories became one of the most evil research centers since the Nazi experiments of World War II.

EVERY MORNING WHEN HE WAS NOT TRAVELING, Wouter Basson descended to his laboratory complex. Exiting from the elevator, he faced a heavy metal door, which only opened when he held his ID card against the wall sensor. Beyond was his office; from floor to ceiling its shelves were filled with books, scientific journals, and papers from all over the world devoted to the subject of germ warfare. Some were already in the public domain; others had been obtained by agents of South African military intelligence traveling on false passports and posing as students, researchers, and science journalists. On his orders, they had trawled their way down through California's Silicon Valley and the campuses of America's leading universities, visited London, Paris, Madrid, and

Munich, and gone to all those places where information on germs was available. Basson had visited Taiwan's CBW facilities and ordered some of its state-of-the-art equipment.

On the shelves were studies of how the Pentagon had once planned to attack Fidel Castro's Cuba with toxins in the run-up to the Cuban Missile Crisis and of how, during the Vietnam War, scientists at Fort Detrick had found a way to preserve the variola virus, smallpox. Using a process called lyophilization, they had successfully freeze-dried the virus so it would remain dormant and then, when returned to room temperature, would be even more virulent.

There were papers on how America and Britain had secretly tested delivery systems to spread germs over entire cities, and books devoted to Venezuelan equine encephalitis, a virus found in horses and mules in South and Central America that leaves humans close to the point of death; manuals devoted to each of the seven different types of botulinum, toxins that are the ultimate killer; a history of the development of ricin, which when weaponized causes vascular collapse and certain death.

Research papers detailed the development of the black pox, the most malignant form of smallpox, which has a fatality rate of 100 percent, and of nanopowder silica, minute fine particles of silica glass that when mixed into a biological weapon enable it to become easily airborne and so more able to penetrate human lungs. More papers dealt with the most infamous bacterial agents in history: bubonic plague, the Black Death of medieval times, and the Spanish flu, which in 1918 had killed many times more victims than the Great War. The papers had come from supposedly highly secure biological warfare centers in countries like the United States, Britain, and Israel. Others had been bought on the black market in Eastern Bloc countries.

Basson's original research, the most secret of all Project Coast's projects, remained in a filing cabinet that only he could open with a code no one else knew. It contained his search for what his apartheid political masters had told him was the ultimate weapon, one that would guarantee the nation's survival, one that would sterilize not only one person but an entire race. It would be a "genetic bomb."

Basson had followed the continuing debate within the scientific community about the feasibility of producing such a weapon. Its supporters pointed out that endemic disease had contributed to the defeat of the Aztecs and Incas by the Spanish conquistadors, who appeared to be often immune to the germs that ravaged Central and South America. The British had launched their own crude "gene bombs" when they distributed blankets infected with smallpox to the Indians in North America and saw their own death rates from the disease were many times lower than the rates within the tribes; the military doctors who accompanied the invading forces believed the redcoats possessed a stronger physical resistance built up over the centuries.

During America's intervention in Nicaragua, the idea of creating a "genetic bomb" had occupied the Central Intelligence Agency geneticists. Substantial sums of money were spent obtaining blood samples of Nicaraguans to be tested in CIA laboratories. No gene specific to Nicaragua was identified. The project was abandoned, only to be resurrected at the time when Cuba posed a growing threat in Washington. The CIA had launched the search for a "Cuban-only gene." Again, the research came to nothing.

Still, the possibility of finding a biological weapon that could target a specific race had continued to engage the talents of biologists in the Soviet Union and finally Wouter Basson. He knew creating an ethnic bomb was no longer a fantasy. It had become what the Nobel Prize–winning scientist Joshua Lederberg called the "monster in our backyard." Anthropologist John Moore, an acknowledged expert on the threat from an ethnic bomb, had predicted its release would unleash genetic variations that could create widespread contagion in the human population and rates of mortality like the fictional Andromeda Strain, sufficient to exterminate the whole species. For Wouter Basson, it would be sufficient to control the black population in South Africa.

IN SEPTEMBER 1992, WOUTER BASSON and one of his assistants, Dr. Jan Lournes, a studious-faced biochemist, flew to London. In their hand luggage was a folding umbrella, two small vials in lead jackets, and a small toolbox containing a set of jeweler's screwdrivers. The vials contained ricin, one of the most deadly weapons in the biological arsenal. The umbrella and screwdrivers were intended to murder two leading members of the African National Congress (ANC) who were based in London. One was Ronnie Kasrils, its senior intelligence officer in Europe; the other was Dr. Pallo Jordan, the ANC senior representative in Britain. Kasrils was to be killed by the method used on the Bulgarian dissident Georgy Markov; as he walked to work in London he was stabbed by an umbrella tip coated with ricin by an agent of his country's secret service. Jordan, whose interest in repairing watches was well known, would die once he handled any of the ricin-coated screwdrivers.

Waiting at Heathrow Airport for Basson and Lournes was Trevor

Floyd, a senior officer with BOSS. He was responsible for monitoring
the activities of the considerable number of ANC leaders who had sought
refuge in Britain, waiting for the collapse of the apartheid regime. Floyd
drove them to a cottage Basson had rented near Ascot in Berkshire to
provide Project Coast with a safe house in Britain. Number One Fair-
cloth Farm in Watersplash Lane was listed as the headquarters of WPW
International Incorporated, registered in the Cayman Islands. In 2007,
the cottage changed hands and the WPW tile motif in the bathroom
had been removed. Neighbors vaguely remembered Basson was a regular visitor and among the guests was a suntanned American with a
friendly manner.

He was Dr. Larry Creed Ford, a forty-nine-year-old Mormon who had
graduated from Brigham Young University, married his Sunday school
sweetheart, Diana, and joined the teaching faculty of UCLA. No one in
the quiet Berkshire backwater realized that the friendly American they
saw walking down the lanes around the cottage had been involved with
the CIA, that his backyard was a repository for a small arsenal of arms,
ammunition, and military explosives, that stashed in a refrigerator in an
outbuilding at his $1 million home was a secret collection of pathogens
stored in baby food jars, or that he had made visits to North Korea to
discuss biological warfare.

On whose authority he had done so would remain one of the many
secrets Dr. Ford would carry to his grave. On a bright spring morning in
March 2002, in Irving, California, dressed in his favorite casual clothes
and high-top basketball shoes, Ford shook his attorney's hand, left the
lawyer's office after a five-hour meeting behind closed doors, drove
home in his new convertible, went upstairs to a bedroom, and shot himself. It would be a year before his link to Wouter Basson would surface.

ON THAT AUTUMN DAY IN BERKSHIRE, Basson would have more
important matters to think about than Ford. He watched carefully as
Floyd took possession of the vials, umbrella, and toolbox. There was,
however, a moment of drama when Lournes's finger touched one of the
screwdrivers in the toolbox. The scientist began to gasp and grabbed a
bottle from his briefcase, swallowed a mouthful, and staggered to the
bathroom, where he vomited into the toilet. Basson gave him a second
drink and then made Lournes drink copious amounts of water. It still
took the biochemist a while to recover.

"Holy Christ," murmured Floyd. "Imagine if you'd actually held that
screwdriver."

"Then you'd have a different problem," Basson replied.

Floyd drove back to London to brief the hit team who would kill the two ANC men, but there was no record of the attempt being made until some details of the plot emerged during the Truth and Reconciliation hearings in Cape Town, held at the request of South Africa's first black president, Nelson Mandela. No explanation was offered why the assassination did not go ahead or what became of the weapons. An MI5 source suggested to the author that Floyd realized the apartheid regime was doomed and President Mandela wanted the transition to power to be kept as peaceful as possible.

ALMOST FROM THE OUTSET, Project Coast came to the attention of MI5 and MI6. Dr. David Kelly alerted them that one of his contacts among his extensive network of scientists had encountered Wouter Basson at an aerospace conference in San Antonio, Texas, describing him as "charming and a big spender at the bar, but seemed to have no interest in any other aspect of aerospace except collecting any paper dealing with airborne delivery systems for germs."

Basson had left the conference with a large briefcase filled with documents and flown to Washington, where he had claimed to be a biochemist to gain entry into a restricted area of the Library of Congress. Among much else, he had photocopied the Centers for Disease Control (CDC) investigation into a religious cult in Oregon, which had in 1984 experimented with biological weapons in an attempt to poison a small neighboring township opposed to its activities. Twelve people had died in what transpired—the first act of bioterrorism in the United States. The CDC had decided not to make its report public so as not to encourage other extremists. Dr. Kelly had wondered why Basson had been interested in such an event.

An MI6 officer in Pretoria, acting on a tip from one of his informers inside SADF, drove out to the Roodeplaat Dam and found that three hundred hectares of scrubland surrounding the farmhouse had been fenced off, mechanical diggers had excavated large holes around the building, and army trucks had unloaded crates marked MEDICAL EQUIPMENT. A further check revealed they had come from Libya. The holes were to house the underground containment laboratories. The officer also learned the University of Pretoria Medical School was recruiting biologists on its staff who were ready to "practice interesting science." The project director was named as Wouter Basson.

Meanwhile, MI5 discovered Basson had visited another medical trade

fair in the Bloomsbury neighborhood of London, and again he had
collected all available literature on biological weapons. His next trip
had been to the World Congress of Forensic Toxicologists in Ghent,
Belgium. He had been followed by an MI6 officer who saw Basson had
registered himself as "Director, Forensic Laboratories, Box X620, Pretoria, South Africa." The officer discovered that there was no such organization and that the box had been set up by Basson. The details
went into the Basson file that had been opened by the Secret Intelligence Service.

Before he had left London for Ghent, Basson rented the cottage in
Watersplash Lane. Every step of the deal had been monitored by MI5: A
South African Embassy diplomat in London had fronted the deal and a
lawyer in Fleet, Hampshire, had notarized the long-term lease. After
Basson flew to Belgium, an MI5 surveillance technician visited the cot-
tage and installed voice-activated bugs.

An MI6 officer in Washington had tracked down Basson's visit to the
Library of Congress and established he had not only photocopied the
CDC document but had left the library laden with copies of documents
relating to the biological research going on in North Korea. The officer
established that after Basson's visits to research centers in and around
the capital, he had FedExed several packages to his Pretoria box. Meanwhile, Dr. Ford had made two visits to Pyongyang, the North Korean
capital, on behalf of a small medical research company in Newport
Beach, California, ostensibly to investigate reports that an institute
there had discovered a cure for baldness. He had also explored the possibility of working with North Korean geneticists to find a cure for
AIDS, already reaching pandemic proportions across Africa. Among
those Dr. Ford had met was Dr. Yi Yong Su. The name had further deepened the interest of the North Korean Desk at MI6.

Dr. Yi ran numerous research projects across North Korea. They included laboratories investigating cellular biology and genetic engineering using human growth hormones. Her scientists had also started
researching the creation of organisms designed to attack food crops and
human immune and nervous systems. The most important research was
done at Institute 398.

It had been left to Dr. Kelly to explain the importance of the center-
piece of Dr. Yi's empire at his next meeting with Britain's intelligence
service. He began by explaining that Institute 398, listed in the North
Korean General Staff manual of the People's Armed Forces, employed
over four hundred of the country's best scientists engaged in developing antidotes and decontamination methods for exposure to radiation,

including protective masks and suits. Located at Sokam-ri in the south of the country, it was ring-fenced by three battalions of troops. That, Dr. Kelly said, provided a clue to what else went on in the underground laboratories.

Dr. Kelly had a gift for reducing complex science to understandable terms and would, for instance, explain that a hundred million viruses could comfortably sit on top of a pinhead, or why the India-1 strain of smallpox was vaccine resistant and had been weaponized in huge quantities by Soviet scientists working in the Biopreparat project. He used the same brisk voice to take his listeners in a JIC office through all he knew about the research at Institute 398. Dr. Yi had ordered it on the command of the country's leader, Kim Jong-il, to "create a biological weapon that would defeat the most powerful enemy we face—the white supremacists of America."

Anthrax developed at the institute had already been tested on prisoners brought from a gulag and placed in a large cage, where they were sprayed with anthrax particles. All developed skin sores, blisters, and bloodstained sputum, a glimpse of the horror of biowarfare. The corpses were burned in the institute's incinerator. Following the testing, the institute's scientists coated the anthrax spores with organic compounds to shield them from ultraviolet rays, so they would not become less potent after exposure to sunlight. Further tests were then conducted on more of the 250,000 North Koreans imprisoned in the country's gulags. How many had died would remain another secret in this country of secrets. All this Dr. Kelly had learned during the weeks he had spent questioning Dr. Vladimir Pasechnik, who had revealed that working at the institute were some of the scientists from the Biopreparat project secretly recruited to work in North Korea's biological program. Others had gone to China, Syria, Libya, and Iran.

Before the end of the meeting, Dr. Kelly had told the intelligence officers he had confirmed Dr. Pasechnik's fears that the latest project the institute was working on was far more potent than anthrax, one for which no scientist in the West could produce an antidote, one that would attack only the genome—the sixty thousand to eighty thousand genes that make up human DNA—of the white population of the world.

The unanswered question, Dr. Kelly had wondered, was how much Dr. Ford knew of this. A decision was made to ask the CIA to have the obstetrician questioned by the FBI. A few days later MI6 chief Colin McColl received a response that Larry Ford was an agency asset and would not be questioned. The response was put in a Y file, where MI6's most secret communications are stored.

IN OCTOBER 1998, the Truth and Reconciliation Commission published its final report, clearly mindful of President Mandela's wish to have a peaceful transition from the apartheid regime to his own government of National Unity that should not be damaged by highly embarrassing revelations about the twelve years when Wouter Basson had secretly run a biological warfare research program. By then he had shredded his secret plan to create an ethnic bomb to attack the black population, along with other incriminating evidence. The commission concluded: "The military High Command of the former government was grossly negligent for approving a biological and chemical warfare program it did not understand."

ON A SUNNY MORNING IN SOUTH AFRICA'S SPRING, Dr. Kelly, two MI6 officers, and a note taker walked into a room in the SADF headquarters in Pretoria. On the opposite side of the table sat Wouter Basson. It was only pressure from the U.K. government on a reluctant President Mandela that had brought him there to answer questions that the Truth and Reconciliation Commission had not asked—and that Mandela had agreed must be answered if South Africa was to regain its place in the world.

Dr. Kelly was struck by Basson's arrogance, "He made it clear he was here on sufferance, and the sooner this was over, the quicker we could all go home," recalled Dr. Kelly.

He well understood such an attitude. He had encountered it in Iraq with Dr. Rihab Taha and used the same approach as he had then, putting his questions in a firm but always polite voice. At first Basson, keeping his answers short, shrugged them aside. Dr. Kelly persisted, following up Basson's response with more probing supplementary questions into Project Coast's production methods and delivery systems. It was a highly technical interrogation that the others in the room did not interrupt. Hour after hour the battle of wills between the no longer arrogant Basson and the relentless Dr. Kelly continued. How had Basson weaponized his germs? Judged their efficacy? Stored them? Had he conducted open-air trials? Where and what were the targets?

Dr. Kelly found the answers were surprising. There had been no aerial dissemination because the climate "was not suitable." Instead, toxins had been placed in food and water supplies. What had been his weapon of choice? Botulinum, anthrax, cholera, or plague? Dr. Kelly later recalled that Basson had sat back and considered his answer. None of those germs had been weaponized "because we could not find suitable ways to introduce them into the food chain," he finally admitted.

Were any of the biological germs left? Basson was dismissive, "We didn't make any BW weapons as you know them." Dr. Kelly had pressed. There was ample evidence some had been produced. Nothing had gone beyond the testing stage, insisted Basson. Had any of those that had formed part of that stage been retained—perhaps hidden? Basson replied, "Dammit, man, we destroyed them." "How?" Dr. Kelly asked. "By heat and bleach," said Basson.

The MI6 team had taken over, questioning him about his trips to Libya. The discussion had been short. The officers merely wanted confirmation of what they already knew. "You understand, Dr. Basson, that you are on a Mossad list. If you ever return to Libya you will never leave alive. Is that clear?" demanded one of the officers. Wouter Basson nodded. The interrogation was over.

The warning was clear-cut. If in the future he attempted to resume his activities, he would be killed by the Kidon, the Mossad unit that specializes in executing the enemies of Israel.

SINCE OCTOBER 4, 1999, Wouter Basson had sat in the dock of the Pretoria High Court for thirty months. On the morning of April 11, 2002, Judge Willie Hartzenberg concluded that the evidence of 153 witnesses, thousands of pages of affidavits by those who had worked for him, and documents that had survived the shredder were still insufficient to convict Wouter Basson on any of the sixty-one charges he had faced. Neither Dr. Kelly nor the transcript of Basson's interrogation had formed part of the prosecution.

To this day, four metal trunks filled with classified information about Project Coast remain locked in a government vault in Pretoria. Only two keys exist that can open the vault. One of them remained in the possession of President Nelson Mandela until his retirement. He has steadfastly refused to discuss Project Coast. Who holds the keys remains unknown.

LONG BEFORE THE END OF THE WOUTER BASSON TRIAL, Teng Cheng, the MSS agent, had been recalled to Beijing to become Qiao Shi's personal aide. In 2007, he was reported to be in charge of security for the Olympic Games in Beijing in 2008.

15

A New World: Adjust or Die

On that March day in 1991 when he celebrated his sixty-seventh birthday with his wife, Lynda, and added another honorary degree to the growing number he had already acquired from colleges and universities, Judge William Webster knew his four-year tenure as CIA director was coming to an end. Soon his awards would be joined by the Distinguished Intelligence Medal, the Presidential Medal of Freedom, and the National Security Medal. His enemies in the White House and the Justice Department and at Langley called the awards Webster's "good-bye baubles." It was a cruel joke about a man who had tried to consistently deliver what President Bush wanted—"good-quality intelligence before I damn well read it on CNN." The sniping had begun after Bush had embarrassed Webster before his own staff by saying he learned more from the TV set, constantly tuned to the news channel in the Oval Office, than he did from his President's Daily Briefing.

"Webster became like a dead man walking. No one wanted to look him in the eye," remembered General Vernon Walters, a former deputy director of the CIA.

There had certainly been a number of bungles laid at Webster's door. One was the agency's failure to anticipate how events would develop after the collapse of the Berlin Wall and the breakup of the Soviet Union. Yet the CIA Soviet Desk, under the direction of Douglas MacEachin, had continued to insist the best way to learn what was happening in the USSR was to read its local newspapers; most arrived in Washington almost a month after publication. To compensate, MacEachin had sent a team to Berlin to buy up shelves of files of the Stasi, the East German secret police, whose headquarters had been looted by Berliners.

There had been the Noriega debacle. For twenty years General Manuel Noriega, Panama's corrupt dictator, had run the country as the final staging post for drugs to be smuggled into the United States. He knew he could count on his contacts in the CIA to warn him of the latest moves by the Drug Enforcement Agency to arrest him. Every month, Noriega's CIA stipend was paid into a Cayman Islands bank account. America's long-serving U.S. ambassador in Panama, Arthur H. Davis, had repeatedly warned the State Department about Noriega's activities and urged the dictator should be overthrown. Four attempts had failed before the Pentagon launched a full-scale invasion of Panama, using smart bombs to reduce large areas of Panama City to rubble before Special Forces captured Noriega and flew him in chains to Miami. Webster was blamed for failing to stop the CIA station chief in Panama, Dan Winter, for turning whistle-blower at Noriega's trial for drug trafficking. Winter revealed that Noriega had been the agency's "best liaison with Fidel Castro" and that his "retainer," totaling $320,000 by the time of his capture, was money well spent.

Now, during March 1991, in what would be his last major decision before leaving office, Webster had ordered the clandestine side of the agency to recruit moles in the boardrooms of Japanese corporations, including Sony, Honda, and Mitsubishi. He had done so after Bush had read a CIA report that described the Japanese as "a people who are amoral, manipulative and operating in a culture which is intent on world economic dominance. Japan is also still a racialist, non-democratic nation." It turned out the report was culled from two books. One was *The Coming War with Japan,* by George Friedman and Meredith Lebard, both conservative-minded economists who argued that economic competition with Japan would "almost certainly end in a war." The second book, by Shintaro Ishibara, a radical Japanese tycoon, claimed Japan would have to "face up to America if it was to survive as a major Pacific power with trading links around the world." The White House had ordered copies of the books to be sent to members of the administration—after dismissing the CIA report as "a poor pastiche of carefully considered views."

Webster, the only American to have served as director of both the FBI and the CIA, retired from public office to join a Washington law firm and gain still further awards.

ON MAY 8, 1991, Air Force One was cruising at thirty-eight thousand feet heading back to its home at Andrews Air Force Base outside Washington, having collected President George H. W. Bush from his Texas ranch. Throughout the flight he had remained closeted in his onboard office with senior advisers helping him to decide who should replace Webster. Names had been considered, discussed, and rejected. Finally, Bush had sent for Bob Gates.

The former deputy director of the CIA had withdrawn his nomination to become Casey's successor after realizing he faced a hostile confirmation hearing because of his role in the Iran arms-for-hostages scandal. Since then he had remained a close friend of Bush and had traveled with him to Texas to have another "brainstorming session" about world events.

The years had treated Gates kindly: He was still trim, his hair only showed the first signs of silvering, and even when sitting in one of the airliner's armchairs, he exuded energy. "A can-do man" was how one CIA officer later described Gates.

Bush came directly to the point. "I want you to run the agency, Bob. You okay with that?" Gates nodded, "thrilled, but slightly terrified," he later recalled.

His reaction was understandable. Running the CIA had been a dream since he had first joined twenty-four years before and had recognized that, in order to survive, the agency must be analysis-led and that consumers of intelligence—the president and his advisers—must be educated on its proper use. He had argued intelligence was not just deciphering the present but projecting the future.

Gates regarded intelligence as more than the cloak-and-dagger activities of the cold war. To be effective it should now be treated as a social science dealing not only with military matters but also with political, economic, and social trends. Intelligence gathering in those areas did not have to be obsessively secret: The fall of Communism in Eastern Europe had opened the doors to vast archives of material, especially in East Germany, enabling important technological and demographic information to become available, which good analysts could interpret to decide how the new world would operate.

Gates knew that as the information age developed, new kinds of officers would be required to handle what would still be the key elements of the CIA: spies to obtain information; counterintelligence to protect the agency's own information; analysts who could use the latest technology to access the acquired information.

Gates had studied how China's MSS increasingly used front companies, student exchange programs, and placement of their agents in commercial and scientific delegations. There was also an increase in Chinese "sleepers," agents trained to identify the latest U.S. technology, who had been sent to live in deep cover. North Korea also had its quota of similar sleepers in its ethnic communities in California to obtain economic and technological information. After Jonathan Pollard had plundered America's military secrets, the Mossad had continued to target Silicon Valley and Boston's Route 128 for high-tech secrets. Gates had reminded President Bush the CIA still listed Israel as one of six foreign countries with "a government-directed, orchestrated, clandestine operation to collect U.S. nonmilitary secrets."

For Gates it would be essential to have analysts who could predict the kind of information a foreign service was seeking. Were the North Korean spies searching for scientific data to insert into its order of battle? Was a friendly nation like Israel focused on obtaining American economic and social data that would enable the Jewish state to deal with its Arab neighbors? And always—*always*—a priority for foreign spies would be looking for data that would indicate America's level of defense against a surprise attack. The analysts would be tasked to decide the reality of a threat, using reports from CIA field agents of lights suddenly burning at night in a defense ministry in the capital of a potentially hostile country. Why were its military commanders taking an unusual number of trips to their bases? Were the signs of stockpiling food and preparations in emergency rooms only part of a military exercise?

The answers had to be factored into the jigsaw, turning snippets of data into a cohesive intelligence picture. That required analysts who could combine their intellectual skills with a proper understanding of modern intelligence assessment. The United States had a better chance of recruiting the right kind of analysts, given its long history of absorbing diverse cultural and religious groups. While the languages of Europe, China, and Japan would remain requirements for the analysis department, a good knowledge of those of Pakistan, Afghanistan, and other Middle East countries was not yet a priority. Richard Clarke, who became America's first antiterrorist czar, later said, "Members of the Bush administration seemed to have not noticed a new international movement continued to grow which did not seek to commit terror for its own sake, only to use it to impose its own interpretation of Islam." Only trained linguists could have seen how far they had gone.

Osama bin Laden, by now rejoicing in the religious title of sheikh, saw al-Qaeda as eventually creating the New Caliphate, the rebirth of the repressive fourteenth-century Muslim theocracy. To do so, he had told his followers, America had to be destroyed.

On that May day in 1991, there was not one analyst on the staff of the CIA who had read, let alone interpreted, the threat bin Laden had made.

AS AIR FORCE ONE BEGAN its descent into Andrews, Bush asked Gates how he would handle the CIA. "There's a new world out there. Adjust or die," came the response. Bush smiled: He had made the right choice.

UNDER STELLA RIMINGTON'S FIRM HAND, MI5 continued to change; its male-dominated culture was no longer the driving force. She appointed more women to important positions in the departments where she had made her own reputation: countersurveillance, counterespionage and counterterrorism. Women became members of surveillance teams and were assigned to often dangerous operations, helping to track IRA terrorists and drug-trafficking criminals, or assigned to implement many of the hundreds of telephone intercept warrants granted by the home secretary. It meant spending long hours in a transit van outside a suspect's office or home, headphones clasped to ears listening for incriminating conversations.

Rimington had herself broken another MI5 taboo by lunching with newspaper editors to promote the successes of the Security Service. Home Secretary Ken Clarke pronounced on television, "It is helpful to have a director-general who is a living, walking, moving human being, who can be met by people, and who can be trusted to talk to newspaper editors."

Sometimes a journalist overstepped the mark. William Rees-Mogg, the former editor of the *Times,* claimed in his column that MI5 had bugged telephone calls by members of the royal family. One senior officer growled, "That's what happens when our lady takes scribblers to lunch." Miranda Ingram, a counterintelligence officer, retorted by saying, "The trouble with our male colleagues is that they want to hang on to the mystery of what we do."

Rimington had told her department chiefs the days were over when they could behave as "barons each representing their own fiefdoms." She wanted a collegial approach to how the Security Service worked, and she wanted them to call in experts from the business community and other organizations beyond Whitehall so MI5 would not be "cut off from the outside world."

She organized weekends in country house hotels to discuss her latest changes and, after a communal dinner, led them in songs around the piano. The gatherings, known as "swots"—discussing strengths, weaknesses, opportunities, and threats—became a feature of her tenure, and from them emerged the idea of producing a booklet about MI5 that had more than the hint of a glossy pamphlet for an annual meeting of company stockholders. The *Times* reminded Rimington, "A wise virgin keeps her veils," to which she riposted to her staff, "An even wiser virgin knew exactly how many veils she could cast off and still remain safe." It was knockabout stuff that encouraged her to extend the feminine atmosphere in MI5. A sword her predecessor had hung on what was now her office wall, after it was presented to him by a European security service, was taken down because it looked too militaristic, and she had given her office a new coat of paint and dotted it with potted plants.

After the booklet was published, following numerous vettings by senior Whitehall civil servants who spent hours agonizing over words and the implication of every sentence, it became the first bestseller produced by any of Britain's intelligence services. Rimington posed for a photo shoot, neatly dressed, with discernible makeup on her face. She managed to smile into the camera, looking like the headmistress of a girls' school, not a spy catcher. Next she gave a televised lecture about security in a democracy. Again, every word was picked over before it was agreed she could use it. For Rimington, it must have seemed that a hint of her last night in Moscow, when she felt she had managed to escape from the villain's lair in a Bond film, permeated the Whitehall air.

For weeks after her lecture, largely for the novelty of seeing a living spy catcher—and a woman at that—emerging from the shadows, she was a talking point in the serious media, and for the tabloids she became a figure of endless interest: What she wore, where she shopped, nothing was too inane to fill column inches. When she hosted a lunch for a parliamentary intelligence oversight committee and offered "Reform Cutlets" to her guests, the menu was widely reproduced in the next day's newspapers.

Behind her headline-gathering behavior, she continued to be deeply immersed in the fight against terrorism as the IRA bombing campaign worsened with devastating attacks on the London Docklands and in the very heart of Manchester.

Sensing the Special Branch was hard-pressed, she sent a team of her best women officers over to Scotland Yard to assist. Many had considerable experience in tracking the IRA. On the day they arrived at the Yard, they found a cool welcome—a campaign of harassment began, to persuade them to go back to MI5. It culminated with one of the women arriving in the branch operations room to find a pile of dirty men's laundry on her desk with a typed order: "Get this washed." The officer picked up the laundry and threw it out a window. After underpants, undershirts, and shirts wafted down onto the pavement, she returned to her desk and started her first calls of the morning. It was the end of the harassment.

ON A MAY DAY IN 1992, a gangly, tousle-haired man wearing a creased suit and scuffed shoes walked into Century House with all the cheeky confidence of the journalist he had pretended to be for the previous week. Richard Tomlinson flashed his ID card at the guard in the foyer and rode the elevator up to the Eastern European Controllerate. Another mission had been completed by Agent D/813317.

Tomlinson had traveled across war-torn Serbia on a British passport describing him as Ben Presley and carrying a press card that said he was a member of the respected National Union of Journalists. Both documents were forged by MI6's Technical Services department.

A cease-fire had been brokered by the European Union only to be followed by hostilities in Bosnia-Herzegovina. Muslims and Croats continued to fight each other. Massacres were a daily occurrence, and starving survivors were interned in prison camps evoking memories of the Holocaust. In the midst of the carnage, spies, informers, and double agents plied their craft everywhere, relaying information, betraying either side of the conflict.

One was a waiter in one of the open-air cafés in the Croatian port of Split. He had recently been recruited by MI6, and Tomlinson had been told in London which table to sit at and what to order. It would be another of the "brush pass" contacts at which he had become adept. When the waiter had served coffee, Tomlinson found in the sugar bowl a folded piece of paper, which he pocketed before returning to his hotel. He locked the door to his room and carefully unfolded the paper. As he had expected, it was blank. From his shaving kit he removed a bottle of aftershave and a cotton ball; he placed the paper on the plastic toilet seat cover, poured some aftershave on the cotton, and gently rubbed the paper. Though he could read French, German, and Spanish, the words that emerged meant nothing to him, but in the year he had operated as a field officer, he had learned that his controller strictly practiced a need-to-know policy. He carefully refolded the paper, massaged the Velcro fastening on his shaving kit to open a small gap, and inserted the paper into it. A further rub and any trace of the gap he had opened was gone.

Returning to Century House, he handed in his forged documents and shaving kit and was debriefed by his controller, who sent him home to get a good night's sleep before reporting back to the controllerate.

TOMLINSON WAS "TAPPED" at Cambridge, where he had studied advanced aerodynamic engineering after graduating as a Kennedy Scholar from the Massachusetts Institute of Technology. The day after Tomlinson received his degree, he was invited to tea by a college instructor and asked if he would like to do "something interesting in the foreign service." He successfully passed through the usual hoops—a fast-track Civil Service Selection Board and the vetting process—followed by a final interview in which he answered the last question by saying he wanted to be a spy "for genuine patriotic reasons."

He had graduated from Fort Monkton, the MI6 training school at Gosport, equipped with such diverse skills as making a brush pass, like the one he had carried off with the café waiter, and expertly executing judo throws. In between he learned how to pose as a pilot, a yachtsman, and a businessman and subtly change his New Zealand accent to the broader twang of South Africa. He could also do passable English regional voices, and his Spanish was good enough to support a cover story of having worked in Latin America. He had been encouraged to use his charm on young women in the local Portsmouth pubs, and more than one had fallen for it. His instructors noted he had good weapons-handling skills, equally able to use a Browning 9 mm or an Israeli Uzi. "It was good fun, but my instructor said he couldn't remember when an officer carried a weapon. That was strictly for Bond," Tomlinson later told the author.

He had been singled out as one of the best in the 1991 intake into the Secret Intelligence Service. He had a flair for using a scanner the size of a television remote control that stored half a million words of documents and transmitted them in short bursts for a satellite to download to GCHQ; he had memorized the MI6 codes that identified information restricted to in-house circulation and other material that could not be shared with the CIA or any other foreign intelligence service. Before each mission, he had memorized a list of names of those who could

be trusted to help in an emergency. On the Balkan assignment, he had
been given a list of journalists working for the British media.

THE DAY AFTER HE RETURNED to the controllerate, Tomlinson
would recall he was summoned to the office of Nicholas Fishwick, identified as P4/Ops/11, the senior target officer for the Balkans. Fishwick's office was identical to all the others on the floor: a battered
government-issue desk, walls covered with maps marking the realignment of the former SovBloc, battleship gray chest-high steel safes with
red stickers reminding that they must be kept locked when the office
was unused. Security guards regularly checked every office in the building, and if a safe was found unlocked, a Security Breach Warning was issued. Three warnings led to a Severe Reprimand ticket being placed in
an officer's personal file, guaranteeing he would be excluded from consideration for an overseas posting. Six warnings usually led to dismissal
from MI6.

The saving grace of Fishwick's office was the view overlooking Lambeth Palace and the Thames, and in between the maps, the walls were
adorned with oil paintings and trinkets Fishwick had picked up on his
foreign trips.

Still some years from the compulsory retirement age of sixty, Fishwick had an engaging chuckle and an eye for a pretty girl among the
secretarial staff. That morning, as they sipped tea, Fishwick had looked
at Tomlinson and asked if he would like to finalize a plan to assassinate
Slobodan Milosevic, the Serbian leader.

Tomlinson was used to Fishwick's offbeat sense of humor about how
to choose a target. In the past he had prefaced a discussion by reminding Tomlinson that MI6 had been involved in various plots to assassinate Hitler as well as one against Saddam Hussein in the Gulf War.
Nevertheless, Tomlinson would recall his sense of shock when Fishwick
tossed a file across the desk and told him to read it, "It was identified as
Most Restricted by the yellow stripe on the cover. Inside was a document,
two typed pages long, with a small yellow card attached to signify it was
an 'accountable account' rather than a draft proposal. Accountable
meant it had a 'ready to act' status. The document was entitled 'A Proposal to Assassinate Serbian President Slobodan Milosevic,'"

The more he read, the more Tomlinson realized how far advanced
the plan was. Three options had been set out. The first called for a Serbian group opposed to Milosevic—Tomlinson wondered whether the
waiter in the Split café was a member—that could be trained to carry

out the killing, much as the SOE had trained Czech agents to assassinate Reinhard Heydrich, the Nazi Deputy Protector for the Realm of Bohemia and Moravia, in 1942. The document judged the possibility of success against Milosevic as "unpredictable." The second proposal was for a joint SAS/SBS team to kill Milosevic with a bomb or by a sniper ambush. While that would guarantee a result, it also carried the risk of not being undeniable: The bomb shrapnel or bullets could be traced, causing what the document called "serious repercussions." The final and "best" option would be to stage a car crash. As Tomlinson remembered it, "A stun device could be used to dazzle the gaze of the driver of Milosevic's car as it passed through one of Geneva's motorway tunnels while the president was attending the international conference on the former Yugoslavia in the city, forcing the car to crash with fatal results. Milosevic always liked to be driven at high speed."

Richard Tomlinson had handed back the file without a word and walked out of the office. Later he came to believe that was the moment his promising career as a G5 officer, the fast-track grade to higher promotion, began to unravel. He still made trips to the Balkans, but they increasingly left him traumatized by the atrocities he saw. He was told the intelligence he brought back was "neither substantial nor of quality." No longer were commendations placed in his personnel file, and a recommendation that he possessed the qualities to one day become a department head was lost beneath other less favorable reports.

After one trip he came home to his London apartment to find his girlfriend had died in the months he had been away. No one at MI6 had thought to tell him. She had been the one person to whom he could unburden himself, even though by doing so he was breaking the Official Secrets Act. He became depressed, remembering all the times he had risked his life on operations that he increasingly perceived as unethical. It led him to conclude "MI6 is not properly accountable and provides a fertile ground for corruption," he told the author.

On a rainy Monday morning, having spent a weekend alone, Tomlinson stood in the line waiting to pass through the staff entrance to the newly opened Vauxhall Cross headquarters. The weather did nothing to lift his spirits especially since he had completed a couple of missions to Brazil and South Africa. On his return he had been told he was being assigned to a new personnel officer.

Personnel, he had learned, was staffed by career officers approaching retirement who had no training in management skills and ran the department "on intrigue and secrecy, using its own network of line managers to settle a person's future. You were not allowed to read or sign

the minutes of an interview, which could make or break an officer's career. In the time I had been there, many a good officer had gone to the
wall, sacked. My new personnel officer was known as the Poison Dwarf,
not only because of his physical appearance but also his gratuitously un-
pleasant manner," recalled Tomlinson.

Their first meeting went badly, "The Poison Dwarf didn't bother
with pleasantries and immediately accused me of not being interested
in my job. He said my performance continued to be dismal." Tomlinson
broke the Official Secrets Act by writing up the interview on his laptop
at home. It was foolish, given that MI6 had the technology to access any
employee's computer.

Waiting in the rain, Tomlinson knew he was due to have another encounter with the Poison Dwarf later that morning. Should he instead go
and see his doctor and explain the sheer pressure of work was getting to
him? Yet to reveal he worked for MI6 would be an even more serious
breach of the Official Secrets Act.

The man ahead of him in the line passed through the security
doors, and it was Tomlinson's turn to place his swipe card into the
groove. He punched in his code on the keypad, six-nine-two-one, and
waited for the familiar green light showing the door was open. Instead
the light turned a bright red. Thinking he had mistyped, he fed in the
code again. The red light reappeared. Behind him in the line, people
were muttering. Tomlinson made a third attempt. This time the red light
was accompanied by an alarm bleeping inside the building. Suddenly
the VIP door beside the staff entrance swung open and two security
guards appeared, quickly moving to either side of a startled Tomlinson.

"Are you a member of staff, sir?" asked one.

"Yes, of course. I am PTCP/7, staff number 813317."

The guards escorted Tomlinson into their room inside the building.
One tapped Tomlinson's staff number into a computer while the other
switched off the alarm. Both men watched a message appear on the
screen announcing that Tomlinson's security pass had been canceled
and he was to be escorted to the personnel department.

"Poison Dwarf was waiting. He told me it was clear my performance
would not improve. I was fired. I was told to go home and make no further attempt to enter the building."

It had taken less than a minute for Richard Tomlinson's career to
end. Angry and bitter, he was about to begin his new life as a whistle-
blower. His formidable memory and his copious notes stored on his laptop would be his weapons. He had no idea why he had been sacked, and
that had furthered his determination to write a book telling the truth

about MI6, at least as he saw it. He would strike back where he believed it would hurt the Secret Intelligence Service the most, "in the glare of the public spotlight."

Nevertheless, he thought it wise to write to MI6 asking "for guidance" on how he should submit a manuscript for security clearance. The response was short and swift. Under no circumstances should he attempt to write a book. Matters then moved quickly. His laptop was stolen from his apartment. Tomlinson was convinced the theft had been organized by MI6. Meanwhile, he had already sent an Australian publisher a synopsis of his book. His plan was to repeat how Peter Wright had succeeded with his *Spycatcher*: publish abroad. "Once my book was in the public domain, MI6 would give up trying to stop me, much as MI5 had done over *Spycatcher*," Tomlinson later said.

He had miscalculated the determination of the Secret Intelligence Service. He was arrested and charged with breaching the Official Secrets Act, convicted, and imprisoned in Britain's high security prison, Belmarsh, for eight months. His fellow prisoners included some of the most dangerous terrorists he had once helped to track. Released, he fled to France and finally put together his book, which found an unlikely publisher in Moscow, one he would share with another whistle-blower, Kim Philby.

For two years Tomlinson drifted around Europe, taking jobs as a snowboard instructor, deckhand, mathematics tutor, and translator, never finding the excitement or sense of purpose he admitted MI6 had provided. Finally he settled in Antibes in the south of France as a salesman for a company that rented yachts for tourists.

EARLY IN THE AFTERNOON OF AUGUST 30, 1997, beneath a cobalt blue sky, a private jet landed at Le Bourget Airport, eight miles northeast of Paris. On board were Diana, Princess of Wales, and her recently acquired lover, Dodi al-Fayed, son of Harrods millionaire Mohammed al-Fayed. It was an unscheduled stopover in Paris, hastily penciled in on the couple's original itinerary after the paparazzi had besieged their Sardinian holiday hideaway the day before. It was to be their final flight together. Twenty-one hours later, at 12:23 A.M. on August 31, the princess was seriously injured in the backseat of the Mercedes in which she was a passenger. Beside her lay Dodi's body; he had been killed instantly when the car glanced off the thirteenth pillar of the Pont de l'Alma tunnel and smashed side-on into its concrete wall. The battle to save the princess was to last a few hours longer before she was pronounced dead at the Pitie-Salpetriere Hospital just after 4:00 A.M.

When he first saw the images of the crash on his television, Tomlinson's initial reaction was "My God, how could that have happened?"

It would be a question echoed by millions of people around the world. Soon one answer had gained popularity over all the others. Diana had been killed by MI6, went the endless mantra, killed on the order of her former father-in-law, Prince Philip, to the Secret Intelligence Service because she planned to marry Dodi, a Muslim, and so create an unprecedented constitutional crisis for the royal family. The claim became the leitmotif for conspiracy theorists the world over—and had sent Tomlinson searching for the aide-mémoire he had written after his meeting with Nick Fishwick, who had shown him the document describing how President Slobodan Milosevic could be assassinated. That plan had not been carried through, but could it have served as a blueprint for the terrible tragedy in the tunnel? Tomlinson had no doubt. "It could well have been. Only a fool would refuse to believe MI6 did not have the resources or had not used them in the past," he told the author.

In the untold billions of words subsequently spoken or written about the deaths of Diana and Dodi, Tomlinson's allegation was the one seized upon by Mohammed al-Fayed to launch an extraordinary and, at times bizarre, campaign alleging that the royal family, led by the Duke of Edinburgh, was behind a plot to kill Diana. She was pregnant with Dodi's child, al-Fayed claimed, and the royals had her killed rather than accept a Muslim stepfather for the future King William.

Tomlinson had remained unshaken through interviews by Scotland Yard detectives in his assertion that the document to assassinate Slobodan Milosevic not only really existed but remained in the highly restricted Y file. The inquiry by Lord Stevens, the former Commissioner of Scotland Yard, confirmed its existence—but insisted it could not be linked to the deaths of Diana and Dodi.

In October 2007, at the outset of the inquest that had finally gone ahead after pressure from Mohammed al-Fayed to hold it in public, the coroner, Lord Justice Scott Baker, said any assassination proposal would have to be examined, as a number of witnesses would claim they saw "flashing lights in the tunnel just before the crash." One witness, Brian Anderson, a passenger in a taxi that was passed by the Mercedes carrying Diana and Dodi, would testify he saw "a flash of great intensity like magnesium igniting shortly before I heard an explosion." For Tomlinson, it was sufficient confirmation that MI6 had been "involved directly in the plot or they had used a surrogate."

There were many observers who believed that no matter what verdict the inquest finally returned, the theory launched by Richard Tomlinson would continue to reverberate. Within MI6, there was an equally entrenched feeling that he had acted out of vindictiveness.

DURING CHRISTMAS OF 1995, no one in MI5 knew Stella Rimington had decided she would resign in the coming April, when she would have served twenty-seven years in the Security Service, four of them as director-general.

The memory of that bright summer morning in 1969, when she had walked into Leconfield House as a junior assistant officer not knowing what to expect but filled with a determination to do her best, had long been replaced by the satisfaction of having been the first woman to head any of Britain's intelligence services and also the conviction she had played an important role in shaping MI5's future. She had worked closely with several prime ministers and home secretaries, sometimes not always easily, and had learned Whitehall was dominated by politicians driven by self-interest and not above stabbing her in the back. She had handled them the way she did anyone who tried to get the better of her, with a cool look followed by a firm response. Her one great personal pleasure had been to see the growing number of women who joined every year, not only as secretaries but eager to use their intellectual abilities to deal with the serious issues of terrorism and crime.

Technology had become part of Rimington's daily life in a way that a decade earlier she would never have thought possible. The Internet and mobile phone systems were absorbed into hundreds of satellite networks, and the computer specialists several floors below her office spoke of "backdoor lists" and "sniffer software." She had battled with the Treasury to ensure MI5 was sufficiently funded to remain in the race for hardware; she had learned that a quantum computer could scan a massive body of intercepts and that by the next millennium the latest computers would be called nanomachines with circulatory systems making them a hundred billion times faster than the laptop she used.

The mandatory age for retirement is sixty years in Britain's public service, and she had given much of them to her working life while other concerns had taken a backseat; her marriage and her friendships outside MI5 had suffered. What would she do when she no longer walked into Thames House, knowing she ultimately controlled everyone and everything that happened in the building? The prospect of sitting in a chair knitting appalled her. She wondered if she should try for a post as master of one of the Cambridge or Oxford colleges from where, over the years, had come so many of her officers. She applied for the vacant mastership of Emmanuel College, Cambridge, but no sooner had she done so than the news leaked to the press, and her application fell by the wayside because of the fear of the college fellows that the security risks she posed were too great for the venerable building; shortly after her application the IRA had detonated a massive truck bomb in the Docklands.

News of her application had triggered the question in MI5: Exactly when would she finally retire, and who would replace her?

The thought had already been in Rimington's mind when she went to another of those duty-calls dinners, this one for the London diplomatic corps. During the meal, an ambassador to one of the former Soviet Bloc countries had turned to the other guests at her table and announced that Rimington knew the names of all his mistresses. She had politely smiled the claim aside, but it made her wonder if that was how some people saw her work, as someone who ordered her staff to pry into people's sexual peccadilloes. Certainly Peter Wright, her bête noire, had claimed such snooping was part of "the fun when we burgled and bugged our way across London for the State, and pompous, bowler-hatted civil servants in Whitehall pretended to look the other way."

There was some truth in that claim. When the 1985 Interception and Communications Act passed through Parliament, giving MI5 and MI6 the right to tap phones and intercept mail, it was deemed to be politically sensitive to include bugging private conversations. But as Rimington knew, it went on: Foreign intelligence services did it; so did detective agencies. To exclude it from the act was one thing, the reality another.

By New Year's 1996, there was speculation in MI5 about whether her decision to retire came after she had been driven to one of her meetings at JIC or the Home Office to sit in on yet another discussion about the need for a government minister of terrorism, an idea that had gained momentum as the IRA bombing campaign intensified. She had opposed the concept because it would politicize the intelligence services; besides, there were sufficient watchdogs in Parliament, the Home Office, and JIC.

How much had her appearance before a Washington oversight national security committee to investigate the situation in Northern Ireland played its part in her decision to go? The committee had no authority to summon her, but she had gone because she wanted to tell them of the very real threat domestic terrorism posed. Her interrogators had been hostile from the outset, often barely concealing their support for the "hard-pressed" Catholic community and the "inevitability" it would seek support from the IRA against "the British Army occupiers."

She had flown home knowing she would have to give an account of herself to the Intelligence and Security Committee. Created in 1994, it consisted of members of Parliament tasked to "examine the expenditure, administration, and policies" of MI5, MI6, and GCHQ. Its nine members met every week in secret session in Room 150 in the Cabinet Office to produce "issue reports," which were hand-carried through a connecting door into the prime minister's office on Downing Street. The last thing Tony Blair did in 2007 before resigning was to sign off on such a report; among the first documents Gordon Brown read on becoming prime minister was an issue report.

The rumors concerning when Rimington would resign had given way to speculation about who would replace her. Two very different candidates had emerged. One was Julian Hansen. In his late forties, he looked and spoke like a classic Whitehall mandarin. He kept his own views on a matter under careful lock and key until he had taken every possible sounding and then he delivered his own verdict in short sentences. He was Rimington's deputy, and, in every way, he was more John le Carré's Smiley than Ian Fleming's Bond. The other front-runner was Stephen Lander. Annie Machon claimed he had a dismissive attitude toward junior officers. After she had spent a morning preparing a terrorist assessment, he had once told her that he didn't bother to read their briefs. Lander had been involved when the SAS shot dead three IRA terrorists on Gibraltar, despite a warning they were not armed. After the incident, Lander had moved steadily up the promotion ladder to become director of corporate affairs in charge of the Registry and ensuring the Security Service had the latest computers and software. One item was the PROMIS system, a surveillance tool developed by a Washington-based specialist company, INSLAW, used by the Security Service to track the movements of the growing numbers of Middle East groups who had set up bases in London and the IRA members who came and went across the border with the Irish Republic. Israel's former national security adviser Ari Ben-Menashe, who had played a role in developing a Mossad version of the program, said that "PROMIS changed the thinking of the entire intelligence world."

With his usual stealth, Lander moved to secure his position to become the next director-general of the Security Service. Diminutive, defensive, quick to blame others, and prickly, he had secured the support of the statuesque Eliza Manningham-Buller, who was then the principal

operations director with overall responsibility for surveillance, telephone tapping, and covert searches. She towered over Lander, but next
to Rimington she had the most comprehensive knowledge of the operational side of MI5. Unlike Lander, she had considerable experience in
agent running, had been involved in the Lockerbie investigation, had
headed the Middle East section, and had served in Washington as MI5's
liaison officer. Forceful, opinionated, and calm under pressure, she was
the antithesis of Lander, but by the beginning of 1996 the "odd couple,"
as they were described to the author by one former MI5 officer, were
displaying what he called the "signs of a plot on the boil." Manningham-
Buller and Lander were spending time in one or the other's office and
supported each other at the weekly staff meetings of heads of department. "There were other small signs, like sitting together in a corner of
the bar, then leaving at the same time and lunching together in the
restaurant. It was all very lovey-dovey, but this was not one of the usual
affairs which flared and faded in Thames House. This was good old-
fashioned plotting."

At some point in January 1996, Lander had requested a meeting
with Rimington. He told her he wanted to make it clear he hoped he
would have her support to become her replacement. If Rimington was
astonished at such blatant lobbying she kept it to herself, not least because she knew the appointment was ultimately in the gift of the incumbent prime minister and she had been careful not to give Downing
Street any indication of her preference. When the time came, all she
could do was recommend.

A few days later, Lander requested a second meeting. This time he
arrived with Manningham-Buller. They both said they had no confidence
that Hansen would have the skills needed to direct MI5 after her departure. He was called "ineffectual" by Lander and "lacking in presence" by
Manningham-Buller.

Behind her closed door, with her secretary given strict instructions
to hold all calls, Rimington listened as both Lander and Manningham-
Buller played their trump card: They would resign if Hansen were appointed director-general. Their departure would not only cause a major
media outcry but would also have a huge impact on morale. By the end
of the meeting, Rimington agreed to ask Hansen to abandon any plan
he had of becoming her successor. In return, she would ensure he remained as deputy director. Hansen gracefully agreed, knowing he had
been outmaneuvered by a powerful new axis within MI5. It subsequently emerged that Lander had promised Manningham-Buller she
would be his deputy and he would support her appointment as next

director-general after his retirement. It was a classic coup d'état plucked from the pages of le Carré.

ON THE DAY STELLA RIMINGTON finally retired in April 1996, she cleared her desktop of photographs of her two daughters and other memorabilia, placing them into a box to take home with the bunch of flowers colleagues had given her, to which she had responded with a short, witty speech, and left Thames House for the last time still with no job to go to but with a thought evolving in her mind. She would write her autobiography. She knew her career had generated considerable interest, and she hoped an account of her life would attract readers. Not for a moment did she anticipate the furor her decision would produce.

After completing her manuscript, Stella Rimington typed a note to her successor, Stephen Lander, saying she would be happy to make any changes that might be required under the Official Secrets Act. She placed the letter with the manuscript and had it hand-delivered by a former colleague to Thames House. Apart from a brief acknowledgment letter, she heard nothing for two months. She was not unduly concerned; she knew how long the process could take.

She was completely unaware of the reaction that had followed the manuscript's arrival in MI5. Lander had personally authorized copies to be made, and within days they were circulating within the Joint Intelligence Committee and the Cabinet Office, being given the same scrutiny as Peter Wright's *Spycatcher*, Tomlinson's book, and the earlier work of Kim Philby. There were at least two meetings at JIC during which Rimington's manuscript was picked over, page by page, and often line by line. There was consensus that Rimington was another whistle-blower and had to be stopped from publishing. So she would clearly understand the seriousness of her position, she had to be brought before the ultimate Whitehall judge of such matters, Sir Richard Wilson, the cabinet secretary.

In the meantime, the usual back door would be used to discourage any publisher in Britain from publishing the book. MI5 would mobilize its friendly journalists—contacts Rimington had been instrumental in creating—who should be told that her book was an attempt to cover up her own incompetence and that, in places, its contents were a "grotesque act of betrayal." A copy of the manuscript was leaked to the mass circulation *Sun*, long the newspaper of choice for the kind of campaign that now followed. The *Sun*, after expressing its anger at the content, returned the manuscript to Downing Street, having made its own copy.

Rimington found herself placed in the same public stocks as other whistle-blowers. She began to feel like a character in a Kafka novel as a stream of abuse was hurled at her. Worse was to come when she appeared before Sir Richard Wilson in his splendid office on Downing Street. Wilson had the cold, incisive manner of a hanging judge. He began by simply asking her to withdraw the book. She explained it was only a draft manuscript and she was ready to have any passages removed that could be construed as breaking the Official Secrets Act. Her offer was the signal for Wilson to launch into his renowned bullying and threatening mode: The book could not be published in its present form. Rimington saw an opening; she would cooperate on any changes required. Wilson stared at her, his belligerence slowly fading. If all the changes required could be agreed on, he would, after all, recommend a truncated book could be published, providing the government concurred.

In the end, the book in its published form was described as "a bland, harmless account." There was no reference to how she saw her meeting with Wilson which Rimington recalled as "a polite bollocking—mostly polite, but sometimes pretty sharp." Neither did the book include his stern reminder that "anything" said by a former director-general of MI5 could be useful to the enemies of the realm. She had maintained her loyalty to the state she had long served only to be rewarded by a media campaign mounted against her.

16

Tango in the Basement

In the first week of July 1997, the atmosphere in the command center in the basement of Vauxhall Cross, the home of the Secret Intelligence Service for the past two years, was not unlike those World War II times when senior officers waited for the signal that a bombing raid on a German target had been successful. There was the same controlled tension, the quick nods, the glances at wristwatches, the looks when someone came or went from the large open-plan room. Otherwise, the center bore little resemblance to its wartime predecessor, where blackboards and maps covered in colored streamers indicated the routes to and from targets starkly clear in the harsh overhead lights.

The center's lights were low, shadowless pools illuminating the workstations, each equipped with a computer and communications console that could reach anyone on a restricted list of names positioned alongside. Those who worked at the stations wore tiny earpieces and throat mikes to listen or speak to anyone as necessary.

At one end of the room was a large electronic plasma screen. It was linked to an NSA satellite, one of the Trumpet series equipped with the latest voice-recognition technology. In a top corner of the screen was a twenty-four-hour clock that gave the local time in Bosnia. The screen could be split to provide alternate views of the same location or images from various locations, which had been downloaded by the satellite to Menwith Hill and relayed directly to the screen.

Trumpet had been targeted to track the whereabouts of Simo Drljaca, a Serbian police chief, and Dr. Milan Kovacevic, an anesthetist;

both had been indicted by the war crimes tribunal in The Hague for "ethnic cleansing" during the war in Bosnia five years previously. So far they had evaded capture.

In a semicircle before the screen sat the controllers of Operation Tango, the code name for kidnapping the two Serbs and flying them to The Hague to stand trial. The order to do so followed a meeting of the Joint Intelligence Committee, chaired by Dame Pauline Neville-Jones, a highflier from the Foreign Office with a go-for-it reputation. Prime Minister Tony Blair had swiftly approved the operation and tasked MI6 to organize it. The first-stage planning had been given to the SAS's Counter-Revolutionary Warfare Wing. It operated from its own war room inside its Regent's Park headquarters in London. Photographs of the two wanted men were acquired from Bosnia and sent to Menwith Hill for uploading into the satellite. Details about their families and friends were obtained by NATO intelligence officers on the ground. The last known movements of the pair were provided, along with a description of the vehicles they were known to use and an estimation of the number of Serb bodyguards they might have; the figure varied between thirty and fifty battle-hardened veterans of the Bosnia war.

When a detailed plan had been drawn up and approved, the SAS team moved into the Vauxhall Cross basement. That had been at the end of June. Now, a week later, the command center was in full operational mode. There were senior SAS officers, including two from the Fourteenth Intelligence Company, which had earned its reputation fighting the IRA in Northern Ireland as the most deadly of all SAS units. Speed and aggression were at the core of all it did, and every new piece of electronic equipment came to the company first. Like the other SAS officers, its members wore no identifying shoulder flashes; everyone in the room knew who they were. The others wore NATO flashes on their shoulder tabs.

THE ONE CIVILIAN AMONG the uniforms was David Spedding, the first chief never to have served in the armed forces. That July week, he was fifty-two years old and in his third year of running the Secret Intelligence Service, the youngest in its history to hold the position. A chain-smoker from his days as head boy at Sherborne School, he had later campaigned against the nuclear bomb, joining the protest marches in London—much to the dismay of his father, who had been a colonel in the Border Regiment. Spedding's background was as distinguished as that of any of the officers in the command center.

Having read medieval history at Oxford and learned French and Spanish in his spare time, he had spent a year at the British Embassy in Santiago, finding stories from the Chilean press to send to London. His selection was enough to bring an offer couched in the usual terms of "doing something a little more interesting." He graduated from Fort Monkton with a sufficiently high grade to be sent to Lebanon to study Arabic at Shenlan, the language school where Kim Philby once studied.

Two years later, Spedding became a member of the MI6 station in Beirut. The city was already becoming a dangerous place, and the tension in the streets was reflected inside the hundred and more mosques during Friday prayers. The imams reminded the faithful that God, not the God of Christendom and Judaism but the Allah-God of the Hezbollah, required them one day soon to avenge the Catastrophe of 1948, that time when more than two million Arabs had been driven from their homeland because the land was needed to form the new Israel.

Among those people, Spedding had created his own network of informers—shoeshine boys, carpet sellers, and businessmen—who kept him apprised of the bubbling tensions. With his ability to speak their language, understand their culture, and sympathize with their bitterness, he learned much when he met those he called "my people" at the Hippodrome, the city racecourse, or one of the street cafés on Corniche Mazraa; to those who wished it of him he spoke French, the second language of Beirut, and sometimes Spanish to the students he had recruited at the American University, but mostly it was his fluent Arabic he relied on to catch the nuances of what was being said.

His reports to London described the growing inflation, the strident editorializing of Hezbollah's two newspapers, the first barricades dividing Christian Beirut from Muslim West Beirut, where the Shiites lived and practiced a faith in which martyrdom promised them a place in paradise. Spedding observed the imams had become increasingly more vociferous in their proclamation that the time was fast approaching to make Lebanon a completely Islamic society from which the West would be excluded. His reports earned him praise, and it was decided by the Middle East Directorate to widen his experience in the Arab world by posting him to Abu Dhabi in the United Arab Emirates. Spedding was all MI6 expected, and his superiors' satisfaction was reflected in that commendation in his personnel file.

It was there Spedding saw Osama bin Laden for the first time, when he witnessed him holding an audience spellbound in the dusty open-air square of Tarif (Murban), a town overlooking the Gulf. The sheikh had traveled from Khartoum to deliver his sermon, which quoted extensively from a book by a militant scholar, Abdallah Azzam, *Defending the Land of the Muslims Is Each Man's Most Important Duty.* Bin Laden had extrapolated from the text to demand that every individual Muslim must commit himself to jihad. Spedding obtained a copy of the book and compared it to bin Laden's own speech, which supporters had distributed after the sermon. While the sheikh's words lacked the subtleties of Azzam's writing, Spedding saw how cleverly bin Laden interpreted the book for his own theme; that the *umma,* the Islamic global community, had been under attack for two centuries: first by the French invasion of Egypt at the end of the eighteenth century, then Britain's occupation of Egypt, followed by the Italian capture of Libya, then the realignment of the entire Middle East after World War I by Britain and France leading to the creation of Israel, and finally the domination of the entire region by America. He had ended with a clear warning America would forever subjugate the *umma* until its people rose. It would not be military might that would lead the faithful to victory. It would be their Islamic faith.

Spedding's report to the Middle East Directorate was the first concise document the Secret Intelligence Service had received about Osama bin Laden's intentions that his war would be a religious one, devoid of the slightest hint of the traditional values of tolerance to the impious, a pitiless war to be waged as a matter of individual obligation by all Muslims as long as the *umma* remained threatened. The warning delivered in that dusty square in the Gulf was simply filed in the directorate with all the other reports about radical Muslim preachers fulminating against their enemies—so many of them had come to nothing.

Two years later Spedding became station commander in Amman, Jordan, and earned a second commendation when he uncovered a plan by Abu Nidal, the leader of a breakaway group from the Palestinian Liberation Front, to assassinate the Queen on her state visit to Jordan. Despite misgivings in the Foreign Office, Spedding advised the trip should go ahead, a view with which the Queen and Prime Minister Thatcher concurred. Her Majesty made him a Commander of the Royal Victorian Order during her visit, the first time she had awarded any MI6 officer during a state trip.

Spedding was now on the fast track to the top: He was appointed controller of all Middle East operations against terrorists from the region, and when the first Gulf War started, he took charge of MI6 operations in Kuwait and Iraq. Afterward, Colin McColl appointed him as his deputy.

When he became chief, the twelfth man to do so, Spedding supervised the move to the new Vauxhall Cross headquarters at 85 Albert Embankment, personally taking charge of the longcase clock that the first chief, Mansfield Cumming, had built. Spedding was glad to move out of Century House after staff members had complained the building was affecting their health and one or two had been diagnosed with cancer. No one knew Spedding had started to develop the first symptoms of the disease—and had been advised by his doctors to stop smoking. He had ignored the warning and, on that first week in July 1997, continued to inhale his forty cigarettes a day as Operation Tango moved to its climax.

THE SAS COUNTER-REVOLUTIONARY WARFARE TEAM, accompanied by a unit from the Fourteenth Intelligence Company, had flown from RAF Brize Norton. With them went an MI6 officer who would act as the liaison with the Vauxhall Cross command center.

Arriving at the multinational headquarters at Sarajevo, the team transferred to American Black Hawk helicopters and, in what was later described as "a perfect fastball operation," had swooped on the town of Prijedor. Police chief Simo Drljaca was hiding out in a police barracks. When he opened fire as the helicopters landed nearby, he was shot dead and his men fled. Minutes later, Dr. Milan Kovacevic was arrested in the town hospital.

The signal to the command center was two letters: "DD." Done and Dusted.

BY JANUARY 1998, eight years had passed since the end of the Soviet occupation of Afghanistan, where Osama bin Laden had fought. His role in that war in a country like no other in the Middle East, with its long tradition of mountain warfare and total resistance to any invader, passed virtually unnoticed against the huge resources of American money and weapons and the full backing of the Pakistani state. While bin Laden was an undoubted hero to the Arabs he had led into battle with American Stinger missiles, which brought down Russian bombers, and American explosives shipped in by the truckload from Pakistan, to the outside world he was still little more than a footnote in a barbaric conflict in which the Russians had lost fifteen thousand lives and suffered close to forty thousand casualties. Nearly two million Afghanis had died, their villages razed and their livestock slaughtered.

For bin Laden it had been a turning point. Already moved by the intoxicating speeches of the Ayatollah Ruhollah Khomeini of Iran, he saw his own role as a committed fighter against all perceived enemies of

Islam, and his interpretation of the Koran continued to provide the theological cover for his repeated cry to those he had led in battle against the Soviets, "The sword is the key to paradise which can be used only by holy warriors."

Even to the CIA officers he fought alongside, he remained a withdrawn figure, speaking to them only through an interpreter and then usually to ask for more vitamins and the drug Arcalion, normally prescribed for weakness and fatigue, a condition that years later led to the reports he had developed kidney failure in Afghanistan. He insisted the drug helped him to concentrate on how he would deal with his enemies. To the officers he was definitely an oddball who lived in a tent in the depths of winter, chewed ice, and bathed in near-frozen rivers. In between he prayed, rolling out his mat five times a day, his rifle close to his left arm, on which he wore a watch he had removed from the body of a Russian officer.

After his ablutions, he sat down and wrote another of the speeches that set out his long-term ambitions, scribbling on a scratch pad with a pen from the box of ballpoints he carried in his rucksack. Not for a moment did the officers realize he was setting down his hatred of what their country represented. Even if copies of his writings had been sent to Langley, the half dozen analysts on the Middle East Desk had more pressing responsibilities to keep track of: what the Arab press was reporting about Yasser Arafat, Hezbollah, and the PLO. Besides, the desk's interpreters did not include fluent native-born linguists for the nineteen languages and dialects of the region.

Before bin Laden had gone to Afghanistan, he had synthesized his attitude, "Because infidels have killed, we must kill you. Our innocents are not less innocent than yours." Yet when Cofer Black, a veteran station chief in Khartoum, had warned Langley of the danger bin Laden posed, he had been told that any such threat was aimed against King Faud of Saudi Arabia for allowing American troops to remain in the kingdom after the Gulf War had liberated Kuwait from Saddam's Iraq. No connection had been made between bin Laden's antipathy to the ruler and the continuous presence of foreign soldiers on the Saudi soil bin Laden held more sacred than any other.

IN LONDON IN 1998, Jonathan Evans, by now the director of MI5's international counterterrorism branch, continued to explore bin Laden's background and the growing influence al-Qaeda had through its cells in Europe, North Africa, and the Gulf. Everywhere in the Muslim world governments found themselves confronting a new generation of not only the urban poor but young intellectuals, while in Germany, France, and Britain—unlike their parents, who complied with the laws and cultures of the countries they chose to settle in—Muslim children often came to believe their hosts were responsible for the failure to provide proper education and jobs and to protect them against racism and police harassment. Those claims became part of the Friday prayers when clerics read out the words of Osama bin Laden, but there were still insufficient linguists in MI5 to translate the words. The priority for them remained translating the Irish-language newsletters that supported the IRA and trying to make sense of what the Arab press published in London. Bin Laden's name never cropped up; it was Arafat and other leaders of Middle East groups who commanded the headlines.

Yet from Bosnia to Chechnya and across the breadth of Europe, a growing number of Muslim youths joined the Community of Believers, mesmerized by the words of Osama bin Laden, who, almost a decade earlier, had set down in the mountain fastness of Afghanistan the utopian aims of al-Qaeda, "To establish the truth, rid the world of infidel evil, and establish an Islamic nation. The way this will come about will be to put aside the education offered by infidels and read only the Holy Book." At every Friday prayer meeting, the words were spoken as a reminder to the faithful of their duty.

Evans had wondered how British Muslims, born in the country, raised, educated, and immersed in its culture, could so easily accept this doctrine. How far would they go to implement it?

IN HIS SEARCH FOR ANSWERS EVANS had read the file on Abu Hamza, the radical imam at the Finsbury Park mosque in London, who ended each of his sermons by announcing a jihad against Jews and the descendants of the Crusaders who had occupied the Al-Aqsa mosque in Jerusalem on July 15, 1099, only to be driven out by Saladin in 1187. Soon the new "battalions of faith" would once more sweep aside the infidels of Britain. Sheikh Osama had promised no less, Hamza had shouted at his followers.

More than any other imam, he had attracted young and often impressionable Muslims: They traveled not only from their homes in London but from cities as far away as Bradford, Birmingham, and Leeds. Hamza had the skill of a born street-corner orator, and they applauded when he praised the militants in Egypt, from where he had fled for his life because of his extremist views, receiving political asylum in Britain.

They nodded in excited agreement when he urged them to go to one of the training camps in Pakistan's Northwest Frontier province to learn how to defend themselves against hated infidels. They clapped even longer when he exulted at the arrival of the Taliban in Afghanistan to use sharia—Koranic law—to end the lawlessness, to make it compulsory for women to wear the burka, and to publicly execute all those who broke the law.

Each week at noon, the heavily bearded Hamza, his squint and a hook in place of his left hand giving him the look of a stage villain, brought more news to his spellbound listeners: how Islamism had gained power in the once Communist republics of Tadjikistan and Chechnya and how young Muslims who had fought in Afghanistan had joined al-Qaeda. When Hamza finished preaching, he urged his congregation to join the fight. Those who had money should donate it—and he would ensure it would be used to pay the fares of those willing to go to be trained in Pakistan. They would be welcomed, he said, by the greatest fighter of them all, Sheikh Osama. His name had echoed around the mosque and had been noted by the MI5 officer sent by Jonathan Evans to begin the slow process of gathering evidence, which would finally, in 2006, result in Abu Hamza being sentenced to seven years' imprisonment for "promoting and taking part in terrorist activities."

By then the Security Service specialists—the psychiatrists, psychologists, behaviorists, scientists, and voice analysts—had begun to make deductions about bin Laden. A behaviorist suggested he could have developed a "messianic madness," a religious psychosis in which death increasingly featured. He had cited bin Laden's response to the car bombing that had killed seven people in the center of Riyadh in November 1995, five of them Americans. Before they were publicly beheaded, the bombers had said they were influenced by the writings of bin Laden. In June 1996, when nineteen American soldiers were killed and hundreds more injured in another attack in Saudi Arabia, he had expressed hope the deaths would make the Saudi ruling family reconsider their policy of allowing infidel soldiers to remain in the country. A psychologist had wondered if the demand was another clue to his personality, "the seemingly devoted husband to his four wives who had given him twenty-four children, who saw the cold-blooded murder of the sons of American mothers as a way to change Saudi foreign policy."

Only a few photographs existed of bin Laden (videos would only start to appear after 9/11), and they had been enlarged and studied intensely by computer experts skilled in the Facial Analysis Comparison

and Elimination System (FACES), which took forty-nine characteristics
to create images of how bin Laden would look in certain states of mind;
angry, uncertain, satisfied, and disappointed were among them. Physically bin Laden was an easy man to spot. With his high cheekbones and
thin lips went a long pepper-and-salt beard and sharp, penetrating eyes.
One of the photographs had caught his smile; it revealed a poor set of
teeth. A specialist had wondered if bin Laden had deliberately ignored
dental care, as he had been raised in a society where healthy teeth were
a sign of wealth. Was this another way to turn his back on the past and
become more identifiable with the impoverished?

Evans had arranged for a City of London banker to study the financial status of the bin Laden family. From near poverty it had risen to be
one of the most powerful in Saudi Arabia and its Saudi–bin Laden
group (SBG) had an estimated worth in 1997 of $8 billion, employing
thirty-three thousand workers in construction projects that included
building a new Hyatt hotel in Amman, Jordan, and a $150 million base
outside Riyadh for four thousand American soldiers. Other SBG projects were distributing American soft drinks across the Middle East and
being licensed by Disney to publish books based on Mickey Mouse and
other animated characters. Yet Osama bin Laden's own share of the
group's annual profits had never been more than twenty-seven million
Saudi riyals, a little over $7 million. While the sum still made him rich,
it did not place him at the same level as the scions of Saudi's other trading families. After the Riyadh bombings, SBG had been ordered by
King Faud to stop paying bin Laden's annual dividend; at the same
time, his assets in Saudi had been frozen, his passport and citizenship
were canceled, and he had been expelled from the kingdom. From
Khartoum he had delivered his defiance, "We are living in dignity and
honor, for which we thank God. It is much better for us to live under a
tree here on these mountains than to live in palaces in the land most sacred to God, yet subjected to the disgrace of not worshipping God even
in the most sacred land on earth, where injustice is so widespread."

The specialists realized the words would have stirred the imagination
of his followers. They would see him as a leader who had rejected the
luxury of his family and his peers to live the life of a holy man. He might
lack the textual subtleties of other Koran exegetes, but he spoke in a
voice from which the impoverished illiterates could draw strength, both
as devout Muslims and as advocates for radical change in the world
where they were forced to live alongside infidels.

In 1998, even Jonathan Evans, by now recognized as the Security

Service's expert on al-Qaeda, was unable to speculate how far Osama bin Laden would go to use his religious authority to launch his own version of Armageddon.

ON A MISTY WEEKDAY MORNING IN FEBRUARY 1998, two cars converged on the crossroads that marked the summit of Sally Gap, a scenic spot in the Wicklow Mountains of the Irish Republic. In one of the vehicles was an MI5 officer who had flown into Dublin on the early morning flight from London. The other car was driven by an IRA terrorist who had crossed over the border from Northern Ireland. He had been given the code name of "Skate," and the officer was traveling under the name of "Wilson"; both aliases would never be used again once the meeting ended.

Its location had been chosen for two reasons: At this time of year there were unlikely to be any tourists driving past the mounds of cut turf; and the weather would reduce visibility for any surveillance operation being conducted by the Gardaí, though it was doubtful its Irish Special Branch had got wind of the meeting. Both the intelligence officer and the IRA terrorist knew the importance of airtight security in what was known in the Security Service as "parallel diplomacy," in which MI5, like other intelligence services, maintained backdoor channels of communication with enemies of the state, contacts that would be politically unthinkable—and even physically dangerous—for other servants of government to consider.

The CIA had established links with the PLO long before Yasser Arafat had been invited to the White House by President Clinton; the Mossad had its own pipeline into Egyptian intelligence and, from time to time, had shared common interests with the KGB and its successor, the FSB; MI6 had maintained contacts with the African National Congress in the run-up to the peaceful transition to black rule in South Africa, sometimes acting as a broker between the ANC and the intelligence service of the apartheid regime.

Meir Amit, a former director-general of the Mossad, widely regarded as one of the best door-openers into the mysterious world of the back channel, described to the author how it works, "We tell the other side what we would like to see happen. Usually these are senior intelligence officers who we know exert influence within their governments. If they are members of a terrorist organization, we make the same assumption. It's a dark world in which a good address book is essential. Contacts often include businessmen and those who operate close to the edge of legality." In the past, Amit had used connections to pave the way for an exchange of prisoners or for building bridges that allowed Israeli diplomats to have working relationships with Jordan and Lebanon.

The kind of meeting that took place in the Irish countryside had once been described by Jonathan Evans as "allowing no stone to be left unturned to advance the cause of peace," and Gerry Adams, the head of Sinn Fein, the political wing of the IRA, who had himself been involved in similar meetings, later admitted a "long line of contact" existed between MI5 and his organization.

William Casey, the former CIA director who once depicted himself as "hooked on the back door," explained to the author why, "The channel evokes mutual trust, which is often not possible through the usual channels. We saw that when the Japanese ambassador in Washington lied to our government over Pearl Harbor. Given what we knew later, if there had been a back channel to Tokyo, things just may have worked out differently. In the back channel you have to maintain a basis of trust. Otherwise there is no point in going there. Both sides visit because they have been asked by their political masters to explore the possibility of moving forward in a delicate situation. While everyone in the channel knows there will be no final conclusion until the diplomats sign off, what the channel offers is exploration, a place where a clear understanding exists that either side can walk away and the discussions never took place. If one side breaks that understanding, it's a hundred percent guaranteed there will be no way back in. In all my time, I never found the other side breaking that rule."

After MI6 was withdrawn from Northern Ireland following the Littlejohn debacle, MI5 had continued to develop its own contacts with the IRA, which took place in IRA safe houses on either side of the Irish border. Those contacts were fraught with problems. MI5 had no mandate from Britain's government to meet the demands of the IRA. The Security Service's brief was, in the words of one officer, "to discover what was possible." Meetings took weeks to set up, and on the IRA side its army council had to meet to finally approve any contact. Many ended in failure after intelligence officers had reported back the demands of the IRA, which were firmly rejected by the government. Still, the back channel continued to remain open, and long after the original hostility had thawed, something close to mutual understanding continued late into the night over more than one bottle of Irish whiskey.

The rules for a meeting remained the same. There would be no surveillance around the meeting place either by the army patrols or helicopters fitted with long distance listening equipment. No more than two MI5 officers would attend, and under no circumstances would any member of the Royal Ulster Constabulary be allowed to be present. There would be no bugging device carried by either side. Notes could be taken to avoid any future dispute over what was discussed and agreed upon. After the meeting, no attempt would be made to follow the IRA negotiators.

Finally came a meeting with Martin McGuinness, then the IRA commander of the Derry Brigade. It began with him reading out a statement to the MI5 officers, first warning, "No word of this is to be changed." There was a moment of silence; then the hard-voiced McGuinness continued, "It is to be understood that we are prepared to enter into dialogue for an unannounced cease-fire and to have a dialogue leading to a lasting peace."

The MI5 officers could not quite hide their smiles. Years of using the back channel had finally led to a major breakthrough. The meeting in the mists of the Sally Gap was the latest to bring closer what finally became known as the Good Friday Agreement, which had been signed in April 1998 to finally bring peace to Northern Ireland.

ON AUGUST 7, 1998—the day between America dropping its nuclear bombs on Hiroshima and on Nagasaki fifty-three years before—Osama bin Laden delivered his latest threat to kill "as many Americans and their allies at every opportunity." The promise had been enshrined in the World Islamic Front, created the previous February by bin Laden and the Egyptian-born Ayman al-Zawahiri, who had become his most trusted strategist in the ever-expanding al-Qaeda, which six previous CIA directors in the past five years had failed to deal with.

Bin Laden had continued to expand his organization while the world's most powerful intelligence agency, which should have been aiming to destroy it, staggered from one disaster to another. During the Bosnian bloodbath, the CIA had not one agent in the country to report on the massacre in Srebernica by the Serbs; it was a full three weeks before Langley's photo analysts confirmed satellite images of the killings. There was the embarrassment of the French government very publicly expelling Dick Holm, the station chief in Paris, and four of his officers for economic espionage. Station chiefs in Latin America had been hauled back to Langley to face charges of stealing substantial sums given to them to fight drug runners; all had been allowed to quietly resign. A procession of DCIs had come and gone, unable to deal with what they saw as an out-of-control agency. Jim Woolsey sent his resignation letter by courier to President Clinton and caught the first plane out of Washington before anyone could try to change his mind. John Deutch survived seventeen months of turmoil before he was fired. Clinton offered the job to his national security adviser, Tony Lake. He didn't even make it to Langley, falling at the confirmation hearing. Watching in the wings was George Tenet, who as deputy director had virtually run the agency while Clinton looked for someone else to pick up the poisoned chalice. There were no takers. So he finally sent for the bull-necked Tenet, who had the swagger of a New York cop. "Fix things in Langley," ordered the president.

From the moment Tenet was appointed, he said, "I felt like I'd been shot out of a cannon. I bounced from meeting to meeting, with people thrusting thick briefing books into my hands and snatching them away almost before I'd had a chance to digest the first page."

Sworn in as the eighteenth director of central intelligence on July 11, 1997, Tenet found himself confronted with yet more problems wherever he looked. The agency was worse off for cash than he suspected and was struggling to keep up with the information age exploding on all fronts, where the Internet made encrypting language into code a simple matter for all college students. Yet another traitor had been discovered in the ranks. Harold Nicholson, the former station chief in Romania, had been recalled to run the Farm, the CIA training school outside Williamsburg, Virginia, until the FBI finally caught up with him. He had provided the Russians with the name of every graduate, making them virtually useless for any overseas posting. He was serving a twenty-three-year sentence. No one knew why Nicholson had carried out his betrayal.

The House Intelligence Committee had castigated the agency for lacking "the depth, breadth, and expertise needed to be a spy in the modern world." Ensconced in his sixth-floor suite at Langley, Tenet had found himself caught up in the CIA's fiftieth anniversary celebrations planned for the coming September. "It turned out," Tenet later admitted, "bin Laden was determined to piss on our parade." One of his first decisions on becoming director was to order a plan to capture bin Laden "if, and it was a big *if,* we can ever find him." He had also been warned by the attorney general, Janet Reno, it would actually be illegal to kill bin Laden before he was brought before an American court.

Mike Scheuer, an innovative veteran of counterterrorism operations, was put in charge of the plan. The first thing he did was to give it the code name Alec Station after his adopted Korean son. Scheuer sent an officer who had served in Afghanistan to contact the few remaining assets the agency had among the tribesmen to try to establish where bin Laden could be. To his delight, Scheuer learned bin Laden had been living for some months in a house on the outskirts of Kandahar. The plan went into top gear. When the time came, the CIA-led Afghanis would storm the house, using silenced weapons to kill anybody who tried to stop them, and grab bin Laden. They would rush him to a preselected cave in one of the mountains outside Kandahar and hold him there gagged, bound, and hooded. From there he would be spirited across the border into Pakistan, where a commercial shipping container would be waiting at a nearby military airport; from there he would be flown to the United States in a C-130 aircraft.

The container had been fitted with a dentist's chair, which Scheuer had specified must be able "to hold a person six feet five inches tall, and the restraints must be sufficiently strong to securely hold his ankles, thighs, and arms." Bin Laden was only six feet one and not known to have undue physical strength. A special linen hood, which would allow him to breathe comfortably and through which he could be fed during the flight, had been made. It would be secured to bin Laden's head with metal straps, giving him the look of Hannibal Lecter. A commode had been adapted to fit beneath the chair. Built into the container would be a small pharmacy with a wide range of sedatives. These would be administered "if required" by a doctor who would be selected from a panel of physicians the CIA kept on tap and travel in the container. There would also be a dialysis machine to handle any kidney problems; Scheuer had read the reports that bin Laden suffered from renal disease.

When the container had been flown to Pakistan, Scheuer had ordered a C-130 to practice flying in and out of the small Pakistani airfield normally only used by fighter planes. A landing strip able to take the C-130 upon its return to the United States had been created on Scheuer's orders at the same Texas ranch where President Lyndon Johnson had captivated his friends by pointing skyward. The final detail of the plan would be just as dramatic. An FBI agent would be waiting when the aircraft landed. The cargo door would be opened, the ramp lowered. To comply with Attorney General Reno's strict orders that "only the FBI or the police have arresting rights," the agent would wait until the dentist's chair was actually touching American soil before he would step forward, remove bin Laden's hood, formally ask his name, arrest him, and then read him his rights. There would be one film camera present to record the undoubtedly historic moment.

But other events intervened. India tested a nuclear bomb. Pakistan reacted by detonating six nuclear weapons under mountains close to the kidnap route Scheuer had chosen to bring out bin Laden. Suddenly the Afghanis recruited to storm the Kandahar house were no longer there. Osama bin Laden had also vanished, and no one in Alec Station had any idea as to where he had gone.

The sense of impending catastrophe that had kept George Tenet awake at nights trying not to disturb his wife, Stephanie, increased. Then came the early hours of August 7, 1998.

AT 5:31 A.M. THAT MORNING, the orderly routine of the CIA Counter-Terrorism Center in Langley was broken by a call from the station chief in Cairo. Moments later came a call from the Tel Aviv station. Both reported that the American embassies in Nairobi, Kenya, and Dar es Salaam, Tanzania, had been car-bombed. The senior duty officer at the center had glanced at the electronic calendar on his workstation: The day was the eighth anniversary of the day U.S. troops had first set foot in Saudi Arabia. The officer remembered the reports in the *Post* and *Time* a few months back, when bin Laden had declared a fatwa on the United States. This was his follow-up. The officer made his first call to George Tenet.

Since he had been appointed director, the basement of Tenet's house in suburban Maryland had been converted into a security command post. Manned around the clock by a two-man armed detail, it included a classified document vault and a communications console.

At 5:32 A.M. the red light on the console began to blink. Moments later Tenet, his first cup of coffee in his hand, walked in to take the call. He listened to the duty officer's report, which now included news that casualties could be high. Tenet then made his first call of the day.

Richard Clarke, who since 1992 had been the White House national coordinator for counterterrorism, was dressing when Tenet's call came. The first casualty estimates indicated at least a hundred dead and maybe a thousand injured. Among them were some Americans, Clarke recalled Tenet saying.

Clarke said he would call the president. Meanwhile, after calling the duty officer at Counter-Terrorism to get people to their crisis positions as soon as possible, Tenet made his way to the secure videoconference center (SVC) in the White House West Wing.

At 5:35 A.M. the console rang on President Clinton's night table. He picked up the handset to listen to Clarke's words. Clinton had found there was no person better than Clarke at reducing a crisis to its essentials. He explained the reason for his call, adding, "It looks like there are over two hundred dead and close to three thousand injured. We may have Americans among them, Mr. President."

"Do we know yet who's behind this?"

"Bin Laden. Has to be, Mr. President. He's declared war on us."

Clarke could imagine the look of horror on the president's face, but nothing showed in his voice.

"Okay, Dick," Clinton said. "Anything you recommend, I will back all the way."

IN NAIROBI, THE FIRST DETAILS OF THE ATTACKS were being pieced together by intelligence officers, including those of MI6, at their embassies in the city. The car bomb that had demolished the American Embassy had been constructed from TNT, aluminum nitrate, and aluminum powder. The ingredients had been mixed together and placed in wooden boxes, the kind in which fruit and vegetables are displayed in open markets, then wired to batteries and locked in a Toyota truck. Given the scale of the destruction, it seemed likely that two thousand pounds of mixed explosives had been used. The Tanzania bomb, though smaller, had the additional impact of being connected to a number of gas cylinders used for domestic cooking; exploded, they would have made effective fragmentation bombs. A gasoline truck had been used to drive into the American Embassy in Dar es Salaam.

For the experienced Mossad officers in both cities, the bombs appeared to have been the work of an expert, perhaps someone who had gained his knowledge providing the suicide bombers of Beirut with their car bombs. What really interested the officers was the manner in which the bombs had been detonated at intervals of two minutes. Was there some significance in that? Or was the decision to virtually explode them simultaneously a determined attempt by al-Qaeda to leave its mark? Not even the Beirut suicide bombers had detonated their bombs in tandem, and, until now, al-Qaeda attacks had been modest compared with those of Hezbollah and Hamas.

Did the double bombings in locations well apart signify not only al-Qaeda's arrival in international terrorism but a modus operandi that no one had predicted?

THE SECURE VIDEOCONFERENCE CENTER (SVC) was a small room paneled with dark wood and fitted with a bank of monitors on one wall. Opposite where Clarke sat at the head of the table was a presidential seal on the wall. Around the table were some of the members of the Counter-terrorism Security Group, chaired by the National Security Council, with each supported by his or her senior staff members. Several looked as if they had jumped out of bed. The exception was Gayle Smith, special assistant to the president for African affairs. In her elegant suit and carefully applied makeup, she could have been on her way to an early evening cocktail party and not attending a crisis meeting before most people in Washington had yet to eat breakfast.

Scattered around the table were plates of bagels and coffeepots. No one touched them; all eyes were on the monitors rapidly filling with familiar faces in their studios in the Pentagon, the State Department, Justice, the FBI, and the Department of Defense. At 6:40 A.M., barely an hour after the first call into the Counter-Terrorism Center, everyone was in place.

Clarke started the meeting with an update. There were now definitely a dozen Americans, including one CIA officer, confirmed dead. Two hundred and fifty of various nationalities had also been killed. The casualty figure now exceeded five thousand; many had severe injuries. Foreign embassies in both cities were doing all they could to help. Members of U.S. Embassy staffs in South Africa, Cairo, and Europe, were being flown in.

Clarke reminded everyone in the room and on the screens that "crisis mode" applied. Microphones were to be switched off unless a person was speaking. If anyone wanted to interrupt, he or she waved a hand. Clarke pointed to a red telephone on the table before him: Anyone who wanted to say something "ultra sensitive" should call him on the phone.

He turned to Gayle Smith. She was going to be in charge of getting heavy-lifting equipment to the devastated sites. That was a priority, to recover the dead and maybe—"just mebbee"—rescue anyone alive. The air force would fly out Nightingale teams from their base in Germany to bring back the wounded in their flying ambulances.

Clarke addressed the screen where Susan Rice, the assistant secretary of state for African affairs, stared intently into her camera. She was to organize medical facilities in Europe for the injured: Spain, France, Britain—anywhere she could find hospital beds, she should reserve them.

He turned to another screen to the face of Louis Freeh, the FBI director, sitting impassively in the video studio beside his office a few blocks away. He would be responsible for sending evidence recovery teams to both sites.

Freeh waved a hand and spoke, "I got John O'Neill in New York. He has a team at an air force base in New Jersey." O'Neill was the FBI agent in charge of New York, a hard-drinking Irishman who handpicked his agents and defended them with a fierce loyalty. Clarke had made him a founding member of the Counterterrorism Security Group.

"Louis, John goes on the first flight."

Clarke turned to the woman on his left, Lisa Gordon-Hegarty, from the National Security Council and his most trusted aide. He told the others she would act as the overall mission controller.

For an hour Clarke, in his calm, quietly authoritative voice, delivered his orders. The air force had three C-141s on standby. The number had to be upped to a dozen with ready-to-go status and another six to follow. The Defense Department would organize midair refueling.

Finally he turned to Tenet. The CIA would handle response. Tenet nodded: There was no more to be said on that.

Clarke looked into the faces around him and at those on the screens. He addressed them all: "After you've dealt with this, we start to plan how to stop the next one."

JONATHAN EVANS SAW THE ATTACKS as an inevitable step-up from bin Laden's months of bluster in the Arab press that al-Qaeda now had a fully equipped army ready to launch jihad, but he still wondered if bin Laden's claim was just another of those boasts made by other terror groups. Were the embassy bombings only an attempt to attract more recruits for al-Qaeda? Given the total surprise of the attacks, the backup team would have been small: Just a few men would have been needed to acquire and bring the explosives to the bomb maker. MI5's own ballistic experts had told Evans that assembling the bombs would have been easy and loading them onto the trucks only required the usual care handling any volatile package would. Evans had asked his officers to try to find out if there were any links between the embassy bombers and someone in Britain's Muslim communities. Recently, immigrants from both Kenya and Tanzania along with Somalia had entered Britain. It was still a long shot.

In Vauxhall Cross, David Spedding had been in a planning meeting when news of the bombings reached him. Since then, he and his director of operations, Richard Dearlove, who had served in Nairobi, had discussed how best to provide assistance from MI6.

Logistically, Americans would want for nothing to run a recovery operation once the "flow" to East Africa was under way. Where MI6 could help was with on-the-ground intelligence. Nairobi had always been a key

African station: From there a veteran officer, Daphne Park, had organized the overthrow of the Congo's pro-Communist prime minister, Patrice Lumumba. The station had led the fight against Soviet penetration of Central Africa by infiltrating subversive organizations and then turning them into informers. It had developed the plans that led to the election of pro-British leaders like Kenya's Tom Mboya, Julius Nyerere of Tanganyika, Nysaland's Hastings Banda, Kenneth Kaunda of Zambia, and Joshua Nkomo of Rhodesia. They had all been given substantial funds to become "agents of influence."

On August 5, 1962, Nelson Mandela, by then a key member of the African National Congress, was arrested near the town of Howick in Natal. It was a time when the country was filled with foreign spies, mostly from MI6 and the CIA, but also a number of French and German intelligence officers. Some were "declared"—their presence announced to the apartheid regime, and so protected by diplomatic immunity; many more were "undeclared" and subject to prosecution if caught. South Africa's own intelligence service, BOSS, had reached into all areas of society: university students, bankers, politicians, and criminal gangs. BOSS had also penetrated the ANC, and a number of its members had been compromised into helping BOSS. It also exploited the postcolonial uncertainty and hypocrisy that colored many reports of MI6 spies and took advantage of the CIA's inability to make direct contact with African political groups. The CIA station chief in 1961 wrote that they were "Communist-motivated."

Between the CIA and MI6 there was intense rivalry, in part because the Secret Intelligence Service saw itself as protecting Britain's prime interest, the Cape shipping route to the empire, while the CIA wanted to obtain control of the country's minerals, especially uranium needed for nuclear weapons.

Sensing the "wind of change" blowing across the country, MI6 had established contacts with Mandela and other talented young ANC politicians, including Oliver Tambo and Walter Sisulu. The intention was to recruit them as "agents of influence," but not one had succumbed to the blandishments of MI6; they had been told by the CIA of the Secret Intelligence Service's close links with BOSS.

The arrest of Mandela halted any recruitment, as the apartheid government subsequently arrested other leaders of the African political party who had not fled into exile. The CIA began to spread the belief in ANC circles, to further disrupt MI6 plans to enlist members of the political group, that MI6 had given out the date, time, and route Mandela would be traveling on that August day.

In 1986, Paul Eckel, who had been a CIA operative in South Africa at the time, revealed details of why Mandela had come to be arrested. In a report to Langley, Eckel wrote, "The arrest of Mandela served the interests of the U.S. because of his Communist leanings." A decade later, Henrik van den Bergh, head of the country's postapartheid intelligence service, SASS, admitted, "Mandela was given to BOSS by the CIA." The allegations barely surfaced in the upheaval that marked the end of the apartheid regime and the emergence of a new ANC government.

Within a year, however, whispers began to circulate among die-hard Afrikaaners that Mandela, the country's first black president, had really been an MI6 informer and that the Secret Intelligence Service had fanned the "wind of change" that ended the apartheid regime. In 2001, the claim was given respectability by the British historian Stephen Dorill and finally unleashed the fury of the Mandela government. Dorill was accused of a "futile attempt to tarnish his image." Dorill denied the assertion but declined to reveal the confidential source for his claim.

In February 2008, Richard Tomlinson, the renegade MI6 officer, gave his testimony at the inquest into the deaths of Princess Diana and Dodi al-Fayed. Shortly after he had done so, two senior intelligence sources in London and Pretoria separately contacted the author and said the claim that Mandela was indeed an MI6 agent had first been made by Tomlinson, who said he had seen the evidence while working for the Secret Intelligence Service. For once, the usually loquacious former spy refused to comment on the matter except to say, "I know the truth and that is enough for me."

Tomlinson also confirmed he had traveled to South Africa in November 1995 after learning that a former colleague in MI6 had been sent to Johannesburg "to handle the two most important agents we have in South Africa." Tomlinson claims his colleague had told him one of those agents was a senior army officer and the other a senior official in the South African government. "They were so senior in their position that he told me no one in MI6 station in Pretoria was allowed to contact them. When I turned up, my old colleague virtually closed the door on me with a warning that if I made any attempt to join South African counterintelligence, I would be in deep trouble. The thought had never crossed my mind." Neither had it been considered by South Africa's secret intelligence service. They made no attempt to approach Tomlinson during his fourteen-day visit to the country.

Tomlinson insists that in making his claims—such as those about the deaths of Diana and Dodi al-Fayed—he is not motivated by financial gain, only by "a need for the truth to come out."

SPEDDING DECIDED THE BEST SUPPORT MI6 could offer was to have Nairobi station activate its still-in-place network of informers to track down the embassy bombers.

Spedding had been told that Prudence Bushnell, the American ambassador, had died in her embassy. Having met her in Washington, he had been about to send a message to the station commander in Nairobi asking for condolences to be expressed on his behalf when news came that Bushnell had survived. Spedding had redrafted his message, "Thank God you are safe."

In Tel Aviv, Efraim Halevy, the ninth director of the Mossad, was a man Tenet had judged on their first meeting to be "someone I can rely on. We had common motives and concerns." The urbane Halevy, only a year away from his pension, had a long and distinguished diplomatic background in Europe and East Africa and had promised to use his contacts.

Mossad analysts had already started to make deductions. The timing of the bombings, ten thirty local time, was when all observant Muslims would be at Friday prayers in their mosques. That was another pointer to al-Qaeda's involvement. Bin Laden had already recently repeated in a speech that as long as Muslims prayed the *shahada*, the belief in the words of Allah and the prophethood of Mohammed, one of the five pillars of Islam, they would come to no harm.

Shortly afterward, bin Laden accepted responsibility for the bombing with chilling words, "By the grace of God Almighty, I have brought happiness to the Islamic world for these strikes against the Americans. There is an enormous wave of joy and happiness spreading across the Islamic world."

PRESIDENT CLINTON SAT BACK in his chair in the Oval Office after Tenet had read aloud the translation. He peered over his half-glasses, and when he spoke there was a quiet seriousness to his tone the CIA chief had not heard before.

"Listen, retaliating for these attacks is all well and good, but we gotta get rid of the guy once and for all. You understand what I'm telling you?"

Tenet nodded and said he had "real-time intelligence" on where bin Laden was going to be—"not where he had been, but where he was *going* to be," he emphasized. "He's due to hold a terrorist summit at a place called Khost." Tenet had unfurled a map and pointed at a dot in Afghanistan, near the border with Pakistan.

Clinton said attacking it would demonstrate the United States was ready to destroy al-Qaeda "anywhere in the world."

On August 20, a salvo of million-dollar missiles launched from U.S. Navy ships in the Gulf obliterated the target. No evidence was later discovered of a "terrorist summit" or that Osama bin Laden had ever been there. The failure would be seen within the later administration of President George W. Bush, whose father had proudly run the CIA, as evidence that the CIA had "just been guessing" about bin Laden's whereabouts. It was a charge the embattled Bush would repeat in 2004 over the way CIA intelligence about Iraq was developing. The accusation was one no incumbent president had ever made. In one of his weekly staff meetings following Bush's claim, John Scarlett, chief of MI6, told his senior staff that for once there was "more than an element of truth in what Bush said."

17

Route Nine Eleven

As David Spedding's cancer began to spread, he continued to ignore the requests of his doctors to give up smoking, and the few senior colleagues who by 1999 had become aware of his progressing illness wondered if it had also begun to affect his judgment; he had started speaking to them of his determination that, when the time came to leave, he wanted to be remembered as a modernist. Some of his decisions had certainly caused raised eyebrows among the traditionalists in Vauxhall Cross. There had been Spedding's decision to allow the makers of the latest James Bond film, *The World Is Not Enough*, to have their cameras linger over the exterior of the building, and he had spent time watching the action on the Thames. Afterward he had invited Dame Judi Dench as his personal guest to the MI6 1999 Christmas party, introducing her to his bemused colleagues as "Bond's M to your C." Later, he had told one of his Monday morning senior staff meetings he was posting a gay intelligence officer and his live-in partner to the Prague station, and from now on he wanted it known that homosexuality was no longer part of positive vetting.

In Whitehall, that decision had finally led Foreign Secretary Robin Cook and Prime Minister Tony Blair—both of whom then knew of Spedding's illness—to conclude it was time to have his replacement ready. "Nobody wanted to push out a sick man, but Spedding needed to be encouraged to retire," recalled one Foreign Office official. In February 1999, Cook sent for Spedding and said it would be "appropriate to have his successor announced so as to try and end the media speculation

which had started," fueled by leaks about Spedding's decisions. Cook
concluded the meeting by saying he intended to name Richard Dearlove
as the thirteenth chief of MI6. Spedding's response would remain between him, his political master, and Cook's note taker. On August 30,
1999, Spedding retired. He would die of cancer twenty-three months
later at the age of fifty-eight. Among the mourners at his memorial service
was George Tenet.

THERE WAS A FEELING INSIDE MI6 that Richard Dearlove had been
a sound choice. He was a good listener, respected by his department
heads and, just as important, by the chiefs of foreign intelligence services. He had served thirty years in MI6 in posts as far apart as Nairobi,
Prague, and Paris. In each country he had either created a network of
informers or developed the existing one. Colleagues spoke of the elegant dinner parties he and his wife, Rosalind, presided over in their
comfortable home in the suburbs.

Early on as chief, Dearlove had shown his negotiating skills by per-
suading the Treasury to add another £4 million to the MI6 budget. A
portion of the money was used in an operation Dearlove had taken over
from Spedding. Code-named Jessant, it became known as "the Mitrokhin
Archive," named after Vasili Mitrokhin, who was recognized by many
within the Secret Intelligence Service as the most important defector
since Oleg Gordievsky. Unlike the former spy, whose exfiltration from
Russia had been handled with all the bravura of a spy novel, Mitrokhin
had politely knocked on the door of the new British Embassy in Latvia
on a cold afternoon in March 1992, put down his suitcase, and announced
to the receptionist that he had been the KGB senior archivist for twelve
years; then, pointing to the suitcase, he added he had some "interesting
documents to show the right person."

The receptionist pushed a button on her phone, and minutes later
the station commander appeared. Mitrokhin once more pointed to the
suitcase and asked, "You like to see here or in your office?"

The officer led the way back into the building, where Mitrokhin elab-
orated a little on his background: He had worked for eight years in the
basement of the Lubyanka, cataloguing a library of documents, many so
secret only the most senior officers in the First Chief Directorate's eleven
departments had seen them. He had opened the suitcase, explaining that
for years he had carefully selected what he thought were the most "histor-
ically interesting" and had brought some samples with him.

Mitrokhin had begun to hand over the documents, stressing they were only a selection of what he possessed. The more he read, the more the officer realized he was looking at what was later described as "pure gold." He asked his first question: Where were the other documents?

"In a safe place. Two milk churns I buried beneath one of my two dachas."

The officer had been unable to conceal his further astonishment, "Two churns? Two dachas?"

Mitrokhin's smile broadened. "I was well paid for my work."

He explained that following the collapse of the KGB, Russia's new intelligence service, FSB, had ordered him to supervise the transfer of the secret library from the Lubyanka to its new headquarters deep inside a birch forest off the highway southeast of Moscow. After the transfer was completed, he had filled each of the churns with paperwork, then driven them to Latvia. The churns were now in another safe place.

The officer's next question had been carefully couched: What did Mitrokhin want for them?

"That you will guarantee to publish them in the West as testimony to the evils of the Soviet system. And that my family and myself can live in England."

The station commander said that he guaranteed both requests would be honored once the documents had been verified. At short notice and without consulting with London, it was a highly unusual promise to give, but the officer had a strong intuition that the documents still in the churns were as genuine as the ones pulled from the suitcase; in any event, the suitcase documents alone made it worthwhile to bring Mitrokhin, his wife, and son to England. Within days the family had been flown to London, along with the two churns packed inside a crate marked as having diplomatic immunity.

In London the arrangements for the safety of the Mitrokhins had been placed in the hands of John Scarlett, who had read in one of the documents details of his own expulsion in January 1994 from Moscow, where he had been station commander. There were many thousands of other secrets, and after they were analyzed and transferred onto computer discs, some were passed on to friendly intelligence services before being culled for material to form the book Mitrokhin would publish. Edited by the Cambridge historian Christopher Andrew, it became required reading in every major intelligence service that had dealt with the KGB. Only a handful of MI6 Soviet experts would ever have complete access to the contents of the two milk churns. Among much else, the documents provided a unique and powerful insight into the mind-set of one of the KGB's former chiefs, Russia's president Vladimir Putin. His fully documented attitude to the West was one of contempt.

WHILE PUBLISHING ARRANGEMENTS for the Mitrokhin Archive were under way, Dearlove had seen the search for the embassy bombers in Nairobi and Dar es Salaam lose its momentum. Part of the problem was the insistence of the Kenyan National Security Intelligence Service (NSIS) on having a major role in the operation. Lacking the experience to provide anything useful in an international manhunt, its investiga-tors failed to understand how to use equipment for fighting a new kind of terrorism; satellite surveillance and the latest technology were be-yond their grasp.

In the critical first days until the CIA and FBI arrived, the NSIS agents focused on finding answers to why so many Kenyans had died. Why had this happened? Why had bin Laden chosen to attack two countries who had no quarrel with al-Qaeda? And where was he now? John O'Neill, in his first call from Nairobi to FBI director Louis Freeh, said, "The locals are still looking in the chicken coop after the fox has long gone."

In one of his regular calls to Tenet, Dearlove had suggested bin Laden was probably back in Afghanistan and to target him would be almost im-possible. Both knew after the Khost debacle, which had produced furi-ous headlines in Pakistani newspapers, that any air attack that involved overflying Pakistani airspace could be seen as coming from India: Ten-sions were high between the two nations, who were each armed with nu-clear weapons. American cruise missiles bound for Afghanistan could be mistaken as coming from India and trigger a nuclear response by Pakistan.

Equally, Dearlove was determined MI6 would not lag behind in the fight against al-Qaeda. Recently retired officers who, in the words of one, had "served in places where the alleys had no names" found them-selves recalled to sit behind a desk in Vauxhall Cross, working alongside other Middle East analysts.

Meanwhile, Osama bin Laden's name and face had become, in the Muslim world, the subject of dozens of television programs and magazine covers, hailed as the new hero of anti-Americanism. His commentary on the hadiths, the sayings and stories of the Prophet, became the fastest-selling tracts in the souks and marketplaces. Versions of his life were ea-gerly bought, and his followers saw a parallel between the Prophet's flight to Medina in Year One of the hegira, before he had recovered Mecca and revealed Islam to the world, and bin Laden's determination to rid the Muslim world of all infidel impurities. In a series of interviews, he himself said the carnage in Nairobi and Dar es Salaam was the first step in that direction. Let the Americans increase the $5 million price on his head. It would make no difference, because he would not be diverted from the True Path of Light. Let them send their rockets and bombs. They would never reach him, thanks to him being allowed to "awaken Islam," and every Muslim must remember, "Jihad is every man's duty—*fard ayn.*"

IN WASHINGTON, THE IMMEDIATE response to the destruction of the embassies had been President Clinton signing Executive Order 13099. It was intended to uncover al-Qaeda's financial networks and, wherever possible, freeze its assets by using the Treasury Department's Office of Foreign Asset Control (OFAC). Richard Clarke, Clinton's antiterrorism czar, could be forgiven his sigh. Despite its imposing title and well-appointed offices, OFAC had achieved little in uncovering the financial operations of the Colombia drug cartels, and their money-laundering operations remained as mysterious as ever. It quickly became clear OFAC would do little better against al-Qaeda. It had almost no information on file about terrorist funding, and its staff had not begun to gather data until the president's executive order landed on their desks.

The wake-up call was swiftly followed by the ever-energetic Clarke laying out his own vision of what he expected. All government departments—from the aloof diplomats of the State Department to the narrowly focused Justice lawyers, from the CIA to the FBI, and all the other agencies who make Washington the largest government town in the world—were to be involved. Clarke had insisted, "Now is not the time to hold back. Everyone must step up to the plate with answers."

Instead he found himself mired in the multitude of bureaucracies that continued to grow in the capital despite its noxious mixture of wasted breath and oxidized hopes. A furious Clarke found that no one had any suggestions of how to discover al-Qaeda's funding; not only that, "they approached the question from their own limited perspective, uninterested in a unified strategy. Some were involved in long-standing turf battles against what they see as competing parts of the government."

The FBI insisted following the money trail was a matter only for them. The CIA provided a "data dump of everything they'd ever come across on the subject and thought that answered the question of how al-Qaeda is financed," fumed Clarke.

It appeared to the genuinely angry counterterrorism czar that "only a handful of people knew anything about how the bad guys move money around the world and that finding out is all a waste of time because it doesn't take much money to blow up two embassies."

When Clarke had cooled his anger, he set up his own network inside his Counterterrorism Security Group. Backed by presidential authority, each man could go where he liked and ask any question. Trampling on egos or walking over mini empires should not deter them. Clarke wanted answers—and he wanted them fast.

In a matter of weeks, his staff provided them. They had moved through the Internet, checking and double-checking, often pretending to be who they were not, to go ever deeper along a money trail that until then was not known to have existed and to discover al-Qaeda was a fund-raising machine, whose operations extended far beyond the Middle East into every place where there were Muslim communities.

There were many millions of Muslims in Indonesia and hundreds of thousands in the Philippines and the northern provinces of China. Other communities in the Amazon amounted to only hundreds. Some Muslims ran legitimate corporations; others were criminals dealing in human trafficking and drugs; several controlled Muslim charities and nongovernmental organizations. All had one common link: They had either received a personal visit from an al-Qaeda fund-raiser or had been reached by phone or fax. No political organization in the West could match such a global money-gathering setup. But had the cash been transferred using banks around the world? The first clues suggested it was moved through financial houses in Cairo, Damascus, the City of London, Paris, Frankfurt, South Africa, Hong Kong, Taiwan, Rangoon, Tokyo, Minsk, Leningrad, and Bucharest. However, it increasingly became clear the global banking system had not been used. So how was it done?

THE QUESTION CONTINUED to engage Richard Dearlove, and he called upon the Bank of England and the Treasury for help. Both had experts in money laundering by organized crime families that sent huge sums—profits from drugs and arms smuggling, and prostitution—around the world.

Dearlove and MI6's financial director had sat in Vauxhall Cross listening to the City experts, who had begun by explaining that an organization the size of al-Qaeda would almost certainly have its own financial experts, bankers who had either been bribed or coerced to "weave and loop" vast sums and make sure their electronic transfer "signature"—

usually a series of onetime figures—remained untraceable. The bankers would also have devised special codes for all the transfers in the name of dozens, if not hundreds, of front companies involved, maybe even a thousand. Some of the codes would be active for no longer than the hours a particular bank opened for business on a particular day. The code could authorize the transfer of a deposit minutes before close of business to some other front company in another part of the world that was about to open. While it was possible to track electronic transfers through CHIPS, an Internet system linked to thirty-six countries, it did not extend to banks in the former Soviet Union or Saudi Arabia.

The senior Bank of England official told Dearlove there was every possibility that to further hide the money, al-Qaeda would have entered into deals with the Russian mafia, Colombian drug cartels, Chinese tongs and triads, and the Japanese Yakuza: all those organizations had front companies across the world.

The MI6 station in Riyadh had established that many Saudi charities were directly linked to their government and promoted a version of Islamic extremism that bin Laden continued to endorse. Though he had been expelled from the country, the Saudi regime had done little to tighten its financial regulations, which would have made it harder for funds to flow in and out to support al-Qaeda.

The Foreign Office planned to call in Saudi Arabia's London ambassador and warn him that any financial support that could provide "material assistance" to al-Qaeda would be unacceptable. Dearlove had already discussed the matter with Tenet, who doubted diplomatic pressure by London or Washington would achieve much. A better way would be to use their own back channels to Prince Turki, the Saudi head of intelligence, and Prince Naif, who ran Mabahith, the country's internal security service. Both royals had high connections in the Saudi banking systems through Prince Bandar, the long-serving Saudi ambassador to the United States, and the country's Crown Prince Abdullah. Tenet proposed, and Dearlove agreed, they could make a joint approach to provide Turki and Naif with evidence that could help them in their own fight against bin Laden, but first they had to guarantee all possible steps would be taken to choke off al-Qaeda's use of Saudi Arabia as a "money box."

Neither spy chief would mention those times when Saudi Arabia's ruling family had sidestepped questions about its role in supporting terrorism, even if only discreetly, but the princes would not fail to understand that President Clinton's executive order had made it clear he would not tolerate any more financial assistance for bin Laden from his Arab friends.

———

MEANWHILE, ONE OF RICHARD CLARKE'S investigators in Washington had gone to the basement of the Treasury building where the Financial Crimes Enforcement Unit worked. An hour later the investigator had left with a rare smile on his lips. In his briefcase was a photocopy of a file about *hawala,* an ancient system in the Muslim world to provide money transfers that left no paper trail. Hundreds of years old, it was the perfect means for al-Qaeda to receive a continuous flow of funds from every Muslim who answered Osama bin Laden's call to support jihad.

The system was simple—and foolproof—and was created by Arab traders on the Silk Road, which had stretched from China to Europe. At the system's center were the *hawaladars.* Every Muslim community had its quota of these unique brokers: taxi drivers, shopkeepers, undertakers, even imams; all were sworn to secrecy, and no one could be admitted until he was vouched for by another *hawaladar.* The only rule the system had was trust; often substantial sums of money were transferred through it. The slightest breach of trust resulted in immediate expulsion and disgrace in a broker's local community.

Any transaction that would end in the coffers of al-Qaeda began with the person wishing to make it visiting a *hawaladar.* He handed over the sum he wished to donate and gave the name and location of the recipient. The *hawaladar* added his fee, usually no more than 0.5 percent of the sum to be transferred. He then contacted a *hawaladar* in the destination country by either phone or fax using his personal code, which allowed him to operate within the system. The recipient's broker knew that next time he and his correspondent broker did business, when the process would be reversed, he would recover the money he had paid out. The system operated on such a high level of trust, no formal banking system could equal it.

When Richard Clarke had read the document his investigator had brought to him, he realized how vast sums of cash could have flowed to al-Qaeda through the system, which, until the aftermath of the embassy bombings, had gone unsuspected. Yet when Clarke had asked to have the FBI find answers to "even basic questions about the number, location, and activities of *hawaladars* in the United States, much less take action," he had been referred back to the original source of the document. The Treasury official who provided it had been fired.

———

THE DAY BEFORE GEORGE W. BUSH was inaugurated in January 2001, he met with President Bill Clinton at 716 Lafayette Park, the building across from the White House where Chinese and American diplomats had found common ground over the Tiananmen massacre. Since the previous November, the building had served as a base for the transition team to prepare the new administration for taking office after a bitterly fought election, which had gone down to the wire in the vote count in Florida.

For two hours Clinton gave the president-elect a personal view of the current world situation. Bin Laden remained the main threat and as elusive from capture as ever. The embassy bombers had vanished, and there was no clue where they were. The residue of the bombing of the Chinese Embassy in Belgrade by B-52 bombers during the Balkans war still continued to blight relations with Beijing; the CIA had provided outdated maps to the Pentagon targeters in the belief the building was a vital Serbian military depot. China had accepted the mistake was genuine, but Washington's relationship with Beijing remained visibly cool. In that final meeting before Bush took office, Clinton had concluded with an updated tour of the trouble spots, among them Iraq, Iran, Pakistan, Afghanistan, and North Korea.

"North Korea," Bush echoed. "That's a new one on the table."

ON A COOL SPRING MORNING IN APRIL 2001, a middle-aged man politely presented himself to the marine on duty at the entrance to the U.S. Embassy in Seoul, the capital of South Korea. He carried a briefcase and gave his name as Ku Kim Bok, explaining he had an appointment. The marine checked his clipboard; the name was there, as it had been ten days before. Nevertheless, he asked Ku to open his briefcase; after the bombings on the embassies in Nairobi and Dar es Salaam, security at all U.S. missions remained at a high level. The briefcase contained only papers written in Korean, a language the marine could neither read nor write.

Waiting in the reception area for Ku was a man identified on the embassy staff list as a protocol officer. His official duties included liaising with the local community, attending cultural functions, and accompanying the ambassador on important visits. The work provided a good cover for his real assignment as a CIA officer. He had introduced himself to Ku at their first meeting as Tim.

In that time, Tim had checked the heartbreak story Ku had unfolded. His heavily pregnant wife had been overheard by an informer, working for the North Korean regime of Kim Jong-il, lamenting that when her child was born she would have little or no food to suckle the infant. She had been taken from their home to the most feared of all the country's prisons, Nongpo, in South Sinuiju.

Ku had continued to tell his story in the precise way of a man trained to present facts: He had returned home after another long week of work as an electrical engineer in missile guidance systems Factory 395, near Najin in the Northeast of the country, to discover the fate of his wife.

Later Ku learned she had been packed into a cell so crowded she could only crouch and there was no room to lie down when she had gone into labor. After delivery a guard had entered the cell, taken the newly born infant, placed it facedown on the concrete floor, and used his boot to crush the child's head. It was the fate of all the childbearing women who went to Nongpo. Ku had said there were a number of similar prisons around the country, but Nongpo had the worst reputation, and he knew his wife would never leave alive.

Sickened and horrified at what he discovered, Ku had made his escape from North Korea into northwest China and eventually to Seoul, helped by some of the human rights organizations engaged in the dangerous work of bringing out refugees from the regime of Kim Jong-il. The helpers included Buddhist and Christian charities, missionaries from all denominations, profit-seeking middlemen, and corrupt officials. Assisting them beyond China's borders were Japanese housewives, Burmese rebels, right-wing South Korean politicians, and diplomats from almost a dozen countries. They all had their reasons for helping: compassion, religious beliefs, and profiteering. Mingled into this mixture were the intelligence agents on the constant lookout for a refugee who could provide information or, even more important, who had worked in the ultra-secret military programs of North Korea.

Not only had Ku done so, but his details about Nongpo and the other prisons killing babies provided an additional bonus for the CIA officer. Tim had contacted the National Security Agency and within hours had received satellite images of Nongpo, together with pictures of factories suspected of producing missile guidance systems.

On that April morning, he escorted Ku to one of the small and featureless offices the CIA station used for interviews. Waiting was an elderly North Korean who would once more act as translator. Laid out on a table was a tray of steamed rice cakes and coffee. Beside them were the satellite images. While Ku ate and drank, the translator produced a small tape recorder. When it was turned on, Tim formally identified the tape as an interview with North Korean defector Ku Kim Bok. He dated the tape and its start time. Tim's New York twang was in marked contrast to Ku's soft tones.

He began to carefully cross-question Ku, each time waiting for the translation to be completed, and from time to time making notes on a pad, brief summaries of what had been recorded. Tim turned to exploring Ku's own work at Factory 395. Ku explained it provided missile guidance systems for rockets capable of delivering nuclear warheads, which could also be equipped with chemical and biological warheads.

His own duties included buying parts for missile guidance systems, which mostly came from Japan. Its salesmen regularly visited the factory to demonstrate the latest equipment. From his briefcase he produced papers and handed them to the translator. They contained the names of the salesmen and the companies they worked for. The calm, considered way he spoke impressed Tim that Ku was providing the kind of important information that made him a comparative rarity, an informer who did not have to be courted, blackmailed, bribed, or coerced.

The details about the salesmen would be passed to the CIA station in Tokyo; the possibility of recruiting one of them as an informer able to get inside Factory 395 was becoming a reality.

Ku had developed the all too familiar story of the regime's oppression that he had outlined on his first interview: dawn roundups, families set to spy on each other, starvation, and abuses of power by those who were favored by the regime. His wife had been an example of how the slightest indiscretion was severely punished. Men had been sent to a gulag after being seen smiling at one of the portraits of the country's leader that adorned every public place. Women had been taken by police to their barracks and gang-raped. Some had committed suicide afterward.

The names of some of the people who had been brutalized, their torturers, and the places where the brutality had occurred had all been carefully set down by Ku in his papers. At the factory he had witnessed a woman being roasted in an electrical oven, a man beaten to death with steel rods. Both had been caught trying to smuggle out food from the factory kitchen.

One day Ku had been summoned to a meeting at the General Staff headquarters in Pyongyang to deliver a report on the latest missile guidance system developed at the factory. He told Tim he suspected much of the technical data would pass over the heads of his audience, but he had taken no chances. His predecessor's failure to provide enough detail at a military conference, where one of the Russian engineers had ridiculed the presentation, had resulted in the factory manager's execution. To be responsible for allowing a slur to be committed against the country's scientific community was another capital offense in the regime.

Tim continued to show Ku images of factory sites. Each time Ku studied them, then shook his head. He did not recognize any. Tim's hopes grew: Some of the images were of sites in South Korea, which Ku could not possibly have known about. It was another sign his claims were genuine. So many refugees lied in the hope it would guarantee them a visa to the United States. Once discovered, they were handed over to the South Korean government to be resettled as it thought fit.

Tim handed over another image. It showed Factory 395 had half a dozen factories clustered around it. Ku identified each one by its number. Tim asked how many they employed. Ku did not hesitate: over ten thousand. Tim knew this was no wild guess; the figure was a current CIA estimate. He probed further: What was the ratio between those working on nuclear, chemical, and biological projects? Ku's reply further satisfied the CIA officer that he was not dealing with another of those asylum seekers who invented what they thought their interrogators wanted to hear. Ku said that while creating nuclear bombs was still the country's largest military priority, the work was also divided between research and production of chemical and biological weapons; each section employed about four hundred thousand people. Again, the figure corresponded with the CIA's.

Tim indicated a snapshot of a woman. Ku confirmed she was Dr. Yi, who had been at the meeting, listening and taking notes while he explained the technicalities of inserting a guidance system into one of the SS-18 missiles that had been acquired from the Soviet Union shortly before its collapse. When he had completed his presentation, Dr. Yi had asked: When would the system be ready to deliver a biological weapon? Within a year? Longer? A stocky, middle-aged general had interjected to say this was not a matter for Ku to judge.

Now, months later when he had completed his account, Ku Kim Bok was promised he would be allowed to travel to the United States, where he would be helped to integrate into the growing population of North Koreans.

AROUND SEVEN THIRTY MOST RUSH-HOUR MORNINGS, George Tenet's government car wove through Washington traffic. Seated beside him on the backseat was a CIA briefer holding a copy of the President's Daily Brief printed on high-quality paper and bound between heavy leather covers. Another copy had already been delivered to Wilma Hall in Room 345 in the Old Executive Office Building directly across from the White House. She had run the CIA "town office" for many years, and for Tenet, the calm, graying, middle-aged woman was a comforting anchor in a sea of changing demands. There had been plenty since Bush had entered the Oval Office. Tenet had handled them with a quick nod and a barked order into a phone with his favorite phrase, "This has gotta be slam dunk." He knew he was in good grace with the new president, not least because Tenet had been instrumental in having Langley renamed the George Bush Center for Intelligence, after George W.'s father. Everyone still called it Langley.

The briefer was a career officer hoping to make his way up through the agency, and his night's work of preparing the PDB was part of that. It called for expert judgment on the flow of reports into his computer and a skill in summarizing the ones he chose for the PDB. A briefer spent no more than a year doing the job before showing signs of burnout. Tenet described it as "a killer job, but a chance to witness history up close and personal."

The briefer's task was to read to Tenet the items he had selected over the phone as he was being driven in for their usual meeting in Wilma's office. Afterward, Tenet would walk across the road to the West Wing of the White House and up the back staircase to the Oval Office. Speculation continued as to whether or not the staircase was used by Monica Lewinsky for her assignations with President Clinton, and Secretary of Defense Donald Rumsfeld was credited with one of the few jokes he was heard to make when he predicted the Clinton era would be known as "sex between the Bushes."

During the drive, the two phones in the car's built-in console rang continuously: calls from Langley operations, calls from senior staff asking for decisions, calls from the White House checking he was on time, calls from the escort car tailgating behind, calls from the security detail positioned outside the Old Executive Office Building double-checking the car's estimated time of arrival. Tenet had long ago tuned his ears to responding to the calls while still listening to the briefer as he ran through the PDB.

At 7:45 A.M., Tenet entered Room 345, where Wilma Hall waited with his steaming mug of coffee along with a CIA analyst who had already studied her copy of the PDB. Tenet recalled, "We immediately began to huddle over 'the book' and tried to find out what questions the president would ask." It was the same every morning.

At 8:00 A.M., Tenet walked over to the Oval Office, trailed by his security men, and entered. In their usual places in the semicircle of armchairs

sat Bush, to his left Vice President Dick Cheney, and to his right Condoleezza Rice, the national security adviser. Each had a copy of the PDB.
As usual, near the top was the latest update on North Korea. Since his
comment to Clinton about "a new one on the table," Bush had made it
clear it was catchup on the secret regime on the other side of the world.

The reality was that the CIA knew little about North Korea and most
of it dated back to the Korean War. The agency had no spies in the
country, and the State Department had no diplomatic representation
with the regime. The few European and Asian diplomats accredited to
Pyongyang had turned out to be virtually impossible to recruit. The majority of refugees who had managed to escape painted the same grim
portrait of horror; while Ku Kim Bok's account had been valuable, it
still left many gaps.

It had been the Mossad and MI6 that had provided valuable insights
about the role played by Abdul Qadeer Khan, the brilliant nuclear scientist who hated the West but rejoiced in being hailed in his homeland,
Pakistan, as "the father of the Islamic bomb."

An MI6 officer in the counterproliferation department had discovered Khan had stolen documents of highly classified technology from
his former workplace, the Physical Dynamic Research Laboratory in Holland. The blueprints were essential for building the centrifuges that
provided enriched uranium. The laboratory—set up by Britain, Germany, and Holland—provided the material for Europe's nuclear reactors to produce energy, and the blueprints had enabled Khan to create
Pakistan's nuclear arsenal. When the news broke, he became a national
hero in the country.

The Mossad had learned, however, that there was a dark and, for Israel, more dangerous side to Khan. Not only was he an anti-Semite, but
he had been holding secret meetings with North Korea. The contacts had
been discovered when a Mossad agent had accessed Khan's hotel suite in
Geneva and photographed documents in the scientist's briefcase, which
provided the first positive proof that, in return for the latest centrifuges
built in his laboratories in Pakistan, Khan had received almost $2 million.
One of the documents showed he had deposited the money in a Swiss
bank account.

An MI6 officer, posing as a magazine writer, had later interviewed
Khan, who described himself as the "world's nuclear bomb peacemaker." The officer had taped Khan reading a passage aloud from a report by the John F. Kennedy School of Government at Harvard University
that included a grim scenario, "A ten-kiloton bomb explodes in New

York. Half-a-million people are killed and the United States suffers $1 trillion in economic damage."

Khan said this should be seen as a timely reminder to America that it was no longer the only supreme nuclear power. The threat was all too clear: Khan could ensure that less powerful nations would also have the weapons to attack America and its allies. "He made it clear he had the organization to do so," noted the officer.

Tenet immediately arranged a meeting with Richard Dearlove and Efraim Halevy. They agreed that while Khan posed a serious threat, to assassinate him would still leave an organization with nuclear scientists, probably recruited from the former Soviet Union, and a sizable support staff to run his laboratories. Until Khan's network could be destroyed, it was best to keep him under close surveillance and see where the trail led beyond North Korea.

It was agreed a team from the CIA, MI6, and the Mossad should be formed to track the organization. Each intelligence chief would select from his own service officers who would disappear into the world where Khan and his cohorts operated to jump-start a rogue state into the nuclear age. George Tenet had returned from the meeting knowing he had become part of a project that would occupy the CIA, MI6, and the Mossad for the foreseeable future. To this day, what the team has achieved has remained one of the most closely guarded secrets in all three services.

IN THE MIDDLE OF JUNE 2001, DR. DAVID KELLY had flown to Washington at the request of MI6 to check on persistent reports that a biological weapons attack was being planned by al-Qaeda. At Fort Detrick, America's research establishment against biological warfare, scientists told him the reports came from CIA sources in the Middle East claiming deadly germs were being weaponized to strike terror in American and European shopping malls, cinemas, Broadway theaters, sports stadiums—anywhere people gathered. The original reports had come from Saudi Arabia but gave few details except that an attack was imminent.

Dr. Kelly knew biological weapons could be created in a laboratory no more sophisticated than one in a high school, but had that actually happened? If so, how had the germs been obtained, and where had they been weaponized, and by whom? No one knew, yet the CIA continued to warn that it was not only a nuclear bomb but pathogens that posed the threat. A half dozen of the world's greatest cities, including New York, London, and Paris, were named as targets for what was being described as "the poor man's hydrogen bomb."

In London, Dr. Kelly had been shown by an MI6 officer an e-mail Richard Clarke had sent Condoleezza Rice on May 29, "When these attacks occur, as they likely will, we will wonder what more we could have done."

Dr. Kelly knew Clarke's reputation as a sound judge of a threat: If he felt an attack was probable, then it must be taken seriously. He also knew, however, that while there are over thirty fungi, bacteria, and viruses capable of being weaponized, they would still require sophisticated delivery systems that would need to take into account the vagaries of weather: Wind strength, rain, and snow would be key factors. Yet if fleas and rodents had been weaponized with the plague, then untold millions would die: One-quarter of the population of Europe had perished from the Black Death in the fourteenth century. A single bite by a weaponized flea could disgorge up to twenty-four thousand plague cells into a person's bloodstream. In a day, the flea could infect thousands of people who would infect thousands more. In a week, a million could be infected.

Dr. Kelly's careful questions at Fort Detrick had produced the admission that not one infected insect or rodent had been found outside the center's Third Level High Containment laboratories. There was no proof of a single case of a biological warfare victim in the United States or anywhere. Still, the stories of an impending attack continued: If not the plague, *Yersinia pestis,* then anthrax or smallpox pathogens had somehow found their way into the hands of terrorists who were waiting to launch them. Both diseases had high mortality rates. Again, there was no proof to support the claim.

Before flying to Washington, Dr. Kelly had discussed the matter with Vladimir Pasechnik, the Russian scientist he had debriefed. The two men had become friends, and Dr. Kelly had helped Pasechnik establish his own research company, Regma, near Porton Down and also arranged for the Russian to have a small laboratory inside the research establishment. Pasechnik had been eager to announce Regma as a new player in the scientific world and had issued a press release. Dr. Kelly had been mildly irritated by the announcement, "It had a sniff of the snake-oil salesman about it, and I made it clear to Vladimir he should not involve Porton Down."

Dr. Kelly knew that the Russian Embassy in London had diplomats assigned to read Britain's scientific publications, and one of them would certainly have passed to their intelligence colleagues details of Pasechnik's plans and his whereabouts. However, he had been told by MI6 that his security protection had been withdrawn as it had been decided he was no longer in danger from the Russians.

Over lunch in the Porton Down cafeteria to discuss the possibility of a biological attack by terrorists, Pasechnik said that unless they had managed to recruit experts capable of building a distribution system for their germs, there was little chance of them launching a successful attack. "A system would require, at minimum, a small rocket equipped with a nose cone filled with the germs," Dr. Kelly recalled Pasechnik saying. He had been reassured to have his own view confirmed. Nevertheless, he had asked if he should see Dr. Ken Alibek while he was in Washington. He had been Pasechnik's boss in Biopreparat. "To my surprise," Dr. Kelly recalled, "Vladimir said, 'It is a matter for you, but when I worked with him he was someone who often made too many claims.'"

KANATJAN ALIBEKOV RAN BIOPREPARAT before defecting to the United States in the autumn of 1992. Soon after arriving in America, Alibekov changed his name to Ken Alibek. "It was my way of integrating into a new life," he told journalists. Under the guiding hand of the CIA, he began to publish articles detailing the threat biological warfare posed and soon became a media favorite, always ready to provide a sound bite in his heavily accented English. His expertise, combined with his dire revelations, solidified his reputation in Langley and on Capitol Hill. His thickset figure sat before congressional committees, their members listening attentively as he revealed how Russian scientists were still working to develop bioweapons in spite of the 1972 international treaty banning all such work, which the Soviet Union had signed.

Alibek offered up the names of scientists who had gone to Iraq, Iran, and North Korea to continue their work on anthrax and smallpox. The virus, he had emphasized, was especially dangerous because once genetically modified, smallpox not only posed a more deadly risk but struck down even those who were vaccinated against it. His claims became an important part of a U.S. decision to eventually spend billions of dollars to counter the two diseases.

Dr. Kelly had also found other scientists who were uncertain whether the Russian scientist was always applying strict scientific judgments before making his claims. Dr. Philip K. Russell, a distinguished physician and a ranking expert on biological warfare whom Dr. Kelly respected, had joined the Bush administration shortly after the president was elected. Russell accepted that while Alibek had "solid information about the former Soviet Union's production of anthrax, when it came to genetically engineered smallpox, I began to think Ken was more fanciful. He would claim that certain things had been done, and then when you came right down to it, he didn't have knowledge of it—he'd heard it from somebody. For example, the issue of putting Ebola genes into smallpox virus. That was somewhat fanciful and probably not true," Dr. Russell recalled in July 2007.

Nevertheless, Ken Alibek's media-promoted expertise in that summer of 2001 ensured he had the powerful support of senators and representatives. Alibek, who had grown up in the harsh surrounds of Almaty, then the capital of impoverished Kazakhstan, found himself dining in expensive Washington restaurants. While he sipped vodka and champagne, he engaged his listeners with descriptions of Biopreparat's lethal arsenal: the Marburg virus, plague, and a virulent "battle strain" of anthrax. He always ended by expressing his great hope of finding money to develop treatments that would bolster the immune system against such terrifying pathogens. Of course, doing so would require huge sums to develop vaccines and drugs that could "filter toxins from blood" and "be rapidly deployed against genetically engineered biowarfare agents." He made it clear he would not only like to be associated with U.S. companies' research as a consultant but, now that the Soviet Union had collapsed, would like to open his own facility in the Ukraine to produce generic versions of antiviral agents or antibiotics that would cost "three, four, five times" less than they would to manufacture in the United States. "It would be a win-win situation for investors and our clients," Alibek said.

Funding was not slow in coming. A Virginia company called Advanced Biosystems, of which Alibek became an executive, won a $3.59 million contract from the government Defense Advanced Projects Research Agency. "It was Ken Alibek's name on its letterhead which would attract the investment," Vladimir Pasechnik told Dr. Kelly after the latter had returned from Washington having failed to get Alibek to meet him. Each time, Dr. Kelly was told that Alibek was in the Ukraine setting up his facility. Dr. Kelly later insisted, "He never returned my calls."

In 2007, Ken Alibek admitted to the author in a telephone interview from the Ukraine, "My research grants in U.S. government contracts now exceed $25 million. My facility in the Ukraine is working to produce antiviral drugs and antibiotics to save hundreds of millions, if not billions, of people from being killed by biological weapons which North Korea and Iran possess."

DR. DAVID KELLY'S OFFICE, off the hallway of his home at South-moor in Oxfordshire, was a book-lined room and part of what his wife, Janice, described as "David's secret world." It was here that his off-hours calls came from MI5, MI6, or any of the other intelligence services that had the unlisted number. It was here that he used the computers that linked him to the Secret Intelligence Service, the Security Service, GCHQ, the Ministry of Defense, and the Foreign Office. Each organiza-tion had installed its own computer for him to use on its behalf and to exchange encrypted messages.

On those computers was stored information that came from all over the world, some what he called "copper-bottomed," some less so. The most important, he would say, smiling, was mentally filed behind his domed forehead beneath his thinning gray hair.

He had typed his report on his Washington visit into the computer designated for MI6. It summarized the views of scientists at Fort Detrick and those employed by the CIA and the FBI, as well as colleagues from the team he had headed in Iraq after the Gulf War, which had ended in a fruitless search for biological weapons of mass destruction. He had de-scribed his meetings at the U.S. Army Medical Research Institute of In-fectious Diseases and discussions with microbiologists at the Centers for Disease Control in Atlanta, one of the two repositories legally allowed to store smallpox. He had also reported on the views of contacts he had in Los Angeles, San Francisco, and Chicago. All concurred a biological at-tack on the United States or in Europe was unlikely in the immediate future.

After the report was automatically encrypted, it was transmitted by the computer to MI6. Later Dr. Kelly had turned to the sixth computer, the one he called "my aide-mémoire," where he stored reminders for birth dates of family and friends, work to be done in the garden, and, oc-casionally, something unusual he came across during one of his walks. Over the years, Dr. Kelly had trodden every countryside footpath around his home.

More recently, his personal computer had included a reminder for him to see his line manager about a salary increase; the extra money would be useful to pay for additional private treatment for Janice, who was suffering from increasingly serious arthritis. On the latest trip to America, he had spoken to friends about the possibility of coming to work in the private sector in the States. He was now fifty-seven years old, and the continuous pressure from the intelligence services and the demands of his work at Porton Down were growing onerous.

Back home, though, enjoying the last days of the summer of 2001 with Janice, he could think of nowhere better to be than in England. He could see nothing in his calendar as September approached that would affect his life.

18

The Day Their Lives Changed

At eight twenty-five on a cloudless summer morning in September 2001, George Tenet's car pulled up outside the St. Regis Hotel in Washington for his breakfast meeting. He could see his security detail was already in place, two men at one door watching the street, and knew Tim Ward, the senior agent, was in the lobby eyeing everyone who came and went. Tenet stepped quickly from the car into the hotel and, with Ward at his side, walked briskly to the restaurant.

Usually at this hour Tenet would be leaving the Oval Office, a copy of the President's Daily Brief in his hand marked with items to be followed up, but George Bush had flown to Florida to speak at an elementary school. On the drive to the hotel, one of the White House Secret Service agents with the president had called on the car phone to say there were no problems; it was a small reminder that Tenet was responsible for the president's personal safety along with being the nation's intelligence supremo. He had on more than one occasion told his wife, Stephanie, that it was quite a step up for the son of working-class Greek immigrants, who had been born and raised in the New York City borough of Queens, to have ended up overseeing "the wilderness of mirrors" of America's intelligence world.

The closing weeks of that summer in 2001 had once more shown Tenet that, while the job was continuously demanding, it remained both thrilling and frustrating. He constantly dealt with the secrets and lies, the unclear and unknown, the machinations of the enemies of the United

States and his determination to thwart them. In his view it was the best job in government.

The one certainty was others were still helping him. MI6 had discovered that a Yemeni group was planning to attack Jordan. Tenet had asked his station chief in Riyadh to check with Saudi intelligence if this was linked to an earlier threat to bomb the U.S. school in Jeddah. DAS, the Colombian intelligence service, had warned that FARC, the country's left-wing terrorist group, was planning to bomb a mall in Bogotá where staff in the city's American Embassy shopped. Tenet had ordered the ambassador to ensure no one went to the mall and had offered to send a team to reinforce the DAS agents. The offer had been politely rejected: He had learned that what DAS lacked in experience, it more than made up for with pride, and the fiery Greek in Tenet sometimes found it hard to deal with Latin American temperaments.

Efraim Halevy had called personally to say the Mossad had solid evidence Hezbollah was in an advanced stage of planning "a large-scale operation" in southern Asia against Jewish-owned banks and companies. The Mossad was tracking it, but the time would come when it might be necessary to launch a preemptive strike against the group. Tenet knew he would need to talk to his counterterrorism staff and probably have a conference call involving Martin Indyk, U.S. ambassador to Israel, and William Burns, assistant secretary of state for Near Eastern affairs, and could have to go all the way to the president before the United States became involved in a strike. Halevy had agreed there were "political considerations" for the United States, but Israel was quite prepared to deal alone with any threat to its interests.

Some of the reports told of success: SISMI, the Italian secret intelligence service, had broken up an Algerian-based terrorist group that had been planning an attack against the U.S. Embassy to the Vatican. Malaysian intelligence, working with CIA officers, had stopped terrorist attacks on U.S. facilities in the country hours before they were launched. In all, nineteen foreign intelligence services continued to funnel reports to the CIA.

Jordan's King Abdullah told his intelligence chief to inform Tenet that Jordan could send two battalions of their Special Forces into Afghanistan to "deal with al-Qaeda." The offer had been put on "the front burner" at Langley, but any decision to finally accept it would need "to be fitted into the wider political picture in the region." Egyptian intelligence had tracked two extremists plotting to bomb an American facility in Cairo. The small but efficient United Arab Emirates intelligence agency had arrested an Arab on his way to Paris to bomb the American

Embassy in the city. Bolivian intelligence had arrested six Pakistanis plotting to hijack an American airliner.

While the threats outnumbered the successes, no one seemed to pay serious attention to the Presidential Daily Brief dated August 6, 2001, warning "Bin Laden determined to attack U.S." As Labor Day came and went in Washington, the city gave all the appearances of normal life. Tenet, after a summer of dealing with the flow of reports, had found an hour to catch up with the man who was his closest friend and mentor, David Boren; the former Oklahoma senator had plucked Tenet from obscurity to serve as chief of staff of the Senate Select Committee on Intelligence, which Boren chaired. It had been Boren who advised him to stay on under the Bush administration for six months before deciding if the way the new White House worked was how he wanted the CIA to operate. The breakfast meeting was to discuss whether Tenet was happy on that front.

AS TENET AND BOREN ORDERED BREAKFAST, Richard Clarke chaired a conference in the Ronald Reagan Building three blocks from the White House. He had run many meetings in his thirty years in government service, working in the State Department, at the Pentagon, and, since President Clinton had appointed him, as the first national coordinator for counterterrorism—a job President Bush had asked him to continue in.

After the embassy bombings in Nairobi and Dar es Salaam, Clarke had placed the Counterterrorism Security Group on five minutes' readiness during business hours and twenty minutes at all other times to get to the West Wing SVC or to one of their approved video stations around the city. He had also insisted on being copied on all the reports Tenet received as well as those from FBI's fifty-six field offices. Most of the reports dealt with drug busts or the activities of organized crime; there were never details about the activities of any Islamic radicals in the area. When he challenged the FBI director, Freeh replied: "Because there are probably none in that particular city."

The one exception was the reports from John O'Neill, the special agent in charge of the FBI's New York office. Since his return from Nairobi and Dar es Salaam, O'Neill had insisted some of those who had helped with the embassy bombings could be living in America, very possibly among one of New York's ethnic communities. His memos to FBI headquarters had met with no response, so the bullish O'Neill had started to copy Clarke. It was another move in their two-handed effort to alert Washington of the al-Qaeda threat they were now convinced was imminent.

At a meeting in the White House with Condoleezza Rice, Donald Rumsfeld, and Dick Cheney on September 4, 2001, Clarke told the author that he had asked Rice, "What will you wish you had already done when al-Qaeda have killed hundreds of Americans?" She had not replied.

Now, the conference Clarke was chairing that morning seven days later was to reinforce that unseen threat. He had begun with a blunt reminder: The further America was from the last al-Qaeda attack, the closer it was to the next.

THREE THOUSAND MILES AWAY FROM WHERE CLARKE spoke with his usual passion, it was one forty in the afternoon in Thames House, five hours ahead of Eastern Standard Time. In his private dining room, MI5's director-general, Stephen Lander, lunched with Eliza Manningham-Buller, his deputy, and continued to forensically dissect the first three months of Tony Blair's second term of office as prime minister. It allowed Lander to display his fixation with detail—where and when Blair had make a particular point, who else had been at one of Blair's Downing Street parties or at one of the weekend soirees Cherie Blair gave at Chequers. Lander had described each moment in long sentences, broken with lengthy pauses. It was the speech pattern of a man regarded by many of his staff as a pedant; certainly he dressed and sounded like a refugee from the Institute of Historical Research at the University of London, where he had once worked before joining MI5: He liked the same tweed suits and could quote from books no one else knew.

Dr. William Sargant, the psychiatrist, once told the author Lander was the "perfect example of a personality who displays no natural authority, but covers it with judgments which sound like a medieval judge handing down a death sentence."

Lander had disliked Blair from their first meeting briefing him on MI5's activities, and his feelings had not changed on that September afternoon. In the corner of the dining room, the television set was turned low as it relayed a report from Brighton, where Tony Blair would shortly give a keynote speech to the Trades Union Congress.

JOHN SCARLETT, CHAIRMAN OF THE JOINT INTELLIGENCE COMMITTEE, sat in his Whitehall office and took a final look at the agenda for the JIC meeting. Items to be discussed included approving the expansion of the joint research and development department so "all offensive equipment designed by the scientists for MI6 at the same time was given to MI5." He knew Manningham-Buller would push for that, another of the turf battles she liked to win at JIC meetings. Time would also be allotted to discuss the latest requests for internal budget allocations for both services to fight terrorism and money laundering. There would be the usual review of the latest trouble spots around the world. The schedule was light, and the meeting would likely take less than an hour from the time it started at two o'clock. There were fifteen minutes to go. It was one forty-five, London time.

A MINUTE LATER ON THE eastern seaboard of America, at 8:46 A.M. Eastern Standard Time on Tuesday, September 11, 2001, a succession of events began that would change forever the lives of George Tenet, Richard Clarke, Stephen Lander, Eliza Manningham-Buller, and John Scarlett, along with untold millions of other people. The first of two hijacked passenger jets flew headlong into the twin towers of the World Trade Center in Manhattan, and minutes later another crashed into the Pentagon, while a fourth, aimed at the White House or Capitol Hill, having failed to reach either target, plunged into a field in Pennsylvania.

The sights of the collapse of the twin towers and the flames engulfing the Pentagon continued to be broadcast all over the world, sending shock waves expanding ever outward. There had been nothing like it: the number of civilian deaths, three thousand, exceeding all others in a modern massacre; the catastrophic hit at America's supremacy as a global commercial and financial power. All this and much more would become deeply ingrained into the collective memory of mankind for future generations, but for the moment on that September day, lost in the impact of what had occurred was the one question: How had this happened on what became known as 9/11?

IN THE ST. REGIS BREAKFAST ROOM, Tenet was about to drink another cup of coffee when he saw Tim Ward, head of his personal security detail, hurrying toward the table. David Boren, Tenet's guest, glanced up as his host stepped from the table to meet the agent. Ward told him about the first airliner flying into the north tower at the World Trade Center.

Tenet turned to Boren and repeated the news. The senator recalled Tenet adding, "It's a terrorist attack, has to be, and has to be bin Laden."

Led by Ward and watched by curious people at other tables, Tenet hurried from the room. In the lobby his security detail joined him, and in a concerted move the group swept out of the hotel to where Tenet's car was already waiting, engine running. Tenet climbed into the backseat and started answering the console phones as the car, lights flashing, began to race to Langley.

ON THE SOUTH COAST OF ENGLAND, it was three minutes past two in the afternoon, British Summer Time, and in his suite in the Grand Hotel, Tony Blair was fine-tuning his speech to the Trades Union Congress. He sipped water and underlined the emphasis he would give to some words and where he needed to pause for applause. His team, led by Anji Hunter, his close aide, and Alastair Campbell, his communications director, had worked on several drafts during the night. Campbell, a former tabloid reporter, had a gift for giving Blair punchy phrases that guaranteed media exposure.

Initially Hunter had wanted to highlight a reference to Labour's readiness to deal with terrorists. Campbell had vetoed the idea: All summer the newspapers had had their fill of terrorist-related stories, and readers were growing tired of their cry-wolf tone. In his view, the prime minister did not need "a bunch of towel heads led by a maniac who lives in a cave" to remind the delegates Blair was a safe pair of hands; his speech should have a feel-good tone that reflected Labour's plans for its next four years in office.

At six minutes past two, Hunter and Campbell ran into the suite, and she switched on one of its television sets. The Sky News channel was relaying live footage from New York.

"It looks like a terrible accident," she said. Hunter would recall how Blair stared at the screen and "said 'Oh my God' in a sort of absent-minded way, then turned to Alastair saying, 'I'll have to refer to this at the top of my speech, won't I, Ali?'" Before Campbell answered, Downing Street's political secretary, Robin Hill, came in. "Reuters has just reported another plane has hit the south tower," he said in a tight voice.

On the screen they could see confirmation of the second hit. One of the Special Branch officers who guarded the prime minister stood in the open door of the suite and said, "They're no accidents. It's terrorism."

BY 9:29 A.M., RICHARD CLARKE had driven from the Ronald Reagan Building to the White House, raced through the corridors of the West

Wing, ignoring the startled looks of staffers, and entered without knocking the office of Vice President Dick Cheney, who was alone with Condoleezza Rice watching the television images from the twin towers. He told them he was certain this was an al-Qaeda attack and reminded Rice that he had warned her that "something big" was coming.

She responded by saying she was appointing him as "crisis manager." Cheney nodded agreement. Through the open door came a Secret Service agent; behind him others were arriving in the outer office. Clarke asked where POTUS—the president of the United States—was. The agent's voice was urgent when he told Cheney he must move now. The vice president picked up a paper from his desk and read aloud, "On my timetable, POTUS is in the middle of his talk to those kindergarten kids in Florida."

The Secret Service agent looked impatient. Cheney began to gather up more papers. In the outer office, several more agents waited to form a protective cordon to escort Cheney to the President's Emergency Operations Center, the bomb shelter.

"You do anything you have to," Cheney said as he departed. Clarke headed for the videoconference center, calling out orders on his cell phone. He wanted a line open to NORAD, the North American Aerospace Defense Command, which had been created during the cold war to warn of a Soviet air attack. He wanted Norman Mineta, the secretary of transportation onscreen and also Jane Garvey, the administrator of the Federal Aviation Administration. And the chairman of the Joint Chiefs. And the attorney general. And he wanted an open line to Navy Captain Deborah Lower, the director of the White House Situation Room, who was traveling with POTUS. She would be the president's briefing officer.

Running behind Clarke came Condoleezza Rice, her high heels clicking over the floor.

IT HAD TAKEN TENET'S DRIVER fifteen minutes to drive down the George Washington Parkway to Langley, where he went directly to the conference room adjoining his sixth-floor suite. He had called ahead for all his senior staff to assemble there, work the phones, and open the video link to the SVC in the White House West Wing. Tenet was given the news that American Flight 77 had crashed into the Pentagon and a fourth passenger plane, which had also been hijacked, was still in the sky, possibly heading toward Washington. It was United Flight 93.

Meanwhile, the rumor mills were starting to spin and their alarmist reports reached into the conference room: A bomb had been discovered in the White House; the Capitol and the State Department were on fire; more planes had been hijacked. All those reports were untrue but reflected the growing panic in Washington and New York, which, fanned by media claims, spread across the country like a brush fire.

However, two of the reports that were true angered Tenet. While the twin towers began to collapse, the head of Pakistan's InterService Intelligence (ISI), Lieutenant General Mahmoud Ahmed, many of whose officers had links to al-Qaeda, was being hosted on Capitol Hill by Representative Porter Goss, who had once worked for the CIA under Allen Dulles and Richard Helms. Tenet wished he knew the purpose of their meeting; Goss had not obliged him with advance warning, which would have given Tenet the chance to have Ahmed questioned about al-Qaeda's activities. There was also another meeting he had only become aware of after arriving in Langley. While he was hurrying from the St. Regis Hotel, Osama bin Laden's brother Shafiq had been attending the annual investment conference of the secretive Carlyle Group at the nearby Ritz-Carlton Hotel. The two brothers were widely reported to be estranged, but talking to Shafiq would have been an opportunity to learn more about his terrorist brother.

By 10:00 A.M. over the video link, Clarke had confirmed the White House was being evacuated, along with the State and Justice departments and the World Bank. In New York, the United Nations building was emptying of its twelve thousand employees. As they were rushing into the street, news came that United Flight 93 had crashed near Shanksville, Pennsylvania.

Dick Cheney called from the White House bunker to ask if there was "any possibility" of another attack. Air Force One was en route from Florida with President Bush to the underground headquarters of the U.S. Strategic Command at Offutt Air Force Base. From his onboard communications system, Bush had asked who was behind the attacks. Tenet told him what he kept telling everyone around him: al-Qaeda. The president said he wanted everybody involved, from bin Laden down, found and brought to justice. Whatever it cost in manpower and resources, it must be done. There must be no limits on what Tenet was authorized to do. It was the beginning of a system that would turn the CIA from being primarily an intelligence-gathering organization into a worldwide military police service with unprecedented power to arrest anyone on the slightest suspicion and to imprison and have them tortured in secret prisons in Egypt, Jordan, and Guantanamo Bay. It was done in the name of a president seeking vengeance. Its methods would be spelled out in the *New York Times*, "American intelligence may have to rely on its liaisons with the world's toughest foreign services, men who can look and think and act like terrorists. If someone is going to interrogate a man in a basement in Cairo or Quella, it will be an Egyptian or a Pakistani officer. American intelligence will take the information without asking a lot of lawyerly questions."

But on that Tuesday morning in the conference room, the mood was: Why wait for help? We have the right to kill him now.

Tenet called General Michael Hayden, the director of the National Security Agency. Could he devise a way to bug any suspected terrorist in the United States? He could.

An officer fished up a report on his computer that Cairo station had sent a year ago about an al-Qaeda cell discussing how to fly a plane into CIA headquarters. It had been dismissed as not possible. How would they get hold of a plane? A pilot to fly it? Chewing furiously on another cigar butt, Tenet had growled: Neither had turned out to be a problem.

Another officer suggested Langley should be evacuated. Tenet compromised. Administrative staff should leave, but all others must remain.

The Counter-Terrorism Center was to send out a global alert to all CIA stations to dig up every shred of information about the attackers.

At five past ten, the Tel Aviv station reported the Popular Front for the Liberation of Palestine had just claimed responsibility for the attacks. Tenet dismissed the claim. "It's al-Qaeda," he repeated one more time.

By ten fifteen, thousands of administrative staff members were leaving the main building while Tenet led his key force to the agency printing plant. He joined in the rush to set up a makeshift operations room among the presses. Phones, databanks, and computers began to come on line.

By 10:40 A.M., all commercial flights in and out of the United States had been grounded and its borders with Canada and Mexico were sealed. Air force jets controlled the sky over America.

At eleven forty-three, the Federal Aviation Authority reported that a passenger jet out of New York to London appeared to have turned off its transponder, the device every aircraft has so it can be tracked by its own electronic signal. The one from the Heathrow-bound jet was silent except for an occasional squawk. Tenet grabbed a phone and dialed Richard Dearlove's direct-line number in Vauxhall Cross. A voice asked him to stay on the line, and a moment later Tenet found himself talking to Stephen Lander, who started to explain that Dearlove was "away" and he was "covering for MI6." Tenet cut Lander short. "I don't care who does it, but someone has to get your air force to intercept that plane," one of the officers in the operations room recalled Tenet saying.

AT MIDAFTERNOON ON THAT TUESDAY, Tony Blair and his aides in the Grand Hotel suite in Brighton watched the unfolding drama from America on television while discussing more pressing questions that directly affected them.

Lander had called with news about the passenger plane with its silent transponder, and the RAF had been scrambled to intercept it. When the plane commenced its descent into Heathrow, its flight plan would bring it close to Brighton. Blair had vetoed the idea of closing London's two airports, but everybody in the suite remembered that the IRA had almost wiped out Margaret Thatcher and her government in 1984 by exploding a massive bomb in the hotel during a Tory Party conference. Suppose the incoming aircraft had been hijacked by terrorists who planned to fly into the Grand? What orders should be given to the RAF? To force it to divert—or even shoot it down?

Neither Blair nor his advisers had come to a decision when Jeremy Heywood, the prime minister's private secretary, called from 10 Downing Street, the official residence of the prime minister, and asked if he should evacuate the building. Anji Hunter told Heywood to call the cabinet secretary, Richard Wilson, who was driving back from Brighton. Their brief conversation reflected the tensions inside the hotel suite. Wilson asked Heywood where he planned to evacuate to. Heywood did not know. Wilson recalled replying, "It's quite a good idea not to evacuate until one knows where one is going." His waspish words ended any idea of emptying Number 10.

The next call was from John Scarlett, to tell Blair the transponder failure had been caused by a cockpit malfunction, which had been corrected by the pilot. Nevertheless, Scarlett asked the RAF to escort the plane into Heathrow. A further indication of the tension in the suite was the ensuing conversation.

Blair asked Scarlett if MI6 had established who was behind the attack and was told they had "nothing firm yet, but the CIA are going with al-Qaeda." Blair wanted to know where Bush was. Scarlett said he was on board Air Force One, but no one knew its destination. It brought Blair to a decision: He was returning to London at once by car. Scarlett told the prime minister he was strongly advising against being driven, "A car convoy would be more of a target," and that the prime minister should take the train.

One of Blair's staff made another attempt to contact the White House. There was no response.

On the train back to London, Alastair Campbell began to draft the public statement he told Blair he would have to make from Downing Street. Once more Campbell's words rang with the tone that would appeal to the tabloids. "This is not a battle between the United States of America and terrorism, but between the free and democratic world and terrorism. We, therefore, here in Britain stand shoulder to shoulder with our American friends in this hour of tragedy, and we, like them, will not rest until this is driven from our world."

Blair had read the words to himself and added a few more, "It is hard even to contemplate the utter carnage and terror which has engulfed so many innocent people."

One of his staff, Tom Kelly, sensed the prime minister "wanted America to know it was not alone."

Shortly before 5:00 P.M., Blair, Campbell, and Hunter headed for the prime minister's small office next to the Cabinet Room in 10 Downing Street. Already seated in armchairs were Scarlett and Lander. In a corner of the room was a note taker. His record once more caught the mood of the day.

Blair asked if MI6 had "firmly confirmed who was responsible." Lander replied there were two possibilities. The more likely was al-Qaeda, "but it could have been a Middle East Islamic group because it was a suicide attack," he added. Blair asked if he should have known about an impending attack. Lander's reply later became quoted as an example of self-protection. "If you have read the JIC material, you would have come across some of the stuff," said the director-general. Blair confined himself to two words: "Fair enough."

IN THE WEST WING SVC, Richard Clarke, his eyes red-rimmed from exhaustion and sometimes anger, listened to another update. Apart from having a sandwich and coffee, he had worked nonstop, listening, noting, and ordering. In a day that would create many heroes, he would be one of them.

The New York Port Authority had closed all the bridges and tunnel connections into Manhattan. The FBI had ordered all landmark buildings to be evacuated; they included the Sears Tower in Chicago, Disney World in Orlando and Disneyland in Anaheim, and the Transamerica Building in San Francisco. NORAD had sent AWACs to fly over New York and Washington. The Air National Guard was patrolling from

Florida to Boston. The first of twenty Coast Guard cutters had converged on New York. Every available city firefighter was down where the twin towers had stood.

From one of the video screens, Dale Watson, the FBI counterterrorism director, waved a hand and indicated that he wished to speak to Clarke privately. Clarke picked up a phone on his desk.

His face betrayed his sudden fury as Watson told him the FBI had obtained the passenger manifests for all four aircraft and they had contained the names of al-Qaeda terrorists the CIA had opened files on after the attack on the World Trade Center on February 26, 1993. Then a bomb had exploded in the south tower's subterranean parking garage, killing six and injuring over a thousand people. The attack had been planned by Omar Abdel Rahman; the blind sheikh had been a hero to the CIA after recruiting thousands of Arab fighters to join bin Laden in fighting the Soviets in Afghanistan. Rahman had later been tried and acquitted in a Cairo court for the assassination of President Anwar Sadat and, three years afterward, had been allowed to live in the United States on a visa issued by the CIA station chief in Khartoum. Watson explained how the names of the bombers on the flight manifests had been acolytes of Rahman. Clarke recalled how he had fumed into the phone, "How was this possible?" Watson replied that the CIA hadn't passed on the names.

The rift between the FBI and the CIA, which had simmered throughout the day, had finally exploded in the high-tension atmosphere of the SVC, but Clarke knew this was not the time to let it run out of control. He silenced his own anger with a crisp reminder there was work to do. The update continued. The FAA had managed to land over four thousand aircraft. Air Force One was now the only noncombat plane in the sky. Aircraft carriers and battle cruisers of the Atlantic Fleet were steaming toward New York. More than a hundred fighters were patrolling over New York and Washington. The Federal Emergency Management Agency (FEMA) had its first rescue teams at the disaster area where Number Seven World Trade Center had also collapsed, burying the city mayor's command post and the New York Secret Service field office.

At 7:30 P.M., Air Force One landed at Andrews Air Force Base and its engine blades were still spinning when President Bush hurried down the steps to where Marine One was waiting. Two identical decoy helicopters were already hovering in the air, and above them flew two F-15s and two F-16s. Minutes later, Marine One touched down on the South Lawn of the White House.

Rumsfeld and Cheney, ringed by guards in body armor with shotguns and MP5 machine guns, had emerged from the White House bunker. Bush asked the vice president for the latest death toll. Cheney said no one really knew: "Perhaps thousands."

As Bush led the way into the White House, Cheney told him the stock markets had all stopped trading and there had been structural damage to the Wall Street Stock Exchange. Bush, without breaking stride, gave his first order. He wanted all the markets open by next day. "The world has to know America is still in business." Cheney said he'd declared a state of emergency in New York state, Virginia, and the District of Columbia. Rumsfeld still had not spoken.

Inside the Oval Office, Karen Hughes, Bush's communications director, handed Bush a draft of the speech he would make to the nation at eight thirty that evening. It included, "We will make no distinction between the terrorists who committed these acts and those who harbor them." It caught the mood of Tony Blair's speech, which CNN had carried earlier from London.

The television screens in the Oval Office, in the West Wing, in the offices of the staff who had returned to the White House, and across Washington, the United States, and the world beyond all carried the same images of horror.

A few minutes before midnight, Condoleezza Rice told Clarke the president had gone to bed, and she suggested everyone should catch a few hours' sleep to be refreshed for the morning.

ON WEDNESDAY, SEPTEMBER 12, Clarke awoke well before dawn to find the horror was still there. He knew it would be the same the day after that and for all the foreseeable days, a horror that would turn into weeks and the weeks into a month and the month into many months.

He had constantly asked himself the same questions: How many more al-Qaeda sleepers remained in America? Where were they planning a new attack? When would they launch it? He had started carrying the .357 the Secret Service had issued him. At each meeting, he insisted the questions remain at the top of the agenda.

Then came October 25, 2001, when Clarke attended a meeting with Secretary of Defense Donald Rumsfeld and Paul Wolfowitz, his deputy. He had listened intently as both men argued that al-Qaeda could not have carried out the attacks by itself and must have had a state sponsor—and that Iraq had to be that sponsor.

Clarke had been startled. All the intelligence he had seen had not once placed Iraq in the frame. Indeed, some reports had claimed

Saddam and bin Laden actively disliked each other on religious grounds; bin Laden was a committed Islamic fundamentalist, while Saddam was an avowed secularist.

Yet Rumsfeld insisted, "Iraq is behind the attacks. It is a world-ranking sponsor of terrorism." Wolfowitz concluded, "Our priority now is to deal with Saddam. Until he is removed, America and our allies can never be safe."

Clarke had felt almost physically sick as he realized the rumors he had heard from friends in the Pentagon were now all too true. The Bush administration really was planning to go to war with Iraq. Hours later Clarke's fears were realized when he walked into the White House Situation Room and found the president looking "like someone who wanted something to do." Clarke recalled how Bush had looked at him and then asked if the bombings could be linked to Saddam Hussein, "See if he was involved. I want to know any shred. Look into Iraq. Saddam."

Without waiting for a response, Bush had strolled out, in Clarke's mind having confirmed the birth of the Gulf War.

AT 12:30 P.M., THE DAY AFTER 9/11, Tony Blair was in his Downing Street den studying the latest JIC document John Scarlett had sent over. Until late the previous evening, Scarlett had taken the prime minister through some of the al-Qaeda briefing papers while the Downing Street switchboard reported it had still been unable to reach the president. Now Bush was on the line.

John Sawers, one of Blair's foreign advisers, recalled "the PM was genuinely pleased" to be told by Bush he was the first foreign leader the president was calling. The "special relationship," to which Blair attached such importance, remained intact. Sawers would later recall that before the phone call, "Blair had made it clear to me that the attacks on New York and Washington, he believed, would be a defining issue for Bush and Blair in the coming years."

In the opening minutes of the call, as Blair expressed his hope Bush would not act "precipitately or disproportionately," Bush had interrupted, "I know what I've got to do. I don't just want to hit cruise missiles into the sand."

Another marker had been laid down on the road to Baghdad.

THROUGHOUT THE AUTUMN AND WINTER OF 2001, Dr. David Kelly found his time divided between meetings with MI5, MI6, and the

Home Office to discuss the possibility of a terrorist attack against Britain, not by crashing planes into buildings but by poisoning rivers, reservoirs, and water purification plants.

The prospect of a biological weapons attack had been given priority by the government, and the skepticism Dr. Kelly had felt on returning from Washington in the summer had gone, but he was equally determined "that reality, not panic, should be the order of the day."

In his calm, authoritative voice, he had spoken to his listeners in closed-door conference rooms, reminding them that since the collapse of the Soviet Union many of its microbiologists had gone to work in Iran, Iraq, and North Korea or could have been recruited by a terrorist organization. The simplicity and low cost of biological weapons, as well as the difficulty of identifying them, made them attractive to extremist organizations, and it was almost impossible to prevent their development because of the ever more sophisticated means of genetic engineering.

He had described the wide choice of weapons that could be used including anthrax, botulinum, tularemia, and yellow fever; all were capable of spreading death throughout the land. Dr. Kelly had helped unravel the genetic code of plague, the Black Death, and despite his urging it should not be published, even in respected scientific journals, it had been. It subsequently appeared on the Internet, and scores of Web sites—a number with links to terror groups—had posted the code along with those for smallpox and cholera. Dr. Kelly reminded his Whitehall listeners there were germs that could produce epidemics of dysentery and other incapacitating illnesses. Weaponized fleas could spread killer germs; five hundred thousand would fit into a shoe box.

While vaccines could be developed, they would only give minimal protection. A microbiologist at Porton Down who had been researching a vaccine that could be used against the plague had actually contracted the disease and died. A secret test by other scientists had shown that "harmless bacteria" released from a Royal Navy ship in the English Channel could cover the "entire country in ten hours." Though that test had taken place in the 1950s at the height of the cold war, there was no reason to believe a terrorist group could not successfully repeat it.

Dr. Kelly reminded his listeners of more recent incidents: how a Tokyo cult had, in March 1995, scattered Sarin from plastic bags into the city subway, killing six people and injuring another five thousand and, in the same year, how a member of a white supremacist group in Ohio had created his own laboratory-headed paper and used it to order up three vials of plague from the American Type Culture Collection— the laboratory Donald Rumsfeld had authorized to send lethal germs to

Iraq for "medical research." The Ohio extremist had only been caught when he began to call the company asking for "urgent delivery." Dr. Kelly had explained a lab technician's suspicions had finally been aroused because any genuine researcher would know it required up to six weeks to process an order for the plague pathogens. The FBI had arrested the supremacist.

In his briefings, Dr. Kelly had said there were more than fifteen hundred microbe banks where strains of deadly germs could be bought for genuine medical research: Tracking, let alone destroying, a biological weapon created by terrorists was virtually impossible. It could be concealed in a bottle, jar, can, or tube of toothpaste or cosmetic cream. No detection system had yet been created to spot it. The simple truth meant there was no way to effectively protect Britain's population.

That remained the position at the time of writing.

BECAUSE OF HIS ROLE AS AN ADVISER on possible biological terrorist attacks, Dr. Kelly received details about other microbiologists, and early in October 2001, he received an intriguing report from MI6.

On October 4, 2001, an Air Sibir passenger plane, Flight 1812 flying from Tel Aviv to Novosibirsk in Siberia, was shot down over the Black Sea by a Ukrainian surface-to-air missile. All on board were killed. The Ukrainian government admitted the missile was "inexplicably" one hundred miles off its computer-controlled course in a test firing range. Among the dead were five microbiologists who had worked at the Russian Center of Virology and Biotechnology. Known as Vector, the institute was about twenty miles east of Novosibirsk. Dr. Kelly had visited Vector when he had been in charge of the team inspecting the dismantling of Russian biological warfare facilities under the trilateral agreement brokered between Britain, America, and Russia. Vladimir Pasechnik had told Dr. Kelly that Vector had resumed its research into DNA sequencing, which could be used to develop pathogens to target genetically related groups. Was that why the microbiologists had gone to Israel?

There had been an international uproar after the CIA had leaked, in 1998, a report to the London *Sunday Times* that Israeli scientists were "trying to exploit medical advances by identifying distinctive genes carried by some Arabs to create a genetically modified bacterium or virus. Still at the early stages, the intention is to exploit the way viruses and certain bacteria can alter the DNA inside their host's living cells." The newspaper claimed the real purpose of the research was "an attempt to create a pigmentation weapon that would target only Arab people." The allegation had been angrily denied by the Israeli government—not least because of the disturbing parallel with genetic experiments conducted by the Nazis. Dedi Zucker, then a member of the Knesset, said, "We of all people must not create such weapons."

Had the Russian microbiologists been involved in the "pigmentation weapon" research? Dr. Kelly had asked MI6 to help obtain their names and find out if they had been working at Israel's own biological warfare establishment in Tel Aviv. For once, however, the Secret Intelligence Service had been unable to discover who the microbiologists were or what they had been doing in Israel. There was a total news blackout on the crash.

The Mossad had sent a team to the Ukraine to investigate. Its report was submitted to the Israeli government. It has never been made public. The names of the five microbiologists and details of their visit to Tel Aviv would remain secret.

On November 12, five weeks after the crash, a cell biologist Dr. Kelly knew slightly, Dr. Benito Que, was found in a coma near his laboratory at the University of Miami Medical School in Florida. The fifty-two-year-old expert on infectious diseases had been investigating how a virus like HIV could be genetically engineered into a biological weapon. His classified work in DNA sequencing was partly financed by the U.S. Department of Defense. A careful researcher who ran his life with clockwork precision, Dr. Que had suddenly left his lab after receiving a phone call. He was found unconscious in the medical school's parking lot and later died. A verdict of "death by natural causes" was returned. Challenged by Dr. Que's family as to why they had not taken in to account sworn testimony that the biologist appeared to have been "repeatedly struck with a baseball bat," the Miami police continued to insist there was no need to reopen the case.

Dr. Don Wiley was one of the foremost microbiologists in the United States. He was a specialist in DNA sequencing and an expert on how the immune system responds to a variety of deadly germs. Dr. Kelly, a friend of Wiley's, knew he had a close connection to the CIA, regularly traveling from his laboratory at the Howard Hughes Medical Institute at Harvard University to Washington. "Dr. Wiley's specialty was deciphering high-resolution images of viruses, a prerequisite of identifying those which could be used as biological weapons. His lab had contracts with the Pentagon to create defenses against Ebola, Marburg fever, and other doomsday germs," Dr. Kelly recalled to the author.

On November 14, the fifty-seven-year-old scientist had traveled to Memphis, Tennessee, to visit Graceland, the home of Elvis Presley. He had told friends he was eager to learn more about the singer. The next day he attended a dinner for medical researchers at the Peabody Hotel in Memphis and left around midnight. His fellow guests remember he was cheerful and had little to drink. When he was reported missing, and the Memphis police were told of his standing as a world-renowned scientist, they began a search. His rental car was found abandoned on a bridge across the Mississippi River. The keys were in the ignition, the gas tank was full, and the hazard lights were not turned on. There was no sign of collision damage. The distance from the Peabody Hotel to where the car was found was only a four-minute drive. The car was pointing toward the Arkansas state border—the opposite direction to where Dr. Wiley had been staying in Memphis with his father. The bridge crossing was a busy one for traffic, even at night. Yet no motorist had reported the parked car was causing an obstruction. The police could not say how long it had stood on the bridge. They searched the area. There was no sign of Dr. Wiley or of any violent crime.

The police thought it was "possible" the scientist had parked on the bridge, perhaps to look down at the river, and had either toppled or jumped into the river. However, only a physically fit man could have climbed over the rail, and Dr. Wiley was not physically fit. There was no evidence in his background of depression or a threat to commit suicide. He was listed as a "missing person."

The FBI later visited his laboratory and examined DNA sequencing paperwork he had been working on. Some of it was removed. The FBI has consistently refused to say why. It was not until December 20 that Dr. Wiley's body was found three hundred miles downstream from Memphis, snagged on a tree on the bank of the Mississippi. The body bore evidence of severe head wounds, but no forensic examination was performed to try to establish the cause. The local medical examiner announced the death was "accidental."

On November 21, 2001, Vladimir Pasechnik left his office at Regma Biotechnologies. He had seemed happy and in good health. Returning home, he had cooked supper, washed up, and went to sleep. He was found dead in bed the next day. There was no obvious cause of death, and the police listed the death as "inexplicable." However, following a post-mortem, the coroner accepted the pathologist's conclusion that Pasechnik had died from a stroke. No details of the autopsy report were made public. While English law demands a coroner's inquest must be open to the public, no prior notice was given to the press of its date or venue. No reporter covered the event. The funeral, which normally would have drawn media attention given who Pasechnik was, went unreported.

He had been buried almost a month before the briefest details of his death were released by Dr. Christopher Davis, his former MI6 briefing officer, who had retired from the service and was living outside Washington in Virginia. He was the proud holder of an Order of the British Empire. He believed it had been awarded for helping to debrief Pasechnik with Dr. Kelly. There had been no award to Dr. Kelly.

Set Van Nyugen, a Vietnamese-born researcher, had worked for fifteen years in Australia's Scientific and Industrial Research Organization at Geelong and was a regular correspondent with Dr. Kelly on DNA sequencing. Scientists at the institute had recently created a new and virulent type of mousepox, a cousin of smallpox, and had wondered if it could be possible for similar genetic manipulation to produce a comparable and more powerful strain of smallpox. On December 11, 2001, Van Nyugen had gone into a refrigeration room at the institute to collect samples of anthrax. He never managed to open the cabinet containing the spores. No one saw what happened; shortly afterward the sixty-one-year-old microbiologist was found dead on the floor. The official verdict was he had been overcome by an unexplained leakage from the room's nitrogen cooling system. Yet such a cause would have produced warning symptoms for the experienced scientist, giving him sufficient time to escape before he was overcome with shortness of breath or fatigue, the two usual side effects from exposure to an excess of nitrogen.

On February 9, 2002, Dr. Kelly received news of another death from the MI6 commander of Moscow station. Viktor Korshunov, the director of the microbiology department at the city's state university, had been found murdered outside his front door clutching his door key in his hand. Dr. Kelly had known Korshunov since they met at a microbiology conference in Stockholm, and they had kept in contact as part of the network of scientists Dr. Kelly had created. In a recent letter, Korshunov had revealed he was working on a vaccine against anthrax. The Moscow police reported he had been attacked with a small axe, which had split open his skull. Though he lived in a busy apartment block, no one had seen or heard anything. His wallet was intact, and no attempt had been made to open his front door with the key. The police had removed all his work files and concluded Korshunov had been the victim of a "hit-and-run" thief.

Another unexplained death that came to Dr. Kelly's attention was that of Dr. Ian Longford, a senior fellow at the University of East Anglia. The campus was where Dr. Rihab Taha had spent five years studying before returning to Iraq to run the country's biological warfare program, and Dr. Kelly had met Longford during his inquiries into her background. Dr. Longford had been found dead on February 19, 2002, in his home in Norwich, where he lived alone. The *Times* reported that all the outside doors to the house had been locked from the inside. When police broke in, they found his seminaked body in a blood-spattered room and partly wedged under a chair. There were signs the house had been searched. An autopsy was unable to determine the cause of death. An "open verdict" was returned at the inquest.

Dr. Kelly was not a superstitious man; all he said and did was within the parameters of a careful scientist. Nevertheless, apart from the five Russian microbiologists who had been killed in the plane crash, he had known all these men. Could all their deaths be somehow related to the persistent rumor he had heard at the various medical conferences he attended that countries like North Korea, China, and Iran had continued to try to recruit microbiologists—and when turned down threatened to have them killed?

Ken Alibek had claimed he was approached by "a representative of the government of South Korea to share any knowledge about North Korea's biowarfare program." Alibek had declined, but since then, he had told Dr. Kelly, he had been approached by other countries. Alibek had hinted his refusals had put his own life in danger.

The longer Dr. Kelly had pondered the question, the more he wondered if the deaths of his fellow microbiologists could be linked to their refusal to work elsewhere. Each man had valuable information that could save months, possibly years, of costly research for any nation trying to develop or improve its biological warfare program. He drew up a list of countries that would be ready to kill the microbiologists, if they refused an offer to work for them. At the top of that list was North Korea, followed by Iran.

19

Back to the Future

On a warm evening in June 2003, Sir Richard Billing Dearlove strolled through the oldest gatehouse of all the university colleges in Cambridge, the entrance to Pembroke College. From inside the gate he had a splendid view of the architectural magnificence before him. The Old Court, the buildings in which the college had been founded almost seven hundred years before; the adjoining chapel designed by Christopher Wren; the gardens said to have more carefully selected vegetation than any other Cambridge college's; the preserved area of semiwild growth that dated from that Christmas Eve in 1347 when Edward III had granted Mary St. Pol, the widow of the earl of Pembroke, the license to found the college; the row of plane trees, each of which had stood for centuries, as impressive as those planted in Vauxhall Cross.

As master of Pembroke College, Dearlove would rule over an academic fiefdom so different from MI6. Instead of spies, he would have the ultimate responsibility for over six hundred graduates and undergraduates. No longer would he have to sign his memos in green ink, send for the most secret of the Y files, or take middle-of-the-night phone calls, attend JIC meetings, or fly to Washington to meet with Tenet.

The two spy chiefs had bonded from the morning after 9/11 when Dearlove had flown into Washington on a private jet accompanied by Eliza Manningham-Buller, then the deputy head of MI5, and Sir David Manning, Tony Blair's foreign affairs adviser. Tenet had been stunned to see them: Almost no aircraft were being admitted into U.S. airspace. Dearlove had smiled and murmured they had come to show their

support. Tenet had been visibly moved, and over dinner he had toasted
the "special relationship between our countries," speaking late into the
night about the threat bin Laden posed. In the early hours Tenet had
driven them past the still smoking Pentagon. The next morning
Dearlove had flown back to London to brief the JIC on what he had
seen and heard in Washington. Since then, Dearlove had participated
in every stage of the fighting back.

Soon, though, he would only be an observer, no longer at the center
of the decisions involving the Secret Intelligence Service striking against
al-Qaeda. Soon he would no longer need a bombproof car, nor be required to leave his special cell phone permanently switched on wherever
he went, nor have to notify a select number of people at 10 Downing
Street and in the Foreign Office of his holiday destination.

There were so many things that would no longer be part of his daily
life: briefing the prime minister and the foreign secretary, meeting Europe's intelligence chiefs, and reading the endless flow of papers, which,
no matter how diligently his staff sorted them out, still left him with a
formidable pile on his desk to work through in a day all devoted in one
way or another to the growing threat of terrorism.

Each time, how to act had been his final decision after he had
weighed the risks involved against the anticipated results, but to win a war
like no other, the war against terrorism, had meant developing even
closer links with Europe's intelligence services. Dearlove had spent time
doing that, particularly with the Spanish and Italian agencies that had not
often figured on previous distribution lists for MI6 intelligence. In turn,
his daily reading had frequently contained high-quality intelligence from
Madrid and Rome.

Soon he would instead be reading reports about the costs of maintaining the college buildings and Pembroke's immaculately kept bowl-
ing green, which was said to be the oldest in continuous use in Europe.

The month before, in May, Dearlove had finally told Tony Blair of
his decision to accept the mastership, one of the most respected posts in
British academia, and he had suggested his deputy, Nigel Inkster, would
make an ideal successor as chief. Inkster had been a contemporary of
Blair's at Oxford before joining MI6 in 1975, and most of his overseas
service had been in Asia. With a good record of making fair but firm decisions, he was a popular figure in Vauxhall Cross. Blair had been noncommittal, saying he wanted to see a "difficult summer through" before
making a decision on who would next run MI6.

For Dearlove, it was a sign Inkster's appointment was not guaranteed, and that left only one contender, John Scarlett. There had been rumors for weeks the chairman of the JIC was eager to return to MI6. Dearlove had every reason to believe the choice would create a public furor because of Scarlett's role in the intelligence presentation that had led to the second Gulf War.

ON MARCH 18, 2003, led by the United States and the United Kingdom, and supported by ground forces from Australia, Poland, and Denmark, the invasion of Iraq began. George Bush and Tony Blair had ordered hostilities because Saddam Hussein had failed to take what they called a "final opportunity" to disarm Iraq of its nuclear, chemical, and biological weapons, which were described as "an immediate and intolerable threat to world peace." The goal was "to end Saddam's support for terrorism and to free the Iraqi people."

When the war ended on May 1, 2003, Saddam Hussein and his Baath Party had been toppled and a new government installed under the occupation by the coalition forces, who had suffered close to eight hundred dead and wounded during the fighting. The Iraqi numbers of killed and injured were set between 65,000 and 650,000. Sectarian violence and then insurgency had broken out and would continue. The opposition to the war had grown, and an estimated thirty-six million people around the world had, by June 2003, taken part in almost three thousand protests. All had focused on the claims that Iraq had possessed weapons of mass destruction, or WMD.

The claim these existed had forcefully been made by Secretary of State Colin Powell when he addressed the United Nations General Assembly on February 5, 2003. His slick slide presentation had included a model vial of anthrax and pictures of vehicles that Powell claimed were "mobile biological agent factories . . . that travel the roads of Iraq every day." Powell had insisted the evidence for his claims was assured by MI6 from its own impeccable sources.

In London, an alarmed Richard Dearlove had written a memo saying that while "Bush wants to remove Saddam through military action, justified by the conjunction of terrorism and weapons of mass destruction, the intelligence facts are being mixed around the politics." (The memo finally surfaced in the *Washington Post* on May 13, 2005.)

The intelligence skewing that Dearlove referred to had been orchestrated by Scarlett in his capacity as chairman of the JIC; he had also supervised the intelligence input of what later became known as "the

sexed-up dossier" claiming Saddam had the capability to launch a nuclear attack within forty-five minutes. It was one of the planks Blair and
Bush had used to justify going to war.

Among those who had been called upon to support that claim was
Dr. David Kelly. Specifically he had been asked to provide evidence that
Iraq had developed a smallpox program and possessed "mobile chemical factories." Dr. Kelly had expressed grave doubts about the existence
of either. Nonetheless, his reservations were not included in the Downing Street final version of the "sexed-up dossier" or in Powell's claims to
the United Nations the previous February. When the war ended and the
cry intensified for proof about the existence of weapons of mass destruction, over a thousand experts were sent to Iraq to search. Among
them was Dr. David Kelly.

WHILE OTHERS HUNTED for evidence of nuclear or chemical
weapons, Dr. Kelly had concentrated on discovering the whereabouts of
shells and missiles with warheads capable of delivering huge quantities
of germs, which he had been told were secretly developed between the
wars and remained buried in dumps under the desert sands. He had ordered thousands of tons of sand to be excavated. Nothing was found.
He was told they had been hidden beneath homes and office buildings,
in the foundations of a school, even in a hospital. Everywhere had been
rigorously searched. Each time no biological weapons were discovered.

Dr. Kelly had returned to London only to be urged to look again. He
had done so. Once more, he had drawn a blank, and increasingly his
conviction grew that if there had been weapons, they were no longer
anywhere in Iraq. He had questioned Dr. Taha for hours in the prison
camp near Baghdad International Airport, where she was being held
awaiting trial for her crimes. She insisted she had supervised the destruction of "what few germs she still had" shortly before the outbreak of war.

From the Ministry of Defense in Whitehall, from the Joint Intelligence Committee, and finally from Downing Street came the same demand: Iraq's biological weapons of mass destruction had to be found.
The hunt for them became all the more urgent when it became clear
Iraq did not possess any nuclear or chemical weapons.

Dr. Kelly had continued his search. He again questioned the scientists
who had worked for Dr. Taha. Nothing. He once more questioned Dr.
Taha. She still adamantly repeated her denials. He had new holes dug beside old ones in the desert. More buildings were searched to their foundations. Nothing. But the pressure on Dr. Kelly continued.

The events of recent weeks had made him conclude that, under the Blair government, intelligence was a tool ministers used to manipulate an increasingly doubting public. He had seen how raw intelligence sent from MI6 to the Foreign Office and the Ministry of Defense, and then assessed by the JIC, had been politicized to support the Downing Street claim Saddam Hussein could launch WMD within forty-five minutes. The final version of that document, earlier drafts of which Dr. Kelly had contributed to, contained a certitude not reflected by the subtle nuances and caveats of the original intelligence on which his own opinions were based. Dr. Kelly shared a view that had led to Robin Cook, the foreign secretary, resigning from the Blair cabinet on the eve of the war with Iraq. "Selected for inclusion were only the scraps of intelligence that fitted the government's case. The net result was a gross distortion," Cook later wrote.

Like Cook, Dr. Kelly felt betrayed. Finally he had told Andrew Gilligan, a BBC reporter on the prestigious radio program *Today,* that he believed the report Downing Street had published on the eve of war that Iraq possessed weapons of mass destruction was untrue. Gilligan's broadcast referred to the report as being "sexed-up" and described the unnamed source for his story as a credible intelligence person.

In the furor that followed, the BBC and the Blair government became increasingly locked in a titanic struggle over the truth of the broadcast. Dr. Kelly went to his line manager at the Ministry of Defense (MOD) and admitted he had spoken to the BBC reporter but claimed he did not recognize "some forty percent" of what had been broadcast. He believed he would be kept out of the public spotlight; instead the MOD leaked his name to the media. He became the story and began to fear that at the age of fifty-nine, less than a year away from retirement, he would lose his pension along with his reputation. Those fears increased when he appeared before the House of Commons Foreign Affairs Committee on Intelligence. He was vigorously questioned by its members, some of whom were known government supporters.

On the evening of Wednesday, July 16, 2003, Dr. Kelly arrived home visibly exhausted and shaken by his ordeal. Janice comforted him as they watched the continuous rerunning on television of his appearance before the parliamentary committee. On screen he cut a sad and lonely figure, the unwilling flag bearer of bitterly divided factions that either supported or opposed the war.

Dr. Kelly was like Rubashov, the helpless hero of *Darkness at Noon,* Arthur Koestler's novel about the Stalinist show trials. Just as in the book, Dr. Kelly had found himself the central figure in a world where hesitation was guilt, silence admission, and blame and stigma opposite sides of the same coin. He may well have pondered how this had come about. His dealing with the BBC reporter had followed his nonattribution rule when talking to the media, which he had done a number of times, usually in what he called "broad brush meetings" to set in context information often already in the public domain. Dr. Kelly had also always made it clear to reporters that while he did have dealings with intelligence services, he was not employed by them. He saw himself as "a consultant, an expert witness, if you like," he once said.

The truth was that he had been used by Whitehall's political fixers and spin doctors as their shuttlecock, finally reducing him to near tears before that parliamentary committee. The sight of such naked emotion had stunned his friends. To them he was still the gentle-voiced man with a fund of stories about his thirty-seven visits to Iraq and how he had matched toast for toast Russian biological scientists as they raised their vodka glasses at a banquet after he had supervised the dismantling of their biological warfare facilities at the end of the cold war. For his friends he was the man who had now been cruelly and publicly humiliated and traduced.

Over lunch with Janice on that Thursday in the kitchen of their home in Southmoor, Dr. Kelly gave no sign of the anger that gripped him regarding the behavior of his superiors at the Ministry of Defense and those he had worked with in the dark world of intelligence. But as a result the Blair government would be rocked as by no other crisis in its existence; the public perception of the BBC would be forever changed; the activities of Britain's intelligence services would be subjected to an unprecedented spotlight. If David Kelly realized any of these consequences, he gave no hint to Janice.

WHILE JANICE PREPARED SANDWICHES IN THE KITCHEN, Dr. Kelly had taken several phone calls in his study from colleagues at Porton Down and the MOD expressing their anger at the way he was being treated. Dr. Kelly had told one caller he would be surprised if "my body isn't one day found in the woods." Were those the words of someone contemplating suicide—or was there something more sinister behind them? Had the fate of those other dead microbiologists begun to haunt him? In the coming week, before he was due once more to return to Iraq to launch yet another search for weapons of mass destruction, he was to be interviewed by an MI6 officer about his contacts with Wouter Basson. Dr. Kelly had thought his report on Project Coast had dealt with that. So why had it surfaced again? Yet any concerns he felt had not been shared with his line manager.

There had also been an incident that perturbed Janice. A few weeks previously, she had been sitting with David in the living room when the phone rang in his office quite late in the evening. This was not unusual, but after taking the call, he had changed into the clothes he only wore for important meetings in Whitehall and left the house without any explanation. "That was so unlike him," Janice later recalled. "When he returned, he did look somewhat worried." She had long known not to question him about such matters: She and their children remained in a box in his brain that had no access to all the other compartments of his mind.

Before joining her for lunch, Dr. Kelly had told a caller he was "basically holding up all right, but Janice is having a difficult time both physically and mentally."

At the kitchen table, Janice had noticed her husband looked "tired and subdued, but not depressed." She had seen him on other occasions like this: after returning from an overseas trip or another long day in London or at Porton Down. In fact, during the meal it was Janice who showed the first signs of strain from the mounting political storm that was engulfing them. She excused herself from the table, saying she was going to lie down because of her arthritis pains and a pounding headache. As she climbed the stairs, the telephone rang again in Dr. Kelly's office. After he answered it, he went upstairs to see if Janice was feeling better. She reassured him, and, satisfied, he said he would take a short walk to help the back pain with which he had suffered for some years.

AT TWO THIRTY THAT THURSDAY AFTERNOON, Detective Chief Inspector Alan Young sat down in his office in Thames Valley Police headquarters in Kidlington, Oxfordshire, and began to create a highly restricted file on his secure computer.

Young was an experienced officer and was used to handling sensitive matters. Senior politicians, members of the security services, and Whitehall civil servants all lived within the force's jurisdiction; for them the commute to London was a necessary evil that let them have their homes in the countryside.

He now knew Dr. Kelly felt the same: Traveling on a rush-hour train to London or driving from home to Porton Down was worthwhile because he and his wife enjoyed the village life of Southmoor. She was a member of the local history society; he would walk to the far end of the village to play cribbage in his local pub, the Wagon and Horses. There, over a pint, he could catch up on the local gossip about rising house prices and the creeping urbanization that saw farmland replaced by housing estates. He was popular at the hostelry, ready to stand his round. He never spoke about his work, but the regulars assumed he was, in the words of one, "somebody important in London."

Across the top of his screen Young typed a code name: *Operation Mason*. Beneath it he added: *Not for Release. Police Operational Information.* Below that he added figures: *14.30* and *17.07.03*. They indicated the file had been opened at two thirty on Thursday, July 17, 2003.

Young's file had begun after a morning of often tense discussions in various government offices in Whitehall. Dr. Kelly's appearance before the Commons Intelligence Committee continued to reverberate in the Foreign Office, the Ministry of Defense, Downing Street, and the Joint Intelligence Committee. John Scarlett, JIC's chairman for the past two years, had taken his share of the calls. On that Thursday afternoon, Scarlett's well-attuned nose for trouble sensed that Dr. Kelly's responses before the parliamentary committee and the continuing government quarrel with the BBC over its broadcast containing the accusation over the "sexed-up" dossier were becoming a problem.

Scarlett had played a key part in producing the document. In doing so, he had discarded the carefully judged input of Dr. Kelly in the early drafts. The original raw intelligence had come from MI6, approved by Richard Dearlove, before it had electronically made its way through the intelligence community, passing across the desk of the Defense intelligence staff. None of them had supported Dr. Kelly's continued assertion that the lack of evidence made it unsafe to claim Saddam had any weapons of mass destruction, but in saying so to the BBC reporter, he had aroused concern among the mandarins of Whitehall.

In the tangled web beginning to ensnare the scientist was a concern that a middle-grade civil servant could do even more serious damage to the government. On that Thursday morning, the question had been asked over the secure telephone lines in Whitehall: What else could Kelly do—*would* he do?

At some point the decision had been taken to launch Operation Mason. Who gave the order would remain a secret, just as would the contents of the file that Detective Chief Inspector Young had opened to commence the police investigation "into the circumstances surrounding Dr. Kelly's death." Most remarkable was that Young had been asked to start his file an hour before Dr. Kelly had set out on his walk.

ON JUNE 30, 2003, MI5 had e-mailed to all police forces in Britain a document headed "Secret Service Espionage Alert." It read, "We are aware that Russian intelligence officers travel widely throughout the U.K. and that some of the activity undertaken by these officers is intelligence related. The Russian Federation Intelligence Services are assessed as posing a SUBSTANTIAL threat to the U.K. Full vehicle registration, date, time and place sighted, direction of travel, description and number of occupants and a description of the vehicle should be noted. Vehicles should not be stopped or followed, nor should their occupants be questioned. Reports should be sent to the Security Service." The alert concluded with a reminder that the vehicles would be bearing the license plate prefix 248D, assigned to all Russian diplomatic vehicles.

A week before Dr. Kelly set out on his walk, a Thames Valley Police car had spotted a Land Rover with those numbers heading toward Southmoor. Details were radioed to the force's traffic headquarters, where they were sent over a secure line to Thames House. Had the vehicle's presence in the area been purely a coincidence, perhaps on the way to take a recently arrived Russian diplomat on a sightseeing tour of Oxford? Or had it been on reconnaissance to establish where Dr. Kelly lived, the road he traveled in and out of Southmoor, and the layout of the countryside around the village?

Despite his work in trying to find biological weapons in Iraq, a decision had been taken not to surround Dr. Kelly with undue protection. While his panic button at home would enable him to call upon the Special Branch officers at Thames Valley Police headquarters if he felt threatened, to provide him with more obvious protection would have been difficult because Dr. Kelly had made it clear he did not want it. However, after his appearance before the parliamentary committee, he had reluctantly agreed to let two police officers accompany him home. At the front door he had thanked them politely and said they should return to London.

Another threat also figured in Dr. Kelly's life. Though the war with Iraq was over, the country was a highly dangerous place for him to continue to search for biological weapons, and he had been warned by his MI5 controller that when he returned to Iraq he would be a target for Saddam Hussein's death squads roaming the country seeking vengeance for his defeat. Dr. Kelly had shrugged the risks aside, "It goes with the territory." He had still not mentioned the threats to Janice as he set off on his walk that Thursday afternoon. Theirs was a loving but loose-fitting marriage, and after thirty-six years, they both knew its boundaries.

TEN MINUTES INTO HIS WALK he passed a neighbor, Ruth Absalom, and they exchanged a few pleasantries before she headed back to Southmoor, he toward the village of Kingston Bagpuize. Before reaching it, he would walk down two country lanes; one petering out into a footpath that eventually led to Harrowdown Hill, a lonely area of woodland with brambles dense enough to deter most people. The one certainty of what followed was that sometime that afternoon Dr. Kelly received two calls on his cell phone.

Later, questions would be asked about the calls by the growing number of journalists who had begun to look into Dr. Kelly's background after his dramatic appearance before the parliamentary committee. Were the callers from the MOD, MI5, or MI6? Newspaper security correspondents had established that Dr. Kelly's relationship with both intelligence services was closer than they realized. Had the calls been to establish his whereabouts and remind him he was to stay in contact due to what was now a rapidly developing story in Whitehall? Or were the calls from an intelligence officer from a foreign service? Ari Ben-Menashe, a former adviser on intelligence to the Israeli government, later claimed that since Dr. Kelly had been identified as the source of the BBC "sexed-up dossier" broadcast, the Mossad's London station had "taken a close interest in Dr. Kelly because of his involvement with those other dead microbiologists." The Internet had continued to carry speculation about their deaths, including claims they were the victims of a Chinese intelligence death squad, killed because they had refused to work in China's own biological warfare program. The claims were dismissed but still found their way into the files, both the ones MI5 and MI6 already had on Dr. Kelly and the one Detective Inspector Young was now busy preparing.

HOURS BEFORE HE SET OUT ON HIS WALK, Dr. Kelly had sent from his office an e-mail to Judith Miller, a *New York Times* reporter and a Pulitzer Prize winner, indicating "there are many dark actors playing games." She was one of a growing number of serious journalists who had begun to feel that not only had he been badly treated, but that he had a story still to tell. Another was Jim Rarey, a respected American investigative reporter, who had discovered Dr. Kelly had been discussing with an Oxford-based specialist publisher the possibility of writing a book about the relationship between government policy and war. In Rarey's view, the prospect "sent the intelligence elite in several countries into a containment mode."

AT HOME, JANICE KELLY lay on their bed, crippled with another bout of arthritis, hoping her husband would return soon. Normally he walked for no more than thirty minutes. When an hour had passed, she began to wonder where he could be. At dusk on that summer evening, she called the police. A search began.

Shortly after 8:00 A.M. on Friday, July 18, 2003, and after a sleepless night, Janice Kelly answered a door knock and found a Thames Valley Police officer and three men in dark suits. In answer to her question, the officer said there was no news of her husband's whereabouts, but a search continued. One of the men explained he and his colleagues had come to "recover" Dr. Kelly's computers. Janice did not query this. She had long been used to the way the MOD behaved. She led the way to her husband's office and left them to get on with their work while waiting in the kitchen. The police officer stood guard over the office. The men were computer experts from MI5's Technical Assessment Unit. They unplugged the six computers and carried them out to a van. It took less than ten minutes to complete what they came to do.

THE SEARCH FOR DR. KELLY had been under way for some time that Friday morning, with police teams assisted by local helpers checking the wooded countryside around Southmoor. Louise Holmes had brought a collie to help check the dense undergrowth as she and Paul Chapman made their way toward Harrowdown Hill. Both were volunteer searchers who had firsthand knowledge of the area. The animal was a little ahead when it started to howl and came running back. "Unusually, he refused to move, as if something had frightened him," Louise later recalled. She and Paul ran to where the dog had come from and found the body of Dr. Kelly "propped up against a tree." Louise used her cell phone to call the police on the number all the searchers had been given and was told not to touch the body and that "support officers" were on the way. In the meantime, she and Paul "should leave the scene so as not to disturb anything."

Walking back to their car, the couple met three men who said they were Thames Valley "detectives." She remembered one flashed an ID card

and asked where the body was. Louise pointed in the direction they had
come from, and she and Paul continued walking to their car. Thirty-five
minutes after Dr. Kelly's body had been found, two ambulance paramedics, David Bartlett and Vanessa Hunt, arrived at the scene. According
to them, the body was lying on its back a little distance from where
Louise and Paul had reported it "propped up against a tree." Both experienced paramedics agreed there was not enough blood at the scene to
indicate the small wound in Dr. Kelly's left wrist was the cause of death—
and doubted he had deliberately slashed it to commit suicide.

THE INTRIGUE SURROUNDING DR. KELLY'S death began inside
the forensic tent the police had erected over his body on Harrowdown
Hill. An MI5 officer had arrived with the pathologist to recover Dr.
Kelly's cell phone, which had been found in his jacket pocket. The officer had immediately left, and what became of the phone would remain
one of the many mysteries of that day.

Before the pathologist began his examination of the body, he asked
for Dr. Kelly's dental records. They turned out to be missing from the
local dentist's practice Dr. Kelly visited for his annual checkup. The dentist reported to the police he had arrived at work that morning to find a
window open; he was certain he had locked it the night before. The
window was large enough for a small person to wriggle through, but no
forensic checks were made by the police to discover evidence of entry.
Two days later the records reappeared in their correct place in the office's filing system, but again no forensic tests were made for finger-
prints. However, their disappearance so alarmed the police that the
pathologist was asked to conduct a DNA test to "confirm it really is Dr.
Kelly." The mystery of the removal and reappearance of the dental records remained unsolved. Had they been removed by one of the MI5
specialists in housebreaking?

Another unsolved question was the thirty-tablet blister pack of the
painkiller co-proxamol the police found on his body. The medicine had
been prescribed for Janice Kelly to help ease the pain of her arthritis. In
their initial body search, the police discovered all but one of the tablets
had been removed from the pack. They reasonably assumed Dr. Kelly
had swallowed them, but no traces of the drug were found in his body
on postmortem examination, and it emerged he had a well-developed
aversion to swallowing pills. Had the blister pack been placed in Dr.
Kelly's jacket to further the idea he had used them to commit suicide?
Was the knife he had owned since childhood that was found near his

body part of a plan to show he had killed himself? The blade showed no trace of blood nor signs it had been wiped clean on his jacket or the grass. Had someone else used a cloth? Again there would be no answers to these troubling questions.

In his final report the pathologist concluded Dr. Kelly had committed suicide by using the knife to sever the ulnar artery on his left wrist. Three doctors—a consultant in trauma, a radiologist, and a vascular surgeon—collectively, and very publicly, concluded the verdict did not substantiate suicide, "If Dr. Kelly had intended to kill himself, he would have cut his radial artery." Such an outright challenge, let alone in a case that was gathering international headlines, was unknown in Britain's conservative medical circles.

Janice Kelly had told the police her husband had converted to the Baha'i religion, a pacifist faith that condemned suicide, and she felt his newfound belief enabled him to cope with the pressures of his work.

Among the three hundred interviews the police would conduct was one with Dr. Julian Perry, a longtime friend who revealed Dr. Kelly had been considering retiring in a year from his £63,000-a-year job and possibly going to America, where a higher salary would pay for the latest available treatment for Janice. Dr. Perry believed "David had all to play for, and suicide would be the last thing on his mind."

Support for this came from a colorful source. She was Mai Pederson, a former belly dancer who had joined the U.S. Army, had been married twice and, according to one of her former husbands, had an "astonishing ability to bewitch men." More certain is that her Arabic linguistic skills had found her a role in the intelligence world, and she had first met Dr. Kelly in Iraq in 1998. After she introduced him to the Baha'i faith, they had remained close friends. During his regular visits to America, he would make a point of seeing her, but she would insist their relationship was "only platonic." They had last been in touch just weeks before his death, and when she heard about it, she was "absolutely positive he did not kill himself."

Meanwhile, in Washington, the idea that Dr. Kelly had actually been murdered began to preoccupy a lawyer, Michael Shrimpton, who briefed the powerful U.S. Senate Intelligence Committee on national security issues. "My own high-level contacts had told me that Kelly was going to be taken down. Within forty-eight hours of his body being found I was telephoned by a British intelligence officer and told that Kelly had been murdered. But he insisted that neither MI5 nor MI6 were involved," he told Tim Shipman, one of the many investigative reporters who had tried to pursue the fate of Dr. Kelly.

While they excavated and burrowed and ran up huge expenses around the drinking dens in Whitehall and the Wagon and Horses in Southmoor, interviewing anyone who had a memory of David Kelly, Tony Blair had appointed a seventy-two-year-old retired judge, Brian Hutton, to preside over a full-blown government inquiry into his death. It was intended to replace the usual inquest into a suicide. The son of middle-class Belfast Protestants, Lord Hutton had made his reputation as a judge in IRA terrorist cases when he had dismissed several charges for lack of evidence. By then he had lost his Ulster vowels, but he continued to bemuse his friends by inviting them to sit with him and watch reruns of *The Lone Ranger*. In many ways the character fitted his own personality. He was also authoritative and enjoyed reading the latest Law Society reports.

Downing Street had let it be known that the appointment of Lord Hutton to replace the Oxfordshire coroner, Nicholas Gardiner, was intended to give the inquiry additional gravitas. Instead it had led to controversy. Experts in coroners' laws pointed out that Hutton, though a senior Law Lord, had no previous experience in conducting an inquest. Other senior lawyers pointed out that his reputation had been made acting for the Crown during his time as a barrister, representing the army in the Bloody Sunday inquiry before becoming Lord Chief Justice of Northern Ireland. Had he been brought out of retirement, in the words of one barrister "to ensure the remit of the inquest remained firmly within the boundary of how David Kelly had died?" Roy Hattersley, the former deputy leader of the Labour Party, publicly speculated, "The choice is tactical. Tony Blair has appointed Hutton so we could be sure there would be no questions about Kelly's failure to uncover weapons of mass destruction in Iraq." As of that Friday morning of course, this would be for the future.

Minutes after the body was found, a call was made to Detective Chief Inspector Young. He made his last entry for Operation Mason. It simply stated: *09.00 18.07.03. Body recovered.*

Later that morning the file was transmitted to the Home Office, the overall authority for Britain's police force, so ending Young's involvement in the case. From the Home Office separate copies of the document were sent to MI5 and Downing Street. Upon his appointment Lord Hutton received a copy. He had read it by the time he visited Janice Kelly at home a week after her husband's death. He spent less than an hour with her, sitting in the chair her husband once occupied. What they spoke about would remain confidential at his request. The existence of the file only emerged during his hearing, when the front page of the Operation Mason file was allowed by Lord Hutton into the public domain. The rest of its contents have remained locked away in the MI5 Registry.

Far from the forest glade where Dr. Kelly had died, in the coming weeks, from the thickets of Whitehall would emerge a procession of its inhabitants, arriving before the Royal Courts of Justice in the Strand in their government high-gleam, state-paid sedans. One by one they were ushered into Court Number 73 to testify under the owlish gaze of Lord Hutton. There was Tony Blair and his Special Branch bodyguard, built like a Hereford bull, the veins on his bald head pulsating, listening as the prime minister revealed that "to know" a document did not mean the same as "to see" it. Behind Blair had followed some of his most senior mandarins: Sir David Ormand, the chief intelligence coordinator in the Cabinet Office; Sir David Manning, the prime minister's chief foreign political adviser; John Scarlett, chairman of the Joint Intelligence Committee, but poised to take over MI6; Jonathan Powell, Tony Blair's chief of staff; and Geoffrey Hoon, who when asked gave his full name, "I am Geoffrey William Hoon." "And you are Secretary of State for Defense, Mr. Hoon?" asked the inquiry's Queen's counsel, James Dingemans. "Yes, I am." At which a stage whisper came from the gallery, "But for how long?"

Sections of the media had already decided Hoon's ministry was culpable in Dr. Kelly's suicide by betraying his name to reporters. Hoon's own special adviser, Richard Taylor, had told an impassive Lord Hutton the Defense secretary had attended a meeting where the decision to reveal Dr. Kelly's identity had been made. One of the sketch artists had described Taylor leaving the court "like a hotel under-manager avoiding an incident in the foyer."

The mandarins had spoken in lawyerly voices, far removed from the way Janice Kelly gave her evidence. Supported by a walking cane and her eldest daughter, Rachel, she had spoken with precise consonants that carried their own convincing truth: A wife so worried about her husband she had tried to shield him from her own health problems, her dignity in the face of his death was far more upsetting than the glottal-stopping language of the procession of witnesses who appeared to have spent hours preparing for their appearance in the spotlight.

Finally the weeks of hearing came to an end. No longer would next morning's command "All rise" ring out from Lord Hutton's lady usher at 10:30 A.M. as he entered the court. Now resembling more than ever a sleepy owl going back to his nest, he left to prepare his judgment on all he had been told.

FOR WEEKS INTO THE NEW YEAR OF 2004, there was mounting
speculation in the media, close to hysteria at times, that Lord Hutton's
report would prove to be the government's nemesis, that the Ulsterman
would be the bringer of truth, the judge who would tell the world how it
was Dr. Kelly had died.

So many journalists wanted to be present to hear his judgment that
Court 76, one of the largest in the Royal Courts of Justice, had been set
aside. By twelve-thirty on Wednesday, January 28, it was crowded and all
eyes were on the high dais where his lordship sat upon his chair, an impassive figure in another of his gray suits, peering over his half-moon
glasses, waiting for complete silence to settle over the public gallery, the
reporters poised with their notebooks, the sharp-suited lawyers at their
table. For a moment longer Lord Hutton bowed his head, staring down
at the paper on his bench containing his summary of thousands of
pages of evidence given by seventy-four witnesses over twenty-five days
into "the circumstances surrounding the death of Dr. David Kelly."

During the hearing he had spoken little, leaving it to the lawyers representing the government, the BBC, the Kelly family, and other "interested parties," as they were described. He had made notes, courteously
thanked each witness for coming, and asked the occasional question.
From these, some of the commentators in the court had concluded he
was "after the truth, the whole truth, and nothing but the truth," which
he had promised to deliver in his opening preamble a month earlier.

Now, when Lord Hutton started to speak, his delivery was magnificent, holding his listeners in thrall. Then looks of surprise and next disbelief spread across an increasing number of faces as it became clear
Lord Hutton was unleashing a cold, calculated attack on the BBC and
its now infamous broadcast on the *Today* program about the "sexed-up
dossier."

Already branded as a crude phrase, it was now consigned to perdi-
tion. "The term 'sexed-up,'" he said, spitting out the *p,* "is a slang expression, the meaning of which lacks clarity in the context of the
discussion of the dossier." From then on he continued to fillet and slice
through the BBC hierarchy, laying out what he saw as a collective vein of
weakness running from the very top of the corporation, where its gover-
nors sat in the same lofty position Lord Hutton now occupied on the
dais, all the way down to Gilligan. Each time he mentioned "Mr. Gilligan," Lord Hutton's pronunciation seemed to grow shorter and more
tinged with distaste. The government—Tony Blair, his officials at Num-

ber 10, those at the Ministry of Defense, and John Scarlett from JIC—
Lord Hutton concluded, had all "acted reasonably" in their decision
making, which had ultimately led to Dr. Kelly's being identified as "Mr.
Gilligan's source." He stared for a long moment at the BBC lawyers.

"Having considered a large volume of evidence, I consider there was
no dishonorable or underhand or duplicitous strategy devised by the
Prime Minister and his officials," continued Lord Hutton.

The stares of incredulity increased as each damning sentence was
made more lethal by Lord Hutton: "unfounded," "at fault," "to be criticized for." When he finished after eighty-five minutes, reporters had
scribbled notes, "This is an affront to the evidence we heard." "Heads
will roll." Gavyn Davis swiftly resigned as chairman of the BBC, along
with Greg Dyke, its director-general.

Lord Hutton had not delivered a definitive explanation of why Dr.
Kelly had committed suicide, nor of why the microbiologist had left no
note, nor of why, if he had killed himself, he had chosen a method so
rare as to be almost unknown. Why had the full report of Operation Mason never been introduced into the hearing, so Lord Hutton could have
delivered his own judgment on a document that had been started a full
hour before Dr. Kelly's death? Neither had Lord Hutton even touched
upon the allegations that David Kelly could have been murdered.

These absences from his judgment would ensure the Hutton Inquiry
would be labeled a travesty—and not just by the conspiracy Web sites
devoted to the subject; these would be dismissed as the ramblings of
fully paid-up members of the lunatic fringe. Soon it would be harder to
dismiss one investigator, Norman Baker, a member of Parliament who
resigned from his front-bench responsibilities as Liberal Democratic
spokesman to begin his own investigation. His reputation for taking on
the establishment was well known. He had uncovered the profligate expenses members of Parliament ran up; he had forced a Labour government minister, Peter Mandelson, to resign; he had campaigned against
vivisection and Chinese persecution in Tibet. The Hutton Report, he
told the author, "attracted me from the beginning as an abuse of
power."

In November 2007, Baker finally published his findings in a closely
argued book, *The Strange Death of David Kelly*. Like so many other people
who had published various theories about Dr. Kelly's death, Baker
found himself branded as a conspiracy theorist. He had fallen by the
wayside in claiming Dr. Kelly had been killed by an Iraqi "hit squad," either vengeful Saddam loyalists or more likely followers of the CIA/MI6-
supported dissidents Ahmed Chalabi and Ayad Allawi, both of whom

had hoped to be installed in positions of power after the successful Anglo-American invasion of Iraq. Dr. Kelly's claim that there were no weapons of mass destruction—which Chalabi and Allawi had insisted did exist to, among others, the author—had effectively ended their hopes of becoming Washington's puppeteers in Iraq. When the findings were published, Baker was invited on to the BBC's Sunday morning prime time television talk show. Waiting to ambush him was the corporation's veteran reporter Tom Mangold, who presented himself as a friend of the Kelly family. He dismissed Baker's book as "rubbish" but admitted he had not read "a word of it." Mangold's trump card was to produce an invitation to David Kelly's funeral, which he used to support his claim the microbiologist had committed suicide. Baker had no chance to highlight an uncontested anecdote in his book that Tony Blair's wife, Cherie, had auctioned a copy of the Hutton Report to raise money for the Labour Party.

In St. Mary's churchyard, which serves Southmoor, Dr. Kelly's grave is in the farthest corner of the cemetery. In the distance are the woods of Harrowdown Hill where he met his death, one now never likely to be resolved. By road, the graveyard is seventy-five miles from Court 76, where Lord Hutton had delivered his verdict. Many critics said it was many miles more from the truth.

ON JULY 7, 2004, George Tenet called, in turn, John Scarlett, now the chief of the Secret Intelligence Service; Meir Dagan, who had replaced Efraim Halevy as head of the Mossad; and Eliza Manningham-Buller, who had take over as director of the Security Service from Stephen Lander. He thanked them all for the help their services had provided in the seven years he had run the CIA and ended each call by wishing them luck in the continuing fight against terrorism. He then told them he was resigning the next day. No one asked why: They knew why. Tenet had been the intelligence chief who had told President Bush, who had told Tony Blair, the CIA had "slam dunk" evidence Iraq possessed weapons of mass destruction. This had provided Bush and Blair with the final reason to go to war. Tenet's claim, perhaps more than any other, had contradicted what David Kelly and all the other doubters had said.

As Tenet made his calls, however, on his desk was a report that mocked his claim about WMD and raised yet further doubts about the Hutton Report. The document had been prepared by his former deputy Richard Kerr, the one man he had trusted to provide a detailed, impartial report about how the WMD claim had emerged. When Kerr delivered it, Tenet was devastated by the information that the CIA's spies, after a decade of trying to discover the truth about Saddam's arsenal, had allowed evidence to be presented from sources that were both misleading and unreliable. When he had read Kerr's findings, Tenet knew he would be judged as incompetent, the DCI who had presided over the ultimate intelligence failure. Nothing else in those seven years would detract from that: America and its allies had gone to war on a massive falsehood. *Slam dunk. Iraq had no weapons of mass destruction.*

ON DECEMBER 30, 2006, at the time the Iraqi court had appointed for Saddam Hussein's execution after his trial for war crimes, he saw the gallows and began to tremble.

One hour before, he had followed the ritual formalities for execution. Saddam ate a meal of boiled chicken and rice. With the food he drank several cups of hot water laced with honey. When invited to use the cell toilet—to avoid the embarrassment of wetting himself in the execution chamber—Saddam refused the offer.

At 2:30 A.M. he performed his final religious ablutions, kneeling and washing his hands, face, and feet. He then sat on the edge of his iron cot and began to read the Koran. It had been a gift from his wife, sent to him at the outset of his trial. But only after the court's death sentence had been passed had Saddam begun to study it.

Meantime in the execution chamber, a sack filled with builder's sand was used to test the gallows trap door. Twice the trap door swung open and the bag plunged into the void. The hangman judged the rope had been fully stretched.

At 2:45 A.M. two mortuary attendants arrived with a plain wooden coffin. They placed it beside the gallows. By 2:50 A.M. the invited witnesses arrived: members of the Iraqi judiciary, clerics, a representative of the Iraqi government, and a doctor. Their whispers stopped as the chamber door opened. Gripped by two hooded Iraqi guards, Saddam Hussein stood blinking in the bright lights switched on by the Iraqi video cameraman.

Gripping him firmly by the elbows, Saddam's guards then motioned him forward toward the twelve steps leading up to the gallows platform. At the foot of the steps an Iraqi government official read out the official death sentence.

An observer recalled, "Saddam's mouth started to work. But no words came. The terror in his eyes was there for us all to see. He started to struggle. But he had no muscular power."

The official withdrew. Gripped even tighter by the guards, Saddam was half-forced up the steps. The executioner—another Iraqi—came forward. In his hand he held a hood. He offered the blindfold up to Saddam. Saddam shook his head. One of his guards quickly pinioned Saddam's hands behind his back. He was maneuvered onto the center of the platform.

Suddenly there was the sound of a lever being pushed down hard. The trap door swung open. Saddam's body plunged through. Saddam, his neck broken, hung suspended for a few minutes. Then the doctor stepped forward and listened through a stethoscope for a heartbeat. There was none. The two morticians cut the body down. The knife they used to slice through the rope looked like the kind a butcher would use.

At 3:14 A.M. Saddam Hussein's body was placed in the plain wooden coffin and taken to a mortuary storage vault while a final decison was taken on the manner of its disposal. His widow had requested for it to be handed over to her for burial in the family cemetery beside his two sons.

20

For the Moment

In Vauxhall Cross, John Scarlett had watched events in Washington with growing astonishment after Tenet's departure was followed by the appointment of J. Porter Goss as his replacement. The former agency spy had once come knocking on the door of MI6 looking for "good information about the KGB" when he was at the CIA London station during the Cold War. Goss had failed to impress the MI6 liaison officer because of his lack of knowledge about Russian intelligence and had soon returned to Washington filled with resentment, which was a marked feature of his character.

Using his political skills, Goss gained a seat in Congress and quickly became the chairman of the House Intelligence Committee, deploying his influence to consistently attack the CIA for "becoming a stilted bureaucracy heading down the road to the proverbial cliff." His words were enough for President Bush to appoint him, and he swept through his Senate confirmation by a massive majority, promptly being driven out to Langley "to get the feel of the place." Shortly after his arrival, many key veteran agents left the agency, including Stephen Kappes, the head of the clandestine service and a former station chief in Moscow, who was a spy Scarlett held in the highest regard. Between them, he and Kappes had recently persuaded Colonel Gadhafi to give up his weapons of mass destruction in return for Libya no longer being treated as a pariah.

Nineteen months later, Bush finally fired Porter Goss on May 5, 2006, after the continued bitterness he had created in the agency threatened to "virtually destroy the CIA. It's so broken that nobody wants to believe it," said Carl Ford, the assistant secretary of state for intelligence. By then, John D. Negroponte, a former U.S. ambassador to Iraq, had been appointed head of a new post, director of national intelligence. It had been one of the first recommendations of the 9/11 Commission looking into the massive intelligence failure of the CIA and FBI. It gave Negroponte supreme authority over the U.S. intelligence community, and the CIA came under the diminished control of General Michael Hayden, the former director of the National Security Agency. His first overseas visit as CIA director was to London to see Scarlett. Both already had a strong belief in electronic surveillance and an understanding it should be used in "hot pursuit" of terrorists—ignoring designated map borders. It was an attitude that ensured their friendship would survive into 2007.

EVEN HIS CRITICS ACKNOWLEDGED JONATHAN EVANS was a workaholic, arriving in Thames House often before dawn broke and returning home when the West End theaters were emptying of their audiences. His staff suspected what drove Evans was his hope that one day he would become director-general of the Security Service, the sixteenth to hold the post. Since the London bombings in July 2005, MI5 had been under fierce criticism; much of it had fallen on the broad shoulders of Eliza Manningham-Buller, and the calls for her resignation had persisted. Only Evans knew that before the bombings she had already made up her mind to retire in April 2007; she had told him then that after four years it would be time for a fresh face at the helm. Though she had not said so, he had sensed the post would be his.

Following his appointment as deputy director in 2005, the staff had long regarded Evans as "a cold fish with few social graces and the funereal manner of an undertaker." Colin Wallace, an officer who had worked alongside him in Northern Ireland recalled, "Evans was the spy's spy. He worked the streets of Belfast like no one else. He knew how to recruit informers and he was ready to take calculated risks in how he used them. But it always worked for him. In the end he had an informer close to Gerry Adams." Stella Rimington, his former boss, had found Evans "a hard man to get to know. But there was no doubting his eye for detail."

After the London bombings, his critics in MI5 realized not only that his vast knowledge and ability to convert it into superb intelligence were vital in tracing the links British-born bombers had with al-Qaeda in

Pakistan but also that he provided a steady flow of data for the twenty-two other intelligence services for whom Osama bin Laden remained a prime target. In those long hours Evans spent at his desk before others arrived at work or had ended their own day, he sat behind the closed door of his office studying every reported sighting and every word bin Laden spoke in praise of the killings made in his name: In Bali there had been two hundred deaths, mostly young British and Australian tourists; in Tunisia, fifty more tourists had died in a truck bomb attack as they emerged from a two-thousand-year-old synagogue; in London, his bombers had killed more than fifty, leaving hundreds scarred and many more people with post-traumatic stress.

Time and again bin Laden had justified the violence and destruction carried out in his name by invoking the same reciprocity, "Just as you kill, so shall you be killed; just as you bomb, so shall you be bombed." Throughout Ramadan and even on the holiest day of the Islamic calendar, Eid-al-Adha, the Feast of Sacrifice, he had called for jihad and promised that the sacrifice of "all warriors of Islam will be rewarded by becoming one of the band of knights dwelling in a high mountain pass to descend to face our enemies."

Evans had come to understand that the mental world of Osama bin Laden allowed no contact in any form with the West other than by destruction, though he had recognized the tremendous opportunities Western technology offered to create havoc on an unprecedented scale. Evans had been the first intelligence officer in MI5 to warn that activists would enroll to study applied sciences and other technologies at British universities, to learn how to stoke the firestorm that bin Laden demanded with carefully crafted words to show the credibility of his threat. *What you have done to us we will do to you.* He had also convinced his growing number of followers this was not the time to merely create a movement that would eventually mobilize the masses. That would come later. What was important *now*, his speeches had continually emphasized, was to believe in the immediacy of violence so great and powerful it would rock the West—the American Great Satan and its disciple, Britain—to its very foundation. Then the Muslim world would rise in jihad.

It had not happened. Evans had told a staff meeting, "It is our job to make sure it never happens."

Eliza Manningham-Buller retired on the April day she had promised. At her farewell party, attended by European and American intelligence chiefs, she graciously conducted Evans around the room to meet all her guests and, in her retirement speech, reminded everyone this was the last time they would hear from her; then, with a final booming laugh, she said they had nothing to fear from her memoirs. They would never be written. Some of her guests saw it as a dig at Stella Rimington for writing her autobiography.

The next morning, Jonathan Evans moved into the director-general's office and spent his first day arranging his library of books and documents devoted to al-Qaeda, working into the evening updating himself on the latest reports about the organization: El Salvador was now the latest country through which al-Qaeda laundered its money on its journey around the world; the FBI had sent an update on the latest U.S. companies—many were leaders in the high-tech industry—in which al-Qaeda was strongly suspected of buying stocks. Several companies had British branches. There were a dozen and more reports that needed his attention. It was close to midnight before he ended his first day.

Early the next morning, Evans was driven to a large, windowless, open-plan room in Central London only accessed by a swipe card, the code of which changed regularly. It was here the Surfers worked, fifty highly trained MI5 operatives who spent their ten-hour shifts with headphones clamped to their ears. Each operative sat at his or her workstation with its computer and recording equipment as they searched the Internet looking for sources of secret chat rooms where jihadists in Britain communicated with one of the most dangerous of Osama bin Laden's recruiters. Omar Bakri Mohammed was banned from the U.K. but reached deep into its two-million-strong Muslim community with his messages of hatred. Bakri had given each of his followers a secret password to log in to his chat rooms. Like the swipe-card codes that allowed the operatives to enter their tracking room, his terror Web sites also had secret codes that changed all the time. The operatives had identified as many as a hundred Web sites Bakri controlled. Each time one was discovered and electronically destroyed by the operators, Bakri opened another one with new passwords.

Buried in the Web sites—between the horrific photographs of British and American soldiers killed in Iraq and Afghanistan—were messages urging British jihadists to be ready to "rise and wage holy war against the infidels." That was the message Omar Bakri reiterated in his broadcasts from one of the Internet cafés in Beirut where, in November 2007, he lived and operated, publishing the addresses of dead soldiers and urging that their families "should be made aware they are not protected from all of you who support our cause."

On her last day in office, Eliza Manningham-Buller had said to her staff, "Unless we stem the rising tide of radical Islamic rhetoric in Britain, then the carnage of Baghdad may well erupt on the streets of cities like Bradford and Leeds or anywhere there are Muslim enclaves filled with disaffected people."

The next morning, Evans listened to some of the recordings Bakri and other radical clerics had made. During the time Evans spent in the room, the Surfers destroyed another dozen Web sites. Soon there would be other sites to hunt down. It was an endless battle fought in cyber-space.

JONATHAN EVANS'S VAST EXPERIENCE in Northern Ireland fighting against the IRA had shown him it was an organization of different groups. Al-Qaeda was similar and was an increasing inspiration for attacks against Western targets by affiliated groups. Evans had decided that if al-Qaeda had a global headquarters, it was probably in the remote mountain fastness of Waziristan, a province in the impregnable northwest area of Pakistan. There, in one of the valleys virtually inaccessible to a modern army, was a secure haven for al-Qaeda after years of fleeing the global manhunt for its leadership. The land was covered in dense vegetation in the summer and deep snowdrifts in winter, its inhabitants screened inside their deep caves from even the most sophisticated satellite surveillance.

Evans had discovered that within this redoubt bin Laden had expanded the *shura,* the al-Qaeda leadership, to twenty-five members. One of his new appointments had been Adam Gadahn, a twenty-eight-year-old Californian who, after converting to Islam, was called "Azzam the American" and was the organization's director of propaganda. MI5 analysts had concluded Gadahn had written and produced bin Laden's latest audiotape, one of sixty cassettes al-Qaeda had issued in 2007.

Another new member of the *shura* was Abu Obaidah al-Masri, who had worked with some of the London bombers when they had visited Pakistan. His new title was external operations chief. One by one, Evans had built his profiles of the key men bin Laden had appointed: Atiyah Abd al-Rashman was in charge of recruiting jihadists in Algeria, Morocco, and Tunisia; Abu Yahya al-Libi became the senior commander in Afghanistan after his predecessor had been killed in an American bombing raid; Khalid Habib was the new liaison for al-Qaeda in Ethiopia.

The most disturbing appointment had been of Abu Jihad al-Masri, a.k.a. Muhammed Khalil al-Hakaymah as al-Qaeda's full-time intelligence chief. His position, according to one of the Islamic Web sites al-Qaeda used, was to "coordinate all future major terrorist attacks and train our warriors to penetrate the intelligence services of our enemies." The site boasted al-Hakaymah would show recruits how to beat lie detector tests.

What concerned Evans was that such claims would attract still more impressionable young British Muslims. His own officers had told him that children as young as fifteen had been recruited, part of an army of "sleepers who have been radicalized, indoctrinated, and groomed to carry out acts of terrorism."

By December 2007, he believed there were over four thousand British-born Muslim extremists who had attended training camps in Afghanistan and Pakistan and were now back in the United Kingdom. The number doubled the estimate Eliza Manningham-Buller had announced shortly before her retirement.

IN THE CLOSING WEEKS OF 2007, yet another operation was under way in Thames House to locate Osama bin Laden. No one had said as much, but if he was captured alive he would be killed at once. To put him on trial would risk huge embarrassment, far greater than there had been over Saddam Hussein's trial, not least because of bin Laden's still heroic standing in the Muslim world and his own powers of eloquence.

Since 9/11, scores of attempts to kill him had been made by the twenty-two Western intelligence services hunting him. The CIA had its own bin Laden desk, well staffed and with a money-no-problem budget. Since the London bombings of July 2005, similar units existed in MI5 and MI6. The services had provided the intelligence that had led to heavy bombing raids on areas where bin Laden was said to be hiding and triggered the ground assaults on his bolt-holes by U.S. Special Forces, Britain's SAS, Australian commandos, and French legionnaires. Each time bin Laden managed to escape through the mountains of Afghanistan into the "badlands" of the Northwest Frontier.

In six years the United States had spent over $300 million trying to locate bin Laden with satellites, pilotless drones, and state-of-the-art electronic tracking equipment. Vast sums had been spent on bribes to encourage his supporters to betray him and collect the $25 million bounty on his head. Not one follower had come forward, as the price of disloyalty was greater than any sum of money; not only would their immediate families be killed, but so would distant relatives and friends. An entire lineage would be wiped out. It was by such methods the ideologue of terror continued to avoid capture.

Now, five thousand miles from where bin Laden was once again believed to be hiding in a sixty-mile-square area of northwest Pakistan, the British end of the operation to find him was in the hands of Jonathan Evans. The plan had been his idea, and he guarded ownership with a possessiveness that confirmed to some colleagues he was, in the words of one, "a bit of an oddball."

The plan had been developed in total secrecy by MI5, MI6, the SAS, the Australian Special Forces, and the CIA. Afghani-speaking intelligence officers had been sent to the mountainous regions bordering the area to act as forward listening posts. Their equipment enabled them to receive images from a hyperspectral satellite geopositioned in the deep black of space, its hundreds of narrow wavelength bands collecting energy from objects on the ground, separating rocks from vegetation, empty caves from those occupied either by animals or any human presence. With the officers were specialist radar operators working SAR, synthetic aperture radar, which received images even during one of the blizzards that swirled through the area. Further back inside Afghanistan awaiting the signal was the joint SAS/U.S./Australian Special Forces group. The two hundred mountain warfare troops had trained in the snowscapes of Norway for their mission. Each of their helicopters was fitted with "whispering technology" which would make their approach to the target area virtually undetectable.

Pakistan's president, Pervez Musharraf, had been deliberately excluded from any of the preparations. Pakistan was in growing turmoil, and he had been forced to resign his army rank as commander in chief of the army. Despite his declaring a state of emergency, his political crisis had worsened in the run-up to the 2008 elections, operating conditions that were ideal for al-Qaeda to exploit; violent demonstrations were a daily occurrence.

Jonathan Evans had decided an attack against bin Laden's hideout should not be launched until there was, he had said, a "high probability" the world's most wanted terrorist was there. So many times bin Laden had somehow managed to slip away through icy ravines and past mountains shrouded in cloud.

Central to the plan was the NSA satellite. The area had been selected after officers in MI5's G-Branch had tracked young jihadists who had returned to Britain from Pakistan during the summer of 2007 having spent time at al-Qaeda training camps in the border areas where the Pakistani government patrols did not operate.

Every day the satellite's unblinking array of cameras downloaded images to the NSA station at Menwith Hill. Computers analyzed the images and sent the results to GCHQ. From there the images were transmitted to Evans's office. Among them were weather reports giving the daily rate of the snowfall at various altitudes in the valleys and on the steep cliffsides under surveillance. Another image pinpointed which of the estimated one thousand cave openings in the area had disappeared after blizzards had hidden them from view. The openings that remained visible indicated there might be people inside. The images were transmitted to the operators on the Afghanistan border so they could use their radars to check. Evans believed it was in some of those caves bin Laden could be developing new targets in Europe, attracting new recruits in Britain, encouraging the Taliban movement in Afghanistan, and restructuring al-Qaeda on the lines of a world-ranking corporation—"Terrorism Incorporated," Evans had called it.

While bin Laden remained the equivalent of a chairman of the board, his deputy al-Zawahiri was the managing director, running the daily business of a core group of departments. These included recruitment, finance, and communications. There was even a "pensions department" to provide for the families of suicide bombers. Terrorism Incorporated funding still came from donations provided by Saudi Arabian princes and wealthy Muslims in Asia. For months Evans had kept abreast of the follow-the-money trail out of the Pacific Rim countries that supported bin Laden. The details had gone into Evans's computer files.

The weather report from the far side of the world had been the first thing Evans studied when he arrived at his desk in those December days in 2007. Soon the number of visible cave mouths would have been reduced to a handful by the snowstorms. Would bin Laden make a break under their cover? He had done so before, many times. An insight into his mind-set had come from his former personal bodyguard, Nasir al-Bahri. On al-Qaeda's Web site, in 2004 he had claimed, "Sheikh Osama has given me a special gun and said if he is attacked and unable to be saved, I must use the gun to kill him." Was this merely propaganda or a further sign of bin Laden's determination to die a martyr's death rather than be left hanging at the end of a rope, the fate of Saddam Hussein?

Evans's own undergraduate student studies had taught him much about posthumous legend, and, no doubt, bin Laden's would survive for a while. Posthumous legends in history is part of Bristol University's study course. Evans extrapolated the course to learn more about bin Laden. But Evans had become more certain generations of Muslim youths would in the future see bin Laden for what he was: obsessive, charismatic, and fanatic, but one who also had failed to understand that terrorism as a credo could not succeed by itself.

Increasingly Evans saw that the 9/11 attack on America, the London bombings, and the attacks in Madrid and on all the other targets bin Laden claimed were necessary to establish the New Caliphate were in reality the very symbol of his failure. Horrific though the massacres had been, they had failed to ignite the global firestorm bin Laden had promised would follow, the precursor to the extremist Islamism that would dominate not only the Muslim world but the globe itself. In the closing days of 2007, his dream would seem as far from realization as ever.

There would be more terrorist attacks for sure, Evans had told his staff, but they would not lead to political power for al-Qaeda any more than they had for the Moscow-backed ultra-radicals of Europe in the 1960s. "For the time being bin Laden continues to create a mystique for jihad, but it will not last for long after his own death. The sooner that comes, the better for those who are deluded by it," Evans had said.

IN THE WEEKS FOLLOWING GENERAL ALI-REZA ASGARI, Iran's spy chief, and his family being successfully exfiltrated to London by MI6, he had undergone a lengthy debriefing in a safe house outside the city, driven there every weekday morning from where he and his family were staying, taking lessons with their English-language tutor; the children, in particular, had made good progress. Asgari already spoke the language well enough to answer questions in English posed by the strategists and analysts. They explored with him the two decades during which Iran had pursued its nuclear program using the international black market, specifically North Korea, as well as its support for terrorism. Some of what Asgari covered his debriefers already knew, but a great deal was new, and Asgari presented the information with the detailed recall of a professional intelligence officer. After his weeks of close questioning, he had then undergone a similar process with CIA and Mossad officers; their focus was on the threat posed to their nations. By June 2007, the last questions had been asked and answered.

Throughout the summer, Asgari and his family were taken by their MI6 minder on visits to London and elsewhere to look at places where they might like to settle. Instead, it was after one of those outings that Asgari announced he and his family would like to make their final home in the United States. From the time they had come to Britain, he had been told the option was open to him. Arrangements were quickly made and approved by the Foreign Office and the State Department. The family was issued with American passports, which contained their new identities, and in August a transition team flew from Washington to accompany them to America. On arrival they were absorbed into the Witness Protection Program and assured that for the foreseeable future they would be among the most protected of all American citizens.

MEANWHILE, ANALYSTS ON THE IRAN DESK in Vauxhall Cross continued to study Israel's plans to launch a preemptive strike against Iran's three prime uranium enrichment facilities: Natanz; a uranium conversion site at Isfahan; and the heavy water reactor at Arak. Low-yield bunker-busting bombs would be used against Natanz, as the facility was buried deep underground. It would be the first time since 1945, when the United States dropped atomic bombs on Hiroshima and Nagasaki, that nuclear weapons would be used. The Israeli bombs would explode a force equivalent to one-fifteenth of that detonated over Hiroshima.

Two squadrons of Israeli F-151 and F-161 jets, based in the Negev Desert south of Tel Aviv, had been training for weeks to carry out the mission. The order to launch would be given by Major General Eliezer Shkedy, a veteran fighter pilot who commanded Israel's air force and who had been tasked by Prime Minister Ehud Olmert to prepare the mission. It would begin with conventional laser-guided bombs designed to burrow deep underground before exploding. Those aimed at Natanz would be followed by mini nukes, which would explode seventy feet belowground to reduce the risk of radioactive fallout. An analyst on the MI6 Iran Desk had asked a scientist at Harwell, Britain's nuclear research center, to compute the level of risk. He was told it would depend on the depth of the explosion and its exit path to the surface, but there would be some fallout.

The possibility of an attack had increased when Israeli jets had been tracked flying the length of the Mediterranean before turning back over Gibraltar to simulate the two-thousand-mile round-trip to Natanz. There were other signs Israel increasingly felt compelled to deal with Iran's threat. Meir Dagan had agreed to remain in office until the end of 2008 to continue to supervise the collection of intelligence from inside Iran. The Mossad had deep-cover agents at the nuclear sites. Israel's Strike 700—its three nuclear-powered submarines—had once more been tasked to lie motionless on the seabed in the Gulf. Each submarine carried twenty-four cruise missiles, which would be guided to their targets by American software. But would President Bush, in the closing year of his administration, allow the attack to go ahead? Or would an attack come down to what Ephraim Sneh, Israel's deputy defense minister, had said, "At the end of the day it is always down to the Jews to deal with the problem of Iran. We now live in the age of preemption, and the Jewish people have not forgotten the last time the world watched and did nothing, and we are determined that shall never happen again." For the analysts on the Iran Desk, there was ultimately a single question: How much longer would Israel wait before it took matters into its own hands?

In London, the question continued to preoccupy the weekly meetings of the JIC, which were briefed by military chiefs and Scarlett on the role the United Kingdom could be asked to play if Gordon Brown's government endorsed a plan his predecessor, Tony Blair, had agreed on with President Bush for massive air strikes to be launched against over one thousand military targets in Iran. The figure had been provided to Scarlett and was a far larger number than any other he had previously given. Meanwhile, Meir Dagan continued to feed Scarlett reports from Mossad's own deep-cover agents in Iran indicating its nuclear enrichment plants had increased their output.

AS GLOBAL WARMING CONTINUED to preoccupy political leaders, MI5 and MI6 found themselves involved in preparations for an unusual possible threat. Government scientists had calculated that over one hundred million tons of helium-3 were buried nine feet beneath the moon's surface, which could provide unlimited power on earth for a thousand years; a mere six metric tons would meet all Britain's energy needs every year into the foreseeable future.

Already NASA, with the support of the European Space Agency, had announced it would have a base at one of the moon's poles by 2014. Space engineers from Britain, the United States, and Europe would then begin the process of extracting the gas, which would be shipped back to earth in giant tanks to space-cargo landing sites, where the gas would be unloaded and conveyed to newly built fusion reactors.

It was at that point MI5 and MI6 had become involved to assess the potential of a terror attack on the landing sites and the reactors, both of which would be based on remote moorlands in Scotland and the west of England. Britain's own nuclear reactors had already been found to have less than secure defenses, and protecting the lunar-cargo landing sites and fusion reactor sites could be even more difficult. Both intelligence services had been tasked to decide how an attack could be mounted and stopped.

In May 2007, MI6 agents in Moscow and Beijing discovered Russia and China had signed an agreement to mine helium-3 on the moon. Both Roscosmos, Russia's Federal Space Agency, and China's Lunar Exploration Agency, predicted they would have a five-year start over their American and European rivals in bringing back cargoes of helium-3. After being landed in Russia and China, the gas would be processed and, once domestic needs were met in both countries, marketed globally at prices Moscow and Beijing would set. It was an extension of the threat Russian president Vladimir Putin had made to use vast oil supplies as a bargaining weapon with the West.

An MI5/MI6 team of computer experts, supported by cyberwarfare specialists at GCHQ, had decided any terrorist attack on Britain's space-cargo landing sites would be carried out by the latest generation of computer systems that Russia and China were developing, which in 2007 were already far in advance of those in the West and were able to evade the most sophisticated firewalls and antivirus software. Those computers could electronically penetrate the landing sites and even be programmed to interdict the space-cargo rockets as they entered the earth's atmosphere, causing them to crash with disastrous results.

Evidence of how far China had advanced in cyberwarfare tactics had surfaced in the Pentagon in the autumn of 2007. The Chinese People's Liberation Army specialists, based in their underground headquarters in the Western Hills outside Beijing, had been discovered to have made seventy thousand "intrusions" into the Pentagon's computers and had scored even more hits on the Pentagon's other six million computer networks around the world. In a briefing paper, Linton Wells, the head of the Pentagon's worldwide computer network, said, "The attacks on our system are part of a plan which ultimately calls for a simultaneous attack on the U.S. carrier fleet in the Pacific and the disabling of communications at its headquarters at Pearl Harbor with the Pentagon. It would mean communications between the Pentagon and its Pacific battle fleet could no longer function properly."

A team working at the Pentagon to protect the United States against a Chinese cyberwarfare attack predicted even a limited attack on America's power supplies could leave the country without electrical power for six months.

In London, the task force investigating the threat computer terrorism would pose to the lunar mining program concluded, "This is in effect an arms race, one in which the West is still playing catch-up. China and Russia both appear to regard launching offensive computer strikes as the first stage of a war."

The threat came closer in November 2007 when Jonathan Evans, in an unprecedented alert, sent a confidential memo to three hundred chief executives and security chiefs at banks, accounting firms, and legal firms warning them they were already "under attack from Chinese state organizations." It was the first time the British government had directly accused China of running Web site espionage.

In Washington, the CIA similarly asserted that Chinese cyberwarfare against the United States "now represents the single greatest risk to the security of American technologies."

CHINA'S INTELLIGENCE MANIPULATIONS were not the only cause for concern as 2007 drew to a close.

MI5 computer experts discovered that terrorists held in Belmarsh Prison, Britain's maximum security jail, had secretly accessed the Internet to contact members of militant Islamic groups. The possibility has led to the Chief Inspector of Prisons, Anne Owen, issuing a warning that inmates at Belmarsh were in danger of becoming radicalized. The revelation came after the Security Service experts intercepted several messages emanating from Belmarsh. Some had come from computers prisoners could use during "education classes," but most were sent via cell phones. Owen said some e-mail messages had been sent to a Web site linked to the Al-Muhajiroun Islamic movement, which was officially banned in Britain under anti-terror laws.

The prison's inmates included Abu Doha and Dhiren Barot, both serving life sentences for planning terror attacks in Britain, including one using a radioactive bomb.

Another prisoner, Abu Hamza, was awaiting extradition to the United States after he completed his seven-year sentence for inciting terrorism. "A quarter of Belmarsh prisoners were Muslim, many of them young and impressionable and open to persuasion by the likes of Hamza," an intelligence source told the author.

After weeks of streaming the Internet, the MI5 experts established that the mastermind behind prisoners' access to the Internet was Mizanur Rahman, a twenty-five-year-old Web site designer who was jailed in 2006 after calling on his site for British troops to be brought back from Iraq in body bags. He was serving a five-year sentence in Belmarsh.

In their search, the experts discovered Rahman had managed to post on an extremist Web site nine hundred e-mails, some attacking homosexuals and Jews. Other messages included his photograph along-side the image of an armed man on horseback—an icon commonly used by terrorist Web sites to represent Osama bin Laden. The Home Office admitted that in 2007 almost 3,500 cell phones were recovered from prisoners in Belmarsh and other jails in Britain.

Meanwhile, MI6 agents based in the Middle East had established that thirteen countries in the region had drawn up new plans—or re-viewed previous ones—to build nuclear stations following Iran's push for an enriched uranium program capable of producing nuclear weapons. The International Institute for Strategic Studies (IISS) con-firmed MI6's findings, and said the other nations "have embarked on their programs in order to give them each the option of building a nu-clear bomb in the future."

According to IISS chief executive, John Chapman, "Iran's program has built on regional rivalry, security concerns, and sheer one-upmanship. These issues have contributed to a regional surge to obtain nuclear en-ergy. The urgent question for Britain, the United States, and other coun-tries with interests in the region is how to confine the expansion to purely nuclear civilian programs. That is exactly what Iran claimed it was doing. We have established the truth is otherwise."

By continuing to create enriched uranium suitable to be weaponized for its latest ballistic missile, the Shahab-3, Iran had already established itself as not only a threat to Israel, but to Turkey, a NATO nation; Egypt, with its pro-West government; Jordan, also pro-West; and the United Arab Emirates. These were all nations where the West has strategic in-terests. With its 1,200-mile range, the Shahab-3 could deliver nuclear warheads to any of these countries.

MI6 agents in Cairo also established that in recent months Egypt, which already possessed a solid grounding in nuclear technology, could be the first country outside Iran to produce a nuclear weapon. The evi-dence about those thirteen countries was given to Israel's Mossad dur-ing a visit to Tel Aviv by MI6 chief, John Scarlett. Israel has had its own nuclear arsenal in the Negev Desert at Dimona for the past forty years where MI6 estimates it has stockpiled between one hundred and two hundred warheads. The Stockholm International Peace Research Insti-tute believes some of the Israeli warheads have been positioned on its frontline airfields ready to launch attacks on Iran should it threaten a preemptive strike against the Jewish state.

"Any escalation of an already tense Middle East would only increase the pressure on other Arab countries to produce their own nuclear weapons—effectively triggering a nuclear-arms race. The worry is that a number of countries have recruited foreign scientists to originally create peaceful nuclear programs. But those same scientists could be switched to military work to produce a nuclear bomb. The growing fear which has triggered the drive in those countries is to create their own nuclear shield. Iran is racing to be the first nation in the region to have a full nuclear weapons capability, possibly by 2010. The Sunni monarchs of the Gulf are increasingly worried, not least because Tehran is stirring deep unrest among their own Shia populations," Chapman told the author.

From Pakistan emerged another chilling revelation: MI6 officers working alongside Pakistani intelligence officers in that nation's remote Northwest province, located a training camp where children, some as young as six years old, were being trained as suicide bombers. The camp outside the village of Spinkai in the mountainous region—one of several al-Qaeda training camps in the region—was under the direct control of the terror group.

An MI6 document described the school as "a classroom equipped with documents and gadgets for the children to learn how to carry out suicide bomber attacks. There was also evidence they had been subjected to intense religious indoctrination. As well as the Koran, there were texts by bin Laden. There was also video footage of successful attacks on targets in Iraq and Afghanistan."

One of the DVDs showed footage of the children receiving instruction from a masked man. He wore a white headband inscribed with verses from the Koran. In the footage he was demonstrating various kinds of hand grenades. MI6 linguists in London revealed the instructor showed the pupils how to plant roadside improvised explosive devices (IEDs).

The discovery that children had been trained as suicide bombers caused consternation in Pakistan. In the closing months of 2007, there had been more than eighty suicide attacks that had killed more than one thousand people across the country.

IN DECEMBER 2007, JOHN SCARLETT, Jonathan Evans, David Pepper, and the new head of the Joint Intelligence Committee, Alex Allan, met for their customary Christmas luncheon to discuss the durable and mutating threats they would have to deal with in the coming year. During the premeal drinks, there was some good-natured joking with Allan about his Web site, on which he had listed his personal hobbies—listening to the U.S. cult band the Grateful Dead, card games, and windsurfing on the Thames during a rail strike. In true Facebook style, Allan had also published his address and phone number, along with those of family friends, which had been quickly deleted after his appointment. At least, Scarlett had joked, it would stop foreign spies from having to find out where Allan lived.

Over lunch the conversation turned to more serious matters. Each had received from MI6 Washington station a classified copy of the 2007 U.S. National Intelligence Estimate (NIE). Months in preparation, it contained the assessment of America's sixteen intelligence services, led by the CIA and the NSA, and contained a wealth of Sensitive Compartmented Information (SCI), itself guarded by special controls and handling, which provided an estimate of the capabilities, vulnerabilities, and probable course of action by foreign nations—friendly, enemy, and neutral—in 2008.

Issued under the signature of the Director of Central Intelligence, the NIE represented the composite view of the U.S. intelligence community. Footnotes indicated where any agency had expressed its dissent from consensus opinion. In addition to national and regional studies, the NIE also produced a section entitled "Estimates of the World Situation." By tradition, the first copy of the report had gone to President Bush; afterward, the heads of Britain's three intelligence services had been among the first to see the contents.

In the weeks before, Scarlett had heard "Chinese whispers" from Washington that the 2007 NIE could contain unusually explosive contents, but not even the chief had guessed it would reveal, "Iran had halted its nuclear program in 2003, and there is no evidence it has enriched uranium to build an atomic bomb; it is less determined to develop nuclear weapons than we have been judging since 2005. The Iranian government decision was guided by a cost-benefit approach rather than a rush to obtain a nuclear weapon irrespective of the political, economic and military costs."

Donald Kerr, the Bush administration's deputy national intelligence director, who oversaw the report, said that the NIE "reflected our understanding of Iran's capabilities has changed," and he agreed to have the portions relating to Iran declassified to ensure "an accurate presentation."

The decision was presented by the White House as "the hope that the Iran problem can be solved diplomatically without the use of force as this administration has been trying to do."

That claim had drawn wry smiles among the staff of MI6. They knew how hard the Pentagon was still pushing for military intervention in Iran, but the window for such an attack had narrowed by the day. In

November 2008, Bush's tenure as president would be effectively over, and it seemed that whoever took his place would be more moderate.

The four men tucking into their Christmas lunch fare agreed it was far too early to reduce the surveillance on Iran—or, for that matter, on Russia. In the new year, Vladimir Putin would end his tenure as Russia's president, but he had indicated he would remain the power broker in the country. Robert Morningstar, an American defense analyst specializing in Russian affairs, had warned that Putin would continue to expand the FSB's collaboration with China's MSS. "Both services will form, in 2008 and in years to come, a powerful force against the West. We must plan to protect freedom and not only for security, but only freedom can make security secure," he said.

The quartet talked about the need to convince the public that terrorism alerts were only issued when threats were assessed as requiring a public warning, as well as to remind people that intelligence services could not assess the total scale of any threat, the range and diversity it presented, and the balance between homegrown terrorism and that launched from overseas.

Jonathan Evans led a discussion about the hopes for capturing Osama bin Laden. As it is a current target, no more can be said here.

The talk turned to budget considerations and the need for recruitment, especially linguists and computer experts.

David Pepper provided his usual succinct overview of how GCHQ and the NSA continued to work in perfect harmony, while at the same time he had maintained close contact with the surveillance arrangements France and Germany had developed to track targets across the world that could directly threaten their nations.

Much of what was said around the lunch table would remain secret, understandably so, but increasingly there are those within that world of secrecy—ruled by its endless cycle of collection, dissemination, analysis, and tasking—who believe mystery for mystery's sake need not always allow security to become an end in itself.

This book has worked within that framework.

IN LATE SEPTEMBER 2008, Sir John Scarlett suddenly announced he would retire on the eve of MI6's one-hundredth anniversary, August 1, 2009. Officially he would have served his term. But it was the first time the head of the Secret Intelligence Service had given so much advance warning of his departure.

Within the intelligence community there was mounting speculation that Scarlett had been forced out by the Brown government due to MI6's failure to deal with the increased terrorist threat to Britain, its mishandling of secret missions in Iraq and Afghanistan, and Scarlett's own failure to outsmart his longtime archrival, Vladimir Putin. Putin, the former head of the Russian Intelligence Service and later prime minister, had continued to orchestrate intelligence operations against the U.K.

"It is no secret that Scarlett's relationship with prime minister Gordon Brown has been uneasy from the outset. Tony Blair had been Scarlett's political protector in the Whitehall jungle," said former MI6 officer Richard Tomlinson.

Scarlett had played a crucial part in preparing the notorious document that claimed Saddam Hussein had weapons of mass destruction—the very reason President Bush and Blair had gone to war. The ensuing public criticism, for what Scarlett was forced to admit were highly dubious intelligence sources in Iraq, had led to calls at the time for his resignation.

He would leave office having created a global organization that in November 2008 employed almost three thousand people. His own salary was over £200,000 a year—more than the prime minister's.

He had recommended his successor should be Charles Farr, a forty-nine-year-old Whitehall mandarin who had made a reputation as the government's head of the Office of Security and Counter-Terrorism. Created in 2007, it was a small force designed to fight al-Qaeda inside Britain.

A PERSONAL NOTE

A book that deals with MI5 and MI6 can have no conclusion. New threats emerge every day from unexpected quarters as you read these words. Peter Hennessy, a lecturer on intelligence at Queen Mary University, London, has said it is impossible to calibrate, let alone control, the ebb and flow of terrorist action/reaction on a national or international basis to any threat. The one certainty is that coping with the new form of international terrorism, as both MI5 and MI6 head toward their century anniversaries in August 2009, will become even more difficult and protracted. Their work will not be so easily labeled as when it was part of the forty-plus years of the cold war or the thirty years of countering Irish terrorism in its seminal period.

The only real identification terrorism has today is with Osama bin Laden. While he has been almost poetic in telling the world he is waging war, his reasons for doing so have nothing to do with freedom, liberty, and democracy. They are contained within his driven belief that he, and he alone, has been called to free the world from imperialism. His is a madness like no other: Hitler, Stalin, and all the other despots of the twentieth century undoubtedly murdered many more, but none possessed the same mental aberration that drives bin Laden.

Gordon Brown, Britain's prime minister in 2008, made it clear he disliked President Bush's label of "War on Terror." Brown found it both simplistic and limiting, as it allowed the focus to remain on the 9/11 attacks when the current world of counterterrorism required a global view of the threat. In Britain, dealing with that threat had led to increasing arguments about the ethics involved. The controversy over "extraordinary rendition"—the process the CIA used to secretly arrest terrorist suspects and fly them to secret prisons beyond the rules of interrogation in the U.S. justice system—had led to an international outcry. One result was that in Britain, an MI5 officer hunting a terrorist would often call in the Security Service's lawyers to ensure his method of gathering evidence would withstand the courtroom cross-examination of a defense lawyer.

Another problem both MI5 and MI6 continue to face is balancing their relationships with European Union intelligence agencies—there are, in 2008, twenty-five of them working within the EU—and yet doing nothing to lose the vital contact with U.S. agencies. If global terrorism is to be defeated, then British, European, and U.S. intelligence services must be more openhanded in sharing their secrets with services that would never have featured on their distribution list prior to 9/11. Few within their world will disagree with defense analyst Michael Smith's judgment, "Intelligence will need to be untainted and, unlike the notorious (sexed-up) dossier on Iraq, both genuine and accurate."

I share his view that while the protection of sources must remain paramount, the intelligence world will have to be more open about what it does. My attitude was summed up by James Angleton, the legendary CIA spymaster, "Secrecy from public scrutiny leads to often uncheckable and different accounts of the same events, which are often contradictory and distorted."

I have authored, lectured, and broadcast for over fifty years on intelligence, met and interviewed many of its officers, and become friends with a number who have devoted, and in many cases still do, their working lives to toiling at the front line of their profession.

My late father-in-law, Joachim Kraner, was one such person; another was Bill Buckley, the former station chief of the CIA in Beirut, where he was captured and eventually murdered by Hezbollah. Through them I came to understand, among much else, the role of intelligence in the cold war and in the emergence of a new strategic era—the birth of the information age, which led to the creation of global terrorism.

They helped me understand that each intelligence service had needed to be placed into a historical context, none more so than MI5 and MI6. Between them their development of techniques and technology has helped to transform intelligence gathering from a game for amateurs to a high-tech professional business.

Many of those who helped me are listed in the front of this book. They helped me because, time and again, they told me the declassification of once secret information from World War II and the cold war, as well as data available from the archives of Eastern Europe and the former KGB, had, if anything, added to the confusion about the intelligence world of claim and counterclaim.

Like all my previous books on intelligence, throughout the text sources are identified by their direct quotations. Those who spoke to me did so because they trusted that I would represent them accurately. Yet writing about the secret world of spies cannot be the entire truth—they themselves do not often know the complete truth of what they are involved in. That is the nature of their work.

Some interviewees who provided information asked for their names to be protected because they work in intelligence but still provided "background" on sensitive matters. The truth is that people in their position often will not discuss security matters without this protection.

During the past half century since I have written on intelligence subjects, there has developed an increasing feeling within the global intelligence community of the need for openness. I have learned this as a speaker at intelligence seminars. One was a conference DAS, the Colombian intelligence service, hosted. It was attended by intelligence officers from forty-two nations, including the CIA, MI5, MI6, the Mossad, and European Services. I was asked to speak on the theme of "The Need for More Openness in Intelligence." I have also lectured in Washington to a conference attended by members of the various U.S. intelligence agencies. My writing was commended for its sourcing and what an officer called "responsibility in handling entrusted material." Meir Amit, the former director of the Mossad, has said, "Thomas tells it like it was—and like it is." It is encouragement like this that has enabled me to fill the gaps in previously published material.

The research for this book spanned some fifty years of my own career, which took me from the Suez Crisis in 1956 to Africa, the Middle East, Asia, and Europe to the present day. In all those continents I picked up the footprints of MI5 and MI6. What I learned enabled me to write more authoritatively on intelligence and how it works. Somewhere along the way the idea took root that, one day, I would attempt to put all that information into a single book. Finally, in 2006, my French publisher, Yannick Dehee, a gifted writer himself, suggested I now had sufficient experience to do this. He felt my book *Gideon's Spies,* which he had published with great success, had put a spotlight on the secret world of the Great Game. From the outset his support contributed enormously to the final manuscript.

I am also indebted to my editor, Rob Kirpatrick, at Thomas Dunne Books for his continued enthusiasm and support for the project, and to India Cooper, a quite brilliant copy editor who, when the manuscript was completed, displayed fact-checking skills that were outstanding.

Others, too, were a major help: Barbara Lowenstein, Madeleine Morel, Norman Kurz, and Zoe Fishman, who between them handled the project from its inception with their accustomed skill. I am also indebted to that fine documentary maker Steve Cole. He saw the potential of the book becoming a major television series and encouraged me to think along those lines; if it does happen, it will be primarily due to the skills of Steve. Among the many journalists whose encouragement I valued are Stuart Winter, Dick Dismore, and Sean Carberry. For many years, Sean has acted as my first reader and made a manuscript all that much better for his advice.

I also express my gratitude to my longtime assistant, Emer Lenehan; her sharp eye was invaluable at a time of pressure. Finally, but by no means least, there was my wife, Edith. She was always there, reading, double-checking, searching for sources, and I dedicate this book to her, not only in memory of her father but also for her patience and help in ensuring the final manuscript left my desk in the best possible shape.

Gordon Thomas
November 2008

SELECT BIBLIOGRAPHY

Adams, James. *The New Spies: Exploring the Frontiers of Espionage*. London: Hutchinson, 1994.

Adams, James, Robin Morgan, and Anthony Bambridge. *Ambush: The War Between the SAS and the IRA*. London: Pan, 1988.

Agee, Philip. *Inside the Company: CIA Diary*. Harmondsworth, England: Penguin Books, 1975.

Aid, Matthew M., and Cees Wiebes. *Secrets of Signals Intelligence During the Cold War and Beyond*. London, England: Frank Cass, 2001.

Aldrich, Richard J. "Britain's Secret Intelligence Service in Asia During the Second World War." *Modern Asian Studies* 32, no. 1 (February 1998): 179–218. 1: 1998.

———. *British Intelligence, Strategy, and the Cold War, 1945–51*. London: Routledge, 1992.

———. *Espionage, Security, and Intelligence in Britain, 1945–70*. Manchester, England: Manchester University Press, 1998.

Aldrich, Richard J., Gary D. Rawnsley, and Ming-Yeh T. Rawnsley, eds. *The Clandestine Cold War in Asia, 1945–65*. London: Frank Cass, 2000.

Alibek, Ken, with Stephen Handelman. *Biohazard: The Chilling True Story of the Largest Covert Biological Weapons Program in the World—Told from Inside by the Man Who Ran It*. London: Random House, 1999.

Allen, Thomas B., and Norman Polmar. *Merchants of Treason: America's Secrets for Sale*. London: Robert Hale, 1988.

Allon, Yigal. *Shield of David*. London: Weidenfeld & Nicolson, 1970.

Alvarez, David. *Secret Messages: Codebreaking and American Diplomacy, 1930–1945.* Lawrence: University Press of Kansas, 2000.

———, ed. *Allied and Axis Signals Intelligence in World War II.* London: Frank Cass, 1999.

Andrew, Christopher. "Churchill and Intelligence." *Intelligence and National Security* 3 no. 3 (April 1998): 181–93.

———. *For the President's Eyes Only.* London: HarperCollins, 1995.

Andrew, Christopher, and David Dilks. *The Missing Dimension: Governments and Intelligence Communities in the Twentieth Century.* London: Macmillan, 1984.

Andrew, Christopher, and Oleg Gordievsky. *Instructions from the Centre: Top Secret Files on KGB Foreign Operations, 1975–1985.* London, England: Hodder & Stoughton, 1991.

———. *KGB: The Inside Story.* London, England: Hodder & Stoughton, 1990.

Andrew, Christopher, and Vasili Mitrokhin. *The Mitrokhin Archive: The KGB and the West.* London: Allen Lane, 1984.

Andrew, Christopher, and Jeremy Noakes. *Intelligence and International Relations, 1909–1945.* Exeter, England: University of Exeter, 1987.

Bainerman, Joel. *Inside the Covert Operations of the CIA and Israel's Mossad.* New York, USA: SPI Books, 1991.

Ball, Desmond. *Soviet Signals Intelligence (SIGINT).* Strategic and Defense Studies Center, Research School of Pacific Studies, Canberra, Australia, 1989.

Bamford, James. *The Puzzle Palace: America's National Security Agency and Its Special Relationship with Britain's GCHQ.* London: Sidgwick & Jackson, 1982.

———. *The Puzzle Palace: A Report on America's Most Secret Agency.* Boston: Houghton Mifflin, 1982.

Barron, John. *KGB Today: The Hidden Hand.* New York: Reader's Digest Press, 1983.

Bar-Zohar, Michel. *Ben-Gurion: A Biography.* London: Weidenfeld & Nicolson, 1977.

———. *Spies in the Promised Land.* London: Davis-Poynter, 1972.

Bell, J. Bowyer. *The Secret Army: The IRA, 1916–1979.* Dublin: Academy Press, 1970.

Ben-Porat, Yeshayahu, et al. *Entebbe Rescue.* New York: Delacorte Press, 1977.

Ben-Shaul, Moshe, ed. *Generals of Israel.* Tel Aviv, Israel: Hadar, 1968.

Beschloss, Michael R., and Strobe Talbott. *At the Highest Levels: The Inside Story of the End of the Cold War.* Boston: Little, Brown, 1993.

Bishop, Patrick, and Eamonn Mallie. *The Provisional IRA.* London: Corgi, 1987.

Black, Ian, and Benny Morris. *Israel's Secret Wars.* London: Hamish Hamilton, 1991.

Blumenthal, Sid, and Harvey Yazijian, eds. *Government by Gunplay: Assassination Conspiracy Theories from Dallas to Today.* New York: Signet, 1976.

Borovik, Genrikh. *The Philby Files.* London: Little, Brown, 1994.

Bower, Tom. *A Perfect English Spy: Sir Dick White and the Secret War, 1935–90.* London: Heinemann, 1995.

———. *The Red Web: MI6 and the KGB Master Coup.* London, England: Aurum Press, 1989.

Boyle, Andrew. *The Climate of Treason.* Rev. Ed. London: Coronet, 1980.

Brown, Anthony Cave. *"C": The Secret Life of Sir Stewart Graham Menzies, Spymaster to Winston Churchill.* New York: Macmillan, 1987.

Brzezinski, Zbigniew. *Power and Principle: Memoirs of the National Security Adviser, 1977–1981.* New York: Farrar, Straus & Giroux, 1983.

Budiansky, Stephen. *Battle of Wits.* London: Viking, 2000.

Cabinet Office. *Central Intelligence Machinery.* London: HMSO, 1993, 1995.

Central Intelligence Agency. *Analysis: Directorate of Intelligence in the 21st Century.* Washington: GPO, 1996.

The CIA's Nicaragua Manual: Psychological Operations in Guerrilla Warfare. With essays by Joanne Omang and Aryeh Neier. New York: Vintage Books, 1985.

Clarke, Richard A. *Against All Enemies.* New York: Free Press, 2004.

Cline, Ray S. *The CIA Under Reagan, Bush, and Casey.* Washington: Acropolis Books, 1981.

———. *Secrets, Spies, and Scholars: Blueprint of the Essential CIA.* Washington: Acropolis Books, 1976.

Cline, Ray S., and Yonah Alexander. *Terrorism: The Soviet Connection.* New York: Crane Russak, 1984.

Constantinides, George C. *Intelligence and Espionage: An Analytical Bibliography.* Boulder, Colo.: Westview Press, 1983.

Cookridge, E. H. *George Blake: Double Agent.* London: Hodder, 1970.

Copeland, Miles. *The Game of Nations.* New York: Simon & Schuster, 1969.

———. *The Real Spy World.* London: Sphere Books, 1978.

Cruickshank, Charles. *SOE in Scandinavia.* Oxford, England: Oxford University Press, 1986.

Curry, John. *The Security Service, 1908–1945.* London: Public Record Office, 1999.

Dandeker, Christopher. *Surveillance, Power, and Modernity.* Cambridge, England: Polity Press, 1990.

Deacon, Richard. *"C": A Biography of Sir Maurice Oldfield.* London: Macdonald, 1985.

———. *A History of the British Secret Service.* London: Muller, 1969.

Dear, I. C. B., ed. *The Oxford Companion to World War II.* Oxford: Oxford University Press, 1995.

Dekel, Efraim. *A History of British Secret Service.* London: Granada, 1980.

———. *Shai: The Exploits of Hagana Intelligence.* Tel Aviv, Israel: Yoseleff, 1959.

Delmer, Sefton. *Black Boomerang*. London: Secker & Warburg, 1962.

De Silva, Peer. *Sub Rosa: The CIA and the Uses of Intelligence*. New York: Times Books, 1978.

Dobson, Christopher, and Ronald Payne. *The Dictionary of Espionage*. London: Harrap, 1984.

Dorril, Stephen. *MI6: Fifty Years of Special Operations*. London: Fourth Estate, 2000.

Drozdov, Yuri. *Zapiski nachal'nika nelegal'noj razvedki [Memoirs of the Head of Illegal Intelligence]*. Moscow: Novosti, 2000.

Dulles, Allen. *The Craft of Intelligence*. Westport, Conn.: Greenwood Press, 1977.

Dziak, John. *Chekisty: A History of the KGB*. New York: Ivy, 1988.

Eisenberg, Dennis, Uri Dan, and Eli Landau. *Meyer Lansky: Mogul of the Mob*. London: Corgi Books, 1980.

———. *The Mossad, Israel's Secret Intelligence Service: Inside Stories*. New York: Signet, 1979.

Elon, Amos. *The Israelis: Founders and Sons*. London: Weidenfeld & Nicolson, 1971.

Epstein, Edward Jay. *Deception: The Invisible War Between the KGB and the CIA*. London: W. H. Allen, 1989.

Faligot, Roger, and Pascal Krop. *La Piscine: The French Secret Service Since 1944*. Oxford, England: Basil Blackwell, 1989.

Farago, Ladislas. *Burn After Reading*. New York: Macfadden, 1963.

Fergusson, Thomas G. *British Military Intelligence, 1870–1914: The Development of a Modern Intelligence Organisation*. London: Arms and Armour Press, 1984.

Foot, M. R. D. *Resistance: An Analysis of European Resistance to Nazism, 1940–1945*. London: Methuen, 1976.

Foot, M. R. D., and J. M. Langley. *MI9: Escape and Evasion, 1939–1945*. London: Bodley Head, 1979.

Fourcade, Marie-Madeleine. *Noah's Ark: The Story of the Alliance Intelligence Network in Occupied France*. London, England: Allen & Unwin, 1973.

Gann, Ernest K. *The Black Watch: The Men Who Fly America's Secret Spy Planes*. New York: Random House, 1989.

Gelb, Norman. *The Berlin Wall*. London: Michael Joseph, 1986.

Geraghty, Tony. *The Irish War*. London: HarperCollins, 1998.

———. *Who Dares Wins: The Special Air Service, 1950 to the Gulf War*. London: Little, Brown, 1992.

Gilbert, Martin. *The Arab-Israeli Conflict*. London: Weidenfeld & Nicolson, 1974.

Godson, Roy, ed. *Intelligence Requirements for the 1980s: Covert Action*. Washington: National Strategy Information Center, 1981.

Golan, Aviezer, and Danny Pinkas. *Shula, Code Name the Pearl*. New York: Delacorte Press, 1980.

Golinkov, David. *The Secret War Against Soviet Russia.* Moscow: Novosti, 1981.

Graham, Bill. *Break-In: Inside the Soviet Trade Delegation.* London: Bodley Head, 1987.

Gulley, Bill, with Mary Ellen Reese. *Breaking Cover.* New York: Warner Books, 1981.

Haig, Alexander M., Jr. *Caveat: Realism, Reagan, and Foreign Policy.* London: Weidenfeld & Nicolson, 1984.

Harel, Isser. *The House on Garibaldi Street.* London: André Deutsch, 1975.

Harris, Robert, and Jeremy Paxman. *A Higher Form of Killing.* London: Triad/Granada, 1983.

Haswell, Jock. *Spies and Spymasters: A Concise History of Intelligence.* London: Thames & Hudson, 1977.

Henze, Paul B. *The Plot to Kill the Pope.* London: Croom Helm, 1984.

Hill, George. *Go Spy the Land.* London: Cassell, 1932.

Hinsley, F. H., E. E. Thomas, C. F. G. Ransom, and R. C. Knight. *British Intelligence in the Second World War: Its Influence on Strategy and Operations.* 4 vols. London: HMSO, 1979–90.

Hinsley, F. H. and Alan Stripp, eds. *Codebreakers: The Inside Story of Bletchley Park.* Oxford: Oxford University Press, 1993.

Hollingsworth, Mark, and Nick Fielding. *Defending the Realm: MI5 and the Shayler Affair.* London: André Deutsch, 1999.

Howard, Michael. *British Intelligence in the Second World War,* vol. 5, *Strategic Deception.* London: HMSO, 1990.

Hyde, H. Montgomery. *The Quiet Canadian: The Secret Service Story of Sir William Stephenson.* London, England: Constable, 1989.

Jeffreys-Jones, Rhodri. *The CIA and American Democracy.* New Haven: Yale University Press, 1989.

Johns, Philip. *Within Two Cloaks: Missions with SIS and SOE.* London: William Kimber, 1979.

Johnson, Loch K. *America's Secret Power: The CIA in a Democratic Society.* New York: Oxford University Press, 1989.

Jones, R. V. *Most Secret War: British Scientific Intelligence, 1939–1945.* London: Hamish Hamilton, 1978.

———. *Reflections on Intelligence.* London: Jonathan Cape, 1989.

Judd, Alan. *The Quest for C: Mansfield Cumming and the Founding of the Secret Service.* London: HarperCollins, 1999.

Kirkpatrick, Lyman B. *The U.S. Intelligence Community: Foreign Policy and Domestic Activities.* New York: Hill & Wang, 1973.

Knightley, Phillip. *Kim Philby: KGB Masterspy.* London: André Deutsch, 1988.

———. *The Second Oldest Profession: The Spy as Bureaucrat, Patriot, Fantasist, and Whore.* London: André Deutsch, 1986.

Kyle, Keith. *Suez*. London: Weidenfeld & Nicolson, 1991.

Landau, Henry. *All's Fair: The Story of the British Secret Service Behind the German Lines*. New York: Putnam, 1934.

Lane, Jan-Erik. *The Public Sector: Concepts, Models, and Approaches*. London: Sage, 1993.

Lanning, Hugh, and Richard Norton-Taylor. *A Conflict of Loyalties: GCHQ, 1984–1991*. Cheltenham, England: New Clarion, 1991.

Laqueur, Walter, ed. *The Israel-Arab Reader*. New York: Bantam, 1969.

———. *The Struggle for the Middle East: The Soviet Union and the Middle East, 1958–1968*. London: Routledge & Kegan Paul, 1969.

Lashmar, Paul. *Spy Flights of the Cold War*. London: Sutton, 1996.

Leigh, David. *The Wilson Plot: The Intelligence Services and the Discrediting of a Prime Minister, 1945–1976*. London: Heinemann, 1988.

Lockhart, Robert Bruce. *Memoirs of a British Agent*. London: Putnam, 1932; rpt. Macmillan, 1985.

Lockhart, Robin Bruce. *Reilly, Ace of Spies*. London: Futura, 1983.

Lotz, Wolfgang. *The Champagne Spy*. London: Vallentine, Mitchell, 1972.

Mangold, Tom. *Cold Warrior: James Jesus Angleton, the CIA's Master Spy Hunter*. London: Simon & Schuster, 1991.

Marchetti, Victor, and John D. Marks. *The CIA and the Cult of Intelligence*. New York: Dell Publishing, 1974.

Martin, David C., and John Walcott. *Best Laid Plans: The Inside Story of America's War Against Terrorism*. New York: Harper & Row, 1988.

Masterman, J. C. *The Double-Cross System in the War of 1939–1945*. New Haven and London: Yale University Press, 1972.

McCall, Gibb. *Flight Most Secret: Air Missions for SOE and SIS*. London: William Kimber, 1981.

McClintock, Michael. *Instruments of Statecraft: U.S. Guerrilla Warfare, Counterinsurgency, and Counterterrorism, 1940–1990*. New York: Pantheon Books, 1992.

McDermott, Geoffrey. *The New Diplomacy and Its Apparatus*. London: Plume, 1973.

McGehee, Ralph W. *Deadly Deceits: My 25 Years in the CIA*. New York: Sheridan Square Publications, 1983.

McGhee, George. *Envoy to the Middle World: Adventures in Diplomacy*. New York: Harper & Row, 1983.

Meir, Golda. *My Life*. London: Weidenfeld & Nicolson, 1975.

Melman, Yossi, and Dan Raviv. *The Imperfect Spies: The History of Israeli Intelligence*. London: Sidgwick & Jackson, 1989.

Modin, Yuri. *My Five Cambridge Friends*. London: Headline, 1994.

Moses, Hans. *The Clandestine Service of the Central Intelligence Agency*. McLean, Va.: Association of Former Intelligence Officers, 1983.

Neave, Airey. *Saturday at MI9*. London: Grafton, 1989.

Neff, Donald. *Warriors at Suez: Eisenhower Takes America into the Middle East.* New York: Linden Press, 1981.

Norton-Taylor, Richard. *In Defence of the Realm?* London: Civil Liberties Trust, 1990.

O'Brien, Terence. *The Moonlight War: The Story of Clandestine Special Operations in Southeast Asia, 1944–5.* London: Collins, 1987.

Occleshaw, Michael. *Armour Against Fate: British Military Intelligence in the First World War.* London: Columbus, 1989.

Offer, Yehuda. *Operation Thunder: The Entebbe Raid, the Israelis' Own Story.* Harmondsworth, England: Penguin Books, 1976.

Office of the Security Service Commissioner. *The Security Service.* London, England: HMSO, 1993.

Ostrovsky, Victor. *The Other Side of Deception.* New York: HarperCollins, 1994.

Ostrovsky, Victor, and Claire Hoy. *By Way of Deception.* New York: St. Martin's Press, 1990.

Parritt, Lt. Col. B. A. H. *The Intelligencers: The Story of British Military Intelligence up to 1914.* Ashford, England: Templer Press, 1971.

Penkovsky, Oleg. *The Penkovsky Papers.* New York: Avon, 1965.

Pincher, Chapman. *The Secret Offensive, Active Measures: A Saga of Deception, Disinformation, Subversion, Terrorism, Sabotage, and Assassination.* London, England: Sidgwick & Jackson, 1985.

Popplewell, Richard. *Intelligence and Imperial Defence: British Intelligence and the Defence of the Indian Empire, 1904–1924.* London: Frank Cass, 1995.

Power, Thomas. *The Man Who Kept the Secrets: Richard Helms and the CIA.* New York: Knopf, 1979.

Prados, John. *Keepers of the Keys: A History of the National Security Council from Truman to Bush.* New York: William Morrow, 1991.

———. *Presidents' Secret Wars: CIA and Pentagon Covert Operations Since World War II.* New York: William Morrow, 1986.

Pugh, Marshall. *Commander Crabb.* London: Macmillan, 1956.

Rabin, Yitzhak. *The Rabin Memoirs.* London: Weidenfeld & Nicolson, 1979.

Ranelagh, John. *The Agency: The Rise and Decline of the CIA, from Wild Bill Donovan to William Casey.* New York: Simon & Schuster, 1986.

Ransom, Harry Howe. *The Intelligence Establishment.* Cambridge, Mass.: Harvard University Press, 1970.

Rathmell, Andrew. *Secret War in the Middle East: The Covert Struggle for Syria, 1949–1961.* London: Tauris, 1995.

Rennie, James. *The Operators: Inside 14 Intelligence Company.* London: Century, 1996.

Richelson, Jeffrey T. *American Espionage and the Soviet Target.* New York: William Morrow, 1987.

———. *Foreign Intelligence Organizations.* Cambridge, Mass.: Ballinger, 1988.

———. *Sword and Shield: The Soviet Intelligence and Security Apparatus.* Cambridge, Mass.: Ballinger, 1986.

———. *The U.S. Intelligence Community.* Cambridge, Mass.: Ballinger, 1985.

Richelson, Jeffrey T., and Desmond Ball. *The Ties That Bind.* 2nd ed. Boston: Unwin Hyman, 1990.

Rimington, Stella. *At Risk.* London, England: Hutchinson, 2004.

———. *Open Secret.* London, England: Hutchinson, 2001.

Robertson, K. G., ed. *British and American Approaches to Intelligence.* London: Macmillan, 1987.

———. *War, Resistance, and Intelligence: Essays in Honour of M. R. D. Foot.* London: Leo Cooper, 1999.

Roosevelt, Kermit. *Countercoup: The Struggle for Control of Iran.* New York: McGraw-Hill, 1979.

Rositzke, Harry. *The KGB: The Eyes of Russia.* London: Sidgwick & Jackson, 1981.

Rusbridger, James. *The Intelligence Game: Illusions and Delusions of International Espionage.* London: Bodley Head, 1989.

Sawatsky, John. *Men in the Shadows: The RCMP Security Service.* Toronto: Doubleday, 1980.

Schechter, Jerrold S., and Peter S. Duriabin. *The Spy Who Saved the World: How a Soviet Colonel Changed the Course of the Cold War.* New York: Charles Scribner's Sons, 1992.

Seth, Ronald. *The Executioners: The Story of SMERSH.* New York: Tempo Books, 1970.

Smith, Colin. *Carlos: Portrait of a Terrorist.* New York: Holt, Rinehart & Winston, 1976.

Smith, Michael. *The Emperor's Codes: Bletchley Park and the Breaking of Japan's Secret Ciphers.* London: Bantam, 2000.

Stafford, David. *Churchill and Secret Service.* London: John Murray, 1997.

Sterling, Claire. *The Terror Network: The Secret War of International Terrorism.* London: Weidenfeld & Nicolson, 1981.

Stevens, Stewart. *The Spymasters of Israel.* London: Hodder & Stoughton, 1981.

Stevenson, William. *90 Minutes at Entebbe.* New York: Bantam Books, 1976.

Stockwell, John. *In Search of Enemies: A CIA Story.* New York: W. W. Norton, 1978.

Suvorov, Viktor. *Soviet Military Intelligence.* London, England: Hamish Hamilton, 1984.

Tenet, George. *At the Center of the Storm: My Years at the CIA.* New York: HarperCollins, 2007.

Tinnin, David B. *The Hit Team.* Boston: Little, Brown, 1976.

Tully, Andrew. *CIA: The Inside Story.* New York: William Morrow, 1962.

———. *The Super Spies: More Secret, More Powerful than the CIA.* New York: William Morrow, 1969.

Turner, Stansfield. *Secrecy and Democracy: The CIA in Transition.* Boston: Houghton Mifflin, 1985.

Weiner, Tim. *Legacy of Ashes.* New York: Doubleday, 2007.

West, Nigel [Rupert Allaston]. *The Friends: British Post-War Secret Intelligence Operations.* London: Weidenfeld & Nicolson, 1988.

———. *GCHQ: The Secret Wireless War, 1900–1986.* London: Weidenfeld & Nicolson, 1986.

———. *A Matter of Trust: MI5, 1945–72.* London: Weidenfeld & Nicolson, 1982.

———. *MI5: British Security Service Operations, 1909–1945.* London, England: Bodley Head, 1981.

West, Nigel. *MI6: British Secret Intelligence Service Operations, 1909–1945.* London: Weidenfeld & Nicolson, 1983.

———. *Secret War.* London, England: Hodder & Stoughton, 1993.

Wiesenthal, Simon. *The Murderers Among Us.* London: William Heinemann, 1967.

Wilkinson, Paul, and A. M. Stewart, eds. *Contemporary Research on Terrorism.* Aberdeen, Scotland: Aberdeen University Press, 1987.

Wilson, F. M. G. *The Organisation of British Central Government.* London: England: Allen & Unwin, 1957.

Wilson, Harold. *Final Term: The Labour Government, 1974–1976.* London: Weidenfeld & Nicolson and Michael Joseph, 1979.

Woodhouse, C. M. *Something Ventured.* London: Granada, 1982.

Woodward, Bob. *Veil: The Secret Wars of the CIA, 1981–1987.* London: Simon & Schuster, 1987.

Wright, Peter. *Spycatcher: The Candid Autobiography of a Senior Intelligence Officer.* Toronto: Stoddart, 1987.

INDEX

A

Abdollahpour, Zahra, 39
Abdullah, Abu, 16
Abramson, Harold, 211
Absalom, Ruth, 370
Acheson, Dean, 112, 143
Adams, Gerry, 171, 309, 382
Adams, James, 254
Adams, Terence George "Terry", 58–61
Admoni, Nahum, 200, 203, 204, 206, 217
Adye, Sir John, 235
African National Congress (ANC), 273, 308
Ahmadinejad, President Mahmoud, 25, 27, 39
Ahmadi, Ziba, 39
Ahmed, Lieutenant General Mahmoud, 348
Aich, Hamid, 20
al-Adel, Saif, 27
al-Bahri, Nasir, 388
Alexander, Field Marshall Lord, 99
al-Fayed, Dodi, 216, 291–292, 318
al-Fayed, Mohamed, 8–9, 291–292
al-Hakaymah, Muhammed Khalil. *see* al-Masri, Abu Jihad, 27, 385
Alibek, Dr. Ken, 337–338, 360
al-Islamiya al-Muqatila, 235
Allawi, Ayad, 377–378

Allen, Alex, 395–396
Allen, Charles, 237
Allen, Mark, 7
al-Libi, Abu Yahya, 385
al-Masri, Abu Jihad, 27, 385
al-Masri, Abu Obaidah, 385
al-Muhajiroun (radical Islamic organization), 50, 53
al-Qaeda, 284, 314, 316, 324, 325–327, 335, 342, 344, 347, 348–350
   and biochemical/nuclear weapons, 15, 22, 27
   and croquet analogy, 66
   in Britain, 49–54, 56–62, 65–67
   and Communist enemies, 69
   and Evans intrigued by, 258–259
   leadership of, 27, 385
   links in Dublin, 19–20
   and 9/11 attacks, 2, 8, 11, 20, 39, 43, 50, 361, 386, 389
   organizations infiltrated by, 54
   and Pakistan, 11, 19, 28
   plot(s), 10, 11–12, 61–63
   and recruitment, 3, 27, 54
   and Saudi Arabia, 15–16
   training, 3, 4, 386, 395
   and WMD, 17
   see also bin Laden, Osama; jihad(ist)
al-Rashman, Abd, 385
Altimimi, Omar, 54

413

al-Zawahiri, Ayman, 27, 258, 310, 388
Amery, John, 104
Ames, Aldrich "Rick," 191–194,
    197–198, 200, 202
Ames, Carlton, 191
Ames, Rob, 203
Amin, Mustafa, 144
Amit, Meir, 38, 39, 55, 308–309
Anastasio, Michael, 18
Anderson, Brian, 292
Andrew, Christopher, 112
Angleton, James, 125, 131
Anglo-French Invasion of Egypt (1956),
    158
Anglo-Iranian Oil Company (AIOC),
    31, 34, 35
An Yue Jiang (cargo ship), 244–245
Apostles Society, 127
Apollo 11, 161
Arad, Ron, 25
Arafat, Yasser, 304
Arms Control Treaty, 215
arms-for-hostages deal. *see* Iran-Contra
    Affair
Armstrong, Neil, 161
Armstrong, Robert, 185
Asgari, General Ali-Reza
    education of, 24
    and Iran, 21–30, 36–41, 389–390
    opinion of bin Laden, 27–28
    reason(s) for defecting to MI6, 26,
    36
Asquith, Viscount, 195–197
"Assassination Methods" manual,
    147–148
atomic bomb(s). *see* nuclear weapon(s)
Atomic Energy Commission, 115
Attlee, Clement, 117
Australian Secret Intelligence Service
    (ASIS), 115
Azzam, Abdallah, 302
Azzam the American. *see* Gadahn,
    Adam

B

Bandar bin Sultan, Prince of Saudi
    Arabia, 218
Baghdad pact, 146–147
Baha'i religion, 373
Bakatin, Vadim, 251–254
Baker, James, 244

Baker, Lord Justice Scott, 292
Baker, Norman, 377–378
Bakri, Sheikh Omar, 50
Barnard, Dr. Christiaan, 268
Barot, Dhiren, 53
Barrass, Gordon, 197
Basson, Wouter, 268–279, 366
Battle, Luke, 142
Bellamy, Kate, 138
Benbow, Christopher, 57–62
Ben-Gurion, David, 153, 155
Ben-Menashe, Ari, 29, 56, 206, 219,
    222, 295, 370
Ben-Tov, Cheryl, 55–56
Ben-Tov, Ofer, 55
Beria, Lavrenti, 98, 254
Bettany, Michael, 194
Bickford, David, 45
bin Laden, Mohammed, 27
bin Laden, Osama, 53–54, 283,
    319–320, 324–325, 327–328, 348,
    354
    behaviorist analysis of, 306–308
    fought for Afghanistan, against
        Soviets, 303
    and hatred of America/infidels, 284,
        310, 314, 362
    health of, 304
    as hero to Muslim people, 49–50,
        301–302, 305
    and his "Base" in Sudan,
        258–259
    founds al-Qaeda, 217
    hunt for/plan to capture, 20,
        312–313
    meets Cheng in Sudan, 267
    on his thirty-fourth birthday,
        252
    recruits of, 27
    remains a prime target, 383–389,
        394, 397
    as sheikh, 283
    threats against the U.S., 284, 310,
        314, 362
    see also al-Qaeda; jihad(ist);
        Taliban/"Talibanized"
bin Laden, Saad, 27
bin Laden, Shafiq, 348
biological/biochemical weapon(s)/
    warfare, 17, 191, 236–238, 241
    and bioterrorism, in the U.S., 275

and al-Qaeda, 259
and antidotes in Britain, 241
"genetic bomb," 272–273
germ warfare used by
 Japanese/Nazis, 269
and Iraq, 259
and Libya, 270
in North Korea, 276–277
and Russia, 259
theoretical defensive use of germ
 warfare, 268–269
see also Basson, Wouter; Kelly, Dr.
 David
Biological and Toxin Weapons
 Convention (1972), 212–213,
 260
Biopreparat. *see under* Russia/Russian
Bishop, Maurice, 188
black art of media manipulation,
 151–154
the Black Chamber, 82–83
Black, Cofer, 304
black propaganda, 153–154
Black September, 174, 175
Blair Crisis Cabinet, 5
Blair, Prime Minister Tony, 4, 295, 300,
 321, 344, 346, 350, 353, 354, 391
 and Dr. Kelly investigation, 376
 and Iraq WMD blunder, 5
 and relationship with Bush, 5
 and relationship with Scarlett, 5,
  7–8, 9, 398
 resignation of, 65
Blake, George, 134–137, 145
Blunkett, David, 51
Blunt, Anthony, 126–128, 132
Boer War of 1899–1902, 79
Bolshevik Revolution in 1917, 82
Booth, Cherie, 8
Boren, David, 343, 345
BOSS, 317
Boursicot, Pierre, 155, 156
Bowes-Lyon, Elizabeth Angela
 Marguerite, 85
Boxer Rebellion, 78
brain drain from Germany, 98
brainwashing, 210–212
Britain/British
 and al-Qaeda, 49–54, 56–62, 65–67,
  69, 386
 aristocracy support of Hitler, 84

atomic energy research center, 115
collaboration/relations with U.S., 23
 112, 113, 152, 228
and control of the Suez Canal,
 141–145, 146–160
government, and Intelligence and
 Security Committee (ISC), 65
government, and Military
 Operations Five (forerunner of
 MI5), 78
and Israel's plan to attack Egypt, 156
jihad in, 50, 51, 53, 57
Secret Intelligence Service. *see* MI6
and SIGINT collaboration with the
 U.S., 112
and Soviet Union, fear of, 18
and surveillance, 14–16
and relations with China, 266–267
the role of information gathering in,
 76–78
servicemen were used as guinea pigs
 for MK-ULTRA, 210–211
spy mania sweeping, 80
British Broadcasting Corporation
 (BBC), 74–75, 89, 213, 365, 370,
 376–377
Brook, Norman, 152
Brown, Prime Minister Gordon, 4, 6, 9,
 247, 295, 391, 398
Brown, Kerry, 246
Browning, Robert, 190, 194
Brynes, James, 122
Buckley, William "Bill," 24, 33, 94, 95,
 126, 127, 163, 188, 189, 200, 206,
 217–219
Bulganin, Nikolai, 158, 159
Bulgaria intelligence service. *see*
 Darzhavna Sigurnost (DS)
Bull, Gerald, assassination of, 238
Bundesnachrichtendienst (BND;
 German Federal Intelligence
 Service), 99, 137, 142, 172, 183, 217
Burgess, Guy, 108, 125–130, 135, 202,
 256
Burns, William, 342
Bushnell, Prudence, 319
Bush, Prescott, 264
Bush, President George H. W., 193,
 236, 280–284
 and China, 242–248
 and Iraq War, 240–244, 248

Bush, President George W., 5, 39, 320,
  329, 341, 348, 352–353, 354, 381,
  391, 397
Bute, Lord, 77
Butler, Lord, 199

C

Caccia, Harold, 148
Campbell, Alastair, 346, 351
Canadian Security Intelligence Service
  (RCMP), 123
Canadian spy ring, 108–111
Canaris, Admiral Wilhelm, 107
Carlos the Jackal, 173–174
Carter, President James "Jimmy,"
  204–205, 243
Casey, Tom, 245
Casey, William "Bill," 197, 203, 206,
  217, 240, 309
  death of, 219, 222
  embarrassment for, 215
  forced resignation, 219, 221
  as Reagan's campaign manager, 206
  and Howard treason debacle,
    200–202
  questions Yurchenko, 209–210, 212
Castro, Fidel, 188, 209, 272, 281
Central Intelligence Agency. see CIA
Chalabi, Ahmed, 377–378
Chamberlain, Neville, 85
Chapman, Eddie, 93, 104
Chapman, John, 394–395
Chapman, Paul, 371–372
Chavez, Hugo, 245
Cheney, Dick, 334, 344, 347, 348,
  352–353
Cheng, Teng, 267, 279
Chuvakhin, Sergei D., 192–193
China/Chinese
  arms sales to Saddam Hussein, 242
  arms sales to Zimbabwe, 244–245
  and Boxer Rebellion, 78
  Central External Liaison
    Department, 262, 265
  and cyberwarfare, 392–393
  defectors, highly unlikely to find,
    263
  executed by government, for their
    organs, 266
  Investigation Bureau, 262–263
  labor camps in, 265

Ministry of State Security (MSS), 18,
  262–268, 279, 397
and nuclear weapons. see under
  nuclear weapon(s)
Olympic Games in, 246, 247
and the People's Liberation Army
  (PLA), 243, 246
and relations with Britain, 266–267
and relations with Israel/Mossad, 18
and relations with MI5. see under MI5
  (relations)
and relations with MI6. see under MI6
  (relations)
and relations with U.S., 242–248
and Sanya (a.k.a. Yulin) naval base,
  245–246
sleepers, use of by, 283
surveillance in, 265–266
and Tiananmen Square Massacre,
  243–244, 264–266
and U.S. company links to, 242
and U.S. trade restrictions, 243–244
Choudrav, Anjem, 53
Churchill, Prime Minister Winston, 78,
  111–112, 240
  fires Kell, 90–91
  and Germany, 94
  and his relationship with Menzies,
    33
  and his warnings about Hitler, 84–85
  protects capital at the expense of the
    East End, 102–104
  quote by, regarding India, 163
  and Stalin, 116
  and Soviet Union, 98–100
  and WWII, 86–90
CIA
  and "black ops," 201
  budget of, 170
  comes into existence, 112–113
  and counterintelligence against
    China, 283
  and dependence on the Mossad, 240
  documents stolen by an ally country,
    240
  double agent. see Ames, Aldrich
    "Rick"
  "expendables," 210–211
  failures of, 280, 379, 382
  and gadgets, 62–63
  and key elements of spies, 282

loses intelligence via bombing in
Lebanon, 203
and MK-ULTRA. *see* brainwashing;
MK-ULTRA experiments
and obsessive fear of the skills of the
KGB, 130
and obsessive pursuit to control
human behavior, 212
precursor to. *see* Office of Strategic
Services (OSS)
recruitment of analysts, 283
recruitment of Japanese moles, 281
relations with MI5. *see under* MI5
relations with MI6. *see under* MI6
and relations with Mossad, 188, 203,
240
and relations with DGSE/SDECE,
156–157, 203, 217
Clarke, Ken, 284
Clarke, Richard, 283, 313, 314–316,
325–326, 328–329, 336, 343–344,
345–347, 348, 351–354
Clinton, President William "Bill," 248,
311, 313, 319–320, 325, 327, 333,
343
Cohen, Eli, 142
Cohen, Yakov, 174–175
Colby, William, 201, 214, 226
Collins, John, 141, 143, 145
Collins, Michael, 82
Columbia
intelligence organization. *see* DAS
terror group(s). *see* FARC
The Coming War with Japan
(Friedman/Lebard), 281
COMINT, 227
Continuity IRA, 28–29
Cook, Robin, 10, 321, 322, 365
Cooper, Chester, 149, 151, 152
Costello, Seamus, 176
coup d'état, and Mossadeq, 35, 36
Cromwell, Oliver, 77
Crowley, Aleister, 83
Cumming, Sir Mansfield Smith, 2, 303
Curwen, Christopher, 195–198, 208,
216
cyberspace, and theft of commercial
info in, 231
cyberterrorism/cyberwarfare, 19,
392–393
cyberware, 15

D
Daily Mail, 54, 79, 80
Daily Mirror, 224
Daily Express, 90
Daily Telegraph, 23
Daily Worker, 105
Dagan, Meir, 17, 37–38, 378, 390, 391
Dalai Lama, 247
Danish intelligence service. *see* PET
Dansey, Sir Claude, 97, 133
Dan, Wang, 244
Darzhavna Sigurnost (DS), 224
DAS (Columbian intelligence), 28–29,
46
Dastych, David, 18–19, 60
Davis, Arthur H., 281
Davis, Christopher, 259, 359
Davis, Gavyn, 377
Dayan, Moshe, 155, 156–157
Dean, Patrick, 155
Dearlove, Richard, 9, 316, 322, 324,
326–327, 335, 361–363
deception of senior officer
discovered by, 196
and memo criticizing lack of hard
evidence and WMD in Iraq, 363
relationship with Tenet, 361–362
resignation of, 7, 361–362
sought collaboration with Spanish/
Italian intelligence agencies, 362
Deep Black Operators, 181
*Defending the Land of the Muslims Is Each
Man's Most Important Duty*, 302
Democratic Republic of Congo, 38–39
Dench, Judi, 321
Dennys, Rodney, 155
Derpaska, Oleg, 9
Deutch, John, 311
Diana, Princess of Whales, 9, 216,
291–292, 318
Dodds-Parker, Douglas, 152
Donovan, William, 86–90, 93–96,
109–110
doodlebug bombs, 103–104
Dorill, Stephen, 318
double agent(s), 93, 102–103, 177, 190,
224
best. *see* Philby, Kim
working for MI6. *see* Asgari, General
Ali-Reza; Lyalin, Oleg; Gordievsky,
Oleg

double agent(s) *(continued)*
    working against CIA/MI6. *see* Ames,
        Aldrich "Rick"; Blake, George;
        Blunt, Anthony; Burgess, Guy;
        Maclean, Donald; Philby, Kim
Drake, Ivan, 109–110
Drljaca, Simo, 299–300, 303
Duff, Antony, 208, 217
Duke of Edinburgh, 292
Dulles, Allen, 33, 36, 94–100, 107, 111,
        120–124, 126, 147, 149, 151–154,
        156, 158, 159
    and black propaganda, 96
    and brainwashing/MK-ULTRA, 210,
        211
    death of, 159
    dislike of Britain/MI5/MI6, 95, 99,
        113, 127, 143
    dislike of Philby, 127
    and his love for India, 163, 164
    as newbie spy, 96
    receives a dagger from Harel,
        139
    schooling of, 95
    sexual drive of, 95
Dulles, Clover, 94
Dulles, John Foster, 35, 95, 101, 147,
        148, 156, 157
Dupuy, Rosario, 192, 193, 194
Durbin, Evan, 68
Dyke, Greg, 377

E
Easter Rising of 1916, 82
ECHELON, 229–231
Eckel, Paul, 318
Economist, 10
Eden, Anthony, 140, 145, 150
    and Suez crisis, 146–159
    resignation of, 159
Egypt
    Israel's plan to attack, 156
    and loan for the Aswan Dam, 148
    and Soviet arms deal, 147
    and Suez crisis, 141–145, 146–160
    and threats of attack against Israel,
        153–154
Egyptian Committee, 144, 145
Eichelberger, James, 143, 149
Eichmann, Adolf, 238
Einstein, Albert, 133

Eisenhower, President Dwight D., 120,
        147, 154, 158
    death of, 159
    and the great betrayal, 156–157
    hailed as the "Prince of Peace,"
        165
Eitan, Rafi, 153, 170–171
Eitner, Horst, 137
Eksund (cargo ship), 171
Elizabeth I, Queen of England, 76–77
Elliott, Nicholas, 153, 159
es-Said, Nuri, 152
Evans, Jonathan, 199
    and al-Qaeda, 43–44, 258–259, 304,
        307–308, 309, 316, 382–389, 393,
        395, 397
    appearance of, 258
    and IRA, 59, 258
    personality of, 258
    plan to find bin Laden, 387–388

F
Falklands War, 195
Faisal, King of Iraq, 152
FARC (Columbian terror group),
        28–29, 342
Farouk, King of Egypt, 140,141
Farr, Charles, 398
Farrell, Terry, 37
Faud, King of Saudi Arabia, 304
Fawzi, Mahmoud, 155
Federal Bureau of Investigation (FBI),
        112, 125
Federal Security Service (FSB; Russian
        security service), 113
Feoktisov, Aleksander, 168
Figures, Colin, 184, 186–188, 195
Fishwick, Nicholas, 288, 292
fledgling democracies, intelligence
        services of, 225
Fleming Ian, 135, 159
Floyd, Trevor, 273–275
Ford, Carl, 382
Ford, Dr. Larry Creed, 274, 276, 277
Ford, Gerald, 200
France/French
    and Israel's plan to attack Egypt, 156
    intelligence (DST), 171, 172, 183
    Operation Musketeer, 155
    SDECE (external intelligence
        agency), 149, 155–157

Franco, General, and his Facist forces, 106
Franks, Arthur Temple, 184, 185–186, 188
Friedman, George, 281
Fuchs, Klaus, 26, 116–119, 122–123, 146
Fuchs, Kristel, 116–117
Fuller, Graham, 218

G

Gadahn, Adam, 385
gadgets, for espionage, 62–63
Gadhafi, Colonel Mu'ammar, 235, 256, 270, 381
Gandhi, Indira, 162
Gandhi, Mohandas Karamchand, 164
Garvey, Jane, 347
Gates, Bill, 189
Gates, Robert "Bob," 219, 242, 282–283, 284
Gehlen, General Reinhard, 99
General Agreement on Tariffs and Trade (GATT), 244
"genetic bomb," 272–273
George VI, King of England, 85, 88
George, Clair, 202, 222
germ warfare. *see* biological/biochemical weapon(s)/warfare
German/Germany
    brain drain from, 98
    declares war on the U.S., 94
    invasion, 86–90, 96
    Nazis, 104
    spies, as a menace to the security of Britain, 78–85
    see also Third Reich
Giligan, Andrew, 365
Global Issues Controllerate (GIC), 12
Goddard, Lord, 118, 138
Goebbels, Dr. Joseph, 85, 97
Goldberg, Moshe, 6, 47
Gold, Harry, 118
Goleniewski, Michael, 137
Gorbachev, President Mikhail, 215, 228, 251–253
Gordievsky, Oleg, 43, 190–191, 194–200, 253, 322
Goss, Porter, 39, 381–382

Gottlieb, Dr. Sidney, 147–148, 150, 211–212
Gouzenko, Igor, 108–111
Government Communications Headquarters (GCHQ), 11, 61–62, 75, 112, 146, 198, 245
    annual budget of, 228
the Grand Alliance, 99
Greene, Graham, 106
GRU (Russian military intelligence), 106, 165
Gunderson, Edward, 221

H

Haas, Kenneth, 203
Habash, Dr. George, 173, 174
Habib, Khalid, 385
Haig, Alexander, 200, 264
Halevy, Efraim, 319, 335, 342, 378
Hall, Admiral Reginald, 83
Hamas, 314
Hammerskjöld, Dag, 155
Hamza, Abu, 16, 50, 305–306, 393
Hanley, Michael, 173, 177, 198, 250
Hanning, August, 45
Hansen, Julian, 295, 296
Harel, Isser, 139–140, 153, 155
Harker, Jasper, 91, 111
Hartzenberg, Judge Willie, 279
Harvey, Bill, 125, 129, 137, 138
Hashemi-Rafsanjani, Ali Akbar, 206
Hattersley, Roy, 374
Haughey, Charles, 168
Hayden, General Michael, 349, 382
Heathcote, Mark, 189
Heath, Prime Minister Edward, 170, 185
Helms, Richard McGarrah, 73, 122, 168, 169–170
    and Kennedy assassination, 209
    and Rennie, differences between, 169
Heydrich, Reinhard, 289
Heywood, Jeremy, 350
Hezbollah, 203, 204, 206, 304, 314
    hijackings, 204
    in Iran, 24, 204
    and Israel, 28, 40
    links to IRA, 170
Hillenkoetter, Admiral Roscoe H., 114–115, 118, 120
Hill, Robin, 346

Hindu beliefs, 164
Hitler, Adolf, 84–85, 87–90, 270, 288
    plan to assassinate, 97–98
    surrender of, 100
Hollis, Sir Roger, 71–72, 105, 109–111,
    115, 117
Holm, Dick, 310
Holmes, Louise, 371–372
Holocaust, 87–90, 104, 140, 240
Holroyd, Fred, 175–176
Hoon, Geoffrey William, 375
Hoover, J. Edgar, 112, 124, 125, 131, 185
Howard, Edward Lee, 201–202
Howe, Geoffrey, 196
Hughes, Karen, 353
Hull, Cordell, 86–88
human rights
    and Amnesty International, 172
    ignored in China, 265–266
    legislation, 64
Hunter, Anji, 346, 350
Hussein, King of Jordan, 218, 237
Hussein, Saddam, 288, 354, 363–380
    and alleged WMD, 363–379
    CIA tracks movements of, 248
    execution of, 379–380
    overthrow of, 21
    and the supergun, 238
    and UN date set for withdrawal from
      Kuwait, 241–242
    uses germ warfare against Kurds,
      236–237
    and war with Iran/Khomeini, 258
Hutton, Brian, 374–377, 378
the Hutton Inquiry, 374–377, 378

I
India
    important posting for MI5/MI6, 162
    Soviet plans to gain control over, 164
Indyk, Martin, 342
Ingram, Miranda, 284
Inkster, Nigel, 7, 362–363
Inman, Bobby, 201
INSLAW, 295
Intelligence and Security Committee
    (ISC), 65, 295
intelligence gathering, human vs.
    technological, 205, 206
Interception and Communications Act,
    294

International Islamic Front for Jihad
    Against Jews and Crusaders, 49
interrogation center(s)
    alternate form of intelligence
      gathering, 89
    in Syria, 40
    Latchmere House, 92
    technique(s), 110
Iran
    and Asgari, 21–30
    and expansion policy in Soviet
      Union, 30–34
    foreign intelligence service. *see*
      VEVAK
    and Hezbollah, 24, 204
    and nuclear weapons. *see under*
      nuclear weapon(s)
    and oil, 31–35, 146
    and relations with Israel, 22–23, 25,
      37, 39, 390–391
    Revolutionary Guards, 24, 36, 37
    security service. *see* SAVAK
Iran-Contra Affair, 206, 221–222, 282
    and buildup of anti-Americanism
      across the Muslim world, 222
Irangate. *see* Iran-Contra Affair
Iran-Iraq War, 236–237, 258
Iraq
    and alleged WMD, 363–379
    and oil, 146
    invades Kuwait, 237–240
    and Hussein. *see* Hussein, Saddam
    suspected biological sites in, 249
    War in, 5, 240–244, 248, 363–380
    weapons inspectors in, 248
    see also Operation Desert Storm
Ireland/Irish
    acts as peacemaker during Cold
      War, 168
    government tolerates presence of
      IRA, 175–176
Irish Republican Army (IRA), 3, 59,
    201, 216, 223, 234–235
    contacts with other terrorist groups,
      170, 172
    and links to Hezbollah, 170
    threat to Britain/MI6, 43, 45, 47, 66,
      215
Irish Republican Brotherhood (IRB), 78
Irish Parliamentary Party, 78
"Iron Curtain," 98

Ishibara, Shintaro, 281
Islamic Fighting Force, 235
Israel/Israeli
    arms sales to Nigeria, in return for
        oil, 175
    Defense Forces (IDF), 153, 157,
        238–239
    and focus on obtaining American
        data, 283
    intelligence. *see* Mossad
    plan to preemptively attack Egypt,
        156
    plan to preemptively attack Iran,
        390–391
    relations with China, 18
    relations with Iran, 22–23, 25, 37, 39,
        390–391
    threats against, 153–154, 170
Italy/Italian
    declares war on the U.S., 94
    Intelligence and Military Security
        Service (SISMI), 217, 342
Izmailovo Organization (Russian mafia
    gang), 9

J
Jacobsen, David, 219
Japan, intent on world economic
    dominance, 281
jihad(ist), 3, 4, 16, 50, 51, 53, 56–57,
    258, 383–385, 389
John, Otto, 107
Johnson, President Lyndon Baines, 72,
    179–180, 209–210, 312
Johnstone, Andrew, 176
Joint Intelligence Committee (JIC), 148,
    186, 208, 235, 241, 277, 297, 300, 362
    and connection to MI5 and MI6, 2
    and the Suez Group, 145
    and the "Surfers," 10, 11
    and terrorism, 13
    and Thatcher, 255
Jones, Martin Furnival, 72, 166, 167
Jones, John Lewis, 207–208
Jong-il, Kim, 277
Jordan, Dr. Pallo, 273
Joyce, William, 104

K
Kai-shek, Chiang, 115
Kappes, Stephen, 381

Kasrils, Ronnie, 273
Kazakhstan, sells uranium to Iran,
    38–39
Kell, Constance, 91
Kell, Vernon, 111, 139
    death of, 91
    firing of, 90–91
    as MI6 chief, 78–84
Kelly, Dr. David, 237–238, 335–337,
    338–340, 355–356, 359–360
    and alleged biological WMD in Iraq,
        241, 248–250, 364–378
    and al-Qaeda WMD, 259
    body found, 371
    death of, 364–378
    and missing dental records, 372
    monitors Project Coast, 275
    and Pasechnik's story, 259–261
    and unknown cause of death, 372
Kelly, Janice, 365–366, 371–375
Kelly, Tom, 351
Kennan, George, 122
Kennedy, President John F.,
    assassination of, and links to KGB,
        209–210
Kerr, Donald, 396
Kerr, Richard, 378
KGB (Komitet Gosudarstvennoi
    Bezopasnosti)
    and Bakatin. *see* Bakatin, Vadim
    and fledgling democracy, 250–255
    reform of, 250–255
    as threat, 6, 17, 26, 71–72, 113, 134,
        136, 136–139, 165, 198, 204,
        209–210, 213, 224
Khalil, General Hassan, 40
Khan, Mohammed Sidique, 3, 57
Khan, Abdul Qadeer, 334
Khomeini, Ayatollah Ruhollah, 23, 36,
    188, 204–205, 258
Kissinger, Henry, 242, 264
Knight, Charles Henry Maxwell,
    83–84
Kolbe, Fritz, 97
Korda, Alexander, 13
Korean War, 188
Korshunov, Viktor, 359
Kouzminov, Dr. Alexander, 17
Kovacevic, Dr. Milan, 299–300, 303
Kringen, John, 11
Kryuchkov, Vladimir, 224, 253

Kuwait
  Iraqi invasion of, 237–240
  abuses of human rights in, 242

L
Labour Party
  and first prime minister, 82
  and rations after WWII, 67–68
  and relations with MI5/MI6, 70, 82,
    111, 198, 234
  victory, 8
Ladell, Dr. "The Sorcerer," 150–151
Laden, Osama bin. *see* bin Laden,
  Osama
Lambton, Ann Katherine Swynford, 30
Lander, Sir Stephen, 45, 295, 296, 297,
    344, 345, 349–350, 351, 378
Latchmere House (interrogation
  center), 92–93, 103
Lawson, Nigel, 255
Lawson, Nigella, 70 , 255
Lebard, Meredith, 281
Lederberg, Joshua, 273
Leger, Paul, 149
Lenin, Vladimir Ilyich, 95, 185
Lewinsky, Monica, 333
Lewis, James, 203
Libya
  arms sales to IRA, 170–171
  and biological weapons, 270
  and Project Coast, 275
  see also Gadhafi, Colonel Mu'ammar
Liddell, Guy, 111, 117, 126–128
  passed over for MI5 director, 132
  as White's mentor, 132, 139
Lilley, James, 242, 264–265
Ling, Kao, 267
Littlejohn, Keith, 175–176
Littlejohn, Kenneth, 175–176
Litvinenko, Alexander, 199
Lloyd, Selwyn, 147, 155
Lockerbie investigation, 296
Lockhart, John Bruce, 131, 154
Lody, Karl, 81
London
  after WWII, 67–68
  bombings, in June 1944, 102–104
  bombings, in July 2005, 3, 14, 48–49,
    51, 63, 65, 382
  Jewish population in, 103–104

London *Observer*, 160
Longford, Dr. Ian, 359, 360
Lotz, Wolfgang, 141–142
Lournes, Dr. Jan, 273–274
Lower, Deborah, 347
Lumumba, Patrice, 317
Lyalin, Oleg, 166–167

M
MacEachin, Douglas, 280
Machon, Annie, 51, 232–236, 295
Macintyre, Ben, 104
Mackenzie, Robert, 125, 127
Maclean, Donald, 108, 125–130, 256
Macmillan, Harold, 130
Mail on Sunday, 199, 236
Makarios, Archbishop, 185
Malan, Magnus, 271
Malenkov, Georgi, 133
Mandela, Nelson, 275, 278, 279,
    317–318
Mandelson, Peter, 8, 9
Mangold, Tom, 378
the Manhattan Project, 110, 116, 119,
    123
Manningham-Buller, Dame Eliza, 12,
    42–46, 47, 50, 65–67, 67–70, 194,
    199–200, 207, 295, 296, 344, 345,
    361, 378, 382
  and al-Qaeda-as-croquet analogy,
    66
  career high points of, 44–45
  education of, 69
  enthusiasm for MI5 work, 76
  family life of, 42
  joined MI5, 73
  as a new spy, 73–76
  retirement of, 67, 383–385
  salary of, 43
  and her teaching career, 70
Manningham-Buller, Reginald, 69
Manning, Sir David, 361
Markov, Georgy, 213, 273
Martin, Arthur, 113, 146
Marwan, Ashraf, 159–160
Marychurch, Peter, 198
Mary, Queen of Scots, 77
Massiter, Cathy, 256
Masterman, Cecil, 102
Maxwell, Robert, 60, 224

MBR (Russian internal security service), 252

McCann, Joe, 176

McColl, Colin, 223–225, 227, 229, 231, 237, 241, 251, 277, 302

McCone, John Alex, 72

McDermott, Geoffrey, 145

McDonald, Ramsay, 82

McGuinness, Martin, 47, 310

Meir, Golda, 174

Menzies, Audrey, 131

Menzies, Pamela, 130–131

Menzies, Stewart
death of, 131
as MI6 chief, 32–34, 89–90, 94, 97, 99, 100, 102, 104, 107, 133, 149
and Soviet spy ring in MI6, 124, 126, 128–131
wives of, 131

Merari, Ariel, 218

MI5 (Britain's Security Service), 2, 42–63
after WWII, 69
annual budget of, 78, 81, 83, 250
and computers and phone systems, 293
directors, list of, ix
emergence of, 78
failure(s)/mistake(s) of, 48–49, 64–67, 82, 117, 118, 122–125, 256
file system, 48
and glass ceiling, 232, 284
growth of, 80, 81
headquarters. see Thames House
and hiring process, 232–233
and homosexuality/lesbianism, 75
and info sharing with France/U.S., 81
and information technology, 48
keeps secrets from Americans to protect itself, 117, 118
lacks the power of arrest, 3
and legal advisors, 64–65
male-dominated culture in, 232, 284
and obsessive fear of the skills of the KGB, 130
and propaganda, 88
questions enemy spies, 92
recruiting and training, 54–55, 70–71, 215, 231

role of women in, 284
staff of, 43, 66
and surveillance, 66, 241
and suspicion of Labour Party, 82, 198, 234
and terrorism, 43–63
and the "Watchers," 49, 51, 65, 71, 82, 146, 166

MI5 (departments and divisions)
the Registry, 48, 79, 81, 91, 92, 107, 114, 117, 124, 147, 177, 178, 219
Technical Operations, 71
and Transcriptions, 71, 74, 91

MI5 (operations and involvements)
and Bradford operation, 51–53
and Canadian spy ring, 108–111
and deportation of Saddam sympathizers, 241
and Forest Gate fiasco, 65
installs bugs in Basson cottage, 276
monitors Basson and Project Coast, 275–279
and Operation Double Cross, 93
and Operation Trinity, 58–62
and Operation Venona/Venona Project, 113–115, 124–125, 146
removes Dr. Kelly's computers from his home, 371
and Soviet spy ring, 120–132

MI5 (relations)
and friendly relations with Moscow, 250–254
relations with the CIA, 10, 44, 72–73, 88, 94, 122
relations with Labour party. see under Labour Party
relations with the Mossad, 10, 139–140
relations with MSS, 266–267

Military Operations Five (forerunner of MI5), 78

Miller, Judith, 370

Milmo, Helenus, 129–130

Milosevic, Slobodan, plans to assassinate, 288, 289, 292

Mineta, Norman, 347

Ministry of State Security (MSS), in China, 18, 262–268, 279

MI6 (Britain's Secret Intelligence Service)
annual budget of, 12, 13, 170
and arrival of CIA, 33–34
Combined Services Interrogation Center, 89
designated name for chief of, 83
directors, list of, ix–x
dismissal from, 288
emergence of, 78
failures of/embarrassing revelations about, 195–196, 398
and homosexuality/lesbianism, 185
and Joint Intelligence Committee (JIC). *see* Joint Intelligence Committee (JIC)
lacks the power of arrest, 3
and links between Iranians and the Communists, 31
mistakes and scandals. *see* double agent(s); Nunn May Canadian spy ring
morale within, 12
and obsessive fear of the skills of the KGB, 130
and opinion(s) of Dulles, 96
and propaganda, 88, 153–154
provides fertile ground for corruption, 289
recruiting and training, 55, 71, 223, 287
Red Book, 195
stresses of, 289, 290
and surveillance, 14–17
use "front" companies in espionage, 13–14
MI6 (operations and involvements)
and al-Qaeda, 11, 15–16
and black propaganda, 153–154
and Canadian spy ring, 108–111
compromises IRA operatives to cause embarrassment to Irish government, 175–176
and CYAS (cover your ass solution), 129
and deportation of Saddam sympathizers, 241
Imperial Hotel Operation, 134
investigation into Marwan's death, 160

Jameah Islamiyah faith school as training camp, 16
monitors Basson and Project Coast, 275–279
monitors terrorism, 2–3
most expensive construction during the Cold War, 136
and Operation Kadesh, 156–157
and Operation Stopwatch, 134–138
plots to assassinate Gadhafi, 235
plots to assassinate Hussein, 288
plots to kill Princess Diana and Dodi al-Fayed, 292
and small victories against terrorism, 11
and Soviet spy ring, 120–132
MI6 (relations)
and relations/sharing of info with the CIA, 2, 10, 12, 13, 33–34, 94, 118–119, 122, 134, 145, 156, 203
and relations/sharing info with DST, 171
and relations/sharing of info with the Mossad, 2, 10, 12, 17, 37, 39, 139–140, 171, 174, 394
and relations with PET, 196
Mitchell, Graham, 145–146
Mitrokhin, Vasili, 322–324
MIT (Turkish intelligence), 40
MK-ULTRA experiments, 62, 210–212
Mogilevich, Semyon Yukovich, 38, 60, 256
Mohammed, Omar Bakri, 384
Mollet, Guy, 153, 154, 155
Montgomery, Bernard, 141
Moore, John, 273
Morning Star, 105, 166, 177
Morningstar, Robert, 397
Mosley, Sir Oswald, 84
the Mossad, 139, 170–171, 283, 319, 334, 357
assassination squad (the Kidon), 142, 151
and black propaganda, 153–154
and Operation Kadesh, 156–157
sends a spy to Iraq, 238–239
reasons people might want to join, 56
recruitment, 55
and relations with China, 18
and relations with CIA, 188, 240

and relations with DST, 171
and relations with MI6. *see under* MI6
(relations)
and sexual entrapment, 55–56
Mossadeq, Prime Minister Mohammed,
31, 32, 34–36
Mountbatten, Lord Louis, 165
Moussaoui, Zacarias, 50
Mugabe, President Robert, 244
Murdoch, Rupert, 247
Musharraf, President Pervez, 11, 28, 387
Muslim beliefs, 164
My Silent War (Philby), 130

N
NASA, 161, 391
Nasser, Gamal Abdel, 140, 143–159
Nasser, Mona, 159
National Iranian Oil Company, 35
National Security Agency (NSA), 12,
113, 115, 116, 156, 201, 217,
225–231, 382
Nazis. *see under* Germany
1948 War of Independence, 140
9/11 attacks, 2, 8, 11, 20, 39, 43, 50,
361, 386, 389
see also al-Qaeda
9/11 Commission, 382
Negroponte, John, 39, 382
Neguib, General Mohammed, 142, 143,
144
Nehru, Jawaharlal, 163
Neill, Alex, 246
Neitzel, Sönke, 90
Nelson, Carl, 138
Neville-Jones, Dame Pauline, 300
New China News Agency (NCNA),
267
Newsome, Sir Frank, 140
New York Times, 370
Nicholson, Harold, 311
Nieuwoudt, Nicol, 269–270
Nigeria, supplies Israel with oil, 175
Nixon, Richard, 219
NKVD (Russian intelligence
service/secret police), 95, 98–99,
113, 122, 142
No Abiding City (Blake), 138
No Other Choice (Blake), 138
Noriega, General Manuel, 281
Northcliffe, Lord, 79

North Korea
biological program. *see*
biological/biochemical
weapon(s)/warfare
experiments done on prisoners in,
277
invades South Korea, 120–121
and nuclear weapons. *see under*
nuclear weapon(s)
Nosenko, Yuri, 209
Nunn May, Alan, 110, 118, 119, 123
Nunn May Canadian spy ring, 108–111,
113, 114
nuclear weapon(s)
and al-Qaeda, 15, 22, 27
and China, 22, 242–245
and Iran, 22, 38, 389–391, 394, 396
and Iraq, 242–243
and Israel, 389–391, 394
and Japan, 114, 133
most accessible, 57–58
and North Korea, 22, 189
and Pakistan, 12, 22
and Russia/Soviet Union, 113,
114–119, 133
and the United States, 110, 114, 189
see also biochemical warfare; the
Manhattan Project; weapons of
mass destruction (WMD)
Nyugen, Set Van, 359

O
Odum, General William, 229
Office of Foreign Asset Control
(OFAC), 325
Office of Strategic Services (OSS), 94,
95, 96, 99, 111, 125, 211
Office of the Coordinator of
Information (COI), 94, 109
Official Secrets Act, 77, 78, 233, 289,
290, 298
Oldfield, Maurice, 184–185, 188
Olson, Frank, 210–212
Omar, Mullah Mohammed, 28
O'Neill, John, 315–316, 324, 343
Open Secret (Rimington), 178, 216
Operation Desert Storm, 240–244, 248
Operation Mason, 367, 374, 377
Ostrovsky, Victor, 151
Oswald, Lee Harvey, 210
Ottawa Journal, 108

P

PAGAD (People Against Gangsterism and Drugs), 29
Pakistan
    and al-Qaeda/Taliban/terrorism, 11, 19, 28
    and Counter Terrorism Center (CTC), 11
    and nuclear program, 12, 22
Pahlevi, Mohammed Reza, 34
Paisley, Ian, 171
Palestine Liberation Organization (PLO), 174
Panama, invasion of, 281
Panorama, 236
Park, Daphne, 317
Park, Trent, 88–90
Parsons, Sir Anthony, 186
Pasechnik, Vladimir, 259–261, 277, 336–337, 356, 358
Patel, Bilal, 16
Paterson, Geoffrey, 128
Patton, George, 120
Pearl Harbor, 94
Pederson, Mai, 373
Pelley, Jean-Marre, 149
the People's Liberation Army (PLA), 243, 245
Pepper, David, 397
Peres, Shimon, 155
Perry, Dr. Julian, 373
PET (Danish intelligence service), 196
Petrie, David, 91–94, 102, 104, 105, 111
Philby, Kim, 13, 97, 105–108, 111, 124–132, 145, 198, 256, 291
    death of, 130
    interrogation of, 129–130
Philby, Sir Harry, 105–106, 162
Philip, Prince, Duke of Edinburgh, 9, 292
Pineau, Christian, 155
Pitt, William, 77
Pollard, Jonathan, 240, 283
Pont de l'Alma tunnel, 291
Pontecorvo, Bruno, 122–124, 133
Popular Front for the Liberation of Palestine (PFLP), 172, 173
Postdam Agreement, 98
Pravda, 168, 178, 254
Price, Ted, 194

Primakov, Yevgeni, 253–255
Privacy International, 265
Project Coast, 269–279, 366
Project 8313, 229
PROMIS, 295
Putin, Vladimir, 9, 198, 392, 397, 398

Q

Qaeda, al-. *see* al-Qaeda
Que, Dr. Benito, 357
Quine, John, 138
Quinn, Frank, 149–150

R

Raborn, Admiral William F., 72–73
radomes, 230
Rahman, Mizanur, 393–394
Rahman, Omar Abdel, 352
Ramsay, Margaret "Meta," 197
Rarey, Jim, 370–371
Reagan, President Ronald, 197, 200, 201, 209, 215, 219, 221, 240
    inauguration of, 205
    and Irangate, 222
    and opinion of Israel, 204
Rees, Lord, 75
Rees-Mogg, William, 284
Reid, John, 65
Reid, Richard ("the shoe bomber"), 3, 8, 50
Rennie, John, 169–170, 171–173, 176, 189
    and Helms, differences between, 169–170
    resignation of, 176
Reno, Janet, 311, 312
Ressam, Ahmed, 50
Rice, Condoleezza, 334, 337, 344, 347, 353
Ricketts, Peter, 7
Rimington, Dame Stella, 44, 45, 47, 71, 161, 177, 207, 208, 215, 231, 234, 284–286, 293–298
    appointed to director-general of MI5, 159
    becomes a full fledged officer, 178
    becomes a full-time spy, 166
    changes MI5's male dominated culture, 241, 284, 293
    collegial approach to the security service, 284

contemplates her autobiography, 297
fears hit by IRA, 257
first position in MI5, 165–166
immersion in the fight against the
 IRA, 285
knowledge of MI5 operations, 296
life in India for, 162
and Moscow trip, 250–252, 254–255
and opinion on Evans, 382
promotes the successes of MI5, 284
promotion of, 241, 257
reorganization of MI5, 285
replacing, 294, 295
resignation of, 293–298
suffering relationships of, 293
teen years of, 162
the Rising Sun (Europe's leading crime
 family), 38, 60, 61, 256
Rodriguez, Carlos, 46
Roosevelt, Kermit, 143–144, 147
Roosevelt, President Franklin D., 85,
 87–88, 93, 94, 100, 101, 111–112,
 116, 143, 240
 death of, 112
Rosenberg, Ethel, 118
Rosenberg, Julius, 118
the royal family, 9
Royal Ulster Constabulary (RUC),
 170–173
"Rule Book Man," 221
Rumsfeld, Donald, 333, 344, 352–353,
 355
 gives germ strains to Iraq, 236–237,
 249, 271
Russell, Dr. Philip K., 337–338
Russell-King, Joan, 146
Russia/Russian
 and arms sales to Iraq, 6
 and arms sales to Syria, 6
 biological warfare program
 (Biopreparat), 17, 212–213, 248,
 260, 277
 Federal Security Service (FSB), 113,
 397
 Foreign Intelligence Service (SUR),
 17, 113
 and hydrogen bomb annoucement,
 133
 internal sercurity service. see MBR
 and KGB. see KGB
 secret police organization. see NKVD

 and SVR (Russian Federal
 Intelligence Service), 253
 see also Soviet Union
Russo-Anglo-American Treaty, 248

S
Sabri, Ali, 151
Sadat, Anwar, 159, 160
Sanchez, Ilich Ramirez. see Carlos the
 Jackal
Sargant, Dr. William, 75, 125, 210–211,
 234, 344
satellite surveillance, 179–183, 386–388
Saudi Arabia
 and al-Qaeda, 15–16
Saud, Ibn, 106
Savage, Sean, 170–171
SAVAK (Iran's security service), 24, 186
Sawers, John, 354
Scarlett, Sir John McLeod, 7, 320, 323,
 344–345, 363, 381, 391, 395, 396
 and calls for resignation of, 398
 as chief of MI6, 1–3
 and Dr. Kelly investigation, 368,
 377
 education/family of, 1
 and "the golden nuggets," 5
 and Gordievsky, 194–200
 and his belief in surveillance, 15–16
 and his office, 37
 and Iraq WMD blunder, 5
 and relationship with Blair, 5, 7–8, 9,
 398
 and relationship with CIA, 39
 and relationship with Dagan, 37–38
 retirement of, 397–398
 salary of, 398
 as a young spy, 6–7
Scheuer, Mike, 311
Schultz, George, 218–219
Schultz, Max, 79–80
Scowcroft, Brent, 242
Secret Service Fund, 77
Senja, Major General Jan, 168
Seven Pillars of Wisdom (T.E. Lawrence),
 36
Shamir, Yitzhak, 240
Shavit, Shabtai, 238–239, 270
Shayler, David, 235, 236, 256
Shepherd, Sir Francis, 31
Shimron, Gad, 159–160

Shipman, Tim, 373
Shi, Qiao, 264–268, 279
Shkedy, Eliezer, 390
Shrimpton, Michael, 373
Shu'bat al-Mukhabarat al-Askariya
    (Syrian military intelligence), 40
Shulikov, Lev Aleksandrovich, 213
Sigint City. *see* National Security Agency
    (NSA)
signals intelligence (SIGINT), 112
Sillitoe, Percy, 111, 117, 126, 132, 138
Sinclair, Hugh, 13
Sinclair, John, 34–35, 133–136
    good relationship with CIA, 134
    kind gesture of, 133–134
Single Unified Vote (secret funding for
    MI5/MI6), 12, 65
Sinn Fein (the political arm of the
    IRA), 47, 82, 167, 223, 309
Sinstov, Vladimir, 6–7
SISMI. *see under* Italy/Italian
Sisulu, Walter, 317
Skardon, Jim, 26, 117–118, 129, 130
Smellie, Craig, 174–175
SMERSH ("Death to Spies,") 99
Smith, Gayle, 315
Smith, General Walter Bedell, 120–124,
    126, 129, 131
Smith, Howard, 171
Smythe, Douglas, 175, 176
Sorocco, Steve, 212
Sorokin, Colonel Vyacheslaw, 224
Somalia, sells uranium to Iran, 38–39
South African Defense Force (SADF),
    268–279
Soviet Order of battle, 99
"Soviet Perception of Nuclear Warfare,"
    197
Soviet Union
    and arms deal with Egypt, 147
    carves up Europe, 100
    launches fifty satellites, 183
    managed to breach the Biological
        Warfare Convention, 260
    MI6 and CIA collaboration against,
        134
    plans to gain control over India, 164
    secret war against the, 136
    spy ring. *see* Blake, George; Blunt,
        Anthony; Burgess, Guy; Maclean,
        Donald; Philby, Kim

    as threat to Britain, 15, 18, 31, 69,
        83–84, 97
    ties to Labour Party, 198
    and WMD, 17, 113
    see also Russia/Russian
Spanish Civil War, 84
Special Operations Executive (SOE), 88
Spedding, David, 300–303, 316, 319,
    321–322
Sputnik, 179–180
Sporting Life, 131
Spycatcher (Wright), 72, 291, 297
Stalin, Joseph, 69, 99, 100, 116,
    121–122, 254
Stalker Inquiry, 216
Stalker, John, 216
Steele, Frank, 167–168, 171–174
Steinhauer, Gustav, 80
Stephenson, William, 109
Stephens, Robin, 92–93, 103
Stern, 176
Stimson, Henry, 83, 87
The Strange Death of David Kelly (Baker),
    377
Strauss, Robert, 252–254
Straw, Jack, 8
Studeman, Vice Admiral William,
    227–228, 231
Su, Dr. Yi Yong, 276–277
Suez Canal 141–145, 146–160, 169
    Nasser announced he would
        nationalize the, 151
    and oil, 142, 148–149
Suez Group, 144, 145
Sunday Times, 9, 254, 257
Sununu, John, 242
SUR (Russian intelligence service). *see
    under* Russia/Russian
SVR (Russian Federal Intelligence
    Service). *see under* Russia/Russian
Syria
    and Hezbollah, 204
    and monitoring/surveillance, 40

T
Taha, Dr. Rihab
    personality of, 249
    studied biological weapons, 359–360
    questioned by Dr. Kelly, 249–250,
        278, 364
    and weapons inspectors, 249–250

Taliban/"Talibanized," 11
Tambo, Oliver, 317
Tanweer, Shehzad, 3
Tehran hostage fiasco, 204–205
TELINT, 227
Tenet, George, 39, 311, 313, 319, 322,
    324, 327, 332–334, 335, 341–343,
    345–348
  relationship with Dearlove, 361–362
  resignation of, 378
  told Bush that Saddam had WMDs,
    378
terrorism/terrorist(s), 216–217
  in Britain, 4
  dream target for, 58
  and hijacking/kidnapping, 170
  and MI6. *see under* MI6
  small victories against, 11
  and WMD. *see* biochemical warfare;
    nuclear weapon(s); weapons of
    mass destruction (WMD)
  see also al-Qaeda; jihad(ist); 9/11
    attacks; Taliban/"Talibanized"
TECHINT. *see* satellite surveillance
Thames House
  branches of, 57
  floor designation for, 62–63
  lawyers, 64
  location/decoration of, 46–48
Thatcher, Prime Minister Margaret, 10,
    72, 127, 185, 189, 195, 208, 215,
    225, 251, 255–257, 302, 350
  close interest in/inspection of MI5,
    255
  concern for the "enemy within,"
    255–256
Third Reich, 96, 97, 270
  see also German invasion
Thomson, Basil, 80
Tiananmen Square Massacre, 243–244,
    264–266
Times of London, 106, 136
Today, 365, 376
Tolkachev, Adolf, 202
Tomlinson, Richard, 7, 20, 224,
    286–288, 289, 290, 293, 318, 398
  and the stresses of MI6, 289,
    290–291
  and the use of informants, 286–287
  assignment of new personnel officer,
    289–290

belief of MI6 involvement in the
    death of Princess Diana, 292
  firing of, 290
  imprisonment of, 291
  and his attempt to write a tell-all
    book, 291
  and meeting the poison dwarf, 290
  recruitment/training of, 287
  theories of, 293
  and the unraveling of his career, 289
torture, 172
The Tower Commission, 222
Tredegar, Lord, 93
Trevelyan, Humphrey, 147, 152
Tripartite Agreement, 154
Truman, President Harry, 33–34, 68, 69,
    97, 112–113, 116, 120–121, 228
  detonates the hydrogen bomb in the
    South Pacific, 132
  and his Marshall Plan, 121–122
Truth and Reconciliation Commission,
    278
Tuobin, Zhang, 244
Turner, Admiral Stansfield, 204–205,
    243
TWA flight 847, 204, 206
Twenty Committee, 102–103

U
UKUSA (secret agreement between
    Britain and U.S.), 228
"Ulster's secret dirty war," 171
United States
  bioterrorism, first act of in the U.S.,
    275
  blind to Iraq threat, 237
  collaboration with Britain, 112, 113,
    228
  companies, links to China, 242
  explodes the hydrogen bomb
    "Mike," 132–133
  as "the Great Satan," 258, 383
  Italy/Germany declare war on, 94
  National Photographic
    Interpretation Center, 182
  National Intelligence Estimate
    (NIE), 396
  as postwar superpower, 68, 113
  pressures invaders of Suez Canal to
    withdraw, 159
  relations with Britain, 23, 152

United States *(continued)*
    relations with China, 242–248
    SIGINT collaboration with Britain,
        112
    and trading American hostages for
        American arms, 204
    and trade restrictions in China,
        243–244
    see also CIA

V
van den Bergh, Henrik, 318
van der Westhuizen, Pieter, 269
the Vatican, 82
    fear that the Holy See was
        pro-German, 82–83
VEVAK (Iran's prime foreign
    intelligence service), 21–22, 25, 36
Viljoen, Constand, 269–270
Volkov, Konstantin, 107–108, 129
von Braun, Werner, 98–99
von Choltitz, General Dietrich, 90
Vopos (East German Police), 135

W
Wallace, Colin, 52, 171, 382
Walker, General Sir Michael, 23
Walker, Patrick, 235, 255–257
Walsingham, Sir Francis, 76–77
Walters, General Vernon, 280
Ward, Tim, 341, 345, 346
Watson, Dale, 352
Wright, Peter, 256, 291, 294, 297
Warsaw Pact, 75, 191
Washington Post, 200, 363
weapons of mass destruction (WMD)
    and al-Qaeda, 17
    and miscalculations in Iraq, 5, 364,
        378, 379
    and Libya, 275
    and Pakistan, 12, 22
    and Soviet Union, 17
    see also biochemical warfare; nuclear
        weapon(s)
Webster, Judge William, 200, 221–223,
    227, 237, 241–242, 248, 280, 281, 282
    finding a replacement for, 282

Weekly News, 79
Weiss, Shalom, 238
White, Dick, 73, 127, 138–140,
    145–148, 151–152, 154–155,
    158–159, 211
    becomes new director for MI5,
        132
    death of, 159
    interrogates Philby, 129
    retirement of, 159
White, George Hunter, 211–212
Whitelaw, William, 173
Wiley, Dr. Don, 357–358
Wilhelm II, Kaiser, 79
Willsher, Kathleen "Kay," 110
Wilson, Sir Richard, 297, 298, 350
Wilson, Harold, 185, 216, 256
Winter, Dan, 281
Wodehouse, P. G., 104
Woodhouse, Christopher Montague
    "Monty," 30, 31, 35
Woodward, Bob, 200
Wright, Peter, 71–72, 75, 151
Wyman, John (a.k.a. Douglas Smythe),
    175–176
Wynter, Gilbert, 58, 60

X
Xioping, Deng, 264

Y
the Yalta Conference, 99–100
Yardley, Herbert, 82
Yeltsin, Boris, 253
Young, Alan, 367, 374, 377
Young, George, 30, 31, 134, 135, 144,
    148, 153, 158
Yom Kippur War, 38
Yurchenko, Colonel Vitali, 207,
    209–210, 212–215

Z
Zamir, Zvi, 174
Zaehner, Robin, 31
Zedong, Mao, 115, 263
Zimbabwe, political crisis in, 244–245
Zucker, Dedi, 357